The B-Book

The B-Book

Assigning Programs to Meanings

J.-R. Abrial

CAMBRIDGE
UNIVERSITY PRESS

Published by the Press Syndicate of the University of Cambridge
The Pitt Building, Trumpington Street, Cambridge CB2 1RP
40 West 20th Street, New York NY 10011-4211, USA
10 Stamford Road, Oakleigh, Melbourne 3166, Australia

© Cambridge University Press 1996

First published 1996

Printed in Great Britain at the University Press, Cambridge

British Library cataloguing in publication data available

Library of Congress cataloging in publication data available

ISBN 0 521 49619 5 (hardback)

to Hélène Villers

Tribute

Those who have the privilege of friendship with Jean-Raymond Abrial have long been aware of the great work in which he has been engaged. It is no less than a complete understanding of the nature of software engineering, from the capture and analysis of requirements, the formalization of specifications, the evolution of designs, the generation of programs and their implementation on computers. The publication of this book is the culmination of his work, and the complete fulfilment of our fondest hopes.

There will now be a much wider class of readers, for whom the book will come as a revelation, their first introduction to the power of its author's innovative intellect, their first appreciation of the clarity and masterful simplicity of his writing. His achievement is to reconcile the concepts of mathematics with the promptings of intuition, and harness both to solve the problems of modern programming practice. There is much to enjoy learning from the text, and even more to be learnt by putting its lessons into practice. Read, learn, enjoy and prosper!

C.A.R. Hoare

Foreword

This book is much more than a new programming manual. It introduces a method in which the program design is included in the global process that goes from understanding the problem to the validation of its solution.

The mathematical basis of the method provides the exactness while the proposed notation eliminates the ambiguities of the vernacular language. At the same time, the process is simple enough for an industrial use. "Industrial" is in fact the key word.

The general aim of formal methods is to provide correctness of the problem specification. Here we can see how the solution can be found, step by step, by a continuously monitored process. The mathematical verification of each step is so closely bound to the refinement activity that it is no longer possible to separate the design choices from the checking process. Imagination is helped by exactness!

But how about the efficiency? Isn't the design too long? Are the design people able to do this work? Are the machines powerful enough to implement the method? The answers are easy to give. Let me tell you.

My company has been involved, since the sixties, in the realisation of train control systems, which must meet stringent safety requirements. As soon as we began to use programmed logic (end of the seventies) we had to solve the problem of software correctness. Together with other methods, we chose to use the program proving method proposed by C.A.R. Hoare. In 1986, J.-R. Abrial introduced us to the B method. We decided to learn it and to use it. The tools did not exist at the time. We contributed to their elaboration by offering a real-world benchmark with our applications, and proposed some improvements. Now the tools can be found on the market, and the method can be used with its full efficiency. What did we learn?

- First, understanding the principles of the method is quite easy and expertise comes in less than a year.
- Then the method encourages and facilitates re-usability, based on use of a growing library of already proven abstract machines.
- The time saved during test and validation phases is very important, resulting in a global economic balance that is quite positive.
- The produced programs are efficient in spite of their structure being organised in layers of increasing abstraction.
- The tools can be implemented on simple workstations.

The use of the method has been a decisive element by increasing our confidence when using software for safety related applications. Moreover, the new international standards recommend the use of formal methods for the specification and design of safety-related software.

Thanks to J.-R. Abrial, we now have an industrial method to build correct programs. We hope that this book will convince the readers to save their money by using this method.

Pierre Chapront
Technical Director
GEC-ALSTHOM Transport

Introduction

This book is a very long discourse explaining how, in my opinion, the task of programming (in the small as well as in the large) can be accomplished *by returning to mathematics*.

By this, I first mean that the precise mathematical definition of what a program does must be present at the *origin* of its construction. If such a definition is lacking, or if it is too complicated, we might wonder whether our future program will mean anything at all. My belief is that a program, in the absolute, means absolutely nothing. A program only means something *relative* to a certain intention, that must predate it, in one form or another. At this point, I have no objection with people feeling more comfortable with the word "English" replacing the word "mathematics". I just wonder whether such people are not assigning themselves a more difficult task.

I also think that this "return to mathematics" should be present in the very process of program construction. Here the task is to assign a program to a well-defined meaning. The idea is to accompany the technical process of *program* construction by a similar process of *proof* construction, which guarantees that the proposed program agrees with its intended meaning.

Simultaneous concerns about the architecture of a program and that of its proof are surprisingly efficient. For instance, when the proof is cumbersome, there are serious chances that the program will be too; and ingredients for structuring proofs (abstraction, instantiation, decomposition) are very similar to those for structuring programs. Ideally, the relationship between the construction of a program and its proof of correctness should be so intimate as to make it impossible to detect which of the two is driving the other. It might then be reasonable to say that constructing a program is just constructing a proof.

Today, very few programs are specified and constructed in this way. Does this correlate with the fact that, today, so many programs are fragile?

Jean-Raymond Abrial

Acknowledgements

The writing of this book spreads over a period of almost fifteen years. During that period, I have met many people, among which certain have had a positive influence on the work presented in this book. I would like to thank them all.

Clearly, the main source of influence, without which this book could not have been brought into existence, lies in the ideas conveyed by C.A.R. Hoare and E.W. Dijkstra. The view of a program as a mathematical object, the concepts of pre- and post-conditions, of non-determinism, of weakest pre-condition, all these ideas are obviously central to what is presented in this book.

The B method, being a "model oriented" method of software construction, is thus close to VDM and to Z. Obviously, many ideas of both these methods can be recognized in B. This is reasonable for Z, since I was one of its originators before and during my visit at the Programming Research Group in Oxford from 1979 to 1981. This is also reasonable for VDM since I shared an office with C.B. Jones during that same period. From him, I learned the idea of program development and the concept of refinement and its practical application, under the form of proof obligations.

Discussions with C.C. Morgan on specification and refinement have had a significant influence on the material of this book. His idea of enlarging the concept of program to embody that of specification has had a seminal effect on this work.

The collective work done at the Programming Research Group during the eighties on the notion of refinement has been directly borrowed in my presentation of refinement. To the best of my knowledge, the people concerned were P. Gardiner, J. He, C.A.R. Hoare, C.C. Morgan, K.A. Robinson, and J.W. Sanders.

During the practical elaboration of the method, certain people have had a significant influence on this work. Belonging to that category are G. Laffitte, F. Mejia,

I. McNeal, P. Behm, J.-M. Meynadier and L. Dufour, whom I thank very warmly.

G. Laffitte influenced this work by his careful reviews, his acccurate criticisms, and the sometimes very serious rearrangements he proposed for some of the mathematical developments of this book.

F. Mejia proposed some important improvements in the area of structuring large software constructions. Together with B. Dehbonei, he developed a complete tool set for B, now commercialized as *Atelier B*.

I. McNeal has made various contributions to the early development of the method. This has had some beneficial influence on the mechanization of proofs.

P. Behm, J.-M. Meynadier and L. Dufour made very interesting suggestions and constructed a prototype prover whose mechanisms are extremely useful.

The magnificient team of DIGILOG, which is industrializing and commercializing *Atelier B*, and developing software systems with it, deserves special congratulations. Their competence, enthusiasm, and kindness make it a real pleasure to work with them. I would like to thank F. Badeau, F. Bustany, E. Buvat, P. Lartigue, J.-Ph. Pitzalis, C. Roques, D. Sabatier, T. Servat, C. Tognetty, and C. Zagoury.

A number of other people have been working indirectly on the B project by reviewing this book, by teaching this work, by applying it, or by promoting it. I would like to thank them all, particularly an anonymous reviewer and also P. Bieber, P. Chartier, J.-Y. Chauvet, C. Da Silva, T. Denvir, P. Desforges, R. Docherty, M. Ducassé, M. Elkoursi, Ph. Facon, H. Habrias, N. Lopez, I. Mackie, L. Mussat, P. Ozello, J.-P. Rubaux, P. Ryan, S. Schuman, M. Simonot, and H. Waeselynk.

Casual meetings and discussions with B. Meyer and M. Sintzoff have had an indirect influence on this work. Meeting them is always an intellectual pleasure, which, to my regret, does not happen often enough.

In the industrial world, a number of institutions have made possible, in one way or another, the writing of this book. I am particularly indebted to ADI, BP, DIGILOG/groupe STERIA, DIGITAL, GEC-ALSTHOM Transport, GIXI, INRETS, INSEE, MATRA Transport, RATP and SNCF. These institutions, at various stages of the many years of the development of this project, supported it in various ways. I would like to thank particularly the following persons: P. Barrier, P. Beaudelaire, J. Betteridge, P. Chapront, A. Gazet, A. Guillon, C. Hennebert, J.-L. Lapeyre, J.-C. Rault, and O. Sebilleau.

The publishing of this book has been a long and sometimes painful process, especially at the end of it, where a number of unusual difficulties emerged. Bertrand Meyer, Cliff Jones, and Tony Hoare played a significant contribution in trying to solve these difficulties. May they be very warmly thanked for their help.

In conclusion, I would like to give many thanks to David Tranah from Cambridge University Press. I am particularly indebted to him for making possible the publication of my book while respecting the independence within which this scientific work has been performed.

What is B?

B is a method for specifying, designing, and coding software systems.

Coverage

The method essentially deals with the central aspects of the software life cycle, namely: the technical specification, the design by successive refinement steps, the layered architecture, and the executable code generation.

Proof

Each of the previous items is envisaged as an activity that involves writing mathematical proofs in order to justify its results. It is, precisely, the collection of such proofs that makes one convinced that the software system in question is indeed correct.

Abstract Machine

The basic mechanism of this approach is that of the abstract machine. This is a concept that is very close to certain notions well-known in programming, under the names of modules, classes or abstract data types.

Data and Operations

A software system conceived with that method is composed of several abstract machines. Each machine contains some data and offers some operations. The data cannot be reached directly; they are always reached through the operations of the machine. They are said to be encapsulated in the machine.

Specification of Data

The data of an abstract machine are specified by means of a number of mathematical concepts such as sets, relations, functions, sequences and trees. The static laws that the data must follow are defined by means of certain conditions, called the invariant.

Specification of Operations

The specification of the operations of an abstract machine is expressed as a non-executable pseudo-code that does not contain any sequencing or loop. In this pseudo-code one describes each operation as a pre-condition and an atomic action. The pre-condition expresses the indispensable condition without which the operation cannot be invoked. The atomic action is formalized by means of a generalization of the notion of substitution. Among these generalized substitutions is the non-deterministic choice that leaves room for some later decision to be taken in the refinement phase. The formal definition of the pseudo-code allows one to prove that the invariant of an abstract machine is always preserved by the operations it offers.

Refinement towards an implementation

The initial model of an abstract machine (its specification) may be refined in an executable module (its code). This passage from specification to code is carried out entirely under the control of the method. It is thus necessarily concluded by some proofs, whose goal is to show that the final code of a machine indeed satisfies its initial specification.

Using refinement as a technique of specification

Besides the previous (classical) one, there exists another practical use of refinement. It consists in using refinement as a means of including more details of the problem into the formal development. Thus the formal translation of the initial problem statement is performed gradually rather than all at once.

Refinement Techniques

Refinement is conducted in three different ways: the removal of the non-executable elements of the pseudo-code (pre-condition and choice), the introduction of the classical control structures of programming (sequencing and loop), and the transformation of the mathematical data structures (sets, relations, functions, sequences and trees) into other structures that might be programmable (simple variables, arrays, or files).

Refinement Steps

In order to carefully control the previous transformations, the refinement of an abstract machine is performed in various steps. During each such step, the initial abstract machine is entirely reconstructed. It keeps, however, the same operations, as viewed by its users, although the corresponding pseudo-code is certainly modified. In the intermediate refinement steps, we have a hybrid construct, which is not a mathematical model any more, but certainly not yet a programming module.

Layered Architecture

Experience shows that it is preferable to have a small number of refinement steps. As soon as its level of complexity becomes too high, it is recommended to decompose a refinement into smaller pieces. The last refinement of a machine is thus implemented using the specification of one, or more, abstract machines that are, themselves, refinable. This is done by means of calls to the operations offered by the machines in question. As you can see, the "user" of an abstract machine is, thus, always the ultimate refinement of another abstract machine. In this way, the layered architecture of our software system (or of its translated informal specification) is constructed piece by piece.

Library

The machines on which the last refinement of a given machine is implemented may exist prior to that refinement. In fact, together with the method, a series of pre-defined abstract machines are proposed, which constitutes a library of machines, whose purpose is to encapsulate the most classical data structures.

Re-use

For a given project, it is advisable to extend that library so as to organize the basis on which the future abstract machines of higher level will be implemented. As you can see, the method allows one to choose either a purely top down design, or a bottom up one, or, better, a mixed approach integrating the re-use of specification and that of code.

Code Generation

The ultimate refinement of a machine may be easily translated into one or several imperative programming languages. By doing so, the method provides a solution to the problem of porting an application from one language to another.

B User Group

There exists a user group, called the BUG, for discussions and exchange of information on **B**. Here is its electronic address: `bug.@estasl.inrets.fr`. A mailing list for this book is also available at `bbook.@estasl.inrets.fr`.

What is the B-Book?

The **B-Book** is the standard reference for the **B** method and its notations.

It contains the mathematical basis on which the method is founded and the precise definition of the notations used. It also contains a large number of examples illustrating how to use the method in practice. The book comprises four parts and a collection of appendices:

Part I	Mathematics
Part II	Abstract Machines
Part III	Programming
Part IV	Refinement

Part I

Part I contains a systematic construction of predicate logic and set theory. It also contains the definition of various mathematical structures that are needed to formalize software systems. A special emphasis is put on the notion of proof. Part I consists of the following chapters:

Chapter 1	Mathematical Reasoning
Chapter 2	Set Notation
Chapter 3	Mathematical Objects

Part II

Part II contains a presentation of the Generalized Substitution Language (GSL) and the Abstract Machine Notation (AMN). These notations are the ones we use in order to specify software systems. They are presented together with a number of examples showing how large specifications can be built systematically. A set-theoretical foundation of GSL and AMN is also presented. Part II consists of the following chapters:

Chapter 4	Introduction to Abstract Machines
Chapter 5	Formal Definition of Abstract Machines
Chapter 6	Theory of Abstract Machines
Chapter 7	Constructing Large Abstract Machines
Chapter 8	Examples of Abstract Machines

Part III

Part III introduces the two basic programming features, namely sequencing and loop. After a theoretical presentation, an important chapter is devoted to the study of the systematic construction of a variety of examples of algorithm developments. Part III consists of the following chapters:

Chapter 9	Sequencing and Loops
Chapter 10	Programming Examples

Part IV

Part IV presents a notion of refinement for both generalized substitutions and abstract machines. Refinement is given a mathematical foundation within set theory. The construction of large software systems by means of layered architectures of modules is also explained. Finally, a number of large examples of complete development are studied with a special emphasis on the methodological approach. Part IV consists of the following chapters:

Chapter 11	Refinement
Chapter 12	Constructing Large Software Systems
Chapter 13	Examples of Refinement

Appendices

A collection of appendices contains a summary of all the logical and mathematical definitions. It also contains a summary of all the rules and proof obligations:

Appendix A	Summary of Notations
Appendix B	Syntax
Appendix C	Definitions
Appendix D	Visibility Rules
Appendix E	Rules and Axioms
Appendix F	Proof Obligations

How to use this book

This book can be used by people having very different concerns.

For instance, you might intend to learn the method *as a formal method practitioner*. In this case, you are probably not (although you might be) interested in the detailed mathematics presented in the book. It is then recommended to read the book as follows:

Appendix A	Summary of Notations
Chapter 2	Set Notation (section 2.7)
Chapter 4	Introduction to Abstract Machines
Chapter 7	Constructing Large Abstract Machines (sections 7.2 and 7.3)
Chapter 8	Examples of Abstract Machines
Chapter 11	Refinement (sections 11.1.1, 11.2.1, 11.2.5, 11.2.7 and 11.2.8)
Chapter 12	Constructing Large Software Systems (sections 12.1 and 12.2)
Chapter 13	Examples of Refinement

At the other extreme of the spectrum, you are a *computer scientist* and you are interested in the mathematical foundation of the method. In that case, you might be reading the book as follows:

Appendix A	Summary of Notations
Chapter 1	Mathematical Reasoning
Chapter 2	Set Notation
Chapter 3	Mathematical Objects
Chapter 6	Theory of Abstract Machines
Chapter 9	Sequencing and Loops
Chapter 11	Refinement
Appendix C	Definitions
Appendix E	Rules and Axioms

In between, there might be people interested in looking at how the method can be used in order to *structure large specifications and large designs.* The following reading can then be recommended:

Appendix A	Summary of Notations
Chapter 4	Introduction to Abstract Machines
Chapter 6	Theory of Abstract Machines
Chapter 7	Constructing Large Abstract Machines

Chapter 11	Refinement
Chapter 12	Constructing Large Software Systems
Chapter 13	Examples of Refinement

People interested in *developing small programs* in a systematic fashion can read the book as follows:

Appendix A	Summary of Notations
Chapter 4	Introduction to Abstract Machines
Chapter 10	Programming Examples

For people interested in the *formal details of the notations*, it is recommended to read the book as follows:

Chapter 5	Formal Definition of Abstract Machines
Chapter 7	Constructing Large Abstract Machines (section 7.4)
Chapter 11	Refinement (section 11.3)
Chapter 12	Constructing Large Software Systems (section 12.6)
Appendix D	Visibility Rules
Appendix F	Proof Obligations

Contents

Mathematics

CHAPTER 1

Mathematical Reasoning

WHEN doing mathematics, people *prove* assertions. This is accomplished with the implicit or explicit help of some *rules of reasoning* admitted, for quite a long time, to be *the* correct rules of reasoning. Our goal, in this chapter, is to make absolutely precise what such rules are, so that, in principle, if not in practice, the activity of proving could be made *checkable* by a robot.

The reason why we insist, in this first chapter, on the very precise definition of what mathematical reasoning is, must be clear. Our eventual aim is to have a significant part of software systems constructed in a way that is guaranteed by proofs. Most of the time such proofs are, mathematically speaking, not very deep; however, there will be many of them. Hence, it will be quite easy to introduce errors in doing them, in very much the same way as people introduce errors in writing programs. There is, clearly, no gain in just shifting the production of errors from programs to proofs. Fortunately, however, there exists an important distinction between programs and proofs. Both are formal texts, but, provided the foundation for proofs is sufficiently elaborate (hence this chapter), then proofs can *always* be checked mechanically for correctness, whereas programs cannot.

This chapter is organized as follows. In the first section, we introduce the way mathematical conjectures are presented and the way such conjectures can be eventually proved. This is done independently of any precise mathematical domain. In the second section, we introduce elementary reasonings known to form what is usually called *Propositional Calculus*. In the third section, we introduce more elaborate reasonings known to form what is usually called *First Order Predicate Calculus*. The next two sections are concerned with *Equality* and with *Ordered Pairs*. The last section contains some exercises.

The presentation of this chapter is certainly influenced by, although not directly connected to, the way Bourbaki introduces similar topics in the first of his encyclopedic treatises. An important influence is also that of the "natural deduction" school as introduced by Gentzen.

1.1. Formal Reasoning

In this section our intention is to make clear the implicit rules we apply when doing a mathematical proof, be it formal or informal. The rules we shall introduce are totally independent of the precise mathematical domain we are working with.

1.1.1. Sequent and Predicate

A conjecture, say P, that you wish to prove, is very rarely given to you in the absolute. Most of the time, what is to be proved depends on a certain number of *hypotheses*, HYP, (also called premisses or assumptions) which one may assume in the course of the proof of P. The conjecture (also called the *goal*) P is then said to be proved *under* the hypotheses HYP. It is also said that the hypotheses HYP *entail* the *conclusion* P. This is represented formally as follows:

$$\text{HYP} \vdash P$$

Such a formal statement is called a *sequent*. In this sequent, each of the hypotheses of the collection HYP, as well as the conjecture P, is a formula, that is called a *Predicate*. In other words, a predicate is a formal statement expressing a certain property that we may assume, or a certain property that we wish to prove. We do not know yet how to write such predicates. Further on in this chapter and in subsequent chapters, we shall build, little by little, a formal *Predicate Language* allowing us to express mathematical statements with a very rich expressive power. All we need for the moment is a simple means to denote predicates in an abstract way. For this we shall simply use upper case letters, such as P, Q, etc. Such letters denote (stand for) any predicate whatsoever. Notice that such letters do not belong to our predicate language, they only give us the possibility to speak of predicates: for this reason, they are called *meta-linguistic* variables.

For example, and anticipating the possibility of using our future predicate language to express arithmetical properties, let us suppose that 8 is greater than 5 (this is the unique hypothesis), then you might be asked to prove that 8 is positive (this is the conclusion). Formally, we have thus the following sequent S to prove:

$$8 > 5 \vdash 8 > 0$$

In this example, we have only one hypothesis. More generally, we can have a (finite) number of such hypotheses, separated by commas, and situated on the left-hand side of the "$\vdash$" symbol, as in the example that follows:

$$8 > 5, \quad 5 > 0 \vdash 8 > 0$$

As a special case, we might also have no hypotheses at all. In that case, we still use the "$\vdash$" symbol with nothing on its left, as in the following sequent:

$$\vdash \quad 5 > 0$$

1.1.2. Rule of Inference

For conducting the proof of a sequent, people, most of the time implicitly, use rules relating (the proof of) certain sequents to each other. Such rules, called *inference* rules, are formally written as follows, where $\Sigma_1, \ldots, \Sigma_n$ and Σ are all supposed to be sequents (that is formal statements of the form $\mathsf{HYP} \vdash P$):

$$\Sigma_1$$
$$\vdots$$
$$\Sigma_n$$
$$\overline{}$$
$$\Sigma$$

The sequents $\Sigma_1, \ldots, \Sigma_n$ are said to be the *antecedents* of the rule, whereas the sequent Σ is said to be the *consequent*. Such a rule can be read as follows: the individual and independent proofs of the sequents $\Sigma_1, \ldots, \Sigma_n$ entitle you to claim that you now have a proof of Σ. In other words, the proof of the consequent can be *derived* from (is a consequence of, or follows from) the proofs of the antecedents of the rule. Alternatively, that rule can be read as follows: the proof of Σ can be *reduced* to the proofs of $\Sigma_1, \ldots, \Sigma_n$. In other words, in order to prove the consequent, it suffices to prove the antecedents. The horizontal bar situated between $\Sigma_1, \ldots, \Sigma_n$ and Σ can thus be understood as a "derivation" symbol or as a "reduction" symbol. This depends on the way one is using the rule. The "derivation" symbol induces a so-called *forward* use of the rule, whereas the "reduction" symbol induces a so-called *backward* use. For instance, we might have been given the following rule:

$$\vdash \ 5 > 0$$
$$8 > 5, \ 5 > 0 \ \vdash \ 8 > 0$$
$$\overline{}$$
$$8 > 5 \ \vdash \ 8 > 0$$

If we choose the backward interpretation, then the proof of our sequent S, that is

$$8 > 5 \ \vdash \ 8 > 0$$

will be established as soon as we have a proof of the two antecedents of that rule. Notice that it is quite possible (and even indispensable) to have inference rules with no antecedents: this simply means that the corresponding consequents of such rules are proved without further work. Such a special rule is called an *axiom*. In that case, we still have an horizontal bar: this is to make a clear distinction between a simple sequent (for which we might have no proof yet) and an axiom (whose proof is "given"). For instance, we might have the following axiom:

$$\overline{}$$
$$\vdash \ 5 > 0$$

We might also have the following axiom, which, together with the previous one, allows us to complete the proof of our original sequent S :

$$
\begin{array}{c}
\hline
8 > 5, \; 5 > 0 \;\vdash\; 8 > 0
\end{array}
$$

1.1.3. Proofs

In the previous section, we have explained, by a short example, how one might perform a very simple proof, from a number of rules of inference. Our intention, in this section, is to make this notion of proof a little more precise.

Proof of a Sequent

Once you have at your disposal a certain collection of inference rules, as described in the previous section, the formal proof of a certain sequent S can then be done in a very systematic fashion. You look for a rule in the collection, with a consequent that is identical to the sequent to prove, and you apply the selected rule in backward mode, yielding a number of new sequents to prove. You then resume the previous step for each new sequent you have obtained, and so on. The process stops at some point when each of the remaining sequents to prove is the consequent of a rule with no antecedent, in other words when the remaining sequents are all axioms of your collection of rules of inference.

Once proved, a sequent is said to be a *theorem*. It can be added to the collection of rules of inference as if it were an axiom. As you can see, the proof of a sequent is always done *relative* to a certain collection of inference rules.

Proof of a Rule of Inference

As a slight generalization of the proof of a sequent, it is also possible to envisage proving an inference rule. Given a collection of rules of inference, the proof of a new rule of inference R consists (1) in adjoining the antecedents of R, as new axioms, to the given collection of rules of inference, and (2) in proving the consequent of R relative to that extended collection, as we have explained in the previous section.

Once proved, a rule of inference is said to be a *derived* rule. It can be added to the original collection of rules of inference.

1.1.4. Basic Rules

In section 1.1.2, and for the sake of our example, we have suggested some trivial rules of inference that depended on a particular domain of mathematics: arithmetic. We might wonder whether there exists some more basic rules of inference, supposed to be completely independent of any particular domain of mathematics. Such rules would formalize the very essence of proving a sequent, that is proving a conjecture under a certain number of hypotheses. In this section, we present four such basic rules of inference.

Our first basic rule of inference (which is in fact an axiom) formalizes the notion of entailment. Given any predicate P denoting a certain conjecture in some domain of mathematics, the rule says that you can always derive the sequent expressing the fact that P is provable under the assumption P itself. A very tautological fact about the notion of assumption: assuming P gives you "automatically" a proof of P. Here is the rule:

$$P \vdash P$$

Our second basic rule of inference has to do with the monotonicity of proofs with regard to hypotheses. That is, once you have got a proof of a certain sequent S, then you "automatically" have proofs of all the sequents obtained by adding more hypotheses to S, while keeping its conclusion. In other words, and quite naturally, the addition of extra hypotheses to a sequent does not destroy the proof you may have already obtained for that sequent: the new hypotheses only play *passive* rôles in the new proofs. Formally, this can be written as follows:

$$\frac{\text{HYP} \vdash P \qquad \text{HYP is included in HYP'}}{\text{HYP'} \vdash P}$$

The above rule does not correspond exactly to the general framework we have given previously for a rule of inference: clearly, the second antecedent is not a sequent. The non-formal statement "HYP is included in HYP' " bears its obvious natural meaning: each individual assumption in HYP is also an individual assumption in HYP'. We use this informal "abuse of language" as a technicality: the previous "rule" stands, in fact, for an infinite number of ad-hoc rules that would correspond to the various ways one can add more hypotheses to a given sequent.

Sometimes, people object to the above rule by saying that if HYP' contains new hypotheses that are *contradictory* with some of the hypotheses of the original collection HYP then the previous rule might be faulty. Of course, at this point we cannot give a proper answer to that remark because we do not know yet what "contradictory" means. At this stage, the answer to that objection is the following: in this book, we shall place ourselves in a logical framework such that a contradictory collection of hypotheses entails *any* conclusion. Thus the potential contradictory hypotheses of HYP' will certainly not make P suddenly unproved. This question will be definitively settled at the end of section 1.2.2.

From the two previous rules, it is easy to deduce the following rule, which may be convenient. Again, the unique antecedent of that rule is not a sequent. It bears its natural meaning: the predicate P is one of the hypotheses of the collection HYP.

$$
\begin{array}{c}
P \quad \text{occurs in} \quad \text{HYP} \\
\hline
\text{HYP} \;\vdash\; P
\end{array}
$$

This rule follows from the first two rules since, obviously, the collection of hypotheses with the single hypothesis P is included in the collection HYP, supposed to contain P as a particular hypothesis.

Our fourth basic rule of inference has to do with the fact that once a sequent of the form HYP $\vdash P$ has been proved, then the conclusion P of that sequent can be used as an extra assumption in another sequent of the form HYP, $P \vdash Q$. This entitles you to claim that you now have a proof of the sequent HYP $\vdash Q$. Here is the correponding rule:

$$
\begin{array}{c}
\text{HYP} \;\vdash\; P \\
\text{HYP}, P \;\vdash\; Q \\
\hline
\text{HYP} \;\vdash\; Q
\end{array}
$$

This rule is normally used in a backward way. It says that, in order to prove Q under the collection of hypotheses HYP, it is sufficient to prove the same Q under HYP, enlarged with a new hypothesis P. This is valid, of course, provided you also have a proof of P under HYP. In practice, one has to guess the new hypothesis P. Provided you have made a good choice for P, then the proof of Q under HYP, enlarged with P, might be easier to do than that of Q under HYP alone. Also the additional proof of P under HYP might be a proof you have already established, or alternatively, it might be a "well-known" fact (an axiom).

In order to present our basic rules in a more synthetic fashion, we put them together in a table as follows:

	Antecedents	Consequent
BR 1		$P \vdash P$
BR 2	$\begin{cases} \text{HYP} \vdash P \\ \\ \text{HYP is included in HYP'} \end{cases}$	$\text{HYP'} \vdash P$
BR 3	P occurs in HYP	$\text{HYP} \vdash P$
BR 4	$\begin{cases} \text{HYP} \vdash P \\ \\ \text{HYP}, P \vdash Q \end{cases}$	$\text{HYP} \vdash Q$

The antecedents of each basic rule (BR) are grouped in the Antecedents box, whereas the consequent is put in the Consequent box. From now on, we shall always present our rules in tables like the above.

So far, we have made only slight allusions to the "mathematical notation" we intend to use throughout this book. In what follows, our intention is to build that language, *incrementally*, in a very systematic fashion.

1.2. Propositional Calculus

Our first attempt at building our mathematical notation consists in defining the syntax of the basic *Predicates* necessary to express elementary logical statements. Then we shall define the few rules of inference allowing us to conduct proofs on these elementary predicates.

1.2.1. The Notation of Elementary Assertions

Elementary predicates introduce the notion of *conjunction*, *implication*, and *negation*. Syntactically, our notation is thus defined (for the moment) as follows:

Syntactic Category	Definition
Predicate	*Predicate* $\wedge$ *Predicate* *Predicate* $\Rightarrow$ *Predicate* $\neg$ *Predicate*

The original notation only contains three logical operators called *conjunction* ($\wedge$), *implication* ($\Rightarrow$), and *negation* ($\neg$). The precise meaning of these operators will be given in the next section, where we shall present the various rules of inference allowing us to prove predicates containing them.

The syntax presented in the previous table is clearly *ambiguous*. For instance, a predicate such as:

$$P \wedge Q \Rightarrow R$$

can be parsed as follows:

$$(P \wedge Q) \Rightarrow R$$

or as follows:

$$P \wedge (Q \Rightarrow R)$$

As usual, the use of pairs of parentheses is allowed in order to disambiguate the parsing of such formulae. Thus parentheses are not part of our formal language, they simply appear as a technicality that can be used freely to disambiguate ambiguous formulae. In the absence of parentheses, however, the binary operators *associate to the left*. This means that a predicate such as:

$$P \wedge Q \wedge R$$

is implicitly parsed as follows:

$$(P \wedge Q) \wedge R$$

As a means of further simplification, we suppose, moreover, that operator $\neg$ has priority over operator $\wedge$ which, itself, has priority over operator $\Rightarrow$. The relative priority of our operators is thus the following, in decreasing order, from left to right:

$$\neg \qquad \wedge \qquad \Rightarrow$$

We remind the reader that, when an operator has a greater priority than another one, the former *attracts* its surrounding formulae more strongly than the latter. For instance, in our case, a *Predicate* such as:

$$P \wedge \neg Q \Rightarrow \neg Q \wedge P$$

is parsed as follows:

$$(P \wedge (\neg Q)) \quad \Rightarrow \quad ((\neg Q) \wedge P)$$

because the priority of $\neg$ is greater than that of $\wedge$ which, itself, has a priority greater than that of $\Rightarrow$.

Our syntax has no base: that is, we have no *given* predicates. This is simply because none are needed *for the moment*, as our present goal is only to formalize the way some general (schematic) mathematical reasonings are performed. But we might wonder, then, whether one can write any predicate at all. For instance, are we allowed to write a predicate such as $P \wedge Q \Rightarrow P$ since in that predicate the letters P and Q do not correspond to any alternative of the syntactic category *Predicate* in our syntax? The answer, again, is that, in such a predicate, the letters P and Q are (meta-linguistic) variables standing for any *Predicate*. This will allow us to develop a so called *schematic* logic. Of course, any mathematical development containing such meta-linguistic variables must be preceded by an informal statement claiming that they stand for (are) *Predicates*: "Let P and Q be two *Predicates*, then ...". I am afraid we shall not do so systematically, however, since it might become a bit heavy.

1.2.2. Inference Rules for Propositional Calculus

Together with the previous logical notation, a number of *rules of inference* are given which allow us to conduct proofs. There are two rules per logical operator. Next are the rules for conjunction and for implication where P and Q are two *Predicates*. These rules are symmetric:

	Antecedents	Consequent
Rule 1	$\left\{\begin{array}{l} \text{HYP} \vdash P \\ \\ \text{HYP} \vdash Q \end{array}\right.$	$\text{HYP} \vdash P \wedge Q$

Rule 1 is called the $\wedge$-introduction rule (for short CNJ). Usually Rule 1 is applied in a backward way since it has the effect of *splitting* a goal of the form $P \wedge Q$ into two *simpler* goals P and Q while keeping the same hypotheses.

	Antecedents	Consequent
Rule 2 Rule 2'	$\text{HYP} \vdash P \wedge Q$	$\left\{\begin{array}{l} \text{HYP} \vdash P \\ \\ \text{HYP} \vdash Q \end{array}\right.$

Rule 2 and Rule 2' are called the ∧-elimination rules. Usually such rules are applied in a forward way. For instance, when a new hypothesis of the form $P \wedge Q$ is added to the already present hypotheses, then, applying BR 2 (end of section 1.1.4) has the effect of deriving $P \wedge Q$, from which P and Q can be derived by applying Rule 2 and Rule 2'. Conversely, $P \wedge Q$ can be derived from P and Q by applying Rule 1. As a consequence, introducing the hypothesis $P \wedge Q$ has the same effect as introducing the two separate hypotheses P and Q in turn.

	Antecedents	Consequent
Rule 3	HYP, $P \vdash Q$	HYP $\vdash P \Rightarrow Q$
Rule 4	HYP $\vdash P \Rightarrow Q$	HYP, $P \vdash Q$

Rule 3 is called the deduction rule (for short DED). Usually, Rule 3 is applied in a backward way since it has the effect of *cutting* a goal of the form $P \Rightarrow Q$ into the simpler goal Q while expanding the collection of hypotheses with P.

Rule 4 is seldom used on its own. Rather, it is used together with the basic rule BR 4 (end of section 1.1.4), yielding the following *derived* rule, called MP (for Modus Ponens):

	Antecedents	Consequent
MP	$\begin{cases} \text{HYP} \vdash P \\ \text{HYP} \vdash P \Rightarrow Q \end{cases}$	HYP $\vdash Q$

Starting from the two antecedents of MP, one can derive the two antecedents of BR 4 by using Rule 4. One can then deduce the consequent of MP by using BR 4. We have thus just shown how MP is derivable from Rule 4 and BR 4. Notice that, by writing MP in the more traditional (vertical) way:

$$\frac{\begin{array}{c} \text{HYP} \vdash P \\ \text{HYP} \vdash P \Rightarrow Q \end{array}}{\text{HYP} \vdash Q}$$

we can observe, within the same rule, the three linguistic levels of "deduction". The horizontal bar denotes the possible derivation of a consequent from some antecedents. The "⊢" symbol denotes the entailment from a collection of hypotheses to some conclusion. Finally, the "⇒" symbols denotes the implication between two predicates.

Next are the two rules for dealing with negation:

	Antecedents	Consequent
Rule 5	$\begin{cases} \text{HYP}, \neg Q \vdash P \\[2mm] \text{HYP}, \neg Q \vdash \neg P \end{cases}$	$\text{HYP} \vdash Q$
Rule 6	$\begin{cases} \text{HYP}, Q \vdash P \\[2mm] \text{HYP}, Q \vdash \neg P \end{cases}$	$\text{HYP} \vdash \neg Q$

Rule 5 and Rule 6 are called the "reductio ad absurdum" rules (or contradiction rules). These rules are used in backward mode. For instance, Rule 5 can be applied when you have a certain goal Q and you have already proved a certain predicate P under $\neg Q$ (or, more simply, when P is a hypothesis). You can then replace your original goal Q by the new goal $\neg P$ to be proved under the new hypothesis $\neg Q$. If you succeed in proving $\neg P$ under $\neg Q$, then it is said that you have *contradicted* P: this is precisely what entitles you, according to Rule 5, to claim that you now have a proof of Q.

We are now in a position to formally define what is called a collection of contradictory hypotheses and to analyze the consequence of such a definition. A collection HYP of hypotheses is said to be contradictory if the following two sequents are provable, for some predicate P:

$$\text{HYP} \vdash P$$

$$\text{HYP} \vdash \neg P$$

Thus by applying BR 2 (end of section 1.1.4), we also have, for any predicate Q:

$$\text{HYP}, \neg Q \vdash P$$

$$\text{HYP}, \neg Q \vdash \neg P$$

$$\text{HYP}, Q \vdash P$$

$$\text{HYP}, Q \vdash \neg P$$

By applying then respectively Rule 5 and Rule 6, we can prove:

$$\text{HYP} \vdash Q$$

$$\text{HYP} \vdash \neg Q$$

In other words, under contradictory hypotheses, you can prove any predicate Q as well as its negation. The "miraculous" world of contradiction, where you can prove anything, is coherent: it always remains contradictory.

1.2.3. Some Proofs

In this section our intention is to present the proofs of some theorems, the use of which will make it possible later to completely mechanize (in section 1.2.4) the simple reasoning presented so far. All such theorems have the general form:

$$\text{HYP} \vdash P \Rightarrow Q$$

where the collection HYP of hypotheses is, a priori, *completely independent* of the two predicates P and Q (so that, for the sake of simplicity, we shall not mention the collection HYP in the forthcoming statement of these theorems). Theorems of this form are very interesting because they can be transformed into derived inference rules of the following form by applying MP in a forward way:

Antecedents	Consequent
$\text{HYP} \vdash P$	$\text{HYP} \vdash Q$

Our first three theorems (once transformed into inference rules) show how a goal of the form $\neg Y$ can be replaced by one (or two) simpler goal(s) X, so that the resulting theorems are all of the form $X \Rightarrow \neg Y$. Because of our syntax, $\neg Y$ can only take one of the three possible forms: $\neg \neg P$, $\neg (P \Rightarrow Q)$, and $\neg (P \wedge Q)$. Here are the statements of the first three theorems:

P	$\Rightarrow$	$\neg \neg P$
$P \wedge \neg Q$	$\Rightarrow$	$\neg (P \Rightarrow Q)$
$(P \Rightarrow \neg Q)$	$\Rightarrow$	$\neg (P \wedge Q)$

Our next three theorems (once transformed into inference rules) show how a goal of the form $\neg Y \Rightarrow R$ can be replaced by one (or two) simpler goal(s) X, so that the resulting theorems are all of the form $X \Rightarrow (\neg Y \Rightarrow R)$. Because of our syntax, $\neg Y$ can only take, again, one of the three possible forms: $\neg \neg P$, $\neg (P \Rightarrow Q)$, and $\neg (P \wedge Q)$. Here are the statements of the next three theorems:

$$(P \;\Rightarrow\; R) \qquad\qquad\qquad \Rightarrow \quad (\neg\neg P \;\Rightarrow\; R)$$

$$(P \;\Rightarrow\; (\neg Q \;\Rightarrow\; R)) \qquad\qquad \Rightarrow \quad (\neg(P \;\Rightarrow\; Q) \;\Rightarrow\; R)$$

$$(\neg P \;\Rightarrow\; R) \wedge (\neg Q \;\Rightarrow\; R) \quad \Rightarrow \quad (\neg(P \wedge Q) \;\Rightarrow\; R)$$

Our final two theorems (once transformed into inference rules) show how a goal of the form $Y \;\Rightarrow\; R$ (where Y is not in negated form) can be replaced by one (or two) simpler goal(s) X, so that the resulting theorems are all of the form $X \;\Rightarrow\; (Y \;\Rightarrow\; R)$. Because of our syntax, the only possible forms for Y are $P \;\Rightarrow\; Q$ and $P \wedge Q$. Here are the statements of the last two theorems:

$$(\neg P \;\Rightarrow\; R) \wedge (Q \;\Rightarrow\; R) \quad \Rightarrow \quad ((P \;\Rightarrow\; Q) \;\Rightarrow\; R)$$

$$(P \;\Rightarrow\; (Q \;\Rightarrow\; R)) \qquad\qquad \Rightarrow \quad (P \wedge Q \;\Rightarrow\; R)$$

We now prove our eight theorems in turn. This will be done in a way which will be less and less formal as we proceed. The idea is to adopt, little by little, certain conventions, so that the proof text becomes more concise (thus more readable) but still remains fully convincing.

HYP $\vdash$ $P \;\Rightarrow\; \neg\neg P$ Theorem 1.2.1

Proof

We have to prove the following sequent:

HYP $\vdash$ $P \;\Rightarrow\; \neg\neg P$ Sequent 1

By applying DED (Rule 3) in a backward way to Sequent 1, it is sufficient to prove:

HYP, P $\vdash$ $\neg\neg P$ Sequent 2

The form of Sequent 2 suggests doing a proof by contradiction by applying Rule 6 in a backward way, so that we have to prove, in turn, the following two sequents, for a predicate X to be discovered:

HYP, P, $\neg P$ $\vdash$ X

HYP, P, $\neg P$ $\vdash$ $\neg X$

Clearly, we can take P for X, since we obviously have the following according to BR 3:

HYP, P, $\neg P$ $\vdash$ P Sequent 3

$$\text{HYP, } P, \ \neg P \ \vdash \ \neg P \qquad\qquad \text{Sequent 4}$$

End of Proof

As you can see, we have adopted a style where informal English texts are mixed with labelled formal statements, which are all sequents. Although the previous text is, we think, convincing as a proof, our opinion is that it is too heavy. For instance, each sequent but the first starts with "HYP, *P*". This is boring to write and also boring to read. In more elaborate proofs, the recurrent writing of such hypotheses might be so heavy that it would completely hide the very difference between two successive sequents. So, in order to lighten the proof text, we might (1) *forget* mentioning HYP, which is thus always implicit, and (2) *factorize the hypotheses*, from the place they are generated by the backward application of some rule. Of course, such a factorization has only a *limited lifetime* corresponding to that of the proof of the corresponding conclusion. Next is a second presentation of the previous proof, according to this new style:

$$\text{HYP} \ \vdash \ P \ \Rightarrow \ \neg\neg P \qquad\qquad \text{Theorem 1.2.1}$$

Proof

We have to prove:

$$P \ \Rightarrow \ \neg\neg P \qquad\qquad \text{Goal 1}$$

By applying DED (Rule 3) in a backward way to Goal 1, we may assume:

$$P \qquad\qquad \text{Hypothesis 1}$$

and then replace Goal 1 by:

$$\neg\neg P \qquad\qquad \text{Goal 2}$$

The form of this new goal suggests doing a proof by contradiction by applying Rule 6 in a backward way, so that we assume:

$$\neg P \qquad\qquad \text{Hypothesis 2}$$

and we have to prove in turn X and then $\neg X$ for some predicate X to be discovered. We can take P for X since, from Hypothesis 1 and by applying BR 3, we derive:

$$P \qquad\qquad \text{Derivation 1}$$

and since, from Hypothesis 2 and by applying BR 3 again, we derive:

$$\neg P \qquad\qquad \text{Derivation 2}$$

End of Proof

Here, again, we have a style where informal English texts are mixed with labelled formal statements. Each of the latter is recorded as a numbered Hypothesis, Goal, or Derivation. A Goal can generate other Goals by applying some rule of inference *in a backward way* and, of course, with the help of some Hypothesis or Derivation.

Likewise, a Derivation can be generated by applying some inference rule *in a forward way* and, of course, with the help of some Hypothesis or Derivation. In fact, as soon as it is generated, a Derivation can be considered a genuine hypothesis (we could thus have called it a Derived Hypothesis). It is, of course, justified by rule BR 4 (section 1.1.4) which says, precisely, that once a predicate is proved under some hypotheses, then that very predicate can be added to the hypotheses in question. Note that in the proposed new style, where hypotheses are factorized, the "lifetime" of a Derivation is, of course, the same as that of the hypotheses that have been used to prove it.

When a Goal meets (is the same as) a Hypothesis or a Derivation, it is said to be *discharged* by it (this is an application of rule BR 3). A Goal can be generated together with a certain corresponding Hypothesis when applying Rule 3, Rule 5, or Rule 6. When that Goal is eventually discharged, the corresponding Hypothesis has, of course, to be discarded together, again, with the various Derivations that could have been generated from it. In the proof text, we have not tried to enforce this practice through indentations or through a structured numbering scheme.

Next are a few conventions that we propose to adopt in what follows in order to lighten the proof text even more.

From now on, when our goal has the form $P \Rightarrow Q$, we shall no longer mention explicitly that we apply DED (Rule 3) in a backward way; we shall instead directly assume the new hypothesis P and generate the new goal Q.

Also, when doing a proof by contradiction by applying Rule 5 or Rule 6, we shall no longer claim that we are going to prove in turn X and $\neg X$ for some predicate X "to be discovered". We shall try, instead, to prove a certain predicate Q, provided $\neg Q$ is a hypothesis or a derivation. Alternatively, we shall try to prove $\neg Q$, provided Q is a hypothesis or a derivation. In the proof text, we shall simply say that our new goal is an attempt at *contradicting* a certain hypothesis or derivation.

Finally, we shall no longer mention the use of BR 3 when this is obvious. We shall instead mention directly the hypothesis concerned.

$(P \wedge \neg Q) \quad \Rightarrow \quad \neg (P \Rightarrow Q)$ Theorem 1.2.2

Proof

We assume

$$P \wedge \neg Q \qquad\qquad \text{Hypothesis 1}$$

and we have to prove

$$\neg (P \Rightarrow Q) \hspace{6cm} \text{Goal 1}$$

From Hypothesis 1, and by applying Rule 2 and Rule 2' in a forward way, we can derive in turn

$$P \hspace{7cm} \text{Derivation 1}$$

$$\neg Q \hspace{6.8cm} \text{Derivation 2}$$

The form of Goal 1 suggests doing a proof by contradiction by applying Rule 6, so that we assume

$$P \Rightarrow Q \hspace{6.2cm} \text{Hypothesis 3}$$

and we try to contradict $\neg Q$ (Derivation 2), which is easy, since from Derivation 1 and Hypothesis 3 and by applying MP we can derive Q, which indeed contradicts Derivation 2.
End of Proof

From now on, when we are about to generate a hypothesis of the form $P \wedge Q$, we shall no longer mention the use of Rule 2 and Rule 2', as we have done in the previous proof text. Instead, we shall generate directly the two separate hypotheses P and Q. Notice that, if $P \wedge Q$ is still needed, it can always be derived by subsequently applying Rule 1 in a forward way.

$$(P \Rightarrow \neg Q) \Rightarrow \neg (P \wedge Q) \hspace{4cm} \text{Theorem 1.2.3}$$

Proof

We assume the following:

$$P \Rightarrow \neg Q \hspace{6cm} \text{Hypothesis 1}$$

and we have to prove

$$\neg (P \wedge Q) \hspace{6cm} \text{Goal 1}$$

The form of this goal suggests doing a proof by contradiction by applying Rule 6, so that we assume $P \wedge Q$, that is both

$$P \hspace{7cm} \text{Hypothesis 2}$$

$$Q \hspace{7cm} \text{Hypothesis 3}$$

and we try to contradict Q (Hypothesis 3) which is easy, since from Hypothesis 2 and Hypothesis 1 and by applying MP we can derive $\neg Q$, which indeed contradicts Hypothesis 3.
End of Proof

$(P \Rightarrow R) \Rightarrow (\neg\neg P \Rightarrow R)$ Theorem 1.2.4

Proof

We assume

$$P \Rightarrow R \qquad \text{Hypothesis 1}$$

and we have to prove

$$\neg\neg P \Rightarrow R \qquad \text{Goal 1}$$

We assume now

$$\neg\neg P \qquad \text{Hypothesis 2}$$

and we have to prove

$$R \qquad \text{Goal 2}$$

The form of Hypothesis 1 suggests trying to derive P, since by applying MP we shall then be able to derive R which is exactly Goal 2. Our new goal is then

$$P \qquad \text{Goal 3}$$

In the absence of any better suggestion, we perform a proof by contradiction by applying Rule 5, so that we assume $\neg P$ which, in fact, contradicts Hypothesis 2. **End of Proof**

From now on, when doing a proof by contradiction, we shall no longer mention which of Rule 5 or Rule 6 we are using, since it should be obvious from the goal: if the goal has a negated form, this is Rule 6 and, in the other case, this is Rule 5. We shall just say that we apply the "rule" CTR.

$(P \Rightarrow (\neg Q \Rightarrow R)) \Rightarrow (\neg(P \Rightarrow Q) \Rightarrow R)$ Theorem 1.2.5

Proof

We assume

$$P \Rightarrow (\neg Q \Rightarrow R) \qquad \text{Hypothesis 1}$$

and we have to prove

$$\neg(P \Rightarrow Q) \Rightarrow R \qquad \text{Goal 1}$$

We assume now

$$\neg(P \Rightarrow Q) \qquad \text{Hypothesis 2}$$

and we have to prove

$$R \qquad \text{Goal 2}$$

In the absence of any better suggestion, we apply CTR, so that we assume

$$\neg R \hspace{6cm} \text{Hypothesis 3}$$

and we try to contradict $\neg (P \Rightarrow Q)$ (Hypothesis 2). In other words, our new goal is

$$P \Rightarrow Q \hspace{6cm} \text{Goal 3}$$

We assume

$$P \hspace{6cm} \text{Hypothesis 4}$$

and we have to prove

$$Q \hspace{6cm} \text{Goal 4}$$

In the absence of any better suggestion, we apply CTR, so that we assume

$$\neg Q \hspace{6cm} \text{Hypothesis 5}$$

and we try to contradict $\neg R$ (Hypothesis 3) which is easy since, by applying now MP to Hypothesis 4 and Hypothesis 1, we can derive $\neg Q \Rightarrow R$ which, together with Hypothesis 5 and by applying again MP, allows us to derive R, which indeed contradicts Hypothesis 3.
End of Proof

$$(\neg P \Rightarrow R) \wedge (\neg Q \Rightarrow R) \quad \Rightarrow \quad (\neg (P \wedge Q) \Rightarrow R) \hspace{2cm} \text{Theorem 1.2.6}$$

Proof

We assume

$$\neg P \Rightarrow R \hspace{6cm} \text{Hypothesis 1}$$

$$\neg Q \Rightarrow R \hspace{6cm} \text{Hypothesis 2}$$

and we have to prove

$$\neg (P \wedge Q) \Rightarrow R \hspace{6cm} \text{Goal 1}$$

We assume now

$$\neg (P \wedge Q) \hspace{6cm} \text{Hypothesis 3}$$

and we have to prove

$$R \hspace{6cm} \text{Goal 2}$$

In the absence of any better suggestion, we apply CTR, so that we assume

$$\neg R \hspace{6cm} \text{Hypothesis 4}$$

and we try to contradict $\neg(P \wedge Q)$ (Hypothesis 3). After CNJ (Rule 1), it is sufficient to prove P and Q in turn. In fact, we shall apply CTR to both of them, so that we may assume first

$$\neg P \qquad\qquad \text{Hypothesis 5}$$

which together with Hypothesis 1, and by applying MP, allows us to derive R, which contradicts Hypothesis 4. Likewise, we assume now $\neg Q$, which, together with Hypothesis 2 and by applying MP, allows us to derive R again.
End of Proof

$$(\neg P \implies R) \wedge (Q \implies R) \implies ((P \implies Q) \implies R) \qquad \text{Theorem 1.2.7}$$

Proof

We assume

$$\neg P \implies R \qquad\qquad \text{Hypothesis 1}$$

$$Q \implies R \qquad\qquad \text{Hypothesis 2}$$

and we have to prove

$$(P \implies Q) \implies R \qquad\qquad \text{Goal 1}$$

We assume now

$$P \implies Q \qquad\qquad \text{Hypothesis 3}$$

and we have to prove

$$R \qquad\qquad \text{Goal 2}$$

In the absence of any better suggestion, we apply CTR, so that we assume

$$\neg R \qquad\qquad \text{Hypothesis 4}$$

and we try to contradict $P \implies Q$ (Hypothesis 3). In view of Theorem 1.2.2, which says that, in order to prove $\neg(P \implies Q)$ (the negation of Hypothesis 3), it is sufficient to prove $P \wedge \neg Q$, we then try the following goal:

$$P \wedge \neg Q \qquad\qquad \text{Goal 3}$$

After CNJ it is sufficient to prove P and $\neg Q$ in turn. Both are proved by applying CTR. We first assume $\neg P$, which, together with Hypothesis 1 and by applying MP, allows us to derive R, which contradicts Hypothesis 4. We then assume Q, which, together with Hypothesis 2 and by applying MP, allows us to derive R again, which contradicts Hypothesis 4.
End of Proof

In the proof of the previous theorem, we have used a previously proved theorem. In doing so, we have followed the standard mathematical practice. In principle, however, this could be completely avoided at the price of incorporating the theorem mentioned within our proof. Alternatively, and anticipating what we shall do in the next section, we could have transformed Theorem 1.2.2 into a derived inference rule.

$(P \Rightarrow (Q \Rightarrow R)) \quad \Rightarrow \quad (P \wedge Q \Rightarrow R)$

Theorem 1.2.8

Proof

We assume

$$P \Rightarrow (Q \Rightarrow R)$$

Hypothesis 1

and we have to prove

$$P \wedge Q \Rightarrow R$$

Goal 1

We assume now

$$P$$

Hypothesis 2

$$Q$$

Hypothesis 3

and we have to prove

$$R$$

Goal2

From Hypothesis 2 and Hypothesis 1, and by applying MP, we derive $Q \Rightarrow R$, which, together with Hypothesis 3 and by applying MP, allows us to derive R.
End of Proof

1.2.4. A Proof Procedure

As we have already noticed at the beginning of the previous section, the eight theorems we have just proved can be transformed into equivalent *derived* inference rules because they are all of the general implicative form $P \Rightarrow Q$. This can be done as shown in the following table where it can be seen that at most one rule at a time can be applied in backward mode.

Also noticeable is the fact that, in this table, the Antecedents boxes contain sequents that are "simpler" than those of the Consequent box. This is clearly the case for rules DR 1 and DR 2. In rule DR 3 the negated conjunction is transformed into an implication. In the other rules, which all have consequents of the implicative form $X \Rightarrow R$, the corresponding antecedent(s) are also of the implicative form $Y \Rightarrow R$, but with Y clearly "simpler" than X.

	Antecedents	Consequent
DR 1	HYP $\vdash P$	HYP $\vdash \neg\neg P$
DR 2	$\begin{cases} \text{HYP} \vdash P \\ \text{HYP} \vdash \neg Q \end{cases}$	HYP $\vdash \neg(P \Rightarrow Q)$
DR 3	HYP $\vdash P \Rightarrow \neg Q$	HYP $\vdash \neg(P \wedge Q)$
DR 4	HYP $\vdash P \Rightarrow R$	HYP $\vdash \neg\neg P \Rightarrow R$
DR 5	HYP $\vdash P \Rightarrow (\neg Q \Rightarrow R)$	HYP $\vdash \neg(P \Rightarrow Q) \Rightarrow R$
DR 6	$\begin{cases} \text{HYP} \vdash \neg P \Rightarrow R \\ \text{HYP} \vdash \neg Q \Rightarrow R \end{cases}$	HYP $\vdash \neg(P \wedge Q) \Rightarrow R$
DR 7	$\begin{cases} \text{HYP} \vdash \neg P \Rightarrow R \\ \text{HYP} \vdash Q \Rightarrow R \end{cases}$	HYP $\vdash (P \Rightarrow Q) \Rightarrow R$
DR 8	HYP $\vdash P \Rightarrow (Q \Rightarrow R)$	HYP $\vdash P \wedge Q \Rightarrow R$

By applying these rules (in backward mode) as much as we can, we obtain either a non-implicative simple goal (made up of a single predicate variable or of its negation) or a goal of an implicative form whose left-hand side reduces to a single predicate variable or to its negation. In the latter case, *and only when it cannot be further simplified*, the left-hand side in question can be transformed into a hypothesis by applying DED and then the reduction process can be resumed on the right-hand side, and so on. In the former case, where the goal reduces to a non-implicative form, either the goal is already a hypothesis and we are done, or the collection of hypotheses is contradictory, or finally nothing else can be done, in which case the proof fails.

The fact that the hypotheses are potentially contradictory can be determined *as early as possible* since hypotheses are entered one at a time. We thus propose to simplify the way we can apply Rule 5 and Rule 6, the "reductio ad absurdum" rules. Let us suppose that we have a situation with a sequent of the form:

$$\text{HYP} \vdash P \Rightarrow R$$

We also suppose that $\neg P$ occurs in HYP. We can then apply DED, in backward mode, to the previous sequent, thus getting the following:

$$\text{HYP}, P \vdash R$$

Applying then Rule 5, in backward mode, may lead to the following two sequents:

$$\text{HYP}, P, \neg R \vdash P$$

$$\text{HYP}, P, \neg R \vdash \neg P$$

which are, clearly, both discharged using BR 3 since we have assumed that $\neg P$ occurs in HYP. A similar simplification can be conducted with Rule 6. This leads to the following two *derived* bases:

	Antecedents	Consequent
DB 1	P occurs in HYP	$\text{HYP} \vdash \neg P \Rightarrow R$
DB 2	$\neg P$ occurs in HYP	$\text{HYP} \vdash P \Rightarrow R$

Finally, we keep rules CNJ and DED, and we split BR 3 into two obvious rules called BS 1 and BS 2 as follows (BS 1 can be deduced from BR 3 after using DED, and BS 2 is another name for BR 3):

	Antecedents	Consequent
BS 1	R occurs in HYP	$\text{HYP} \vdash P \Rightarrow R$
BS 2	P occurs in HYP	$\text{HYP} \vdash P$

The principle of the proof procedure, mentioned earlier, comes from a systematic use of these rules in the following order and *at each step of the proof*:

$$\text{BS1, BS2, DB1, DB2, DR1, } \ldots \text{, DR8, CNJ, DED}$$

The rule DED is selected when no other rule can be applied. As a consequence, only the most simple predicates (or their negations) are entered as hypotheses. This sequence of rules constitutes the *tactics* of the proof procedure.

As an example of using it, we now prove the following theorem. Here we have reverted to the more mechanistic style with only one kind of formal statement: the sequent. Each sequent is labelled with a structured numbering scheme showing the tree-structured nature of such proofs (and of any proof whatsoever).

$(\neg P \Rightarrow Q) \wedge R \quad \Rightarrow \quad (\neg(P \wedge R) \Rightarrow (Q \wedge R))$ Theorem 1.2.9

Proof

We have the following sequent to prove

$$\vdash (\neg P \Rightarrow Q) \wedge R \quad \Rightarrow \quad (\neg(P \wedge R) \Rightarrow (Q \wedge R)) \qquad \text{sequent 1}$$

sequent 1 can be transformed into the following by DR 8

$$\vdash (\neg P \Rightarrow Q) \Rightarrow (R \Rightarrow (\neg(P \wedge R) \Rightarrow (Q \wedge R))) \qquad \text{sequent 1.1}$$

sequent 1.1 can be transformed into the following two sequents by DR 7

$$\vdash \neg\neg P \Rightarrow (R \Rightarrow (\neg(P \wedge R) \Rightarrow (Q \wedge R))) \qquad \text{sequent 1.1.1}$$

$$\vdash Q \Rightarrow (R \Rightarrow (\neg(P \wedge R) \Rightarrow (Q \wedge R))) \qquad \text{sequent 1.1.2}$$

Applying DR 4 and then DED twice to sequent 1.1.1 leads to

$$P, R \vdash \neg(P \wedge R) \Rightarrow (Q \wedge R) \qquad \text{sequent 1.1.1.1}$$

Applying DR 6 to sequent 1.1.1.1 leads to the following two sequents

$$P, R \vdash \neg P \Rightarrow (Q \wedge R) \qquad \text{sequent 1.1.1.1.1}$$

$$P, R \vdash \neg R \Rightarrow (Q \wedge R) \qquad \text{sequent 1.1.1.1.2}$$

Both previous sequents are discharged according to DB 1. Applying now DED twice to sequent 1.1.2 leads to

$$Q, R \vdash \neg(P \wedge R) \Rightarrow (Q \wedge R) \qquad \text{sequent 1.1.2.1}$$

Applying DR 6 to sequent 1.1.2.1 leads to the following two sequents

$$Q, R \vdash \neg P \Rightarrow (Q \wedge R) \qquad \text{sequent 1.1.2.1.1}$$

$$Q, R \vdash \neg R \Rightarrow (Q \wedge R) \qquad \text{sequent 1.1.2.1.2}$$

sequent 1.1.2.1.2 is discharged according to DB 1. Applying DED and CNJ to sequent 1.1.2.1.1 leads to

$$Q, R, \neg P \vdash Q \qquad\qquad \text{sequent 1.1.2.1.1.1}$$

$$Q, R, \neg P \vdash R \qquad\qquad \text{sequent 1.1.2.1.1.2}$$

which are both discharged according to **BS 2**.
End of Proof

In the above proof, the heaviness of the sequents does not bother us too much as, now, such proofs can be completely mechanized, according to the proof procedure we have presented in this section.

1.2.5. Extending the Notation

The notation is now extended by means of two syntactic rewriting rules introducing the other classical logical operators: *disjunction* ($\vee$) and *equivalence* ($\Leftrightarrow$)

Syntax	Definition
$P \vee Q$	$\neg P \Rightarrow Q$
$P \Leftrightarrow Q$	$(P \Rightarrow Q) \wedge (Q \Rightarrow P)$

The relative priority of all our operators is now assumed to be the following, in decreasing order and from left to right:

$$\neg \qquad\qquad \begin{matrix} \wedge \\ \vee \end{matrix} \qquad\qquad \Rightarrow \qquad\qquad \Leftrightarrow$$

An interesting application of the disjunction operator concerns the possibility of proving by cases. This is based on the following theorem:

$$(P \Rightarrow R) \wedge (Q \Rightarrow R) \wedge (P \vee Q) \;\Rightarrow\; R \qquad\qquad \text{Theorem 1.2.10}$$

The following proof is another example of using the proof procedure of the previous section.

Proof

After applying the above rewriting rule, we obtain the following sequent to prove:

$$(P \Rightarrow R) \wedge (Q \Rightarrow R) \wedge (\neg P \Rightarrow Q) \;\Rightarrow\; R \qquad\qquad \text{sequent 1}$$

Applying DR 8 twice and then DR 7 leads to the two following sequents:

$$\neg P \;\Rightarrow\; ((Q \Rightarrow R) \;\Rightarrow\; ((\neg P \Rightarrow Q) \Rightarrow R)) \qquad \text{sequent 1.1}$$

$$R \;\Rightarrow\; ((Q \Rightarrow R) \;\Rightarrow\; ((\neg P \Rightarrow Q) \Rightarrow R)) \qquad \text{sequent 1.2}$$

sequent 1.2 is discharged after applying DED, DR 7 and then BS 1 twice. Applying DED and DR 7 to sequent 1.1 leads to the two following sequents:

$$\neg P \vdash \neg Q \;\Rightarrow\; ((\neg P \Rightarrow Q) \Rightarrow R) \qquad \text{sequent 1.1.1}$$

$$\neg P \;\vdash\; R \;\Rightarrow\; ((\neg P \Rightarrow Q) \Rightarrow R) \qquad \text{sequent 1.1.2}$$

sequent 1.1.2 is discharged after applying DED and BS 1. Applying DED and DR 7 to sequent 1.1.1 leads to the two following sequents:

$$\neg P, \neg Q \vdash \neg\neg P \Rightarrow R \qquad \text{sequent 1.1.1.1}$$

$$\neg P, \neg Q \vdash Q \Rightarrow R \qquad \text{sequent 1.1.1.2}$$

which are discharged using DB 1 and DB 2 respectively.

End of Proof

This gives rise to the following proof rule which can be applied in a backward way in some proofs. Of course, the difficult bit might be to invent the two "cases" P and Q (sometimes good candidates are simply P and $\neg P$, for some predicate P):

		Antecedents	Consequent
CASE	$\left\{\begin{array}{l} \\ \\ \\ \end{array}\right.$	HYP $\vdash P \vee Q$ HYP, $P \vdash R$ HYP, $Q \vdash R$	HYP $\vdash R$

1.2.6. Some Classical Results

With the help of the proof procedure of section 1.2.4, we can now derive a number of classical results showing many interesting properties:

$P \vee Q \;\Leftrightarrow\; Q \vee P$ $P \wedge Q \;\Leftrightarrow\; Q \wedge P$ $(P \Leftrightarrow Q) \;\Leftrightarrow\; (Q \Leftrightarrow P)$	commutativity
$P \vee Q \vee R \;\Leftrightarrow\; P \vee (Q \vee R)$ $P \wedge Q \wedge R \;\Leftrightarrow\; P \wedge (Q \wedge R)$ $(P \Leftrightarrow Q \Leftrightarrow R) \;\Leftrightarrow\; (P \Leftrightarrow (Q \Leftrightarrow R))$	associativity
$R \wedge (P \vee Q) \;\Leftrightarrow\; (R \wedge P) \vee (R \wedge Q)$ $R \vee (P \wedge Q) \;\Leftrightarrow\; (R \vee P) \wedge (R \vee Q)$ $R \Rightarrow (P \wedge Q) \;\Leftrightarrow\; (R \Rightarrow P) \wedge (R \Rightarrow Q)$	distributivity
$P \vee \neg P$	law of excluded middle
$P \vee P \;\Leftrightarrow\; P$ $P \wedge P \;\Leftrightarrow\; P$	idempotence
$(P \vee Q) \wedge P \;\Leftrightarrow\; P$ $(P \wedge Q) \vee P \;\Leftrightarrow\; P$	absorption
$\neg(P \vee Q) \;\Leftrightarrow\; \neg P \wedge \neg Q$ $\neg(P \wedge Q) \;\Leftrightarrow\; \neg P \vee \neg Q$ $\neg(P \wedge Q) \;\Leftrightarrow\; (P \Rightarrow \neg Q)$ $\neg(P \Rightarrow Q) \;\Leftrightarrow\; P \wedge \neg Q$	de Morgan laws
$(P \Rightarrow Q) \;\Leftrightarrow\; (\neg Q \Rightarrow \neg P)$ $(\neg P \Rightarrow Q) \;\Leftrightarrow\; (\neg Q \Rightarrow P)$ $(P \Rightarrow \neg Q) \;\Leftrightarrow\; (Q \Rightarrow \neg P)$	contraposition
$P \;\Leftrightarrow\; \neg\neg P$	double negation
$(P \Rightarrow Q) \wedge (Q \Rightarrow R) \;\Rightarrow\; (P \Rightarrow R)$	transitivity

$(P \Rightarrow Q)$ $\Rightarrow$ $(P \wedge R \Rightarrow Q \wedge R)$ $(P \Rightarrow Q)$ $\Rightarrow$ $(P \vee R \Rightarrow Q \vee R)$ $(P \Rightarrow Q)$ $\Rightarrow$ $((R \Rightarrow P) \Rightarrow (R \Rightarrow Q))$ $(P \Rightarrow Q)$ $\Rightarrow$ $((Q \Rightarrow R) \Rightarrow (P \Rightarrow R))$ $(P \Rightarrow Q)$ $\Rightarrow$ $(\neg Q \Rightarrow \neg P)$		monotonicity
$(P \Leftrightarrow Q)$ $\Rightarrow$ $(P \wedge R \Leftrightarrow Q \wedge R)$ $(P \Leftrightarrow Q)$ $\Rightarrow$ $(P \vee R \Leftrightarrow Q \vee R)$ $(P \Leftrightarrow Q)$ $\Rightarrow$ $(R \Rightarrow P \Leftrightarrow R \Rightarrow Q)$ $(P \Leftrightarrow Q)$ $\Rightarrow$ $(P \Rightarrow R \Leftrightarrow Q \Rightarrow R)$ $(P \Leftrightarrow Q)$ $\Rightarrow$ $(\neg P \Leftrightarrow \neg Q)$		equivalence

The last series of properties shows that when two predicates have been proved
to be equivalent then replacing one by the other in any predicate preserves
equivalence (this can be proved by induction on the syntactic structure of the
predicate notation). In other words, once proved, an equivalence assertion can
be used operationally as if it were a *rewriting rule*. In what follows we shall feel
free to use these properties in proofs just by naming them.

1.3. Predicate Calculus

1.3.1. The Notation of Quantified Predicates and Substitutions

In this section, we introduce the Predicate Calculus. This is first done by
extending our basic syntax as it was first introduced in section 1.2.1. We now
have two extra syntactic categories: *Expression* and *Variable*. Here is the new
(still temporary) syntax:

Syntactic Category	Definition
Predicate	*Predicate* $\wedge$ *Predicate* *Predicate* $\Rightarrow$ *Predicate* $\neg$ *Predicate* $\forall$ *Variable* $\cdot$ *Predicate* [*Variable* := *Expression*] *Predicate*

Syntactic Category	Definition
Expression	*Variable* *[Variable := Expression] Expression*
Variable	*Identifier*

More on Parsing

In this syntax, the dot binary operator, as it is used in *Predicates* of the form $\forall x \cdot P$ and contrary to the two other binary operators, is supposed to *associate to the right*. Moreover, it has a priority greater than that of the negation operator, so that the eventual priority ordering is now the following:

$$\cdot \qquad \neg \qquad \begin{array}{c} \wedge \\ \vee \end{array} \qquad \Rightarrow \qquad \Leftrightarrow$$

As a consequence a *Predicate* such as the following:

$$\neg \, \forall x \cdot \forall y \cdot P \quad \Rightarrow \quad Q$$

is parsed as follows:

$$\neg (\forall x \cdot (\forall y \cdot P)) \quad \Rightarrow \quad Q$$

Notice that the fact that the dot has the highest priority is an arbitrary choice of ours, a choice that may be different from one author to another.

In a formula such as $[x := E]F$, we may think that we have a *hidden binary operator* situated between $[x := E]$ and F. This operator, although hidden, has a priority which is the *same* as that of the dot. It also associates to the *right* like the dot. For instance, the following predicate:

$$\forall x \cdot [y := E] \, [z := F] \, \forall t \cdot P$$

is parsed as follows:

$$\forall x \cdot ([y := E] \, ([z := F] \, (\forall t \cdot P)))$$

and the predicate:

$$\forall x \cdot \forall z \cdot [y := E]P \quad \Rightarrow \quad Q$$

is parsed as follows:

$$(\forall x \cdot (\forall z \cdot ([y := E]P))) \quad \Rightarrow \quad Q$$

About the Syntax

As can be seen in the above table, we have extended the *Predicate* syntactic category with two more clauses. The first one defines the syntax for *universal quantification* (∀)(section 1.3.2) and the other one introduces a special notation for *substitution* (:=) (section 1.3.4). A second (embryonic for the moment) syntactic category is that of *Expression*, which can be either a simple *Variable* or a *Substituted Expression*. Finally, our last syntactic category, *Variable*, is just defined for the moment to be a simple *Identifier*.

Predicate and Expression

It is important to notice immediately that an *Expression* is quite different in nature from what a *Predicate* is. As we have already seen, a *Predicate* is a formula that is subject to proof. In other words, a *Predicate* is a statement which says things about a certain state of (mathematical) affairs which can be proved rigorously. A *Predicate* does not denote anything: it cannot be evaluated.

On the contrary, there is nothing like the "proof" of an *Expression*. An *Expression* is rather seen as a formula that *denotes a (mathematical) object* such as, say, a set, a relation, a natural number, a sequence, or a tree; as we shall construct in subsequent chapters.

Variable, Universal Quantification and Substitution

A *Variable* is an identifier that denotes an *unknown* object (a *Variable* is thus an *Expression*) and when it occurs in a *Predicate* it makes it a more general statement than just a simple assertion about some constants. For instance, when writing an arithmetical predicate such as the following, which says that, provided n is a natural number (belongs to the set $\mathbb{N}$), then 0 is smaller than or equal to n:

$$n \in \mathbb{N} \quad \Rightarrow \quad 0 \leq n$$

we do not compare the natural number 0 to another specific member of the set $\mathbb{N}$ of natural numbers, we rather compare 0 to an *unknown* natural number n. Quite naturally, the identifier n is said to be a *Variable*.

A statement such as the previous one can be transformed into other statements in two different (and, in a sense, opposite) ways. In both cases the *Variable n* is "removed". The first way consists in *generalizing* the previous predicate by prefixing it with a *universal quantification*. This yields the following:

$$\forall n \cdot (n \in \mathbb{N} \quad \Rightarrow \quad 0 \leq n)$$

This says that whatever the natural number n is, then 0 is smaller than or equal to it. The second way consists in *specializing* the original predicate by prefixing it with the application of a *Substitution*:

$$[n := 3](n \in \mathbb{N} \quad \Rightarrow \quad 0 \leq n)$$

Here it is said that the original property involving n holds when n is replaced by the natural number 3. As you can see, universal quantification and substitution are two complementary features.

1.3.2. Universal Quantification

As we now have the notions of *Variable* and *Expression*, we can introduce the notion of *Quantifier*. Given a *Variable* x and a predicate P, the construct $\forall x \cdot P$ is said to be a *Universally Quantified Predicate*. The *Variable* x is said to be the *Quantified Variable* and the *Predicate P* is the *Scope* of that *Variable* within our quantified predicate. The symbol $\forall$ is the universal quantifier. In section 1.3.8, we shall introduce another quantifier, the existential quantifier $\exists$. Since we have introduced a new form of *Predicate*, we have to explain, through some new rules of inference, how we can assert sequents of the form

$$\mathsf{HYP} \vdash \forall x \cdot P$$

Such a statement is intended to be read "whatever the *Expression* substituted for occurrences of x in P, the corresponding sequent is indeed asserted". From that informal understanding, it must be clear that the particular *Variable* x we are using can be replaced by another *fresh* one, say y, as long as we also replace each occurrence of x in P by y. For that reason, the variable x is said to be a *Dummy Variable* in the formula $\forall x \cdot P$. It is also said to be *non-free* in the formula $\forall x \cdot P$ since there is no point in replacing it by any *Expression*.

1.3.3. Non-freeness

As mentioned in the previous section, the *Variable* x is said to be *non-free* in the predicate $\forall x \cdot P$. This notion of non-freeness is very important when we deal with substitution (next section) since what are substituted are only the *free* occurrences of the *Variables*, the non-free ones being just *dummies* that could have been different.

In this section our intention is first to make precise this notion of non-freeness. Then we shall present the syntactic rules allowing us to express this notion in a formal way.

Definition

A *Variable* is said to have a *free* occurrence in a *Predicate* or in an *Expression* if: (1) it is present in such a formula and (2) it is present in a sub-formula which is not under the scope of a quantifier introducing that same variable as its quantified variable.

Conversely, a *Variable* is said to have *no free* occurrences in a *Predicate* or in an *Expression* if: (1) it is not present in such a formula or (2) it is only present in sub-formulae which are within the scope of some quantifiers introducing that same variable as their quantified variable.

For instance, the variable x has a free occurrence in the following predicate, whereas the variables n and y have no free occurrences:

$$\forall n \cdot (n \in \mathbb{N} \; \Rightarrow \; n > x)$$

This is true for y because it does not appear at all, and for n because it appears only in a formula that is within the scope of a quantifier introducing precisely n as its quantified variable.

Syntactic Rules for Non-freeness

We first present a syntactic notation for non-freeness and then we give the corresponding rules.

Given a *Variable* x and a *Formula* F, the syntactic construct $x \setminus F$ is to be read "*Variable* x is non-free in *Formula* F" (notice that, from now on, the syntactic category *Formula* denotes either that of *Predicate* or that of *Expression*).

The following syntactic rules allow us to mechanically check for non-freeness. We are given two *Variables* x and y, two *Predicates* P and Q, a *Formula* F, and an *Expression* E

	Non-freeness	Condition
NF 1	$x \setminus y$	x and y are distinct
NF 2	$x \setminus (P \wedge Q)$	$x \setminus P$ and $x \setminus Q$
NF 3	$x \setminus (P \Rightarrow Q)$	$x \setminus P$ and $x \setminus Q$
NF 4	$x \setminus \neg P$	$x \setminus P$
NF 5	$x \setminus \forall x \cdot P$	
NF 6	$x \setminus \forall y \cdot P$	$x \setminus y$ and $x \setminus P$
NF 7	$x \setminus [x := E] F$	$x \setminus E$
NF 8	$x \setminus [y := E] F$	$x \setminus y$ and $x \setminus E$ and $x \setminus F$

Rule NF 1, clearly, is the basis of non-freeness as it indicates that variable x is non-free in variable y if x and y are *typographically distinct*. Notice that to say that x and y are typographically distinct is not a tautology since, in fact, x and y are meta-linguistic variables standing for *Variables*. Clearly x and y, as letters, are typographically distinct, but as meta-linguistic variables they can denote *Variables* that are (or are not) typographically distinct. The last four rules convey the intuitive idea we have of non-freeness for quantified predicates and for substituted formulae.

In what follows, we shall use conditions such as $x \setminus F$ in the statement of theorems. These are called *Side Conditions*.

1.3.4. Substitution

In this section, we formally define the notion of substitution. First we present the corresponding notation, then we give some syntactic rewriting rules. Given a *Variable x*, an *Expression E*, and a *Formula F*, we denote by

$$[x := E] F$$

the *Formula* obtained by replacing all *free* occurrences of x in F by E. The syntactic rewriting rules of substitutions are now defined by case. We are given two *Variables x* and y, two *Predicates P* and Q, and an *Expression E*

	Substitution	Definition
SUB 1	$[x := E] x$	E
SUB 2	$[x := E] y$	y if $x \setminus y$
SUB 3	$[x := E] (P \wedge Q)$	$[x := E] P \wedge [x := E] Q$
SUB 4	$[x := E] (P \Rightarrow Q)$	$[x := E] P \Rightarrow [x := E] Q$
SUB 5	$[x := E] \neg P$	$\neg [x := E] P$
SUB 6	$[x := E] \forall x \cdot P$	$\forall x \cdot P$
SUB 7	$[x := E] \forall y \cdot P$	$\forall y \cdot [x := E] P$ if $y \setminus x$ and $y \setminus E$

The first of these rules, clearly, is the basis of substitution, since it states that the result of substituting E for x in x is precisely E. In rule SUB 7, the side condition $y \setminus E$ is very important indeed. Should this condition be missing then the potential free occurrences of y in E would have been *captured* by the quantification $\forall y$. Here is an example of what could happen when the side condition is violated. The following predicate:

$$n \in \mathbb{N} \ \Rightarrow \ \neg \forall m \cdot (m \in \mathbb{N} \ \Rightarrow \ m = n)$$

says that, provided n is a natural number, then it is not the case that each natural number m is equal to it. We have the intuitive idea that this predicate can be proved (since, "clearly", there is more than one natural number). Suppose now that we perform the following substitution:

$$[n := m]\,(n \in \mathbb{N} \;\Rightarrow\; \neg\,\forall m \cdot (m \in \mathbb{N} \;\Rightarrow\; m = n))$$

If we violate the side condition requiring that the quantified variable m is non-free in the right-hand expression of the substitution (this side condition is indeed false since the expression in question is exactly m), we obtain the following which, clearly, no longer holds:

$$m \in \mathbb{N} \;\Rightarrow\; \neg\,\forall m \cdot (m \in \mathbb{N} \;\Rightarrow\; m = m)$$

because it says that provided m is a natural number there is no natural number that is equal to itself. In order to get around this problem in a substitution of the form:

$$[x := E]\,\forall y \cdot P$$

where y would be free in E, it is always possible to perform a *change of variable* consisting: (1) in replacing the quantified variable y by another one, say z, provided, of course, z is non-free in E as well as in P, and (2) in replacing free occurrences of y by z in P. In other words, the previous statement would become equivalently:

$$[x := E]\,\forall z \cdot [y := z]\,P$$

The rules SUB 8 to SUB 11 in the table below are rules that may be derived from the previous ones. This can be done by induction on the structure of our notation. In these rules, x and y are *Variables*, F is a *Formula*, and D and E are *Expressions*.

SUB 8	$[x := x]\,F$	F
SUB 9	$[x := E]\,F$	F if $x \setminus F$
SUB 10	$[y := E]\,[x := y]\,F$	$[x := E]\,F$ if $y \setminus F$
SUB 11	$[x := D]\,[y := E]\,F$	$[y := [x := D]E]\,[x := D]\,F$ if $y \setminus D$

1.3.5. Inference Rules for Predicate Calculus

We now extend our rules of inference, as introduced in section 1.2.2. The two new rules deal with universal quantification and substitution.

	Antecedents	Consequent
Rule 7	$\begin{cases} x \setminus H \quad \text{for each } H \text{ of HYP} \\ \\ \text{HYP} \vdash P \end{cases}$	$\text{HYP} \vdash \forall x \cdot P$
Rule 8	$\text{HYP} \vdash \forall x \cdot P$	$\text{HYP} \vdash [x := E] P$

Rule 7 is called the $\forall$-introduction (or generalization) rule (for short **GEN**). It is mostly used in the backward way since it has the effect of simplifying a universally quantified goal by removing the quantifier. As you may have noticed, the quantified variable x should be non-free in all the hypotheses of the collection of hypotheses HYP. This is because, clearly, for the proof of P under HYP to replace safely that of $\forall x \cdot P$ we do not want to take advantage of any property of x that could be already assumed in HYP (remember, x is just a *dummy* variable in a predicate such as $\forall x \cdot P$). In other words, a proof of $\forall x \cdot P$ can be replaced by a proof of P as long as x is not already *known*. In the case where x is free in some hypotheses of HYP then it is always possible to perform a *change of variable* transforming the goal $\forall x \cdot P$ into the new goal $\forall y \cdot [x := y] P$, provided, of course, y is non-free in P and in all the hypotheses composing HYP.

Rule 8 is called the $\forall$-elimination rule (**ELIM** for short). It is used in forward mode. Clearly, once you have got a proof of $\forall x \cdot P$ then you are entitled to claim that you have a proof of $[x := E] P$, that is a proof of P with all free occurrences of the variable x replaced by *any* expression E. In particular, if you have a hypothesis of the form $\forall x \cdot P$ then you can derive P (that is, $[x := x] P$) by applying Rule 8.

1.3.6. Some Proofs

In this section, as we have already done in section 1.2.3, we shall prove some basic theorems that will help us to mechanize the Predicate Calculus as much as we can. Notice that in this proof we revert to the more verbose style.

$$\forall x \cdot (\neg P \Rightarrow R) \quad \Rightarrow \quad (\neg \forall x \cdot P \Rightarrow R) \quad \text{if } x \setminus R \qquad \text{Theorem 1.3.1}$$

Proof

We have to prove the following:

$$\forall x \cdot (\neg P \Rightarrow R) \quad \Rightarrow \quad (\neg \forall x \cdot P \Rightarrow R) \qquad \text{Goal 1}$$

under the following side condition:

$$x \setminus R \qquad\qquad \text{Side Condition}$$

We assume

$$\forall x \cdot (\neg P \Rightarrow R) \qquad\qquad \text{Hypothesis 1}$$

and we have to prove

$$\neg \forall x \cdot P \Rightarrow R \qquad\qquad \text{Goal 2}$$

We now assume

$$\neg \forall x \cdot P \qquad\qquad \text{Hypothesis 2}$$

and we are left to prove

$$R \qquad\qquad \text{Goal 3}$$

In the absence of any better suggestion, we apply CTR, so that we assume

$$\neg R \qquad\qquad \text{Hypothesis 3}$$

and we try to contradict Hypothesis 2. In other words, our new goal is

$$\forall x \cdot P \qquad\qquad \text{Goal 4}$$

We can check that x is non-free in the pending hypotheses: we have $x \setminus \forall x \cdot (\neg P \Rightarrow R)$ according to NF 5; we have $x \setminus \neg \forall x \cdot P$ according to NF 4 and NF 5; finally, we have $x \setminus \neg R$ according to NF 4 and our assumed Side Condition. As a consequence, we can apply GEN (Rule 7) in a backward way, so that our goal becomes

$$P \qquad\qquad \text{Goal 5}$$

By applying ELIM (Rule 8) in a forward way to Hypothesis 1 we can derive $[x := x](\neg P \Rightarrow R)$, that is according to SUB 8

$$\neg P \Rightarrow R \qquad\qquad \text{Derivation 1}$$

which, by contraposition, is equivalent to

$$\neg R \Rightarrow P \qquad\qquad \text{Derivation 2}$$

which, according to Hypothesis 3 and by applying MP, leads to Goal 5.
End of Proof

In the forthcoming proofs, we shall not always feel obliged to explicitly check formally for the non-freeness conditions (we shall rely on the reader doing the checking mentally). We shall do the same with the substitution rewriting rules. The proof of our second theorem is left to the reader:

$$[x := E]\neg P \Rightarrow \neg \forall x \cdot P \qquad\qquad \text{Theorem 1.3.2}$$

1.3.7. Extending the Proof Procedure

We now extend our collection of *derived* rules, as presented in section 1.2.4. Besides rule GEN, which we keep, we propose the following three rules:

	Antecedents	Consequent
DR 9	$\begin{cases} x \setminus R \\ x \setminus H \quad \text{for each } H \text{ of HYP} \\ \text{HYP} \vdash \neg P \Rightarrow R \end{cases}$	$\text{HYP} \vdash \neg \forall x \cdot P \Rightarrow R$
DR 10	$\text{HYP} \vdash [x := E] \neg P$	$\text{HYP} \vdash \neg \forall x \cdot P$
DR 11	$\begin{cases} \forall x \cdot P \quad \text{occurs in HYP} \\ \text{HYP} \vdash [x := E] P \Rightarrow R \end{cases}$	$\text{HYP} \vdash R$

Rule DR 9 is a direct consequence of Theorem 1.3.1 and GEN. Rule DR 10 is a consequence of Theorem 1.3.2. The third rule, DR 11, is a consequence of ELIM and MP.

By putting together the previous rules with those of section 1.2.4, we obtain a new procedure to be performed with the following *tactics*:

BS1, BS2, DB1, DB2, DR1, ..., DR11, CNJ, DED

As you can see, the use of these derived rules in backward mode has the effect of completely removing the universal quantifier from the goal unless it has a negated form (it is important to notice that the rule DED is still applied when no other rules can be applied). This is done either by applying rules DR 9 or GEN, or by pushing universally quantified predicates into the collection of hypotheses, by applying DED. After this is done, we reach a point where the goal may have a negated universally quantified form and where we may have some universally quantified hypotheses. In order to proceed, we have then to apply DR 10 or DR 11. *This requires some invention*, since we have to provide an expression E, which constitutes the *creative part* of the proof. After applying such rules, we can return to the more mechanistic style, until we again have to apply again DR 10 or DR 11, and so on.

Notice that in rule DR 11, the substitution $[x := E] P$ performed on the universally quantified hypothesis $\forall x \cdot P$ does not immediately result in a new hypothesis. Instead, $[x := E] P$ takes the left-hand place of a new implicative goal whose right-hand place is the previous goal. As a consequence, once the substitution is performed on $[x := E]\,P$, the resulting predicate can be further decomposed by using the proof procedure of section 1.2.4 as enlarged in this section.

As an example of using these rules, together with the one given in section 1.2.4, we now prove a few more theorems.

$$\forall x \cdot (P \Rightarrow Q) \;\Rightarrow\; (\forall x \cdot P \;\Rightarrow\; \forall x \cdot Q) \qquad\qquad \text{Theorem 1.3.3}$$

Proof

We have the following sequent to prove

$$\forall x \cdot (P \Rightarrow Q) \;\Rightarrow\; (\forall x \cdot P \;\Rightarrow\; \forall x \cdot Q) \qquad\qquad \text{sequent 1}$$

By applying DED twice, and then GEN, we obtain

$$\forall x \cdot (P \Rightarrow Q), \forall x \cdot P \vdash Q \qquad\qquad \text{sequent 1.1}$$

By applying now DR 11 to hypothesis $\forall x \cdot P$, we get

$$\forall x \cdot (P \Rightarrow Q), \forall x \cdot P \vdash P \Rightarrow Q \qquad\qquad \text{sequent 1.1.1}$$

By applying now DED and then DR 11 to hypothesis $\forall x \cdot (P \Rightarrow Q)$, we get

$$\forall x \cdot (P \Rightarrow Q), \forall x \cdot P, P \vdash (P \Rightarrow Q) \Rightarrow Q \qquad \text{sequent 1.1.1.1}$$

leading to the two following sequents by applying DR 7

$$\forall x \cdot (P \Rightarrow Q), \forall x \cdot P, P \vdash \neg P \Rightarrow Q \qquad\qquad \text{sequent 1.1.1.1.1}$$
$$\forall x \cdot (P \Rightarrow Q), \forall x \cdot P, P \vdash Q \Rightarrow Q \qquad\qquad \text{sequent 1.1.1.1.2}$$

which are both easily discharged by using DB 1 for the former and DED followed by BS 2 for the latter.

End of Proof

1.3.8. Existential Quantification

We now extend the notation once again by introducing the *Existential Quantifier* as follows:

Syntax	Definition
$\exists x \cdot P$	$\neg \forall x \cdot \neg P$

Applying this rewriting rule allows us to extend the derived rules as follows, by transforming rules DR 9 and DR 10 into rules DR 12 and DR 13. This can be done by means of rule DR 16, which transforms the negation of a universal quantification into an existential quantification. We also have two obvious rules, DR 14 and DR 15, dealing with the negation of existential predicates.

	Antecedents	Consequent
DR 12	$\begin{cases} x \setminus R \\ x \setminus H \ \text{ for each } H \text{ of HYP} \\ \text{HYP} \vdash P \Rightarrow R \end{cases}$	$\text{HYP} \vdash \exists x \cdot P \Rightarrow R$
DR 13	$\text{HYP} \vdash [x := E]\,P$	$\text{HYP} \vdash \exists x \cdot P$
DR 14	$\text{HYP} \vdash \forall x \cdot \neg P \Rightarrow R$	$\text{HYP} \vdash \neg \exists x \cdot P \Rightarrow R$
DR 15	$\text{HYP} \vdash \forall x \cdot \neg P$	$\text{HYP} \vdash \neg \exists x \cdot P$
DR 16	$\text{HYP} \vdash \exists x \cdot \neg P$	$\text{HYP} \vdash \neg \forall x \cdot P$

In the proof procedure, as extended in this section, the tactics still consist of using the rule DED when no other rules are applicable. By doing so, we always end up with hypotheses that are either simple predicates or universally quantified predicates (*no existentially quantified hypotheses*). Likewise, the goal is either a simple predicate or an existentially quantified predicate (*never a universally quantified predicate*). As already pointed out, the proof then proceeds by doing some instantiations either on universally quantified hypotheses (rule DR 11) or on an existentially quantified goal (rule DR 13). As an example of using the extended procedure, here is a theorem showing an interesting relationship between the two quantifiers:

$$\exists x \cdot (P \Rightarrow Q) \ \Leftrightarrow \ (\forall x \cdot P \Rightarrow \exists x \cdot Q) \qquad\qquad \text{Theorem 1.3.4}$$

Let us only prove the second half of it, that is $(\forall x \cdot P \Rightarrow \exists x \cdot Q) \Rightarrow \exists x \cdot (P \Rightarrow Q)$

Proof

We have the following sequent to prove:

$$(\forall x \cdot P \Rightarrow \exists x \cdot Q) \ \Rightarrow \ \exists x \cdot (P \Rightarrow Q) \qquad\qquad \text{sequent 1}$$

By applying DR 7, we obtain the following two sequents:

$$\neg \forall x \cdot P \quad \Rightarrow \quad \exists x \cdot (P \Rightarrow Q)$$

sequent 1.1

$$\exists x \cdot Q \quad \Rightarrow \quad \exists x \cdot (P \Rightarrow Q)$$

sequent 1.2

By applying DR 9 and DED to sequent 1.1, we obtain

$$\neg P \vdash \exists x \cdot (P \Rightarrow Q)$$

sequent 1.1.1

By applying DR 13 to sequent 1.1.1, we obtain

$$\neg P \vdash P \Rightarrow Q$$

sequent 1.1.1.1

which is discharged by DB 2. By applying DR 12 and DED to sequent 1.2, we obtain

$$Q \vdash \exists x \cdot (P \Rightarrow Q)$$

sequent 1.2.1

Applying DR 13 to sequent 1.2.1, we obtain

$$Q \vdash P \Rightarrow Q$$

sequent 1.2.1.1

which is discharged by BS 1.

End of Proof

1.3.9. Some Classical Results

With the help of the extended proof procedure of the previous section, we can easily prove the following classical properties:

$\forall x \cdot \forall y \cdot P \ \Leftrightarrow \ \forall y \cdot \forall x \cdot P$ $\exists x \cdot \exists y \cdot P \ \Leftrightarrow \ \exists y \cdot \exists x \cdot P$	commutativity
$\forall x \cdot (P \wedge Q) \ \Leftrightarrow \ \forall x \cdot P \ \wedge \ \forall x \cdot Q$ $\exists x \cdot (P \vee Q) \ \Leftrightarrow \ \exists x \cdot P \ \vee \ \exists x \cdot Q$	associativity

$P \lor \forall x \cdot Q \ \Leftrightarrow \ \forall x \cdot (P \lor Q) \quad$ if $\ x \setminus P$ $P \land \exists x \cdot Q \ \Leftrightarrow \ \exists x \cdot (P \land Q) \quad$ if $\ x \setminus P$ $P \Rightarrow \forall x \cdot Q \ \Leftrightarrow \ \forall x \cdot (P \Rightarrow Q) \quad$ if $\ x \setminus P$	distributivity
$\neg \forall x \cdot P \ \Leftrightarrow \ \exists x \cdot \neg P$ $\neg \exists x \cdot P \ \Leftrightarrow \ \forall x \cdot \neg P$ $\neg \forall x \cdot (P \Rightarrow Q) \ \Leftrightarrow \ \exists x \cdot (P \land \neg Q)$ $\neg \exists x \cdot (P \land Q) \ \Leftrightarrow \ \forall x \cdot (P \Rightarrow \neg Q)$	de Morgan laws
$\forall x \cdot (P \Rightarrow Q) \ \Rightarrow \ (\forall x \cdot P \ \Rightarrow \ \forall x \cdot Q)$ $\forall x \cdot (P \Rightarrow Q) \ \Rightarrow \ (\exists x \cdot P \ \Rightarrow \ \exists x \cdot Q)$	monotonicity
$\forall x \cdot (P \Leftrightarrow Q) \ \Rightarrow \ (\forall x \cdot P \ \Leftrightarrow \ \forall x \cdot Q)$ $\forall x \cdot (P \Leftrightarrow Q) \ \Rightarrow \ (\exists x \cdot P \ \Leftrightarrow \ \exists x \cdot Q)$	equivalence

1.4. Equality

In this section we develop the classical theory of equality. For this, we first have to extend our syntax once more by adding one clause to the *Predicate* syntactic category (the previous version of the syntax was that of section 1.3.1). This is done as follows:

Syntactic Category	Definition
Predicate	. . . *Expression* $=$ *Expression*

We have now our first given *Predicate*, expressing the equality of two *Expressions*. Of course, we have to enlarge accordingly the syntactic rules of non-freeness with the following rule:

	Non-freeness	Condition
NF 9	$x \setminus (E = F)$	$x \setminus E$ and $x \setminus F$

and we also have to add one more syntactic rewriting rule for substitution:

	Substitution	Definition
SUB 12	$[x := C](D = E)$	$[x := C]D = [x := C]E$

In the same spirit as for the Propositional and Predicate Calculi of the previous sections, we now give the inference rules to allow us to reason about equality. We have two such rules:

	Antecedents	Consequent
Rule 9	$\begin{cases} \text{HYP} \vdash E = F \\ \\ \text{HYP} \vdash [x := E]P \end{cases}$	$\text{HYP} \vdash [x := F]P$
Rule 10		$\text{HYP} \vdash E = E$

Rule 9 is called the **Leibnitz Law**. It says, quite naturally, that once two expressions E and F have been proved to be equal, then anything that has been proved of one, say $[x := E]P$, is also *ipso facto* proved of the other, $[x := F]P$. Rule 9 is used mostly in the forward way.

Rule 10 is called the **Equality Rule** (for short **EQL**). It shows, also quite naturally, that equality is reflexive: in other words, every *Expression* is equal to itself.

With the help of these rules, we can prove the classical properties of equality, namely symmetry and transitivity. Let us prove now these properties in turn:

$E = F \quad \Rightarrow \quad F = E$ Theorem 1.4.1

Proof

We assume

$$E = F$$ Hypothesis 1

and we have to prove

$$F = E$$ Goal 1

According to rule EQL, we already have

$$E = E \qquad \qquad \text{Derivation 1}$$

Given a variable x which is supposed to be such that

$$x \setminus E \qquad \qquad \text{Side Condition}$$

we can get the following from Derivation 1 and by applying SUB 12, SUB 1, and SUB 9

$$[x := E](x = E) \qquad \qquad \text{Derivation 2}$$

Applying now Rule 9 in a forward way to Hypothesis 1 and Derivation 2, we obtain

$$[x := F](x = E) \qquad \qquad \text{Derivation 3}$$

that is according again to SUB 12, SUB 1 and SUB 9

$$F = E \qquad \qquad \text{Derivation 4}$$

which is exactly Goal 1.
End of Proof

From the previous result, we obtain immediately

$$E = F \ \Leftrightarrow \ F = E \qquad \qquad \text{Theorem 1.4.2}$$

We now prove the transitivity of equality

$$E = F \ \wedge \ F = G \ \Rightarrow \ E = G \qquad \qquad \text{Theorem 1.4.3}$$

Proof

We assume

$$E = F \qquad \qquad \text{Hypothesis 1}$$

$$F = G \qquad \qquad \text{Hypothesis 2}$$

and we have to prove

$$E = G \qquad \qquad \text{Goal 1}$$

Given a variable x which is supposed to be such that

$$x \setminus E \qquad \qquad \text{Side Condition}$$

we can get the following from Hypothesis 1 and by applying SUB 12, SUB 1 and SUB 9

$$[x := F](E = x) \qquad \qquad \text{Derivation 1}$$

Applying now Rule 9 to Hypothesis 2 and Derivation 1, we obtain

$$[x := G](E = x)$$ Derivation 2

that is according to SUB 12, SUB 1 and SUB 9

$$E = G$$ Derivation 3

which is exactly Goal 1.
End of Proof

The next two theorems show an interesting connection between equality, substitution and universal quantification:

$$\forall x \cdot (x = E \ \Rightarrow \ P) \quad \Rightarrow \quad [x := E]P \quad \text{if} \ \ x \setminus E \qquad \text{Theorem 1.4.4}$$

Proof
We assume

$$\forall x \cdot (x = E \ \Rightarrow \ P)$$ Hypothesis 1

and we have to prove

$$[x := E]P$$ Goal 1

under the following

$$x \setminus E$$ Side Condition

From Hypothesis 1 and by applying ELIM we obtain

$$[x := E](x = E \ \Rightarrow \ P)$$ Derivation 1

that is according to SUB 4, SUB 12, SUB 1 and SUB 9

$$E = E \ \Rightarrow \ [x := E]P$$ Derivation 2

leading to Goal 1 after applying MP together with $E = E$ derived from EQL.
End of Proof

$$[x := E]P \quad \Rightarrow \quad \forall x \cdot (x = E \ \Rightarrow \ P) \quad \text{if} \ \ x \setminus E \qquad \text{Theorem 1.4.5}$$

Proof
We assume

$$[x := E]P$$ Hypothesis 1

and we have to prove

$$\forall x \cdot (x = E \ \Rightarrow \ P)$$ Goal 1

under the following

$$x \setminus E \hspace{6cm} \text{Side Condition}$$

which can be transformed into the following, by applying GEN (which we can do thanks to NF 7 defined in section 1.3.3):

$$x = E \;\Rightarrow\; P \hspace{6cm} \text{Goal 2}$$

We assume

$$x = E \hspace{6cm} \text{Hypothesis 2}$$

that is equivalently (according to Theorem 1.4.2)

$$E = x \hspace{6cm} \text{Derivation 1}$$

and we have to prove

$$P \hspace{6cm} \text{Goal 3}$$

By applying the Leibnitz Law to Hypothesis 1 and Derivation 1, we obtain

$$[x := x]\,P \hspace{6cm} \text{Derivation 2}$$

which is obviously the same as Goal 3 according to SUB 8.
End of Proof

Put together, the two previous results constitute the One Point Rule for universal quantification which we can state as follows:

$$\forall x \cdot (x = E \;\Rightarrow\; P) \;\Leftrightarrow\; [x := E]\,P \hspace{1cm} \text{if} \;\; x \setminus E \hspace{2cm} \text{Theorem 1.4.6}$$

We have the following similar One Point Rule for existential quantification:

$$\exists x \cdot (x = E \wedge P) \;\Leftrightarrow\; [x := E]\,P \hspace{1cm} \text{if} \;\; x \setminus E \hspace{2cm} \text{Theorem 1.4.7}$$

In order to facilitate further proofs dealing with equality, we now propose to enlarge our collection of derived rules as follows:

	Antecedents	Consequent
EQL 1	$\begin{cases} E = F \quad \text{occurs in HYP} \\ \\ P \quad \text{occurs in HYP} \\ \\ P \;\Leftrightarrow\; [x := E]Q \\ \\ \text{HYP} \;\vdash\; [x := F]Q \;\Rightarrow\; R \end{cases}$	$\text{HYP} \;\vdash\; R$
EQL 2	$\begin{cases} E = F \quad \text{occurs in HYP} \\ \\ R \;\Leftrightarrow\; [x := E]P \\ \\ \text{HYP} \;\vdash\; [x := F]P \end{cases}$	$\text{HYP} \;\vdash\; R$
EQL 3	$\begin{cases} E = F \quad \text{occurs in HYP} \\ \\ \text{HYP}, F = E \;\vdash\; R \end{cases}$	$\text{HYP} \;\vdash\; R$
EQL		$\text{HYP} \;\vdash\; E = E$

Rules EQL 1 and EQL 2 show the effect of an equalitarian hypothesis on another hypothesis and on the goal respectively. Both of them are obvious consequences of the Leibnitz Law. Notice how, in the case of rule EQL 1, the transformed hypothesis is put back in the goal for possible further transformations.

1.5. Ordered Pairs

In this section we extend our notation once more by introducing the concept of an *ordered pair*.

An ordered pair is an *Expression* made of two *Expressions* separated by the comma symbol or by the "maplet" symbol $\mapsto$. The reason why we have two ways of denoting ordered pairs is that the first form is very traditional. However, it is sometimes ambiguous and would thus require a large number of parentheses. When this is the case, we shall use the second form. A *Variable* can be made of a list of *Variables*. In that case, *distinct Identifiers* are required and the corresponding "variable" is said to be a *multiple* variable. For instance, we may now build predicates of the form

$$\forall\,(x,y) \cdot P$$
$$C,D = E,F$$
$$[x,y := E,F]\,P$$

In the first case, we have a *multiple* quantification on the "variable" x, y. In the second case, we have an example of the equality of ordered pairs. In the third case, we have the *multiple* substitution of x and y by E and F in P. Here is the new syntax for *Expressions* and *Variables*:

Expression	Variable [*Variable* := *Expression*] *Expression* *Expression, Expression*
Variable	*Identifier* *Variable, Variable*

together with the mentioned syntactic extension:

Syntax	Definition
$E \mapsto F$	E, F

Notice that the operators "," and "$\mapsto$", like every operator (unless otherwise stated explicitly as in section 1.3.1), *associate to the left*. In other words the triples

$$x,\,y,\,z \qquad \text{and} \qquad (x,\,y),\,z$$

denote the same triple, and this triple is different from the following one:

$$x,\,(y,\,z)$$

Before proving properties of such predicates, we first have to enlarge the syntactic rules of non-freeness with the following four rules:

	Non-freeness	Condition
NF 10	$(x, y) \setminus E$	$x \setminus E$ and $y \setminus E$
NF 11	$x \setminus (E, F)$	$x \setminus E$ and $x \setminus F$
NF 12	$x \setminus \forall (y, z) \cdot P$	$x \setminus \forall y \cdot \forall z \cdot P$

and we also have to add one more syntactic rule for (multiple) substitution:

	Substitution	Definition
SUB 13	$[x, y := C, D] F$	$[z := D] [x := C] [y := z] F$ if $x \setminus y$ and $z \setminus (x, y, C, D, F)$

Next is an example of the use of the previous rewriting rule (remember that substitution associates to the right) where we suppose that x is distinct from y and z.

$$[x, y := y, x](x = y)$$
$$\Leftrightarrow$$
$$[z := x] [x := y] [y := z](x = y)$$
$$\Leftrightarrow$$
$$[z := x] [x := y] (x = z)$$
$$\Leftrightarrow$$
$$[z := x] (y = z)$$
$$\Leftrightarrow$$
$$y = x$$

Contrary to what has been done for equality in the previous section, we do not have to introduce extra rules of inference for ordered pairs. This is because we implicitly extend the ones we already have, that deal with simple variables, to deal now with multiple variables. This concerns Rule 7 and Rule 8, as introduced in section 1.3.5, and Rule 9, as introduced in section 1.4. Next are a few more proofs.

$\forall (x, y) \cdot P \quad \Rightarrow \quad \forall x \cdot \forall y \cdot P \qquad$ if $\ x \setminus y \qquad\qquad$ Theorem 1.5.1

Proof

We assume

$$\forall\,(x,y)\cdot P \qquad\qquad\qquad \text{Hypothesis 1}$$

and we have to prove

$$\forall\,x\cdot\forall\,y\cdot P \qquad\qquad\qquad \text{Goal 1}$$

Applying GEN twice leads to the following

$$P \qquad\qquad\qquad \text{Goal 2}$$

Applying ELIM to Hypothesis 1 allows one to derive

$$[x,y := x,y]\,P \qquad\qquad\qquad \text{Derivation 1}$$

which is exactly Goal 2 according to SUB 8.
End of Proof

Our next theorem is the following:

$$\forall\,x\cdot\forall\,y\cdot P \quad\Rightarrow\quad \forall\,(x,y)\cdot P \qquad \text{if}\ \ x\setminus y \qquad\qquad \text{Theorem 1.5.2}$$

Proof

We assume

$$\forall\,x\cdot\forall\,y\cdot P \qquad\qquad\qquad \text{Hypothesis 1}$$

and we have to prove

$$\forall\,(x,y)\cdot P \qquad\qquad\qquad \text{Goal 1}$$

Applying GEN leads to the following:

$$P \qquad\qquad\qquad \text{Goal 2}$$

Applying ELIM to Hypothesis 1 allows one to derive

$$[x := x]\,\forall\,y\cdot P \qquad\qquad\qquad \text{Derivation 1}$$

that is

$$\forall\,y\cdot P \qquad\qquad\qquad \text{Derivation 2}$$

Applying then ELIM again leads to

$$[y := y]\,P \qquad\qquad\qquad \text{Derivation 3}$$

which is exactly Goal 2.
End of Proof

Putting together the two previous theorems, we obtain:

$$\forall\,(x,y)\cdot P \;\;\Leftrightarrow\;\; \forall\,x\cdot\forall\,y\cdot P \qquad \text{if } x \setminus y \qquad\qquad \text{Theorem 1.5.3}$$

and we have the following similar theorem for multiple existential quantifications:

$$\exists\,(x,y)\cdot P \;\;\Leftrightarrow\;\; \exists\,x\cdot\exists\,y\cdot P \qquad \text{if } x \setminus y \qquad\qquad \text{Theorem 1.5.4}$$

Our final theorem is concerned with the equality of ordered pairs.

$$C,D = E,F \;\;\Rightarrow\;\; C = E \,\wedge\, D = F \qquad\qquad \text{Theorem 1.5.5}$$

Proof

We assume

$$C,D = E,F \qquad\qquad \text{Hypothesis 1}$$

and we have to prove

$$C = E \,\wedge\, D = F \qquad\qquad \text{Goal 1}$$

As we have, according to EQL, $C = C$ and $D = D$, we also have according to Rule 1 applied in a forward way

$$C = C \,\wedge\, D = D \qquad\qquad \text{Derivation 1}$$

Considering now the two distinct variables x and y such that

$$(x,y)\setminus(C,D) \qquad\qquad \text{Side Condition}$$

we obtain the following from Derivation 1 and by applying SUB 3, SUB 12, SUB 13, SUB 1 and SUB 9:

$$[x,y := C,D]\,(C = x \,\wedge\, D = y) \qquad\qquad \text{Derivation 2}$$

Applying now the Leibnitz Law to Hypothesis 1 and Derivation 2, we obtain

$$[x,y := E,F]\,(C = x \,\wedge\, D = y) \qquad\qquad \text{Derivation 3}$$

which is exactly Goal 1 by applying SUB 3, SUB 12, SUB 13, SUB 1 and SUB 9.
End of Proof

1.6. Exercises

1. Given three predicates P, Q and R, prove the following:

$$(P \;\Rightarrow\; Q) \,\wedge\, (\neg P \;\Rightarrow\; R) \;\;\Leftrightarrow\;\; (P \wedge Q) \,\vee\, (\neg P \wedge R)$$

2. Given two predicates P and Q, prove the following:

$$(P \Leftrightarrow Q) \quad \Leftrightarrow \quad (P \wedge Q) \vee (\neg P \wedge \neg Q)$$

3. Prove some of the "classical" results of section 1.2.6.

4. Check the rule SUB 11 by induction on the structure of the notation.

5. Given two distinct variables x and y and two predicates P and Q together with the side conditions $x \setminus Q$ and $y \setminus P$, prove the following:

$$\forall (x, y) \cdot (P \wedge Q) \quad \Leftrightarrow \quad \forall x \cdot P \wedge \forall y \cdot Q$$

6. Given two distinct variables x and y and three predicates P, Q and R together with the side conditions $x \setminus Q$ and $y \setminus P$, prove that the following predicates are all equivalent to each other:

$$\forall (x, y) \cdot (P \wedge R \Rightarrow Q)$$
$$\forall y \cdot (\exists x \cdot (P \wedge R) \Rightarrow Q)$$
$$\forall x \cdot (P \Rightarrow \neg \exists y \cdot (\neg Q \wedge R))$$
$$\forall x \cdot (\exists y \cdot (\neg Q \wedge R) \Rightarrow \neg P)$$
$$\forall (x, y) \cdot (P \wedge R \Rightarrow R \wedge Q)$$
$$\forall (x, y) \cdot (R \Rightarrow \neg P \vee Q)$$
$$\neg \exists (x, y) \cdot (P \wedge R \wedge \neg Q)$$

7. Given three distinct variables x, y and z, and three predicates P, Q and R together with the side condition $x \setminus R$, prove the following:

$$\forall (x, y, z) \cdot (P \wedge Q \Rightarrow R) \quad \Leftrightarrow \quad \forall (y, z) \cdot (\exists x \cdot (P \wedge Q) \Rightarrow R)$$

8. Prove some of the "classical" results of section 1.3.9.

9. Given two distinct variables y and z, and three predicates P, Q and R together with the side conditions $z \setminus P$ and $y \setminus R$, prove the following:

$$\exists y \cdot (P \wedge \exists z \cdot (Q \wedge R)) \quad \Leftrightarrow \quad \exists z \cdot (R \wedge \exists y \cdot (P \wedge Q))$$

10. Given a variable x and three predicates P, Q and R, prove the following:

$$\exists x \cdot (R \wedge (P \vee Q)) \quad \Leftrightarrow \quad \exists x \cdot (R \wedge P) \vee \exists x \cdot (R \wedge Q)$$
$$\exists x \cdot (R \wedge P \wedge Q) \quad \Rightarrow \quad \exists x \cdot (R \wedge P) \wedge \exists x \cdot (R \wedge Q)$$
$$\exists x \cdot (R \wedge P) \wedge \neg \exists x \cdot (R \wedge Q) \quad \Rightarrow \quad \exists x \cdot (R \wedge P \wedge \neg Q)$$

11. Prove the one point rule with existential quantification. That is, given a variable x, a predicate P, and an expression E such that $x \setminus E$, prove the following:

$$\exists x \cdot (x = E \wedge P) \quad \Leftrightarrow \quad [x := E] P$$

12. Given two distinct variables x and y, two expressions E and F, and a predicate P such that $x \setminus P$, check that the predicate $[x, y := E, F] P$ is the same as $[y := F] P$.

13. Given a variable x and a predicate of the form r_x, prove the following:

$$\exists x \cdot r_x \quad \wedge$$
$$\forall (x, y) \cdot (r_x \wedge r_y \;\Rightarrow\; x = y)$$
$$\Rightarrow$$
$$\exists x \cdot (r_x \wedge \forall y \cdot (r_y \;\Rightarrow\; x = y))$$

14. Given a variable x and three predicates of the form r_x, p_x and q_x, prove the following:

$$\forall (x, y) \cdot (r_x \wedge r_y \;\Rightarrow\; x = y)$$
$$\Rightarrow$$
$$\exists x \cdot (r_x \wedge p_x \wedge q_x) \;\Leftrightarrow\; \exists x \cdot (r_x \wedge p_x) \wedge \exists x \cdot (r_x \wedge q_x)$$

15. Given a variable x and three predicates of the form r_x, p_x and q_x, prove the following:

$$\forall (x, y) \cdot (r_x \wedge r_y \;\Rightarrow\; x = y)$$
$$\Rightarrow$$
$$\exists x \cdot (r_x \wedge p_x) \wedge \neg \exists x \cdot (r_x \wedge q_x) \;\Leftrightarrow\; \exists x \cdot (r_x \wedge p_x \wedge \neg q_x)$$

CHAPTER 2

Set Notation

THE main objective of this chapter, and of the next one, is to make precise part of the notation that we intend to use in order to specify and design software systems. As a matter of fact, this notation is nothing but the one used, more or less formally, by every scientist: that of set theory.

Clearly, in order to perform our subsequent formal developments, we could have stayed within some extensions of the logic introduced in the previous chapter. For the following three reasons it is my view that set theory is a better choice.

First, when using set theory, one *remains within first order logic* while it is clearly possible to manipulate objects of "high order" such as sets and relations of any depth (that is, sets and relations built themselves on sets and relations, and so on). In any case, such constructs are *objects* (not predicates) and are thus licit candidates for first order quantifications.

Second, and more importantly, the use of set theory allows one, very often, to *eliminate quantifiers*. In fact, most of the set-theoretic concepts are introduced precisely because they hide some quantifications. Typical examples are: set inclusion, relational composition, and generalized intersection or union of sets of sets.

Third, set theory has the (apparently innocent but, in fact, very important) property of *handling negation in a very controlled way*: it is simply because the complement of a set is still a set. That is, negation does not extend beyond certain limits. On the contrary, in logic, the negation of a predicate might correspond sometimes to a property that is "too large".

The notation defined hereafter is described not only *syntactically* but also, and more importantly, *axiomatically*. We make this latter choice because we intend to *prove* (formally) the properties of our software systems, and to do so as part of the very process of constructing them: we must then have at our disposal a notation capable of helping us to produce formal descriptions, and also capable of being used to express and prove theorems.

The axiomatic construction presented here is a simplification of classical set theory. The reason for using a simplified theory is that we are interested in the notation, not as professional mathematicians ([1], [2], and [3]), but rather as practitioners of formalisms.

In what follows, we shall explain briefly to the mathematically oriented reader which axioms of classical set theory we can discard and why. As we shall not deal with the concept of *ordinal number*, the Replacement Axiom is not needed. Another simplification comes from the fact that the concept of *ordered pair*, which we have introduced in the previous chapter (section 1.5), is defined outside set theory. As a consequence, the Pairing Axiom, which, normally, is necessary to construct ordered pairs within set theory is not needed either. We also found that the Union Axiom was not indispensable. Finally, the Foundation Axiom, which is needed in order to prove that certain sets do not "exist", will not be necessary. This is so because we shall require that each predicate involving set-theoretic constructs be *type-checked* before being proved (section 2.2).

As a consequence, the *only* basic set theoretic constructs we shall axiomatize (section 2.1) are the most natural ones: cartesian product, power-set, and set comprehension. To the three axioms corresponding to these three basic constructs, we shall add only three more axioms: the Axiom of Extensionality defining set equality, a special form of the Axiom of Infinity and a special form of the Axiom of Choice (the two latter axioms will allow us to construct the Natural Numbers formally in the next chapter). All other classical constructs (in particular, the construction of sets defined *in extension*) will be *derived* from the basic constructs (section 2.3).

In this chapter we introduce the well-known basic concepts of set theory: sets, binary relations, and functions. The next chapter is devoted to the study of the construction of *Mathematical Objects*: that is, finite sets, natural numbers, finite sequences, and various trees.

This chapter comprises eight sections. The first one is devoted to the introduction of the basic constructs of set theory and to the corresponding axiomatization. Section 2.2 deals with the concept of type-checking. Section 2.3 deals with the classical set operators (union, intersection, etc.). Sections 2.4 and 2.5 are devoted to binary relations and functions. In section 2.6, we present a catalogue of laws that can be deduced from the previous material and that we shall use freely in the book. Finally, section 2.7 contains an example using most of the set notations, and section 2.8 contains a number of exercises.

The notation presented here is by no means a closed body. Rather it forms an open basis from which other notations can be built at will.

2.1. Basic Set Constructs

When introducing set theory, most authors start their presentation with an intuitive definition explaining what sets are. The trouble with such definitions is that they contain other (undefined) concepts such as those of *collections* or of *objects having certain common properties*; concepts which are all supposed to *explain* sets without being themselves at all defined. The reader, usually, feels a bit uncomfortable.

Here, we adopt a somewhat different approach: this is a *linguistic* approach consisting of explaining first how sets can be *denoted*. More precisely, we define various constructs making clear how set denotations can be built from *already known* set denotations. There exists only three such constructs called *cartesian product*, *power-set*, and *set comprehension*.

Since we have adopted a linguistic approach, we have to give a *formal meaning* to each of these constructs: this will be done under the form of a *Predicate* formalizing the concept of *set membership*.

Of course, one could question the origin of the *already known* sets, alluded to above. Most of the time, we shall not bother too much and simply consider that they have been *given*. For instance, when using set theory for building mathematical models, people usually start their construction informally by writing down statements such as: "Let S, T, U be three sets ...", and nobody complains that the *generic* model thus built is not well-defined. In fact, and as already pointed out for predicates in section 1.1.1, S, T and U are meta-linguistic variables standing for sets.

However, in order to construct formally the *Mathematical Objects* (natural numbers, sequences, etc.) in the next chapter, we shall have no choice but to postulate the *existence* of at least one *infinite set*. This existential axiom will take the linguistic form of a set constant, BIG, that denotes the infinite set in question. Notice, of course, that the concept of infinity has thus to be defined rigorously beforehand (section 3.4). We shall also need the concept of a set choice that corresponds to a simple linguistic variant of the *Axiom of Choice*.

2.1.1. Syntax

The syntax of our basic set constructs is now presented as an extension of the syntax introduced in the previous chapter.

Syntactic Category	Definition
Predicate	*Predicate* $\land$ *Predicate* *Predicate* $\Rightarrow$ *Predicate* $\neg$ *Predicate* $\forall$ *Variable* $\cdot$ *Predicate* [*Variable* := *Expression*] *Predicate* *Expression* = *Expression* *Expression* $\in$ *Set*

Syntactic Category	Definition
Expression	*Variable* [*Variable* := *Expression*] *Expression* *Expression, Expression* choice (*Set*) *Set*
Variable	*Identifier* *Variable, Variable*
Set	*Set* × *Set* $\mathbb{P}$(*Set*) {*Variable* | *Predicate*} BIG

As you can see, to the *Predicate* syntactic category, as defined in the previous chapter, we have added a new clause introducing set *membership* ($\in$). In the *Expression* syntactic category too, some new clauses are added: the choice construct and a reference to the *Set* syntactic category, which is a new syntactic category made of four clauses: the *cartesian product* ($\times$), the *power-set* ($\mathbb{P}$), the *set comprehension* ({ \| }), and, finally, the set BIG.

One of the most important aspects of this syntax is that, contrary to what happens in classical set theory, here it is not the case that every expression denotes a set. In particular, as we have said previously, an ordered pair is *not* a set. In fact, the classical technique of representing the pair $E \mapsto F$ by the "set" {{E}, {E, F}} just appears to be an "ad-hoc" coding trick that is used only because one can then prove that the equality of ordered pairs distributes through the two components of the pair. We find that this is a perversion of the concept of membership. For instance, to be thus able to say that the set {E, F} is a "member" of the pair $E \mapsto F$ is, we feel, a non-sense. Also notice that, in this case, when E and F are the same, then the coding of the pair $E \mapsto E$ reduces to {{E}}, which is rather counter-intuitive since the "pair" has then disappeared (this was pointed out to me by Michel Sintzoff).

In what follows, we shall very often write statements starting with: "Let s be a set, then ...". There should be no misinterpretation of that statement. It simply means that s is a formula, which belongs to the syntactic category *Set* (again, s is thus a meta-linguistic variable standing for a set). In the chapter 1, we used similar wording with predicates. For instance, we often wrote statements starting as follows: "Let P be a *Predicate*, then ...". In fact, in order to be absolutely clear, we should have written: "Let *s* be a *Set*, then ...", thus emphasizing the syntactic nature of that announcement. I am afraid we shall not do so systematically, however.

Before proceeding, we have to enlarge our set of syntactic rules concerning non-freeness. This is done in a straightforward way in the following table where *x* and *y* are *Variables*, *E* is an *Expression*, *s* and *t* are *Sets*, and *P* is a *Predicate*:

	Non-freeness	Condition
NF 13	$x \setminus (E \in s)$	$x \setminus E$ and $x \setminus s$
NF 14	$x \setminus \text{choice}(s)$	$x \setminus s$
NF 15	$x \setminus (s \times t)$	$x \setminus s$ and $x \setminus t$
NF 16	$x \setminus \mathbb{P}(s)$	$x \setminus s$
NF 17	$x \setminus \{ y \mid P \}$	$x \setminus \forall y \cdot P$
NF 18	$x \setminus \text{BIG}$	

Likewise, we have to enlarge our set of syntactic rules concerning substitution. In the following table, *x* is a simple *Variable* and *y* is a *Variable*, *E* and *F* are *Expressions*, *s* and *t* are *Sets*, and *P* is a *Predicate*:

	Substitution	Definition
SUB 14	$[x := E](F \in s)$	$[x := E]F \in [x := E]s$
SUB 15	$[x := E]\text{choice}(s)$	$\text{choice}([x := E]s)$
SUB 16	$[x := E](s \times t)$	$[x := E]s \times [x := E]t$
SUB 17	$[x := E]\mathbb{P}(s)$	$\mathbb{P}([x := E]s)$
SUB 18	$[x := E]\{ y \mid P \}$	$\{ y \mid P \}$ if x occurs in y
SUB 19	$[x := E]\{ y \mid P \}$	$\{ y \mid [x := E]P \}$ if $y \setminus (x, E)$
SUB 20	$[x := E]\text{BIG}$	BIG

2.1.2. Axioms

We now present informally the basic constructs of set theory we have just introduced syntactically in the previous section. We shall then state and comment on the statements of the six axioms of set theory.

In what follows, we present our constructs by using statements such as "(a certain construct) denotes the set whose *members* are ...". Of course, this is just a non-formal and non-rigorous style. Again, only the formal definition of the concept of set membership will give a rigorous definition to our constructs.

The *cartesian product* of two sets s and t is the set whose members are all the *ordered pairs* whose two components are members of s and t respectively. This is denoted by:

$$s \times t$$

The *power-set* of a set s is the set whose members are all the sets whose members belong to s (these are called the subsets of s). This is denoted by:

$$\mathbb{P}(s)$$

A set is defined *in comprehension* with respect to another set s when the members of the former are exactly the members of s satisfying a certain predicate P. Notice that in the following expression, x is a non-free quantified variable:

$$\{ x \mid x \in s \wedge P \}$$

Given a set s with some member, the choice construct denotes a *distinguished* member of that set. It is denoted by:

$$\text{choice}(s)$$

The last set-theoretic construct is the constant set

$$\text{BIG}$$

As already stated, the meanings of the first three constructs above are given by means of a predicate formalizing the concept of *set membership*. More precisely, we use the construct

$$x \in s$$

to express formally that x is a *member* of s, or an *element* of s (x is also said to *belong* to s). Membership is axiomatized by using the notations of the Propositional and Predicate Calculi as introduced in the previous chapter. Set theory just appears then to be an extension of these logical theories. Let us now present the six axioms of set theory. In the following table, s and t are *Sets*, E and F are *Expressions*, P is a *Predicate*, and x is a *Variable*:

	Axiom of Set Theory	Condition
SET 1	$(E, F) \in (s \times t) \quad \Leftrightarrow \quad (E \in s \;\wedge\; F \in t)$	
SET 2	$s \in \mathbb{P}(t) \quad \Leftrightarrow \quad \forall x \cdot (x \in s \;\Rightarrow\; x \in t)$	$x \setminus (s, t)$
SET 3	$E \in \{x \mid x \in s \;\wedge\; P\} \quad \Leftrightarrow \quad (E \in s \;\wedge\; [x := E]\,P)$	$x \setminus s$
SET 4	$\forall x \cdot (x \in s \;\Leftrightarrow\; x \in t) \quad \Rightarrow \quad s = t$	$x \setminus (s, t)$
SET 5	$\exists x \cdot (x \in s) \quad \Rightarrow \quad \text{choice}\,(s) \in s$	$x \setminus s$
SET 6	infinite (BIG)	

Axiom **SET 1** tells us that the membership of an ordered pair in a cartesian product can be equivalently decomposed into the two memberships of each component of the pair in the corresponding component of the cartesian product.

Axiom **SET 2** tells us that the membership of a set s in the power-set of a set t is equivalent to the fact that each member of s is also a member of t. The set s is thus said to be a subset of t and, thanks to the forthcoming axiom of extensionality, $\mathbb{P}(t)$ is exactly the set made up of all such subsets of t. We shall see below that the predicate $s \in \mathbb{P}(t)$ will be given the simplified form $s \subseteq t$.

Axiom **SET 3**, the *comprehension* axiom, is also called the *separation* or the *selection* axiom. It tells us how we can construct a subset of a set s by "selecting" those members of s that correspond to a certain predicate. Notice that we use here the substitution notation as introduced in the previous chapter. You may have noticed that the set expression used in axiom **SET 3** is slightly less general than that allowed by the syntax. This means that the other forms allowed by the syntax are not axiomatized. For instance, a predicate such as $E \in \{x \mid x \notin x\}$ is not decomposable by axiom **SET 3**. In section 2.2, we shall see that the notation will be given more constraints due to our requirement for type-checking.

As already stated, *a set is characterized by its elements*. As a consequence, axiom **SET 4**, the *extensionality* axiom, explains formally under which circumstances two sets are equal (or better, under which circumstances two set denotations denote the *same* set).

Axiom **SET 5** tells us that, provided a set has some member, then the choice operator applied to that set denotes a certain member of that set. However, we do not know more about that special member. The non-algorithmic nature of that axiom contrasts strongly with the constructive nature of the previous axioms.

Finally, axiom **SET 6** tells us that the set **BIG** denotes an *infinite* set. The definition of the predicative operator "infinite" is postponed for the moment. It will be defined with full rigour in section 3.4.

Set Inclusion

We now present various forms of *set inclusion* ($\subseteq$, $\subset$) as simple syntactic definitions. In the following table, s and t are *Sets*.

Syntax	Definition
$s \subseteq t$	$s \in \mathbb{P}(t)$
$s \subset t$	$s \subseteq t \ \wedge \ s \neq t$

2.1.3. Properties

From the above definitions and axioms, a number of classical properties can be derived as shown in the following table where s, t and u are *Sets*, x is a *Variable*, P is a *Predicate*, and E is an *Expression*:

$s \subseteq s$	reflexivity
$s \subseteq t \ \wedge \ t \subseteq u \ \Rightarrow \ s \subseteq u$	transitivity
$s \subseteq t \ \wedge \ t \subseteq s \ \Rightarrow \ s = t$	anti-symmetry
$u \subseteq s \ \wedge \ v \subseteq t \ \Rightarrow \ u \times v \subseteq s \times t$ $s \subseteq t \ \Rightarrow \ \mathbb{P}(s) \subseteq \mathbb{P}(t)$ $s \subseteq t \ \Rightarrow \ \{x \mid x \in s \ \wedge \ P\} \subseteq \{x \mid x \in t \ \wedge \ P\} \quad$ if $x \setminus s,t$	monotonicity
$\{x \mid x \in s \ \wedge \ P\} \subseteq s \quad$ if $x \setminus s$ $E \in s \ \wedge \ s \subseteq t \ \Rightarrow \ E \in t$	inclusion

Each of the previous properties can be proved by translating the corresponding statement into the predicate notation, and then using the rules of the previous chapter. For instance, let us prove the following where s and t are *Sets*:

$$s \subseteq t \quad \Rightarrow \quad \mathbb{P}(s) \subseteq \mathbb{P}(t)$$ Property 2.1.1

According to the definition of set inclusion ($\subseteq$), we obtain the following first translation:

$$s \in \mathbb{P}(t) \quad \Rightarrow \quad \mathbb{P}(s) \in \mathbb{P}(\mathbb{P}(t))$$

That is, according to axiom **SET 2** used twice:

$$\forall x \cdot (x \subset s \;\rightarrow\; x \in t)$$
$$\Rightarrow$$
$$\forall y \cdot (y \in \mathbb{P}(s) \;\Rightarrow\; y \in \mathbb{P}(t))$$

where the variables x and y are supposed to be non-free in s and t. The previous statement can be further translated by using axiom **SET 2** twice more:

$$\forall x \cdot (x \in s \;\Rightarrow\; x \in t)$$
$$\Rightarrow$$
$$\forall y \cdot (\forall x \cdot (x \in y \;\Rightarrow\; x \in s) \;\Rightarrow\; \forall x \cdot (x \in y \;\Rightarrow\; x \in t))$$

where the variable y is supposed to be non-free in (distinct from) x. Once this mechanical translation is performed, we can proceed with the proof.

Proof

We have the following side conditions:

$$x \setminus s, t$$
$$y \setminus s, t \qquad\qquad \text{Side conditions}$$
$$y \setminus x$$

We assume

$$\forall x \cdot (x \in s \;\Rightarrow\; x \in t) \qquad\qquad \text{Hypothesis 1}$$

and we have to prove

$$\forall y \cdot (\forall x \cdot (x \in y \;\Rightarrow\; x \in s) \;\Rightarrow\; \forall x \cdot (x \in y \;\Rightarrow\; x \in t)) \text{Goal 1}$$

We can remove the universal quantification. We assume then

$$\forall x \cdot (x \in y \;\Rightarrow\; x \in s) \qquad\qquad \text{Hypothesis 2}$$

and we have to prove

$$\forall x \cdot (x \in y \;\Rightarrow\; x \in t) \qquad\qquad \text{Goal 2}$$

We can remove the universal quantification. We assume then

$$x \in y \qquad\qquad \text{Hypothesis 3}$$

and we have to prove

$$x \in t$$ Goal 3

According to Hypothesis 1, it is then sufficient to prove

$$x \in s$$ Goal 4

which is obvious according to Hypothesis 2 and Hypothesis 3.

End of Proof

2.2. Type-checking

As mentioned in the introduction of this chapter, we shall require that any predicate involving set-theoretic constructs be *type-checked* before being proved. For instance, this will have the effect of not even trying to prove a predicate such as $\exists x \cdot (x \in x)$, as it cannot be type-checked.

More precisely, we cannot claim that there "exists" a set x which is a member of itself since that very statement (as well as its negation) is, in fact, *not part of our allowed discourse*. In other words, such a statement "does not make sense". This constrasts with *Zermelo-Fraenkel* set theory, within which the negation of such a statement is provable thanks to the Foundation Axiom.

Besides those already dictated by the syntactic structure of our notation, type-checking will thus put more limitations on the kind of discourse we can use. What is important to emphasize here is that these limitations can be mechanically checked.

Type-checking is essentially based on the monotonicity and inclusion properties presented in the previous section. For instance, suppose we have an *Expression E* and a *Set s* such that $E \in s$ and also a set t such that $s \subseteq t$; we have then $E \in t$. If we can further include t in a larger set u, then E will also belong to u, and so on.

The idea of type-checking is that, within the framework of a certain predicate to be proved, there is an *upper limit* for such set containments. This upper limit is said to be the *super-set* of s and the *type* of E. Clearly these concepts are very close to each other since the type of a set is nothing but the power-set of its super-set. However, as some *Expressions* are not *Sets* (ordered pairs) the concept of super-set only applies to those *Expressions* that are *Sets* whereas the concept of type applies to all *Expressions*.

In order to proceed formally we have introduced in the following table the two syntactic categories of *Type* and of *Type_Predicate*. These are introduced in order to avoid confusing the two linguistic levels of proving and of type-checking.

Syntactic Category	Definition
Type	type (*Expression*) super (*Set*) *Type* × *Type* $\mathbb{P}$ (*Type*) *Identifier*
Type_Predicate	check (*Predicate*) *Type* ≡ *Type*

A *Type_Predicate* is either defined as the construct check (*Predicate*) or as the construct *Type* ≡ *Type*. The former is the one we use to start the type-checking of a *Predicate*. It will be transformed little by little into the latter which will eventually be discharged if type-checking succeeds.

In a predicate to be proved, involving set-theoretic constructs, each *Expression* will eventually be assigned a *Type* which will reduce either to a simple identifier (see the concept of "given set" presented below), or to the power-set of a *Type*, or to the cartesian product of two *Types*. Likewise, each *Set* will be assigned a *Type*, which will be the power-set of a *Type*. For instance, suppose that *s* is a type, then the following is also a type:

$$\mathbb{P}\,(s \times \mathbb{P}\,(s \times s))$$

The process of type-checking resembles that of proving. As a matter of fact, we shall use exactly the same concepts of *sequent* and of *rule of inference* as presented in the previous chapter. Only the informal interpretation will differ. In the context of type-checking, a sequent such as

$$\text{ENV} \vdash \text{check}(P)$$

is to be read: "Within the environment ENV, the predicate *P* type-checks". The environment, like the hypotheses in the previous chapter, is a finite collection of *Predicates*. In an environment, however, each predicate has the following simple form:

$$x \in s$$

where *x* is a *Variable* supposed to be non-free in the *Set s*. In fact, each free variable occuring in *P* should be represented by such a predicate in the environment.

When submitting a statement for type-checking, we might wonder what the initial environment is. We shall always suppose that our submitted statement has a *closed* form. This means that it should not contain any free variables. As a consequence, we could think that the initial environment is then just empty. However, it might happen that we would like to prove some *generic* statement involving a certain set *s* (to be more precise, a certain meta-linguistic variable *s*). Usually such a statement is informally announced by some surrounding prose such as: "Given a *Set s*, ...". Of course, *s* has to participate in the type-checking but we wonder what its super-set could be. The answer is simple: it is *s* itself. In order to be able to deal with such a given set *s*, we shall record it in the initial environment in the following form:

$$given\,(s)$$

We present now a decision-procedure for type-checking. It consists of a collection of inference rules that have to be tried (in a backward way) in numeric order. In what follows, we shall introduce and comment on these rules gradually.

Our first three rules indicate how the type-checking of simple predicates can be decomposed in a straightforward manner. In the following table, *P* and *Q* are *Predicates*:

	Antecedents	Consequent
T 1	$\begin{cases} \text{ENV} \ \vdash \ \text{check}\,(P) \\[1em] \text{ENV} \ \vdash \ \text{check}\,(Q) \end{cases}$	$\text{ENV} \ \vdash \ \text{check}\,(P \wedge Q)$
T 2	$\begin{cases} \text{ENV} \ \vdash \ \text{check}\,(P) \\[1em] \text{ENV} \ \vdash \ \text{check}\,(Q) \end{cases}$	$\text{ENV} \ \vdash \ \text{check}\,(P \Rightarrow Q)$
T 3	$\text{ENV} \ \vdash \ \text{check}\,(P)$	$\text{ENV} \ \vdash \ \text{check}\,(\neg P)$

The next three rules deal with universally quantified predicates. In order to allow for the type-checking of such predicates, we require that their form be slightly less general than what is allowed by the syntax. First, the inside of the universally quantified predicate should always be an implication. Second, we require that the quantified variable is introduced by means of a membership predicate which should be the first predicate situated on the left-hand side of the implication. In other words, a quantified predicate should have the following general form where *x* is a *Variable* supposed to be non-free in the *Set s* and where *P* is a *Predicate*:

$$\forall x \cdot (x \in s \ \wedge \ \cdots \ \Rightarrow \ P\,)$$

In the case of an existential quantifier, the general form is thus:

$$\exists x \cdot (x \in s \ \wedge \ \cdots \ \wedge \ P)$$

As already seen in the formulation of axiom SET 3, we also require for the purpose of type-checking that the sets defined in comprehension are of the following similar shape:

$$\{x \mid x \in s \ \wedge \ \cdots \ \wedge \ P\}$$

Notice that, as special cases, we might consider $\exists x \cdot (x \in s)$ and $\{x \mid x \in s\}$ as being shorthands for $\exists x \cdot (x \in s \ \wedge \ x = x)$ and $\{x \mid x \in s \ \wedge \ x = x\}$ respectively. In the following table, x and y are *Variables*, s and t are *Sets*, and P, Q and R are *Predicates*:

	Antecedents	Consequent
T 4	$x \backslash s$ $x \backslash R$ for each R occuring in ENV ENV, $x \in s$ $\vdash$ check(P)	ENV $\vdash$ check$(\forall x \cdot (x \in s \ \Rightarrow \ P))$
T 5	ENV $\vdash$ check$(\forall x \cdot (x \in s \ \Rightarrow \ \forall y \cdot (y \in t \ \Rightarrow \ P)))$	ENV $\vdash$ check$(\forall (x,y) \cdot (x,y \in s \times t \ \Rightarrow \ P))$
T 6	ENV $\vdash$ check$(\forall x \cdot (P \ \Rightarrow \ Q \wedge R))$	ENV $\vdash$ check$(\forall x \cdot (P \wedge Q \ \Rightarrow \ R))$

Rule T4 has a close relationship with rule GEN of Predicate Calculus as presented in section 1.3.5. Applied in a backward way, it has the similar effect of removing the quantifier of the goal and enlarging the environment, together with a number of non-freeness conditions. Rule T5 indicates how a multiple quantified variable is decomposed little by little. Finally, rule T6 shows how extra predicates situated on the left-hand side of the implication are moved to the right-hand side.

The next three rules deal with the remaining kinds of *Predicates*, namely equality, membership and inclusion. This is where the typing system starts to enter into action. In the following table, E and F are *Expressions*, and s and t are *Sets*.

	Antecedents	Consequent
T 7	$\text{ENV} \;\vdash\; \text{type}(E) \equiv \text{type}(F)$	$\text{ENV} \;\vdash\; \text{check}(E = F)$
T 8	$\text{ENV} \;\vdash\; \text{type}(E) \equiv \text{super}(s)$	$\text{ENV} \;\vdash\; \text{check}(E \in s)$
T 8'	$\text{ENV} \;\vdash\; \text{super}(s) \equiv \text{super}(t)$	$\text{ENV} \;\vdash\; \text{check}(s \subseteq t)$

Rule **T 7**, applied in a backward way, transforms the goal $\text{check}(E = F)$ into the corresponding equivalence of the types of E and F. The operator type will be given its meaning through the forthcoming rules. Rule **T 8**, applied in a backward way, transforms a goal of the form $E \in s$ into the corresponding equivalence of the type of E with the super-set of the set s. The operator super will be given its meaning through the forthcoming rules. Rule **T 8'**, applied in a backward way, transforms a goal of the form $s \subseteq t$ into the corresponding equivalence of the super-set of s with the super-set of the set t. That rule is not indispensable since inclusion is already a shorthand for the membership in the power-set. It is just given here because of its simplicity.

The next five rules show how the types of *Expressions* can be computed once encountered in a typing equivalence. In the following table, x is a *Variable*, s is a *Set*, U is a *Type* and E and F are *Expressions*:

	Antecedents	Consequent
T 9	$\left\{ \begin{array}{l} x \in s \;\; \text{occurs in ENV} \\[1em] \text{ENV} \;\vdash\; \text{super}(s) \equiv U \end{array} \right.$	$\text{ENV} \;\vdash\; \text{type}(x) \equiv U$
T 10	$\text{ENV} \;\vdash\; \text{type}(E) \times \text{type}(F) \equiv U$	$\text{ENV} \;\vdash\; \text{type}(E \mapsto F) \equiv U$
T 11	$\text{ENV} \;\vdash\; \text{super}(s) \equiv U$	$\text{ENV} \;\vdash\; \text{type}(\text{choice}(s)) \equiv U$
T 12	$\text{ENV} \;\vdash\; \mathbb{P}(\text{super}(s)) \equiv U$	$\text{ENV} \;\vdash\; \text{type}(s) \equiv U$

Rule T 9 deals with the type of a variable. This should be provided by the environment. Quite naturally, rule T 10 tells us that the type of an ordered pair is the cartesian product of the types of its components. Rule T 11 tells us that the type of the choice of a set is the super-set of that set. Finally, rule T 12 tells us that the type of a set is the power-set of the super-set of that set.

Notice that similar rules dealing with the right-hand side of a typing equivalence should also be proposed (such rules are named with the same numbers primed).

Our next series of rules shows how the super-set of a *Set* can be computed. In the following table, x is a *Variable*, s and t are sets, P is a *Predicate*, U is a *Type*, and I is an *Identifier*.

	Antecedents	Consequent
T 13	$\begin{cases} x \in s \text{ occurs in ENV} \\[1ex] \text{ENV} \vdash \text{super}(s) \equiv \mathbb{P}(U) \end{cases}$	$\text{ENV} \vdash \text{super}(x) \equiv U$
T 14	$\text{ENV} \vdash$ $\text{super}(s) \times \text{super}(t) \equiv U$	$\text{ENV} \vdash \text{super}(s \times t) \equiv U$
T 15	$\text{ENV} \vdash \mathbb{P}(\text{super}(s)) \equiv U$	$\text{ENV} \vdash \text{super}(\mathbb{P}(s)) \equiv U$
T 16	$\begin{cases} \text{ENV} \vdash \\ \quad \text{check}(\forall x \cdot (x \in s \Rightarrow P)) \\[1ex] \text{ENV} \vdash \text{super}(s) \equiv U \end{cases}$	$\text{ENV} \vdash$ $\text{super}(\{ x \mid x \in s \wedge P \}) \equiv U$
T 17	$\begin{cases} \text{given}(I) \text{ occurs in ENV} \\[1ex] \text{ENV} \vdash I \equiv U \end{cases}$	$\text{ENV} \vdash \text{super}(I) \equiv U$
T 18	$\text{ENV} \vdash \text{super}(s) \equiv \mathbb{P}(U)$	$\text{ENV} \vdash \text{super}(\text{choice}(s)) \equiv U$

Rule T 13 deals with the super-set of a (set) variable. This should be provided by the environment. Rule T 14 tells us that the super-set of a cartesian product is the cartesian product of the super-set of the sets composing that cartesian product. Rule T 15 tells us that the super-set of the power-set of a set is the power-set of the super-set of the set in question. Rule T 16 deals with the super-set of a set defined in comprehension from a certain set s. Clearly the super-set in question is the same as that of s. But we also have to type-check the predicate involved in the "selection": this is the purpose of the first sequent of the rule. Rule T 17 tells us that the super-set of a given set (as mentioned in the environment) is that set itself. Finally, rule T 18 concerns the (possible) super-set of a set (of sets) choice. Notice that similar rules dealing with the right-hand side of a typing equivalence should also be proposed (such rules are named with the same numbers primed).

Our next four rules show how type equivalence can be decomposed in a straightforward manner. In the following table, T, U, V, and W are *Types* and I is an *Identifier*.

	Antecedents	Consequent
T 19	$\text{ENV} \vdash T \equiv U$	$\text{ENV} \vdash \mathbb{P}(T) \equiv \mathbb{P}(U)$
T 20	$\begin{cases} \text{ENV} \vdash T \equiv U \\ \\ \text{ENV} \vdash V \equiv W \end{cases}$	$\text{ENV} \vdash T \times V \equiv U \times W$
T 21	$\text{given}(I)$ occurs in ENV	$\text{ENV} \vdash I \equiv I$

As an example, we show the mechanical type-checking of the following predicate where s is a (given) *Set*, and a, b and x are supposed to be distinct *Variables* that are non-free in s:

$$\forall (a,b) \cdot (a,b \in \mathbb{P}(s) \times \mathbb{P}(s) \;\Rightarrow\; \{x \mid x \in s \,\wedge\, (x \in a \,\wedge\, x \in b)\} \subseteq s)$$

Type-checking
We have the following sequent:

$$\text{given}(s) \vdash$$
$$\text{check}(\forall (a,b) \cdot (a,b \in \mathbb{P}(s) \times \mathbb{P}(s) \;\Rightarrow$$
$$\{x \mid x \in s \,\wedge\, (x \in a \,\wedge\, x \in b)\} \subseteq s))$$

Applying T 5, we obtain

$$\text{given}(s) \vdash$$
$$\text{check}(\forall a \cdot (a \in \mathbb{P}(s) \;\Rightarrow\; \forall b \cdot (b \in \mathbb{P}(s) \;\Rightarrow$$
$$\{x \mid x \in s \,\wedge\, (x \in a \,\wedge\, x \in b)\} \subseteq s)))$$

Applying T 4, we obtain

> given (s), $a \in \mathbb{P}(s)$ $\vdash$
> check $(\forall b \cdot (b \in \mathbb{P}(s) \Rightarrow \{x \mid x \in s \wedge (x \in a \wedge x \in b)\} \subseteq s))$

Applying T 4 again, we obtain

> given (s), $a \in \mathbb{P}(s)$, $b \in \mathbb{P}(s)$ $\vdash$
> check $(\{x \mid x \in s \wedge (x \in a \wedge x \in b)\} \subseteq s)$

Applying T 8', we obtain

> given (s), $a \in \mathbb{P}(s)$, $b \in \mathbb{P}(s)$ $\vdash$
> super $(\{x \mid x \in s \wedge (x \in a \wedge x \in b)\}) \equiv$ super (s)

Applying T 17', we obtain

> given (s), $a \in \mathbb{P}(s)$, $b \in \mathbb{P}(s)$ $\vdash$
> super $(\{x \mid x \in s \wedge (x \in a \wedge x \in b)\}) \equiv s$

Applying T 16, we obtain both

> given (s), $a \in \mathbb{P}(s)$, $b \in \mathbb{P}(s)$ $\vdash$
> check $(\forall x \cdot (x \in s \Rightarrow (x \in a \wedge x \in b)\}))$

> given (s), $a \in \mathbb{P}(s)$, $b \in \mathbb{P}(s)$ $\vdash$ super $(s) \equiv s$

The latter is discharged according to T 17 and T 21. Applying T 4 and then T 1 to the former yields both

> given (s), $a \in \mathbb{P}(s)$, $b \in \mathbb{P}(s)$, $x \in s$ $\vdash$ check $(x \in a)$

> given (s), $a \in \mathbb{P}(s)$, $b \in \mathbb{P}(s)$, $x \in s$ $\vdash$ check $(x \in b)$

As these sequents are essentially the same, we only treat the first of them. We apply T 8 yielding

> given (s), $a \in \mathbb{P}(s)$, $b \in \mathbb{P}(s)$, $x \in s$ $\vdash$ type $(x) \equiv$ super (a)

We apply T 13' yielding

> given (s), $a \in \mathbb{P}(s)$, $b \in \mathbb{P}(s)$, $x \in s$ $\vdash$ $\mathbb{P}($type $(x)) \equiv$ super $(\mathbb{P}(s))$

We apply then T 15', T 19 and T 17' yielding

> given (s), $a \in \mathbb{P}(s)$, $b \in \mathbb{P}(s)$, $x \in s$ $\vdash$ type $(x) \equiv s$

Applying T 9, we obtain

> given (s), $a \in \mathbb{P}(s)$, $b \in \mathbb{P}(s)$, $x \in s$ $\vdash$ super $(s) \equiv s$

which is now discharged according to T 17 and T 21.
End of Type-checking

2.3. Derived Constructs

2.3.1. Definitions

We now define various classical constructs that will be derived from the basic constructs of the previous section: first the *union, intersection,* and *difference* of two sets, then the *empty set,* then the notion of sets defined *in extension* and, finally, the set of non-empty subsets of a set. Note that, in principle, these constructs are not indispensable. In other words, it would always be possible to come back to the basic constructs we have defined in the previous section but, of course, this would turn out to be very unpractical. As a result, as we proceed, we will use less and less the logical calculi introduced in the previous chapter and more and more the notation of set theory introduced in this chapter. Notice that the notations introduced in this and subsequent sections are very close (if not identical) to similar notations defined in Z [4] and VDM [5].

All such derived concepts are introduced in the following table where u is a *Set*, a is a *Variable*, E is an *Expression* supposed to belong to u, L is a list of *Expressions* separated by commas and all supposed to belong to u, and s and t are sets both supposed to be included in u.

Syntax	Definition
$s \cup t$	$\{a \mid a \in u \wedge (a \in s \vee a \in t)\}$
$s \cap t$	$\{a \mid a \in u \wedge (a \in s \wedge a \in t)\}$
$s - t$	$\{a \mid a \in u \wedge (a \in s \wedge a \notin t)\}$
$\{E\}$	$\{a \mid a \in u \wedge a = E\}$
$\{L, E\}$	$\{L\} \cup \{E\}$
$\varnothing$	BIG $-$ BIG
$\mathbb{P}_1(s)$	$\mathbb{P}(s) - \{\varnothing\}$

The definition of the empty set, $\varnothing$, seems to indicate that it is only defined for the set BIG. In fact, it is easy to prove, using the axiom of extensionality SET 4, that the empty set is equal to the difference of *any* set with itself.

2.3.2. Examples

In order to illustrate the previous constructs, we shall now present some examples. In all the forthcoming examples we use sets defined in extension whose members all are natural numbers. Although we have not yet defined the set $\mathbb{N}$ of natural numbers (this will be done rigorously in section 3.5), we feel free to do so. In fact, we do not make use of any property of the natural numbers, we just consider them here as "tokens". Here are the examples:

$$
\begin{aligned}
a &= \{1, 2, 3, 4, 5\} \\
b &= \{4, 5, 6, 7\} \\
a \cup b &= \{1, 2, 3, 4, 5, 6, 7\} \\
a \cap b &= \{4, 5\} \\
a - b &= \{1, 2, 3\}
\end{aligned}
$$

2.3.3. Type-checking

The type-checking laws have to be enlarged as follows. In the following table, a and b are *Sets*, U is a *Type*, E is an *Expression* and L is a list of *Expressions* separated by commas. As things are now clear enough, in what follows we shall always remove the leading "ENV $\vdash$" from the various sequents.

	Antecedents	Consequent
T 22	$\begin{cases} \operatorname{super}(a) \equiv U \\ \operatorname{super}(b) \equiv U \end{cases}$	$\operatorname{super}(a \cup b) \equiv U$
T 23	$\begin{cases} \operatorname{super}(a) \equiv U \\ \operatorname{super}(b) \equiv U \end{cases}$	$\operatorname{super}(a \cap b) \equiv U$
T 24	$\begin{cases} \operatorname{super}(a) \equiv U \\ \operatorname{super}(b) \equiv U \end{cases}$	$\operatorname{super}(a - b) \equiv U$

	Antecedents	Consequent
T 25	$\text{type}(E) \equiv U$	$\text{super}(\{E\}) \equiv U$
T 26	$\begin{cases} \text{type}(E) \equiv U \\ \\ \text{super}(\{L\}) \equiv U \end{cases}$	$\text{super}(\{L, E\}) \equiv U$
T 27	$\text{given}(I)$ occurs in ENV	$\text{super}(\varnothing) \equiv I$
T 28	$\text{super}(\mathbb{P}(s)) \equiv U$	$\text{super}(\mathbb{P}_1(s)) \equiv U$

Among the above rules, T 27 is of particular interest. It shows that the super-set of the empty set can be *any* given set. In other words, depending on the context where they are, various occurrences of the empty set might have different interpretations, as far as typing is concerned. We might wonder whether that poses some problems. For instance, what is the super-set of $\{\varnothing\}$? of $\{\varnothing, \{\varnothing\}\}$? Are we allowed to "write" such sets at all? In order to answer such questions, we first leave the reader to type-check the following predicates (where s is a given set):

$$\varnothing \subseteq s$$

$$\{\varnothing\} \subseteq \mathbb{P}(s)$$

$$\{\varnothing, \{\varnothing\}\} \subseteq \mathbb{P}(\mathbb{P}(s))$$

In fact, in the above predicates, the right-hand sides of the expressions involving s are the minimal ones. In other words, there could have been more $\mathbb{P}$ operators but certainly no less. For instance, the following predicate does type-check:

$$\{\varnothing, \{\varnothing\}\} \subseteq \mathbb{P}(\mathbb{P}(\mathbb{P}(s)))$$

On the other hand, the status of the following predicate

$$\varnothing \in \{\varnothing, \{\varnothing\}\}$$

should be quite clear: *it does not type-check.* This is the case simply because there is no given set to relate to the various occurrences of "$\varnothing$". This means that the empty set, in the absolute, does not make sense. Within our framework, an occurrence of the empty set in an expression must always be the empty set of *something*, and the something in question must be a *Type*.

Note also that, given a set s, none of the following predicates:

$$s \cup \{s\} \subseteq s$$

$$s \cup \{s\} \subseteq \mathbb{P}(s)$$

type-check. All this, of course, will have a certain influence on our definition of the set $\mathbb{N}$ of natural numbers in the next chapter. What is already certain is that, within our framework, the classical definition of $\mathbb{N}$, namely

$$\{\varnothing, \{\varnothing, \{\varnothing\}\}, \{\varnothing, \{\varnothing, \{\varnothing\}\}\}, \ldots\}$$

does not make sense.

2.3.4. Properties

From the definitions given in section 2.3.1, we can easily deduce the following well-known algebraic properties, where a, b, and c are all supposed to be subsets of a given set s. Moreover, for any subset u of s, $\overline{u}$ is a shorthand for $s - u$.

$a \cup b = b \cup a$ $a \cap b = b \cap a$	commutativity
$a \cup b \cup c = a \cup (b \cup c)$ $a \cap b \cap c = a \cap (b \cap c)$	associativity
$a \cap (b \cup c) = (a \cap b) \cup (a \cap c)$ $a \cup (b \cap c) = (a \cup b) \cap (a \cup c)$ $a - (b \cup c) = (a - b) \cap (a - c)$ $a - (b \cap c) = (a - b) \cup (a - c)$ $a - (b - c) = (a - b) \cup (a \cap c)$ $(a \cup b) - c = (a - c) \cup (b - c)$ $(a \cap b) - c = (a - c) \cap b$ $(a \cup b) \times t = (a \times t) \cup (b \times t)$ $(a \cap b) \times t = (a \times t) \cap (b \times t)$ $(a - b) \times t = (a \times t) - (b \times t)$ $t \times (a \cup b) = (t \times a) \cup (t \times b)$ $t \times (a \cap b) = (t \times a) \cap (t \times b)$ $t \times (a - b) = (t \times a) - (t \times b)$	distributivity and pseudo-distributivity

$a \cup \bar{a} = s$ $a \cap \bar{a} = \emptyset$	law of excluded middle
$a \cup a = a$ $a \cap a = a$	idempotence
$a \cup \emptyset = a$ $a \cap s = a$	neutral element
$a \cap (a \cup b) = a$ $a \cup (a \cap b) = a$ $\emptyset \cap a = \emptyset$ $s \cup a = s$ $\emptyset - a = \emptyset$ $a - \emptyset = a$	absorption
$s - s = \emptyset$	empty set
$a = \bar{\bar{a}}$	double complementation
$b \subseteq c \quad \Rightarrow \quad a \cap b \subseteq a \cap c$ $b \subseteq c \quad \Rightarrow \quad a \cup b \subseteq a \cup c$ $b \subseteq c \quad \Rightarrow \quad b - a \subseteq c - a$ $b \subseteq c \quad \Rightarrow \quad a - c \subseteq a - b$ $b \subseteq c \quad \Rightarrow \quad \bar{c} \subseteq \bar{b}$	monotonicity
$\overline{a \cup b} = \bar{a} \cap \bar{b}$ $\overline{a \cap b} = \bar{a} \cup \bar{b}$	de Morgan law
$a \subseteq (a \cup b)$ $(a \cap b) \subseteq a$ $(a \cap b) \subseteq c \Leftrightarrow a \subseteq (\bar{b} \cup c)$	inclusion

Each of the above properties can be proved within Predicate Calculus after performing a systematic translation. For instance, the statement

$$a - (b - c) = (a - b) \cup (a \cap c)$$

can be translated as follows (we have already removed the universal quantification over the variable x)

$$x \in s \, \wedge \, x \in a \, \wedge \, x \notin b - c$$
$$\Leftrightarrow$$
$$x \in s \, \wedge \, (x \in a - b \, \vee \, x \in a \cap c)$$

that is

$$x \in s \, \wedge \, x \in a \, \wedge \, (x \notin s \, \vee \, x \notin b \, \vee \, x \in c)$$
$$\Leftrightarrow$$
$$x \in s \, \wedge \, ((x \in s \, \wedge \, x \in a \, \wedge \, x \notin b) \, \vee \, (x \in s \, \wedge \, x \in a \, \wedge \, x \in c))$$

that is, in a more schematic way

$$S \, \wedge \, A \, \wedge \, (\neg S \, \vee \, \neg B \, \vee \, C)$$
$$\Leftrightarrow$$
$$S \, \wedge \, ((S \, \wedge \, A \, \wedge \, \neg B) \, \vee \, (S \, \wedge \, A \, \wedge \, C))$$

which we can now prove easily using the proof procedure of section 1.2.4.

2.4. Binary Relations

In this section we enlarge our notation once again to cope with the very important concept of *binary relation*. We are going to introduce the corresponding operators in two separate series. In each series, the operators will first be introduced syntactically, and then we shall give an informal explanation of each of them. We group all the examples in a separate subsection. Finally, in the last subsection, we present all the typing rules of the binary relation constructs.

2.4.1. Binary Relation Constructs: First Series

We introduce the set of binary relations from one set to another ($\leftrightarrow$), then the notion of *inverse* ($^{-1}$) of a relation (also called *converse*), then the notions of *domain* (dom) and *range* (ran) of a relation, then relational *composition* (;), the *identity relation* (id)), and, finally, various forms of relational *restrictions* ($\lhd, \rhd, \lhd\!\!\!-, -\!\!\!\rhd$). In the following table, u, v and w are *Sets*, a, b and c are distinct *Variables*, and p, q, s and t are as follows:

$$p \in u \leftrightarrow v \qquad q \in v \leftrightarrow w \qquad s \subseteq u \qquad t \subseteq v$$

We have then the following definitions:

Syntax	Definition
$u \leftrightarrow v$	$\mathbb{P}(u \times v)$
p^{-1}	$\{\, b, a \mid (b, a) \in v \times u \;\wedge\; (a, b) \in p \,\}$
$\mathrm{dom}\,(p)$	$\{\, a \mid a \in u \;\wedge\; \exists b \cdot (b \in v \;\wedge\; (a, b) \in p \,)\}$
$\mathrm{ran}\,(p)$	$\mathrm{dom}\,(p^{-1})$
$p\,;q$	$\{\, a, c \mid (a, c) \in u \times w \;\wedge$ $\qquad \exists b \cdot (b \in v \;\wedge\; (a, b) \in p \;\wedge\; (b, c) \in q \,)\}$
$q \circ p$	$p\,;q$
$\mathrm{id}\,(u)$	$\{\, a, b \mid (a, b) \in u \times u \;\wedge\; a = b \,\}$
$s \lhd p$	$\mathrm{id}\,(s)\,;p$
$p \rhd t$	$p\,;\mathrm{id}\,(t)$
$s \mathbin{\lhd\!\!\!-} p$	$(\mathrm{dom}\,(p) - s) \lhd p$
$p \mathbin{-\!\!\!\rhd} t$	$p \rhd (\mathrm{ran}\,(p) - t)$

As you can see, we have managed to give the smallest number of genuine definitions. In fact, most of the introduced constructs are defined in terms of other constructs. This principle of economy might be misleading at times, so that in the following table we also give the more basic definitions that are missing in the previous table:

Syntax	Definition
$\mathrm{ran}\,(p)$	$\{\, b \mid b \in v \;\wedge\; \exists a \cdot (a \in u \;\wedge\; (a, b) \in p \,)\}$
$s \lhd p$	$\{\, a, b \mid (a, b) \in p \;\wedge\; a \in s \,\}$
$p \rhd t$	$\{\, a, b \mid (a, b) \in p \;\wedge\; b \in t \,\}$
$s \mathbin{\lhd\!\!\!-} p$	$\{\, a, b \mid (a, b) \in p \;\wedge\; a \notin s \,\}$

Syntax	Definition
$p \rhd t$	$\{\, a,b \mid (a,b) \in p \,\wedge\, b \notin t \,\}$

In words, a relation from a *source u* to a *destination v* (for short, a relation from u to v) is a set of pairs constructed from members of u and v respectively.

The inverse, p^{-1}, of a relation p is that relation with each pair of the form $a \mapsto b$ turned into the pair $b \mapsto a$.

The domain, $\mathsf{dom}\,(p)$, of a relation p from u to v is the subset of u whose members are related to at least one member of v under the relation p.

The range, $\mathsf{ran}\,(p)$, of a relation p from u to v is the subset of v whose members are related to at least one member of u under the relation p.

The forward composition, $p \,;\, q$, of two relations p and q is a certain relation from the source of p to the destination of q. A pair, $a \mapsto c$, belongs to that relation when its first component a is the first component of some pair of p and when its second component is the second component of some pair of q with the added constraint that the two chosen pairs in p and q are such that the second component of the first one and the first component of the second one are the same.

The identity relation, $\mathsf{id}\,(u)$, built on a set u is the relation from u to u whose pairs are built from identical elements.

The domain restriction, $s \lhd p$, of a relation p by a set s is the relation obtained by considering only the pairs of p whose first elements are members of s.

Likewise, the range restriction, $p \rhd t$, of a relation p by a set t is the relation obtained by considering only the pairs of p whose second elements are members of t.

The domain subtraction, $s \blacktriangleleft p$, of a relation p by a set s is the relation obtained by considering only the pairs of p whose first elements are *not* members of s.

Finally, the range subtraction, $p \blacktriangleright t$, of a relation p by a set t is the relation obtained by considering only the pairs of p whose second elements are *not* members of t.

In section 2.4.3, we shall give examples of such constructs.

2.4.2. Binary Relation Constructs: Second Series

We now introduce more relational constructs such as the *image* ([ ]) of a set under a relation, the *overriding* ($\mathbin{<\!\!+}$) of a relation by another one, the *direct product* ($\otimes$) of two relations, the two classical *projections* for ordered pairs ($\mathsf{prj}_1, \mathsf{prj}_2$), and the *parallel product* ($\|$) of two relations. These concepts, together with the previous ones, allow us to develop a very rich *Relational Calculus* which proves to be extremely convenient in writing most of our abstract specifications. In the following table, s, t, u and v are *Sets*, a, b and c are distinct *Variables*, and p, w, q, f, g, h, and k are as follows:

$$p \in s \leftrightarrow t \qquad w \subseteq s \qquad q \in s \leftrightarrow t \qquad f \in s \leftrightarrow u$$
$$g \in s \leftrightarrow v \qquad h \in s \leftrightarrow u \qquad k \in t \leftrightarrow v$$

We have then the following definitions:

Syntax	Definition
$p[w]$	$\mathrm{ran}(w \lhd p)$
$q \mathbin{\lhd\!\!\!-} p$	$(\mathrm{dom}(r) \mathbin{\lhd\!\!-} q) \cup r$
$f \otimes g$	$\{a,(b,c) \mid a,(b,c) \in s \times (u \times v) \ \wedge\ (a,b) \in f \ \wedge\ (a,c) \in g\}$
$\mathrm{prj}_1(s,t)$	$(\mathrm{id}(s) \otimes (s \times t))^{-1}$
$\mathrm{prj}_2(s,t)$	$((t \times s) \otimes \mathrm{id}(t))^{-1}$
$h \parallel k$	$(\mathrm{prj}_1(s,t); h) \otimes (\mathrm{prj}_2(s,t); k)$

As for the previous collection of relational constructs, we have managed to give the smallest number of genuine definitions. In fact, most of the introduced constructs are defined in terms of other constructs. This principle of economy might be misleading at times, so that in the following table we also give the more basic definitions that are missing in the previous table:

Syntax	Definition
$p[w]$	$\{b \mid b \in t \ \wedge\ \exists a \cdot (a \in w \ \wedge\ (x,y) \in r)\}$
$q \mathbin{\lhd\!\!\!-} p$	$\{a,b \mid (a,b) \in s \times t \ \wedge$ $\qquad (((a,b) \in q \ \wedge\ a \notin \mathrm{dom}(p)) \ \vee\ (a,b) \in p)\}$
$\mathrm{prj}_1(s,t)$	$\{a,b,c \mid (a,b,c) \in s \times t \times s \ \wedge\ c = a\}$
$\mathrm{prj}_2(s,t)$	$\{a,b,c \mid (a,b,c) \in s \times t \times t \ \wedge\ c = b\}$
$h \parallel k$	$\{(a,b),(c,d) \mid ((a,b),(c,d)) \in (s \times t) \times (u \times v) \ \wedge$ $\qquad (a,c) \in h \ \wedge\ (b,d) \in k\}$

In words, the image, $p[w]$, of a set w under a relation p from s to t is the subset of t whose members are the second elements of those pairs of p whose first elements are members of w.

The overriding, $q \triangleleft\!+ p$, of a relation q by a relation p is the relation obtained by taking all the pairs of p and by removing from q those pairs whose first elements are also the first elements of some pairs of p. Such a construct is of particular interest when p and q are functions (section 2.5) since it will have the effect of forming a new function made up of p and that part of q whose domain does not overlap with that of p (i.e. changing q only at those points in the domain of p).

The direct product, $f \otimes g$, of two relations f and g is the relation made up of pairs of the form $x \mapsto (y, z)$ where (x, y) and (x, z) are pairs belonging to f and g respectively. As we shall see, this construct might be very interesting when f and g are functions. In that case, we might insist that their direct product is an *injective* (i.e. one-one) function. Thus, when a pair of the form $x \mapsto (y, z)$ belongs to $f \otimes g$, then (y, z) determines x *uniquely* and vice-versa.

The two projections $\mathsf{prj}_1 (s, t)$ and $\mathsf{prj}_2 (s, t)$ are relations (in fact functions) mapping pairs of the form (x, y) (built from s and t) to x and y respectively.

Finally, the parallel product, $h \mid\mid k$, of two relations h and k is the relation obtained by forming pairs of the form $((x, y), (z, w))$ where (x, z) and (y, w) are pairs of h and k respectively.

In the following diagram we show the relationship between the type of the direct product operator and that of both projection operators:

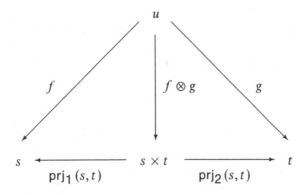

The above diagram has no precise meaning; its only purpose is to illustrate the relationship between the types of the various elements labelling the arrows. In fact, each element labelling an arrow is a binary relation with source the object situated at the beginning of the arrow and with destination the object situated at the end of the arrow.

Likewise, the following diagram shows the relationship between the type of the parallel product operator and that of both projection operators:

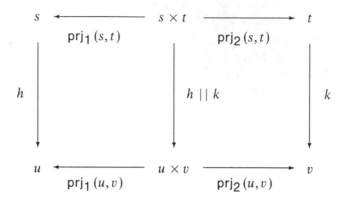

2.4.3. Examples of Binary Relation Constructs

We now give a few examples using the above constructs. Here are examples corresponding to the first series:

$$
\begin{array}{rcl}
p & = & \{\, 3 \mapsto 5,\ 3 \mapsto 9,\ 6 \mapsto 3,\ 9 \mapsto 2 \,\} \\[2mm]
p^{-1} & = & \{\, 5 \mapsto 3,\ 9 \mapsto 3,\ 3 \mapsto 6,\ 2 \mapsto 9 \,\} \\[2mm]
\mathrm{dom}\,(p) & = & \{\, 3,\ 6,\ 9 \,\} \\[2mm]
\mathrm{ran}\,(p) & = & \{\, 5,\ 9,\ 3,\ 2 \,\} \\[2mm]
q & = & \{\, 2 \mapsto 7,\ 3 \mapsto 4,\ 5 \mapsto 1,\ 9 \mapsto 5 \,\} \\[2mm]
p\,;q & = & \{\, 3 \mapsto 1,\ 3 \mapsto 5,\ 6 \mapsto 4,\ 9 \mapsto 7 \,\} \\[2mm]
u & = & \{\, 1,\ 2,\ 3 \,\} \\[2mm]
\mathrm{id}\,(u) & = & \{\, 1 \mapsto 1,\ 2 \mapsto 2,\ 3 \mapsto 3 \,\} \\[2mm]
s & = & \{\, 4,\ 7,\ 3 \,\} \\[2mm]
t & = & \{\, 4,\ 8,\ 1 \,\}
\end{array}
$$

$$
\begin{aligned}
s \lhd p &= \{3 \mapsto 5,\ 3 \mapsto 9\} \\[6pt]
p \rhd t &= \varnothing \\[6pt]
s \mathbin{\lhd\!\!\!-} p &= \{6 \mapsto 3,\ 9 \mapsto 2\} \\[6pt]
p \mathbin{-\!\!\!\rhd} t &= \{3 \mapsto 5,\ 3 \mapsto 9,\ 6 \mapsto 3,\ 9 \mapsto 2\}
\end{aligned}
$$

And here are examples corresponding to the second series:

$$
\begin{aligned}
p &= \{3 \mapsto 5,\ 3 \mapsto 9,\ 6 \mapsto 3,\ 9 \mapsto 2\} \\[6pt]
w &= \{1,\ 2,\ 3\} \\[6pt]
p[w] &= \{5,\ 9\} \\[6pt]
q &= \{2 \mapsto 7,\ 3 \mapsto 4,\ 5 \mapsto 1,\ 9 \mapsto 5\} \\[6pt]
q \mathbin{<\!\!\!+} p &= \{3 \mapsto 5,\ 3 \mapsto 9,\ 6 \mapsto 3,\ 9 \mapsto 2,\ 2 \mapsto 7,\ 5 \mapsto 1\} \\[6pt]
f &= \{8 \mapsto 10,\ 7 \mapsto 11,\ 2 \mapsto 11,\ 6 \mapsto 12\} \\[6pt]
g &= \{1 \mapsto 20,\ 7 \mapsto 20,\ 2 \mapsto 21,\ 1 \mapsto 22\} \\[6pt]
f \otimes g &= \{7 \mapsto (11, 20),\ 2 \mapsto (11, 21)\} \\[6pt]
s &= \{1,\ 4\} \\[6pt]
t &= \{2,\ 3\} \\[6pt]
\mathsf{prj}_1\,(s, t) &= \{(1, 2) \mapsto 1,\ (1, 3) \mapsto 1,\ (4, 2) \mapsto 4,\ (4, 3) \mapsto 4\} \\[6pt]
\mathsf{prj}_2\,(s, t) &= \{(1, 2) \mapsto 2,\ (1, 3) \mapsto 3,\ (4, 2) \mapsto 2,\ (4, 3) \mapsto 3\} \\[6pt]
h &= \{1 \mapsto 11,\ 4 \mapsto 12\} \\[6pt]
k &= \{2 \mapsto 21,\ 7 \mapsto 22\} \\[6pt]
h \parallel k &= \{(1, 2) \mapsto (11, 21),\ (1, 7) \mapsto (11, 22), \\
&\qquad (4, 2) \mapsto (12, 21),\ (4, 7) \mapsto (12, 22)\}
\end{aligned}
$$

2.4.4. Type-checking of Binary Relation Constructs

We have to enlarge our typing rules as follows:

	Antecedents	Consequent
T 29	$\mathsf{super}(r) \equiv U \times \mathsf{super}(\varnothing)$	$\mathsf{super}(\mathsf{dom}(r)) \equiv U$
T 30	$\mathsf{super}(r) \equiv \mathsf{super}(\varnothing) \times U$	$\mathsf{super}(\mathsf{ran}(r)) \equiv U$
T 31	$\mathsf{super}(\mathsf{ran}(r)) \times \mathsf{super}(\mathsf{dom}(r)) \equiv U$	$\mathsf{super}(r^{-1}) \equiv U$
T 32	$\begin{cases} \mathsf{super}(u) \equiv \mathsf{super}(\mathsf{dom}(r)) \\ \mathsf{super}(r) \equiv U \end{cases}$	$\mathsf{super}(u \lhd r) \equiv U$
T 33	$\begin{cases} \mathsf{super}(\mathsf{dom}(p)) \times \mathsf{super}(\mathsf{ran}(q)) \equiv U \\ \mathsf{super}(\mathsf{ran}(p)) \equiv \mathsf{super}(\mathsf{dom}(q)) \end{cases}$	$\mathsf{super}(p\,;q) \equiv U$
T 34	$\mathsf{super}(s) \times \mathsf{super}(s) \equiv U$	$\mathsf{super}(\mathsf{id}(s)) \equiv U$
T 35	$\begin{cases} \mathsf{super}(v) \equiv \mathsf{super}(\mathsf{ran}(r)) \\ \mathsf{super}(r) \equiv U \end{cases}$	$\mathsf{super}(r \rhd v) \equiv U$
T 36	$\begin{cases} \mathsf{super}(u) \equiv \mathsf{super}(\mathsf{dom}(r)) \\ \mathsf{super}(r) \equiv U \end{cases}$	$\mathsf{super}(u \mathbin{\lhd\mkern-9mu-} r) \equiv U$
T 37	$\begin{cases} \mathsf{super}(v) \equiv \mathsf{super}(\mathsf{ran}(r)) \\ \mathsf{super}(r) \equiv U \end{cases}$	$\mathsf{super}(r \mathbin{-\mkern-9mu\rhd} v) \equiv U$

To deal with our second series of operators, we have to enlarge our typing rules as follows:

	Antecedents	Consequent
T 38	$\left\{\begin{array}{l} \mathsf{super}\,(w) \equiv \mathsf{super}\,(\mathsf{dom}\,(r)) \\[1ex] \mathsf{super}\,(\mathsf{ran}\,(r)) \equiv U \end{array}\right.$	$\mathsf{super}\,(r\,[w]) \equiv U$
T 39	$\left\{\begin{array}{l} \mathsf{super}\,(q) \equiv U \\[1ex] \mathsf{super}\,(r) \equiv U \end{array}\right.$	$\mathsf{super}\,(q \lessdot r) \equiv U$
T 40	$\left\{\begin{array}{l} \mathsf{super}\,(\mathsf{dom}\,(f)) \equiv \mathsf{super}\,(\mathsf{dom}\,(g)) \\[1ex] \mathsf{super}\,(\,\mathsf{dom}\,(f) \times (\mathsf{ran}\,(f) \times \mathsf{ran}\,(g))) \equiv U \end{array}\right.$	$\mathsf{super}\,(f \otimes g) \equiv U$
T 41	$\mathsf{super}\,(s \times t \times s) \equiv U$	$\mathsf{super}\,(\mathsf{prj}_1\,(s,t)) \equiv U$
T 42	$\mathsf{super}\,(s \times t \times t) \equiv U$	$\mathsf{super}\,(\mathsf{prj}_2\,(s,t)) \equiv U$
T 43	$\mathsf{super}\,(\,(\mathsf{dom}\,(f) \times \mathsf{dom}\,(g)) \times$ $(\mathsf{ran}\,(f) \times \mathsf{ran}\,(g))\,) \equiv U$	$\mathsf{super}\,(f \;||\; g) \equiv U$

2.5. Functions

In this section we present the concept of function, a special case of relation. More precisely, a function is a relation where no two points of the range can be related to a single point of the domain. That special property of a function gives rise to the concept of *function application*, as opposed to that of *relational image* for a general relation. For instance, here is a function f:

$$f \;=\; \{\,1 \mapsto 2,\; 5 \mapsto 7,\; 8 \mapsto 2\,\}$$

The image of the singleton $\{5\}$ under f is as follows:

$$f\,[\{5\}] \;=\; \{7\}$$

As shown, that image has only one element. This is, by definition, always the case for the image of a singleton under a function. This is why it is possible, as we shall see in section 2.5.2, to define the notion of application of a function at a given point of its domain by considering that single element. Here is the application of the function f at 5:

$$f(5) \; = \; 7$$

We are going to introduce the function related constructs in two separate series (sections 2.5.1 and 2.5.2). We shall then group all the examples in section 2.5.3. In section 2.5.4 some important properties of functions are presented. Finally, in section 2.5.5, we have all the typing rules.

2.5.1. Function Constructs: First Series

Our first series of concepts is that of partial and total *functions*, partial and total *injections*, partial and total *surjections*, and partial and total *bijections*. Again, these notations are identical to those defined in Z [4]. In the following table, s and t are *Sets* and r and f are *Variables*.

Syntax	Definition
$s \nrightarrow t$	$\{\, r \mid r \in s \leftrightarrow t \;\wedge\; (r^{-1}\,;r) \subseteq \mathrm{id}\,(t)\,\}$
$s \rightarrow t$	$\{\, f \mid f \in s \nrightarrow t \;\wedge\; \mathrm{dom}\,(f) = s \,\}$
$s \nrightarrowtail t$	$\{\, f \mid f \in s \nrightarrow t \;\wedge\; f^{-1} \in t \nrightarrow s \,\}$
$s \rightarrowtail t$	$s \nrightarrowtail t \;\cap\; s \rightarrow t$
$s \twoheadrightarrow t$	$\{\, f \mid x \in s \nrightarrow t \;\wedge\; \mathrm{ran}\,(f) = t \,\}$
$s \twoheadrightarrow t$	$s \twoheadrightarrow t \;\cap\; s \rightarrow t$
$s \rightarrowtail\!\!\!\rightarrow t$	$s \nrightarrowtail t \;\cap\; s \twoheadrightarrow t$
$s \rightarrowtail\!\!\!\rightarrow t$	$s \rightarrowtail t \;\cap\; s \twoheadrightarrow t$

A partial function ($\nrightarrow$) is a relation that does not contain two distinct pairs with the same first element: the definition we have given in the above table is, in fact, equivalent to this informal definition, which we now formalize as follows:

$$\{\, r \mid r \in s \leftrightarrow t \;\wedge$$
$$\forall\,(x,y,z) \cdot (\, x,y,z \in s \times t \times t \;\wedge\; (x,y) \in r \;\wedge\; (x,z) \in r \;\;\Rightarrow\;\; y = z \,)\,\}$$

A total function ($\rightarrow$) from s to t is a partial function whose domain is exactly s (rather than being only included in s as is the case for a partial function).

A partial injection ($\rightarrowtail$) from s to t is a partial function from s to t whose inverse is a partial function from t to s. We have a similar concept of total injection ($\rightarrowtail$).

A partial surjection ($\twoheadrightarrow$) from s to t is a partial function from s to t whose range is exactly t. We have a similar concept of total surjection ($\rightarrow$).

Finally, a partial bijection ($\rightarrowtail\!\!\!\!\twoheadrightarrow$) is a partial injection and partial surjection at the same time. We have a similar concept of total bijection ($\rightarrowtail\!\!\!\!\twoheadrightarrow$).

The following diagram indicates the inclusion relationship that exists between these operators. Each object situated at the origin of an arrow is supposed to be included in the object situated at the extremity of the same arrow.

$$s \leftrightarrow t$$

$$\uparrow$$

$$s \twoheadrightarrow t$$

$$\nearrow \qquad \uparrow \qquad \nwarrow$$

$$s \rightarrowtail t \qquad\qquad s \rightarrow t \qquad\qquad s \twoheadrightarrow t$$

$$\uparrow \qquad \nearrow \qquad\qquad\qquad \nwarrow \qquad \uparrow$$

$$s \rightarrowtail t \qquad\qquad\qquad\qquad s \rightarrow t$$

$$\nwarrow \qquad\qquad\qquad \nearrow$$

$$s \rightarrowtail t$$

At this point, we prove a simple result that we shall need in the next chapter. It concerns an equivalent statement about total function membership. Here is the result in question:

$$f \in s \rightarrow t \;\Leftrightarrow\; \forall x \cdot (x \in s \;\Rightarrow\; \{x\} \lhd f \in \{x\} \rightarrow t) \qquad\qquad \text{Property 2.5.1}$$

Proof
We prove first

$$f \in s \rightarrow t \;\Rightarrow\; \forall x \cdot (x \in s \;\Rightarrow\; \{x\} \lhd f \in \{x\} \rightarrow t) \qquad\qquad \text{Goal 1}$$

We assume $f \in s \rightarrow t$, that is

$$f^{-1} ; f \subseteq \text{id}(t) \qquad\qquad \text{Hypothesis 1}$$

$$\text{dom}(f) = s \qquad\qquad \text{Hypothesis 2}$$

And we have to prove

$$\forall x \cdot (x \in s \;\Rightarrow\; \{x\} \lhd f \in \{x\} \to t)$$
Goal 2

We assume then

$$x \in s$$
Hypothesis 3

and we have to prove $\{x\} \lhd f \in \{x\} \to t$, that is

$$(\{x\} \lhd f)^{-1} ; (\{x\} \lhd f) \subseteq \operatorname{id}(t)$$
Goal 3

$$\operatorname{dom}(\{x\} \lhd f) = \{x\}$$
Goal 4

Goal 4 is obvious according to Hypothesis 2 and Hypothesis 3. Goal 3 can be transformed into the following:

$$f^{-1} ; (\{x\} \lhd f) \subseteq \operatorname{id}(t)$$
Goal 5

which holds according to Hypothesis 1, the monotonicity of composition and the transitivity of inclusion. We now prove the following:

$$\forall x \cdot (x \in s \;\Rightarrow\; \{x\} \lhd f \in \{x\} \to t) \;\Rightarrow\; f \in s \to t$$
Goal 6

We assume

$$\forall x \cdot (x \in s \;\Rightarrow\; \{x\} \lhd f \in \{x\} \to t)$$
Hypothesis 4

and we have to prove $f \in s \to t$, that is

$$f^{-1} ; f \subseteq \operatorname{id}(t)$$
Goal 7

$$\operatorname{dom}(f) = s$$
Goal 8

From Hypothesis 4, we deduce easily

$$\forall x \cdot (x \in s \;\Rightarrow\; \operatorname{dom}(\{x\} \lhd f) = \{x\})$$
Derivation 1

$$\forall x \cdot (x \in s \;\Rightarrow\; (\{x\} \lhd f)^{-1} ; (\{x\} \lhd f) \subseteq \operatorname{id}(t))$$
Derivation 2

Derivation 1 can be transformed into

$$\forall x \cdot (x \in s \;\Rightarrow\; x \in \operatorname{dom}(f))$$
Derivation 3

from which Goal 8 follows. Derivation 2 can be transformed as follows into Goal 7:

$$\forall x \cdot (x \subset s \;\Rightarrow\; (\{x\} \lhd f)^{-1} ; (\{x\} \lhd f) \subseteq \mathsf{id}(t))$$

$\Leftrightarrow$

$$\forall x \cdot (x \in s \;\Rightarrow\; f^{-1} ; (\{x\} \lhd f) \subseteq \mathsf{id}(t))$$

$\Leftrightarrow$

$$\forall x \cdot (x \in s \;\Rightarrow\; \forall (y,y') \cdot ((y,y') \in (f^{-1} ; (\{x\} \lhd f)) \;\Rightarrow\; y = y'))$$

$\Leftrightarrow$

$$\forall x \cdot (x \in s \;\Rightarrow\; \forall (y,y') \cdot ((y,x) \in f^{-1} \wedge (x,y') \in f \;\Rightarrow\; y = y'))$$

$\Leftrightarrow$

$$\forall (y,y') \cdot \forall x \cdot (x \in s \wedge (x,y) \in f \wedge (x,y') \in f \;\Rightarrow\; y = y')$$

$\Leftrightarrow$

$$\forall (y,y') \cdot (\exists x \cdot (x \in s \wedge (x,y) \in f \wedge (x,y') \in f) \;\Rightarrow\; y = y')$$

$\Leftrightarrow$

$$f^{-1} ; f \subseteq \mathsf{id}(t)$$

End of Proof

2.5.2. Function Constructs: Second Series

We now introduce the concept of *functional abstraction* and the notion of *function evaluation*. The latter allows us to use the classical notation $f(x)$ to stand for the value of the function f at some point x. In the following table x is a *Variable*, s and t are *Sets*, E is an *Expression*, and P is a *Predicate*. Moreover, x and y are distinct *Variables* that are non-free in s and t and also y is non-free in E.

Syntax	Definition	Condition
$\lambda x \cdot (x \in s \mid E)$	$\{x,y \mid (x,y) \in s \times t \wedge y = E\}$	$\forall x \cdot (x \in s \Rightarrow E \in t)$
$\lambda x \cdot (x \in s \wedge P \mid E)$	$\{x,y \mid (x,y) \in s \times t \wedge P \wedge \\ y = E\}$	$\forall x \cdot (x \in s \wedge P \Rightarrow \\ E \in t)$
$f(E)$	$\mathsf{choice}(f[\{E\}])$	$f \in s \twoheadrightarrow t \wedge \\ E \in \mathsf{dom}(f)$

The first two definitions introduce functional abstraction. Such constructs are also called lambda abstractions. Their rôle is to provide a way of constructing a function given an expression E supposed to depend on the variable x and intended to denote the value of the function at the point x. Notice that the variable x is a quantified variable in these definitions. The pre-condition of these definitions is very important indeed since, by requiring that the expression

E belongs to a certain set, it guarantees that the functional abstraction is a well-defined function from one set to another. The last construct introduces a linguistic way of denoting the *unique* value of a function at a given point. We have used here the choice operator to denote directly the only member of the set $f[\{E\}]$. In section 2.5.4, we shall relate the value of a functional abstraction to substitution.

2.5.3. Examples of Function Constructs

Here are some examples of the previous constructs:

$$f = \{1 \mapsto 2,\ 2 \mapsto 3,\ 3 \mapsto 4\}$$

$$f \in \{1,\ 2,\ 3,\ 4\} \nrightarrow \{1,\ 2,\ 3,\ 4\}$$

$$f \in \{1,\ 2,\ 3\} \rightarrow \{1,\ 2,\ 3,\ 4\}$$

$$f \in \{1,\ 2,\ 3,\ 4\} \rightarrowtail\!\!\!\rightarrow \{1,\ 2,\ 3,\ 4\}$$

$$f \in \{1,\ 2,\ 3\} \rightarrowtail \{1,\ 2,\ 3,\ 4\}$$

$$f \in \{1,\ 2,\ 3,\ 4\} \twoheadrightarrow\!\!\!\rightarrow \{2,\ 3,\ 4\}$$

$$f \in \{1,\ 2,\ 3\} \twoheadrightarrow \{2,\ 3,\ 4\}$$

$$f \in \{1,\ 2,\ 3,\ 4\} \rightarrowtail\!\!\!\twoheadrightarrow \{2,\ 3,\ 4\}$$

$$f \in \{1,\ 2,\ 3\} \rightarrowtail\!\!\!\twoheadrightarrow \{2,\ 3,\ 4\}$$

and also

$$f(2) = \mathsf{choice}\,(f[\{2\}]) = \mathsf{choice}\,(\{3\}) = 3$$

2.5.4. Properties of Function Evaluation

This section is especially devoted to proving some important properties of function evaluation. To begin with, we propose two simple properties. The first property states that the pair $(x, f(x))$ is a member of the function f, provided x is a member of the domain of f, formally:

$f \in s \nrightarrow t$
$x \in \mathrm{dom}(f)$
$\Rightarrow$
$(x, f(x)) \in f$

Property 2.5.2

Proof

We assume

$$f \in s \nrightarrow t \qquad \text{Hypothesis 1}$$

$$x \in \mathrm{dom}(f) \qquad \text{Hypothesis 2}$$

and we have to prove

$$(x, f(x)) \in f \qquad \text{Goal 1}$$

According to the definition of $f(x)$ and Hypothesis 1 and Hypothesis 2, Goal 1 can be transformed into the following:

$$(x, \mathrm{choice}\,(f[\{x\}])) \in f \qquad \text{Goal 2}$$

As we have the following, according to Hypothesis 1 and Hypothesis 2 (the proof that from the two assumptions $r \in s \leftrightarrow t$ and $x \in \mathrm{dom}(r)$ one can deduce $\exists y \cdot (y \in r[\{x\}])$) is left to the reader):

$$\exists y \cdot (y \in f[\{x\}]) \qquad \text{Derivation 1}$$

We thus have, according to axiom SET 5

$$\mathrm{choice}\,(f[\{x\}]) \in f[\{x\}] \qquad \text{Derivation 2}$$

that is, after the definition of the image of a set under a relation,

$$\exists z \cdot (z \in \{x\} \,\wedge\, (z, \mathrm{choice}\,(f[\{x\}])) \in f) \qquad \text{Derivation 3}$$

that is, according to Hypothesis 2 and to the definition of $\{x\}$,

$$\exists z \cdot (x \in \mathrm{dom}(f) \,\wedge\, z = x \,\wedge\, (z, \mathrm{choice}\,(f[\{x\}])) \in f) \quad \text{Derivation 4}$$

that is, according to the one-point rule proved in section 1.4,

$$x \in \mathrm{dom}(f) \,\wedge\, (x, \mathrm{choice}\,(f[\{x\}])) \in f \qquad \text{Derivation 5}$$

This leads directly to Goal 2.
End of Proof

Our next property (whose proof is left to the reader) tells us that the first form of functional abstraction indeed defines a total function.

$$\forall x \cdot (x \in s \;\Rightarrow\; E \in t)$$
$$\Rightarrow$$
$$\lambda x \cdot (x \in s \mid E) \in s \rightarrow t$$

Property 2.5.3

We now come to the fundamental property of the evaluation of a functional abstraction. It expresses the fact that the evaluation of such a function at a point denoted by an expression V is equal to the result of the replacement, by V, of the free occurrences of the formal parameter of the function in the expression defining the function. In the following statement, x is a *Variable*, s and t are *Sets*, and E and V are *Expressions*.

$$\forall x \cdot (x \in s \;\Rightarrow\; E \in t)$$
$$V \in s$$
$$\Rightarrow$$
$$\lambda x \cdot (x \in s \mid E)(V) \;=\; [x := V]E$$

Theorem 2.5.1

Proof

Let f be our function

$$f \;=\; \lambda x \cdot (x \in s \mid E) \qquad\qquad \text{Definition 1}$$

We assume

$$\forall x \cdot (x \in s \;\Rightarrow\; E \in t) \qquad\qquad \text{Hypothesis 1}$$

$$V \in s \qquad\qquad \text{Hypothesis 2}$$

and we have to prove

$$f(V) \;=\; [x := V]E \qquad\qquad \text{Goal 1}$$

From the two previous hypotheses, and from **Property 2.5.3**, we easily deduce the following:

$$f \in s \rightarrow t \qquad\qquad \text{Derivation 1}$$

$$V \in \mathrm{dom}\,(f) \qquad\qquad \text{Derivation 2}$$

As a consequence and according to **Property 2.5.2**, we have

$$(V, f(V)) \in f \qquad\qquad \text{Derivation 3}$$

yielding, according to the definition of f as a functional abstraction:

$$(V, f(V)) \in \{x, y \mid x, y \in s \times t \;\wedge\; y = E\} \qquad\qquad \text{Derivation 4}$$

As a consequence and according to axiom **SET 3**, we have

$$[x, y := V, f(V)](y = E) \qquad\qquad \text{Derivation 5}$$

After distributing substitution over the $=$ operator, we have equivalently

$$[x,y := V,f(V)]y \;=\; [x,y := V,f(V)]E \qquad\qquad \text{Derivation 6}$$

Since y is distinct from x and is also non-free in E, we eventually obtain Goal 1 after "performing" the substitutions

$$f(V) \;=\; [x := V]E \qquad\qquad \text{Derivation 7}$$

End of Proof

Here is an example of applying the previous result:

$$f = \lambda x \cdot (x \in \mathbb{N} \mid x + x)$$

$$f(3) = [x := 3] (x + x) = 3 + 3$$

In the other case of functional abstraction, we have the following similar theorem:

$\forall x \cdot (x \in s \ \wedge \ P \ \Rightarrow \ E \in t)$
$V \in s$
$[x := V]P$ Theorem 2.5.2
$\Rightarrow$
$\lambda x \cdot (x \in s \ \wedge \ P \mid E)(V) \ = \ [x := V]E$

Our last property (whose proof is left to the reader) is the following:

$f \in s \nrightarrow t$
$\Rightarrow$ Property 2.5.4
$(x,y) \in f \ \Leftrightarrow \ (x \in \mathrm{dom}\,(f) \ \wedge \ y = f(x))$

This property is important in that it asserts that the predicate $y = f(x)$ alone is *not sufficient* to guarantee that the pair (x,y) belongs to f. In fact, we also have to be sure that x belongs to $\mathrm{dom}\,(f)$.

2.5.5. Type-checking of Function Constructs

We have to enlarge our typing rules as follows. Notice that in rule T 45 we have presented the full sequent because the environment ENV is modified by that rule.

	Antecedents	Consequent
T 44	$\left\{\begin{array}{l} \text{check}\,(\forall\, x \cdot (x \in s \;\Rightarrow\; P\,)) \\[1.5ex] \text{super}\,(\lambda\, x \cdot (x \in s \mid E\,)) \equiv U \end{array}\right.$	$\text{super}\,(\lambda\, x \cdot (x \in s \wedge P \mid E\,)) \equiv U$
T 45	$\left\{\begin{array}{l} x \setminus s \\[1.5ex] x \setminus R \quad \text{for each } R \text{ occuring in ENV} \\[1.5ex] \text{ENV},\, x \in s \;\vdash \\ \quad \text{super}\,(s) \times \text{type}\,(E\,) \equiv U \end{array}\right.$	$\text{ENV} \;\vdash$ $\text{super}\,(\lambda\, x \cdot (x \in s \mid E\,)) \equiv U$
T 46	$\left\{\begin{array}{l} \text{type}\,(E\,) \equiv \text{super}\,(\text{dom}\,(f\,)) \\[1.5ex] \text{super}\,(\text{ran}\,(f\,)) \equiv U \end{array}\right.$	$\text{type}\,(f(E\,)) \equiv U$
T 47	$\left\{\begin{array}{l} \text{type}\,(E\,) \equiv \text{super}\,(\text{dom}\,(f\,)) \\[1.5ex] \text{super}\,(\text{ran}\,(f\,)) \equiv \mathbb{P}(U) \end{array}\right.$	$\text{super}\,(f(E\,)) \equiv U$

2.6. Catalogue of Properties

In this section, our intention is to present a catalogue of the most useful properties that can be of some interest for proving predicates involving the set-theoretic constructs we have presented in the previous sections. Hence it is given mainly for reference purposes. This catalogue is by no means exhaustive. Its construction is essentially an experimental process, which has been conducted little by little. The idea is that other proofs can then be done by systematically exploring the catalogue rather than by translating the statement to be proved into predicate calculus. We have tried to organize the catalogue in a systematic fashion by grouping together laws that have some common flavour.

Most of the laws we are proposing are stated without proofs. Such proofs are left as exercises for the reader. However, some interesting laws are proved. This is done by translating them into the corresponding predicate calculus statements and by using the techniques developed in the previous chapter. Alternatively, some laws are proved by using other laws. In any case, the proof style we have adopted for doing these proofs is a little less precise than the one we have used so far. We leave readers fill in by themselves the gaps that may exist between some of the proof steps.

2.6.1. Membership Laws

Our first set of laws involves membership. More precisely, we present below a number of valid predicates corresponding to the membership of each construct to various sets of relations or functions.

Membership Property	Condition
$r^{-1} \in t \leftrightarrow s$	$r \in s \leftrightarrow t$
$f^{-1} \in t \;⤀\; s$	$f \in s \;↣\; t$
$f^{-1} \in t \;↣\; s$	$f \in s \;⤀\; t$
$f^{-1} \in t \;⤖\; s$	$f \in s \;⤖\; t$
$\mathrm{dom}(r) \subseteq s$	$r \in s \leftrightarrow t$
$\mathrm{ran}(r) \subseteq t$	$r \in s \leftrightarrow t$
$(p\,;q) \in s \leftrightarrow u$	$p \in s \leftrightarrow t \;\land\; q \in t \leftrightarrow u$
$(f\,;g) \in s \;⇸\; u$	$f \in s \;⇸\; t \;\land\; g \in t \;⇸\; u$
$(f\,;g) \in s \;⤔\; u$	$f \in s \;⤔\; t \;\land\; g \in t \;⤔\; u$
$(f\,;g) \in s \;⤀\; u$	$f \in s \;⤀\; t \;\land\; g \in t \;⤀\; u$
$(f\,;g) \in s \;→\; u$	$f \in s \;→\; t \;\land\; g \in t \;→\; u$
$(f\,;g) \in s \;↣\; u$	$f \in s \;↣\; t \;\land\; g \in t \;↣\; u$
$(f\,;g) \in s \;↠\; u$	$f \in s \;↠\; t \;\land\; g \in t \;↠\; u$
$(f\,;g) \in s \;⤖\; u$	$f \in s \;⤖\; t \;\land\; g \in t \;⤖\; u$
$\mathrm{id}(s) \in s \;⤖\; s$	
$(u \lhd r) \in u \leftrightarrow t$	$u \subseteq s \;\land\; r \in s \leftrightarrow t$
$(r \rhd v) \in s \leftrightarrow v$	$r \in s \leftrightarrow t \;\land\; v \subseteq t$
$(u ⩤ r) \in (s - u) \leftrightarrow t$	$u \subseteq s \;\land\; r \in s \leftrightarrow t$
$(r ⩥ v) \in s \leftrightarrow (t - v)$	$r \in s \leftrightarrow t \;\land\; v \subseteq t$
$r[u] \subseteq t$	$r \in s \leftrightarrow t \;\land\; u \subseteq s$
$(p \mathbin{<\!+} q) \in s \leftrightarrow t$	$p \in s \leftrightarrow t \;\land\; q \in s \leftrightarrow t$
$(f \mathbin{<\!+} g) \in s \;⇸\; t$	$f \in s \;⇸\; t \;\land\; g \in s \;⇸\; t$
$(f \mathbin{<\!+} g) \in s \;⤔\; t$	$f \in s \;⤔\; t \;\land\; g \in s \;⤔\; t \;\land$ $\mathrm{ran}(g) \cap \mathrm{ran}(\mathrm{dom}(g) ⩤ f) = \varnothing$
$(f \mathbin{<\!+} g) \in s \;⤀\; t$	$f \in s \;⇸\; t \;\land\; g \in s \;⤀\; t$
$(f \mathbin{<\!+} g) \in s \;→\; t$	$f \in s \;⇸\; t \;\land\; g \in s \;→\; t$
$(f \mathbin{<\!+} g) \in s \;→\; t$	$f \in s \;→\; t \;\land\; g \in s \;⇸\; t$
$(f \mathbin{<\!+} g) \in s \;↠\; t$	$f \in s \;⇸\; t \;\land\; g \in s \;↠\; t$
$(p \otimes q) \in s \leftrightarrow (t \times u)$	$p \in s \leftrightarrow t \;\land\; q \in s \leftrightarrow u$

Membership Property	Condition
$(f \otimes g) \in s \nrightarrow (t \times u)$	$f \in s \nrightarrow t \; \wedge \; g \in s \nrightarrow u$
$(f \otimes g) \in s \nrightarrowtail (t \times u)$	$f \in s \nrightarrowtail t \; \wedge \; g \in s \nrightarrowtail u$
$(f \otimes g) \in s \rightarrow (t \times u)$	$f \in s \rightarrow t \; \wedge \; g \in s \rightarrow u$
$(f \otimes g) \in s \rightarrowtail (t \times u)$	$f \in s \rightarrowtail t \; \wedge \; g \in s \rightarrowtail u$
$(f \otimes g) \in s \twoheadrightarrow (t \times u)$	$f \in s \twoheadrightarrow t \; \wedge \; g \in s \twoheadrightarrow u$
$(f \otimes g) \in s \rightarrowtail\!\!\!\rightarrow (t \times u)$	$f \in s \rightarrowtail\!\!\!\rightarrow t \; \wedge \; g \in s \rightarrowtail\!\!\!\rightarrow u$
$\mathrm{prj}_1 (s,t) \in (s \times t) \rightarrow s$	
$\mathrm{prj}_2 (s,t) \in (s \times t) \rightarrow t$	
$(p \parallel q) \in (s \times u) \leftrightarrow (t \times v)$	$p \in s \leftrightarrow t \; \wedge \; q \in u \leftrightarrow v$
$(f \parallel g) \in (s \times u) \nrightarrow (t \times v)$	$f \in s \nrightarrow t \; \wedge \; g \in u \nrightarrow v$
$(f \parallel g) \in (s \times u) \nrightarrowtail (t \times v)$	$f \in s \nrightarrowtail t \; \wedge \; g \in u \nrightarrowtail v$
$(f \parallel g) \in (s \times u) \twoheadrightarrow\!\!\!\!\! (t \times v)$	$f \in s \twoheadrightarrow t \; \wedge \; g \in u \twoheadrightarrow v$
$(f \parallel g) \in (s \times u) \rightarrow (t \times v)$	$f \in s \rightarrow t \; \wedge \; g \in u \rightarrow v$
$(f \parallel g) \in (s \times u) \rightarrowtail (t \times v)$	$f \in s \rightarrowtail t \; \wedge \; g \in u \rightarrowtail v$
$(f \parallel g) \in (s \times u) \twoheadrightarrow (t \times v)$	$f \in s \twoheadrightarrow t \; \wedge \; g \in u \twoheadrightarrow v$
$(f \parallel g) \in (s \times u) \rightarrowtail\!\!\!\rightarrow (t \times v)$	$f \in s \rightarrowtail\!\!\!\rightarrow t \; \wedge \; g \in u \rightarrowtail\!\!\!\rightarrow v$
$(f \cup g) \in s \nrightarrow t$	$f \in s \nrightarrow t \; \wedge \; g \in s \nrightarrow t \; \wedge$ $(\mathrm{dom}\,(g) \lhd f) = (\mathrm{dom}\,(f) \lhd g)$
$(f \cup g) \in s \nrightarrowtail t$	$f \in s \nrightarrowtail t \; \wedge \; g \in s \nrightarrowtail t \; \wedge$ $(\mathrm{dom}\,(g) \lhd f) = (\mathrm{dom}\,(f) \lhd g) \; \wedge$ $(f \rhd \mathrm{ran}\,(g)) = (g \rhd \mathrm{ran}\,(f))$
$(f \cap g) \in s \nrightarrow t$	$f \in s \nrightarrow t \; \wedge \; g \in s \leftrightarrow t$
$(f \cap g) \in s \nrightarrowtail t$	$f \in s \nrightarrowtail t \; \wedge \; g \in s \leftrightarrow t$
$(f - g) \in s \nrightarrowtail t$	$f \in s \nrightarrowtail t \; \wedge \; g \in s \leftrightarrow t$
$\{x \mapsto y\} \in s \nrightarrow t$	$x \in s \; \wedge \; y \in t$
$(s \times t) \in s \leftrightarrow t$	
$f(x) \in t$	$f \in s \nrightarrow t \; \wedge \; x \in \mathrm{dom}\,(f)$

2.6.2. Monotonicity Laws

Most of the constructs introduced are monotonic with respect to set inclusion.

Monotonicity Property
$u \subseteq s \; \wedge \; v \subseteq t \quad \Rightarrow \quad u \leftrightarrow v \subseteq s \leftrightarrow t$
$u \subseteq s \; \wedge \; v \subseteq t \quad \Rightarrow \quad u \nrightarrow v \subseteq s \nrightarrow t$
$u \subseteq s \; \wedge \; v \subseteq t \quad \Rightarrow \quad u \nrightarrowtail v \subseteq s \nrightarrowtail t$

Monotonicity Property	Condition
$v \subseteq t \quad \Rightarrow \quad s \rightarrow v \subseteq s \rightarrow t$	
$v \subseteq t \quad \Rightarrow \quad s \rightarrowtail v \subseteq s \rightarrowtail t$	
$u \subseteq s \quad \Rightarrow \quad u \twoheadrightarrow t \subseteq s \twoheadrightarrow t$	
$r \subseteq p \quad \Rightarrow \quad r^{-1} \subseteq p^{-1}$	$p \in s \leftrightarrow t$
$r \subseteq p \quad \Rightarrow \quad \mathrm{dom}\,(r) \subseteq \mathrm{dom}\,(p)$	$p \in s \leftrightarrow t$
$r \subseteq p \quad \Rightarrow \quad \mathrm{ran}\,(r) \subseteq \mathrm{ran}\,(p)$	$p \in s \leftrightarrow t$
$p \subseteq h \,\wedge\, q \subseteq k \quad \Rightarrow \quad (p\,;q) \subseteq (h\,;k)$	$h \in s \leftrightarrow t \,\wedge\, k \in t \leftrightarrow u$
$u \subseteq s \quad \Rightarrow \quad \mathrm{id}\,(u) \subseteq \mathrm{id}\,(s)$	
$u \subseteq v \,\wedge\, r \subseteq p \quad \Rightarrow \quad u \triangleleft r \subseteq v \triangleleft p$	$p \in s \leftrightarrow t \,\wedge\, v \subseteq s$
$r \subseteq p \,\wedge\, u \subseteq v \quad \Rightarrow \quad r \triangleright u \subseteq p \triangleright v$	$p \in s \leftrightarrow t \,\wedge\, v \subseteq t$
$v \subseteq u \,\wedge\, r \subseteq p \quad \Rightarrow \quad u \ntriangleleft r \subseteq v \ntriangleleft p$	$p \in s \leftrightarrow t \,\wedge\, u \subseteq s$
$r \subseteq p \,\wedge\, v \subseteq u \quad \Rightarrow \quad r \ntriangleright u \subseteq p \ntriangleright v$	$p \in s \leftrightarrow t \,\wedge\, u \subseteq t$
$r \subseteq p \,\wedge\, u \subseteq v \quad \Rightarrow \quad r\,[u] \subseteq p[v]$	$p \in s \leftrightarrow t \,\wedge\, v \subseteq s$
$p \subseteq h \quad \Rightarrow \quad (p \mathbin{\lessdot} q) \subseteq (h \mathbin{\lessdot} q)$	$h \in s \leftrightarrow t \,\wedge\, q \in s \leftrightarrow t$
$p \subseteq h \,\wedge\, q \subseteq k \quad \Rightarrow \quad (p \otimes q) \subseteq (h \otimes k)$	$h \in s \leftrightarrow t \,\wedge\, k \in s \leftrightarrow u$
$u \subseteq s \,\wedge\, v \subseteq t \quad \Rightarrow \quad \mathrm{prj}_1\,(u,v) \subseteq \mathrm{prj}_1\,(s,t)$	
$u \subseteq s \,\wedge\, v \subseteq t \quad \Rightarrow \quad \mathrm{prj}_2\,(u,v) \subseteq \mathrm{prj}_2\,(s,t)$	
$p \subseteq h \,\wedge\, q \subseteq k \quad \Rightarrow \quad (p \mid\mid q) \subseteq (h \mid\mid k)$	$h \in s \leftrightarrow t \,\wedge\, k \in u \leftrightarrow v$

2.6.3. Inclusion Laws

We now present laws that deal with set inclusion. We first present the inclusion laws that are concerned with the various sets of functions as presented in section 2.5.1 (such laws were already pictorially presented in that section). Most of the other laws are concerned with the intersection and difference of relations. Similar laws dealing with union of relations are not presented here since they are equality laws (not just inclusion laws) and will thus be presented in subsequent sections.

Inclusion Property
$s \twoheadrightarrow t \subseteq s \rightarrow t$
$s \rightarrowtail t \subseteq s \rightarrow t$
$s \rightarrow t \subseteq s \twoheadrightarrow t$
$s \rightarrowtail t \subseteq s \twoheadrightarrowtail t$

Inclusion Property	Condition
$s \twoheadrightarrow t \subseteq s \to t$	
$s \rightarrowtail t \subseteq s \to t$	
$s \twoheadrightarrow t \subseteq s \nrightarrow t$	
$s \rightarrowtail t \subseteq s \nrightarrow t$	
$s \to t \subseteq s \nrightarrow t$	
$s \nrightarrow t \subseteq s \leftrightarrow t$	
$\mathrm{id}(\mathrm{dom}(r)) \subseteq (r\,;r^{-1})$	$r \in s \leftrightarrow t$
$\mathrm{id}(\mathrm{ran}(r)) \subseteq (r^{-1}\,;r)$	$r \in s \leftrightarrow t$
$(u \lhd r) \subseteq r$	$u \subseteq s \;\wedge\; r \in s \leftrightarrow t$
$(r \rhd v) \subseteq r$	$r \in s \leftrightarrow t \;\wedge\; v \subseteq t$
$(u ⩤ r) \subseteq r$	$u \subseteq s \;\wedge\; r \in s \leftrightarrow t$
$(r ⩥ v) \subseteq r$	$r \in s \leftrightarrow t \;\wedge\; v \subseteq t$
$r\,;(p \cap q) \subseteq (r\,;p) \cap (r\,;q)$	$r \in s \leftrightarrow t \;\wedge\; p \in t \leftrightarrow u \;\wedge\; q \in t \leftrightarrow u$
$(r\,;p) - (r\,;q) \subseteq r\,;(p-q)$	$r \in s \leftrightarrow t \;\wedge\; p \in t \leftrightarrow u \;\wedge\; q \in t \leftrightarrow u$
$(p \cap q)\,;r \subseteq (p\,;r) \cap (q\,;r)$	$p \in s \leftrightarrow t \;\wedge\; q \in s \leftrightarrow t \;\wedge\; r \in t \leftrightarrow u$
$(p\,;r) - (q\,;r) \subseteq (p-q)\,;r$	$p \in s \leftrightarrow t \;\wedge\; q \in s \leftrightarrow t \;\wedge\; r \in t \leftrightarrow u$
$r[u \cap v] \subseteq r[u] \cap r[v]$	$r \in s \leftrightarrow t \;\wedge\; u \subseteq s \;\wedge\; v \subseteq s$
$r[u] - r[v] \subseteq r[u-v]$	$r \in s \leftrightarrow t \;\wedge\; u \subseteq s \;\wedge\; v \subseteq s$
$\mathrm{dom}(p \cap q) \subseteq \mathrm{dom}(p) \cap \mathrm{dom}(q)$	$p \in s \leftrightarrow t \;\wedge\; q \in s \leftrightarrow t$
$\mathrm{dom}(p) - \mathrm{dom}(q) \subseteq \mathrm{dom}(p-q)$	$p \in s \leftrightarrow t \;\wedge\; q \in s \leftrightarrow t$
$\mathrm{ran}(p \cap q) \subseteq \mathrm{ran}(p) \cap \mathrm{ran}(q)$	$p \in s \leftrightarrow t \;\wedge\; q \in s \leftrightarrow t$
$\mathrm{ran}(p) - \mathrm{ran}(q) \subseteq \mathrm{ran}(p-q)$	$p \in s \leftrightarrow t \;\wedge\; q \in s \leftrightarrow t$
$(p \cap q)[u] \subseteq p[u] \cap q[u]$	$p \in s \leftrightarrow t \;\wedge\; q \in s \leftrightarrow t \;\wedge\; u \subseteq s$
$p[u] - q[u] \subseteq (p-q)[u]$	$p \in s \leftrightarrow t \;\wedge\; q \in s \leftrightarrow t \;\wedge\; u \subseteq s$

We prove the law concerning the subtraction of domains:

$$p \in s \leftrightarrow t$$
$$q \in s \leftrightarrow t$$
$$\Rightarrow$$
$$\mathrm{dom}(p) - \mathrm{dom}(q) \subseteq \mathrm{dom}(p-q)$$

Property 2.6.1

In the forthcoming proofs and as said at the beginning of section 2.6, we shall justify proof steps in a more general way than before. We rely on the reader to supply the missing steps. For example, we might justify a step simply by writing **Predicate Calculus** meaning that some logical steps are missing.

Proof

We assume

$$p \in s \leftrightarrow t$$ Hypothesis 1
$$q \in s \leftrightarrow t$$ Hypothesis 2

and we have to prove

$$\mathrm{dom}\,(p) - \mathrm{dom}\,(q) \subseteq \mathrm{dom}\,(p - q)$$ Goal 1

Given a fresh variable x, it is sufficient to prove

$$x \in \mathrm{dom}\,(p) - \mathrm{dom}\,(q)$$
$$\Rightarrow$$ Goal 2
$$x \in \mathrm{dom}\,(p - q)$$

The proof goes as follows:

$$x \in \mathrm{dom}\,(p) - \mathrm{dom}\,(q)$$
$$\Leftrightarrow$$ Definition of Domain
$$x \in s \;\wedge\; \exists y \cdot (y \in t \;\wedge\; (x,y) \in p) \;\wedge\; \neg\, \exists y \cdot (y \in t \;\wedge\; (x,y) \in q)$$
$$\Leftrightarrow$$ Predicate Calculus
$$x \in s \;\wedge\; \exists y \cdot (y \in t \;\wedge\; (x,y) \in p) \;\wedge\; \forall y \cdot (y \in t \;\Rightarrow\; (x,y) \notin q)$$
$$\Rightarrow$$ Predicate Calculus
$$x \in s \;\wedge\; \exists y \cdot (y \in t \;\wedge\; (x,y) \in p \;\wedge\; (x,y) \notin q)$$
$$\Leftrightarrow$$ Definition of Domain
$$x \in \mathrm{dom}\,(p - q)$$

End of Proof

2.6.4. Equality Laws

In this section, we present equality laws. They are organized as independent series concerning specific operators. Most such laws are essentially distributive in nature. In other words, the main operator is distributed (sometimes with an alteration) among other operators.

Our first series of equality laws deals with the inverse operator. All such laws are straightforward.

Inverse Property	Condition
$r^{-1-1} = r$	$r \in s \leftrightarrow t$
$(p\,;q)^{-1} = q^{-1}\,;p^{-1}$	$p \in s \leftrightarrow t \;\wedge\; q \in t \leftrightarrow u$
$\mathrm{id}\,(s)^{-1} = \mathrm{id}\,(s)$	
$(u \vartriangleleft r)^{-1} = r^{-1} \vartriangleright u$	$u \subseteq s \;\wedge\; r \in s \leftrightarrow t$
$(r \vartriangleright v)^{-1} = v \vartriangleleft r^{-1}$	$r \in s \leftrightarrow t \;\wedge\; v \subseteq t$
$(u \blacktriangleleft r)^{-1} = r^{-1} \blacktriangleright u$	$u \subseteq s \;\wedge\; r \in s \leftrightarrow t$
$(r \blacktriangleright v)^{-1} = v \blacktriangleleft r^{-1}$	$r \in s \leftrightarrow t \;\wedge\; v \subseteq t$
$(p \nleftrightarrow q)^{-1} = (p^{-1} \blacktriangleright \mathrm{dom}\,(q)) \cup q^{-1}$	$p \in s \leftrightarrow t \;\wedge\; q \in s \leftrightarrow t$
$(p \parallel q)^{-1} = p^{-1} \parallel q^{-1}$	$p \in s \leftrightarrow t \;\wedge\; q \in u \leftrightarrow v$
$(p \cup q)^{-1} = p^{-1} \cup q^{-1}$	$p \in s \leftrightarrow t \;\wedge\; q \in s \leftrightarrow t$
$(p \cap q)^{-1} = p^{-1} \cap q^{-1}$	$p \in s \leftrightarrow t \;\wedge\; q \in s \leftrightarrow t$
$(p - q)^{-1} = p^{-1} - q^{-1}$	$p \in s \leftrightarrow t \;\wedge\; q \in s \leftrightarrow t$
$\{x \mapsto y\}^{-1} = \{y \mapsto x\}$	$x \in s \;\wedge\; y \in t$
$r^{-1} = \varnothing$	$r \in s \leftrightarrow t \;\wedge\; r = \varnothing$
$(s \times t)^{-1} = t \times s$	

We now present some laws concerning the domain of relations.

Domain Property	Condition
$\mathrm{dom}\,(f) = s$	$f \in s \rightarrow t$
$\mathrm{dom}\,(r^{-1}) = \mathrm{ran}\,(r)$	$r \in s \leftrightarrow t$
$\mathrm{dom}\,(p\,;q) = p^{-1}[\mathrm{dom}\,(q)]$	$p \in s \leftrightarrow t \;\wedge\; q \in t \leftrightarrow u$
$\mathrm{dom}\,(p\,;q) = \mathrm{dom}\,(p)$	$p \in s \leftrightarrow t \;\wedge\; q \in t \leftrightarrow u \;\wedge$ $\mathrm{ran}\,(p) \subseteq \mathrm{dom}\,(q)$
$\mathrm{dom}\,(\mathrm{id}\,(s)) = s$	
$\mathrm{dom}\,(u \vartriangleleft r) = u \cap \mathrm{dom}\,(r)$	$u \subseteq s \;\wedge\; r \in s \leftrightarrow t$
$\mathrm{dom}\,(r \vartriangleright v) = r^{-1}[v]$	$r \in s \leftrightarrow t \;\wedge\; v \subseteq t$
$\mathrm{dom}\,(u \blacktriangleleft r) = \mathrm{dom}\,(r) - u$	$u \subseteq s \;\wedge\; r \in s \leftrightarrow t$
$\mathrm{dom}\,(f \blacktriangleright v) = \mathrm{dom}\,(f) - f^{-1}[v]$	$f \in s \nrightarrow t \;\wedge\; v \subseteq t$
$\mathrm{dom}\,(p \nleftrightarrow q) = \mathrm{dom}\,(p) \cup \mathrm{dom}\,(q)$	$p \in s \leftrightarrow t \;\wedge\; q \in s \leftrightarrow t$
$\mathrm{dom}\,(p \otimes q) = \mathrm{dom}\,(p) \cap \mathrm{dom}\,(q)$	$p \in s \leftrightarrow t \;\wedge\; q \in s \leftrightarrow u$
$\mathrm{dom}\,(p \parallel q) = \mathrm{dom}\,(p) \times \mathrm{dom}\,(q)$	$p \in s \leftrightarrow t \;\wedge\; q \in u \leftrightarrow v$
$\mathrm{dom}\,(p \cup q) = \mathrm{dom}\,(p) \cup \mathrm{dom}\,(q)$	$p \in s \leftrightarrow t \;\wedge\; q \in s \leftrightarrow t$
$\mathrm{dom}\,(f \cap g) = \mathrm{dom}\,(f) \cap \mathrm{dom}\,(g)$	$f \in s \nrightarrow t \;\wedge\; g \in s \nrightarrow t \;\wedge$ $\mathrm{dom}\,(f) \vartriangleleft g = \mathrm{dom}\,(g) \vartriangleleft f$

Domain Property	Condition
$\mathrm{dom}\,(f - g) = \mathrm{dom}\,(f) - \mathrm{dom}\,(g)$	$f \in s \nrightarrow t \ \wedge\ g \in s \nrightarrow t \ \wedge$ $\mathrm{dom}\,(f) \lhd g = \mathrm{dom}\,(g) \lhd f$
$\mathrm{dom}\,(\{x \mapsto y\}) = \{x\}$	$x \in s \ \wedge\ y \in t$
$\mathrm{dom}\,(r) = \varnothing$	$r \in s \leftrightarrow t \ \wedge\ r = \varnothing$
$\mathrm{dom}\,(s \times t) = s$	$t \neq \varnothing$

We prove the law concerning the distributivity of domain over difference.

$f \in s \nrightarrow t$
$g \in s \nrightarrow t$
$\mathrm{dom}\,(f) \lhd g = \mathrm{dom}\,(g) \lhd f$ Property 2.6.2
$\Rightarrow$
$\mathrm{dom}\,(f - g) = \mathrm{dom}\,(f) - \mathrm{dom}\,(g)$

Proof

We assume

$\quad f \in s \nrightarrow t$ Hypothesis 1
$\quad g \in s \nrightarrow t$ Hypothesis 2
$\quad \mathrm{dom}\,(f) \lhd g = \mathrm{dom}\,(g) \lhd f$ Hypothesis 3

and we have to prove

$\quad \mathrm{dom}\,(f - g) = \mathrm{dom}\,(f) - \mathrm{dom}\,(g)$ Goal 1

As the reverse inclusion already holds (this is Property 2.6.1), we only have to prove

$\quad \mathrm{dom}\,(f - g) \subseteq \mathrm{dom}\,(f) - \mathrm{dom}\,(g)$ Goal 2

Given a fresh variable x, it is then sufficient to prove

$\quad x \in \mathrm{dom}\,(f - g)$ Goal 3
$\quad \Rightarrow$
$\quad x \in \mathrm{dom}\,(f) - \mathrm{dom}\,(g)$

The proof goes as follows:

$$x \in \mathsf{dom}\,(f - g)$$

$\Leftrightarrow$ Definition of Domain

$$x \in s \;\wedge\; \exists\,y \cdot (y \in t \;\wedge\; (x,y) \in f \;\wedge\; (x,y) \notin g)$$

$\Leftrightarrow$ Property 2.5.4

$$x \in s \;\wedge\; \exists\,y \cdot (y \in t \;\wedge\; x \in \mathsf{dom}\,(f) \;\wedge\; y = f(x) \;\wedge\; (x,y) \notin g)$$

$\Leftrightarrow$ One Point Rule

$$f(x) \in t \;\wedge\; x \in \mathsf{dom}\,(f) \;\wedge\; (x,f(x)) \notin g$$

$\Leftrightarrow$ Membership

$$x \in \mathsf{dom}\,(f) \;\wedge\; (x,f(x)) \notin g$$

$\Leftrightarrow$ Property 2.5.4

$$x \in \mathsf{dom}\,(f) \;\wedge\; (x \in \mathsf{dom}\,(g) \;\Rightarrow\; f(x) \neq g(x))$$

But from the three hypotheses, we have

$$x \in \mathsf{dom}\,(f) \;\wedge\; x \in \mathsf{dom}\,(g) \;\Rightarrow\; f(x) = g(x) \qquad \text{Derivation 1}$$

As a consequence, and according to the following general law provable using the decision procedure of the previous chapter and valid for any *Predicate A, B,* and *C*

$$A \,\wedge\, B \;\;\Rightarrow\;\; C$$
$$\Rightarrow$$
$$A \,\wedge\, (B \,\Rightarrow\, \neg C) \;\;\Rightarrow\;\; A \,\wedge\, \neg B$$

we have then

$$x \in \mathsf{dom}\,(f) \;\wedge\; (x \in \mathsf{dom}\,(g) \;\Rightarrow\; f(x) \neq g(x))$$
$$\Rightarrow$$
$$x \in \mathsf{dom}\,(f) \;\wedge\; x \notin \mathsf{dom}\,(g)$$
$$\Leftrightarrow$$
$$x \in \mathsf{dom}\,(f) - \mathsf{dom}\,(g)$$

End of Proof

Here are some laws concerning the range of a relation:

Range Property	Condition
$\mathsf{ran}\,(f) = t$	$f \in s \twoheadrightarrow t$
$\mathsf{ran}\,(r^{-1}) = \mathsf{dom}\,(r)$	$r \in s \leftrightarrow t$
$\mathsf{ran}\,(p\,;q) = q[\mathsf{ran}\,(p)]$	$p \in s \leftrightarrow t \;\wedge\; q \in t \leftrightarrow u$
$\mathsf{ran}\,(p\,;q) = \mathsf{ran}\,(p)$	$p \in s \leftrightarrow t \;\wedge\; q \in t \leftrightarrow u$
	$\mathsf{dom}\,(q) \subseteq \mathsf{ran}\,(p)$
$\mathsf{ran}\,(\mathsf{id}\,(s)) = s$	
$\mathsf{ran}\,(u \triangleleft r) = r[u]$	$u \subseteq s \;\wedge\; r \in s \leftrightarrow t$

Range Property	Condition
$\mathrm{ran}\,(r \triangleright v) \;=\; \mathrm{ran}\,(r) \cap v$	$r \in s \leftrightarrow t \;\wedge\; v \subseteq t$
$\mathrm{ran}\,(u \triangleleft r) \;=\; \mathrm{ran}\,(r) - r\,[u]$	$u \subseteq s \;\wedge\; r^{-1} \in t \twoheadrightarrow s$
$\mathrm{ran}\,(r \triangleright v) \;=\; \mathrm{ran}\,(r) - v$	$r \in s \leftrightarrow t \;\wedge\; v \subseteq t$
$\mathrm{ran}\,(p \triangleleft\!\!+ q) \;=\; \mathrm{ran}\,(\mathrm{dom}\,(q) \triangleleft p) \cup \mathrm{ran}\,(q)$	$p \in s \leftrightarrow t \;\wedge\; q \in s \leftrightarrow t$
$\mathrm{ran}\,(p \otimes q) \;=\; p^{-1}\,;q$	$p \in s \leftrightarrow t \;\wedge\; q \in s \leftrightarrow u$
$\mathrm{ran}\,(p \parallel q) \;=\; \mathrm{ran}\,(p) \times \mathrm{ran}\,(q)$	$p \in s \leftrightarrow t \;\wedge\; q \in u \leftrightarrow v$
$\mathrm{ran}\,(p \cup q) \;=\; \mathrm{ran}\,(p) \cup \mathrm{ran}\,(q)$	$p \in s \leftrightarrow t \;\wedge\; q \in s \leftrightarrow t$
$\mathrm{ran}\,(p \cap q) \;=\; \mathrm{ran}\,(p) \cap \mathrm{ran}\,(q)$	$p^{-1} \in t \twoheadrightarrow s \;\wedge\; q^{-1} \in t \twoheadrightarrow s$
	$q \triangleright \mathrm{ran}\,(p) = p \triangleright \mathrm{ran}\,(q)$
$\mathrm{ran}\,(p - q) \;=\; \mathrm{ran}\,(p) - \mathrm{ran}\,(q)$	$p^{-1} \in t \twoheadrightarrow s \;\wedge\; q^{-1} \in t \twoheadrightarrow s$
	$q \triangleright \mathrm{ran}\,(p) = p \triangleright \mathrm{ran}\,(q)$
$\mathrm{ran}\,(\{\,x \mapsto y\,\}) \;=\; \{\,y\,\}$	$x \in s \;\wedge\; y \in t$
$\mathrm{ran}\,(r) \;=\; \varnothing$	$r \in s \leftrightarrow t \;\wedge\; r = \varnothing$
$\mathrm{ran}\,(s \times t) \;=\; t$	$s \neq \varnothing$

We prove that the ran operator distributes over set difference if the inverses of the relations concerned are functional and if they agree on the common part of their ranges.

$$p^{-1} \in t \twoheadrightarrow s$$
$$q^{-1} \in t \twoheadrightarrow s$$
$$q \triangleright \mathrm{ran}\,(p) \;=\; p \triangleright \mathrm{ran}\,(q) \qquad\qquad \text{Property 2.6.3}$$
$$\Rightarrow$$
$$\mathrm{ran}\,(p - q) \;=\; \mathrm{ran}\,(p) - \mathrm{ran}\,(q)$$

Proof

We assume

$$p^{-1} \in t \twoheadrightarrow s \qquad\qquad \text{Hypothesis 1}$$
$$q^{-1} \in t \twoheadrightarrow s \qquad\qquad \text{Hypothesis 2}$$
$$q \triangleright \mathrm{ran}\,(p) = p \triangleright \mathrm{ran}\,(q) \qquad\qquad \text{Hypothesis 3}$$

and we have to prove

$$\mathrm{ran}\,(p - q) \;=\; \mathrm{ran}\,(p) - \mathrm{ran}\,(q) \qquad\qquad \text{Goal 1}$$

The proof goes as follows:

$$\text{ran}\,(p - q)$$
$$=$$ Definition of Range
$$\text{dom}\,((p - q)^{-1})$$
$$=$$ Inverse
$$\text{dom}\,(p^{-1} - q^{-1})$$
$$=$$ Domain
$$\text{dom}\,(p^{-1}) - \text{dom}\,(q^{-1})$$
$$=$$ Definition of Range
$$\text{ran}\,(p) - \text{ran}\,(q)$$

End of Proof

Here are some laws concerning the composition of relations.

Composition Property	Condition
$p = q$	$p \in t \leftrightarrow u \,\wedge\, q \in t \leftrightarrow u \,\wedge\, r \in s \twoheadrightarrow t \,\wedge$ $r\,;p = r\,;q$
$p = q$	$p \in s \leftrightarrow t \,\wedge\, q \in s \leftrightarrow t \,\wedge\, r^{-1} \in u \twoheadrightarrow t \,\wedge$ $p\,;r = q\,;r$
$r\,;(p\,;q) = r\,;p\,;q$	$r \in s \leftrightarrow t \,\wedge\, p \in t \leftrightarrow u \,\wedge\, q \in u \leftrightarrow v$
$r\,;\text{id}\,(v) = r \rhd v$	$r \in s \leftrightarrow t \,\wedge\, v \subseteq t$
$r\,;\text{id}\,(t) = r$	$r \in s \leftrightarrow t$
$r\,;(v \lhd p) = (r \rhd v)\,;p$	$r \in s \leftrightarrow t \,\wedge\, v \subseteq t \,\wedge\, p \in t \leftrightarrow u$
$r\,;(p \rhd w) = (r\,;p) \rhd w$	$r \in s \leftrightarrow t \,\wedge\, p \in t \leftrightarrow u \,\wedge\, w \subseteq u$
$r\,;(v \ntriangleleft p) = (r \ntriangleright v)\,;p$	$r \in s \leftrightarrow t \,\wedge\, v \subseteq t \,\wedge\, p \in t \leftrightarrow u$
$r\,;(p \ntriangleright w) = (r\,;p) \ntriangleright w$	$r \in s \leftrightarrow t \,\wedge\, p \in t \leftrightarrow u \,\wedge\, w \subseteq u$
$f\,;(p \lessdot q) = (f\,;p) \lessdot (f\,;q)$	$f \in s \twoheadrightarrow t \,\wedge\, p \in t \leftrightarrow u \,\wedge\, q \in t \leftrightarrow u$
$r\,;(p \cup q) = (r\,;p) \cup (r\,;q)$	$r \in s \leftrightarrow t \,\wedge\, p \in t \leftrightarrow u \,\wedge\, q \in t \leftrightarrow u$
$f\,;(p \cap q) = (f\,;p) \cap (f\,;q)$	$f \in s \twoheadrightarrow t \,\wedge\, p \in t \leftrightarrow u \,\wedge\, q \in t \leftrightarrow u$
$f\,;(p - q) = (f\,;p) - (f\,;q)$	$f \in s \twoheadrightarrow t \,\wedge\, p \in t \leftrightarrow u \,\wedge\, q \in t \leftrightarrow u$
$r\,;\{x \mapsto y\} = r^{-1}[\{x\}] \times \{y\}$	$r \in s \leftrightarrow t \,\wedge\, x \in s \,\wedge\, y \in u$
$r\,;p = \varnothing$	$r \in s \leftrightarrow t \,\wedge\, p \in t \leftrightarrow u \,\wedge\, p = \varnothing$
$r\,;(u \times v) = r^{-1}[u] \times v$	$r \in s \leftrightarrow t \,\wedge\, u \subseteq t$
$f\,;(p \otimes q) = (f\,;p) \otimes (f\,;q)$	$f \in s \twoheadrightarrow t \,\wedge\, p \in t \leftrightarrow u \,\wedge\, q \in t \leftrightarrow v$
$\text{id}\,(u)\,;r = u \lhd r$	$u \subseteq s \,\wedge\, r \in s \leftrightarrow t$
$\text{id}\,(s)\,;r = r$	$r \in s \leftrightarrow t$
$(u \lhd p)\,;r = u \lhd (p\,;r)$	$u \subseteq s \,\wedge\, p \in s \leftrightarrow t \,\wedge\, r \in t \leftrightarrow u$
$(p \rhd v)\,;r = p\,;(v \lhd r)$	$p \in s \leftrightarrow t \,\wedge\, v \subseteq t \,\wedge\, r \in t \leftrightarrow u$

Composition Property	Condition
$(u \triangleleft p) ; r = u \triangleleft (p ; r)$	$u \subseteq s \ \wedge \ p \in s \leftrightarrow t \ \wedge \ r \in t \leftrightarrow u$
$(p \triangleright v) ; r = p ; (v \triangleleft r)$	$p \in s \leftrightarrow t \ \wedge \ v \subseteq t \ \wedge \ r \in t \leftrightarrow u$
$(p \triangleleft^{+} q) ; r = (p ; r) \triangleleft^{+} (q ; r)$	$p \in s \leftrightarrow t \ \wedge \ q \in s \leftrightarrow t \ \wedge \ r \in t \leftrightarrow u \ \wedge$ $\mathrm{ran}\,(q) \subseteq \mathrm{dom}\,(r)$
$(p \cup q) ; r = (p ; r) \cup (q ; r)$	$p \in s \leftrightarrow t \ \wedge \ q \in s \leftrightarrow t \ \wedge \ r \in t \leftrightarrow u$
$(p \cap q) ; r = (p ; r) \cap (q ; r)$	$p \in s \leftrightarrow t \ \wedge \ q \in s \leftrightarrow t \ \wedge \ r^{-1} \in u \rightarrow\!\!\!\rightarrow t$
$(p - q) ; r = (p ; r) - (q ; r)$	$p \in s \leftrightarrow t \ \wedge \ q \in s \leftrightarrow t \ \wedge \ r^{-1} \in u \rightarrow\!\!\!\rightarrow t$
$\{x \mapsto y\} ; r = \{x\} \times r[\{y\}]$	$x \in s \ \wedge \ y \in t \ \wedge \ r \in t \leftrightarrow u$
$p ; r = \varnothing$	$p \in s \leftrightarrow t \ \wedge \ r \in t \leftrightarrow u \ \wedge \ p = \varnothing$
$(u \times v) ; r = u \times r[v]$	$v \subseteq s \ \wedge \ r \in s \leftrightarrow t$
$f^{-1} ; f = \mathrm{id}\,(\mathrm{ran}\,(f))$	$f \in s \rightarrow\!\!\!\rightarrow t$
$r ; r^{-1} = \mathrm{id}\,(\mathrm{dom}\,(r))$	$r^{-1} \in t \rightarrow\!\!\!\rightarrow s$
$\mathrm{id}\,(u) ; \mathrm{id}\,(v) = \mathrm{id}\,(u \cap v)$	$u \subseteq s \ \wedge \ v \subseteq s$
$(p \parallel q) ; (h \parallel k) = (p ; h) \parallel (q ; k)$	$p \in s \leftrightarrow t \ \wedge \ q \in u \leftrightarrow v \ \wedge$ $h \in t \leftrightarrow w \ \wedge \ k \in v \leftrightarrow z$
$(p \otimes q) ; (h \parallel k) = (p ; h) \otimes (q ; k)$	$p \in s \leftrightarrow t \ \wedge \ q \in s \leftrightarrow u \ \wedge$ $h \in t \leftrightarrow v \ \wedge \ k \in u \leftrightarrow w$

We prove the following property:

$f \in s \rightarrow\!\!\!\rightarrow t$
$p \in t \leftrightarrow u$
$q \in t \leftrightarrow u$
$\Rightarrow$
$f ; (p \triangleleft^{+} q) = (f ; p) \triangleleft^{+} (f ; q)$

Property 2.6.4

Proof

We assume

$$f \in s \rightarrow\!\!\!\rightarrow t \qquad \text{Hypothesis 1}$$
$$p \in t \leftrightarrow u \qquad \text{Hypothesis 2}$$
$$q \in t \leftrightarrow u \qquad \text{Hypothesis 3}$$

and we have to prove

$$f ; (p \triangleleft^{+} q) = (f ; p) \triangleleft^{+} (f ; q) \qquad \text{Goal 1}$$

Given two fresh variables x and z, it is sufficient to prove

$$(x,z) \in f \,;(p \lessdot q)$$

$$\Leftrightarrow$$

$$(x,z) \in (f\,;p) \lessdot (f\,;q)$$

Goal 2

The proof goes as follows:

$$(x,z) \in f\,;(p \lessdot q)$$

$$\Leftrightarrow$$

$$(x,z) \in f\,;(\mathrm{dom}\,(q) \vartriangleleft p \,\cup\, q)$$

Definition of $\lessdot$

$$\Leftrightarrow$$

$$(x,z) \in f\,;(\mathrm{dom}\,(q) \vartriangleleft p) \,\cup\, f\,;q$$

Composition

$$\Leftrightarrow$$

$$(x,z) \in (f \vartriangleright \mathrm{dom}\,(q))\,;p \,\cup\, f\,;q$$

Composition

$$\Leftrightarrow$$

$$(x,z) \in (f^{-1}[\mathrm{dom}\,(q)] \vartriangleleft f)\,;p \,\cup\, f\,;q$$

Property 2.6.7

$$\Leftrightarrow$$

$$(x,z) \in (\mathrm{dom}\,(f\,;q) \vartriangleleft f)\,;p \,\cup\, f\,;q$$

Domain

$$\Leftrightarrow$$

$$(x,z) \in \mathrm{dom}\,(f\,;q) \vartriangleleft (f\,;p) \,\cup\, f\,;q$$

Composition

$$\Leftrightarrow$$

$$(x,z) \in f\,;p \lessdot f\,;q$$

Definition of $\lessdot$

End of Proof

We now present the proof of the law expressing the distributivity of composition over direct product when the first relation is functional.

$$f \in s \nrightarrow t$$
$$p \in t \leftrightarrow u$$
$$q \in t \leftrightarrow v$$
$$\Rightarrow$$
$$f\,;(p \otimes q) = (f\,;p) \otimes (f\,;q)$$

Property 2.6.5

Proof

We assume

$$f \in s \nrightarrow t$$ Hypothesis 1
$$p \in t \leftrightarrow u$$ Hypothesis 2
$$q \in t \leftrightarrow v$$ Hypothesis 3

and we have to prove

$$f\,;(p \otimes q) = (f\,;p) \otimes (f\,;q)$$

Goal 1

Given three fresh variables x, a and b it is sufficient to prove

$$(x,(a,b)) \in f\,;(p \otimes q)$$ Goal 2
$$\Leftrightarrow$$
$$(x,(a,b)) \in (f\,;p) \otimes (f\,;q)$$

The proof goes as follows:

$$(x,(a,b)) \in f\,;(p \otimes q)$$
$$\Leftrightarrow$$ Definition of Composition
$$(x,(a,b)) \in s \times (u \times v) \;\wedge$$
$$\exists y \cdot (y \in t \;\wedge\; (x,y) \in f \;\wedge\; (y,(a,b)) \in p \otimes q\,)$$
$$\Leftrightarrow$$ Property 2.5.4
$$(x,(a,b)) \in s \times (u \times v) \;\wedge$$
$$\exists y \cdot (y \in t \;\wedge\; x \in \mathsf{dom}\,(f) \;\wedge\; y = f(x) \;\wedge\; (y,(a,b)) \in p \otimes q\,)$$
$$\Leftrightarrow$$ One Point Rule
$$(x,(a,b)) \in s \times (u \times v) \;\wedge$$
$$f(x) \in t \;\wedge\; x \in \mathsf{dom}\,(f) \;\wedge\; (f(x),(a,b)) \in p \otimes q$$
$$\Leftrightarrow$$ Definition of Direct Product
$$(x,(a,b)) \in s \times (u \times v) \;\wedge$$
$$f(x) \in t \;\wedge\; x \in \mathsf{dom}\,(f) \;\wedge\; (f(x),a) \in p \;\wedge\; (f(x),b) \in q$$
$$\Leftrightarrow$$ Property 2.5.4 and One Point Rule
$$(x,a) \in s \times u \;\wedge\; \exists y \cdot (y \in t \;\wedge\; (x,y) \in f \;\wedge\; (y,a) \in p\,) \;\wedge$$
$$(x,b) \in s \times v \;\wedge\; \exists y \cdot (y \in t \;\wedge\; (x,y) \in f \;\wedge\; (y,b) \in q\,)$$
$$\Leftrightarrow$$ Definitions of Composition and Direct Product
$$(x,(a,b)) \in (f\,;p) \otimes (f\,;q)$$

End of Proof

Here are some results concerning the identity relation:

Identity Property	Condition
$\mathsf{id}\,(u \cup v) = \mathsf{id}\,(u) \cup \mathsf{id}\,(v)$	$u \subseteq s \;\wedge\; v \subseteq s$
$\mathsf{id}\,(u \cap v) = \mathsf{id}\,(u) \cap \mathsf{id}\,(v)$	$u \subseteq s \;\wedge\; v \subseteq s$
$\mathsf{id}\,(u - v) = \mathsf{id}\,(u) - \mathsf{id}\,(v)$	$u \subseteq s \;\wedge\; v \subseteq s$
$\mathsf{id}\,(\{x\}) = \{x \mapsto x\}$	$x \in s$
$\mathsf{id}\,(u) = \varnothing$	$u \subseteq s \;\wedge\; u = \varnothing$

We now present some laws concerning domain restriction.

Restriction Property	Condition
$u \lhd r = r$	$u \subseteq s \ \land \ r \in s \leftrightarrow t \ \land \ \mathrm{dom}\,(r) \subseteq u$
$u \lhd r = r \rhd r[u]$	$u \subseteq s \ \land \ r^{-1} \in t \nrightarrow s$
$u \lhd (r\,;p) = (u \lhd r)\,;p$	$u \subseteq s \ \land \ r \in s \leftrightarrow t \ \land \ p \in t \leftrightarrow u$
$u \lhd \mathrm{id}\,(v) = \mathrm{id}\,(u \cap v)$	$u \subseteq s \ \land \ v \subseteq s$
$u \lhd (v \lhd r) = (u \cap v) \lhd r$	$u \subseteq s \ \land \ v \subseteq s \ \land \ r \in s \leftrightarrow t$
$u \lhd (r \rhd w) = (u \lhd r) \rhd w$	$u \subseteq s \ \land \ r \in s \leftrightarrow t \ \land \ w \subseteq t$
$u \lhd (v \ntriangleleft r) = (u - v) \lhd r$	$u \subseteq s \ \land \ v \subseteq s \ \land \ r \in s \leftrightarrow t$
$u \lhd (r \ntriangleright w) = (u \lhd r) \ntriangleright w$	$u \subseteq s \ \land \ r \in s \leftrightarrow t \ \land \ w \subseteq t$
$u \lhd (p \ntriangleleft q) = (u \lhd p) \ntriangleleft (u \lhd q)$	$u \subseteq s \ \land \ p \in s \leftrightarrow t \ \land \ q \in s \leftrightarrow t$
$u \lhd (p \otimes q) = (u \lhd p) \otimes (u \lhd q)$	$u \subseteq s \ \land \ p \in s \leftrightarrow t \ \land \ q \in s \leftrightarrow v$
$(u \times v) \lhd (p \parallel q) = (u \lhd p) \parallel (v \lhd q)$	$u \subseteq s \ \land \ v \subseteq t \ \land \ p \in s \leftrightarrow w \ \land \ q \in t \leftrightarrow z$
$u \lhd (p \cup q) = (u \lhd p) \cup (u \lhd q)$	$u \subseteq s \ \land \ p \in s \leftrightarrow t \ \land \ q \in s \leftrightarrow t$
$u \lhd (p \cap q) = (u \lhd p) \cap (u \lhd q)$	$u \subseteq s \ \land \ p \in s \leftrightarrow t \ \land \ q \in s \leftrightarrow t$
$u \lhd (p - q) = (u \lhd p) - q$	$u \subseteq s \ \land \ p \in s \leftrightarrow t \ \land \ q \in s \leftrightarrow t$
$u \lhd \{x \mapsto y\} = \{x \mapsto y\}$	$u \subseteq s \ \land \ x \in s \ \land \ y \in t \ \land \ x \in u$
$u \lhd \{x \mapsto y\} = \varnothing$	$u \subseteq s \ \land \ x \in s \ \land \ y \in t \ \land \ x \notin u$
$u \lhd r = \varnothing$	$u \subseteq s \ \land \ r \in s \leftrightarrow t \ \land \ \mathrm{dom}\,(r) \cap u = \varnothing$
$u \lhd (v \times t) = (u \cap v) \times t$	$u \subseteq s \ \land \ v \subseteq s$
$(u \cup v) \lhd r = (u \lhd r) \cup (v \lhd r)$	$u \subseteq s \ \land \ v \subseteq s \ \land \ r \in s \leftrightarrow t$
$(u \cap v) \lhd r = (u \lhd r) \cap (v \lhd r)$	$u \subseteq s \ \land \ v \subseteq s \ \land \ r \in s \leftrightarrow t$
$(u - v) \lhd r = (u \lhd r) - (v \lhd r)$	$u \subseteq s \ \land \ v \subseteq s \ \land \ r \in s \leftrightarrow t$
$\mathrm{dom}\,(r) \lhd r = r$	$r \in s \leftrightarrow t$
$f^{-1}[v] \lhd f = f \rhd v$	$f \in s \nrightarrow t \ \land \ v \subseteq t$
$\{x\} \lhd r = \{x\} \times r[\{x\}]$	$x \in s \ \land \ r \in s \leftrightarrow t$
$\varnothing \lhd r = \varnothing$	$r \in s \leftrightarrow t$

We prove the following law:

$f \in s \nrightarrow t$

$v \subseteq t$

$\Rightarrow$ Property 2.6.6

$f^{-1}[v] \lhd f = f \rhd v$

Proof

We assume

$\qquad f \in s \nrightarrow t$ Hypothesis 1

$\qquad v \subseteq t$ Hypothesis 2

and we have to prove

$$f^{-1}[v] \vartriangleleft f = f \vartriangleright v \hspace{4cm} \text{Goal 1}$$

Given two fresh variables x and y, it is sufficient to prove the following

$$(x,y) \in f^{-1}[v] \vartriangleleft f \iff (x,y) \in f \vartriangleright v \hspace{2cm} \text{Goal 2}$$

The proof goes as follows:

$\quad (x,y) \in f^{-1}[v] \vartriangleleft f$
$\quad \iff$ $\hspace{4cm}$ Definition of Domain Restriction
$\quad (x,y) \in f \ \wedge \ x \in f^{-1}[v]$
$\quad \iff$ $\hspace{4cm}$ Definition of Image
$\quad (x,y) \in f \ \wedge \ x \in s \ \wedge$
$\quad \exists z \cdot (z \in v \ \wedge \ (x,z) \in f)$
$\quad \iff$ $\hspace{4cm}$ Property 2.5.4
$\quad (x,y) \in f \ \wedge \ x \in s \ \wedge$
$\quad \exists z \cdot (z \in v \ \wedge \ x \in \mathrm{dom}\,(f) \ \wedge \ z = f(x))$
$\quad \iff$ $\hspace{4cm}$ One Point Rule
$\quad (x,y) \in f \ \wedge \ f(x) \in v \ \wedge \ x \in \mathrm{dom}\,(f)$
$\quad \iff$ $\hspace{4cm}$ Property 2.5.4
$\quad y = f(x) \ \wedge \ x \in \mathrm{dom}\,(f) \ \wedge \ f(x) \in v$
$\quad \iff$ $\hspace{4cm}$ Equality
$\quad y = f(x) \ \wedge \ x \in \mathrm{dom}\,(f) \ \wedge \ y \in v$
$\quad \iff$ $\hspace{4cm}$ Property 2.5.4
$\quad (x,y) \in f \ \wedge \ y \in v$
$\quad \iff$ $\hspace{4cm}$ Definition of Range Restriction
$\quad (x,y) \in f \vartriangleright v$

End of Proof

Subtraction Property	Condition
$u \vartriangleleft r = r$	$u \subseteq s \ \wedge \ r \in s \leftrightarrow t \ \wedge \ \mathrm{dom}\,(r) \cap u = \varnothing$
$u \vartriangleleft r = r \vartriangleright r[u]$	$u \subseteq s \ \wedge \ r^{-1} \in t \nrightarrow s$
$u \vartriangleleft (r \,;p) = (u \vartriangleleft r)\,;p$	$u \subseteq s \ \wedge \ r \in s \leftrightarrow t \ \wedge \ p \in t \leftrightarrow u$
$u \vartriangleleft \mathrm{id}\,(v) = \mathrm{id}\,(v - u)$	$u \subseteq s \ \wedge \ v \subseteq s$
$u \vartriangleleft (v \vartriangleleft r) = (v - u) \vartriangleleft r$	$u \subseteq s \ \wedge \ v \subseteq s \ \wedge \ r \in s \leftrightarrow t$
$u \vartriangleleft (r \vartriangleright w) = (u \vartriangleleft r) \vartriangleright w$	$u \subseteq s \ \wedge \ r \in s \leftrightarrow t \ \wedge \ w \subseteq t$
$u \vartriangleleft (v \vartriangleleft r) = (u \cup v) \vartriangleleft r$	$u \subseteq s \ \wedge \ v \subseteq s \ \wedge \ r \in s \leftrightarrow t$
$u \vartriangleleft (r \vartriangleright w) = (u \vartriangleleft r) \vartriangleright w$	$u \subseteq s \ \wedge \ r \in s \leftrightarrow t \ \wedge \ w \subseteq t$
$u \vartriangleleft (p \vartriangleleft\!\!+ q) = (u \vartriangleleft p) \vartriangleleft\!\!+ (u \vartriangleleft q)$	$u \subseteq s \ \wedge \ p \in s \leftrightarrow t \ \wedge \ q \in s \leftrightarrow t$

Subtraction Property	Condition
$(u \lhd p) \otimes (u \lhd q) = u \lhd (p \otimes q)$	$u \subseteq s \ \wedge \ p \in s \leftrightarrow t \ \wedge \ q \in s \leftrightarrow v$
$(p \rhd u) \otimes (q \rhd v) \subseteq (p \otimes q) \rhd (u \times v)$	$u \subseteq t \ \wedge \ v \subseteq z \ \wedge \ p \in s \leftrightarrow t \ \wedge \ q \in s \leftrightarrow z$
$(u \lhd p) \mathbin{\|\|} (v \lhd q) \subseteq (u \times v) \lhd (p \mathbin{\|\|} q)$	$u \subseteq s \ \wedge \ v \subseteq t \ \wedge \ p \in s \leftrightarrow w \ \wedge \ q \in t \leftrightarrow z$
$u \lhd (p \cup q) = (u \lhd p) \cup (u \lhd q)$	$u \subseteq s \ \wedge \ p \in s \leftrightarrow t \ \wedge \ q \in s \leftrightarrow t$
$u \lhd (p \cap q) = (u \lhd p) \cap (u \lhd q)$	$u \subseteq s \ \wedge \ p \in s \leftrightarrow t \ \wedge \ q \in s \leftrightarrow t$
$u \lhd (p - q) = (u \lhd p) - q$	$u \subseteq s \ \wedge \ p \in s \leftrightarrow t \ \wedge \ q \in s \leftrightarrow t$
$u \lhd \{x \mapsto y\} = \{x \mapsto y\}$	$u \subseteq s \ \wedge \ x \in s \ \wedge \ y \in t \ \wedge \ x \notin u$
$u \lhd \{x \mapsto y\} = \varnothing$	$u \subseteq s \ \wedge \ x \in s \ \wedge \ y \in t \ \wedge \ x \in u$
$u \lhd r = \varnothing$	$u \subseteq s \ \wedge \ r \in s \leftrightarrow t \ \wedge \ \mathrm{dom}\,(r) \subseteq u$
$u \lhd (v \times t) = (v - u) \times t$	$u \subseteq s \ \wedge \ v \subseteq s$
$(u \cup v) \lhd r = (u \lhd r) \cap (v \lhd r)$	$u \subseteq s \ \wedge \ v \subseteq s \ \wedge \ r \in s \leftrightarrow t$
$(u \cap v) \lhd r = (u \lhd r) \cup (v \lhd r)$	$u \subseteq s \ \wedge \ v \subseteq s \ \wedge \ r \in s \leftrightarrow t$
$(u - v) \lhd r = (u \lhd r) \cup (v \lhd r)$	$u \subseteq s \ \wedge \ v \subseteq s \ \wedge \ r \in s \leftrightarrow t$
$\mathrm{dom}\,(r) \lhd r = \varnothing$	$r \in s \leftrightarrow t$
$f^{-1}[v] \lhd f = f \rhd v$	$f \in s \nrightarrow t \ \wedge \ v \subseteq t$
$\varnothing \lhd r = r$	$r \in s \leftrightarrow t$

We prove the last but one law:

$f \in s \nrightarrow t$
$v \subseteq t$
$\Rightarrow$
$f^{-1}[v] \lhd f = f \rhd v$ Property 2.6.7

Proof

We assume

$$f \in s \nrightarrow t \qquad \text{Hypothesis 1}$$
$$v \subseteq t \qquad \text{Hypothesis 2}$$

and we have to prove

$$f^{-1}[v] \lhd f = f \rhd v \qquad \text{Goal 1}$$

The proof goes as follows:

$f^{-1}[v] \lhd f$
$=$ Definition of $\lhd$
$(\mathrm{dom}\,(f) - f^{-1}[v]) \lhd f$
$=$ Domain Restriction

$$(\mathrm{dom}\,(f) \lhd f) - (f^{-1}[v] \lhd f)$$

=   Domain Restriction

$$f - (f^{-1}[v] \lhd f)$$

=   Property 2.6.6

$$f - (f \rhd v)$$

=   Range Restriction

$$(f \rhd \mathrm{ran}\,(f)) - (f \rhd v)$$

=   Range Restriction

$$f \rhd (\mathrm{ran}\,(f) - v)$$

=   Definition of $\lhd$

$$f \rhd v$$

End of Proof

We now present some results concerning the image of a set under a relation.

Image Property	Condition
$(p\,;q)[u] = q[p[u]]$	$p \in s \leftrightarrow t \;\wedge\; q \in t \leftrightarrow v \;\wedge\; u \subseteq s$
$(r\,;r^{-1})[u] = u$	$r^{-1} \in t \twoheadrightarrow s \;\wedge\; u \subseteq \mathrm{dom}\,(r)$
$\mathrm{id}\,(u)[v] = u \cap v$	$u \subseteq s \;\wedge\; v \subseteq s$
$(u \lhd r)[v] = r[u \cap v]$	$u \subseteq s \;\wedge\; r \in s \leftrightarrow t \;\wedge\; v \subseteq s$
$(r \rhd v)[u] = r[u] \cap v$	$r \in s \leftrightarrow t \;\wedge\; v \subseteq t \;\wedge\; u \subseteq s$
$(u \ntriangleleft r)[v] = r[u - v]$	$u \subseteq s \;\wedge\; r \in s \leftrightarrow t \;\wedge\; v \subseteq s$
$(r \ntriangleright v)[u] = r[u] - v$	$r \in s \leftrightarrow t \;\wedge\; v \subseteq t \;\wedge\; u \subseteq s$
$(p \lessdot q)[u] = (\mathrm{dom}\,(q) \ntriangleleft p)[u] \cup q[u]$	$p \in s \leftrightarrow t \;\wedge\; q \in s \leftrightarrow t \;\wedge\; u \subseteq s$
$(p \otimes q)[u] = p^{-1}\,;(u \lhd q)$	$p \in s \leftrightarrow t \;\wedge\; q \in s \leftrightarrow v \;\wedge\; u \subseteq s$
$(p \,\|\, q)[u \times v] = p[u] \times q[v]$	$p \in s \leftrightarrow t \;\wedge\; q \in w \leftrightarrow z \;\wedge\; u \subseteq s \;\wedge\; v \subseteq w$
$(\mathrm{id}\,(s) \,\|\, q)[p] = p\,;q$	$p \in s \leftrightarrow t \;\wedge\; q \in t \leftrightarrow u$
$(p \cup q)[u] = p[u] \cup q[u]$	$p \in s \leftrightarrow t \;\wedge\; q \in s \leftrightarrow t$
$(p \cap q)[u] = p[u] \cap q[u]$	$p^{-1} \in t \twoheadrightarrow s \;\wedge\; q^{-1} \in t \twoheadrightarrow s \;\wedge\; u \subseteq s \;\wedge\;$ $(p \rhd \mathrm{ran}\,(q)) = (q \rhd \mathrm{ran}\,(p))$
$(p - q)[u] = p[u] - q[u]$	$p^{-1} \in t \twoheadrightarrow s \;\wedge\; q^{-1} \in t \twoheadrightarrow s \;\wedge\; u \subseteq s \;\wedge\;$ $(p \rhd \mathrm{ran}\,(q)) = (q \rhd \mathrm{ran}\,(p))$
$\{x \mapsto y\}[u] = \{y\}$	$x \in s \;\wedge\; y \in t \;\wedge\; u \subseteq s \;\wedge\; x \in u$
$\{x \mapsto y\}[u] = \varnothing$	$x \in s \;\wedge\; y \in t \;\wedge\; u \subseteq s \;\wedge\; x \notin u$
$r[u] = \varnothing$	$r \in s \leftrightarrow t \;\wedge\; (\mathrm{dom}\,(r) \cap u) = \varnothing$
$(u \times t)[v] = t$	$u \subseteq s \;\wedge\; v \subseteq s \;\wedge\; u \cap v \neq \varnothing$
$(u \times t)[v] = \varnothing$	$u \subseteq s \;\wedge\; v \subseteq s \;\wedge\; u \cap v = \varnothing$
$r[u \cup v] = r[u] \cup r[v]$	$r \in s \leftrightarrow t \;\wedge\; u \subseteq s \;\wedge\; v \subseteq s$
$r[u \cap v] = r[u] \cap r[v]$	$r^{-1} \in t \twoheadrightarrow s \;\wedge\; u \subseteq s \;\wedge\; v \subseteq s$
$r[u - v] = r[u] - r[v]$	$r^{-1} \in t \twoheadrightarrow s \;\wedge\; u \subseteq s \;\wedge\; v \subseteq s$

Image Property	Condition
$f[\{x\}] = \{f(x)\}$	$f \in s \nrightarrow t \;\wedge\; x \in \mathrm{dom}\,(f)$
$r[\varnothing] = \varnothing$	$r \in s \leftrightarrow t$
$r[\mathrm{dom}\,(r)] = \mathrm{ran}\,(r)$	$r \in s \leftrightarrow t$
$r^{-1}[\mathrm{ran}\,(r)] = \mathrm{dom}\,(r)$	$r \in s \leftrightarrow t$

We first prove the rather surprising law relating the parallel product, the image and the composition operators:

$$p \in s \leftrightarrow t$$
$$q \in t \leftrightarrow u$$
$$\Rightarrow$$
$$(\mathrm{id}\,(s) \,||\, q)[p] = p\,;q$$

Property 2.6.8

Proof

We assume

$$p \in s \leftrightarrow t \qquad\qquad \text{Hypothesis 1}$$
$$q \in t \leftrightarrow u \qquad\qquad \text{Hypothesis 2}$$

and we have to prove

$$(\mathrm{id}\,(s) \,||\, q)[p] = p\,;q \qquad\qquad \text{Goal 1}$$

Given two fresh variables a and b, we shall then prove

$$(a,b) \in (\mathrm{id}\,(s) \,||\, q)[p] \qquad\qquad \text{Goal 2}$$
$$\Leftrightarrow$$
$$(a,b) \in p\,;q$$

The proof goes as follows:

$$(a,b) \in (\mathrm{id}\,(s) \,||\, q)[p]$$
$$\Leftrightarrow \qquad\qquad\qquad \text{Definition of Image}$$
$$\exists(x,y)\cdot((x,y) \in p \;\wedge\; (x,y),(a,b) \in \mathrm{id}\,(s) \,||\, q)$$
$$\Leftrightarrow \qquad\qquad\qquad \text{Predicate Calculus}$$
$$\exists y\cdot\exists x\cdot((x,y) \in p \;\wedge\; (x,y),(a,b) \in (\mathrm{id}\,(s) \,||\, q))$$
$$\Leftrightarrow \qquad\qquad\qquad \text{Definition of } ||$$
$$\exists y\cdot\exists x\cdot((x,y) \in p \;\wedge\; (x,a) \in \mathrm{id}\,(s) \;\wedge\; (y,b) \in q)$$
$$\Leftrightarrow \qquad\qquad\qquad \text{Definition of id}$$

$$\exists y \cdot \exists x \cdot ((x,y) \in p \ \wedge \ (x,a) \in s \times s \ \wedge \ x = a \ \wedge \ (y,b) \in q)$$
$$\Leftrightarrow \qquad \qquad \qquad \qquad \qquad \qquad \qquad \text{One Point Rule}$$
$$\exists y \cdot ((a,y) \in p \ \wedge \ (a,a) \in s \times s \ \wedge \ (y,b) \in q)$$
$$\Leftrightarrow$$
$$a \in s \ \wedge \ b \in u \ \wedge \ \exists y \cdot (y \in t \ \wedge \ (a,y) \in p \ \wedge \ (y,b) \in q)$$
$$\Leftrightarrow \qquad \qquad \qquad \qquad \qquad \qquad \qquad \text{Definition of ;}$$
$$(a,b) \in p\,;q$$

End of Proof

We prove the distributivity of the difference of two relations over image in the case where the inverses of both relations are functional and agree on the common part of their range.

$$p^{-1} \in t \twoheadrightarrow s$$
$$q^{-1} \in t \twoheadrightarrow s$$
$$u \subseteq s$$
$$(u \lhd p \rhd \mathsf{ran}\,(q)) = (u \lhd q \rhd \mathsf{ran}\,(p)) \qquad \qquad \text{Property 2.6.9}$$
$$\Rightarrow$$
$$(p - q)[u] \ = \ p[u] - q[u]$$

Proof

We assume

$$p^{-1} \in t \twoheadrightarrow s \qquad \qquad \qquad \text{Hypothesis 1}$$
$$q^{-1} \in t \twoheadrightarrow s \qquad \qquad \qquad \text{Hypothesis 2}$$
$$u \subseteq s \qquad \qquad \qquad \qquad \qquad \text{Hypothesis 3}$$
$$(u \lhd p \rhd \mathsf{ran}\,(q)) = (u \lhd q \rhd \mathsf{ran}\,(p)) \qquad \text{Hypothesis 4}$$

and we have to prove

$$(p - q)[u] \ = \ p[u] - q[u] \qquad \qquad \qquad \text{Goal 1}$$

The proof goes as follows:

$$(p - q)[u]$$
$$= \qquad \qquad \qquad \qquad \qquad \qquad \text{Definition of Image}$$
$$\mathsf{ran}\,(u \lhd (p - q))$$
$$= \qquad \qquad \qquad \qquad \qquad \qquad \text{Domain Restriction}$$
$$\mathsf{ran}\,((u \lhd p) - (u \lhd q))$$
$$= \qquad \qquad \qquad \qquad \qquad \qquad \text{Range}$$
$$\mathsf{ran}\,(u \lhd p) - \mathsf{ran}\,(u \lhd q)$$
$$= \qquad \qquad \qquad \qquad \qquad \qquad \text{Definition of Image}$$
$$p[u] - q[u]$$

End of Proof

Here are some results concerning overriding.

Overriding Property	Condition
$p \Leftarrow (q \Leftarrow r) = p \Leftarrow q \Leftarrow r$ $p \Leftarrow q = p \cup q$ $\varnothing \Leftarrow r = r$ $r \Leftarrow \varnothing = r$ $(\{x\} \times v) \Leftarrow \{x \mapsto y\} = \{x \mapsto y\}$ $(u \times \{y\}) \Leftarrow \{x \mapsto y\} = (u \cup \{x\}) \times \{y\}$	$p \in s \leftrightarrow t \land q \in s \leftrightarrow t \land r \in s \leftrightarrow t$ $p \in s \leftrightarrow t \land q \in s \leftrightarrow t \land$ $\text{dom}(q) \lhd p = \text{dom}(p) \lhd q$ $r \in s \leftrightarrow t$ $r \in s \leftrightarrow t$ $x \in s \land v \subseteq t \land y \in t$ $u \subseteq s \land y \in t \land x \in s$

We now prove the associativity of overriding.

$p \in s \leftrightarrow t$
$q \in s \leftrightarrow t$
$r \in s \leftrightarrow t$ Property 2.6.10
$\Rightarrow$
$p \Leftarrow (q \Leftarrow r) = p \Leftarrow q \Leftarrow r$

Proof

We assume

$p \in s \leftrightarrow t$ Hypothesis 1
$q \in s \leftrightarrow t$ Hypothesis 2
$r \in s \leftrightarrow t$ Hypothesis 3

and we have to prove

$p \Leftarrow (q \Leftarrow r) = p \Leftarrow q \Leftarrow r$ Goal 1

The proof goes as follows:

$p \Leftarrow (q \Leftarrow r)$
$=$ Definition of $\Leftarrow$
$\text{dom}(q \Leftarrow r) \lhd p \cup (\text{dom}(r) \lhd q \cup r)$
$=$ Domain
$(\text{dom}(q) \cup \text{dom}(r)) \lhd p \cup \text{dom}(r) \lhd q \cup r$
$=$ Domain Subtraction
$(\text{dom}(r) \lhd (\text{dom}(q) \lhd p) \cup \text{dom}(r) \lhd q) \cup r$
$=$ Domain Subtraction
$\text{dom}(r) \lhd (\text{dom}(q) \lhd p \cup q) \cup r$
$=$ Definition of $\Leftarrow$

$$(\text{dom}\,(q)\lhd p \ \cup\ q)\mathbin{<\!\!\!\!\!\!+}\, r$$

$$=$$ Definition of $\mathbin{<\!\!\!\!\!\!+}$

$$p\mathbin{<\!\!\!\!\!\!+}\, q\mathbin{<\!\!\!\!\!\!+}\, r$$

End of Proof

We present, finally, some results concerning functional evaluation.

Evaluation Property	Condition
$f^{-1}(f(x)) = x$	$f \in s \rightarrowtail t \ \wedge\ x \in \text{dom}\,(f)$
$(p\,;q)(x) = q(p(x))$	$p \in s \rightarrowtail t \ \wedge\ q \in t \twoheadrightarrow u \ \wedge\ x \in \text{dom}\,(p\,;q)$
$\text{id}\,(s)(x) = x$	$x \in s$
$(u \lhd f)(x) = f(x)$	$u \subseteq s \ \wedge\ f \in s \rightarrowtail t \ \wedge\ x \in u \cap \text{dom}\,(f)$
$(f \rhd v)(x) = f(x)$	$f \in s \rightarrowtail t \ \wedge\ v \subseteq t \ \wedge\ x \in f^{-1}[v]$
$(u \mathbin{\lhd\!\!\!-} f)(x) = f(x)$	$u \subseteq s \ \wedge\ f \in s \rightarrowtail t \ \wedge\ x \in \text{dom}\,(f) - u$
$(f \mathbin{\rhd\!\!\!-} v)(x) = f(x)$	$f \in s \rightarrowtail t \ \wedge\ v \subseteq t \ \wedge\ x \in \text{dom}\,(f) - f^{-1}[v]$
$(f \mathbin{<\!\!\!\!\!+} g)(x) = f(x)$	$f \in s \rightarrowtail t \ \wedge\ g \in s \rightarrowtail t \ \wedge$ $x \in \text{dom}\,(f) - \text{dom}\,(g)$
$(f \mathbin{<\!\!\!\!\!+} g)(x) = g(x)$	$f \in s \rightarrowtail t \ \wedge\ g \in s \rightarrowtail t \ \wedge\ x \in \text{dom}\,(g)$
$(f \otimes g)(x) = f(x) \mapsto g(x)$	$f \in s \rightarrowtail t \ \wedge\ g \in s \rightarrowtail u \ \wedge$ $x \in \text{dom}\,(f) \cap \text{dom}\,(g)$
$\text{prj}_1\,(s,t)(x,y) = x$	$x \in s \ \wedge\ y \in t$
$\text{prj}_1\,(s,t)(x,y) = y$	$x \in s \ \wedge\ y \in t$
$(f \parallel g)(x,y) = f(x) \mapsto g(y)$	$f \in s \rightarrowtail t \ \wedge\ g \in u \rightarrowtail v \ \wedge$ $x \in \text{dom}\,(f) \ \wedge\ y \in \text{dom}\,(g)$
$(f \cup g)(x) = f(x)$	$f \in s \rightarrowtail t \ \wedge\ g \in s \rightarrowtail t \ \wedge$ $\text{dom}\,(g) \lhd f = \text{dom}\,(f) \lhd g \ \wedge\ x \in \text{dom}\,(f)$
$(f - g)(x) = f(x)$	$f \in s \rightarrowtail t \ \wedge\ g \in s \leftrightarrow t \ \wedge\ x \in \text{dom}\,(f - g)$
$\{x \mapsto y\}(x) = y$	$x \in s \ \wedge\ y \in t$
$(u \times \{y\})(x) = y$	$u \subseteq s \ \wedge\ x \in u \ \wedge\ y \in t$

2.7. Example

In this section, we develop a short example showing the practical use we can make of the various concepts we have introduced in this chapter.

Our intention is to formally describe certain relationships that may exist between people of the same family (i.e. *parents, children, brother, wife*, etc.). In order to capture interesting situations, we place ourselves in a very "strict" society with special laws governing the way people can behave. These laws can be stated informally as follows:

(1)   No person can be a man and a woman at the same time
(2)   However, every person is either a man or a woman
(3)   Only women have husbands, who must be men
(4)   Women have at most one husband
(5)   Likewise, men have at most one wife
(6)   Moreover, mothers are married women

In order to formalize these laws, we suppose that we have been given an abstract set, called *PERSON*, which denotes all the people we are interested in. Then, we use the four variables *men, women, mother, husband* together with the following constraints:

$$men \subseteq PERSON$$

$$women = PERSON - men$$

$$husband \in women \rightarrowtail men$$

$$mother \in PERSON \nrightarrow \text{dom}(husband)$$

Example

$$PERSON = \{adam, eve, cain, abel\}$$
$$men = \{adam, cain, abel\}$$
$$women = \{eve\}$$
$$husband = \{eve \mapsto adam\}$$
$$mother = \{cain \mapsto eve, \ abel \mapsto eve\}$$

We can now define the following concepts:

Concept	Definition
wife	$husband^{-1}$
spouse	$husband \cup wife$
father	$mother \ ; husband$
parents	$mother \otimes father$

Concept	Definition
children	$(mother \cup father)^{-1}$
daughter	$children \rhd women$
sibling	$(children^{-1} ; children) - \text{id}(PERSON)$
brother	$sibling \rhd women$
sibling_in_law	$(sibling ; spouse) \cup (spouse ; sibling) \cup$ $(spouse ; sibling ; spouse)$
nephew_or_niece	$(sibling \cup sibling\_in\_law) ; children$
uncle_or_aunt	$nephew\_or\_niece^{-1}$
cousin	$uncle\_or\_aunt ; children$

The following laws to prove are left as exercises to the reader:

$$mother = father ; wife$$

$$spouse = spouse^{-1}$$

$$\text{ran}(parents) = husband$$

$$sibling = sibling^{-1}$$

$$sibling\_in\_law = sibling\_in\_law^{-1}$$

$$cousin = cousin^{-1}$$

The following laws are a little more complicated:

$$father ; father^{-1} = mother ; mother^{-1}$$

$$father ; mother^{-1} = \varnothing$$

$$mother \, ; father^{-1} \; = \; \varnothing$$

$$father \, ; children \; = \; mother \, ; children$$

We now prove the last four properties.

$father \, ; father^{-1} \; = \; mother \, ; mother^{-1}$ Property 2.7.1

Proof

The proof goes as follows:

$father \, ; father^{-1}$

$=$ Definition of *father*

$(mother \, ; husband) \, ; (mother \, ; husband)^{-1}$

$=$ Inverse

$(mother \, ; husband) \, ; (husband^{-1} \, ; mother^{-1})$

$=$ Composition

$mother \, ; (husband \, ; husband^{-1}) \, ; mother^{-1}$

$=$ Composition

$mother \, ; \mathrm{id} \, (\mathrm{dom} \, (husband)) \, ; mother^{-1}$

$=$ Definition of $\triangleright$

$mother \triangleright \mathrm{dom} \, (husband) \, ; mother^{-1}$

$=$ Range Restriction

$mother \, ; mother^{-1}$

End of Proof

$father \, ; mother^{-1} \; = \; \varnothing$ Property 2.7.2

Proof

The proof goes as follows:

$father \, ; mother^{-1}$

$=$ Definition of *father*

$mother \, ; husband \, ; mother^{-1}$

$=$ Domain and Range Restrictions

$mother \, ; (husband \triangleright men) \, ; (women \triangleleft mother^{-1})$

$=$ Range Restrictions

$mother \, ; husband \, ; (men \triangleleft women \triangleleft mother^{-1})$

$=$ Domain Restriction

$mother \mathbin{;} husband \mathbin{;} ((men \cap women) \vartriangleleft mother^{-1})$
$=$ Definition of *women*
$mother \mathbin{;} husband \mathbin{;} ((men \cap (PERSON - men)) \vartriangleleft mother^{-1})$
$=$ Law of Excluded Middle

$mother \mathbin{;} husband \mathbin{;} (\varnothing \vartriangleleft mother^{-1})$
$=$ Domain Restriction
$mother \mathbin{;} husband \mathbin{;} \varnothing$
$=$ Composition
$\varnothing$

End of Proof

$mother \mathbin{;} father^{-1} = \varnothing$ Property 2.7.3

Proof

The proof goes as follows:

$mother \mathbin{;} father^{-1}$
$=$ Inverse
$(mother \mathbin{;} father^{-1})^{-1-1}$
$=$ Inverse
$(father^{-1-1} \mathbin{;} mother^{-1})^{-1}$
$=$ Inverse
$(father \mathbin{;} mother^{-1})^{-1}$
$=$ Property 2.7.2
$\varnothing^{-1}$
$=$ Inverse
$\varnothing$

End of Proof

$father \mathbin{;} children = mother \mathbin{;} children$ Property 2.7.4

Proof

The proof goes as follows:

$father \mathbin{;} children$
$=$ Definition of *children*
$father \mathbin{;} (mother \cup father)^{-1}$
$=$ Inverse
$father \mathbin{;} (mother^{-1} \cup father^{-1})$
$=$ Composition

$$(\textit{father} \,;\, \textit{mother}^{-1}) \cup (\textit{father} \,;\, \textit{father}^{-1})$$
$$=$$ Property 2.7.2
$$\varnothing \cup (\textit{father} \,;\, \textit{father}^{-1})$$
$$=$$ Union
$$\textit{father} \,;\, \textit{father}^{-1}$$
$$=$$ Property 2.7.1
$$\textit{mother} \,;\, \textit{mother}^{-1}$$
$$=$$ Union
$$(\textit{mother} \,;\, \textit{mother}^{-1}) \cup \varnothing$$
$$=$$ Property 2.7.3
$$(\textit{mother} \,;\, \textit{mother}^{-1}) \cup (\textit{mother} \,;\, \textit{father}^{-1})$$
$$=$$ Composition
$$\textit{mother} \,;\, (\textit{mother}^{-1} \cup \textit{father}^{-1})$$
$$=$$ Inverse
$$\textit{mother} \,;\, (\textit{mother} \cup \textit{father})^{-1}$$
$$=$$ Definition of *children*
$$\textit{mother} \,;\, \textit{children}$$

End of Proof

2.8. Exercises

1. Prove some of the properties of section 2.1.3.

2. Given a set s and two subsets u and v of s, prove the following:

$$\mathbb{P}(u) \subseteq \mathbb{P}(v) \quad \Rightarrow \quad u \subseteq v$$

3. Given a set s and two subsets a and b of s and also a set t and two subsets c and d of t, prove the following:

$$a \neq \varnothing \,\wedge\, c \neq \varnothing \quad \Rightarrow \quad ((a \times c) \subseteq (b \times d) \quad \Rightarrow \quad a \subseteq b \,\wedge\, c \subseteq d)$$

4. Prove some of the properties of section 2.3.4.

5. Given a set s and two subsets u and v of s, prove the following equivalences:

$$u \subseteq v \;\Leftrightarrow\; u \cup v = v \;\Leftrightarrow\; u \cap v = u \;\Leftrightarrow\; u - v = \varnothing$$

6. Given a set s and two subsets u and v of s, prove the following equivalences:

$$u \cup v = s \;\Leftrightarrow\; s - u \subseteq v \;\Leftrightarrow\; s - v \subseteq u$$

7. Given a set s and three subsets u, v and w of s, prove the following separate equivalences:

$$u \subseteq w \,\wedge\, v \subseteq w \;\Leftrightarrow\; (u \cup v) \subseteq w$$
$$w \subseteq u \,\wedge\, w \subseteq v \;\Leftrightarrow\; w \subseteq (u \cap v)$$

8. Given a set s and two subsets u and v of s, prove the following two separate results:

$$\mathbb{P}(u \cap v) = \mathbb{P}(u) \cap \mathbb{P}(v)$$
$$\mathbb{P}(u) \cup \mathbb{P}(v) \subseteq \mathbb{P}(u \cup v)$$

9. Given a set s and two subsets u and v of s, define the symmetric difference operator $\triangle$ between u and v as follows:

$$u \triangle v \; \hat{=} \; (u - v) \cup (v - u)$$

Given a third subset w of s, prove then the following separate results:

$$w \cap (u \triangle v) \; = \; (w \cap u) \triangle (w \cap v)$$
$$w \triangle (u \triangle v) \; = \; (w \triangle u) \triangle v$$

10. In sections 2.4.1 and 2.4.2, some set-theoretic operators have been given two distinct definitions. Prove that the two definitions of such operators are indeed equivalent.

11. Given two sets s and t, a relation r from s to t, a subset p of s and a subset q of t, prove the following equivalences where $\overline{p}$ and $\overline{q}$ stand for $s - p$ and $t - q$ respectively:

$$r[p] \subseteq q \; \Leftrightarrow \; r^{-1}[\overline{q}] \subseteq \overline{p} \; \Leftrightarrow \; (p \triangleleft r) \subseteq (r \triangleright q) \; \Leftrightarrow$$
$$r \subseteq (\overline{p} \times t) \cup (s \times q) \; \Leftrightarrow \; p \triangleleft r \triangleright q = \varnothing$$

12. Given two sets s and t, prove that the definitions of the set $s \nrightarrow t$ given in section 2.5.1 are indeed equivalent.

13. Prove some of the laws of the catalogue of section 2.6.

14. Given a set s, a relation r from s to s is said to be an *equivalence relation* on s if the domain of r is s and if the following three conditions hold:

$$\forall x \cdot (x \in s \; \Rightarrow \; (x, x) \in r)$$
$$\forall (x, y) \cdot ((x, y) \in s \times s \; \wedge \; (x, y) \in r \; \Rightarrow \; (y, x) \in r)$$
$$\forall (x, y, z) \cdot ((x, y, z) \in s \times s \times s \; \wedge \; (x, y) \in r \; \wedge \; (y, z) \in r \; \Rightarrow \; (x, z) \in r)$$

Prove that these conditions are respectively equivalent to the following simpler conditions:

$$\text{id}(s) \subseteq r$$
$$r = r^{-1}$$
$$r \, ; r \subseteq r$$

Given then a total function f from s to s, prove that the relation $f \, ; f^{-1}$ is an equivalence relation on s.

15. Given two sets s and t, a partial function f from s to t and two distinct members y and z of t, prove the following:

$$f^{-1}[\{y\}] \cap f^{-1}[\{z\}] = \varnothing$$

Also prove that every member of $\text{dom}(f)$ belongs to a set of the form $f^{-1}[\{y\}]$ for some y in $\text{ran}(f)$, formally

$$\forall x \cdot (x \in \text{dom}(f) \; \Rightarrow \; \exists y \cdot (y \in \text{ran}(f) \wedge x \in f^{-1}[\{y\}]))$$

The sets of the form $f^{-1}[\{y\}]$ for some y in $\text{ran}(f)$ are thus said to form a *partition* of $\text{dom}(f)$.

REFERENCES

[1] N. Bourbaki. *Théorie des Ensembles* (Hermann, 1970)

[2] A. Levy. *Basic Set Theory* (Springer-Verlag, 1979)

[3] H. Enderton. *Elements of Set Theory* (Academic Press, 1970)

[4] J.M. Spivey. *Understanding Z* (Cambridge University Press, 1988)

[5] C.B. Jones. *Systematic Software Development using VDM* (Prentice-Hall, 1990)

CHAPTER 3

Mathematical Objects

THIS chapter contains the second part of our presentation of set notation. It is devoted to the study of the construction of *mathematical objects*: that is, finite sets, natural numbers, finite sequences, and finite trees. All such constructions are realized by using the same inductive method based on the *fixpoint theorem* of Knaster and Tarski. We shall also describe the way recursive functions on these objects can be formally defined.

At the beginning of the chapter generalized intersection and union are presented, then we introduce the framework that we shall use in order to construct our objects. Then the construction of each of the mentioned objects follows in separate sections. Finally, at the end of the chapter, we present the concept of well-foundedness, which unifies completely each of the previous constructs.

Hurried readers, who are not interested in the details of these formal constructions, can skip them. They can go to Appendix A, where the notations are all listed.

3.1. Generalized Intersection and Union

Before presenting the framework that will allow us to construct mathematical objects in a systematic manner (section 3.2), we need first to introduce two important set theoretic concepts called *generalized intersection* and *generalized union*.

As usual, we first introduce our concepts syntactically, then we give an informal explanation and some examples, and finally we state and prove their basic properties. We now present the syntax of the new constructs. In the following table, s and t are *Sets*, and x and y are distinct *Variables*:

Syntax	Definition	Condition
inter (u)	$\{x \mid x \in s \,\wedge\, \forall y \cdot (y \in u \,\Rightarrow\, x \in y)\}$	$u \in \mathbb{P}_1(\mathbb{P}(s))$
union (u)	$\{x \mid x \in s \,\wedge\, \exists y \cdot (y \in u \,\wedge\, x \in y)\}$	$u \in \mathbb{P}(\mathbb{P}(s))$

Given a set s and a non-empty subset u of $\mathbb{P}(s)$ (u is thus a set of sets), the generalized intersection of u, denoted by inter (u), is the subset of s whose members share the property of being members of each member of u. Similarly, the generalized union of a set u of subsets of s, denoted by union (u), is the subset of s made up of all the members of s belonging to at least one member of u. We notice that, this time, u might be empty. As an example, let u be the following set

$$u \;=\; \{\{0,\, 5,\, 2,\, 4\},\, \{2,\, 4,\, 5\},\, \{2,\, 1,\, 7,\, 5\}\}$$

The numbers 2 and 5 are the only numbers which are members of each member of u, and each one of the numbers 0, 1, 2, 4, 5, and 7 appears in at least one member of u. As a consequence, we have

$$\text{inter}\,(u) \;=\; \{2,\, 5\}$$

$$\text{union}\,(u) \;=\; \{0,\, 1,\, 2,\, 4,\, 5,\, 7\}$$

We also define two special quantifiers, $\bigcup$ and $\bigcap$, allowing us to form the generalized union or the generalized intersection of well-defined set-theoretic expressions. Notice that, in the following table, x is the quantified *Variable* of the quantifiers $\bigcap$ and $\bigcup$. Moreover x must be non-free in the two *Sets* s, t. Likewise y is a quantified *Variable* that must be distinct from x and non-free in the two *Sets* s, t and in the *Expression* E.

Syntax	Definition	Condition
$\bigcap x \cdot (x \in s \mid E)$	$\{y \mid y \in t \,\wedge\, \forall x \cdot (x \in s \,\Rightarrow\, y \in E)\}$	(1)
$\bigcap x \cdot (x \in s \,\wedge\, P \mid E)$	$\{y \mid y \in t \,\wedge\, \forall x \cdot (x \in s \,\wedge\, P \,\Rightarrow\, y \in E)\}$	(2)
$\bigcup x \cdot (x \in s \mid E)$	$\{y \mid y \in t \,\wedge\, \exists x \cdot (x \in s \,\wedge\, y \in E)\}$	(3)
$\bigcup x \cdot (x \in s \,\wedge\, P \mid E)$	$\{y \mid y \in t \,\wedge\, \exists x \cdot (x \in s \,\wedge\, P \,\wedge\, y \in E)\}$	(4)

The numbered conditions are as follows:

	Condition
(1)	$\forall x \cdot (x \in s \;\Rightarrow\; E \subseteq t) \;\wedge\; s \neq \varnothing$
(2)	$\forall x \cdot (x \in s \wedge P \;\Rightarrow\; E \subseteq t) \;\wedge\; \{ x \mid x \in s \wedge P \} \neq \varnothing$
(3)	$\forall x \cdot (x \in s \;\Rightarrow\; E \subseteq t)$
(4)	$\forall x \cdot (x \in s \wedge P \;\Rightarrow\; E \subseteq t)$

Note that we shall also use the following alternative denser syntax for $\bigcap x \cdot (x \in s \mid E)$ and $\bigcup x \cdot (x \in s \mid E)$:

$$\bigcap_{x \in s} E \qquad\qquad \bigcup_{x \in s} E$$

It can also be said that these expressions denote the generalized intersection (resp. union) of all the sets E that are *indexed* by the members of the set s. The expression E is thus clearly, most of the time, an expression depending on the variable x. The condition, requiring that E is a subset of a certain set t, is necessary to allow us to type this form of generalized intersection (resp. union). Note, finally, that in the case of the generalized intersection quantifier, the set s must not be empty. As an example of using these quantifiers, consider a relation r typed as follows (with s not empty):

$$r \in s \leftrightarrow t$$

The following expression denotes the intersection of all the sets of the form $r[\{x\}]$, for x in s:

$$\bigcap_{x \in s} r[\{x\}]$$

By using the corresponding definition, we obtain

$$\{ y \mid y \in t \wedge \forall x \cdot (x \in s \;\Rightarrow\; y \in r[\{x\}]) \}$$

that is equivalently

$$\{ y \mid y \in t \wedge \forall x \cdot (x \in s \;\Rightarrow\; (x, y) \in r) \}$$

It is thus the set of members of t that are related (through r) to every member of s. Likewise, the expression

$$\bigcup_{x \in s} r[\{x\}]$$

can be translated as follows, using the corresponding definition:

$$\{ y \mid y \in t \ \wedge \ \exists x \cdot (x \in s \ \wedge \ y \in r[\{x\}])\}$$

that is equivalently

$$\{ y \mid y \in t \ \wedge \ \exists x \cdot (x \in s \ \wedge \ (x,y) \in r)\}$$

It is thus the set of members of t that are related (through r) to at least one member x of s; in other words, it is exactly $\mathsf{ran}\,(r)$. The two forms of generalized unions and generalized intersections we have introduced are not independent of each other. In fact, it is possible (proof left to the reader) to establish the following relationship between them.

$$
\begin{aligned}
\mathsf{inter}\,(u) \quad &= \quad \bigcap y \cdot (y \in u \mid y) \\[2mm]
\mathsf{union}\,(u) \quad &= \quad \bigcup y \cdot (y \in u \mid y) \\[2mm]
\bigcap x \cdot (x \in s \mid E) \quad &= \quad \mathsf{inter}\,(\mathsf{ran}\,(\lambda x \cdot (x \in s \mid E))) \\[2mm]
\bigcup x \cdot (x \in s \mid E) \quad &= \quad \mathsf{union}\,(\mathsf{ran}\,(\lambda x \cdot (x \in s \mid E)))
\end{aligned}
$$

We leave it to the reader to prove the following *associativity* properties. Notice that in the following table, to simplify matters, we have omitted the preconditions as they can easily be deduced from those of the previous definitions. For the same reason, we shall do so for future properties when such preconditions are simple.

$$
\begin{aligned}
\mathsf{inter}\,(\bigcup x \cdot (x \in s \mid E)) \quad &= \quad \bigcap x \cdot (x \in s \mid \mathsf{inter}\,(E)) \\[2mm]
\mathsf{union}\,(\bigcup x \cdot (x \in s \mid E)) \quad &= \quad \bigcup x \cdot (x \in s \mid \mathsf{union}\,(E)) \\[2mm]
\bigcap y \cdot (y \in \bigcup x \cdot (x \in s \mid E) \mid F) \quad &= \quad \bigcap x \cdot (x \in s \mid \bigcap y \cdot (y \in E \mid F)) \\[2mm]
\bigcup y \cdot (y \in \bigcup x \cdot (x \in s \mid E) \mid F) \quad &= \quad \bigcup x \cdot (x \in s \mid \bigcup y \cdot (y \in E \mid F))
\end{aligned}
$$

We also have the following *distributivity* properties:

$$\bigcap x \cdot (x \in s \mid E) \; \cup \; \bigcap y \cdot (y \in t \mid F) \;=\; \bigcap (x,y) \cdot ((x,y) \in s \times t \mid E \cup F)$$

$$\bigcup x \cdot (x \in s \mid E) \; \cap \; \bigcup y \cdot (y \in t \mid F) \;=\; \bigcup (x,y) \cdot ((x,y) \in s \times t \mid E \cap F)$$

$$\bigcap x \cdot (x \in s \mid E) \; \times \; \bigcap y \cdot (y \in t \mid F) \;=\; \bigcap (x,y) \cdot ((x,y) \in s \times t \mid E \times F)$$

$$\bigcup x \cdot (x \in s \mid E) \; \times \; \bigcup y \cdot (y \in t \mid F) \;=\; \bigcup (x,y) \cdot ((x,y) \in s \times t \mid E \times F)$$

We finally have the following various properties:

$\mathsf{inter}(\{a\})$	$=$	a
$\mathsf{union}(\{a\})$	$=$	a
$\mathsf{inter}(\{a, b\})$	$=$	$a \cap b$
$\mathsf{union}(\{a, b\})$	$=$	$a \cup b$
$\mathsf{inter}(a \cup b)$	$=$	$\mathsf{inter}(a) \cap \mathsf{inter}(b) \quad$ if $a \neq \varnothing \wedge b \neq \varnothing$
$\mathsf{union}(a \cup b)$	$=$	$\mathsf{union}(a) \cup \mathsf{union}(b)$
$\mathsf{inter}(a \cup b)$	$=$	$\mathsf{inter}(\{\, \mathsf{inter}(a), \mathsf{inter}(b)\,\}) \quad$ if $a \neq \varnothing \wedge b \neq \varnothing$
$\mathsf{union}(a \cup b)$	$=$	$\mathsf{union}(\{\, \mathsf{union}(a), \mathsf{union}(b)\,\})$

The Generalized Intersection is a Lower Bound

Since each member of $\mathsf{inter}(u)$ is, by definition, also a member of each member of u, it is clearly the case that $\mathsf{inter}(u)$ is included in each member of u. Notice that this does not necessarily mean that $\mathsf{inter}(u)$ itself is a member of u although this can be the case in certain circumstances. As a consequence, $\mathsf{inter}(u)$ is said to be a *lower bound* of members of u. This can be formalized as follows:

$u \in \mathbb{P}_1(\mathbb{P}(s))$
$t \in u$
$\Rightarrow$ Theorem 3.1.1
$\mathsf{inter}(u) \subseteq t$

Proof
We assume

$u \in \mathbb{P}_1(\mathbb{P}(s))$ Hypothesis 1

$t \in u$ Hypothesis 2

and we have to prove

$\mathrm{inter}(u) \subseteq t$ Goal 1

that is, according to the definition of set inclusion,

$\forall x \cdot (x \in \mathrm{inter}(u) \;\;\Rightarrow\;\; x \in t)$ Goal 2

Since x is obviously non-free in Hypothesis 1 and Hypothesis 2, we can remove the universal quantification. We assume now $x \in \mathrm{inter}(u)$, which is equivalent, according to the definition of $\mathrm{inter}(u)$, to the following two hypotheses:

$x \in s$ Hypothesis 3

$\forall t \cdot (t \in u \;\;\Rightarrow\;\; x \in t)$ Hypothesis 4

And we are left to prove $x \in t$ which is obvious according to Hypothesis 2 and Hypothesis 4.
End of Proof

The Generalized Intersection is the Greatest Lower Bound

As we have just seen, $\mathrm{inter}(u)$ is a lower bound of members of u. In fact, among the various lower bounds, $\mathrm{inter}(u)$ has a special position: it includes all of them. As a consequence, $\mathrm{inter}(u)$ is said to be the *greatest lower bound* (glb for short) of members of u. This second property is formalized as the following theorem:

$u \in \mathbb{P}_1(\mathbb{P}(s))$
$v \subseteq s$
$\forall t \cdot (t \in u \;\;\Rightarrow\;\; v \subseteq t)$ Theorem 3.1.2
$\Rightarrow$
$v \subseteq \mathrm{inter}(u)$

Proof

We assume

$u \in \mathbb{P}_1(\mathbb{P}(s))$ Hypothesis 1

$v \subseteq s$ Hypothesis 2

$\forall t \cdot (t \in u \;\;\Rightarrow\;\; v \subseteq t)$ Hypothesis 3

and we have to prove

$v \subseteq \mathrm{inter}(u)$ Goal 1 that is equivalently

$$\forall x \cdot (x \in v \quad \Rightarrow \quad x \in \text{inter}(u)) \qquad \text{Goal 2}$$

Since x is non-free in Hypothesis 1, Hypothesis 2 and Hypothesis 3, we can remove the universal quantifier. We assume

$$x \in v \qquad \text{Hypothesis 4}$$

And we are left to prove

$$x \in \text{inter}(u) \qquad \text{Goal 3}$$

that is, according to the definition of inter

$$x \in s \;\land\; \forall t \cdot (t \in u \quad \Rightarrow \quad x \in t) \qquad \text{Goal 4}$$

As the first statement is obvious (according to Hypothesis 4 and Hypothesis 2), we are left to prove the second one only. As t is non-free in Hypothesis 1, Hypothesis 2, Hypothesis 3 and Hypothesis 4, we can remove the universal quantifier. We assume

$$t \in u \qquad \text{Hypothesis 5}$$

And we have to prove

$$x \in t \qquad \text{Goal 5}$$

From Hypothesis 5 and Hypothesis 3 we can deduce $v \subseteq t$, yielding

$$\forall x \cdot (x \in v \quad \Rightarrow \quad x \in t) \qquad \text{Derivation 1}$$

As a consequence, our goal, $x \in t$, follows from Hypothesis 4.
End of Proof

The form of the previous theorems makes them good candidates for proving statements involving the inclusion operator with a generalized intersection situated either on its left (Theorem 3.1.1) or on its right (Theorem 3.1.2).

The Generalized Union is an Upper Bound

Similarly, the set union (u) includes each member of u. As a consequence, it is said to be an *upper bound* of members of u. This can be formalized as follows:

$u \in \mathbb{P}(\mathbb{P}(s))$
$t \in u$
$\Rightarrow$ Theorem 3.1.3
$t \subseteq \text{union}(u)$

The Generalized Union is the Least Upper Bound

Moreover, union (u) is included in each such upper bound. As a consequence, it is said to be the *least upper bound* (lub for short) of members of u. This can be formalized as follows:

$u \in \mathbb{P}(\mathbb{P}(s))$

$v \subseteq s$

$\forall t \cdot (t \in u \;\Rightarrow\; t \subseteq v)$ Theorem 3.1.4

$\Rightarrow$

union $(u) \subseteq v$

The proofs of Theorem 3.1.3 and Theorem 3.1.4 are left to the reader as exercises.

3.2. Constructing Mathematical Objects

3.2.1. Informal Introduction

In Mathematics, objects with (apparently) *circular* definitions are frequently encountered. For instance, a finite set is either the empty set or the set obtained by adding a single element to an already given finite set. A natural number is either 0 or the number obtained by adding 1 to an already given natural number. A finite sequence is either the empty sequence or the sequence obtained by inserting an element at the beginning of an already given sequence. A finite tree is obtained by putting together a finite sequence of already given finite trees. In each of the above cases, the intuitive implicit idea is that the *entire set* of corresponding objects can be "generated" in this way. The trouble with these definitions, however, is that they do not lead naturally to formal expressions based on set comprehension. The best we can do is write down the properties stated informally. For instance, in the case of the set $\mathbb{N}$ of natural numbers, we have

$$0 \in \mathbb{N}$$

$$\forall n \cdot (n \in \mathbb{N} \;\Rightarrow\; \mathsf{succ}\,(n) \in \mathbb{N})$$

where succ is supposed to be the function that *adds one to a number*. Since we "know" that all natural numbers are characterized in this way, we can simplify the previous properties by using the *image* concept defined in the previous chapter. This yields

$$\mathbb{N} \;=\; \{0\} \cup \mathsf{succ}\,[\mathbb{N}]$$

Thus the set $\mathbb{N}$ appears to be a *solution of an equation* of the general form

$$x = f(x)$$

where f is supposed to be a certain *set function*. An equation of this form is said to be a *fixpoint equation* because the unknown x is a "point" that remains "fixed" when the function f is applied to it. As all the examples above (and many others) follow this general scheme, it is certainly worth investigating how to solve such fixpoint equations. In what follows, we shall show that, under certain circumstances, the fixpoint equation has a well-defined solution. This is the purpose of the **Knaster-Tarski theorems** stated and proved in the next section. From this result, we will be able to build various sets (of *mathematical objects*) such as the set of finite subsets of a set (section 3.3), the set of natural numbers (section 3.5), the set of finite sequences built on a given set (section 3.7), and finally various sets of trees (sections 3.8, 3.9, and 3.10).

3.2.2. Fixpoints

Rationale

As indicated in the previous section, the fixpoint of a set function (also called *set transformer*) is the concept we need in order to build our mathematical objects. Clearly, a fixpoint of the set function f such that

$$f \in \mathbb{P}(s) \to \mathbb{P}(s)$$

is a subset x of s that is *stable* under f, formally

$$f(x) = x$$

Since x is a set, the previous condition can be equivalently decomposed as follows:

$$f(x) \subseteq x \quad \wedge \quad x \subseteq f(x)$$

We can see immediately that the set s certainly fulfils the first sub-condition and that the empty set, $\varnothing$, certainly fulfils the second sub-condition. More generally, it is tempting to consider the set made up of all the sets corresponding to the first sub-condition and alternatively the set made up of all the sets corresponding to the second sub-condition, since the fixpoints, if any, are exactly the members of their intersection. This corresponds to the following sets ϕ and Φ:

$$\phi = \{ x \mid x \in \mathbb{P}(s) \wedge f(x) \subseteq x \}$$

$$\Phi = \{ x \mid x \in \mathbb{P}(s) \wedge x \subseteq f(x) \}$$

Since we have here some sets of sets, we might consider their generalized intersection and generalized union and ask ourselves whether these objects still have the corresponding properties. If this is the case then they might be candidates for fixpoints. The generalized union of ϕ is not very interesting since it is clearly s. Likewise, the generalized intersection of Φ is not very interesting since it is clearly $\varnothing$. So, we are led to consider inter(ϕ) and union(Φ) only. Before even studying, say, inter(ϕ) we might first consider the intersection of two members of ϕ and see whether this intersection still belongs to ϕ because, in case it does not, then there is no point in generalizing the intersection to more members of ϕ. So, given any two members of ϕ, namely two subsets x_1 and x_2 of s such that

$$f(x_1) \subseteq x_1$$

$$f(x_2) \subseteq x_2$$

we wonder whether we also have

$$f(x_1 \cap x_2) \subseteq x_1 \cap x_2$$

Clearly, we already have

$$f(x_1) \cap f(x_2) \subseteq x_1 \cap x_2$$

Therefore, it is *sufficient* (according to the transitivity of inclusion) to have

$$f(x_1 \cap x_2) \subseteq f(x_1) \cap f(x_2)$$

And for this to happen, it is *sufficient* to have both

$$f(x_1 \cap x_2) \subseteq f(x_1)$$

$$f(x_1 \cap x_2) \subseteq f(x_2)$$

But we obviously already have the following:

$$x_1 \cap x_2 \subseteq x_1$$

$$x_1 \cap x_2 \subseteq x_2$$

so that a very general, and again *sufficient*, condition for the set ϕ to be closed under intersection is that f preserves set containment. In other words, given any two subsets a and b of s we should have

$$a \subseteq b \quad \Rightarrow \quad f(a) \subseteq f(b)$$

Likewise, we can easily prove that, under the same *monotonicity property*, the set Φ is closed under union. But we can now prove more, namely not only the following :

$$\text{inter}\,(\phi) \in \phi$$

$$\text{union}\,(\Phi) \in \Phi$$

but also

$$\text{inter}\,(\phi) \in \Phi$$

$$\text{union}\,(\Phi) \in \phi$$

In other words, and quite surprisingly, both $\text{inter}\,(\phi)$ and $\text{union}\,(\Phi)$ are fixpoints, formally

$$f(\text{inter}(\phi)) \;=\; \text{inter}(\phi)$$

$$f(\text{union}(\Phi)) \;=\; \text{union}(\Phi)$$

Finally, we can also prove that inter (ϕ) is the least fixpoint and union (Φ) is the greatest of them. This is essentially the purpose of the Knaster-Tarski theorems that we shall state and prove in what follows.

Definition

We now define the sets ϕ and Φ of the previous sub-section for any function f and we replace inter (ϕ) and union (Φ) by fix (f) and FIX (f) respectively. These are first defined syntactically and then we shall state and prove their fixpoint properties.

Syntax	Definition	Condition
fix (f)	inter $(\{\, x \mid x \in \mathbb{P}(s) \,\wedge\, f(x) \subseteq x \,\})$	$f \in \mathbb{P}(s) \to \mathbb{P}(s)$
FIX (f)	union $(\{\, x \mid x \in \mathbb{P}(s) \,\wedge\, x \subseteq f(x) \,\})$	$f \in \mathbb{P}(s) \to \mathbb{P}(s)$

We notice that the generalized intersection fix (f) is well-defined since the set $\{\, x \mid x \in \mathbb{P}(s) \,\wedge\, f(x) \subseteq x \,\}$ is not empty (s belongs to it). The following two theorems are immediate consequences of these definitions. The first one is a simple transcription of **Theorem 3.1.1**:

$f \in \mathbb{P}(s) \to \mathbb{P}(s)$
$t \subseteq s$
$f(t) \subseteq t$ Theorem 3.2.1
$\Rightarrow$
fix $(f) \subseteq t$

And the next one is a simple transcription of **Theorem 3.1.2**:

$f \in \mathbb{P}(s) \to \mathbb{P}(s)$
$v \subseteq s$
$\forall t \cdot (t \in \mathbb{P}(s) \wedge f(t) \subseteq t \;\Rightarrow\; v \subseteq t)$ Theorem 3.2.2
$\Rightarrow$
$v \subseteq$ fix (f)

We have similar theorems for FIX. Again, the first one is a simple transcription of **Theorem 3.1.3**:

$$f \in \mathbb{P}(s) \rightarrow \mathbb{P}(s)$$
$$t \subseteq s$$
$$t \subseteq f(t) \qquad\qquad\qquad \text{Theorem 3.2.3}$$
$$\Rightarrow$$
$$t \subseteq \mathsf{FIX}(f)$$

And the next one is a simple transcription of Theorem 3.1.4:

$$f \in \mathbb{P}(s) \rightarrow \mathbb{P}(s)$$
$$v \subseteq s$$
$$\forall t \cdot (t \in \mathbb{P}(s) \wedge t \subseteq f(t) \;\Rightarrow\; t \subseteq v) \qquad \text{Theorem 3.2.4}$$
$$\Rightarrow$$
$$\mathsf{FIX}(f) \subseteq v$$

These theorems are important because they can be used to prove statements involving the inclusion operator with an expression of the form $\mathrm{fix}(f)$ or $\mathsf{FIX}(f)$ disposed either on its left or on its right.

The Knaster-Tarski Theorems

We now present the theorems of Knaster and Tarski which state that both expressions $\mathrm{fix}(f)$ and $\mathsf{FIX}(f)$ indeed denote fixpoints of f whenever the set transformer f is monotonic, that is when it preserves set containment. The first theorem concerns the operator fix:

$$f \in \mathbb{P}(s) \rightarrow \mathbb{P}(s)$$
$$\forall (x, y) \cdot ((x, y) \in \mathbb{P}(s) \times \mathbb{P}(s) \wedge x \subseteq y \;\Rightarrow$$
$$f(x) \subseteq f(y)) \qquad\qquad\qquad \text{Theorem 3.2.5}$$
$$\Rightarrow$$
$$f(\mathrm{fix}(f)) = \mathrm{fix}(f)$$

Proof

We assume

$$f \in \mathbb{P}(s) \rightarrow \mathbb{P}(s) \qquad\qquad\qquad \text{Hypothesis 1}$$

Hypothesis 2

$$\forall (x, y) \cdot ((x, y) \in \mathbb{P}(s) \times \mathbb{P}(s) \wedge x \subseteq y \;\Rightarrow\; f(x) \subseteq f(y))$$

And we have to prove

$$f(\mathrm{fix}(f)) = \mathrm{fix}(f) \qquad\qquad\qquad \text{Goal 1}$$

Goal 1 can be transformed into the following two separate goals which we shall prove in turn:

$$f\,(\text{fix}\,(f)) \subseteq \text{fix}\,(f) \qquad \qquad \text{Goal 2}$$

$$\text{fix}\,(f) \subseteq f\,(\text{fix}\,(f)) \qquad \qquad \text{Goal 3}$$

The form of Goal 2 suggests applying Theorem 3.2.2. As a consequence, it is sufficient to prove the following three conditions:

$$f \in \mathbb{P}(s) \rightarrow \mathbb{P}(s) \qquad \qquad \text{Goal 4}$$

$$f\,(\text{fix}\,(f)) \subseteq s \qquad \qquad \text{Goal 5}$$

$$\forall t \cdot (t \in \mathbb{P}(s) \land f\,(t) \subseteq t \quad \Rightarrow \quad f\,(\text{fix}\,(f)) \subseteq t) \qquad \qquad \text{Goal 6}$$

Goal 4 is exactly Hypothesis 1, and Goal 5 is obvious (according to Hypothesis 1). We shall then prove only Goal 6. As t is non-free in Hypothesis 1 and Hypothesis 2, we can remove the universal quantifier. We assume

$$t \in \mathbb{P}(s) \qquad \qquad \text{Hypothesis 3}$$
$$f\,(t) \subseteq t \qquad \qquad \text{Hypothesis 4}$$

And we have to prove

$$f\,(\text{fix}\,(f)) \subseteq t \qquad \qquad \text{Goal 7}$$

But from Hypothesis 1, Hypothesis 3, Hypothesis 4 and Theorem 3.2.1, we deduce

$$\text{fix}\,(f) \subseteq t \qquad \qquad \text{Derivation 1}$$

From the monotonicity property of f (that is, Hypothesis 2), and from the previous derivation, we then deduce

$$f(\text{fix}\,(f)) \subseteq f(t) \qquad \qquad \text{Derivation 2}$$

From here, we easily deduce Goal 7 according to Hypothesis 4 and the transitivity of inclusion. Now, we prove Goal 3. Again, the very form of this goal suggests applying Theorem 3.2.1. As a consequence, it is sufficient to prove the following three conditions:

$$f \in \mathbb{P}(s) \rightarrow \mathbb{P}(s) \qquad \qquad \text{Goal 8}$$

$$f\,(\text{fix}\,(f)) \subseteq s \qquad \qquad \text{Goal 9}$$

$$f\,(f\,(\text{fix}\,(f))) \subseteq f\,(\text{fix}\,(f)) \qquad \qquad \text{Goal 10}$$

Goal 8 is exactly Hypothesis 1, Goal 9 is obvious (according to Hypothesis 1) and Goal 10 is also valid according to the monotonicity property of f and according to Goal 2 which we have already proved.
End of Proof

The second theorem (whose proof is left to the reader) concerns FIX:

$f \in \mathbb{P}(s) \rightarrow \mathbb{P}(s)$

$\forall (x, y) \cdot ((x, y) \in \mathbb{P}(s) \times \mathbb{P}(s) \ \wedge \ x \subseteq y \quad \Rightarrow$
$\quad f(x) \subseteq f(y))$ Theorem 3.2.6

$\Rightarrow$

$f(\text{FIX}(f)) \ = \ \text{FIX}(f)$

We leave it as an exercise for the reader to also prove that under the conditions of the two previous theorems, fix (f) is the *least* fixpoint and FIX (f) is the *greatest* one. We now have a slight embarrassment in that we do not know which of the two special fixpoints is the best choice for constructing our mathematical objects. In fact, we shall see in the next section that the least of them enjoys a *very interesting property* allowing us to prove universal conditions on its members *by induction*. As a consequence, we shall choose the least fixpoint rather than the greatest one. The latter, however, will be used in chapter 9, which is concerned with the theory of loops.

3.2.3. Induction Principle

Definition

An interesting outcome of the definition of fix (f) given in the previous section is that it gives us the possibility to prove universal properties of the members of the fixpoint *by induction*. More precisely, suppose that we want to prove that all members of fix (f) enjoy a certain property P, formally

$$\forall x \cdot (x \in \text{fix}(f) \ \Rightarrow \ P)$$

that is, equivalently

$$\forall x \cdot (x \in \text{fix}(f) \ \Rightarrow \ x \in \text{fix}(f) \ \wedge \ P)$$

that is, equivalently

$$\text{fix}(f) \subseteq \{x \mid x \in \text{fix}(f) \ \wedge \ P\}$$

Consequently, according to Theorem 3.2.1, it is sufficient to prove both statements

$$\{x \mid x \in \text{fix}(f) \ \wedge \ P\} \subseteq s$$

$$f(\{x \mid x \in \text{fix}(f) \ \wedge \ P\}) \subseteq \{x \mid x \in \text{fix}(f) \ \wedge \ P\}$$

Since the former statement is obvious because, by definition, fix (f) is included in s, it is sufficient to prove the latter. This justifies the following theorem which constitutes a very general Induction Principle:

$$f \in \mathbb{P}(s) \rightarrow \mathbb{P}(s)$$
$$f\,(\{x \mid x \in \mathsf{fix}\,(f) \;\wedge\; P\}) \;\subseteq\; \{x \mid x \in \mathsf{fix}\,(f) \;\wedge\; P\}$$
$$\Rightarrow$$
$$\forall x \cdot (x \in \mathsf{fix}\,(f) \;\Rightarrow\; P)$$

Theorem 3.2.7

In what follows, we study two cases corresponding to special forms of the set function f. Additionally we shall see how the induction principle corresponding to Theorem 3.2.7 can then be simplified accordingly.

First Special Case

As a first case, let s be a set, a an element of s, and g a total function from s to s, formally

$$a \in s$$

$$g \in s \rightarrow s$$

We consider the following function f:

$$f \;=\; \lambda z \cdot (z \in \mathbb{P}(s) \mid \{a\} \cup g\,[z])$$

Clearly, this function resembles the one we envisaged for constructing $\mathbb{N}$ in our informal introduction (remember, we considered a function of z, say, constructed around an expression of the form $\{0\} \cup \mathsf{succ}[z]$). Coming back to our function f, we can see that it is obviously a function from $\mathbb{P}(s)$ to $\mathbb{P}(s)$. Moreover, this function is monotonic. This results immediately from the monotonicity of $g\,[z]$ in z and from that of the operator $\cup$ (section 2.3.4). Therefore, the function f has a least fixpoint $\mathsf{fix}\,(f)$ and, consequently, we have

$$\mathsf{fix}\,(f) \;=\; \{a\} \cup g\,[\mathsf{fix}\,(f)]$$

We deduce immediately a first property

$$a \in \mathsf{fix}\,(f)$$

Property 3.2.1

and a second property

$$\forall x \cdot (x \in \mathsf{fix}\,(f) \;\Rightarrow\; g\,(x) \in \mathsf{fix}\,(f))$$

Property 3.2.2

The induction principle corresponding to Theorem 3.2.7 can then be simplified as follows. Let z be the following set:

$$z \;=\; \{x \mid x \in \mathsf{fix}\,(f) \;\wedge\; P\}$$

Our intention is to have a more operational form for the predicate

$$f(z) \subseteq z$$

which constitutes the main antecedent of **Theorem** 3.2.7. We have

$f(z) \subseteq z$	
$\Leftrightarrow$	Definition of f
$\{a\} \cup g[z] \subseteq z$	
$\Leftrightarrow$	Set Theory
$a \in z \ \wedge \ g[z] \subseteq z$	
$\Leftrightarrow$	Definition of z
$a \in \text{fix}(f) \ \wedge \ [x := a] \, P \ \wedge \ g[z] \subseteq z$	
$\Leftrightarrow$	Property 3.2.1
$[x := a] \, P \ \wedge \ g[z] \subseteq z$	
$\Leftrightarrow$	Set Theory
$[x := a] \, P \ \wedge \ \forall x \cdot (x \in z \ \Rightarrow \ g(x) \in z)$	
$\Leftrightarrow$	Definition of z
$[x := a] \, P \ \wedge$	
$\forall x \cdot (x \in \text{fix}(f) \ \wedge \ P \ \Rightarrow \ g(x) \in \text{fix}(f) \ \wedge \ [x := g(x)] \, P)$	
$\Leftrightarrow$	Property 3.2.2
$[x := a] \, P \ \wedge$	
$\forall x \cdot (x \in \text{fix}(f) \wedge P \ \Rightarrow \ [x := g(x)] \, P)$	

By substituting this in **Theorem** 3.2.7, we easily obtain the following:

$[x := a] \, P$	
$\forall x \cdot (x \in \text{fix}(f) \ \wedge \ P \ \Rightarrow \ [x := g(x)] \, P)$	
$\Rightarrow$	Theorem 3.2.8
$\forall x \cdot (x \in \text{fix}(f) \ \Rightarrow \ P)$	

This means that whenever we have to prove a universal property of the form

$$\forall x \cdot (x \in \text{fix}(f) \ \Rightarrow \ P)$$

we can do a so-called *inductive proof* by using the previous result. In practice, this means that it is sufficient to prove first

$$[x := a] \, P$$

which constitutes the **Base Case** of our induction proof. And then we have to prove

$$[x := g(x)] \, P$$

under the Induction Hypothesis

$$x \in \text{fix}(f) \ \wedge \ P$$

This constitutes the **Induction Step** of our induction proof. In other words, we first prove that our property P (supposed to depend on the free variable x) is valid at the point a, and then that it is valid at the point $g(x)$ provided that it is valid at x. One could already recognize a slight generalization of the very classical technique used to prove properties of natural numbers *by mathematival induction*.

Second Special Case

As a second case, let s and t be two sets, a an element of s, and g a total function from $t \times s$ to s, formally

$$a \in s$$

$$g \in (t \times s) \rightarrow s$$

We consider the following function f:

$$f = \lambda z \cdot (z \in \mathbb{P}(s) \mid \{a\} \cup g[t \times z])$$

This is obviously a function from $\mathbb{P}(s)$ to $\mathbb{P}(s)$ whose monotonicity results from that of $g[t \times z]$ in $t \times z$ and that of $t \times z$ in z. Therefore, the function f has a least fixpoint $\mathsf{fix}(f)$ and, consequently, we have

$$\mathsf{fix}(f) = \{a\} \cup g[t \times \mathsf{fix}(f)]$$

From this, we deduce immediately a first property

$a \in \mathsf{fix}(f)$ Property 3.2.3

---

and a second property

$\forall (u, x) \cdot ((u, x) \in t \times \mathsf{fix}(f) \Rightarrow g(u, x) \in \mathsf{fix}(f))$ Property 3.2.4

The induction principle corresponding to Theorem 3.2.7 can then be simplified as follows. Let z be the following set:

$$z = \{x \mid x \in \mathsf{fix}(f) \wedge P\}$$

Our intention again is to have a more operational form for the predicate

$$f(z) \subseteq z$$

which constitutes the main antecedent of **Theorem 3.2.7**. We have:

$$f(z) \subseteq z$$
$$\Leftrightarrow \qquad\qquad\qquad\qquad\qquad\qquad\qquad \text{Definition of } f$$
$$\{a\} \cup g[t \times z] \subseteq z$$
$$\Leftrightarrow \qquad\qquad\qquad\qquad\qquad\qquad\qquad \text{Set Theory}$$
$$a \in z \ \wedge \ g[t \times z] \subseteq z$$
$$\Leftrightarrow \qquad\qquad\qquad\qquad\qquad\qquad\qquad \text{Definition of } z$$
$$a \in \mathsf{fix}(f) \ \wedge \ [x := a] P \ \wedge \ g[t \times z] \subseteq z$$
$$\Leftrightarrow \qquad\qquad\qquad\qquad\qquad\qquad\qquad \text{Property 3.2.3}$$
$$[x := a] P \ \wedge \ g[t \times z] \subseteq z$$
$$\Leftrightarrow \qquad\qquad\qquad\qquad\qquad\qquad\qquad \text{Set Theory}$$
$$[x := a] P \ \wedge$$
$$\forall(u, x) \cdot ((u, x) \in t \times z \ \Rightarrow \ g(u, x) \in z)$$
$$\Leftrightarrow \qquad\qquad\qquad\qquad\qquad\qquad\qquad \text{Definition of } z$$
$$[x := a] P \ \wedge$$
$$\forall(u, x) \cdot ((u, x) \in t \times \mathsf{fix}(f) \ \wedge \ P \ \Rightarrow$$
$$g(u, x) \in \mathsf{fix}(f) \ \wedge \ [x := g(u, x)] P)$$
$$\Leftrightarrow \qquad\qquad\qquad\qquad\qquad\qquad\qquad \text{Property 3.2.4}$$
$$[x := a] P \ \wedge$$
$$\forall(u, x) \cdot ((u, x) \in t \times \mathsf{fix}(f) \ \wedge \ P \ \Rightarrow \ [x := g(u, x)] P)$$
$$\Leftrightarrow \qquad\qquad\qquad\qquad\qquad\qquad\qquad \text{Predicate Calculus}$$
$$[x := a] P \ \wedge$$
$$\forall x \cdot (x \in \mathsf{fix}(f) \ \wedge \ P \ \Rightarrow \ \forall u \cdot (u \in t \ \Rightarrow \ [x := g(u, x)] P))$$

Notice that in these derivations we have supposed implicitly that the variable u can always be chosen so as to be non-free in $x \in \mathsf{fix}(f) \wedge P$. By substituting this in **Theorem 3.2.7**, we obtain the following induction principle:

$$[x := a] P$$
$$\forall x \cdot (x \in \mathsf{fix}(f) \ \wedge \ P \ \Rightarrow \ \forall u \cdot (u \in t \ \Rightarrow$$
$$[x := g(u, x)] P)) \qquad\qquad\qquad\qquad \text{Theorem 3.2.9}$$
$$\Rightarrow$$
$$\forall x \cdot (x \in \mathsf{fix}(f) \ \Rightarrow \ P)$$

Applying this result to prove a universal property of the fixpoint leads again to the possibility of performing inductive proofs. The ***Base Case*** is the same as that of the previous case. The ***Induction step*** is slightly more complicated: we assume the same Induction Hypothesis as before but the goal to be proved has now a universal form.

3.3. The Set of Finite Subsets of a Set

We now use the general theory developed in the previous section to construct our first set of *Mathematical Objects*, namely the set of *finite* subsets of a set s. The set $\mathbb{F}(s)$ should enjoy the following two properties: (1) the empty set is a finite subset of s and (2) if we add a member of s to a finite subset of s we obtain yet another finite subset of s, formally

$$\varnothing \in \mathbb{F}(s)$$

$$\forall (u, x) \cdot ((u, x) \in s \times \mathbb{F}(s) \ \Rightarrow \ (\{u\} \cup x) \in \mathbb{F}(s))$$

This is clearly a situation that corresponds the second special case studied in section 3.2.3. We define a function add (s) (to add an element to a subset of s) and also a set function genfin (s) which is obviously a monotonic function from $\mathbb{P}(\mathbb{P}(s))$ to itself.

Syntax	Definition
add (s)	$\lambda (u, x) \cdot ((u, x) \in s \times \mathbb{P}(s) \mid \{u\} \cup x \,)$
genfin (s)	$\lambda z \cdot (z \in \mathbb{P}(\mathbb{P}(s)) \mid \{\varnothing\} \cup \text{add}\,(s)[s \times z])$

For instance we have

$$\text{add}\,(\{1, 2, 3\})\,(3, \{1\}) \ = \ \{1, 3\}$$

$$\text{genfin}\,(\{1, 2, 3\})\,(\{\varnothing, \{1\}, \{2\}, \{3\}\}) \ = \ \{\varnothing, \{1\}, \{2\}, \{3\}, \{1, 2\}, \{1, 3\}, \{2, 3\}\}$$

The set $\mathbb{F}(s)$ is then defined to be the least fixpoint of the function genfin (s). We also define formally the set of finite *non-empty* subsets of a set.

Syntax	Definition
$\mathbb{F}(s)$	fix $(\text{genfin}\,(s))$
$\mathbb{F}_1(s)$	$\mathbb{F}(s) - \{\varnothing\}$

Since the function genfin (s) is clearly monotone, $\mathbb{F}(s)$ is a fixpoint and we have

$$\mathbb{F}(s) \ = \ \{\varnothing\} \cup \text{add}\,(s)[s \times \mathbb{F}(s)]$$

That is

$\varnothing \in \mathbb{F}(s)$ Property 3.3.1

---

and also

$\forall (u, x) \cdot ((u, x) \in s \times \mathbb{F}(s) \;\Rightarrow\; (\{u\} \cup x) \in \mathbb{F}(s))$ Property 3.3.2

These are exactly the desired properties. The induction principle becomes, according to Theorem 3.2.9

$[x := \varnothing]\, P$
$\forall x \cdot (x \in \mathbb{F}(s) \wedge P \;\Rightarrow\; \forall u \cdot (u \in s \;\Rightarrow\; [x := \{u\} \cup x]\, P))$
$\Rightarrow$ Theorem 3.3.1
$\forall x \cdot (x \in \mathbb{F}(s) \;\Rightarrow\; P)$

This induction principle is very intuitive. In order to prove a universal property valid for all the finite subsets of s, we first prove that our intended property P is valid for the empty set and then that it is valid for the set $\{u\} \cup x$, provided it is already valid for the finite set x and for any member u of s. For example, we can prove the following three properties by using this induction principle. The first property tells us that the union of two finite sets is finite.

$\forall (x, y) \cdot ((x, y) \in \mathbb{F}(s) \times \mathbb{F}(s) \;\Rightarrow\; (x \cup y) \in \mathbb{F}(s))$ Property 3.3.3

Notice that, in order to use the finite set induction principle to prove the above property, we obviously have to restate it as follows:

$$\forall x \cdot (x \in \mathbb{F}(s) \;\Rightarrow\; \forall y \cdot (y \in \mathbb{F}(s) \;\Rightarrow\; (x \cup y) \in \mathbb{F}(s)))$$

The second property tells us that the intersection of two finite sets is finite.

$\forall (x, y) \cdot ((x, y) \in \mathbb{F}(s) \times \mathbb{F}(s) \;\Rightarrow\; (x \cap y) \in \mathbb{F}(s))$ Property 3.3.4

And the third property states that the image of a finite set under a partial function is also a finite set.

$f \in s \rightarrowtail t \;\Rightarrow\; \forall x \cdot (x \in \mathbb{F}(s) \;\Rightarrow\; f[x] \in \mathbb{F}(t))$ Property 3.3.5

Proof

We assume

$$f \in s \rightarrowtail t \qquad\qquad \text{Hypothesis 1}$$

and we have to prove

$$\forall x \cdot (x \in \mathbb{F}(s) \;\Rightarrow\; f[x] \in \mathbb{F}(t)) \qquad\qquad \text{Goal 1}$$

We shall do so by induction on x.

Base Case: We have to prove the following

$$[x := \varnothing] f[x] \in \mathbb{F}(t) \qquad\qquad \text{Goal 2}$$

that is

$$f[\varnothing] \in \mathbb{F}(t) \qquad\qquad \text{Goal 3}$$

which is obvious since $f[\varnothing]$ is equal to $\varnothing$. Goal 3 then follows according to Property 3.3.1.

Induction Step: We assume

$$x \in \mathbb{F}(s) \qquad\qquad \text{Hypothesis 2}$$

$$f[x] \in \mathbb{F}(t) \qquad\qquad \text{Hypothesis 3}$$

and we have to prove

$$\forall u \cdot (u \in s \;\Rightarrow\; f[\{u\} \cup x] \in \mathbb{F}(t)) \qquad\qquad \text{Goal 4}$$

We remove the universal quantifier (since we can always suppose that the variable u is non-free in each of the pending hypotheses). We assume then

$$u \in s \qquad\qquad \text{Hypothesis 4}$$

and we are left to prove

$$f[\{u\} \cup x] \in \mathbb{F}(t) \qquad\qquad \text{Goal 5}$$

that is, since image distributes equivalently through set union,

$$(f[\{u\}] \cup f[x]) \in \mathbb{F}(t) \qquad\qquad \text{Goal 6}$$

We now have two exclusive cases to consider: either u belongs to dom (f) or it does not (but still belongs to s according to Hypothesis 4). In the latter case, $f[\{u\}]$ is empty so that $f[\{u\}] \cup f[x]$ is equal to $f[x]$ and Goal 5 follows acoording to Hypothesis 3. If u belongs to dom (f) then, according to Hypothesis 1, we can transform Goal 6 equivalently as follows:

$$(\{f(u)\} \cup f[x]) \in \mathbb{F}(t) \qquad\qquad \text{Goal 7}$$

which is obvious according to Property 3.3.2, Hypothesis 1 and Hypothesis 3.

End of Proof

3.4. Finite and Infinite Sets

In general, a set is said to be *finite* if and only if it is a member of its finite subsets. Conversely, a set which is not finite is said to be *infinite*. We thus define the two predicates finite (s) and infinite (s) as follows:

Syntax	Definition
finite (s)	$s \in \mathbb{F}(s)$
infinite (s)	$\neg\, \text{finite}\,(s)$

As stated in section 2.1.2, the set BIG is our first (and only) given set. Axiom SET 6 asserted that BIG is infinite. We now have a formal definition of this notion of infiniteness. Notice that BIG is *by no means* a (hypothetical) "set of all sets": in fact, there exist many sets *larger* than BIG such as $\mathbb{P}(\text{BIG})$, $\mathbb{P}(\mathbb{P}(\text{BIG}))$, $\mathbb{P}(\text{BIG}\times\mathbb{P}(\text{BIG}))$, etc. Every infinite set s has an important property: the difference between s and one of its finite subsets is not empty. In other words and quite intuitively, we cannot exhaust an infinite set by finite means. This is so because otherwise the finite part that we removed from s would be equal to it and thus be infinite, which would be contradictory, formally

---

$$\text{infinite}\,(s) \ \wedge\ t \in \mathbb{F}(s) \ \Rightarrow\ s - t \neq \varnothing \qquad\qquad \text{Property 3.4.1}$$

Another definition of infinite sets was given by *Dedekind*. He characterizes an infinite set s as one that is such that there exists a bijection from s to a proper subset of s. For instance and intuitively for the moment, there exists a bijection from the set $\mathbb{N}$ of natural numbers to the set of *even* natural numbers, which is clearly a proper subset of $\mathbb{N}$. The situation would not have been the same if we only considered the finite subset of $\mathbb{N}$ comprising, say, the first ten numbers. In this section, we propose to prove half of the equivalence between Dedekind's definition of infinity and the inductive definition presented here, formally

---

$$\exists f \cdot (f \in s \rightarrowtail s \ \wedge\ \text{ran}\,(f) \neq s) \ \Rightarrow\ \text{infinite}\,(s) \qquad\qquad \text{Theorem 3.4.1}$$

We leave the proof of this theorem as an exercise to the reader (hint: transform the statement by contraposing it and then prove a slightly more general result by finite set induction).

3.5. Natural Numbers

The set of natural numbers is our second set of *Mathematical Objects*. The rôle of this section is to build the natural numbers in a completely formal way. For doing this (section 3.5.1), we shall use the fixpoint technique developed previously. We then prove that the set $\mathbb{N}$ obeys the axioms of *Peano* (section 3.5.2). Next are the definitions of the minimum and maximum of a set of natural numbers (sections 3.5.3, 3.5.4, and 3.5.5). We then justify the possibility of defining recursive functions on natural numbers (section 3.5.6). This will allow us to build the conventional arithmetic operations (section 3.5.7). Then, we define the iterate of binary relations (sections 3.5.8). We also study the definition of the cardinal of finite sets (section 3.5.9). Finally, we define the transitive closures of a binary relation (section 3.5.10).

3.5.1. Definition

Let us recall the characteristic properties that we have in mind for specifying the natural numbers: 0 is a natural number and the *successor* of a natural number is also a natural number, formally

$$
\begin{array}{l}
0 \in \mathbb{N} \\[2mm]
\forall n \cdot (n \in \mathbb{N} \;\Rightarrow\; \mathsf{succ}\,(n) \in \mathbb{N})
\end{array}
$$

As will be noticed immediately, this is a case that corresponds to the first special situation depicted in section 3.2.3. It remains for us to define the corresponding general function, as we did for the construction of the set $\mathbb{F}(s)$. The problem, however, is more complicated than the one encountered for defining $\mathbb{F}(s)$ because here we have to construct the constant 0 and the function succ from scratch. The only set we have at our disposal is the infinite set BIG. It might then seem "natural" to define 0 as the empty set, that is as the difference between BIG and itself. As a consequence, 0 is a genuine subset of BIG. We then define the function succ for all finite subsets of BIG. More precisely, the *successor* of a finite part n of BIG is obtained by adding to n an element of BIG that belongs to the set $\mathrm{BIG} - n$ (in what follows, to simplify matters, we shall systematically replace $\mathrm{BIG} - n$ by $\overline{n}$). Notice that this *successor* operation is well-defined since, according to Property 3.4.1, we know that $\overline{n}$ is not empty (since, after axiom SET 6, BIG is infinite and since, by definition, n is one of its finite subsets). The last pending problem is that of the *choice* of the element we are going to add to n. For this we use, of course, the choice operator as introduced and axiomatized in the previous chapter.

Syntax	Definition
0	BIG $-$ BIG
succ	$\lambda n \cdot (n \in \mathbb{F}(\text{BIG}) \mid \{\text{choice}(\overline{n})\} \cup n)$

We finally define a set function **genat** which is obviously monotonic and whose least fixpoint is exactly our definition of $\mathbb{N}$.

Syntax	Definition
genat	$\lambda s \cdot (s \in \mathbb{P}(\mathbb{F}(\text{BIG})) \mid \{0\} \cup \text{succ}[s])$
$\mathbb{N}$	fix (genat)

As the function **genat** is clearly monotonic, the set $\mathbb{N}$ is indeed a fixpoint and we have

$$\mathbb{N} = \{0\} \cup \text{succ}[\mathbb{N}]$$

that is

$0 \subseteq \mathbb{N}$ Property 3.5.1

---

and also

$\forall n \cdot (n \in \mathbb{N} \;\Rightarrow\; \text{succ}(n) \in \mathbb{N})$ Property 3.5.2

These are exactly the required properties. The induction principle (Theorem 3.2.8) becomes the following, which is known as the **Principle of Mathematical Induction**.

$[n := 0]P$
$\forall n \cdot (n \in \mathbb{N} \wedge P \;\Rightarrow\; [n := \text{succ}(n)]P)$
$\Rightarrow$ Theorem 3.5.1
$\forall n \cdot (n \in \mathbb{N} \;\Rightarrow\; P)$

We now introduce three more constants: 1, $\mathbb{N}_1$ and **pred**.

Syntax	Definition
1	$\text{succ}(0)$
$\mathbb{N}_1$	$\mathbb{N} - \{0\}$
pred	$\text{succ}^{-1} \rhd \mathbb{N}$

We end this section by introducing the classical relational operator:

Syntax	Definition	Condition
$n \leq m$	$n \subseteq m$	$m \in \mathbb{N} \wedge n \in \mathbb{N}$
$n < m$	$n \neq m \wedge n \leq m$	$m \in \mathbb{N} \wedge n \in \mathbb{N}$
$n \geq m$	$m \leq n$	$m \in \mathbb{N} \wedge n \in \mathbb{N}$
$n > m$	$m < n$	$m \in \mathbb{N} \wedge n \in \mathbb{N}$

Notice that the operator $\leq$, being a renaming of $\subseteq$, induces a *partial order* on $\mathbb{N}$. We also introduce the following binary relations between natural numbers:

Syntax	Definition
gtr	$\{\, m, n \mid (m, n) \in \mathbb{N} \times \mathbb{N} \wedge m < n \,\}$
geq	$\{\, m, n \mid (m, n) \in \mathbb{N} \times \mathbb{N} \wedge m \leq n \,\}$
lss	$\{\, m, n \mid (m, n) \in \mathbb{N} \times \mathbb{N} \wedge m > n \,\}$
leq	$\{\, m, n \mid (m, n) \in \mathbb{N} \times \mathbb{N} \wedge m \geq n \,\}$

3.5.2. Peano's "Axioms"

There exists a conventional axiomatic construction of the natural numbers known as the "Peano Axiomatization". It is done through the following five axioms:

$0 \in \mathbb{N}$	Peano 1
$\forall n \cdot (n \in \mathbb{N} \implies \mathrm{succ}(n) \in \mathbb{N})$	Peano 2
$\forall n \cdot (n \in \mathbb{N} \implies \mathrm{succ}(n) \neq 0)$	Peano 3
$\forall n \cdot (n \in \mathbb{N} \wedge m \in \mathbb{N} \wedge \mathrm{succ}(n) = \mathrm{succ}(m) \implies n = m)$	Peano 4
$[n := 0]P$ $\forall n \cdot (n \in \mathbb{N} \wedge P \implies [n := \mathrm{succ}(n)]P)$ $\implies$ $\forall n \cdot (n \in \mathbb{N} \implies P)$	Peano 5

In the present context, it is obviously fundamental to prove that these "axioms" are mere theorems. We have already proved Peano 1, Peano 2, and Peano 5: these are exactly Property 3.5.1, Property 3.5.2 and Theorem 3.5.1. Peano 3 is an obvious consequence of the definition of succ, that is

$$\mathrm{succ}(n) = \{\mathrm{choice}(\bar{n})\} \cup n$$

consequently, we have

$$\mathrm{choice}(\bar{n}) \in \mathrm{succ}(n)$$

therefore

$$\mathrm{succ}(n) \neq \varnothing$$

that is, according to the definition of 0,

$$\mathrm{succ}(n) \neq 0$$

It remains for us to prove Peano 4, which states that the restriction of succ to $\mathbb{N}$ is an injective function. Alternatively, pred is a bijection from $\mathbb{N}$ to $\mathbb{N}_1$. Formally

---

$\mathrm{pred} \in \mathbb{N} \rightarrowtail\mathrel{\mkern-14mu}\rightarrow \mathbb{N}_1$ Property 3.5.3

In order to prove **Peano 4**, we need two more properties. We consider first the following property:

$$\forall\,(m,n)\cdot((m,n) \in \mathbb{N} \times \mathbb{N} \;\Rightarrow\; (n < m) \;\vee\; (n = m) \;\vee\; (m < n))$$ **Property 3.5.4**

This property, sometimes called the *trichotomy law*, states that two natural numbers are either equal to each other or else one is strictly smaller than the other. The application of this property leads naturally to *proofs by cases*. It also makes the partial order, induced by $\leq$ on $\mathbb{N}$, a *total order*: in other words, any two natural numbers are always comparable by $\leq$. We also consider the following property:

$$\forall\,(m,n)\cdot((m,n) \in \mathbb{N} \times \mathbb{N} \;\wedge\; n < m \;\Rightarrow\; \mathsf{succ}\,(n) \leq m)$$ **Property 3.5.5**

This property states that, provided a natural number is strictly smaller than another one, then the successor of the former is smaller than or equal to the latter. Provided these two properties are proved, then, as we shall see, the proof of **Peano 4** is easy. Let us first prove these two properties. We notice that **Property 3.5.4** can be put equivalently in the following form

$$\forall m \cdot (m \in \mathbb{N} \;\Rightarrow\; \forall n \cdot (n \in \mathbb{N} \;\Rightarrow\; (n \leq m) \;\vee\; (m \leq n)))$$

It is then sufficient to prove the following (since, according to the definition of succ, we obviously have $m < \mathsf{succ}\,(m)$):

$$\forall m \cdot (m \in \mathbb{N} \;\Rightarrow\; \forall n \cdot (n \in \mathbb{N} \;\Rightarrow\; (n \leq m) \;\vee\; (\mathsf{succ}\,(m) \leq n)))$$

In order to prove this predicate, we shall remove the universal quantifier and prove

$$m \in \mathbb{N}$$
$$\Rightarrow$$
$$\forall n \cdot (n \in \mathbb{N} \;\Rightarrow\; (n \leq m) \;\vee\; (\mathsf{succ}\,(m) \leq n))$$

In order to prove this statement, we are going to assume an extra hypothesis immediately derivable from (the still unproved) **Property 3.5.5**. Formally, this yields the following property to be proved:

$$m \in \mathbb{N}$$
$$\forall n \cdot (n \in \mathbb{N} \;\wedge\; n < m \;\Rightarrow\; \mathsf{succ}\,(n) \leq m)$$
$$\Rightarrow$$
$$\forall n \cdot (n \in \mathbb{N} \;\Rightarrow\; (n \leq m) \;\vee\; (\mathsf{succ}\,(m) \leq n))$$

  Property 3.5.6

Proof
We assume

$$m \in \mathbb{N} \qquad\qquad \text{Hypothesis 1}$$

$$\forall n \cdot (n \in \mathbb{N} \;\wedge\; n < m \;\;\Rightarrow\;\; \mathsf{succ}(n) \le m) \qquad\qquad \text{Hypothesis 2}$$

and we have to prove

$$\forall n \cdot (n \in \mathbb{N} \;\;\Rightarrow\;\; n \le m \;\vee\; \mathsf{succ}(m) \le n) \qquad\qquad \text{Goal 1}$$

The proof is by induction on n.
Base Case: We have to prove

$$0 \le m \;\vee\; \mathsf{succ}(m) \le 0 \qquad\qquad \text{Goal 2}$$

which is obvious according to the definition of 0 and the definition of $\le$.
Induction Step: We assume

$$n \in \mathbb{N} \qquad\qquad \text{Hypothesis 3}$$

$$n \le m \;\vee\; \mathsf{succ}(m) \le n \qquad\qquad \text{Hypothesis 4}$$

and we have to prove

$$\mathsf{succ}(n) \le m \;\vee\; \mathsf{succ}(m) \le \mathsf{succ}(n) \qquad\qquad \text{Goal 3}$$

The form of Hypothesis 4 suggests a proof by cases. We shall assume successively $n < m$, $n = m$ and $\mathsf{succ}(m) \le n$. We assume then first

$$n < m \qquad\qquad \text{Case 1}$$

Then, according to Hypothesis 3 and Hypothesis 2, we derive the following from which Goal 3 is easily deducible

$$\mathsf{succ}(n) \le m \qquad\qquad \text{Derivation 1}$$

Next is our second case

$$n = m \qquad\qquad \text{Case 2}$$

Then we obviously have the following from which Goal 3 is easily deductible:

$$\mathsf{succ}(m) \le \mathsf{succ}(n) \qquad\qquad \text{Derivation 2}$$

Finally, we have the third case

$$\mathsf{succ}(m) \le n \qquad\qquad \text{Case 3}$$

According to the definition of succ, we have $n \le \mathsf{succ}(n)$; consequently, according to the transitivity of inclusion (hence that of $\le$), we have the following, from which Goal 3 is again easily deducible:

$$\mathsf{succ}(m) \le \mathsf{succ}(n) \qquad\qquad \text{Derivation 3}$$

End of Proof

We now prove **Property 3.5.5** which we restate as follows:

$$\forall m \cdot (m \in \mathbb{N} \;\Rightarrow\; \forall n \cdot (n \in \mathbb{N} \,\wedge\, n < m \;\Rightarrow\; \mathsf{succ}(n) \leq m\,))$$

Proof
The proof is by induction on m.
Base Case: We have to prove

$$\forall n \cdot (n \in \mathbb{N} \,\wedge\, n < 0 \;\Rightarrow\; \mathsf{succ}(n) \leq 0) \qquad\qquad \text{Goal 1}$$

which is obviously true since $n < 0$ is trivially false.
Induction Step: We assume

$$m \in \mathbb{N} \qquad\qquad \text{Hypothesis 1}$$

$$\forall n \cdot (n \in \mathbb{N} \,\wedge\, n < m \;\Rightarrow\; \mathsf{succ}(n) \leq m) \qquad\qquad \text{Hypothesis 2}$$

and we have to prove

$$\forall n \cdot (n \in \mathbb{N} \,\wedge\, n < \mathsf{succ}(m) \;\Rightarrow\; \mathsf{succ}(n) \leq \mathsf{succ}(m)) \qquad \text{Goal 2}$$

We remove the universal quantifier and we assume

$$n \in \mathbb{N} \qquad\qquad \text{Hypothesis 3}$$

$$n < \mathsf{succ}(m) \qquad\qquad \text{Hypothesis 4}$$

and we have to prove

$$\mathsf{succ}(n) \leq \mathsf{succ}(m) \qquad\qquad \text{Goal 3}$$

From Hypothesis 1, Hypothesis 2, Hypothesis 3, and Property 3.5.6, we can deduce

$$n \leq m \;\vee\; \mathsf{succ}(m) \leq n \qquad\qquad \text{Derivation 1}$$

which reduces to the following since the second alternative contradicts Hypothesis 4:

$$n \leq m \qquad\qquad \text{Derivation 2}$$

The proof now proceeds by cases. We assume successively $n < m$ and $n = m$. Here is our first case:

$$n < m \qquad\qquad \text{Case 1}$$

From this we deduce the following according to Hypothesis 2 and Hypothesis 3:

$$\mathsf{succ}(n) \leq m \qquad\qquad \text{Derivation 3}$$

As a consequence, and after the definition of succ yielding $m < \mathsf{succ}(m)$, we have indeed the following, which is exactly Goal 3:

$$\mathsf{succ}(n) \leq \mathsf{succ}(m) \qquad\qquad \text{Derivation 4}$$

Our second case

$$n = m \qquad \qquad \text{Case 2}$$

immediately yields the following, which, again, is exactly Goal 3:

$$\text{succ}(n) \le \text{succ}(m) \qquad \qquad \text{Derivation 5}$$

End of Proof

As already stated, Property 3.5.4 is now easily deducible from Property 3.5.6 and Property 3.5.5. We are now ready to prove Peano 4. We shall do so under its contrapositive form Peano 4'

$$n \in \mathbb{N} \ \wedge \ m \in \mathbb{N} \ \wedge \ n \neq m \quad \Rightarrow \quad \text{succ}(n) \neq \text{succ}(m)$$

Proof
We assume

$$n \in \mathbb{N} \qquad \qquad \text{Hypothesis 1}$$

$$m \in \mathbb{N} \qquad \qquad \text{Hypothesis 2}$$

$$n \neq m \qquad \qquad \text{Hypothesis 3}$$

and we have to prove

$$\text{succ}(n) \neq \text{succ}(m) \qquad \qquad \text{Goal 1}$$

Our intention is to prove this statement *by cases* using Property 3.5.4. Since we already have $n \neq m$ according to Hypothesis 3, it is sufficient to prove our statement under the two remaining cases, namely $n < m$ and $m < n$ (we notice that, in Goal 1, m and n play symmetric rôles so that the proof of the second case will be similar to that of the first one after exchanging m and n). Let us then assume

$$n < m \qquad \qquad \text{Hypothesis 4}$$

Consequently, according to Hypothesis 1, Hypothesis 2, Hypothesis 4, and Property 3.5.5, we have

$$\text{succ}(n) \le m \qquad \qquad \text{Derivation 1}$$

that is, by definition

$$\text{succ}(n) \subseteq m \qquad \qquad \text{Derivation 2}$$

From this, we deduce

$$\text{choice}(\overline{m}) \notin \text{succ}(n) \qquad \qquad \text{Derivation 3}$$

But, according to the definition of succ, we have

$$\text{choice}(\overline{m}) \in \text{succ}(m) \qquad\qquad \text{Derivation 4}$$

Putting together Derivation 3 and Derivation 4, we obtain

$$\text{succ}(n) \neq \text{succ}(m) \qquad\qquad \text{Derivation 5}$$

which is exactly Goal 1. The other case, corresponding to $m < n$, is proved by similar arguments.

End of Proof

3.5.3. Minimum

We now define the minimum of a *non-empty* set s of natural numbers. It is denoted by $\min(s)$ and it is simply defined to be the generalized intersection of s, formally

Syntax	Definition	Condition
$\min(s)$	$\text{inter}(s)$	$s \in \mathbb{P}_1(\mathbb{N})$

Of course $\min(s)$, being a lower bound, is included in (that is, smaller than or equal to) all members of s (remember Theorem 3.1.1). We thus have

---

$$s \in \mathbb{P}_1(\mathbb{N}) \;\Rightarrow\; \forall n \cdot (n \in s \;\Rightarrow\; \min(s) \leq n) \qquad\qquad \text{Property 3.5.7}$$

But, in this case, we can prove more: namely that $\min(s)$ is also a member of s (which is not always the case with a glb). In order to prove this property, we first prove the following "paradoxical" result telling us that, in case $\min(s)$ does not belong to s, then every natural number is smaller than or equal to each member of s, formally

---

$$\begin{aligned} &s \in \mathbb{P}_1(\mathbb{N}) \\ &\min(s) \notin s \\ &\Rightarrow \\ &\forall n \cdot (n \in \mathbb{N} \;\Rightarrow\; \forall m \cdot (m \in s \;\Rightarrow\; n \leq m)) \end{aligned} \qquad\qquad \text{Property 3.5.8}$$

Proof

We assume

$$s \in \mathbb{P}_1(\mathbb{N}) \qquad\qquad \text{Hypothesis 1}$$
$$\min(s) \notin s \qquad\qquad \text{Hypothesis 2}$$

and we have to prove

$$\forall n \cdot (n \in \mathbb{N} \;\Rightarrow\; \forall m \cdot (m \in s \;\Rightarrow\; n \le m)) \hspace{3cm} \text{Goal 1}$$

The proof is by induction on n.

Base Case: We have to prove the following, which is obvious:

$$\forall m \cdot (m \in s \;\Rightarrow\; 0 \le m) \hspace{3cm} \text{Goal 2}$$

Induction Step: We assume

$$n \in \mathbb{N} \hspace{3cm} \text{Hypothesis 3}$$
$$\forall m \cdot (m \in s \;\Rightarrow\; n \le m) \hspace{3cm} \text{Hypothesis 4}$$

and we have to prove

$$\forall m \cdot (m \in s \;\Rightarrow\; \mathsf{succ}\,(n) \le m) \hspace{3cm} \text{Goal 3}$$

We remove the universal quantifier and we assume

$$m \in s \hspace{3cm} \text{Hypothesis 5}$$

We now have to prove

$$\mathsf{succ}\,(n) \le m \hspace{3cm} \text{Goal 4}$$

This goal suggests applying Property 3.5.5 (that is, $n < m \;\Rightarrow\; \mathsf{succ}\,(n) \le m$). We have then just to prove

$$n < m \hspace{3cm} \text{Goal 5}$$

The proof is by cases. We assume first $n \in s$ then $n \notin s$. Next is our first case

$$n \in s \hspace{3cm} \text{Case 1}$$

From Hypothesis 4, from the definition of $\min(s)$ as a generalized intersection and according to Theorem 3.1.2 telling us that $\min(s)$ is indeed a glb, we deduce

$$n \le \min(s) \hspace{3cm} \text{Derivation 1}$$

But from Hypothesis 1, Case 1 and Property 3.5.7, we deduce

$$\min(s) \le n \hspace{3cm} \text{Derivation 2}$$

Consequently, we have

$$n = \min(s) \hspace{3cm} \text{Derivation 3}$$

yielding, according to Case 1

$$\min(s) \in s \hspace{3cm} \text{Derivation 4}$$

which contradicts Hypothesis 2. We assume now

$$n \notin s \hspace{3cm} \text{Case 2}$$

From Hypothesis 5 and Hypothesis 4, we deduce immediately

$$n \le m \hspace{3cm} \text{Derivation 5}$$

Putting together Case 2 and Hypothesis 5, we deduce

$$n \neq m \qquad\qquad\qquad \text{Derivation 6}$$

Putting together Derivation 5 and Derivation 6 we obtain the following which is exactly Goal 5:

$$n < m \qquad\qquad\qquad \text{Derivation 7}$$

End of Proof

Equipped with the previous property, we can now prove the following:

$$s \in \mathbb{P}_1(\mathbb{N}) \;\Rightarrow\; \min(s) \in s \qquad\qquad\qquad \text{Property 3.5.9}$$

Proof

We assume

$$s \in \mathbb{P}_1(\mathbb{N}) \qquad\qquad\qquad \text{Hypothesis 1}$$

And we have to prove

$$\min(s) \in s \qquad\qquad\qquad \text{Goal 1}$$

Since s is certainly not empty, we deduce immediately the following:

$$\exists k \cdot (k \in \mathbb{N} \wedge k \in s) \qquad\qquad\qquad \text{Derivation 1}$$

As our desired goal does not depend on k, we can then assume

$$k \in \mathbb{N} \qquad\qquad\qquad \text{Hypothesis 2}$$
$$k \in s \qquad\qquad\qquad \text{Hypothesis 3}$$

The proof proceeds by contradiction. We assume

$$\min(s) \notin s \qquad\qquad\qquad \text{Hypothesis 4}$$

From Hypothesis 1, Hypothesis 4 and Property 3.5.8, we deduce

$$\forall n \cdot (n \in \mathbb{N} \;\Rightarrow\; \forall m \cdot (m \in s \;\Rightarrow\; n \leq m)) \qquad\qquad\qquad \text{Derivation 2}$$

From Hypothesis 2 and Peano 2 we deduce

$$\text{succ}(k) \in \mathbb{N} \qquad\qquad\qquad \text{Derivation 3}$$

Applying this to Derivation 2, we obtain

$$\forall m \cdot (m \in s \;\Rightarrow\; \text{succ}(k) \leq m) \qquad\qquad\qquad \text{Derivation 4}$$

From this, and according to Hypothesis 3, we then deduce the following, which is an obvious contradiction:

$$\text{succ}(k) \leq k$$

End of Proof

We have thus finally established the classical properties of the minimum of a non-empty subset of natural numbers. This shows that the relation induced by the operator $\leq$ on $\mathbb{N}$ is a *well-order* relation. We remind the reader that a partial order relation is said to well-order a set s if every non-empty subset of s has a least member. From the previous definition of min and according to the property of inter as given in section 3.1, we easily deduce the following properties:

$$
\begin{array}{lll}
\min(\{a\}) & = & a \\[2ex]
\min(\{a, b\}) & = & a \quad \text{if } a \leq b \\[2ex]
\min(\{a, b\}) & = & b \quad \text{if } b \leq a \\[2ex]
\min(u \cup v) & = & \min(\{\min(u), \min(v)\}) \quad \text{if } u \neq \varnothing \wedge v \neq \varnothing \\[2ex]
\min(u \cup \{x\}) & = & \min(\{\min(u), x\}) \quad \text{if } u \neq \varnothing
\end{array}
$$

3.5.4. Strong Induction Principle

The definition and properties of $\min(s)$ lead to another induction principle called the Strong Induction Principle, formally

---

$$
\begin{aligned}
&\forall n \cdot (n \in \mathbb{N} \wedge \forall m \cdot (m \in \mathbb{N} \wedge m < n \Rightarrow \\
&\qquad [n := m]P) \Rightarrow P) \\
&\Rightarrow \\
&\forall n \cdot (n \in \mathbb{N} \Rightarrow P)
\end{aligned}
$$

Theorem 3.5.2

In other words, if one can prove that a property P holds for a natural number n under the assumption that it holds for every natural number m strictly smaller than n, then the property P holds for all natural numbers n.

Proof
We assume

$$\forall n \cdot (n \in \mathbb{N} \wedge \forall m \cdot (m \in \mathbb{N} \wedge m < n \Rightarrow [n := m]P) \Rightarrow P) \quad \text{Hypothesis 1}$$

and we have to prove

$$\forall n \cdot (n \in \mathbb{N} \Rightarrow P) \quad \text{Goal 1}$$

The proof is by contradiction. That is, we assume the negation of the goal and we try to derive a contradiction

$$\exists n \cdot (n \in \mathbb{N} \wedge \neg P) \quad \text{Hypothesis 2}$$

that is equivalently

$$\{n \mid n \in \mathbb{N} \ \wedge \ \neg P\} \neq \varnothing \qquad\qquad \text{Derivation 1}$$

To simplify matters, we define z as follows

$$z = \{n \mid n \in \mathbb{N} \ \wedge \ \neg P\} \qquad\qquad \text{Definition 1}$$

From Derivation 1, Definition 1 and Property 3.5.9, we deduce

$$\min(z) \in \mathbb{N} \qquad\qquad \text{Derivation 2}$$

Our intention is to exhibit a member of the non-empty set z which is *strictly smaller* than its own minimum:, an obvious contradiction according to Property 3.5.7. We deduce the following by instantiating n by $\min(z)$ in Hypothesis 1:

$$\begin{aligned} & \forall m \cdot (m \in \mathbb{N} \ \wedge \ m < \min(z) \quad \Rightarrow \quad [n := m]P) \\ & \Rightarrow \\ & [n := \min(z)]P \end{aligned} \qquad \text{Derivation 3}$$

By contraposition, we obtain equivalently

$$\begin{aligned} & [n := \min(z)] \neg P \\ & \Rightarrow \\ & \exists m \cdot (m \in \mathbb{N} \ \wedge \ m < \min(z) \ \wedge \ [n := m]\neg P) \end{aligned} \qquad \text{Derivation 3}$$

which can be rewritten equivalently as follows (according to Definition 1):

$$\begin{aligned} & [n := \min(z)] \neg P \\ & \Rightarrow \\ & \exists m \cdot (m \in z \ \wedge \ m < \min(z)) \end{aligned} \qquad \text{Derivation 4}$$

But, according to Property 3.5.9, we have

$$\min(z) \in z \qquad\qquad \text{Derivation 5}$$

Consequently, according to Definition 1, we have

$$[n := \min(z)] \neg P \qquad\qquad \text{Derivation 6}$$

therefore, from Derivation 4 and Derivation 6, we deduce

$$\exists m \cdot (m \in z \ \wedge \ m < \min(z)) \qquad\qquad \text{Derivation 7}$$

In other words, there exists indeed a member m of the non-empty set z which is strictly smaller than the minimum of that set, again an obvious contradiction according to Property 3.5.7.
End of Proof

There exists a more advanced proof of the previous theorem (Exercise 37). It uses the theory of well-founded relations introduced in section 3.11.

3.5.5. Maximum

We now define the maximum of a finite set s of natural numbers. It is denoted by $\max(s)$ and it is defined to be the generalized union of s, formally

Syntax	Definition	Condition
$\max(s)$	$\mathrm{union}(s)$	$s \in \mathbb{F}_1(\mathbb{N})$

And we have results similar to those obtained in the previous section for the minimum. Firstly, the maximum of a non-empty finite set is greater than or equal to every member of that set:

$$s \in \mathbb{F}_1(\mathbb{N}) \;\Rightarrow\; \forall n \cdot (n \in s \;\Rightarrow\; n \leq \max(s)) \qquad\qquad \text{Property 3.5.10}$$

And the maximum of a set belongs to that set:

$$s \in \mathbb{F}_1(\mathbb{N}) \;\Rightarrow\; \max(s) \in s \qquad\qquad \text{Property 3.5.11}$$

We leave it as an exercise for the reader to prove Property 3.5.11. Hint: use the Finite Set Induction Principle (Theorem 3.3.1). From the above definition of max, and from various properties established in section 3.1, we can deduce the following properties, where u and v are supposed to be finite sets:

$$
\begin{aligned}
\max(\{a\}) &= a \\[4pt]
\max(\{a, b\}) &= a \quad && \text{if } b \leq a \\[4pt]
\max(\{a, b\}) &= b \quad && \text{if } a \leq b \\[4pt]
\max(u \cup v) &= \max(\{\max(u), \max(v)\}) \quad && \text{if } u \neq \varnothing \wedge v \neq \varnothing \\[4pt]
\max(u \cup \{x\}) &= \max(\{\max(u), x\}) \quad && \text{if } u \neq \varnothing
\end{aligned}
$$

3.5.6. Recursive Functions on Natural Numbers

We turn now our attention to the study of *recursion* on natural numbers. Given a member a of a set s, and a total function g from s to s,

$$a \in s$$

$$g \in s \to s$$

we would like to know whether it is possible to build a total function f from $\mathbb{N}$ to s satifying the following conditions (provided, of course, they make sense) supposed to hold for each natural number n:

$$f(0) = a$$

$$f(\text{succ}(n)) = g(f(n))$$

If this is the case, then f is said to have been defined recursively or *by recursion*. There are many examples of functions defined in this way. Usually this is done by using a large left bracket as in the following definition of $\text{plus}(m)$, the function that adds m to a number:

$$\begin{cases} \text{plus}(m)(0) = 0 \\ \text{plus}(m)(\text{succ}(n)) = \text{succ}(\text{plus}(m)(n)) \end{cases}$$

In section 3.5.7, we shall define in this way the other two basic arithmetic operations, namely multiplication and exponentiation. In order to construct our recursive function f formally, we use the following method: first, we define a certain binary relation from $\mathbb{N}$ to s, and then we prove that this relation is indeed a total function enjoying both stated properties. For this, we define the following set function:

Syntax	Definition
$\text{genf}(a,g)$	$\lambda h \cdot (h \in \mathbb{P}(\mathbb{N} \times s) \mid \{0 \mapsto a\} \cup (\text{pred}\,;h\,;g))$

Obviously genf is a monotonic function from $\mathbb{P}(\mathbb{N} \times s)$ to itself. This results from the monotonicity of composition and union. Consequently, we have a least fixpoint and we thus define f as follows:

$$f = \text{fix}(\text{genf}(a,g))$$

We then have

$$f = \{0 \mapsto a\} \cup (\text{pred}\,;f\,;g) \qquad\qquad \text{Property 3.5.12}$$

As a consequence, and provided f is a *total function* from $\mathbb{N}$ to s (a fact that remains to be proved; we only know for the moment that f is a *binary relation* from $\mathbb{N}$ to s), then f indeed enjoys the two stated conditions. It then remains for us to prove that f is a total function. According to Property 2.5.1, this can be expressed formally as follows:

$$\forall n \cdot (n \in \mathbb{N} \;\Rightarrow\; \{n\} \lhd f \in \{n\} \to s\,) \qquad\qquad \text{Theorem 3.5.3}$$

Proof

The proof is by mathematical induction on n.

Base Case: We have to prove

$$\{0\} \lhd f \in \{0\} \to s \qquad\qquad \text{Goal 1}$$

that is

$$\{0\} \lhd (\{0 \mapsto a\} \cup (\mathsf{pred};f\,;g)) \in \{0\} \to s \qquad\qquad \text{Goal 2}$$

that is the following, which is obvious:

$$\{0\} \lhd \{0 \mapsto a\} \in \{0\} \to s \qquad\qquad \text{Goal 3}$$

Induction step: We assume

$$n \in \mathbb{N} \qquad\qquad \text{Hypothesis 1}$$

$$\{n\} \lhd f \in \{n\} \to s \qquad\qquad \text{Hypothesis 2}$$

and we have to prove

$$\{\mathsf{succ}\,(n)\} \lhd f \in \{\mathsf{succ}\,(n)\} \to s \qquad\qquad \text{Goal 4}$$

that is

$$\{\mathsf{succ}\,(n)\} \lhd (\{0 \mapsto a\} \cup (\mathsf{pred};f\,;g)) \in \{\mathsf{succ}\,(n)\} \to s \qquad \text{Goal 5}$$

that is

$$\{\mathsf{succ}\,(n)\} \lhd (\,\mathsf{pred};f\,;g\,) \in \{\mathsf{succ}\,(n)\} \to s \qquad\qquad \text{Goal 6}$$

We have the following:

$$\{\mathsf{succ}\,(n)\} \lhd (\,\mathsf{pred};f\,;g\,)$$
$$=$$
$$\{\mathsf{succ}\,(n)\} \times (\,g \circ f \circ \mathsf{pred}\,)\,[\,\{\mathsf{succ}\,(n)\}\,]$$
$$=$$
$$\{\mathsf{succ}\,(n)\} \times (\,g \circ f\,)\,[\{n\}]$$
$$= \qquad\qquad\qquad\qquad\qquad\qquad\qquad\qquad \text{Hypothesis 2}$$
$$\{\mathsf{succ}\,(n)\} \times g\,[\{f\,(n)\}]$$
$$=$$
$$\{\mathsf{succ}\,(n)\} \times \{g(f\,(n))\}$$
$$=$$
$$\{\mathsf{succ}\,(n) \mapsto g(f\,(n))\}$$

As a consequence, Goal 6 is clearly valid.

End of Proof

3.5.7. Arithmetic

Arithmetic is the construction and study of the six classical operations on natural numbers: addition, multiplication and exponentiation; and subtraction, division and logarithm (the inverses of the previous ones).

Addition, Multiplication and Exponentiation

Addition, multiplication and exponentiation are defined by means of the following three functions of intended type:

$$\text{plus} \in \mathbb{N} \rightarrow (\mathbb{N} \rightarrow \mathbb{N})$$

$$\text{mult} \in \mathbb{N} \rightarrow (\mathbb{N} \rightarrow \mathbb{N})$$

$$\text{exp} \in \mathbb{N} \rightarrow (\mathbb{N} \rightarrow \mathbb{N})$$

Given a natural number m, the recursive definitions of the functions $\text{plus}\,(m)$, $\text{mult}\,(m)$ and $\text{exp}\,(m)$ are as follows:

Syntax	Recursive Definition	Condition
$\text{plus}\,(m)(0)$ $\text{plus}\,(m)(\text{succ}\,(n))$	m $\text{succ}\,(\text{plus}\,(m)(n))$	$m \in \mathbb{N}$ $n \in \mathbb{N}$
$\text{mult}\,(m)(0)$ $\text{mult}\,(m)(\text{succ}\,(n))$	0 $\text{plus}\,(m)(\text{mult}\,(m)(n))$	$m \in \mathbb{N}$ $n \in \mathbb{N}$
$\text{exp}\,(m)(0)$ $\text{exp}\,(m)(\text{succ}\,(n))$	1 $\text{mult}\,(m)(\text{exp}\,(m)(n))$	$m \in \mathbb{N}$ $n \in \mathbb{N}$

And we now define the more conventional binary operators as follows:

Syntax	Definition	Condition
$m + n$	plus $(m)(n)$	$m \in \mathbb{N} \wedge n \in \mathbb{N}$
$m \times n$	mult $(m)(n)$	$m \in \mathbb{N} \wedge n \in \mathbb{N}$
m^n	exp $(m)(n)$	$m \in \mathbb{N} \wedge n \in \mathbb{N}$

The following properties can be proved by mathematical induction:

$$m + 0 = m$$

$$m + \operatorname{succ}(n) = \operatorname{succ}(m + n)$$

$$m \times 0 = 0$$

$$m \times \operatorname{succ}(n) = m + (m \times n)$$

$$m + 1 = \operatorname{succ}(m)$$

$$1 + m = \operatorname{succ}(m)$$

$$0 + m = m$$

$$m + n = n + m$$

$$m + (n + p) = m + n + p$$

$$0 \times m = 0$$

$$m \times 1 = m$$

$$1 \times m = m$$

$$m \times n = n \times m$$

$$m \times (n \times p) = m \times n \times p$$

$$m \times (n + p) = (m \times n) + (m \times p)$$

$$n \neq 0 \;\Rightarrow\; 0^n = 0$$

$$1^n = 1$$

$$m^1 = m$$

$$m^{n+p} = m^n \times m^p$$

$$m^{n \times p} = (m^n)^p$$

$$(m \times n)^p = m^p \times n^p$$

Subtraction

Given a natural number m, the function plus (m) can be proved to be a bijection from $\mathbb{N}$ to the subset of $\mathbb{N}$ whose members are exactly those numbers that are greater than or equal to m, formally

---

plus $(m) \in \mathbb{N} \rightarrowtail \{ n \mid n \in \mathbb{N} \;\wedge\; m \leq n \}$ Property 3.5.13

We then define subtraction as the inverse of this function:

Syntax	Definition	Condition
$n - m$	plus $(m)^{-1}(n)$	$m \in \mathbb{N} \;\wedge\; n \in \mathbb{N} \;\wedge\; m \leq n$

Given a natural number n and a natural number m smaller than or equal to n, we have $n = m + (n - m)$. This is shown as follows:

$$n - m = n - m$$
$$\Leftrightarrow$$
$$\text{plus}\,(m)^{-1}(n) = n - m$$
$$\Leftrightarrow$$
$$(n, (n - m)) \in \text{plus}\,(m)^{-1}$$
$$\Leftrightarrow$$
$$((n - m), n) \in \text{plus}\,(m)$$
$$\Leftrightarrow$$
$$n = \text{plus}\,(m)(n - m)$$
$$\Leftrightarrow$$
$$n = m + (n - m)$$

We can also define a unary subtraction function minus (m) whose value at n is $m - n$.

Division

Defining natural number division is slightly more complicated than subtraction. Given a natural number n and a *positive* natural number m the natural number division q of these two numbers is specified by means of the following two classical properties:

$$m \times q \; \leq \; n \qquad (1)$$

$$n \; < \; m \times \mathsf{succ}\,(q) \qquad (2)$$

In other words, either n is a multiple of m, and q is then the just number by which we have to multiply m in order to obtain n or, alternatively, n is situated *in between* two successive multiples of m. In this second case, q is the number by which we have to multiply m in order to obtain the *smaller* of these two successive multiples. The quantity q is said to be the *quotient* of the natural number division and the quantity $n - m \times q$ is said to be its *remainder*. For denoting these quantities we use the operators / and mod respectively. They are defined as follows:

Syntax	Definition	Condition
n/m	$\min(\{\, x \mid x \in \mathbb{N} \;\wedge\; n < m \times \mathsf{succ}\,(x)\,\})$	$n \in \mathbb{N} \;\wedge\; m \in \mathbb{N}_1$
$n \;\mathsf{mod}\; m$	$n - m \times (n/m)$	$n \in \mathbb{N} \;\wedge\; m \in \mathbb{N}_1$

It remains for us to verify that the given definition of n/m indeed satisfies our proposed specification. Let s be the following set:

$$s \; = \; \{\, x \mid x \in \mathbb{N} \;\wedge\; n < m \times \mathsf{succ}\,(x)\,\}$$

We leave it to the reader to prove (by induction) that the set s is not empty so that its minimum, n/m, is well defined. The quotient q of n by m, being the minimum of s, belongs to s, so that we have:

$$n \; < \; m \times \mathsf{succ}\,(q)$$

which is exactly our condition (2). The quantity q, being the minimum of s, is smaller than or equal to any member x of s, so that we have

$$\forall x \cdot (x \in \mathbb{N} \;\wedge\; n < m \times \mathsf{succ}\,(x) \; \Rightarrow \; q \leq x)$$

that is, by contraposition,

$$\forall x \cdot (x \in \mathbb{N} \ \wedge \ x < q \ \Rightarrow \ m \times \mathsf{succ}\,(x) \leq n)$$

If q is positive, then we can instantiate x to $\mathsf{pred}\,(q)$ which, obviously, is strictly smaller than q, yielding

$$m \times \mathsf{succ}\,(\mathsf{pred}\,(q)) \ \leq \ n$$

that is

$$m \times q \ \leq \ n$$

As this property clearly holds when q is equal to 0, we have our condition (1). We can also define a unary division function $\mathsf{div}\,(m)$ and a unary remainder function $\mathsf{rem}\,(m)$ whose values at n are m/n and $m \ \mathrm{mod} \ n$ respectively.

Logarithms

By analogy with what we have done for natural number division, we now define the natural number logarithm of n in the base m, $\log_m(n)$, as follows:

Syntax	Definition	Condition
$\log_m(n)$	$\min(\{\, x \mid x \in \mathbb{N} \ \wedge \ n < m^{\mathsf{succ}\,(x)} \,\})$	$m > 1$

Let l be equal to $\log_m(n)$. From the previous definition, we can derive the following properties (proof left to the reader):

$$
\begin{aligned}
l = 0 \quad &\Rightarrow \quad n < m \\
l > 0 \quad &\Rightarrow \quad m^l \leq n < m^{l+1}
\end{aligned}
$$

This shows clearly that $\log_m(n)$ is indeed a natural number logarithm *by defect*. So that we might also envisage another natural number logarithm, namely the logarithm *by excess*. For instance, this will be the logarithm, $\mathrm{LOG}_m(n)$, needed in order to determine the smallest number of digits necessary for encoding a number, n, of distinct discrete values in a numeric system of base m. The definition of this second logarithm is the following:

Syntax	Definition	Condition
$\mathrm{LOG}_m(n)$	$\min(\{\, x \mid x \in \mathbb{N} \ \wedge \ n \leq m^x \,\})$	$m > 1$

Let L be equal to $\text{LOG}_m(n)$. This time, we obtain the following property (proof left to the reader):

$$L = 0 \quad \Rightarrow \quad n \leq 1$$

$$L > 0 \quad \Rightarrow \quad m^{L-1} < n \leq m^L$$

The relationship between l and L is as follows:

$$L = l = 0 \qquad \text{when} \quad n = 0$$

$$L = l \qquad \text{when} \quad m^l = n$$

$$L = l + 1 \qquad \text{when} \quad m^l < n$$

As an example, in the following table we show some values of $\log_3(n)$ and $\text{LOG}_3(n)$ in terms of n.

n	0	1	2	3	4	5	6	7	8	9	10	11
$\log_3(n)$	0	0	0	1	1	1	1	1	1	2	2	2
$\text{LOG}_3(n)$	0	0	1	1	2	2	2	2	2	2	3	3

3.5.8. Iterate of a Relation

Given a set s, the nth iterate, $\text{iter}(r)(n)$, of a relation r from s to s is also a relation from s to s, recursively defined as follows:

Syntax	Recursive Definition	Condition
$\text{iter}(r)(0)$ $\text{iter}(r)(\text{succ}(n))$	$\text{id}(s)$ $r \,;\, \text{iter}(r)(n)$	$r \in s \leftrightarrow s$ $n \in \mathbb{N}$

We also define the following more conventional notation:

Syntax	Definition
r^n	$\text{iter}(r)(n)$

The following properties can be proved by induction:

$$f \in s \rightarrowtail s \quad \Rightarrow \quad f^n \in s \rightarrowtail s$$

$$f \in s \rightarrow s \quad \Rightarrow \quad f^n \in s \rightarrow s$$

$$f \in s \rightarrowtail\!\!\!\!\rightarrow s \quad \Rightarrow \quad f^n \in s \rightarrowtail\!\!\!\!\rightarrow s$$

$$f \in s \twoheadrightarrow s \quad \Rightarrow \quad f^n \in s \twoheadrightarrow s$$

$$r^1 = r$$

$$r^{\text{succ}(n)} = r^n ; r$$

$$(r^n)^{-1} = (r^{-1})^n$$

$$r^m ; r^n = r^{m+n}$$

$$(r^m)^n = r^{m \times n}$$

$$p \subseteq q \quad \Rightarrow \quad p^n \subseteq q^n$$

$$r[a] \subseteq a \quad \Rightarrow \quad r^n[a] \subseteq a$$

3.5.9. Cardinal of a Finite Set

We can, at last, define the cardinal of a finite subset t of a set s. This is denoted by $\text{card}(t)$. The definition we are going to present is a direct consequence of the following property whose proof is left as an exercise to the reader (this property uses the function $\text{genfin}(s)$ which we have defined in section 3.3):

$$\mathbb{F}(s) = \bigcup n \cdot (n \in \mathbb{N} \mid \text{genfin}(s)^n(\{\varnothing\})) \qquad \text{Property 3.5.14}$$

As a consequence, we have

$$t \in \mathbb{F}(s)$$

$$\Leftrightarrow$$

$$\exists n \cdot (n \in \mathbb{N} \wedge t \in \mathsf{genfin}\,(s)^n(\{\varnothing\}))$$

$$\Leftrightarrow$$

$$\{n \mid n \in \mathbb{N} \wedge t \in \mathsf{genfin}\,(s)^n(\{\varnothing\})\} \neq \varnothing$$

Given a finite subset t of s, the set $\{n \mid n \in \mathbb{N} \wedge t \in \mathsf{genfin}\,(s)^n(\{\varnothing\})\}$ is then not empty. It thus has a well-defined minimum which is our definition of $\mathsf{card}\,(t)$. In other words, $\mathsf{card}\,(t)$ is the *smallest number of iterations* of the function $\mathsf{genfin}\,(s)$ that we have to perform in order to *generate* the set t from the set containing the empty set only, formally

Syntax	Definition	Condition
$\mathsf{card}\,(t)$	$\min(\{n \mid n \in \mathbb{N} \wedge t \in \mathsf{genfin}\,(s)^n(\{\varnothing\})\})$	$t \in \mathbb{F}(s)$

For example, let s be the set

$$s = \{3, 4, 6\}$$

We then have

$$\mathsf{genfin}\,(s)^0\,(\{\varnothing\}) = \{\varnothing\}$$

$$\mathsf{genfin}\,(s)^1\,(\{\varnothing\}) = \{\varnothing, \{3\}, \{4\}, \{6\}\}$$

$$\mathsf{genfin}\,(s)^2\,(\{\varnothing\}) = \{\varnothing, \{3\}, \{4\}, \{6\}, \{3, 4\}, \{3, 6\}, \{4, 6\}\}$$

$$\mathsf{genfin}\,(s)^3\,(\{\varnothing\}) = \{\varnothing, \{3\}, \{4\}, \{6\}, \{3, 4\}, \{3, 6\}, \{4, 6\}, \{3, 4, 6\}\}$$

As a consequence, we have

$$\mathsf{card}\,(\{3, 6\}) = 2$$

3.5.10. Transitive Closures of a Relation

The transitive *and reflexive* closure, r^*, of a relation r from s to s is a relation from s to s which has the following property:

$$r^* = \mathsf{id}\,(s) \cup (r\,;r^*)$$

This suggests a fixpoint construction. We define the following set function, $\mathsf{genr}\,(s)$, of which r^* is the least fixpoint:

Syntax	Definition
genr (s)	$\lambda h \cdot (h \in \mathbb{P}(s \times s) \mid \text{id}\,(s) \cup (r\,;h))$
r^*	$\text{fix}\,(\text{genr}\,(s))$

The following properties result from the above definition:

$$r^* = \bigcup n \cdot (n \in \mathbb{N} \mid r^n)$$

$$r^* = r^*\,;r^*$$

$$r^* = r^{**}$$

$$(r^*)^{-1} = (r^{-1})^*$$

$$p \subseteq q \;\; \Rightarrow \;\; p^* \subseteq q^*$$

$$r^*[a] = \text{fix}\,(\lambda x \cdot (x \in \mathbb{P}(s) \mid a \cup r[x]))$$

$$r^*[a] = a \cup (r^*\,;r)\,[a]$$

$$r^*[a] = \bigcup n \cdot (n \in \mathbb{N} \mid r^n[a])$$

$$r[a] \subseteq a \;\; \Rightarrow \;\; r^*[a] = a$$

Likewise, the transitive *and not reflexive* closure, r^+, of a relation r from s to s is a relation from s to s which has the following property:

$$r^+ = r \cup (r\,;r^+)$$

This suggests a fixpoint construction. We define the following set function, genrp (s), of which r^+ is the least fixpoint.

Syntax	Definition
genrp (s)	$\lambda h \cdot (h \in \mathbb{P}(s \times s) \mid r \cup (r\,;h))$
r^+	$\text{fix}\,(\text{genrp}\,(s))$

The following properties result from the above definition:

$$r^+ = \bigcup n \cdot (n \in \mathbb{N}_1 \mid r^n)$$

$$r^+ ; r^+ \subseteq r^+$$

$$r^+ = r^{++}$$

$$(r^+)^{-1} = (r^{-1})^+$$

$$p \subseteq q \;\Rightarrow\; p^+ \subseteq q^+$$

$$r^+[a] = \text{fix}(\lambda x \cdot (x \in \mathbb{P}(s) \mid r[a] \cup r[x]))$$

$$r^+[a] = r[a] \cup (r^+ ; r)[a]$$

$$r^+[a] = \bigcup n \cdot (n \in \mathbb{N}_1 \mid r^n[a])$$

$$r[a] \subseteq a \;\Rightarrow\; r^+[a] \subseteq a$$

We can now express the following relationships concerning the relational operators defined on natural numbers in section 3.5.1:

$$\text{gtr} = \text{succ}^+$$

$$\text{geq} = \text{succ}^*$$

$$\text{lss} = \text{pred}^+$$

$$\text{leq} = \text{pred}^*$$

$$\text{gtr} = \text{lss}^{-1}$$

$$\text{geq} = \text{leq}^{-1}$$

3.6. The Integers

It is definitely outside the scope of this book to reconstruct the other classical sets that are useful in mathematics, namely the integers, the rationals and the reals (and now the hyper-reals). Clearly, however, the construction of these sets could be done without any special difficulties within the framework we have

established so far. What we intend to do in this section is just to introduce
some notations for the integers and extend existing notations valid so far for
the natural numbers to be valid for the integers as well. The set of integers is
denoted, as usual, as follows:

$$\mathbb{Z}$$

And we have

$$\mathbb{N} \subseteq \mathbb{Z}$$

The set of negative integers, that is $\mathbb{Z} - \mathbb{N}$, is denoted by

$$\mathbb{Z}_1$$

Given a member of n of $\mathbb{N}_1$, we can transform it into a member of $\mathbb{Z}_1$ (and
vice-versa) by means of the unary minus function uminus. And uminus (0) is 0.
So that we have

$$\text{uminus} \in \mathbb{Z} \rightarrowtail\!\!\!\rightarrow \mathbb{Z}$$

together with the following properties:

$$\mathbb{Z}_1 \vartriangleleft \text{uminus} \; \in \; \mathbb{Z}_1 \rightarrowtail\!\!\!\rightarrow \mathbb{N}_1$$

$$\mathbb{N}_1 \vartriangleleft \text{uminus} \; = \; (\mathbb{Z}_1 \vartriangleleft \text{uminus})^{-1}$$

We can also use the unary operator $-$, and we have, for any integer n,

$$-n \; = \; \text{uminus}\,(n)$$

In the following table, we show the various constructs whose meaning is extended
from $\mathbb{N}$ to $\mathbb{Z}$:

succ (n)	$n \in \mathbb{Z}$
pred (n)	$n \in \mathbb{Z}$
$n \leq m$	$n \in \mathbb{Z} \land m \in \mathbb{Z}$
$n < m$	$n \in \mathbb{Z} \land m \in \mathbb{Z}$
$n \geq m$	$n \in \mathbb{Z} \land m \in \mathbb{Z}$
$n > m$	$n \in \mathbb{Z} \land m \in \mathbb{Z}$

$(m, n) \in \text{gtr}$	$m \in \mathbb{Z} \land n \in \mathbb{Z}$
$(m, n) \in \text{geq}$	$m \in \mathbb{Z} \land n \in \mathbb{Z}$
$(m, n) \in \text{lss}$	$m \in \mathbb{Z} \land n \in \mathbb{Z}$
$(m, n) \in \text{leq}$	$m \in \mathbb{Z} \land n \in \mathbb{Z}$
$\text{plus}(m)(n)$	$n \in \mathbb{Z} \land m \in \mathbb{Z}$
$\text{mult}(m)(n)$	$n \in \mathbb{Z} \land m \in \mathbb{Z}$
$\text{minus}(m)(n)$	$n \in \mathbb{Z} \land m \in \mathbb{Z}$
$\text{div}(m)(n)$	$n \in \mathbb{Z} \land m \in \mathbb{Z} - \{0\}$
$m + n$	$n \in \mathbb{Z} \land m \in \mathbb{Z}$
$m \times n$	$n \in \mathbb{Z} \land m \in \mathbb{Z}$
$n - m$	$n \in \mathbb{Z} \land m \in \mathbb{Z}$
n / m	$n \in \mathbb{Z} \land m \in \mathbb{Z} - \{0\}$

In the following table, we make precise the extension of the various constructs:

$-(-n)$	$=$	n	$n \in \mathbb{N}$
$\text{succ}(-n)$	$=$	$-\text{pred}(n)$	$n \in \mathbb{N}$

$\mathrm{pred}\,(-n)$	$=$	$-\mathrm{succ}\,(n)$	$n \in \mathbb{N}$
$(-n) \leq m$			$n \in \mathbb{N} \wedge m \in \mathbb{N}$
$n \leq (-m)$	$\Leftrightarrow$	$n = 0 \wedge m = 0$	$n \in \mathbb{N} \wedge m \in \mathbb{N}$
$(-n) \leq (-m)$	$\Leftrightarrow$	$m \leq n$	$n \in \mathbb{N} \wedge m \in \mathbb{N}$
$(-m) + n$	$=$	$n - m$	$n \in \mathbb{N} \wedge m \in \mathbb{N}$
$m + (-n)$	$=$	$m - n$	$n \in \mathbb{N} \wedge m \in \mathbb{N}$
$(-m) + (-n)$	$=$	$-(m + n)$	$n \in \mathbb{N} \wedge m \in \mathbb{N}$
$(-m) \times n$	$=$	$-(m \times n)$	$n \in \mathbb{N} \wedge m \in \mathbb{N}$
$m \times (-n)$	$=$	$-(m \times n)$	$n \in \mathbb{N} \wedge m \in \mathbb{N}$
$(-m) \times (-n)$	$=$	$m \times n$	$n \in \mathbb{N} \wedge m \in \mathbb{N}$
$(-m) - n$	$=$	$-(m + n)$	$n \in \mathbb{N} \wedge m \in \mathbb{N}$
$m - (-n)$	$=$	$m + n$	$n \in \mathbb{N} \wedge m \in \mathbb{N}$
$(-m) - (-n)$	$=$	$n - m$	$n \in \mathbb{N} \wedge m \in \mathbb{N}$
$m - n$	$=$	$-(n - m)$	$n \in \mathbb{N} \wedge m \in \mathbb{N} \wedge n > m$
$(-n)/m$	$=$	$-(n/m)$	$n \in \mathbb{N} \wedge m \in \mathbb{N}_1$
$n/(-m)$	$=$	$-(n/m)$	$n \in \mathbb{N} \wedge m \in \mathbb{N}_1$
$(-n)/(-m)$	$=$	n/m	$n \in \mathbb{N} \wedge m \in \mathbb{N}_1$

We have only mentioned the relational operator $\leq$. This is because the other relational operators can be defined in terms of that one as before. The only other constructs that can be extended to the integers are min and max.

$\min(s)$	$s \in \mathbb{P}_1(\mathbb{Z}) \;\wedge\; s \cap \mathbb{Z}_1 \in \mathbb{F}(\mathbb{Z}_1)$
$\max(s)$	$s \in \mathbb{P}_1(\mathbb{Z}) \;\wedge\; s \cap \mathbb{N} \in \mathbb{F}(\mathbb{N})$

Notice that min and max have become completely symmetrical. We have

$$s \cap \mathbb{Z}_1 \neq \varnothing \;\;\Rightarrow\;\; \min(s) \;=\; -\max(\text{uminus}\,[s \cap \mathbb{Z}_1])$$

$$\max(s) \;=\; -\min(\text{uminus}\,[s])$$

3.7. Finite Sequences

We now construct another set of Mathematical Objects, that of the finite sequences built on a given set. Intuitively, the concept of finite sequence is very simple: it is just a finite and ordered collection of (not necessarily) distinct objects. In other words, sequences are "finite sets" in which the order is significant. So, although the sets $\{1,2\}$ and $\{2,1\}$ are equal, the sequences $[1,2]$ and $[2,1]$ are different. We shall construct the finite sequences by means of two distinct methods: first (section 3.7.1) by an inductive method like the one we have already used to define $\mathbb{F}(s)$ or $\mathbb{N}$: this will result, by arguments very similar to the ones used for the set $\mathbb{N}$, in an Induction Principle and also in a technique for constructing recursive functions on sequences. Second (section 3.7.2), we propose a direct method by which sequences are defined as particular partial functions on natural numbers. The reason for proposing these two methods is essentially pragmatic: sometimes, it is more convenient to use the first approach; sometimes, the second one is more fruitful. We shall see corresponding examples in section 3.7.3 where we define a number of classical operators on sequences.

3.7.1. Inductive Construction

Definition

A sequence built on a certain set s is either the empty sequence, or the sequence obtained by inserting an element x of s at the beginning of an already given sequence. Before proceeding, we have first to make clear this idea of *inserting*. Let f be a partial function from $\mathbb{N}_1$ to a set s, and x an element of s. We define the insertion, $x \to f$, as follows:

Syntax	Definition	Condition
$x \to f$	$\{1 \mapsto x\} \cup (\text{pred}\,;f)$	$x \in s \,\wedge\, f \in \mathbb{N}_1 \twoheadrightarrow s$

As an example, we have

$$3 \to \{1 \mapsto 5,\; 2 \mapsto 6\} \;=\; \{1 \mapsto 3,\; 2 \mapsto 5,\; 3 \mapsto 6\}$$

Denoting the empty sequence (which is just the empty set) by [ ] and the set of sequences built on s by seq (s), we can formalize our two desired properties as follows:

$$[\,] \in \mathsf{seq}\,(s)$$

$$\forall\,(x,t) \cdot ((x,t) \in s \times \mathsf{seq}\,(s) \;\Rightarrow\; (x \to t) \in \mathsf{seq}\,(s))$$

Obviously, we are in a situation corresponding to the second special case described in section 3.2.3. It remains for us to define both corresponding functions. This can be done as follows:

Syntax	Definition
insert (s)	$\lambda\,(x,t) \cdot ((x,t) \in s \times (\mathbb{N}_1 \nrightarrow s)\,\|\,x \to t)$
genseq (s)	$\lambda\,z \cdot (z \in \mathbb{P}(\mathbb{N}_1 \nrightarrow s)\,\|\,\{[\,]\} \cup \mathsf{insert}\,(s)[s \times z])$
seq (s)	fix (genseq (s))

Since seq (s) is a fixpoint, we have

$$\mathsf{seq}\,(s) \;=\; \{[\,]\} \cup \mathsf{insert}\,(s)[s \times \mathsf{seq}\,(s)]$$

That is

[ ] $\in$ seq (s) Property 3.7.1

---

and also

$\forall\,(x,t) \cdot ((x,t) \in s \times \mathsf{seq}\,(s) \;\Rightarrow\; (x \to t\,) \in \mathsf{seq}\,(s))$ Property 3.7.2

We have obtained our desired properties. We finally present the definitions of a few special sequences: first the non-empty sequences (seq$_1$), then the injective sequences (iseq) and finally the permutations (perm), which are bijective sequences constructed on finite sets.

Syntax	Definition
$\text{seq}_1(s)$	$\text{seq}(s) - \{[\,]\}$
$\text{iseq}(s)$	$\text{seq}(s) \cap (\mathbb{N}_1 \rightarrowtail s)$
$\text{perm}(s)$	$\text{iseq}(s) \cap (\mathbb{N}_1 \twoheadrightarrow s)$

Induction

According to **Theorem 3.2.9**, we have the following Induction Principle:

$$[t := [\,]\,]\,P$$
$$\forall t \cdot (t \in \text{seq}(s) \wedge P \Rightarrow$$
$$\forall x \cdot (x \in s \Rightarrow [t := x \rightarrow t]\,P)) \qquad\qquad \text{Theorem 3.7.1}$$
$$\Rightarrow$$
$$\forall t \cdot (t \in \text{seq}(s) \Rightarrow P)$$

Recursion

As for natural numbers, it is possible to define a recursive function on sequences by defining its value at $[\,]$ and also its value at $x \rightarrow t$ in terms of x and its value at t. We leave the formal justification of this construction as an exercise to the reader. We shall see examples of such functions in section 3.7.3.

3.7.2. Direct Construction

In this section, we give a direct definition of the set $\text{seq}(s)$. For this, we first define the concept of *interval*, then we define a finite sequence as a function whose domain is an interval of the form $1 .. n$ where n is a natural number.

Syntax	Definition	Condition
$m .. n$	$\{p \mid p \in \mathbb{Z} \wedge m \le p \wedge p \le n\}$	$m \in \mathbb{Z} \wedge n \in \mathbb{Z}$
$\text{seq}(s)$	$\bigcup n \cdot (n \in \mathbb{N} \mid (1 .. n) \rightarrow s)$	

3.7.3. Operations on Sequences

In this section, we propose two series of operators on sequences. In the first series, the operators are defined *recursively*, whereas in the second series they are defined *directly*. Note that this is just a question of style: either series could be defined with either method (we encourage readers to do so as an exercise).

Operations Defined Recursively

We define the size ($\text{size}(t)$) of a sequence t, the concatenation ($t \frown u$) of two sequences t and u, the insertion ($t \leftarrow y$) of an element y at the end of a sequence t, the reverse ($\text{rev}(t)$) of a sequence t, the generalized concatenation ($\text{conc}(t)$) of a sequence t of sequences, the generalized composition ($\text{comp}(t)$) of a sequence t of relations, and the sum ($\text{sum}(t)$) and product ($\text{prod}(t)$) of a sequence t of integers:

Syntax	Recursive Definition	Condition
$\text{size}([\,])$ $\text{size}(x \rightarrow t)$	0 $\text{size}(t) + 1$	 $x \in s \,\wedge\, t \in \text{seq}(s)$
$[\,] \frown u$ $(x \rightarrow t) \frown u$	u $x \rightarrow (t \frown u)$	$u \in \text{seq}(s)$ $x \in s \,\wedge\, t \in \text{seq}(s)$
$[\,] \leftarrow y$ $(x \rightarrow t) \leftarrow y$	$y \rightarrow [\,]$ $x \rightarrow (t \leftarrow y)$	$y \in s$ $x \in s \,\wedge\, t \in \text{seq}(s)$
$\text{rev}([\,])$ $\text{rev}(x \rightarrow t)$	$[\,]$ $\text{rev}(t) \leftarrow x$	 $x \in s \,\wedge\, t \in \text{seq}(s)$
$\text{conc}([\,])$ $\text{conc}(x \rightarrow t)$	$[\,]$ $x \frown \text{conc}(t)$	 $x \in \text{seq}(s) \,\wedge\, t \in \text{seq}(\text{seq}(s))$
$\text{comp}([\,])$ $\text{comp}(r \rightarrow t)$	$\text{id}(s)$ $r \,;\, \text{comp}(t)$	 $r \in s \leftrightarrow s \,\wedge\, t \in \text{seq}(s \leftrightarrow s)$
$\text{sum}([\,])$ $\text{sum}(x \rightarrow t)$	0 $x + \text{sum}(t)$	 $x \in \mathbb{N} \,\wedge\, t \in \text{seq}(\mathbb{Z})$
$\text{prod}([\,])$ $\text{prod}(x \rightarrow t)$	1 $x \times \text{prod}(t)$	 $x \in \mathbb{N} \,\wedge\, t \in \text{seq}(\mathbb{Z})$

Sequences Defined in Extension

We can now present the concept of *extensive* definition of sequences. A sequence is defined in extension by means of an explicit listing of its elements. In the following table, E is an *Expression* and L is a list of *Expressions* separated by commas.

Syntax	Definition	Condition
$[E]$	$\{1 \mapsto E\}$	$E \in s$
$[L, E]$	$[L] \leftarrow E$	$[L] \in \text{seq}(s) \wedge E \in s$

For instance, the following is a sequence defined in extension:

$$[4, 7, 4] = \{1 \mapsto 4,\ 2 \mapsto 7,\ 3 \mapsto 4\}$$

Examples

Next are some examples of the application of the above operators to sequences defined in extension.

$$\text{size}([5, 8, 5, 3]) = 4$$

$$[5, 4, 5, 3] \frown [1, 3, 3] = [5, 4, 5, 3, 1, 3, 3]$$

$$[5, 4, 5, 3] \leftarrow 1 = [5, 4, 5, 3, 1]$$

$$\text{rev}([5, 4, 5, 3]) = [3, 5, 4, 5]$$

$$\text{conc}[[5, 4, 5, 3], [\ ], [1, 3, 3], [4, 5]] = [5, 4, 5, 3, 1, 3, 3, 4, 5]$$

$$\text{sum}([1, 2, 3, 4]) = 10$$

$$\text{prod}([1, 2, 3, 4]) = 24$$

The following properties can be proved by induction:

$$\text{size}\,(t) \quad = \quad \text{card}\,(\text{dom}\,(t))$$

$$t \frown [\,] \quad = \quad t$$

$$t \frown (u \frown v) \quad = \quad (t \frown u) \frown v$$

$$\text{size}\,(t \frown u) \quad = \quad \text{size}\,(t) + \text{size}\,(u)$$

$$t \frown (u \leftarrow x) \quad = \quad (t \frown u) \leftarrow x$$

$$(t \leftarrow x) \frown u \quad = \quad t \frown (x \rightarrow u)$$

$$\text{size}\,(t \leftarrow x) \quad = \quad \text{size}\,(t) + 1$$

$$\text{rev}\,(t \leftarrow x) \quad = \quad x \rightarrow \text{rev}\,(t)$$

$$\text{rev}\,(t \frown u) \quad = \quad \text{rev}\,(u) \frown \text{rev}\,(t)$$

$$\text{size}\,(\text{rev}\,(t)) \quad = \quad \text{size}\,(t)$$

$$\text{rev}\,(\text{rev}\,(t)) \quad = \quad t$$

$$\text{rev}\,(t)\,;f \quad = \quad \text{rev}\,(t\,;f)$$

$$\text{conc}\,(u \frown v) \quad = \quad \text{conc}\,(u) \frown \text{conc}\,(v)$$

$$\text{rev}\,(\text{conc}\,(t)) \quad = \quad \text{conc}\,(\text{rev}\,(t\,;\text{rev}))$$

$$\text{sum}\,(u \frown v) \quad = \quad \text{sum}\,(u) + \text{sum}\,(v)$$

$$\text{sum}\,(\text{rev}\,(t)) \quad = \quad \text{sum}\,(t)$$

$$\text{prod}\,(u \frown v) \quad = \quad \text{prod}\,(u) \times \text{prod}\,(v)$$

$$\text{prod}\,(\text{rev}\,(t)) \quad = \quad \text{prod}\,(t)$$

Operations on Finite Functions

We close this subsection with the definition of operations on partial finite functions of integers. These operations define the sum and product of the elements of such functions. This is done by transforming the functions into sequences and then using the operations sum and prod. In order to transform a finite function into a sequence, it suffices to compose that function with a permutation of its domain (that is a bijective sequence built on its domain). Since the sum and product of integers are commutative and associative operations, the choice of the permutation is irrelevant (we shall thus use the operator **choice**).

Syntax	Definition	Condition
sumf (f)	sum (choice (perm (dom (f))) ; f)	$f \in s \nrightarrow \mathbb{Z} \wedge$ finite (f)
prodf (f)	prod (choice (perm (dom (f))) ; f)	$f \in s \nrightarrow \mathbb{Z} \wedge$ finite (f)

When the function f is a finite function defined by a functional abstraction, we can use the following quantifiers:

Syntax	Definition	Condition
$\sum x \cdot (x \in s \mid E)$	sumf $(\lambda x \cdot (x \in s \mid E))$	$\forall x \cdot (x \in s \ \Rightarrow \ E \in \mathbb{Z})$ finite (s)
$\sum x \cdot (x \in s \wedge P \mid E)$	sumf $(\lambda x \cdot (x \in s \wedge P \mid E))$	$\forall x \cdot (x \in s \wedge P \ \Rightarrow \ E \in \mathbb{Z})$ finite (s)
$\prod x \cdot (x \in s \mid E)$	prodf $(\lambda x \cdot (x \in s \mid E))$	$\forall x \cdot (x \in s \ \Rightarrow \ E \in \mathbb{Z})$ finite (s)
$\prod x \cdot (x \in s \wedge P \mid E)$	prodf $(\lambda x \cdot (x \in s \wedge P \mid E))$	$\forall x \cdot (x \in s \wedge P \ \Rightarrow \ E \in \mathbb{Z})$ finite (s)

Operations Defined Directly

We give now the direct definitions of some other operations on sequences. We first define the *low restriction* ($\downarrow$) and the *high restriction* ($\uparrow$). Then, we define the first and last element of non-empty sequences and their tail and front. We finally define the composition, cmp, with a total function and then the concatenation, cat, with a sequence.

Syntax	Definition	Condition
$t \uparrow n$	$(1 .. n) \lhd t$	$t \in \mathsf{seq}\,(s) \;\wedge\; n \in (0 .. \mathsf{size}\,(t))$
$t \downarrow n$	$\mathsf{plus}\,(n)\,;\,((1 .. n) \lhd t)$	$t \in \mathsf{seq}\,(s) \;\wedge\; n \in (0 .. \mathsf{size}\,(t))$
$\mathsf{first}\,(t)$	$t(1)$	$t \in \mathsf{seq}_1(s)$
$\mathsf{last}\,(t)$	$t(\mathsf{size}\,(t))$	$t \in \mathsf{seq}_1(s)$
$\mathsf{tail}\,(t)$	$t \downarrow 1$	$t \in \mathsf{seq}_1(s)$
$\mathsf{front}\,(t)$	$t \uparrow (\mathsf{size}\,(t) - 1)$	$t \in \mathsf{seq}_1(s)$
$\mathsf{cmp}\,(f)$	$\lambda t \cdot (t \in \mathsf{seq}\,(s) \mid t\,;f)$	$f \in s \to u$
$\mathsf{cat}\,(u)$	$\lambda t \cdot (t \in \mathsf{seq}\,(s) \mid u \frown t)$	$u \in \mathsf{seq}\,(s)$

Next are some examples of the previous operators:

$$[4,5,4,7,2,7,7] \uparrow 4 \;=\; [4,5,4,7]$$

$$[4,5,4,7,2,7,7] \downarrow 4 \;=\; [2,7,7]$$

$$\mathsf{first}\,([1,3,4,9]) \;=\; 1$$

$$\mathsf{last}\,([1,3,4,9]) \;=\; 9$$

$$\mathsf{tail}\,([1,3,4,9]) \;=\; [3,4,9]$$

$$\mathsf{front}\,([1,3,4,9]) \;=\; [1,3,4]$$

$$\mathsf{cmp}\,(\mathsf{succ})([1,3,4,9]) \;=\; [2,5,4,10]$$

$$\mathsf{cat}\,([5,3,8])([1,3,4,9]) \;=\; [5,3,8,1,3,4,9]$$

The following properties can be proved as exercises:

$$\text{size}\,(t \uparrow n) \;=\; n$$

$$\text{size}\,(t \downarrow n) \;=\; \text{size}\,(t) - n$$

$$(t \uparrow n) ^\frown (t \downarrow n) \;=\; t$$

$$\text{rev}\,(\text{rev}\,(t) \uparrow (\text{size}\,(t) - n)) \;=\; t \downarrow n$$

$$m \le n \quad \Rightarrow \quad t \uparrow n \uparrow m \;=\; t \uparrow m$$

$$n + m \in 0 \,..\, \text{size}\,(t) \quad \Rightarrow \quad t \downarrow n \downarrow m \;=\; t \downarrow (m + n)$$

$$m \le n \quad \Rightarrow \quad t \uparrow n \downarrow m \;=\; t \downarrow m \uparrow (n - m)$$

$$\text{first}\,(x \rightarrow t) = x$$

$$\text{last}\,(t \leftarrow x) = x$$

$$\text{tail}\,(x \rightarrow t) = t$$

$$\text{front}\,(t \leftarrow x) = t$$

$$\text{cmp}\,(f) \in \text{seq}\,(s) \rightarrow \text{seq}\,(u)$$

$$\text{cat}\,(u) \in \text{seq}\,(s) \rightarrowtail \text{seq}\,(s)$$

3.7.4. Sorting and Related Topics

Since it is an important concept, this section is entirely devoted to the abstract definition of the sorting of a sequence of integers and to other related topics.

Sorting a Sequence of Integers

Our intention is to define a certain function sort that maps the set of sequences of integers to itself:

$$\text{sort} \in \text{seq}\,(\mathbb{Z}) \rightarrow \text{seq}\,(\mathbb{Z})$$

Given a sequence u of integers, sort(u) denotes a permuted sorted sequence of u. We shall not immediately give a definition of the function sort; we shall rather introduce its properties gradually. The two properties that sort(u) must satisfy are well known: sort(u) is a permutation of u (has exactly the same elements as u), and sort(u) is sorted. We define these two notions as follows:

Syntax	Definition	Condition
u prm v	$\exists t \cdot (t \in \text{perm}(\text{dom}(u)) \wedge v = t\,;u)$	$u \in \text{seq}(s) \wedge v \in \text{seq}(s)$
sorted(v)	$(v \parallel v)[\text{geq}] \subseteq \text{geq}$	$v \in \text{seq}(\mathbb{Z})$

In other words, a sequence u is a permuted sequence of another sequence v, if there exists a permutation (a bijective sequence), built on the domain u, mapping, by composition, v to u. Likewise, a sequence v is said to be sorted if, for any i and j in the domain of s, $s(i)$ is less than or equal to $s(j)$ when i is less than or equal to j. This condition can be given (exercise) a denser, quantifier-free and variable-free form expressing that the image of the relation geq under the parallel composition of v with itself is included in geq. From the above definitions, we can deduce (exercises) a number of interesting properties. First a property concerning the range of permuted sequences:

---

a prm a'

$\Rightarrow$ Property 3.7.3

ran(a) = ran(a')

Then a property concerning the concatenation of permuted sequences:

---

a prm a'
b prm b'

$\Rightarrow$ Property 3.7.4

$(a \frown b)$ prm $(a' \frown b')$

Then the following obvious transitivity property of permuted sequences:

---

a prm b
b prm c

$\Rightarrow$ Property 3.7.5

a prm c

And finally the following property:

$(a \frown b)$ prm u

$\Rightarrow$ Property 3.7.6

$(x \rightarrow u)$ prm $(a \frown [x] \frown b)$

The three previous properties can be easily proved by exhibiting, in each case, a permutation derived from the existing permutations implied by the various hypotheses. Concerning the sorted predicate, we have the following property:

---

sorted (a)

sorted (b)

ran $(a) \times$ ran $(b) \subseteq$ geq   Property 3.7.7

$\Leftrightarrow$

sorted $(a \frown b)$

This very intuitive property expresses that a sequence of the form $a \frown b$ is sorted if and only if both sequences a and b are sorted and the ranges of a and b follow the obvious order relationship. From the previous property, we can easily deduce the following one:

---

sorted (a)

sorted (b)

ran $(a) \times \{x\} \subseteq$ geq

$\{x\} \times$ ran $(b) \subseteq$ geq   Property 3.7.8

$\Rightarrow$

sorted $(a \frown [x] \frown b)$

Given a sequence u of integers, nothing guarantees, of course, that there exists a sequence sort (u) such that the following holds:

$$u \quad \text{prm} \quad \text{sort}(u) \quad \wedge \quad \text{sorted}(\text{sort}(u))$$

Our intention is to propose a recursive definition of the function sort such that the above condition is satisfied. According to the classical recursion scheme (section 3.7.1), we have thus to define the function sort at the empty sequence [] and then at the sequence $x \rightarrow u$. We shall not, however, follow the classical recursion scheme completely. More precisely, sort $(x \rightarrow u)$ will not be defined in terms of sort (u). We shall rather use a "stronger" scheme (presented in section 3.11.3), allowing us to define sort $(x \rightarrow u)$ in terms of the values of the function sort at any sequence that is strictly "smaller" than $x \rightarrow u$. In what follows, we shall justify intuitively the proposed definition of sort $(x \rightarrow u)$. Clearly, the sequence sort $(x \rightarrow u)$ does contain the element x in it, so that it necessarily has the following form:

$$\mathrm{sort}\,(x \to u) \;=\; a' \frown [x] \frown b'$$

where a' and b' are two sequences such that the following holds:

> sorted (a')
> sorted (b')
> ran $(a') \times \{x\} \subseteq$ geq   (1)
> $\{x\} \times$ ran $(b') \subseteq$ geq
> $(a' \frown b')$ prm u

Property 3.7.6 and Property 3.7.8 can then be used to prove immediately our desired result, that is

$$(x \to u) \quad \mathrm{prm} \quad \mathrm{sort}\,(x \to u) \qquad \wedge \qquad \mathrm{sorted}\,(\mathrm{sort}\,(x \to u))$$

The idea is now to suppose that we have at our disposal two, *not necessarily sorted*, sequences a and b, such that the following holds:

> ran $(a) \times \{x\} \subseteq$ geq
> $\{x\} \times$ ran $(b) \subseteq$ geq   (2)
> $(a \frown b)$ prm u

According to Property 3.7.3, Property 3.7.4 and Property 3.7.5, it is easy to prove that the conditions (2) are kept when a and b are replaced by sort(a) and sort(b) respectively. So that the sorted sequences a' and b' of conditions (1) can be replaced by the two sorted sequences sort(a) and sort(b). Clearly, however, the sequences a and b are not unique. We shall thus define a binary relation partition (x) between u and the pair (a, b) as follows:

$$(u \mapsto (a, b) \ \in \ \mathrm{partition}\,(x)) \quad \Leftrightarrow \quad \left(\begin{array}{l} \mathrm{ran}\,(a) \times \{x\} \subseteq \mathrm{geq} \\ \{x\} \times \mathrm{ran}\,(b) \subseteq \mathrm{geq} \\ (a \frown b) \ \mathrm{prm} \ u \end{array} \right)$$

And now, we can define the function sort recursively as follows:

$$\left\{ \begin{array}{l} \mathrm{sort}\,([]) \;=\; [] \\[2ex] \mathrm{sort}\,(x \to u) \;=\; \mathrm{sort}\,(a) \frown [x] \frown \mathrm{sort}\,(b) \end{array} \right.$$

$$\mathrm{where} \quad u \mapsto (a, b) \ \in \ \mathrm{partition}\,(x)$$

And we have the following:

$\forall u \cdot (\ u \in \text{seq}(\mathbb{Z})$

$\Rightarrow$ Theorem 3.7.2

$u \quad \text{prm} \quad \text{sort}(u) \quad \wedge \quad \text{sorted}(\text{sort}(u)))$

With the help of the previous properties and the previous informal explanations, we can prove this theorem by strong induction (section 3.5.4) on the size of the sequence u. That is, we can suppose that it holds for all sequences of size up to n and then prove that it holds for all sequences of size $n + 1$. Alternatively, we can prove it by using the Well-founded Induction Principle that we shall present in section 3.11.2. The function **sort** we have just proposed is still "generic" in that it depends on the existence of a function satisfying the conditions implied by the binary relation partition(x). We thus propose the following functional "implementation", called separate(x), of the binary relation partition(x). It is typed as follows:

$$\text{separate}(x) \ \in \ \text{seq}(\mathbb{Z}) \rightarrow \text{seq}(\mathbb{Z}) \times \text{seq}(\mathbb{Z})$$

and it is defined recursively as follows:

$$\begin{cases} \text{separate}(x)([]) \ = \ [],[] \\ \\ \text{separate}(x)(y \rightarrow u) \ = \ \begin{cases} (y \rightarrow a), b & \text{if } y < x \\ \\ a, (y \rightarrow b) & \text{if } y \geq x \end{cases} \end{cases}$$

$$\text{where} \quad (a, b) \ = \ \text{separate}(x)(u)$$

Note that in section 10.4.6 of chapter 10, we shall propose another "implementation" of the relation partition(x). It is then easy to prove the following property:

$\forall x \cdot (x \in \mathbb{Z} \ \Rightarrow \ \text{separate}(x) \ \subseteq \ \text{partition}(x))$ Property 3.7.9

Sorting a Finite Set of Integers

By a similar, and simpler, construction we can define a function **sortset** mapping finite sets of integers to sequences of integers:

$$\text{sortset} \in \mathbb{F}(\mathbb{Z}) \rightarrow \text{seq}(\mathbb{Z})$$

Given a finite set s of integers, sortset(s) is the sorted bijective sequence built on s (that is, the sorted permutation built on s), formally

$$\text{sortset}(s) \ \in \ \text{perm}(s) \quad \wedge \quad \text{sorted}(\text{sortset}(s))$$

Squashing a Finite Function with Integer Domain

The previous function allows us to define our last function in this section, namely a function that transforms a finite partial function built on $\mathbb{Z}$ into a sequence by "squashing" its domain (this concept is borrowed from the specification language Z). Here is the type of this function, called squash:

$$\text{squash} \in (\mathbb{Z} \nrightarrow s) \nrightarrow \text{seq}(s)$$

Here is its definition:

Syntax	Definition	Condition
squash(f)	sortset$(\text{dom}(f))\,;f$	$f \in \mathbb{Z} \nrightarrow s \;\wedge\; \text{finite}(f)$

For example, we have:

$$\text{squash}(\{\,2 \mapsto a,\, 5 \mapsto c,\, 7 \mapsto b\,\}) = [\,a, c, b\,]$$

This is because

$$\text{dom}(\{\,2 \mapsto a,\, 5 \mapsto c,\, 7 \mapsto b\,\}) = \{\,2, 5, 7\,\}$$

$$\text{sortset}(\{\,2, 5, 7\,\}) = [\,2, 5, 7\,]$$

$$[\,2, 5, 7\,]\,;\{\,2 \mapsto a,\, 5 \mapsto c,\, 7 \mapsto b\,\} = [\,a, c, b\,]$$

The main property of squash(f) is that it preserves the order of the values of f. More precisely, for any two members i and j of the domain of f where $i \leq j$, there exists two members i' and j' of the domain of squash(f), where $i' \leq j'$, such that $f(i) = \text{squash}(f)(i')$ and $f(j) = \text{squash}(f)(j')$ and vice-versa. This can be expressed formally as follows:

$$(\text{squash}(f) \,||\, \text{squash}(f))\,[\,\text{geq}\,] \;=\; (f \,||\, f)\,[\,\text{geq}\,] \qquad\qquad \text{Property 3.7.10}$$

3.7.5. Lexicographical Order on Sequences of Integers

Consider two sequences s and t *of the same size* built on integers:

$$s \in \text{seq}(\mathbb{Z}) \;\wedge\; t \in \text{seq}(\mathbb{Z}) \;\wedge\; \text{size}(s) = \text{size}(t)$$

The sequence s is said to be lexicographically strictly smaller than the sequence t (in symbols $s \prec t$), if and only if s and t are distinct and $s(i) < t(i)$, where i is the smallest index of their common domain where they are distinct. By extension, $s \preceq t$ means that either s is equal to t or s is lexicographically strictly smaller than t. Formally:

Syntax	Definition	Condition
$s < t$	$s \neq t \;\wedge$ $\text{size}(s) = \text{size}(t) \;\wedge$ $s(i) < t(i)$	$s \in \text{seq}(\mathbb{Z})$ $t \in \text{seq}(\mathbb{Z})$ where $\; i = \min(\{\, n \mid n \in \text{dom}(s) \;\wedge$ $s(i) \neq t(i)\,\})$
$s \leq t$	$s = t \;\vee\; s < t$	

It can be proved that the relation $\leq$ between sequences of integers of the same size is an *order* relation:

$$s \leq s$$

$$s \leq t \wedge t \leq u \;\Rightarrow\; s \leq u$$

$$s \leq t \wedge t \leq s \;\Rightarrow\; s = t$$

Moreover it can be proved that the relation $\leq$ between sequences of the same size built on *natural numbers* is a *well-ordering* relation (this is not the case, of course, for sequences built on integers). In other words, every non-empty set of such sequences has a "smallest" element. As a consequence, the relation $>$ (defined in an obvious way) is *well-founded* (this notion will be defined in section 3.11).

3.8. Finite Trees

In this section, we shall construct our fourth kind of *Mathematical Object*: the finite trees. Such trees will *not* be the ones we are going to use in practice. In subsequent sections we shall introduce two more useful kinds of trees: the labelled trees (section 3.9) and the labelled binary trees (section 3.10). The reason why we introduce the trees of this section is because their construction is simpler and thus serves as a model for the construction of the others, which we shall only present very briefly. The hurried reader can skip this section.

3.8.1. Informal Introduction

A tree is a mathematical structure that is best depicted by a figure such as the one below. In this figure, each dot is called a *node*. The node situated at the top of the tree is called the *root* of the tree. Each node has zero or a finite number of other nodes situated just below it, and connected to it: these are the *sons* of the node in question. The number of sons of a node is called the *arity* of the node. A node with no sons is called a *leaf*. The order of the sons of a node is significant. They form a (possibly empty) sequence of nodes. Conversely, each node *n*, except the root, has a unique *father* of which *n* is one of the sons. The line linking a node to one of its sons is called a *branch*. Each branch can be labelled with a number representing its *rank* as shown.

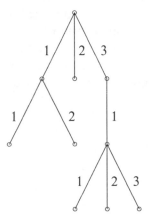

Each node of a tree can be labelled with the sequence of branch ranks one has to follow in order to reach the node in question from the root. This is shown in the next figure, where the root is labelled with the empty sequence.

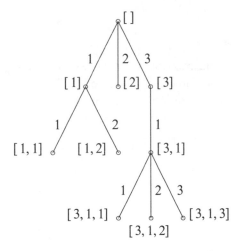

As can be seen, the rank of a branch arriving at a certain son node corresponds to the last element of the sequence labeling the node. Likewise, the father of a node is labelled with the front of that node. As a consequence, the set *ss* of sequences labeling the nodes is *prefix closed*: that is, once a sequence *s* belongs to *ss* then all the prefixes of *s* also belong to *ss*. Moreover, all the sequences of positive natural numbers that are lexicographically smaller than *s* also belong to *ss*.

3.8.2. Formal Construction

From now on, we shall identify each node of a tree with the corresponding sequence of ranks. We also identify the entire tree with the set of its nodes, so that a tree is just a finite set of sequences of positive natural numbers.

As a consequence, the set T of all trees is included in the set of finite subsets of the set of sequences built on positive natural numbers. It remains for us to characterize the set T precisely. For this, we notice that in order to build a new tree, we can use a sequence of existing trees and put them together *in a certain order* as indicated in the next figure (where the second tree in the sequence is a tree consisting of just one root).

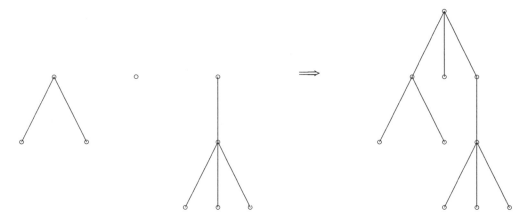

Conversely, by cutting the root of a tree *t* we obtain a (possibly empty) sequence of trees that corresponds to the sons of *t*. The trees, say t_1, t_2 and t_3, of the left part of the above figure are the following:

$$t_1 = \{\,[\,], [1], [2]\,\}$$

$$t_2 = \{\,[\,]\,\}$$

$$t_3 = \{\,[\,], [1], [1,1], [1,2], [1,3]\,\}$$

In order to construct the tree *t* of the right-hand part of the above figure, one has clearly to insert 1 at the beginning of each sequence of t_1, 2 at the beginning of each sequence of t_2 and 3 at the beginning of each sequence of t_3. More generally, we insert the number *i* at the beginning of each sequence of t_i. We have then to put all these new sequences together and finally add to them the empty sequence. In order to formalize this process, we first define the function ins to insert a number at the beginning of a sequence and then the function cns which is the formal counterpart of the informal construction we have just presented. In order to simplify matters we also abbreviate the set $\mathbb{F}(\mathsf{seq}\,(\mathbb{N}_1))$ by FSN.

Syntax	Definition
FSN	$\mathbb{F}(\mathsf{seq}\,(\mathbb{N}_1))$
ins	$\lambda\,i \cdot (i \in \mathbb{N} \mid \lambda\,s \cdot (s \in \mathsf{seq}\,(\mathbb{N}) \mid i \to s\,))$
cns	$\lambda\,t \cdot (t \in \mathsf{seq}\,(\mathsf{FSN}) \mid \{[\,]\} \cup \bigcup i \cdot (i \in \mathsf{dom}\,(t) \mid \mathsf{ins}\,(i)[t(i)]\,))$

We leave it to the reader to prove that cns is an injective function, formally

$\mathsf{cns} \in \mathsf{seq}\,(\mathsf{FSN}) \rightarrowtail \mathsf{FSN}$ Property 3.8.1

The property we would like the set T to have corresponds to the fact that every sequence of members of T can give rise to another member of T, formally

$$\forall\,s \cdot (s \in \mathsf{seq}\,(\mathsf{T}) \implies \mathsf{cns}\,(s) \in \mathsf{T}\,)$$

In other words, we should have

$$\mathsf{T} = \mathsf{cns}\,[\,\mathsf{seq}\,(\mathsf{T})\,]$$

Here again, we have a fixpoint equation so that the final formalities are now the following:

Syntax	Definition
gentree (s)	$\lambda\,z \cdot (z \in \mathbb{P}(\mathsf{FSN}) \mid \mathsf{cns}\,[\,\mathsf{seq}\,(z)\,]\,)$
T	fix $(\mathsf{gentree}\,(s))$

We notice that gentree (s) is a *monotonic* function from $\mathbb{P}(\mathsf{FSN})$ to itself (proof left to the reader) so that T is indeed a fixpoint, and we have

$$\mathsf{T} = \mathsf{cns}\,[\,\mathsf{seq}\,(\mathsf{T})\,]$$

that is

$$\forall s \cdot (s \in \text{seq}(T) \implies \text{cns}(s) \in T) \qquad\qquad \text{Property 3.8.2}$$

---

which is the desired property. In fact, we have more: a very interesting property that says that the function cns restricted to seq(T) is actually a *bijection* from seq(T) to T. In other words, each member of T comes from a *unique* sequence of members T, formally

---

$$\text{seq}(T) \lhd \text{cns} \in \text{seq}(T) \rightarrowtail T \qquad\qquad \text{Property 3.8.3}$$

Proof
We shall prove that seq(T) $\lhd$ cns is a total surjection and an injection at the same time. The function seq(T) $\lhd$ cns is clearly already a total surjection form seq(T) to *T*. This results from Property 3.8.1 and the fixpoint property. But seq(T) $\lhd$ cns, being included in cns, is also an injection since cns is one according to Property 3.8.1.
End of Proof

As there exists a bijection between them, the two sets T and seq(T) are said to be *isomorphic*. In other words, speaking of a tree *t* is the same thing as speaking of a sequence of trees. And the sequence of trees in question is the sequence of sons of the root of *t*. We thus define the function sns as follows

Syntax	Definition
sns	$\text{cns}^{-1} \rhd \text{seq}(T)$

and we have the following property:

$$\text{sns} \in T \rightarrowtail \text{seq}(T) \qquad\qquad \text{Property 3.8.4}$$

3.8.3. Induction

Definition
The fixpoint definition of T induces an induction principle derivable from Theorem 3.2.7. In our case, the main antecedent of that theorem translates to:

$$\text{gentree}(s)(\{t \mid t \in T \land P\}) \subseteq \{t \mid t \in T \land P\}$$

that is, according to the definition of gentree(*s*)

$$\text{cns}\,[\text{seq}\,(\{\,t \mid t \in \text{T} \,\wedge\, P\,\})] \;\subseteq\; \{\,t \mid t \in \text{T} \,\wedge\, P\,\}$$

that is

$$\forall\,t \cdot (t \in \text{cns}\,[\text{seq}\,(\{\,t \mid t \in \text{T} \,\wedge\, P\,\})] \;\Rightarrow\; t \in \text{T} \,\wedge\, P\,)$$

that is

$$\forall\,t \cdot (t \in \text{T} \,\wedge\, \exists\,s \cdot (s \in \text{seq}\,(\{\,t \mid t \in \text{T} \,\wedge\, P\,\}) \,\wedge\, t = \text{cns}\,(s)) \;\Rightarrow\; t \in \text{T} \,\wedge\, P\,)$$

that is, according to the definition of sns

$$\forall\,t \cdot (t \in \text{T} \,\wedge\, \exists\,s \cdot (s \in \text{seq}\,(\{\,t \mid t \in \text{T} \,\wedge\, P\,\}) \,\wedge\, s = \text{sns}\,(t)) \;\Rightarrow\; P\,)$$

that is, according to the **One Point Rule**

$$\forall\,t \cdot (t \in \text{T} \,\wedge\, \text{sns}\,(t) \in \text{seq}\,(\{\,t \mid t \in \text{T} \,\wedge\, P\,\}) \;\Rightarrow\; P\,)$$

This results in the following induction principle:

$$\forall\,t \cdot (t \in \text{T} \,\wedge\, \text{sns}\,(t) \in \text{seq}\,(\{\,t \mid t \in \text{T} \,\wedge\, P\,\}) \;\Rightarrow\; P\,)$$
$$\Rightarrow \qquad\qquad\qquad\qquad\qquad\qquad\qquad\qquad\qquad\qquad\qquad \text{Theorem 3.8.1}$$
$$\forall\,t \cdot (t \in \text{T} \;\Rightarrow\; P\,)$$

In other words, in order to prove a property P for each member t of T, it suffices to prove that P holds at t under the assumption that it holds for each son of t. We notice that, in this induction scheme, we only have one "step", which, in fact, contains the hidden special case where the tree t has no sons. We now consider two special cases that will result in some simplifications of the above induction principle. Both these special cases correspond to special forms of the predicate P to be proved by induction.

First Special Case

As our first case, we consider a certain function f from T to a given set s, and a certain subset a of s, formally

$$f \in \text{T} \to s$$

$$a \subseteq s$$

We now suppose that the predicate P to be proved is as follows:

$$f(t) \in a$$

In this case, we can prove the following equivalence:

$$\text{sns}\,(t) \in \text{seq}\,(\{\,t \mid t \in \text{T} \,\wedge\, f(t) \in a\,\}) \;\Leftrightarrow\; (\text{sns}\,(t);f) \in \text{seq}\,(a)$$

and the Induction Principle thus becomes

$f \in T \to s$
$a \subseteq s$
$\forall t \cdot (t \in T \wedge (\text{sns}\,(t);f) \in \text{seq}\,(a) \;\Rightarrow\; f(t) \in a\,)$ Theorem 3.8.2
$\Rightarrow$
$\forall t \cdot (t \in T \;\Rightarrow\; f(t) \in a)$

Second Special Case

As our second case, we consider two functions f and g as follows:

$$f \in T \to s$$
$$g \in T \to s$$

We now suppose that the predicate P to be proved is as follows:

$$f(t) = g(t)$$

In this case, we can prove the following equivalence:

$$\text{sns}\,(t) \in \text{seq}\,(\{\,t \mid t \in T \wedge f(t) = g(t)\,\}) \;\Leftrightarrow\; (\text{sns}\,(t);f) = (\text{sns}\,(t);g)$$

and the Induction Principle thus becomes:

$f \in T \to s$
$g \in T \to s$
$\forall t \cdot (t \in T \wedge (\text{sns}\,(t);f) = (\text{sns}\,(t);g) \;\Rightarrow\; f(t) = g(t))$ Theorem 3.8.3
$\Rightarrow$
$\forall t \cdot (t \in T \;\Rightarrow\; f(t) = g(t))$

3.8.4. Recursion

We turn now our attention to the problem of *recursion* on trees. Given a certain set s and a function g from $\text{seq}\,(s)$ to s

$$g \in \text{seq}\,(s) \to s$$

we would like to know whether it is possible to build a total function f of the following type:

$$f \in T \to s$$

satisfying the following condition (provided it makes sense) supposed to hold for each member t of T:

$$f(t) \;=\; g\,(\text{sns}\,(t);f)$$

In other words, the value of the function f at t depends on the sequence obtained by applying f to each element composing the sequence $\text{sns}(t)$. In order to construct f formally, we shall use a technique very similar to the one we used in section 3.5.6 for defining recursion on $\mathbb{N}$. We first define a certain binary relation from T to s, and then we prove that that relation is indeed a total function enjoying the previous property. The problem is to eliminate the variable t from the above condition so that a fixpoint equation on f can be exhibited. To do this, and given a binary relation r from T to s, we define a certain binary relation, $\text{tcmp}(r)$, holding between sequences built on T and s respectively. Formally:

$$\text{tcmp} \in (\text{T} \leftrightarrow s) \rightarrow (\text{seq}(\text{T}) \leftrightarrow \text{seq}(s))$$

We thus propose the following definition:

Syntax	Definition
$\text{tcmp}(r)$	$\{a, b \mid (a, b) \in \text{seq}(\text{T}) \times \text{seq}(s) \wedge \text{size}(a) = \text{size}(b) \wedge b \subseteq (a \,;\, r)\}$

When a sequence a built on T is such that r is functional on its range, that is:

$$\text{ran}(a) \lhd r \in \text{ran}(a) \rightarrow s$$

then there is *exactly one* sequence b such that $b \subseteq (a \,;\, r)$ and that sequence is clearly $(a \,;\, r)$. This can be formalized in the following property:

$$\text{ran}(a) \lhd r \in \text{ran}(a) \rightarrow s \quad \Rightarrow \quad \text{tcmp}(r)[\{a\}] = \{(a \,;\, r)\} \qquad \text{Property 3.8.5}$$

Coming back to our main problem, we can see that our recursive definition of $f(t)$ can be put into the following form (since when f is functional then $\text{sns}(t) \,;\, f$ is equal to $\text{tcmp}(f)(\text{sns}(t))$):

$$f(t) = g(\text{tcmp}(f)(\text{sns}(t)))$$

We can eliminate t, thus obtaining the following fixpoint equation:

$$f = g \circ \text{tcmp}(f) \circ \text{sns}$$

We then define the following:

Syntax	Definition
genft (g)	$\lambda h \cdot (h \in \mathbb{P}(\mathsf{T} \times s) \mid g \, \circ \, \text{tcmp}\,(h) \, \circ \, \text{sns}\,)$

The function genft is a *monotonic* function from $\mathbb{P}(\mathsf{T} \times s)$ to itself (proof left to the reader). Consequently, we have a least fixpoint and we thus define f as follows:

$$f \;=\; \text{fix}\,(\text{genft}\,(g))$$

As a consequence, we have

$f \;=\; g \, \circ \, \text{tcmp}\,(f) \, \circ \, \text{sns}$ Property 3.8.6

Of course, at this point, nothing guarantees that the f that has just been defined by a fixpoint is a total function. According to **Property 2.5.1**, we are thus led to prove the following property:

$\forall t \cdot (t \in \mathsf{T} \;\Rightarrow\; \{t\} \lhd f \in \{t\} \to s\,)$ Property 3.8.7

Proof

The proof is by induction. According to **Theorem 3.8.1**, we assume

$t \in \mathsf{T}$ Hypothesis 1
$\text{sns}\,(t) \in \text{seq}\,(\{\,u \mid u \in \mathsf{T} \;\wedge\; \{u\} \lhd f \in \{u\} \to s\,\})$ Hypothesis 2

and we have to prove

$\{t\} \lhd f \in \{t\} \to s$ Goal 1

From **Hypothesis 2**, we deduce the following:

$\text{ran}\,(\text{sns}\,(t)) \lhd f \in \text{ran}\,(\text{sns}\,(t)) \to s$ Derivation 1

Thus, according to **Property 3.8.5**, we have

$\text{tcmp}\,(f)[\{\text{sns}\,(t)\}] \;=\; \{(\text{sns}\,(t);f)\}$ Derivation 2

We have then

$$\{t\} \triangleleft f$$
$$=$$
$$\{t\} \triangleleft (g \,\circ\, \mathsf{tcmp}\,(f) \,\circ\, \mathsf{sns})$$
$$=$$
$$\{t\} \times (g \,\circ\, \mathsf{tcmp}\,(f) \,\circ\, \mathsf{sns})[\{t\}]$$
$$=$$
$$\{t\} \times (g \,\circ\, \mathsf{tcmp}\,(f))[\{\mathsf{sns}\,(t)\}]$$
$$=$$
$$\{t\} \times (g\,[\,\mathsf{tcmp}\,(f)\,[\{\mathsf{sns}\,(t)\}]\,])$$
$$=$$
$$\{t\} \times (g\,[\,\{(\mathsf{sns}\,(t)\,;f)\}\,])$$ Derivation 2
$$=$$
$$\{t\} \times \{g\,(\mathsf{sns}\,(t)\,;f)\}$$

This proves that Goal 1 holds.
End of Proof

From here on, we shall feel free to define functions on T by recursion.

3.8.5. Operations

In this section, we define a number of operations on T by recursion. First a function sizt yielding the number of nodes of a tree. Then, a function mir yielding the mirror image of a tree.

Syntax	Recursive Definition	Condition
$\mathsf{sizt}\,(t)$	$\mathsf{succ}\,(\mathsf{sum}\,(\mathsf{sns}\,(t)\,;\,\mathsf{sizt}))$	$t \in \mathsf{T}$
$\mathsf{mir}\,(t)$	$\mathsf{cns}\,(\mathsf{rev}\,(\mathsf{sns}\,(t)\,;\,\mathsf{mir}))$	$t \in \mathsf{T}$

We have the following property:

---

mir ; sizt = sizt   Property 3.8.8

Proof
We shall prove the following by induction:

$$\forall t \cdot (t \in \mathsf{T} \;\Rightarrow\; \mathsf{sizt}\,(\mathsf{mir}\,(t)) = \mathsf{sizt}\,(t))$$

We are in the presence of the second special case considered in section 3.8.3 (Theorem 3.8.3). As a consequence, we assume

$$t \in \mathsf{T}$$ Hypothesis 1
$$\mathsf{sns}\,(t)\,;\mathsf{mir}\,;\mathsf{sizt} \;=\; \mathsf{sns}\,(t)\,;\mathsf{sizt}$$ Hypothesis 2

and we have to prove

$$\mathsf{sizt}\,(\mathsf{mir}\,(t)) = \mathsf{sizt}\,(t)$$ Goal 1

that is, according to the definition of mir,

$$\mathsf{sizt}\,(\mathsf{cns}\,(\mathsf{rev}\,(\mathsf{sns}\,(t)\,;\mathsf{mir}))) = \mathsf{sizt}\,(t)$$ Goal 2

that is, according to the definition of sizt,

$$\mathsf{succ}\,(\mathsf{sum}\,(\mathsf{sns}\,(\mathsf{cns}\,(\mathsf{rev}\,(\mathsf{sns}\,(t)\,;\mathsf{mir})))\,;\mathsf{sizt})) = \mathsf{sizt}\,(t)$$ Goal 3

that is, since sns is the inverse of cns,

$$\mathsf{succ}\,(\mathsf{sum}\,(\mathsf{rev}\,(\mathsf{sns}\,(t)\,;\mathsf{mir})\,;\mathsf{sizt})) = \mathsf{sizt}\,(t)$$ Goal 4

that is, since $\mathsf{rev}\,(a)\,;f \;=\; \mathsf{rev}\,(a\,;f)$ (section 3.7.3),

$$\mathsf{succ}\,(\mathsf{sum}\,(\mathsf{rev}\,(\mathsf{sns}\,(t)\,;\mathsf{mir}\,;\mathsf{sizt}))) = \mathsf{sizt}\,(t)$$ Goal 5

that is, according to Hypothesis 2,

$$\mathsf{succ}\,(\mathsf{sum}\,(\mathsf{rev}\,(\mathsf{sns}\,(t)\,;\mathsf{sizt}))) = \mathsf{sizt}\,(t)$$ Goal 6

that is, since $\mathsf{sum}\,(\mathsf{rev}\,(a)) \;=\; \mathsf{sum}\,(a)$ (section 3.7.3),

$$\mathsf{succ}\,(\mathsf{sum}\,(\mathsf{sns}\,(t)\,;\mathsf{sizt})) = \mathsf{sizt}\,(t)$$ Goal 7

which is obvious according to the definition of sizt.
End of Proof

We also have the following property:

   $$\mathsf{mir}\,;\mathsf{mir} = \mathsf{id}\,(\mathsf{T})$$ Property 3.8.9

Proof

We shall prove the following by induction:

$$\forall t \cdot (t \in \mathsf{T} \;\Rightarrow\; \mathsf{mir}\,(\mathsf{mir}\,(t)) = t\,)$$

We are in the presence of the second special case considered in section 3.8.3 (Theorem 3.8.3). As a consequence, we assume

$$t \in \mathsf{T}$$ Hypothesis 1
$$\mathsf{sns}\,(t)\,;\mathsf{mir}\,;\mathsf{mir} \;=\; \mathsf{sns}\,(t)$$ Hypothesis 2

and we have to prove

$$\mathsf{mir}\,(\mathsf{mir}\,(t)) = t$$ Goal 1

that is, according to the definition of mir,

$$\mathsf{mir}\,(\mathsf{cns}\,(\mathsf{rev}\,(\mathsf{sns}\,(t)\,;\mathsf{mir}))) = t$$ Goal 2

that is, according to the definition of mir,

$$\mathsf{cns}\,(\mathsf{rev}\,(\mathsf{sns}\,(\mathsf{cns}\,(\mathsf{rev}\,(\mathsf{sns}\,(t)\,;\mathsf{mir})))\,;\mathsf{mir})) = t$$ Goal 3

that is, since sns is the inverse of cns,

$$\mathsf{cns}\,(\mathsf{rev}\,(\mathsf{rev}\,(\mathsf{sns}\,(t)\,;\mathsf{mir})\,;\mathsf{mir})) = t$$ Goal 4

that is, since, $\mathsf{rev}\,(\mathsf{rev}\,(a)) = a$ (section 3.7.3),

$$\mathsf{cns}\,(\mathsf{sns}\,(t)\,;\mathsf{mir}\,;\mathsf{mir}) = t$$ Goal 5

that is, according to Hypothesis 2,

$$\mathsf{cns}\,(\mathsf{sns}\,(t)) = t$$ Goal 6

which is obvious.
End of Proof

3.8.6. Representing Trees

In this section, it is our intention to present an unambiguous represention of
trees in terms of certain sequences of parentheses. For instance, the following
figure shows a tree together with the corresponding parenthetical representation.
The other representation is a rewriting of the previous one where left and right
parentheses are encoded with ones and zeros respectively.

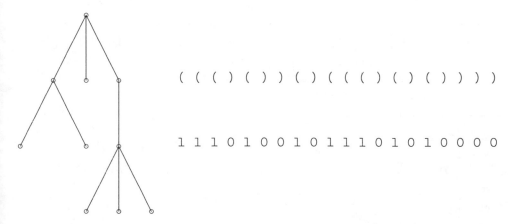

$$(\; (\; (\;) \; (\;) \;) \; (\;) \; (\; (\;) \; (\;) \; (\;) \;) \;) \;)$$

$$1 \; 1 \; 1 \; 0 \; 1 \; 0 \; 0 \; 1 \; 0 \; 1 \; 1 \; 1 \; 0 \; 1 \; 0 \; 1 \; 0 \; 0 \; 0 \; 0$$

The idea of this representation is that each tree is encoded by a pair of
(open, closed) parentheses enclosing the inner representation of the son trees. In
order to formalize such a representation, we first define the following set BRK
of brackets (again, (is 1 and) is 0):

$$\mathsf{BRK} = \{\,(,\,)\,\}$$

Then we define recursively a function rep from T to seq_1 (BRK) as follows:

Syntax	Recursive Definition	Condition
$\mathsf{rep}\,(t)$	$(\ \rightarrow \mathsf{conc}\,(\mathsf{sns}\,(t)\,;\,\mathsf{rep})\ \leftarrow\ )$	$t \in \mathsf{T}$

Our intention is to prove that the function rep is *injective*. For that, we first study the structure of its range. Our claim is that the range of rep consists of all the members of seq (BRK) which are such that the count of open parentheses (the ones) is the same as that of closed parentheses (the zeros). Moreover, every genuine and non-empty prefix of such sequences is a sequence where the count of open parentheses *exceeds* that of closed parentheses. Let BPR (for balanced parentheses) be the following set:

$$\mathsf{BPR} \;=\; \{\, s \mid s \in \mathsf{seq}\,(\mathsf{BRK}) \,\wedge\, \mathsf{opn}\,(s) = \mathsf{clo}\,(s) \,\wedge\, s \neq [\,] \;\wedge$$
$$\forall t \cdot (t \in \mathsf{seq}\,(\mathsf{BRK}) \,\wedge\, t \subset s \,\wedge\, t \neq [\,] \;\Rightarrow\; \mathsf{opn}\,(t) > \mathsf{clo}\,(t))\,\}$$

where

$$\begin{aligned} \mathsf{opn}\,(s) &= \mathsf{card}\,(s^{-1}[\{\,1\,\}]) \\ \mathsf{clo}\,(s) &= \mathsf{card}\,(s^{-1}[\{\,0\,\}]) \end{aligned}$$

Our first property states that rep is a function from T to BPR

$\mathsf{rep} \in \mathsf{T} \rightarrow \mathsf{BPR}$ Property 3.8.10

We leave the proof of this property as an exercise to the reader (hint: use one of the special induction principles defined in section 3.8.3). Our second property states that the function conc applied to sequences of members of BPR is injective. Formally this reduces to proving

---

$s_1 \in \mathsf{seq}\,(\mathsf{BPR})$
$s_2 \in \mathsf{seq}\,(\mathsf{BPR})$
$\mathsf{conc}\,(s_1) = \mathsf{conc}\,(s_2)$ Property 3.8.11
$\Rightarrow$
$s_1 = s_2$

Proof
We assume

$\quad\quad\quad s_1 \in \mathsf{seq}\,(\mathsf{BPR})$ Hypothesis 1
$\quad\quad\quad s_2 \in \mathsf{seq}\,(\mathsf{BPR})$ Hypothesis 2
$\quad\quad\quad \mathsf{conc}\,(s_1) = \mathsf{conc}\,(s_2)$ Hypothesis 3

and we have to prove

$$s_1 = s_2 \hspace{4cm} \text{Goal 1}$$

The proof is by contradiction, so that we assume

$$s_1 \neq s_2 \hspace{4cm} \text{Hypothesis 4}$$

and we try to derive a contradiction. We first observe that say, s_1, cannot be a genuine prefix of s_2 (and vice-versa) since then $\text{conc}(s_1)$ would not be equal to $\text{conc}(s_2)$ as required by Hypothesis 3. As a consequence, we can assume that s_1 and s_2 can be decomposed as follows, where a, b, and c are sequences of members of BPR and x and y are *distinct* members of BPR:

$$s_1 = a \frown [x] \frown b \hspace{3cm} \text{Hypothesis 5}$$
$$s_2 = a \frown [y] \frown c \hspace{3cm} \text{Hypothesis 6}$$

In other words, x and y are the first *distinct* elements of s_1 and s_2 respectively. We have then, according to Hypothesis 3,

$$x \frown \text{conc}(b) = y \frown \text{conc}(c) \hspace{2cm} \text{Derivation 1}$$

and also, since x and y are members of BPR

$$\text{opn}(x) = \text{clo}(x) \hspace{3cm} \text{Derivation 2}$$
$$\text{opn}(y) = \text{clo}(y) \hspace{3cm} \text{Derivation 3}$$

We obviously have either $x \subset y$ or $y \subset x$ since x and y are both distinct prefixes of the same sequence. Suppose that we have $x \subset y$, then Derivation 2 is contradictory with the fact that y is a member of BPR. A similar contradiction arises in the case where $y \subset x$.
End of Proof

We now prove the following:

$$\text{rep} \in T \rightarrowtail \text{BPR}, \hspace{3cm} \text{Property 3.8.12}$$

This property is equivalent to the following (proof left to the reader):

$$\forall n \cdot (n \in \mathbb{N} \Rightarrow$$
$$\text{rep} \triangleright \{s \mid s \in \text{BPR} \wedge \text{size}(s) = n\} \in T \twoheadrightarrow \text{BPR}) \hspace{1cm} \text{Property 3.8.13}$$

Proof
The proof is by strong induction on n (section 3.5.4). We assume

$$n \in \mathbb{N} \hspace{4cm} \text{Hypothesis 1}$$

$$\forall m \cdot (\ m \in \mathbb{N}$$
$$m < n$$
$$\Rightarrow$$
$$\mathsf{rep} \rhd \{s \mid s \in \mathsf{BPR} \ \wedge \ \mathsf{size}\,(s) = m\} \in \mathsf{T} \rightarrowtail \mathsf{BPR} \,) \qquad \text{Hypothesis 2}$$

And we have to prove

$$\mathsf{rep} \rhd \{s \mid s \in \mathsf{BPR} \ \wedge \ \mathsf{size}\,(s) = n\} \in \mathsf{T} \rightarrowtail \mathsf{BPR} \qquad \text{Goal 1}$$

For proving Goal 1, it is sufficient to assume the following:

$$t_1 \in \mathsf{T} \qquad\qquad\qquad\qquad\qquad\qquad\qquad \text{Hypothesis 3}$$
$$t_2 \in \mathsf{T} \qquad\qquad\qquad\qquad\qquad\qquad\qquad \text{Hypothesis 4}$$
$$\mathsf{rep}\,(t_1) \in \{s \mid s \in \mathsf{BPR} \ \wedge \ \mathsf{size}\,(s) = n\} \qquad \text{Hypothesis 5}$$
$$\mathsf{rep}\,(t_1) = \mathsf{rep}\,(t_2) \qquad\qquad\qquad\qquad\quad \text{Hypothesis 6}$$

and we have to prove

$$t_1 = t_2 \qquad\qquad\qquad\qquad\qquad\qquad\qquad \text{Goal 2}$$

From Hypothesis 6, and according to the recursive definition of rep, we have:

$$\mathsf{conc}\,(\mathsf{sns}\,(t_1); \mathsf{rep}) \ = \ \mathsf{conc}\,(\mathsf{sns}\,(t_2); \mathsf{rep}) \qquad \text{Derivation 1}$$

According to Property 3.8.10 and Property 3.8.11, we have then

$$\mathsf{sns}\,(t_1); \mathsf{rep} \ = \ \mathsf{sns}\,(t_2); \mathsf{rep} \qquad\qquad \text{Derivation 2}$$

From which we deduce the following, according to Hypothesis 2 and since the size of $\mathsf{rep}\,(u)$ for each son u of either t_1 or t_2 is certainly smaller than n (that is, the size of $\mathsf{rep}\,(t_1)$):

$$\mathsf{sns}\,(t_1) \ = \ \mathsf{sns}\,(t_2) \qquad\qquad\qquad \text{Derivation 3}$$

Now Goal 2 follows from the injectivity of the function sns as stated in Property 3.8.4.

End of Proof

3.9. Labelled Trees

The trees we have defined in the previous sections are not very interesting because they are too abstract. We have introduced them, however, in order to study the general structure of trees. In practice, we would like to have trees conveying more information. These are the labelled trees. For instance, the following figure shows a tree labelled with natural numbers.

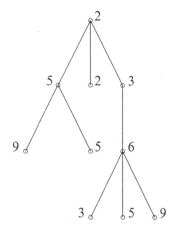

3.9.1. Direct Definition

As shown in the figure of the previous section, each node of a labelled tree is assigned "information" so that the labelled tree can be seen as a function of its nodes to the pieces of information in question. More precisely, a member of the set, tree (s), of labelled trees built on a set s is defined to be a function whose domain is a member of T and whose range is included in s, formally

Syntax	Definition
tree (s)	$\bigcup t \cdot (t \in \mathsf{T} \mid t \rightarrow s)$

3.9.2. Inductive Definition

We now give another definition involving an inductive construction. We first recognize that the set tree (s) is a subset of the set of all partial functions from seq $(\mathbb{N}_1)$ to s, formally

$$\mathsf{tree}\,(s) \subseteq (\mathsf{seq}\,(\mathbb{N}_1) \nrightarrow s)$$

We now define a function cons such that

$$\mathsf{cons} \in s \times \mathsf{seq}\,(\mathsf{seq}\,(\mathbb{N}_1) \nrightarrow s) \rightarrow (\mathsf{seq}\,(\mathbb{N}_1) \nrightarrow s)$$

as follows:

Syntax	Definition
cons	$\lambda(x,t)\cdot((x,t)\in s\times \text{seq}(\text{seq}(\mathbb{N}_1)\twoheadrightarrow s)\mid$ $\{[]\mapsto x\}\cup\bigcup i\cdot(i\in\text{dom}(t)\mid\text{ins}(i)^{-1};t(i)))$

For instance, let t_1, t_2 and t_3 be the following three functions:

$$t_1 = \{[]\mapsto 5,\ [1]\mapsto 9,\ [2]\mapsto 5\}$$

$$t_2 = \{[]\mapsto 2\}$$

$$t_3 = \{[]\mapsto 3,\ [1]\mapsto 6,\ [1,1]\mapsto 3,\ [1,2]\mapsto 5,\ [1,3]\mapsto 9\}$$

We have then

$$\text{cons}(2,[t_1,t_2,t_3]) =$$
$$\{[]\mapsto 2,$$
$$[1]\mapsto 5,\ [1,1]\mapsto 9,\ [1,2]\mapsto 5,$$
$$[2]\mapsto 2,$$
$$[3]\mapsto 3,\ [3,1]\mapsto 6,\ [3,1,1]\mapsto 3,\ [3,1,2]\mapsto 5,\ [3,1,3]\mapsto 9\}$$

We can prove (exercise) that the function cons is injective, formally

---

$$\text{cons}\in s\times\text{seq}(\text{seq}(\mathbb{N}_1)\twoheadrightarrow s)\rightarrowtail(\text{seq}(\mathbb{N}_1)\twoheadrightarrow s)\qquad\text{Property 3.9.1}$$

We then define the following function genltree (s) and its fixpoint tree (s):

Syntax	Definition
genltree (s)	$\lambda z\cdot(z\in\mathbb{P}(\text{seq}(\mathbb{N}_1)\twoheadrightarrow s)\mid\text{cons}[s\times\text{seq}(z)])$
tree (s)	fix (genltree (s))

As a consequence, we have

$$\text{tree}(s) = \text{cons}[s\times\text{seq}(\text{tree}(s))]\qquad\text{Property 3.9.2}$$

As for non-labelled trees in section 3.8.2, we can prove that cons is a bijection provided it is adequately restricted. More formally, we have

---

$(s \times \text{seq}\,(\text{tree}\,(s))) \lhd \text{cons} \;\in\; s \times \text{seq}\,(\text{tree}\,(s)) \rightarrowtail \text{tree}\,(s)$ Property 3.9.3

We now define the two inverses of this function, namely top and sons.

Syntax	Definition
top	$\text{cons}^{-1}\,;\,\text{prj}_1\,(s,\text{seq}\,(\text{tree}\,(s)))$
sons	$\text{cons}^{-1}\,;\,\text{prj}_2\,(s,\text{seq}\,(\text{tree}(s)))$

And we have the following:

$$\text{top} \in \text{tree}\,(s) \rightarrow s$$

$$\text{sons} \in \text{tree}\,(s) \rightarrow \text{seq}\,(\text{tree}\,(s))$$

Conversely, we have the following property:

$\text{top} \otimes \text{sons} \;=\; \text{cons}^{-1} \rhd (s \times \text{seq}\,(\text{tree}\,(s)))$ Property 3.9.4

3.9.3. Induction

As for the set T in section 3.8.3, we can define an induction principle for the set tree (s). By a development very similar to the one we have already done in section 3.8.3, we can deduce the following:

$\forall\, t \cdot (t \in \text{tree}\,(s) \;\wedge$
$\quad \text{sons}\,(t) \in \text{seq}\,(\{\, t \mid t \in \text{tree}\,(s) \;\wedge\; P \,\}) \;\Rightarrow\; P\,)$

$\Rightarrow$

$\forall\, t \cdot (t \in \text{tree}\,(s) \;\Rightarrow\; P)$ Theorem 3.9.1

And, again as in section 3.8.3, we have the following first special case:

$f \in \text{tree}\,(s) \rightarrow u$
$a \subseteq u$
$\forall\, t \cdot (t \in \text{tree}\,(s) \;\wedge\; (\text{sons}\,(t)\,;f) \in \text{seq}\,(a) \;\Rightarrow\; f(t) \in a\,)$ Theorem 3.9.2
$\Rightarrow$
$\forall\, t \cdot (t \in \text{tree}\,(s) \;\Rightarrow\; f(t) \in a)$

---

and the following second special case:

$f \in \text{tree}\,(s) \rightarrow u$

$g \in \text{tree}\,(s) \rightarrow u$

$\forall t \cdot (t \in \text{tree}\,(s) \;\wedge\; (\text{sons}\,(t);f) = (\text{sons}\,(t);g) \;\Rightarrow$
    $f(t) = g(t))$

$\Rightarrow$

$\forall t \cdot (t \in \text{tree}\,(s) \;\Rightarrow\; f(t) = g(t))$

                                                           Theorem 3.9.3

3.9.4. Recursion

Recursion is now defined on $\text{tree}\,(s)$ in a way that is very similar to what has been done in section 3.8.4 for T. More precisely, given two sets s and u and a function g such that

$$g \in s \times \text{seq}\,(u) \rightarrow u$$

we would like to know whether it is possible to build a total function f of the following type:

$$f \in \text{tree}\,(s) \rightarrow u$$

satisfying the following condition (provided it makes sense) valid for each member t of $\text{tree}\,(s)$:

$$f(t) \;=\; g\,(\text{top}\,(t), (\text{sons}\,(t);f))$$

In other words, the value of the function f at t depends on $\text{top}\,(t)$ and on the sequence obtained by applying f to each element composing the sequence $\text{sons}\,(t)$. The construction of the function f follows exactly the same method as the one we have used to construct recursive functions on T in section 3.8.4. We leave it to the reader to carry out the construction of recursion on $\text{tree}\,(s)$.

3.9.5. Operations Defined Recursively

In this section, we define a number of recursive functions on $\text{tree}\,(s)$. These are the prefixed and postfixed flattening of trees. We also redefine the size and the mirror image of a tree.

Syntax	Recursive Definition	Condition
pre (t)	top $(t) \rightarrow$ conc (sons (t) ; pre)	$t \in$ tree (s)
post (t)	conc (sons (t) ; post) $\leftarrow$ top (t)	$t \in$ tree (s)
sizet (t)	succ (sum (sons (t) ; sizet))	$t \in$ tree (s)
mirror (t)	cons (top (t), rev (sons (t) ; mirror))	$t \in$ tree (s)

We have the following property:

mirror ; pre $=$ post ; rev   Property 3.9.5

Proof
We shall prove the following by induction:

$$\forall t \cdot (t \in \text{tree} \,(s) \;\Rightarrow\; \text{pre}\,(\text{mirror}\,(t)) = \text{rev}\,(\text{post}\,(t)))$$

We assume (Theorem 3.9.3)

sons (t) ; mirror ; pre $=$ sons (t) ; post ; rev   Hypothesis 1

And we have to prove

pre (mirror (t)) $=$ rev (post (t))   Goal 1

The proof goes as follows:

pre (mirror (t))
=   definition of pre
top (mirror (t)) $\rightarrow$ conc (sons (mirror (t)) ; pre)
=   definition of mirror
top $(t) \rightarrow$ conc (rev (sons (t) ; mirror) ; pre)
=   since rev (a) ; $f \,=\,$ rev $(a ; f)$
top $(t) \rightarrow$ conc (rev (sons (t) ; mirror ; pre))
=   according to Hypothesis 1
top $(t) \rightarrow$ conc (rev (sons (t) ; post ; rev))
=   since conc (rev $(s ;$ rev)) $=$ rev (conc (s))
top $(t) \rightarrow$ rev (conc (sons (t) ; post))
=   definition of rev
rev (conc (sons (t) ; post) $\leftarrow$ top (t))
=   definition of post
rev (post (t))

End of Proof

We also have the following related property (to be proved by the reader):

---

mirror ; post = pre ; rev   Property 3.9.6

3.9.6. Operations Defined Directly

In this last subsection, we define directly a number of operations on trees. All such operations are concerned with a tree t and a certain node n in it. The first operation yields the rank (rank) of n, then we have an operation yielding the father (father) of n, then the ith son node (son) of n, then the subtree (subt) with root n, and finally the arity (arity) of n.

Syntax	Definition	Condition
rank $(t)(n)$	last (n)	$t \in \text{tree}(s) \ \wedge \ n \in \text{dom}(t) - \{[\,]\}$
father $(t)(n)$	front (n)	$t \in \text{tree}(s) \ \wedge \ n \in \text{dom}(t) - \{[\,]\}$
son $(t)(n)(i)$	$n \leftarrow i$	$t \in \text{tree}(s) \ \wedge \ (n \leftarrow i) \in \text{dom}(t)$
subt $(t)(n)$	cat $(n) ; t$	$t \in \text{tree}(s) \ \wedge \ n \in \text{dom}(t)$
arity $(t)(n)$	size $(\text{sons}(\text{subt}(t)(n)))$	$t \in \text{tree}(s) \ \wedge \ n \in \text{dom}(t)$

3.10. Binary Trees

Binary trees are special case of labelled trees, namely those trees where each node has either no son nodes or exactly two son nodes. The binary trees constructed on a set s, denoted by bin (s), form a subset of the set tree (s). In a binary tree, the arity of each node may only have the value 0 or the value 2. Formally

Syntax	Definition
bin (s)	$\{ t \mid t \in \text{tree}(s) \ \wedge \ \forall n \cdot (n \in \text{dom}(t) \ \Rightarrow \ \text{arity}(t)(n) \in \{0, 2\}) \}$

3.10.1. Direct Operations

Notice first that, since binary trees are labelled trees, all the notations and results we have introduced in section 3.9 are still valid for binary trees. A member of $\text{bin}(s)$ is either a *singleton* binary tree with no son or a *normal* binary tree with exactly two sons. If the information at the top of the tree is x then, in the former case, the tree is denoted by $\langle x \rangle$ and in the latter case it is denoted by $\langle l, x, r \rangle$ where l and r are suppposed to be the two (and exactly two) sons of $\langle l, x, r \rangle$. Conversely, given a normal binary tree t, the first subtree of t is called the left (left) subtree and the second one is called the right (right) subtree. Formally, we have the following definition:

Syntax	Definition	Condition
$\langle x \rangle$	$\text{cons}(x, [\,])$	$x \in s$
$\langle l, x, r \rangle$	$\text{cons}(x, [l, r])$	$x \in s \ \wedge\ l \in \text{bin}(s) \ \wedge\ r \in \text{bin}(s)$
$\text{left}(t)$	$\text{first}(\text{sons}(t))$	$t \in \text{bin}(s) \ \wedge\ \text{sons}(t) \neq [\,]$
$\text{right}(t)$	$\text{last}(\text{sons}(t))$	$t \in \text{bin}(s) \ \wedge\ \text{sons}(t) \neq [\,]$

3.10.2. Induction

In order to perform induction proofs on binary trees, one can of course use the general induction principles presented in section 3.9.3, since binary trees are labelled trees. We propose here another induction scheme specially tailored for binary trees. In order to prove a universal property P for the members of the set $\text{bin}(s)$, we first prove that the property holds for any singleton tree $\langle x \rangle$; this is the **Base Case**. Second, we prove that the property also holds for the normal tree $\langle l, x, r \rangle$ (whatever x) under the hypotheses that it holds for the two trees l and r; this is the **Induction Step**. Formally,

$$
\begin{aligned}
&\forall x \cdot (x \in s \ \Rightarrow\ [t := \langle x \rangle]\, P\,) \\
&\forall (l, r) \cdot ((l, r) \in \text{bin}(s) \times \text{bin}(s) \\
&\qquad\quad [t := l]\, P \\
&\qquad\quad [t := r]\, P \\
&\qquad\quad \Rightarrow \\
&\qquad\quad \forall x \cdot (x \in s \ \Rightarrow\ [t := \langle l, x, r \rangle]\, P\,)) \\
&\Rightarrow \\
&\forall t \cdot (t \in \text{bin}(s) \ \Rightarrow\ P\,)
\end{aligned}
$$

Theorem 3.10.1

We leave it to readers to prove this induction principle for themselves.

3.10.3. Recursion

Likewise, we can define recursive functions on binary trees by using the general scheme developed for labelled trees in section 3.9.4. But there also exists a special recursion scheme for binary trees, which we now quickly present. We are given two sets s and u, and two total functions h and g such that

$$h \in s \to u$$

$$g \in u \times s \times u \to u$$

We would like to construct a function f such that

$$f \in \mathsf{bin}(s) \to u$$

satisfying the following property (if it makes sense):

$$f(\langle x \rangle) = h(x)$$

$$f(\langle l, x, r \rangle) = g(f(l), x, f(r))$$

We leave it to the reader to construct recursive functions on binary trees.

3.10.4. Operations Defined Recursively

Besides the recursive operations we have already introduced for labelled trees in section 3.9.5, which remain valid for binary trees, we can also introduce recursive operations that are specific to binary trees. We also redefine **pre** and **post**.

Syntax	Recursive Definition	Condition
infix $(\langle x \rangle)$	$[x]$	$x \in s$
infix $(\langle l, x, r \rangle)$	infix $(l) \frown [x] \frown$ infix (r)	$l \in \mathsf{bin}(s) \wedge r \in \mathsf{bin}(s)$
pre $(\langle x \rangle)$	$[x]$	$x \in s$
pre $(\langle l, x, r \rangle)$	$[x] \frown$ pre $(l) \frown$ pre (r)	$l \in \mathsf{bin}(s) \wedge r \in \mathsf{bin}(s)$
post $(\langle x \rangle)$	$[x]$	$x \in s$
post $(\langle l, x, r \rangle)$	post $(l) \frown$ post $(r) \frown [x]$	$l \in \mathsf{bin}(s) \wedge r \in \mathsf{bin}(s)$

3.11. Well-founded Relations

In the previous sections of this chapter, we have constructed a number of so-called mathematical objects in a very systematic fashion: in each case, we have used a specific fixpoint (inductive) definition. As a by-product, we have obtained a systematic way of proving universal properties (induction), as well as a systematic way of constructing total functions (recursion). We might wonder whether this can be further generalized so that each of the previous constructions could just appear as a special case of a more general paradigm: this is the subject of this section.

Intuitively, each set s of mathematical objects we have considered in this chapter is characterized by two properties.

First, each "non-basic" member x of s can be constructed (not necessarily in a unique way) by means of other members of s, that are all, in a certain sense, strictly "smaller" than x. For instance, a non-empty finite set can be constructed by adding a *new* element to another finite set; this latter set is thus certainly strictly included in the former (thus strictly "smaller" than the former). The form of the relationship, that holds between "successive" members of the set thus rules out the possibility of "circuits": starting from x and iterating the construction process, we are sure that we will never reach x again. For instance, the process by which we apply iteratively the function succ to a natural number x, never leads to x again (that process, however, can be continued indefinitely).

Second, and contrary to what may happen to the previous construction process, the (not necessarily unique) destruction (the inverse of construction) process by which a member x of s is decomposed into its constituent parts, is characterized by the fact that it cannot be continued for ever: at some point in the destruction process (that is, after a *finite* number of destructions), we necessarily reach some "basic" members that cannot be further destroyed. In other words, we have no infinite "destruction" chains. For instance, the process by which we apply iteratively the function pred (the inverse of succ) to a natural number x, necessarily leads to 0 (a non-destructible element of $\mathbb{N}$) after a finite number of iterations. Likewise, the process by which we remove an element from a non-empty finite set cannot be continued indefinitely: we shall necessarily reach the empty set (which is not further destructible) after a finite number of iterations.

We notice that the second property includes the first one, because, in case the first one did not hold, then the possibility of having "constructive" circuits would certainly rule out the finiteness of the destruction process (since we would then obviously have some "destructive" circuits).

After what we have emphasized in the previous paragraphs, it turns out that we are not so much interested in the set s itself, but rather in the "destructive" relationship, say r, that holds between the elements of s. What we would like to formalize is this idea that the destruction process *cannot be applied for ever*. Of course, we would like to perform this formalization without any reference to the notion of "finiteness", or, of course, to the iterates of the relation r, because such concepts have themselves been defined inductively.

A relation r (from s to s) that has the above property is said to be a *well-founded* relation. By extension, the set s is said to be well-founded by the relation r. In what follows, we shall define these notions rigorously. Then we shall prove that well-founded sets have the induction and recursion properties we mentioned at the begining of this section. Finally, we shall propose a sufficient condition for proving that a set is well-founded (once we already have at our disposal another well-founded set).

3.11.1. Definition

Consider a set s and a relation r from s to s:

$$r \in s \leftrightarrow s$$

If the relation r is *not* well-founded then there should certainly exist a non-empty subset p of s:

$$p \subseteq s \wedge p \neq \varnothing$$

such that for all x in p there exists a y in p such that $(x, y) \in r$:

$$\forall x \cdot (x \in p \Rightarrow \exists y \cdot (y \in p \wedge (x, y) \in r))$$

This simply means that all members of p are members of infinite chains of elements related through r. After the definition of the inverse image of a set under a relation, the above condition can be made more concise as follows:

$$p \subseteq r^{-1}[p]$$

We notice that the empty set clearly bears that property. As a consequence, r is a well-founded relation (that is, wfd (r)) if and only if the only subset p of s bearing the above property is the empty set, formally:

Syntax	Definition	
wfd (r)	$\forall p \cdot (p \in \mathbb{P}(s) \wedge p \subseteq r^{-1}[p] \Rightarrow p = \varnothing)$	(1)

We then have the following alternative definitions whose equivalence with the previous is easy to establish:

Syntax	Definition	
wfd (r)	$\text{union}(\{p \mid p \in \mathbb{P}(s) \;\wedge\; p \subseteq r^{-1}[p]\}) = \varnothing$	(2)
wfd (r)	$\text{inter}(\{p \mid p \in \mathbb{P}(s) \;\wedge\; \overline{p} \subseteq r^{-1}[\overline{p}]\}) = s$	(3)

In formula (3) (as well as in the remaining part of this section), $\overline{p}$ is a short-hand for $s - p$. These three conditions equally characterize well-founded relations and, by extension, well-founded sets.

3.11.2. Proof by Induction on a Well-founded Set

Given a set s, that is supposed to be well-founded by a relation r, we shall propose a sufficient condition for proving a universal property of the following form:

$$\forall x \cdot (x \in s \;\Rightarrow\; P(x))$$

where $P(x)$ is a certain predicate depending upon the variable x. The above property to be proved can be rewritten equivalently as follows:

$$\forall x \cdot (x \in s \;\Rightarrow\; x \in s \wedge P(x))$$

that is

$$s \subseteq \{x \mid x \in s \wedge P(x)\}$$

that is

$$\{x \mid x \in s \wedge \neg P(x)\} = \varnothing$$

After definition (1) of the previous section, this last condition is implied by the following one:

$$\{x \mid x \in s \wedge \neg P(x)\} \;\subseteq\; r^{-1}[\{x \mid x \in s \wedge \neg P(x)\}]$$

that is

$$\forall x \cdot (x \in s \wedge \neg P(x) \;\Rightarrow\; \exists y \cdot (y \in s \wedge \neg P(y) \wedge (x,y) \in r))$$

that is

$$\forall x \cdot (x \in s \wedge \neg \exists y \cdot (y \in s \wedge \neg P(y) \wedge (x,y) \in r) \;\Rightarrow\; P(x))$$

that is

$$\forall x \cdot (x \in s \wedge \forall y \cdot (y \in s \wedge (x,y) \in r \;\Rightarrow\; P(y)) \;\Rightarrow\; P(x))$$

that is

$$\forall x \cdot (x \in s \;\wedge\; \forall y \cdot (y \in r[\{x\}] \;\Rightarrow\; P(y)) \;\Rightarrow\; P(x))$$

To summarize, we thus have the following Induction Rule:

$$\forall x \cdot (x \in s \;\wedge\; \forall y \cdot (y \in r[\{x\}] \;\Rightarrow\; P(y)) \;\Rightarrow\; P(x))$$
$$\Rightarrow$$
$$\forall x \cdot (x \in s \;\Rightarrow\; P(x))$$

The Well-founded Set Induction Rule

In other words, in order to prove that a certain property $P(x)$ holds for each member x of a set s, supposed to be well-founded by a relation r, it is sufficient to prove that $P(x)$ holds under the assumption that it already holds for each member of the set $r[\{x\}]$.

3.11.3. Recursion on a Well-founded Set

In this section, we show how to construct "recursively" a certain total function f on a set s, that is well-founded by a relation r. We have already encountered that mechanism for the set of natural numbers (section 3.5.6), that of finite sequences (section 3.7.3) and that of trees (sections 3.8.4, 3.9.4, 3.10.3): in each case, the idea was to consider the "definition" of a certain total function in terms of its value at the "basic" elements and also at some "constructed" points in terms of the corresponding "constructing" points. We now generalize the previous approaches to well-founded sets: the idea is to suppose, quite naturally, that the value of the function, at some point x of the well-founded set s, depends on the values of the function at the (constructing) points of x: these are exactly those points that are the members of the set $r[\{x\}]$. More precisely, we suppose that we are given a set t and a certain function g of the following type:

$$g \in (s \twoheadrightarrow t) \rightarrow t$$

We shall then show that there exists a certain function f, of the following type:

$$f \in s \rightarrow t$$

such that we have, for each member x of s:

$$f(x) \;=\; g\,(r[\{x\}] \lhd f)$$

In order to eliminate the variable x, we define the function image (r), which is such that the following holds:

$$\text{image}\,(r)(x) \;=\; r[\{x\}]$$

Clearly, image (r) is a well-defined function of the following type:

$$\mathsf{image}\,(r) \in s \to \mathbb{P}(s)$$

We have thus

$$f(x) \;=\; g(\mathsf{image}\,(r)(x) \lhd f)$$

We now rewrite $\mathsf{image}\,(r)(x) \lhd f$ as follows:

$$\mathsf{res}\,(f)(\mathsf{image}\,(r)(x))$$

Note that $\mathsf{res}\,(f)$ is not yet defined formally. It is just, for the moment, a device to allow the elimination of x. In fact, we obtain

$$f(x) \;=\; g(\mathsf{res}\,(f)(\mathsf{image}\,(r)(x)))$$

That is, by eliminating x

$$\boxed{\; f \;=\; g \;\circ\; \mathsf{res}\,(f) \;\circ\; \mathsf{image}\,(r) \;}$$

As expected, we obtain a fixpoint equation. It now remains for us to define $\mathsf{res}\,(f)$ more rigorously. For the moment, we shall suppose that f is a binary relation (later, we shall prove that f is, in fact, a total function). We have thus

$$f \;\in\; s \leftrightarrow t$$

Since we already have

$$\mathsf{image}\,(r) \;\in\; s \to \mathbb{P}(s)$$

and we also have

$$g \;\in\; (s \nrightarrow t) \to t$$

then, a priori, $\mathsf{res}\,(f)$ is a binary relation, connecting the range of $\mathsf{image}\,(r)$ to the domain of g. It is thus typed as follows:

$$\mathsf{res}\,(f) \;\in\; \mathbb{P}(s) \leftrightarrow (s \nrightarrow t)$$

Note that this typing is only dictated by the shape of the fixpoint equation

$$f \;=\; \mathsf{image}\,(r);\ \mathsf{res}\,(f);\ g$$

We then define $\mathsf{res}\,(f)$ as follows:

Syntax	Definition
$\mathsf{res}\,(f)$	$\{\,a, h \mid (a, h) \in \mathbb{P}(s) \times (s \nrightarrow t) \;\wedge\; h \in a \to t \;\wedge\; h \subseteq (a \lhd f)\,\}$

In other words, res (f) connects every subset a of s with each total function h from a to t such that h is included in the relation r restricted to a. Clearly, if $a \triangleleft f$ is a *total function* from a to t, then the corresponding h is unique (it is exactly $a \triangleleft f$). We thus have the following result:

$$(a \triangleleft f) \in a \to t \quad \Rightarrow \quad \text{res}\,(f)[\{a\}] = \{a \triangleleft f\}$$ Property 3.11.1

After Knaster-Tarski theorem (that is Theorem 3.2.5), which we can apply since the expression $g \circ \text{res}\,(f) \circ \text{image}\,(r)$ is clearly monotone in f, the equation

$$f = g \circ \text{res}\,(f) \circ \text{image}\,(r)$$

has a least solution, which is, a priori, a binary relation from s to t. We now show that this solution is also a total function from s to t. In other words, we would like to prove the following:

$$f \in s \to t$$

that is (according to Property 2.5.1)

$$\forall x \cdot (x \in s \quad \Rightarrow \quad (\{x\} \triangleleft f) \in \{x\} \to t\,)$$

This will be proved by means of the Well-founded Set Induction Rule proposed at the end of the previous section. It thus suffices to prove the following:

$$\begin{aligned} \forall x \cdot (\; & x \in s \;\; \wedge \\ & \forall y \cdot (y \in \text{image}\,(r)(x) \;\; \Rightarrow \;\; \{y\} \triangleleft f \in \{y\} \to t\,) \\ & \Rightarrow \\ & \{x\} \triangleleft f \in \{x\} \to t\,) \end{aligned}$$

Since the condition

$$\forall y \cdot (y \in \text{image}\,(r)(x) \;\; \Rightarrow \;\; \{y\} \triangleleft f \in \{y\} \to t\,)$$

is clearly equivalent to

$$(\text{image}\,(r)(x) \triangleleft f) \in \text{image}\,(r)(x) \to t$$

it suffices to prove the following:

$$\begin{aligned} \forall x \cdot (\; & x \in s \;\; \wedge \\ & (\text{image}\,(r)(x) \triangleleft f) \in \text{image}\,(r)(x) \to t \\ & \Rightarrow \\ & \{x\} \triangleleft f \in \{x\} \to t\,) \end{aligned}$$ Property 3.11.2

Proof
We assume

$$x \in s$$ Hypothesis 1

$$(\text{image}\,(r)(x) \triangleleft f) \in \text{image}\,(r)(x) \to t$$ Hypothesis 2

According to Property 3.11.1 (equating a with image $(r)(x)$), we can deduce the following from Hypothesis 2:

$$\text{res}\,(f)\,[\{\,\text{image}\,(r)(x)\,\}] \;=\; \{\text{image}\,(r)(x)\lhd f\} \qquad\qquad \text{Derivation 1}$$

And we have to prove

$$\{x\}\lhd f \;\in\; \{x\}\rightarrow t \qquad\qquad\qquad\qquad\qquad \text{Goal 1}$$

We have the following:

$$\{x\}\lhd f$$
$$=$$
$$\{x\}\lhd(g\circ\text{res}\,(f)\circ\text{image}\,(r))$$
$$=$$
$$\{x\}\times(g\circ\text{res}\,(f)\circ\text{image}\,(r))\,[\{x\}]$$
$$=$$
$$\{x\}\times g\,[\text{res}\,(f)[\text{image}\,(r)\,[\{x\}]]]$$
$$=$$
$$\{x\}\times g\,[\text{res}\,(f)[\{\,\text{image}\,(r)(x)\,\}]]$$
$$= \qquad\qquad\qquad\qquad\qquad\qquad\qquad\qquad\qquad \text{Derivation 1}$$
$$\{x\}\times g\,[\{\,\text{image}\,(r)(x)\lhd f\,\}]$$
$$=$$
$$\{x\}\times\{\,g(\text{image}\,(r)(x)\lhd f)\,\}$$

As a consequence, we have then indeed:

$$\{x\}\lhd f \;\in\; \{x\}\rightarrow t$$

End of Proof

Notice that the result established in this section can be further generalized (exercise 36) so that the value of the function f at some point x also depends on x. For this, we need a certain function g of the following type:

$$g \;\in\; s\times(s\twoheadrightarrow t)\;\rightarrow\;t$$

so that the recursive definition of f is the following:

$$\boxed{\quad f(x) \;=\; g\,(x,(r[\{x\}]\lhd f))\quad}$$

3.11.4. Proving Well-foundedness

In this section we shall prove an important result which states how a certain relation can be proved to be well-founded, provided we already know that another relation is well-founded. As we shall see, this result has very strong connections with the theory of loops (chapter 9) and with that of refinement (chapter 11). We are given a well-founded relation r from a certain set s to itself. Given another relation r' from a certain set s' to itself, we wonder whether there exists a possible connection between the two so that the well-foundedness of r implies that of r'. The idea is to have a certain link between the two sets s' and s under the form of a *total* binary relation v:

$$v \in s' \leftrightarrow s \quad \wedge \quad \mathrm{dom}\,(v) = s'$$

Moreover, the following condition linking r, r' and v should hold:

$$v^{-1}\,;r' \subseteq r\,;v^{-1}$$

The complete formal result is thus the following:

$r \in s \leftrightarrow s$
$r' \in s' \leftrightarrow s'$
$v \in s' \leftrightarrow s$
$\mathrm{dom}\,(v) = s'$ Theorem 3.11.1
$v^{-1}\,;r' \subseteq r\,;v^{-1}$
$\mathrm{wfd}\,(r)$
$\Rightarrow$
$\mathrm{wfd}\,(r')$

Proof

We have the following hypotheses:

$$\mathrm{dom}\,(v) = s' \qquad\qquad\qquad \text{Hypothesis 1}$$

$$v^{-1}\,;r' \subseteq r\,;v^{-1} \qquad\qquad\qquad \text{Hypothesis 2}$$

Hypothesis 2 is obviously equivalent to

$$r'^{-1}\,;v \subseteq v\,;r^{-1} \qquad\qquad\qquad \text{Derivation 1}$$

Since r is well-founded, we also have (according to definition (1) of section 3.11.1)

$$\forall p \cdot (p \in \mathbb{P}(s) \ \wedge \ p \subseteq r^{-1}\,[p] \ \Rightarrow \ p = \varnothing) \qquad \text{Hypothesis 3}$$

And we have to prove that r' is well-founded, that is

$$\forall p' \cdot (p' \in \mathbb{P}(s') \ \wedge \ p' \subseteq r'^{-1}\,[p'] \ \Rightarrow \ p' = \varnothing) \qquad \text{Goal 1}$$

We assume

$$p' \subseteq r'^{-1}\,[p'] \qquad\qquad\qquad \text{Hypothesis 4}$$

And we have to prove the following:

$$p' = \varnothing \qquad\qquad\qquad \text{Goal 2}$$

From Hypothesis 4, we deduce

$$v[p'] \subseteq v[r'^{-1}\,[p']] \qquad\qquad\qquad \text{Derivation 2}$$

From Derivation 2, Derivation 1, and the transitivity of inclusion, we deduce

$$v[p'] \subseteq r^{-1}[v[p']]$$ Derivation 3

As a consequence, and according to Hypothesis 3, we deduce

$$v[p'] = \varnothing$$ Derivation 4

And now, Goal 2 follows, according to Hypothesis 1.
End of Proof

3.11.5. An Example of a Well-founded Relation

As an example of a well-founded relation, we consider a relation r typed as follows:

$$r \in \mathbb{N} \times \mathbb{N} \leftrightarrow \mathbb{N} \times \mathbb{N}$$

such that the following holds:

$$(a, b), (c, d) \in r \;\;\Leftrightarrow\;\; (a > c) \vee (a = c \wedge b > d)$$

Clearly, this relation is well-founded. For this we have to exhibit, for each non-empty subset s of $\mathbb{N} \times \mathbb{N}$, an element that is not related, through r, to any element of s. Notice that the set s is a binary relation from $\mathbb{N}$ to $\mathbb{N}$. Here is the element in question:

$$x, \min(s[\{x\}]) \qquad \text{where} \qquad x = \min(\mathrm{dom}(s))$$

A classical example of a recursive function defined on the set $\mathbb{N} \times \mathbb{N}$, well-founded by the above relation, is the Ackermann function:

$$
\mathrm{ack}(n, m) = \begin{cases}
m + 1 & \text{if } n = 0 \\
\mathrm{ack}(n - 1, 1) & \text{if } n \neq 0 \wedge m = 0 \\
\mathrm{ack}(n - 1, \mathrm{ack}(n, m - 1)) & \text{if } n \neq 0 \wedge m \neq 0
\end{cases}
$$

This definition indeed obeys the recursion scheme of section 3.11.3: the value of ack at the point (n, m), is defined in terms of various values of ack at various points that are certainly "strictly smaller" than (n, m), according to the definition of r.

3.11.6. Other Examples of Non-classical Recursions

Usually, recursive functions on sequences are defined "from the left". That is, one defines the function at the point $x \rightarrow s$ (the sequence obtained by inserting x at the beginning of the sequence s) in terms of the value of the function at s. One might also consider recursion "from the right" where one would define the function at the point $s \leftarrow x$ (the sequence obtained by appending x to the sequence s) in terms of the value of the function at s. A third way is one where the recursive function is defined "from both sides". For example, we can define the following function for reversing a sequence:

$$
\begin{cases}
\text{revlr}\,([\,]) & = \quad [\,] \\
\text{revlr}\,([\,x\,]) & = \quad [\,x\,] \\
\text{revlr}\,(x \rightarrow s \leftarrow y) & = \quad y \rightarrow \text{revlr}\,(s) \leftarrow x
\end{cases}
$$

And we can define the following function for partitioning an integer sequence by means of a certain integer n:

$$
\begin{cases}
\text{partlr}\,(n)(\,[\,]) & = \quad [\,] \\
\text{partlr}\,(n)(\,[\,x\,]) & = \quad [\,x\,] \\
\text{partlr}\,(n)(x \rightarrow s \leftarrow y) & = \begin{cases}
x \rightarrow \text{partlr}\,(n)(s \leftarrow y) & \text{if } x \leq n \,\wedge\, y \leq n \\
\text{partlr}\,(n)(x \rightarrow s) \leftarrow y & \text{if } n < x \,\wedge\, n < y \\
y \rightarrow \text{partlr}\,(n)(s) \leftarrow x & \text{if } n < x \,\wedge\, y \leq n \\
x \rightarrow \text{partlr}\,(n)(s) \leftarrow y & \text{if } x \leq n \,\wedge\, n < y
\end{cases}
\end{cases}
$$

As a third example, we can define as follows a function looking for the smallest element of a non-empty integer sequence:

$$
\begin{cases}
\text{minlr}\,([\,x\,]) & = \quad x \\
\text{minlr}\,(x \rightarrow s \leftarrow y) & = \begin{cases}
\text{minlr}\,(s \leftarrow y) & \text{if } y \leq x \\
\text{minlr}\,(x \rightarrow s) & \text{if } x < y
\end{cases}
\end{cases}
$$

According to what we have presented in this section, these rewriting rules constitute perfectly rigorous definitions of total functions on sequences: the well-founded relation we consider is that relating a sequence with all the sequences of strictly smaller sizes (clearly a well-founded relation). In section 10.4.6, we shall study such functions again and see how we can implement them by means of loops. Proofs that these definitions indeed define what we expect can be conducted using the well-founded induction rule.

3.12. Exercises

1. Prove the following equivalence between the two generalized intersection operators. Prove similar results for generalized union.

$$\mathsf{inter}\,(u) \;=\; \bigcap y \cdot (\,y \in u \mid y\,)$$
$$\bigcap x \cdot (\,x \in s \mid E\,) \;=\; \mathsf{inter}\,(\,\mathsf{ran}\,(\lambda x \cdot (\,x \in s \mid E\,)))$$

2. Prove the distributivity and associativity properties of the generalized intersection and union operators as presented in section 3.1.

3. Given a set s and two non-empty subsets a and b of $\mathbb{P}(s)$, prove the following:

$$\mathsf{inter}\,(a \cup b) \;=\; \mathsf{inter}\,(a) \cap \mathsf{inter}\,(b)$$
$$\mathsf{union}\,(a \cup b) \;=\; \mathsf{union}\,(a) \cup \mathsf{union}\,(b)$$

4. Prove Theorem 3.1.3 and Theorem 3.1.4 establishing that $\mathsf{union}\,(u)$ is a least upper bound of the set (of sets) u.

5. Given a monotone function f from $\mathbb{P}(s)$ to itself. Prove that $\mathsf{fix}\,(f)$ and $\mathsf{FIX}\,(f)$ are respectively the least and greatest fixpoint of f.

6. In this exercise we are given a set s, and any subset of s of the form $s - u$ is denoted by $\bar{u}$. Moreover, given a function f from $\mathbb{P}(s)$ to itself, we define the function $\mathsf{dual}\,(f)$ as follows:

$$\mathsf{dual}\,(f) \;=\; \lambda x \cdot (\,x \in \mathbb{P}(s) \mid \overline{f(\bar{x})}\,)$$

Prove then that the operator FIX can be defined in terms of the operator fix as follows:

$$\mathsf{FIX}\,(f) \;=\; \overline{\mathsf{fix}\,(\mathsf{dual}\,(f))}$$

7. We are given two sets s and t, an injective function f from s to t and an injective function g from t to s. Prove that there exists a bijection from s to t. Hint: Find a subset x of s and a subset y of t such that $(x \lhd f) \cup (g^{-1} \rhd y)$ is indeed a bijection from s to t; then eliminate, say y, and prove that the remaining variable x is the solution of a certain fixpoint equation. This result is called the Cantor-Schroeder-Bernstein theorem.

8. Given two finite subsets a and b of a set s, prove that $a \cup b$ and $a \cap b$ are finite.

9. Prove Theorem 3.4.1 stating that a set that is Dedekind-infinite is indeed infinite.

10. Prove that the set $\mathbb{N}$ is infinite.

11. Prove the reciprocal of Theorem 3.4.1 stating that an infinite set is Dedekind-infinite.

12. Prove Property 3.5.11 stating that the maximum of a finite subset of $\mathbb{N}$ belongs to it.

13. Given a natural number n, prove that there does not exist any natural number m situated in between n and $\mathsf{succ}(n)$.

14. Given two natural numbers m and n, prove the following:

$$m + n = \mathsf{succ}^m(n)$$
$$m \times n = (\mathsf{succ}^m)^n(0)$$

15. Given two natural numbers m and n, prove the following:

$$\forall k \cdot (k \in \mathbb{N} \ \wedge \ m < n \ \Rightarrow \ m + k < n + k)$$
$$\forall k \cdot (k \in \mathbb{N}_1 \ \wedge \ m < n \ \Rightarrow \ m \times k < n \times k)$$
$$\forall k \cdot (k \in \mathbb{N} \ \wedge \ m + k = n + k \ \Rightarrow \ m = n)$$
$$\forall k \cdot (k \in \mathbb{N}_1 \ \wedge \ m \times k = n \times k \ \Rightarrow \ m = n)$$

16. Given a set s, an element a and a function g such that:

$$a \in s$$
$$g \in \mathbb{N} \times s \rightarrow s$$

construct a function f from $\mathbb{N}$ to s obeying the following properties (hint: first construct a certain recursive function obeying the classical recursion presented in section 3.5.6):

$$f(0) = a$$
$$\forall n \cdot (n \in \mathbb{N} \ \Rightarrow \ f(n+1) = g(n, f(n)))$$

Apply this extended recursive scheme to the definition of various functions.

17. Prove some of the properties of the arithmetic operators of section 3.5.7.

18. Prove Property 3.5.13, namely

$$\mathsf{plus}(m) \in \mathbb{N} \rightarrowtail \{n \mid n \in \mathbb{N} \ \wedge \ m \leq n\}$$

19. Given a natural number n and a positive natural number m, prove the following:

$$\{x \mid x \in \mathbb{N} \ \wedge \ n < m \times \mathsf{succ}(x)\} \neq \varnothing$$

20. Prove the stated properties of section 3.5.7 concerning the logarithms.

21. Prove the stated properties of section 3.5.8. concerning the iterate of a relation.

22. We are given a set s and two total functions f and g from s to s such that:

$$f \, ; g \, = \, g \, ; f$$

Given then two natural numbers m and n, prove the following properties:

$$f^m \, ; g^n \, = \, g^n \, ; f^m$$
$$(f \, ; g)^n \, = \, f^n \, ; g^n$$

23. Prove the following for each natural number n:

$$n = \mathsf{succ}^n \, (0)$$

24. Prove Property 3.5.14, namely:

$$\mathbb{F}(s) \, = \, \bigcup n \cdot (n \in \mathbb{N} \mid \mathsf{genfin}\,(s)^n(\{\varnothing\}))$$

25. Given two finite subsets a and b of a set s, prove the following

$$\mathsf{card}\,(a \cup b) \, = \, \mathsf{card}\,(a) \cup \mathsf{card}\,(b) - \mathsf{card}\,(a \cap b)$$

26. Given two finite sets s and t, prove the following:

$$\mathsf{card}\,(s \times t) \, = \, \mathsf{card}\,(s) \times \mathsf{card}\,(t)$$

27. Prove the properties of section 3.5.10 concerning the closure of a relation.

28. Justify the construction of recursion on finite sequences (section 3.7.1).

29. Prove the properties of section 3.7.3 concerning the proposed recursively defined operations on finite sequences.

30. Prove the properties of section 3.7.3 concerning the proposed directly defined operations on finite sequences.

31. Prove Property 3.8.3.

32. Given two members t_1 and t_2 of the set T of trees, prove that $t_1 \cup t_2$ and $t_1 \cap t_2$ are also members of T.

33. Prove Property 3.9.1.

34. Prove Property 3.9.3.

35. Justify the construction of recursion on labelled trees (section 3.9.4).

36. Given a well-founded relation r from a certain set s to itself, given another set t and a certain function g of type:

$$g \, \in \, s \times (s \nrightarrow t) \, \rightarrow \, t$$

prove that there exists a total function f from s to t such that the following holds at each point x of s:

$$f(x) \;=\; g\,(x,r[\{x\}] \lhd f)$$

37. Given a well-founded relation r from s to s, prove that the relation r^+ (the transitive, non-reflexive, closure of r) is also well founded (Hint: use Theorem 3.11.1). By applying this result to the relation pred, give another proof of the strong induction principle for natural numbers (Theorem 3.5.2).

38. Prove that the recursive definitions given in section 3.11.6 for revlr, partlr and minlr indeed define what they are supposed to define: the reversing, the partitionning, and the minimal element of a sequence respectively.

PART TWO

Abstract Machines

CHAPTER 4

Introduction to Abstract Machines

THE intention of this chapter is to present a notation for *specifying* programs to be written later in imperative programming languages such as PASCAL, C, MODULA, ADA, BASIC, or even in assembly code. Put together, the elements of this notation form a very simple *pseudo-programming* language.

The pseudo-programs that we shall write using this notation will not be executed on a computer nor, a fortiori, be submitted to any kind of tests. Rather, and more importantly, they will be able to be submitted to a *mathematical analysis* and this will be made possible because each construct of the notation receives a precise axiomatic definition. For doing so, we shall use the technique of the *weakest pre-condition* as introduced by Dijkstra [1].

The notation contains a number of constructs that look like the ones encountered in every imperative programming language, namely assignment and conditionals. But it also contains unusual features such as pre-condition, multiple assignment, bounded choice, guard, and even unbounded choice, which are very important for specifying and designing programs although, and probably because, they are not always executable or even implementable.

Although it might seem strange at first glance, the notation does not contain any form of sequencing or loop. Yet the use of such features forms the basis of any decent imperative program. The reason for not having these constructs here is that our problem is not, *for the moment*, that of writing programs, rather it is that of specifying them: sequencing and loop certainly pertain to the *how* domain which characterizes programs, but not to the *what* domain which characterizes specifications. In fact, both these features (sequencing and loop) will be introduced in chapter 9, and in chapter 11 the foundations of the techniques to transform *pseudo*-programs into *real* ones (refinement) will be described.

A very central feature of the notation is that of an *abstract machine*. This is a concept that receives various names in various programming contexts. For instance, some related concepts are those of *class* (SIMULA), *abstract data type* (CLUE), *module* (MODULA-2), *package* (ADA), *object* (EIFFEL), etc. This concept is important because it allows us to organize large specifications as independent pieces having well-defined interfaces.

In sections 4.1 to 4.7, we introduce the main components of the Abstract Machine Notation (AMN): variables, invariant, and operations. We also introduce the first two constructs of the Generalized Substitution Language (GSL): simple substitution and its first generalization, the pre-conditioned substitution. We also insist on the notion of proof obligation. In sections 4.8, 4.9 and 4.10 we explain how abstract machines can be parameterized and initialized and also how operations can themselves be parameterized. In section 4.11, we develop some ideas about various specification styles.

In sections 4.12 to 4.21, we introduce the remaining parts of GSL, namely multiple substitution, bounded choice, guard, conditional substitution and unbounded choice. We also present the notion of contextual information. Finally, we present a feature by which we can explicitly introduce some macro-definitions to be used in a specification.

Our intention in the present chapter is only to give a *practical and semi-formal* introduction to AMN and GSL as well as some rationale behind the choices that have been made. For the moment, we give a rather intuitive presentation so that the reader feels more comfortable. The notations will be introduced in full, together with the complete corresponding formal apparatus, in the next chapter.

4.1. Abstract Machines

When given the task of formally specifying a software system, one is usually confronted with some basic but difficult questions: How and where do we start? What kind of filter should we apply to our reading of the usually enormous documentation describing the system requirements? What is and what isn't important in this documentation?

In order to give the beginning of an answer to questions of this sort, it is fundamental to have at one's disposal a simple general model of what software systems are supposed to be. Using this model, we can read the description of a given system more easily; that is, we can try to fill in the components of our general model with the specific material we are analyzing.

Our model is the *abstract machine*, and it is very simple: whatever the size of a system (or sub-system), we claim that we can always regard it as a sort of pocket calculator. What characterizes such a pocket calculator is the presence of an invisible memory and a number of keys. The memory (or better the values stored in it) forms the *state* of this machine, whereas the various keys are the *operations* that a user is able to activate in order to modify the state in question.

From now on, the expression *software system* will be understood in terms of the abstract machine model: that is, in terms of a state and of various operations modifying that state. The analysis of such systems consists in studying their *statics* and *dynamics*. The statics corresponds to the definition of the state whereas the dynamics corresponds to that of the operations.

4.2. The Statics: Specifying the State

For defining the state of a software system, we have, among others, to determine two kinds of things: first, the *variables* which constitute the various components of the state; second, the *invariant* which is a logical statement making clear what the static laws of the system are. The invariant is defined in terms of the variables by means of the formal languages of *Predicate Calculus* and *Set Theory* as presented in chapters 1, 2 and 3.

As an elementary example, suppose that we want to specify a seat reservation system for, say, a one night event. Our state is very elementary: we have one variable, say *seat*, which corresponds to the number of available seats. The invariant simply states that *seat* must be a natural number. Note that this is a very simplistic model indeed: for instance, seats have no specific serial number (they are all alike), and the maximum number of seats is not specified; more details will be introduced later. This model can be described formally as follows:

```
MACHINE

    booking

VARIABLES

    seat

INVARIANT

    seat ∈ ℕ

END
```

As can be seen, our abstract machine is formally described by means of a number of clauses. In this example, we have only three clauses (later, of course, we shall have more), which are the following:

1. The MACHINE clause introduces the name of the machine. This will be extended to parameterized names in section 4.8.

2. The VARIABLES clause introduces the variables (components) of the state of the machine. In our example, we only have one variable; later we shall present machines with several variables. Such variables will be introduced as a list of identifiers separated by commas.

3. The INVARIANT clause introduces the invariant property of the state of the machine. The invariant consists of a number of *Predicates* (chapters 1 and 2) separated by the conjunction operator ∧ (section 1.2.1). In our example we have

just one conjunct. The invariant must contain enough conjuncts to allow for the *typing* of each of the variables (section 2.2). There is no separation between the typing conjuncts and the other conjuncts as is the case in a Z schema [2].

4.3. The Dynamics: Specifying the Operations

As explained in section 4.1, the dynamics of an abstract machine is expressed through its operations. The rôle of an operation, as later executed by the computer, is to *modify the state* of the abstract machine, and this, of course, *within the limits of the invariant*, as we shall explain in section 4.5. For example, in the case of our little booking system, we might define two operations: one to make a reservation, say book, and the other to cancel a reservation, say cancel. The identifiers book and cancel are the names of the corresponding operations whose specification is supposed to be the formal text that follows the '$\widehat{=}$' sign.

```
MACHINE

    booking

VARIABLES

    seat

INVARIANT

    seat ∈ ℕ

OPERATIONS

    book  ≘  ··· ;

    cancel  ≘  ···

END
```

We have added an extra clause, the OPERATIONS clause, which contains a list of the various operation specifications.

Note that the definition of an abstract machine only gives its potential "user" the ability to activate the operations, *not to access its state directly*. This so-called *Hiding Principle* [3] is very important because it will allow us (the designers) to *refine* the machine by making changes of variables and corresponding changes in the operations, while keeping their names (chapter 11).

Consequently, although he has the *illusion* of using the machine operations as described by their specifications, the "user" is in fact using their ultimate refinements in the form of programs written in a conventional programming language. This approach will be described and justified in chapters 11 and 12.

As a rule of thumb, when defining the operations of an abstract machine, do not reason in terms of an "external user" activating the operations you have in mind. Rather think in terms of constructing a relevant Instruction Set that you might like to have at your disposal in order to build some interface that would be closer to the "end-user". In this way, your machine will be more adaptable to the *unintended* use that might come later. It might also be *simpler to refine* (chapter 11).

In fact, as we shall see in chapter 12, the "user" of an abstract machine will always be *yet another abstract machine*.

4.4. Before-after Predicates as Specifications

The specification of an operation is a description of certain *relevant properties* that the intended state modification, as implied by the operation, must fulfil. Later (chapter 11) we shall see how such a specification will be *refined* so that these original relevant properties are kept unchanged. Ultimately, we shall obtain some running code whose execution will thus be guaranteed to satisfy the original specification (chapter 13).

For expressing formally such relevant properties of the state modification, a very popular technique consists in writing down a logical statement, a predicate, relating the values of the state variables, as they are just before the operation takes place, to the values of the same variables, as they will be just after it. In what follows, we call such a logical statement a *before-after* predicate. This technique is the one used in VDM [4] and in Z [2].

In order to write down a *before-after* predicate, a typical convention is to denote the values of the variables just after the operation has been "executed" by priming the corresponding identifiers. For instance, in our previously defined seat reservation system, the operation cancel can be specified by the following *before-after* predicate

$$seat' = seat + 1$$

This is so because we are interested in a subsequent operation whose execution will change the state in such a way that there is one more available seat *after* the operation has taken place in comparison to the number of available seats just *before*.

Note that this form of specification, where the *after-value* is functionally dependent on the *before-value*, is by no means the most general case. The most general case is the one where the before-value and the after-value are related in a *non-deterministic* way. For instance, the following before-after predicate simply specifies that the after-value is greater than the before-value, and thus is clearly not deterministically defined in terms of the before-value:

$$seat' > seat$$

4.5. Proof Obligation

Once an operation has been specified, we have to prove that its specification *preserves the invariant*. In other words, we have to prove that the operation does not violate the static laws of the system. If this is the case, and provided the operation satisfies its specification, then the operation will also preserve the invariant at run-time. In this section, we study the form taken by such a proof obligation in the case of our simple example dealing with the operation cancel of the simple abstract machine *booking*.

We have to prove that, provided the invariant holds before the operation cancel is "executed", that is, in our case, if the predicate $seat \in \mathbb{N}$ holds, then it also holds after the operation, that is for all $seat'$ related to $seat$ by the *before-after* predicate $seat' = seat + 1$. Formally, we obtain the following logical statement which obviously holds:

$$seat \in \mathbb{N} \quad \Rightarrow \quad \forall\, seat' \cdot (seat' = seat + 1 \quad \Rightarrow \quad seat' \in \mathbb{N})$$

As can be seen, the right-hand side predicate of this implication is a predicate of the *before-value only*: it is the minimal (weakest) condition that should hold *before* the operation takes place, in order for that operation, as specified by the before-after predicate, to (re-)establish the invariant. The overall proof obligation then states that the condition $seat \in \mathbb{N}$ is *stronger* than the condition guaranteeing that the invariant is re-established.

4.6. Substitutions as Specifications

This section is intended to show that, in our little example and as far as the proof obligation for invariance preservation is concerned, the specification we have provided could have been equally well formalized by means of a *substitution* (section 1.3.4). We first quickly remind the reader of the concept of substitution. Second, we show how the introduction of that concept will allow us to *simplify* the proof obligation, as provided in the previous section.

Let P be a *Formula*, x be a *Variable* and E an *Expression*, then the following construct:

$$[x := E]P$$

denotes the formula obtained after replacing all free occurrences of x in P by E. Here is an example:

$$[x := x + 1]\,(x \in \mathbb{N})$$

This obviously reduces to the following after performing the substitution:

$$x + 1 \in \mathbb{N}$$

In the previous section, we obtained the following logical statement as a proof obligation for invariance preservation in our little example:

$$seat \in \mathbb{N} \ \Rightarrow \ \forall\, seat' \cdot (\, seat' = seat + 1 \ \Rightarrow \ seat' \in \mathbb{N})$$

We now show that this statement can be simplified by using a substitution instead of a *before-after* predicate. The simplification is due to the following general law of Predicate Calculus called the **One Point Rule** (section 1.4) where x is a *Variable*, E is an *Expression* and P is a *Predicate*:

$$\forall\, x \cdot (x = E \ \Rightarrow \ P) \ \Leftrightarrow \ [x := E]P \qquad \text{if } x \text{ has no free occurrence in } E$$

Applying this law to our case, we obtain the following (since $seat'$ is obviously not a free variable of the formula $seat + 1$):

$$seat \in \mathbb{N} \ \Rightarrow \ [seat' := seat + 1]\,(seat' \in \mathbb{N})$$

yielding

$$seat \in \mathbb{N} \ \Rightarrow \ seat + 1 \in \mathbb{N}$$

that is

$$\boxed{seat \in \mathbb{N} \ \Rightarrow \ [seat := seat + 1]\,(seat \in \mathbb{N})}$$

This new statement is interesting because it does not contain any explicit reference to the *primed* variable (that is, the after-value), nor does it contain any quantifier. In fact, it is worth comparing it with the *equivalent* statement we presented in the previous section. Clearly, it is shorter and more readable.

More generally, let the invariant $seat \in \mathbb{N}$ be denoted by I and the substitution $seat := seat + 1$ be denoted by S, then the previous proof obligation can be rewritten simply as

$$\boxed{I \ \Rightarrow \ [S]\,I}$$

That statement can be read: "If the invariant I holds then the substitution S *establishes* the predicate I". It simply means that the invariant I is stronger than the condition which *guarantees* that the substitution S establishes I. In other words, if we place ourselves in a situation where the invariant I holds, then we can be sure that S establishes I. That is, having "performed" substitution S, our resulting state still satisfies I.

In this section, we have shown, *at least in our little example and as far as the proof obligation is concerned*, that the specification of an operation can be equivalently stated either as a *before-after* predicate or as a *substitution*. From here on, we shall adopt the latter formulation.

Here then is the eventual specification of our operation *cancel*:

$$\text{cancel} \;\;\hat{=}\;\; \text{BEGIN} \quad seat := seat + 1 \quad \text{END}$$

We have enclosed the substitution describing the specification of the operation within a BEGIN ... END parenthetical structure.

In what follows, our intention is to *generalize* this concept of substitution (hence the term *generalized substitution*) and thus envisage various systematic ways of constructing the formal specifications of abstract machine operations.

4.7. Pre-conditioned Substitution (Termination)

In this section we turn our attention to another kind of problem, namely that of specifying an operation that is *not necessarily always usable*. For instance, suppose we would like to specify the booking of a (single) seat in our little booking system. Written without special care, the specification is simply

$$\text{book} \;\;\hat{=}\;\; \text{BEGIN} \quad seat := seat - 1 \quad \text{END}$$

This is so because the number of available seats should be one less after the booking has taken place. However, if we try to state the proof obligation as before, we obtain

$$seat \in \mathbb{N} \;\; \Rightarrow \;\; [seat := seat - 1]\,(seat \in \mathbb{N})$$

that is, equivalently

$$seat \in \mathbb{N} \;\; \Rightarrow \;\; seat - 1 \in \mathbb{N}$$

This is obviously not valid when *seat* is equal to 0. In this case, the effect of the operation, as specified by the substitution $seat := seat - 1$, might be to *break the invariant* and, as a probable consequence, to break the (real) machine (in other words, to crash the program).

In order to make this specification work, we have to add to it an "ad-hoc" *pre-condition* explaining in which case (and in which case only) one is entitled to *activate* the corresponding operation. Obviously, in our case, the book operation can only be activated when the number of available seats is positive (in fact, this is even the essence of the concept of reservation). As a consequence, the specific pre-condition to be added is

$$0 < seat$$

We thus propose to *generalize* simple substitutions by giving the possibility of having such ad-hoc pre-conditions incorporated in them. We first define a notation for this generalization, and then we give a meaning to it. Given a predicate P and a substitution S, we denote our generalization by the following construct (pronounced "P pre S"):

$$P \mid S$$

Note that, in practice, we adopt the following notation which can also be presented vertically:

Syntax	Definition
PRE P THEN S END	$P \mid S$

With this definition in mind, we can now write the specification of our **book** operation as follows:

$$
\begin{array}{l}
\textbf{book} \quad \widehat{=} \\
\quad \text{PRE} \\
\qquad 0 < seat \\
\quad \text{THEN} \\
\qquad seat := seat - 1 \\
\quad \text{END}
\end{array}
$$

Informally speaking, we read this specification as follows: "The operation **book** is to be activated only when $0 < seat$. Activating this operation while $\neg\,(0 < seat)$ holds *may result in an incorrect behaviour*". This interpretation should not be confused with the one we shall give below to the following "conditional" substitution:

$$
\begin{array}{l}
\textbf{book} \quad \widehat{=} \\
\quad \text{IF} \quad 0 < seat \quad \text{THEN} \\
\qquad seat := seat - 1 \\
\quad \text{END}
\end{array}
$$

In the latter case, as we shall see in section 4.13, the interpretation of the formal text of the operation is similar to that of the corresponding conditional statement of programming languages: if the predicate $0 < seat$ holds then the specification is defined by means of the substitution $seat := seat - 1$, and if the predicate $0 < seat$ does not hold then the specification is defined (implicitly) by the substitution $seat := seat$. So in this case the "user" of the substitution has *nothing to prove* before using the operation, whereas in the former case the operation must only be used if the pre-condition has been *proved* to hold.

It remains for us to make precise what it means for a substitution of the form $P \mid S$ to establish a post-condition R. We propose the following decomposition:

$$[P \mid S] R \iff P \wedge [S] R$$

When the pre-condition P does not hold, the operation specified by the (generalized) substitution $P \mid S$ is not guaranteed to achieve anything, say R, since $P \wedge [S]R$ never holds (whatever R), a fact in accordance with our intuition of what a crash is: whatever the expected outcome, it cannot be established. Such a substitution, which is not able to establish anything is said to be a *non-terminating* substitution. In section 6.3.1, we shall give a more formal status to this notion.

We have now to adjust our proof obligation since, obviously, when an operation has a non-trivial pre-condition, the invariant preservation should only be proved *under the extra hypothesis of the pre-condition*, formally

$$I \wedge P \quad \Rightarrow \quad [P \mid S] I$$

Note that this reduces to

$$I \wedge P \quad \Rightarrow \quad [S] I$$

In other words, the *active* part, S, of the generalized substitution $P \mid S$ should establish the invariant I under the conjunction of I and the pre-condition P. For instance, in the case of our book operation, the proof obligation becomes

$$seat \in \mathbb{N} \ \wedge \ 0 < seat \quad \Rightarrow \quad [seat := seat - 1] \, (seat \in \mathbb{N})$$

that is, equivalently, the following statement which clearly holds:

$$seat \in \mathbb{N} \ \wedge \ 0 < seat \quad \Rightarrow \quad seat - 1 \in \mathbb{N}$$

4.8. Parameterization and Initialization

In this section we present two more features of abstract machines: namely, parameterization and initialization. As our first feature, we introduce a mechanism allowing us to *parameterize* abstract machines. The rôle of abstract machine parameters is to *leave open* a number of *finite dimensions* of the machine, dimensions which we might later *instantiate* (section 7.2.3 and section 12.1.4).

Such parameters are understood to be either simple *scalars*, or finite and non-empty *sets*. These are the *implicit constraints* of the parameters. In order to make clear which parameters are scalars and which are sets, we agree to write the latter with *upper case* letters only. In practice, parameters are disposed between brackets situated just after the name of the machine.

We also have the possibility to introduce some *explicit constraints* to hold between the parameters of an abstract machine: this will be done by means of a new clause, the CONSTRAINTS clause. Within such a clause, the constraints are expressed in the form of a number of conjoined predicates. This clause will allow us to make precise the types of the scalar formal parameters and a number of extra constraints for the set formal parameters. Notice that the set formal parameters are *independent* sets. For instance, no constraint can state that one set formal parameter is a subset of another one. A scalar formal parameter, however, can be a member of a set formal parameter. In order to be able to type the formal scalar parameter, we suppose that the following universal constants minint and maxint are implicitly defined, together with the abreviations INT, NAT and NAT$_1$:

$$maxint \in \mathbb{N}$$

$$minint \in \mathbb{Z}$$

$$INT \;\hat{=}\; minint \mathbin{..} maxint$$

$$NAT \;\hat{=}\; 0 \mathbin{..} maxint$$

$$NAT_1 \;\hat{=}\; 1 \mathbin{..} maxint$$

In section 5.2.6, we shall give more details about such pre-defined constants.

As a second feature for this section, we now introduce the INITIALIZATION clause. Its purpose is to make possible the assignment of initial values to the variables of the machine. Such values, of course, must be proved to be such that the invariant holds. The initialization takes the form of a substitution. As we shall see below, such an initialization can be non-deterministic. Examples of abstract machines with non-deterministic initialization are shown in section 4.19.

MACHINE

booking (*max_seat*)

CONSTRAINTS

max_seat $\in$ NAT

VARIABLES

  seat

INVARIANT

  $seat \in 0 \,..\, max\_seat$

INITIALIZATION

  $seat := max\_seat$

OPERATIONS

  book $\widehat{=}$
      PRE
          $0 < seat$
      THEN
          $seat := seat - 1$
      END;

  cancel $\widehat{=}$
      PRE
          $seat < max\_seat$
      THEN
          $seat := seat + 1$
      END

END

In this example, we parameterize our previous *booking* machine by taking the maximum number of available seats, *max_seat*, to be a (scalar) parameter of the machine. Obviously then, the *seat* variable is initialized to *max_seat*.

4.9. Operations with Input Parameters

In order to introduce our next topic, parameterized operations, we extend our example machine as we had it in the previous section. Both operations, book and cancel, in that example are certainly too primitive. An obvious generalization consists in offering "users" of the machine the possibility to book or cancel several seats at a time. In order to do so, we enlarge the concept of a simple operation name, such as cancel or book, to that of a *parameterized* name such as cancel(*nbr*) or book(*nbr*): here *nbr* is a *formal input parameter* supposed to denote the number of seats we intend to book or cancel. For instance, cancel(*nbr*) is now the name of an operation specified as follows:

cancel(*nbr*) $\hat{=}$

    PRE

        $nbr \in \mathsf{NAT} \;\; \wedge \;\; seat + nbr \leq max\_seat$

    THEN

        $seat := seat + nbr$

    END

As can be seen, the pre-condition of this parameterized operation contains quite naturally the condition which the formal parameter *nbr* must fulfil for the operation to be meaningful: in our case $seat + nbr$ must obviously be smaller than or equal to max_seat. We can figure that out by writing down the corresponding proof obligation

$$seat \in 0 \mathinner{.\,.} max\_seat$$
$$nbr \in \mathsf{NAT}$$
$$seat + nbr \leq max\_seat$$
$$\Rightarrow$$
$$[seat := seat + nbr]\,(seat \in 0 \mathinner{.\,.} max\_seat)$$

yielding the obviously valid statement

$$seat \in 0 \mathinner{.\,.} max\_seat$$
$$nbr \in \mathsf{NAT}$$
$$seat + nbr \leq max\_seat$$
$$\Rightarrow$$
$$seat + nbr \in 0 \mathinner{.\,.} max\_seat$$

Similarly, book(*nbr*) is the name of an operation specified as follows:

book(*nbr*) $\hat{=}$

    PRE

        $nbr \in \mathsf{NAT} \;\;\; \wedge$

        $nbr \leq seat$

    THEN

        $seat := seat - nbr$

    END

Note that for both these new versions of the operations, the pre-condition is exactly the one that is needed in order to preserve the invariant. In some cases, however, stronger conditions are required by the very semantics of the operation.

For instance, we could have insisted on the user having the possibility to book no more than, say five, seats at a time, and this would be specified as follows:

$$
\begin{aligned}
&\text{book}(nbr) \quad \hat{=} \\
&\quad \text{PRE} \\
&\qquad nbr \in \text{NAT} \quad \wedge \\
&\qquad nbr \leq seat \quad \wedge \\
&\qquad nbr \leq 5 \\
&\quad \text{THEN} \\
&\qquad seat := seat - nbr \\
&\quad \text{END}
\end{aligned}
$$

It is important to note that the *parameterization mechanism* we have introduced in this section does not give an operation specification the status of what is usually called a *procedure* in an ordinary programming language. It can certainly be the case that an operation will be later implemented as a *procedure*, but it can also be implemented by an "in-line" expansion. The only requirement we have is of a syntactic nature: the formal parameter of a parameterized operation should be a (list of distinct) variable(s) distinct from the state variables of the machine.

4.10. Operations with Output Parameters

In this section we introduce the concept of an operation providing results. If we look at our previous example, it is clear that our machine *booking*(*max_seat*) lacks an operation telling us what the number of available seats is. Clearly, we need that information to be able to use our machine in a safe way, that is to test the various pre-conditions *on the user's side*. Otherwise we run the risk of calling one of the operations *outside its pre-condition*. But, remember, no abstract machine "user" can access the state of a machine directly (again, this is so according to the Hiding Principle). One thus has to have an operation yielding (part of) the state value in order to (indirectly) access it. In our case, this can be done in a very simple way through an operation whose header is the following:

$$
value \longleftarrow \text{val\_seat}
$$

As can be seen, we have extended the concept of an operation name one step further. Here *value* is the formal result of the operation. As for formal input parameters in the previous section, our only requirement about formal output parameters is of a syntactic nature: the formal output parameter(s) of an operation must be a (list of distinct) variable(s) distinct from the input parameters (if any) and also distinct from the state variables of the machine. The complete specification of this operation is thus the following:

$$\boxed{value \longleftarrow \mathsf{val\_seat} \;\;\widehat{=}\;\; \text{BEGIN}\;\; value := seat \;\;\text{END}}$$

The output parameter, *value*, is used in the left-hand part of a simple substitution as if it were a normal state variable. One might think that such a trivial operation would induce some very inefficient running code. In fact, this is not the case as the operation might be implemented "in line". The reader has to remember that the question of efficiency must *not* be our concern *for the moment*. Specifying only consists of building *understandable models*, not *executable programs*.

4.11. Generous versus Defensive Style of Specification

In this section we would like to explore two distinct style of specification: the so-called *generous* style and the so-called *defensive* style.

The generous style corresponds to what we have done in the previous sections with our *booking(max_seat)* machine. In this case, operations are defined together with "elaborate" pre-conditions depending on the machine state: namely $seat + nbr \le max\_seat$ for the cancel operation and $nbr \le seat$ for the book operation. As we know, the invariant is preserved provided the operations are called within their pre-conditions. Since these pre-conditions *depend on the value of the state variable*, we need some *inquiry* operations in order to be able to verify beforehand and from the "user's side" that the pre-condition holds before calling an operation. In other words, the correctness of the machine depends on the "user's code" being *proved* to effectively call the various operations within their pre-condition. This style is called "generous" simply because it does not suspect the "user" of being lax in doing such proofs.

Contrary to what we have described in the previous paragraph, in the defensive style the pre-conditions of the operations do *not* depend on the machine state. As a consequence, in order to be safe the operation specifications have to contain some *internal test*. In other words, in order to preserve the invariant, the specification does not rely on any elaborate proof made on the "user's code". The specification "defends" itself against bad usage.

We do not claim here that one style is "better" than the other. We think, however, that the generous style is more in the spirit of the constructive method presented here. The defensive style corresponds to the classical style of people programming directly without prior specification and design. However, sometimes we shall have no choice but to use the defensive style: this will occur when some limitations will not be known before the implementation is reached. In section 4.14, we give an example showing how this can be done. For the moment, let us illustrate the defensive style by re-specifying our two previous operations.

In our previous version of the little booking system, we have stated that the operation book could crash if activated with a parameter *nbr* whose value is larger than that of the number, *seat*, of available seats. We now suppose instead that the user is interested in being able to generate some sort of "error report" in this case. As the exact content of the message is certainly not a concern for the abstract machine itself, we simply require that our operation book delivers a result telling us whether the operation has been successful or not. We therefore suppose that we have at our disposal a set *REPORT* defined as follows: $REPORT = \{good, bad\}$. In section 4.17, we shall see where such a set has to be defined.

The result of our operation will be a value from this set. The "user" of the operation then only needs to consult the result of the operation to know whether the call has been successful or not. He can then generate a message whose exact content is up to him. Now the new specification of our operation book will be like this:

$$
\begin{array}{l}
report \longleftarrow \mathsf{book}(nbr) \quad \hat{=} \\
\quad \text{PRE} \\
\qquad nbr \in \mathsf{NAT} \\
\quad \text{THEN} \\
\qquad \text{IF} \quad nbr \leq seat \quad \text{THEN} \\
\qquad\qquad report,\ seat := good,\ seat - nbr \\
\qquad \text{ELSE} \\
\qquad\qquad report := bad \\
\qquad \text{END} \\
\quad \text{END}\ ;
\end{array}
$$

Likewise, the new specification of the operation cancel is as follows:

$$
\begin{array}{l}
report \longleftarrow \mathsf{cancel}(nbr) \quad \hat{=} \\
\quad \text{PRE} \\
\qquad nbr \subset \mathsf{NAT} \\
\quad \text{THEN} \\
\qquad \text{IF} \quad seat + nbr \leq max\_seat \quad \text{THEN} \\
\qquad\qquad report,\ seat := good,\ seat + nbr \\
\qquad \text{ELSE} \\
\qquad\qquad report := bad \\
\qquad \text{END} \\
\quad \text{END}
\end{array}
$$

In these operations we have a number of new features. First a new construct, the

IF ... THEN ... ELSE ... END construct, and second the use of a multiple substitution. In the forthcoming sections, we shall introduce these features gradually.

4.12. Multiple Simple Substitution

In this section, we re-introduce the concept of *multiple* substitution (section 1.5). This will be done by considering the THEN part of our last version of the book operation.

$$report,\ seat := good,\ seat - nbr$$

Here, we have specified part of our operation in the form of a multiple substitution. We remind the reader that a construct such as

$$[x,\ y := E,\ F]\,P$$

where x and y are two distinct *Variables*, E and F two *Expressions* and P a *Formula* (that is, either a *Predicate* or an *Expression*), denotes P where free occurrences of x and y are replaced *simultaneously* by E and F respectively. Note that multiple substitution is not a genuinely new concept since it can be defined as follows in terms of simple substitutions. This definition can be extended to more variables.

$$[x,\ y := E,\ F]\,P \quad \Leftrightarrow \quad [z := F][x := E][y := z]\,P$$

In this equivalence, the variable z is supposed to be distinct from x and y and non-free in P, E and F. Such a variable is said to be *fresh*.

Next is an example where we can see how two variables x and y are swapped:

$$[x,\ y := y,\ x]\,(x > y)$$
$$\Leftrightarrow$$
$$[z := x][x := y][y := z]\,(x > y)$$
$$\Leftrightarrow$$
$$[z := x][x := y]\,(x > z)$$
$$\Leftrightarrow$$
$$[z := x]\,(y > z)$$
$$\Leftrightarrow$$
$$y > x$$

As can be seen, we have indeed got the intuitive effect, namely the multiple (simultaneous) replacement of x by y and vice-versa.

Sometimes, large multiple substitutions become unreadable. In this case, we adopt the following alternative notation, which can also be presented vertically:

Syntax	Definition
$x := E \ \ \|\| \ \ y := F$	$x, y := E, F$

4.13. Conditional Substitution

Our previous version of the book operation shows a *conditional substitution* defined by means of the IF ... THEN ... ELSE ... END construct:

$$\text{IF} \quad nbr \leq seat \quad \text{THEN}$$
$$report, seat := good, seat - nbr$$
$$\text{ELSE}$$
$$report := bad$$
$$\text{END}$$

Although such a construct might seem to be self explanatory, we regard it as already too complicated. In fact, we have here two independent concepts. First, the concept of a *choice* between two substitutions. Second, the concept of a substitution "performed" under an *assumption*. For instance, the first substitution is performed under the assumption that *nbr* is smaller than or equal to *seat*, whereas the second substitution is performed under the negation of the previous assumption. We would like to capture these two concepts separately. This is what we are going to do in the two subsequent sections.

4.14. Bounded Choice Substitution

We first have to give a notation to express the *choice* between two substitutions S and T. We borrow the notation invented by Dijkstra in the slightly different context of guarded commands, namely (pronounced "S *choice* T")

$$S \ [] \ T$$

In order to define this construct (that is, to define what it means to establish a certain post-condition R), we have to understand that it introduces a certain kind of *bounded non-determinism*.

More precisely, if an operation is *specified* as the choice between S or T, this does not necessarily mean (although it might) that a corresponding implementation must be executed on a kind of random device choosing at the last moment which statement to execute. It may mean instead that the future *implementer* of this specification has the freedom to choose to implement either the operation corresponding to substitution S or that corresponding to substitution T. This understanding gives us a clue: whatever the future choice of the implementer, the corresponding substitution must achieve the post-condition R. As a consequence, we define

$$[S \,[]\, T]\, R \quad \Leftrightarrow \quad [S]\, R \,\wedge\, [T]\, R$$

In practice, we adopt the following alternative notation which can also be presented vertically:

Syntax	Definition
CHOICE S OR T OR $\cdots$ OR U END	$S \,[]\, T \,[]\, \cdots \,[]\, U$

As an example, we now present a machine encapsulating a sequence and offering various operations. Among them the push operation (the only one we present) adds an element at the end of the sequence: this will clearly augment the size of the encapsulated sequence.

In this machine, the maximum size of the sequence is not limited by any fixed or parameterized value. However, clearly, the future implementation of this machine will have some practical limitations. As we have no idea what this limitation could be *now*, our only possibility is to have the operation push returning a *report* telling us whether the operation has been successful or not. In the case it has not been successful, then the sequence must not be modified. The assignment of any value to *report* is done in a non-deterministic way since we have no clue to how the implementation will ever limit the size of the sequence.

In this example, a new clause can be seen: the SETS clause. This will be explained in more detail in section 4.17.

MACHINE

    Sequence(VALUE)

SETS

    REPORT $=$ {*good*, *bad*}

```
VARIABLES

    sequence

INVARIANT

    sequence ∈ seq(VALUE)

INITIALIZATION

    sequence := [ ]

OPERATIONS

    report ⟵ push(vv)  ≙
        PRE
            vv ∈ VALUE
        THEN
            CHOICE
                report := good   ||
                sequence := sequence ← vv
            OR
                report := bad
            END
        END

    ...

END
```

4.15. Guarded Substitution (Feasibility)

A substitution to be performed under the *assumption* of a predicate P is said (after E.W. Dijkstra) to be *guarded* by P. As a notation for the guarded substitution, we have also borrowed the one invented by Dijkstra in the slightly different context of guarded commands, namely (pronounced "*P guards S*")

$$P \implies S$$

where P is a predicate and S is a substitution. Here S is performed under the assumption P, and we consequently define

$$[P \Longrightarrow S]\,R \quad \Leftrightarrow \quad (P \;\Rightarrow\; [S]\,R)$$

Note that we have an implication sign here. As a consequence, when P does not hold, the substitution $P \Longrightarrow S$ is able to establish anything. Such a substitution is said to be *non-feasible*. In section 6.3.2, we shall give a more formal status to this notion.

It is important to see clearly the distinction between the pre-conditioned substitution $P\,|\,S$ and the guarded substitution $P \Longrightarrow S$. In the former case, in order to establish a post-condition, you must also prove P. In the latter case, in order to establish a post-condition, you may assume P. For instance, in the former case, when P does not hold, the substitution is said to abort because it cannot establish anything. In the latter case, when P does not hold, the substitution is said to be non-feasible because it is able to establish anything.

As a shorthand, we can now define the conditional substitution as follows:

Syntax	Definition
IF P THEN S ELSE T END	$(P \Longrightarrow S) \;[\!]\; (\neg P \Longrightarrow T)$

Consequently, we have the following property

$$[\text{IF } P \text{ THEN } S \text{ ELSE } T \text{ END}]\,R \quad \Leftrightarrow \quad (P \;\Rightarrow\; [S]\,R) \wedge (\neg P \;\Rightarrow\; [T]\,R)$$

It is also very convenient to define the *small* conditional, namely

$$\text{IF} \quad P \quad \text{THEN} \quad S \quad \text{END}$$

We would like to define this construct as a special case of the *large* conditional, that is, as one where we *do nothing* when the predicate P does not hold. However, such a substitution does not exist yet: it will be defined in the next section.

4.16. A Substitution with no Effect

We use the classical symbol skip to denote the substitution that "does" nothing. Obviously, for any post-condition R, we have

$$[\text{skip}]\,R \quad \Leftrightarrow \quad R$$

We can now define the *small* conditional as follows

Syntax	Definition
IF P THEN S END	IF P THEN S ELSE skip END

Consequently, we have the following property

$$[\text{IF } P \text{ THEN } S \text{ END}] R \quad \Leftrightarrow \quad (P \Rightarrow [S] R) \wedge (\neg P \Rightarrow R)$$

4.17. Contextual Information: Sets and Constants

In this section we introduce more features of abstract machines: such features will allow us to define *given sets* (types) within an abstract machine, and also *constants*, and finally *properties* built on those sets and constants.

A given set is first introduced by its *name*. Then we may find an *enumeration* of its distinct elements. Alternatively, the set is left unspecified: it is only implicitly assumed to be *finite* and non-empty. In the former case the set is said to be *enumerated*, whereas in the latter case, it is said to be *deferred*. In section 12.1.7, we shall see how deferred sets can be instantiated. Given sets are introduced by means of the sets clause.

Given sets, be they enumerated or deferred, as well as abstract machine parameters which are sets, all denote *independent types*. As a consequence, no predicate in the properties clause can impose any equality or inclusion relationships between them. Likewise enumerated sets must have *distinct* elements.

Constants are simply listed in a CONSTANTS clause in exactly the same way that variables are listed in the VARIABLES clause.

Finally, properties take the form of various conjoined predicates involving the constants and the given sets. This is done in a PROPERTIES clause which plays, with regard to the constants, the same rôle as the INVARIANT clause plays with regard to the variables. Note that the explicit value of each constant is not necessarily determined in the property clause: constants are thus possibly defined *non-deterministically* as is normal in a specification. As for the deferred sets, we shall see in section 12.1.7 how constants will be given their eventual values.

The formal parameter of a machine cannot be referenced in the PROPERTIES clause. The rationale for this limitation will appear clearly in the sequel (section 12.1.7): this is essentially to avoid circularities. The only thing that one has to remember at this level is that constants and deferred sets are valued *from the inside*, whereas machine formal parameters are valued *from the ouside*.

The constants are either scalar constants of a set, or total functions from a set (or a cartesian product of sets) to a set, or else subsets of a scalar set. In other words, the constants should all be declared within the PROPERTIES clause in one of the following ways:

$$T \qquad\qquad A \rightarrow T \qquad\qquad A \times \cdots \times B \rightarrow T \qquad\qquad \mathbb{P}(S)$$

where each of T, A, ..., B, S can be either a deferred set, an enumerated set or an interval built from numeric constants or literals.

The reason for these special constraints on constants comes from their *visibility rule*. In fact, contrary to what happens for the variables of an abstract machine, the constants of an abstract machine *do not obey the Hiding Principle*. That is, constants are not encapsulated within the machine where they are declared. This means that constants cannot be refined, as the variables are (section 11.2). Constants can only be given final values (section 12.1.7). As a consequence, the constants will thus be implemented in the executable code either as initialized *scalar constants* or as initialised *array constants*.

If more elaborate constants are needed, abstract (hidden) constants can always be defined as will be explained in section 4.21. In that section, we shall also define the so-called concrete variables.

We now present another example. Its first purpose is to illustrate the features we have introduced in this section. Its second purpose is to prepare for the introduction of our last generalized substitution, the unbounded choice substitution, which we shall present in the next section.

In this example, we describe a data-base machine whose function is to keep information about people in a population of individuals. The individuals present in the data-base are supposed to have a sex, *male* or *female*, and a status, *living* or *dead*. So, quite naturally, we have a SETS clause comprising the two enumerated sets SEX and $STATUS$ and also a deferred set, $PERSON$, denoting the persons that are now (or will be later) part of the data-base. We also define a constant that is used to define the cardinal of the deferred set $PERSON$ in the PROPERTIES clause.

MACHINE

    Data_Base

SETS

    $PERSON$;
    $SEX = \{male, female\}$;
    $STATUS = \{living, dead\}$

CONSTANTS

max_pers

PROPERTIES

$max\_pers \in NAT_1$ $\wedge$
$card(PERSON) = max\_pers$

The abstract machine comprises three variables called *person*, *sex* and *status*. The variable *person* is supposed to be a subset of the set *PERSON* corresponding to the individuals whose information is effectively recorded in the data-base. The variables *sex* and *status* are supposed to be total functions from the set *person* to the sets *SEX* and *STATUS* respectively. Note that the complement of the set *person* with respect to *PERSON* represents the "individuals" which are not yet recorded in the data base.

VARIABLES

person, *sex*, *status*

INVARIANT

$person \subseteq PERSON$ $\wedge$
$sex \in person \rightarrow SEX$ $\wedge$
$status \in person \rightarrow STATUS$

INITIALIZATION

$person, sex, status := \varnothing, \varnothing, \varnothing$

Our machine has two operations. The first operation, death(pp), is parameterized and its formal parameter, pp, is specified quite naturally in the pre-condition: it should be a *person* that is of status *living*. The second operation, *baby* $\longleftarrow$ newborn(sx), has a formal result, *baby*, which is the new-born (as chosen *somehow* by the machine). The input parameter sx denotes the sex of the new-born. For the moment, we only define the first operation completely.

```
OPERATIONS

    death(pp)  ≙
        PRE
            pp ∈ person      ∧
            status(pp) = living
        THEN
            status(pp) := dead
        END;

    baby ⟵ newborn(sx)  ≙  ···

END
```

Note that the "substitution"

$$status(pp) := dead$$

in the death operation is a convenient shorthand for

$$status := status ⧦ \{pp \mapsto dead\}$$

where $⧦$ is the relation *overrriding* operator (section 2.4.2). In other words, we only change the value of the function *status* for the argument *pp*. More generally, given a relational variable r, we have

Syntax	Definition
$r(x) := E$	$r := r ⧦ \{x \mapsto E\}$

Let us prove that the specification of the operation $death(pp)$ preserves the invariant. This can be stated formally as follows:

$STATUS = \{living, dead\}$
$SEX = \{male, female\}$
$person \subseteq PERSON$
$sex \in person \rightarrow SEX$
$status \in person \rightarrow STATUS$
$pp \in person$
$status(pp) = living$
$\Rightarrow$
$[status := status ⧦ \{pp \mapsto dead\}]$
$\quad (person \subseteq PERSON \wedge sex \in person \rightarrow SEX \wedge status \in person \rightarrow STATUS)$

Note that the definitions of the sets $STATUS$ and SEX are extra assumptions in the proof obligation. By performing the substitution and removing unnecessary hypotheses or obvious conclusions, we are left with the following to be proved (by the reader)

$$STATUS = \{living, dead\}$$
$$status \in person \rightarrow STATUS$$
$$pp \in person$$
$$\Rightarrow$$
$$status \Leftarrow \{pp \mapsto dead\} \in person \rightarrow STATUS$$

In order to specify the operation $baby \longleftarrow$ newborn(sx), we need an extra generalized substitution, the unbounded choice substitution, which we introduce in the next section.

4.18. Unbounded Choice Substitution

In section 4.14 we defined the bounded choice substitution $S [\!] T$ together with the following:

$$[S [\!] T] R \quad \Leftrightarrow \quad [S] R \wedge [T] R$$

The underlying idea of the *unbounded choice* substitution is to generalize the choice substitution. Let S be a substitution depending on a variable z (a variable which does not appear anywhere in the invariant), and suppose that we would like to describe a new substitution standing for all possible substitutions S whatever the value of z. In other words, we offer the implementer the possibility to choose *any* specific value of z for a future implementation of the operation. We will use the following notation for such a substitution (pronounced "*any* z S"):

$$@z.S$$

Establishing a post-condition R (containing no free occurrence of z) of this substitution is obviously defined as the establishment of R by S whatever z (whatever the future choice), formally

$$[@z \cdot S] R \quad \Leftrightarrow \quad \forall z \cdot [S] R$$

As can be seen, we have generalized the conjunction appearing in the case of the choice operator to a universal quantifier. We now have unbounded non-determinism. Note that this unbounded choice substitution corresponds to a weaker form of the "specification statement" of C. Morgan [5] which combines the notion of pre-condition and that of unbounded choice. Note that, in practice, we adopt the following first notation which can also be presented horizontally. The second notation, introducing the operator $:\in$ (pronounced "becomes a member of"), is a convenient way to express a non-deterministic choice in a set:

Syntax	Definition	Condition
ANY z WHERE P THEN S END	$@z \cdot (P \implies S)$	
$x :\in E$	ANY z WHERE $z \in E$ THEN $x := z$ END	$z \setminus E$

We are now in a position to specify the operation $baby \longleftarrow newborn(sx)$ of our little data-base. The purpose of this operation is to introduce a new living individual. Besides the obvious fact that he is *not yet present* in the data-base, we impose no special constraint about the new individual. Since the definition of the abstract machine does not say anything about the particular nature of the set $PERSON$, we cannot specify any particular value for the new individual: we have no choice but to use an unbounded choice substitution.

$baby \longleftarrow \mathsf{newborn}(sx) \;\; \widehat{=}$
    PRE
        $PERSON - person \neq \varnothing \;\; \wedge$
        $sx \in SEX$
    THEN
        ANY $angel$ WHERE
            $angel \in PERSON - person$
        THEN
            $person := person \cup \{angel\} \;\; \|$
            $sex(angel) := sx \;\; \|$
            $status(angel) := living \;\; \|$
            $baby := angel$
        END
    END

As can be seen, we have required in the pre-condition of this operation that the set *PERSON* − *person* be non-empty. As a consequence, the non-deterministic choice of any element in that set is indeed *feasible*.

Our purpose is now to present another example where unbounded choice will be used for specifying an operation. We show a machine encapsulating an array formalized as a total function, *table*, from a set *INDEX* to a set *VALUE*, both of which are parameters of the machine.

MACHINE

    Array (*INDEX* , *VALUE*)

VARIABLES

    table

INVARIANT

    table $\in$ *INDEX* $\rightarrow$ *VALUE*

INITIALIZATION

    table $:\in$ *INDEX* $\rightarrow$ *VALUE*

The machine first offers two operations, one for entering a new value into the array at a specific index and one for accessing the value stored in the array at a given index. These operations are called enter and access.

OPERATIONS

    enter(*index*, *value*) $\hat{=}$
        PRE
            index $\in$ *INDEX* $\wedge$
            value $\in$ *VALUE*
        THEN
            table(*index*) := *value*
        END ;

OPERATIONS   (*Cont'd*)

$value \longleftarrow$ access(*index*) $\hat{=}$
    PRE
        $index \in INDEX$
    THEN
        $value := table(index)$
    END ;

The next operation *index* $\longleftarrow$ search(*value*) yields an index of the array at which a certain value is stored. The operation is specified as a non-deterministic choice in the set of indices corresponding to the stored value. The pre-condition of this operation is that the value in question is indeed stored in the array. Finally, the fact that a certain value is stored in the array can be tested by the last offered operation called *report* $\longleftarrow$ test(*value*).

OPERATIONS   (*cont'd*)

$index \longleftarrow$ search(*value*) $\hat{=}$
    PRE
        $value \in$ ran(*table*)
    THEN
        $index :\in table^{-1}[\{value\}]$
    END ;

$res \longleftarrow$ test(*value*) $\hat{=}$
    PRE
        $value \in VALUE$
    THEN
        $res :=$ bool($value \in$ ran(*table*))
    END

END

Notice that in the last operation we have used the construct bool together with a substitution. It is defined as follows:

Syntax	Definition
$x :=$ bool(P)	IF P THEN $x :=$ true ELSE $x :=$ false END

where the enumerated set BOOL is predefined as BOOL = {true, false}

At first glance, the fact that we have two operations, one for testing (test) and one for searching (search), seems to be very inefficient since we probably have to test before we can start to search (because of the pre-condition of the operation search). So, it seems that we might have to search twice. Again, efficiency must not be our concern for the moment: we are specifying, *not programming*. In fact, nothing will prevent us from later have a corresponding "intelligent" implementation by which the evidence of a positive test (that is, any index corresponding to the stored value) can be stored so that it can be re-used by the search operation.

Finally, notice that the specification of the operation search is a *genuine* specification. It says absolutely nothing about *how* the search can be done. It only says *what* the result of the search should be in order to be acceptable.

4.19. Explicit Definitions

In this section we present a feature by which we can factorize some definitions: this is done by means of the DEFINITIONS clause. This last feature is best presented by some examples. In our first example, the proposed machine encapsulates a *paged memory*. It offers two operations: one for modifying the memory and the other for accessing its contents. The formal parameters, *memorysize* and *pagesize*, have an *explicit* constraint: *memorysize* must be a multiple of *pagesize*.

```
MACHINE

    Paged_Memory(VALUE, memorysize, pagesize)

CONSTRAINTS

    memorysize ∈ NAT1   ∧
    pagesize ∈ NAT1   ∧
    memorysize mod pagesize = 0
```

The DEFINITIONS clause allows one to introduce some useful, possibly parameterized, aliases.

DEFINITIONS

$ADDRESS \;\hat{=}\; 0\mathinner{\ldotp\ldotp}(memorysize - 1);$
$PAGE \;\hat{=}\; 0\mathinner{\ldotp\ldotp}((memorysize/pagesize) - 1);$
$INDEX \;\hat{=}\; 0\mathinner{\ldotp\ldotp}(pagesize - 1);$
$addr(pp, ii) \;\hat{=}\; (pp \times pagesize) + ii$

VARIABLES

memory

INVARIANT

$memory \in ADDRESS \rightarrow VALUE$

INITIALIZATION

$memory :\in ADDRESS \rightarrow VALUE$

OPERATIONS

$\mathsf{modify}(page, index, value) \;\hat{=}$
    PRE
        $page \in PAGE \quad \wedge$
        $index \in INDEX \quad \wedge$
        $value \in VALUE$
    THEN
        $memory(addr(page, index)) := value$
    END;

$value \longleftarrow \mathsf{access}(page, index) \;\hat{=}$
    PRE
        $page \in PAGE \quad \wedge$
        $index \in INDEX$
    THEN
        $value := memory(addr(page, index))$
    END

END

Notice that such DEFINITIONS are mere "macros" that are supposed to be applied to the text of the abstract machine. As a consequence, the position of the DEFINITIONS clause within the machine *is irrelevant*. That is, although perhaps situated before the VARIABLES clause in a certain machine, the DEFINITIONS can very well use some of the variables of the machine in question.

As our second example, we rewrite another, more complete, version of the data-base abstract machine we have already presented in sections 4.17 and 4.18. We have added a number of useful definitions in order to facilitate the reading of the specification.

MACHINE

   Data_Base

SETS

   $PERSON$;
   $SEX = \{male, female\}$;
   $STATUS = \{living, dead\}$

CONSTANTS

   max_pers

PROPERTIES

   $max\_pers \in \mathsf{NAT}_1 \quad \wedge$
   $\mathrm{card}(PERSON) = max\_pers$

VARIABLES

   person, sex, status, mother, husband, wife

DEFINITIONS

   $MAN \;\hat{=}\; sex^{-1}[\{man\}]$;
   $WOMAN \;\hat{=}\; sex^{-1}[\{woman\}]$;
   $LIVING \;\hat{=}\; status^{-1}[\{living\}]$;
   $DEAD \;\hat{=}\; status^{-1}[\{dead\}]$;
   $MARRIED \;\hat{=}\; \mathrm{dom}(husband \cup wife)$;
   $SINGLE \;\hat{=}\; person - MARRIED$;
   $ANGEL \;\hat{=}\; PERSON - person$

We have also added some variables in order to handle relationships between people: *mother, husband, wife*. A corresponding marriage operation is offered.

INVARIANT

    $person \subseteq PERSON \quad \wedge$
    $sex \in person \rightarrow SEX \quad \wedge$
    $status \in person \rightarrow STATUS \quad \wedge$
    $mother \in person \nrightarrow (MARRIED \cap WOMAN) \quad \wedge$
    $husband \in WOMAN \rightarrowtail MAN \quad \wedge$
    $wife = husband^{-1}$

INITIALIZATION

    $person := \varnothing \quad ||$
    $sex := \varnothing \quad ||$
    $status := \varnothing \quad ||$
    $mother := \varnothing \quad ||$
    $husband := \varnothing \quad ||$
    $wife := \varnothing$

OPERATIONS

    death(pp) $\hat{=}$
        PRE
            $pp \in LIVING$
        THEN
            $status(pp) := dead$
        END ;

    marriage($bride, groom$) $\hat{=}$
        PRE
            $bride \in SINGLE \cap WOMAN \quad \wedge$
            $groom \in SINGLE \cap MAN$
        THEN
            $husband(bride) := groom \quad ||$
            $wife(groom) := bride$
        END ;

    $report \longleftarrow$ saturated $\hat{=}$
        BEGIN
            $report :=$ bool$(ANGEL = \varnothing)$
        END ;

Finally, we have added a number of inquiry operations allowing "users" to test for the pre-conditions of some operations.

$baby \longleftarrow \mathsf{newborn}(sx, mm) \quad \widehat{=}$
   PRE
      $ANGEL \neq \varnothing \quad \wedge$
      $sx \in SEX \quad \wedge$
      $mm \in MARRIED \cap WOMAN$
   THEN
      ANY *angel* WHERE
        $angel \in ANGEL$
      THEN
        $person := person \cup \{angel\} \quad ||$
        $status(angel) := living \quad ||$
        $sex(angel) := sx \quad ||$
        $mother(angel) := mm \quad ||$
        $baby := angel$
      END
   END ;

$report \longleftarrow \mathsf{is\_present}(pp) \quad \widehat{=}$
   PRE $pp \in PERSON$ THEN $b := \mathsf{bool}(pp \in person)$ END ;

$report \longleftarrow \mathsf{is\_living}(pp) \quad \widehat{=}$
   PRE $pp \in person$ THEN $report := \mathsf{bool}(status(pp) \in living)$ END ;

$report \longleftarrow \mathsf{is\_woman}(pp) \quad \widehat{=}$
   PRE $pp \in person$ THEN $report := \mathsf{bool}(pp \in WOMAN)$ END ;

$report \longleftarrow \mathsf{is\_married}(pp) \quad \widehat{=}$
   PRE $pp \in person$ THEN $report := \mathsf{bool}(pp \in MARRIED)$ END

END

4.20. Assertions

In this section we present a new abstract machine clause: the ASSERTIONS clause. This is a clause that resembles an INVARIANT clause (section 4.2) or a PROPERTIES clause (section 4.17). Like these clauses, it is made up of a number of conjoined predicates.

The predicates of an ASSERTIONS clause are supposed to be deducible from those of the INVARIANT or PROPERTIES clauses (this supposition, of course, is guaranteed by a proof obligation). Thus, they need not be proved to be established by the initialization or preserved by the operations of the machine.

The purpose of the predicates of the ASSERTIONS clause is simply to ease the invariant preservation proofs. This is so because such predicates can be entered as extra assumptions in these proofs.

4.21. Concrete Variables and Abstract Constants

As we have seen in section 4.2 and in section 4.17, variables and constants are not treated alike as far as *visibility* is concerned: variables are always hidden, whereas constants are always visible. The fact that variables are hidden is fundamental since it is our intention to refine them. On the contrary, constants being always visible, cannot be refined. It is, by the way, the reason why we have restricted constants to be either scalars, total functions, or subsets of scalar sets (that will not be implemented). The first two of them are clearly implementable directly either by simple variables or by "arrays".

This asymmetric "visibility" treatment of variables and constants is perhaps too drastic. After all, some variables might already be very "concrete" so that no refinement will be necessary in order to implement them. On the other hand, we might sometimes need very abstract and refinable constants.

So, in order to have a completely symmetric treatment, we introduce in this section the following two clauses: CONCRETE_VARIABLES and ABSTRACT_CONSTANTS (these mechanisms have been suggested by Patrick Behm and Jean-Marc Meynadier). The contents of such clauses are simple lists of concrete variables and of abstract constants, respectively. Of course, concrete variables are restricted, as we expect, to scalars or total functions, whereas abstract constants are not restricted.

The typing and the special conditions governing concrete variables and abstract constants are expressed, as for (abstract) VARIABLES and (concrete) CONSTANTS, in the INVARIANT and PROPERTIES clauses, respectively.

As an example, here is a little machine introducing a abstract constant, for defining the square root function:

```
MACHINE

    Square_Root_Operation

ABSTRACT_CONSTANTS

    f
```

PROPERTIES

$$f \in \mathbb{N} \to \mathbb{N} \quad \wedge$$
$$\forall n \cdot (n \in \mathbb{N} \;\Rightarrow\; f(n)^2 \leq n < (f(n) + 1)^2)$$

OPERATIONS

$r \longleftarrow$ square(n) $\;\widehat{=}\;$

    PRE

       $n \in \mathbb{N}$

    THEN

       $r := f(n)$

    END

END

4.22. Exercises

Each exercise in this section corresponds to the realization of some abstract machine. For each of them, when it is relevant, try to write three versions: one in the generous style (section 4.11), one in the deterministic defensive style (section 4.11), and one in the non-deterministic defensive style (see example in section 4.14). You can also try some mixed styles.

1. Define an abstract machine encapsulating a single scalar vv. The variable is supposed to belong to a certain set which is a parameter of the machine. The operations of the machine should be relevant operations modifying, accessing, and testing the variable vv.

2. Define an abstract machine encapsulating a single set ss. The set ss is supposed to be a subset of a certain set which itself is a parameter of the machine. Besides the set ss itself, the machine encapsulates an injective sequence iss whose range is exactly ss. This injective sequence is supposed to represent a certain *ordering* of ss. The machine has operations to add a member to ss, to remove a member from ss, to clear ss, to test for the membership of an element in ss, and to ask for the cardinality of ss. It also has an operation to access the ith element of ss and another one able to modify the ith element of ss. Notice that the operations modifying ss (except the last one) also modify the ordering of ss in a non-deterministic way. On the other hand, operations inquiring about the set (or modifying its ith element) are guaranteed not to change the ordering of the set. In other words, from the specification, we know that there exists an ordering of ss and that it remains the same as long as we do

not change the set except by modifying a member accessed through the ordering.

3. Define an abstract machine encapsulating a single relation. The source and destination of the relation are supposed to be parameters of the machine. The operations of the machine should be relevant operations modifying, accessing, and testing the relation.

4. Define an abstract machine encapsulating a single partial function. The source and destination of the partial function are supposed to be parameters of the machine. The operations of the machine should be relevant operations enlarging, shrinking, modifying, accessing, and testing the function. Such a partial function could be used to model what is called a "record" in programming languages.

5. Define an abstract machine encapsulating a single sequence. The set on which the sequence is supposed to be built is a parameter of the machine. The operations of the machine should be relevant operations enlarging, shrinking, modifying, accessing, and testing the sequence.

6. Define an abstract machine encapsulating an array. The set on which the sequence is supposed to be built is a parameter of the machine. The indices of the array are supposed to be a certain interval from 1 to *max_index*. This identifier is supposed to be a scalar parameter of the machine. The operations of the machine should be relevant operations modifying, accessing, and testing the array.

7. It is possible to have machines *without variables*. All the operations of such machines must have output parameters. Such abstract machines are used to define some useful operations on certain sets. In a sense, such machines represents concrete models for abstract data types. For instance, you can define (1) an arithmetic machine, (2), a boolean machine, (3) a 32-bit string machine.

8. Define an abstract machine encapsulating a certain data-base of objects. In this exercise, we are not interested in what such objects are. All that interests us is that such objects can come into existence, or alternatively can disappear from the data-base. The presence of an object in the data-base can also be tested. All such objects are supposed to be members of a certain set, *OBJECT*, which is supposed to be a deferred set of the machine (in other words, it is genuinely the case that we are not interested in what these objects are: this is left as an implementation issue). One of the variables of the machine, called *object*, is a subset of the deferred set *OBJECT*: it represents the objects that are present in the data-base at a given moment. Try to understand how this contrasts with the set machine defined in Exercise 2. As in Exercise 2, define another variable representing a non-deterministic ordering of the objects that are present in the data-base. Define the corresponding operations.

9. Enlarge Exercise 8 so that the objects are now understood to be scalars as defined in the machine of Exercise 1.

10. Enlarge Exercise 8 so that the objects are now understood to be sets as defined in the machine of Exercise 2.

11. Enlarge Exercise 8 so that the objects are now understood to be "records" as defined in the machine of Exercise 4.

12. Enlarge Exercise 8 so that the objects are now understood to be sequences as defined in the machine of Exercise 5.

13. Enlarge Exercise 8 so that the objects are now understood to be either scalar, sets, partial functions, arrays, or sequences. The nature of each object in the data base can be changed, so the machine must keep track of it.

14. Enlarge Exercise 8 so that the objects are now understood to be composite objects made of various attributes. And, whatever the object, each attribute has a constant "kind" which could be one of: scalar, set, partial function, array, or sequence. Define generic operations to be applicable to the attribute of the objects according to their "kind".

15. Enlarge the machine of Exercise 6 so that we now have an array built on a certain finite subset of $\mathbb{N}$ (i.e.an interval from 0 to a certain maximum value). Have new operations for performing arithmetical modifications on the array. Have new operations for searching for the maximal (minimal) index whose corresponding value in the array satisfies a certain arithmetical test (equality with a number, comparison with a number). Have operations for sorting the array according to various criteria.

REFERENCES

[1] E.W. Dijkstra. *A Discipline of Programming* (Prentice Hall, 1976)

[2] I. Hayes (ed.). *Specification Case Studies* (Prentice Hall, 1985)

[3] D.L. Parnas. *A Technique for Software Module Specification with Examples* (CACM 15,5, May 1972)

[4] C.B. Jones. *Software Development. A Rigorous Approach* (Prentice Hall, 1980)

[5] C. Morgan. *Programming From Specifications* (Prentice Hall, 1990)

CHAPTER 5

Definition of Abstract Machines

IN the previous chapter we presented an informal (and incomplete) introduction to the Generalized Substitution Language and the Abstract Machine Notation. The purpose of this chapter is to give a completely formal definition of the same material. For each of the previous notations, we present in turn, its syntax, its type-checking rules and its axioms.

5.1. Generalized Substitution

5.1.1. Syntax

In the previous chapter we extended the concept of substitution as it was first introduced in section 1.3.4. As a consequence, we have to introduce an extra syntactic construct, the *Substitution*, to replace the now too primitive form of substitution

$$Variable := Expression$$

In particular, in the syntactic category *Predicate* as defined in section 1.3.1, the clause [*Variable := Expression*] *Predicate* is to be replaced by the clause [*Substitution*] *Predicate*. Here is the definition of the *Substitution* syntactic category:

Syntactic Category	Definition
Substitution	*Variable := Expression* skip *Predicate | Substitution* *Substitution* [] *Substitution* *Predicate* $\Longrightarrow$ *Substitution* @*Variable · Substitution*

We now present a few syntactic extensions that we have already presented informally in the previous chapter. They, essentially, are facilities used to ease the writing of large specifications. In the following table, S and T are *Substitutions*, P is a *Predicate*, x and y are distinct *Variables*, E and F are *Expressions*, U is a *Set* such that y is non-free in U, and f is a *Set* which is supposed to be a (partial) function:

Syntax	Definition
BEGIN S END	S
PRE P THEN S END	$P \mid S$
IF P THEN S ELSE T END	$(P \Longrightarrow S)$ [] $(\neg P \Longrightarrow T)$
IF P THEN S END	IF P THEN S ELSE skip END
$x := \text{bool}(P)$	IF P THEN $x := \text{true}$ ELSE $x := \text{false}$ END
$x := E \mid\mid y := F$	$x, y := E, F$
CHOICE S OR $\cdots$ OR T END	S [] $\cdots$ [] T

Syntax	Definition
ANY x WHERE P THEN S END	$@x \cdot (P \implies S)$
$x :\in U$	ANY y WHERE $y \in U$ THEN $x := y$ END
$f(x) := E$	$f := f \lessdot \{x \mapsto E\}$

We now present a few more syntactic extensions. First the classical ELSIF. In the following table, P and Q are *Predicates*, and S, T and U are *Substitutions*.

Syntax	Definition
IF P THEN S ... ELSIF Q THEN T ELSE U END	IF P THEN S ELSE ... IF Q THEN T ELSE U END ... END
IF P THEN S ... ELSIF Q THEN T END	IF P THEN S ... ELSIF Q THEN T ELSE skip END

Then we introduce two more forms of bounded choice: the SELECT and the CASE constructs. The first one, presented in the following table, where P and Q

are *Predicates* and *S* and *T* are *Substitutions*, might be non-deterministic and non-feasible (section 6.3.2).

Syntax	Definition
SELECT P THEN S END	$P \Longrightarrow S$
SELECT P THEN S . . . WHEN Q THEN T END	CHOICE $P \Longrightarrow S$ OR . . . OR $Q \Longrightarrow T$ END

The following second form provides the ELSE clause:

Syntax	Definition
SELECT P THEN S . . . WHEN Q THEN T ELSE U END	SELECT P THEN S . . . WHEN Q THEN T WHEN $\neg (P \vee \cdots \vee Q)$ THEN U END

Next are two forms of CASE substitutions. Here *E* is an *Expression*, *l* and *p* are lists of distinct *Identifiers* or literal numbers, and *S*, *T*, and *U* are *Substitutions*. The next construct is *deterministic* since the various cases are supposed to be *disjoint*. Also notice that, in contrast with the above SELECT substitution, the first form of the present CASE substitution contains an implicit ELSE part which makes it a *feasible* substitution.

Syntax	Definition

CASE E OF
    EITHER l THEN
      S
    ...
    OR p THEN
      T
    END
END
	SELECT $E \in \{l\}$ THEN
	    S
	    ...
	WHEN $E \in \{p\}$ THEN
	    T
	ELSE
	    skip
	END

CASE E OF
    EITHER l THEN
      S
    ...
    OR p THEN
      T
    ELSE
      U
    END
END
	SELECT $E \in \{l\}$ THEN
	    S
	    ...
	WHEN $E \in \{p\}$ THEN
	    T
	ELSE
	    U
	END

Finally, we present a few more syntactic extensions corresponding to the unbounded choice substitution.

Syntax	Definition	Side-Condition
VAR x IN S END	$@x \cdot S$	

LET $x,\ldots,y$ BE
    $x = E \wedge$
    ...
    $y = F$
IN
    S
END
	ANY $x,\cdots,y$ WHERE
	    $x = E \wedge$
	    ...
	    $y = F$
	THEN
	    S
	END
		$x, y \setminus E, F$

In the above table, x and y are distinct *Variables*, S is a *Substitution*, and E and F are *Expressions*. As can be seen, the second construct departs from the ANY construct only because of the presence of the non-freeness conditions. The third construct to come is a simplified form of the *Specification Statement* of C. Morgan [1] (pronounced "any x such that P holds"). In the predicate P the before-value can be denoted by indexing the variable x with 0.

Syntax	Definition	Side-Condition
$x : P$	ANY x' WHERE $$[x_0, x' := x, x']\, P$$ THEN $$x := x'$$ END	$y \setminus P$

5.1.2. Type-checking

In this section we extend the type-checking rules, as defined in chapter 2 for *Predicates* and *Expressions*, to be applied to *Substitutions* as well. Of course, we shall only present the rules corresponding to the basic substitution constructs presented in the previous section since the other constructs can be reduced to the basic constructs. Notice that we extend the construct check to apply to *Substitutions* as well as to *Predicates*.

Antecedents	Consequent
$\begin{cases} x \in s \text{ occurs in } ENV \\ ENV \vdash \text{super}(s) \equiv \text{type}(E) \end{cases}$	$ENV \vdash \text{check}(x := E)$
$\begin{cases} x \setminus y \\ ENV \vdash \text{check}(x := E) \\ ENV \vdash \text{check}(y := F) \end{cases}$	$ENV \vdash \text{check}(x, y := E, F)$

Antecedents	Consequent
	$ENV \;\vdash\; \text{check}\,(\text{skip})$
$\begin{cases} ENV \;\vdash\; \text{check}\,(P) \\ ENV \;\vdash\; \text{check}\,(S) \end{cases}$	$ENV \;\vdash\; \text{check}\,(P \mid S)$
$\begin{cases} ENV \;\vdash\; \text{check}\,(S) \\ ENV \;\vdash\; \text{check}\,(T) \end{cases}$	$ENV \;\vdash\; \text{check}\,(S \; [] \; T)$
$\begin{cases} ENV \;\vdash\; \text{check}\,(P) \\ ENV \;\vdash\; \text{check}\,(S) \end{cases}$	$ENV \;\vdash\; \text{check}\,(P \implies S)$
$ENV \;\vdash\; \text{check}\,(\forall x \cdot (P \Rightarrow S))$	$ENV \;\vdash\; \text{check}\,(@x \cdot (P \implies S))$

These rules are straightforward. Notice that the first one requires that the variable x, involved in the simple substitution, be declared in the environment. Such a declaration will be made, as shown in section 5.2.3 dealing with the type-checking of abstract machines. However, such a previous declaration will not always be possible (for instance, for an operation output parameter), so we shall give below (section 5.2.3) an extra rule for the type-checking of simple substitutions. Notice that in the last rule, we have taken some liberty with the syntax since we have allowed the implication operator to connect a predicate to a substitutiton. This is just to minimize the number of rules.

5.1.3. Axioms

In this section, we summarize the various axioms concerning generalized substitutions. In the following table, P and R are *Predicates*, S and T are *Substitutions*, and x is a *Variable*.

Axiom	Condition
[skip] R $\Leftrightarrow$ R	
$[P \mid S]R$ $\Leftrightarrow$ $(P \wedge [S]R)$	
$[S \; [] \; T]R$ $\Leftrightarrow$ $([S]R \wedge [T]R)$	
$[P \Longrightarrow S]R$ $\Leftrightarrow$ $(P \Rightarrow [S]R)$	
$[@x \cdot S]R$ $\Leftrightarrow$ $\forall x \cdot [S]R$	$x \setminus R$

5.2. Abstract Machines

5.2.1. Syntax

Here is the syntax of Abstract Machines:

Syntactic Category	Definition

Machine	MACHINE
	    Machine_Header
	CONSTRAINTS
	    Predicate
	SETS
	    Sets
	CONSTANTS
	    Id_List
	ABSTRACT_CONSTANTS
	    Id_List
	PROPERTIES
	    Predicate

Syntactic Category	Definition
Machine (*Cont'd*)	VARIABLES *Id_List* CONCRETE_VARIABLES *Id_List* INVARIANT *Predicate* ASSERTIONS *Predicate* DEFINITIONS *Definitions* INITIALIZATION *Substitution* OPERATIONS *Operations* END
Machine_Header	*Identifier* *Identifier* (*Id_list*)
Sets	*Sets* ; *Set_Declaration* *Set_Declaration*
Set_Declaration	*Identifier* *Identifier* = {*Id_List*}
Definitions	*Definitions* ; *Definition_Declaration* *Definition_Declaration*
Definition_Declaration	*Identifier* $\widehat{=}$ *Formal_Text* *Identifier* (*Id_List*) $\widehat{=}$ *Formal_Text*
Operations	*Operations* ; *Operation_Declaration* *Operation_Declaration*

Syntactic Category	Definition
Operation_Declaration	*Operation_Header* $\hat{=}$ *Substitution*
Operation_Header	*Id_List* ⟵ *Identifier* (*Id_List*) *Identifier* (*Id_List*) *Id_List* ⟵ *Identifier* *Identifier*

Each clause introduced in the syntax is, in practice, optional; although a number of dependencies are required as shown below:

- a (ABSTRACT_) CONSTANTS clause requires a PROPERTIES clause and vice-versa.

- a (CONCRETE_) VARIABLES clause requires an INVARIANT clause and vice-versa.

- a (CONCRETE_) VARIABLES clause requires an INITIALIZATION clause and vice-versa.

- a (CONCRETE_) VARIABLES clause requires an OPERATIONS clause. Not vice-versa, however, since it is perfectly possible to have variableless machines with pure operations.

5.2.2. Visibility Rules

In this section we make precise the visibility rules of an Abstract Machine. These are best represented in the following table showing how each relevant clause of a machine (in columns) can access (in case of a √) or not access (blank) corresponding "objects" of the machine:

	CONSTRAINTS	PROPERTIES	INVARIANT	OPERATIONS
parameters	√		√	√
sets		√	√	√

	CONSTRAINTS	PROPERTIES	INVARIANT	OPERATIONS
constants		√	√	√
variables			√	√

It is worth noticing again that a PROPERTIES clause cannot access the formal parameters of the machine (section 4.17).

5.2.3. Type-checking

We now give the rule of Abstract Machine type-checking. Notice that we extend the construct check to apply to machines, lists of operations and operations. In order to simplify matters, we shall use a machine M, built of the following elements:

- The machine has two parameters X and x. X, a supposed upper case parameter, is thus a (given) set, and x, a supposed lower case parameter, is thus a scalar (recall section 4.8).

- The parameters have a number of CONSTRAINTS denoted by the predicate C.

- The SETS clause is supposed to introduce two (given) sets: S which is a deferred set, and T which is an enumerated set with two elements a and b.

- The machine has a number of CONSTANTS and ABSTRACT_CONSTANTS whose lists are together denoted by c.

- These constants have a number of PROPERTIES denoted by the predicate P.

- The machine has a number of VARIABLES and CONCRETE_VARIABLES whose lists are together denoted by v.

- These variables have an INVARIANT denoted by the predicate I.

- The INITIALIZATION of the machine is a substitution denoted by U.

- Finally, the OPERATIONS of the machine are collectively denoted by O.

Antecedents	Consequent

X, x, S, T, a, b, c, v are all distinct
 	
Operation names of O are all distinct
 	
$S, T, a, b, c, v \setminus C$
 	
$v, X, x \setminus P$
 	
given (X),
given (S),
given (T),
$a \in T$,
$b \in T$
$\vdash$
check $(\forall x \cdot (C \Rightarrow$
$\forall c \cdot (P \Rightarrow \forall v \cdot (I \wedge J \Rightarrow U \wedge O))))$
	check (
	MACHINE
	    $M(X, x)$
	CONSTRAINTS
	    C
	SETS
	    S ;
	    $T = \{a, b\}$
	(ABSTRACT_)CONSTANTS
	    c
	PROPERTIES
	    P
	(CONCRETE_)VARIABLES
	    v
	INVARIANT
	    I
	ASSERTIONS
	    J
	INITIALIZATION
	    U
	OPERATIONS
	    O
	END)

A number of obvious distinctness and non-freeness conditions have to be checked before the genuine type-checking can take place (in particuler, notice that the machine parameters must not occur in the PROPERTIES clause). The type-checking is done under an environment resulting from the analysis of the machine parameters and of the SETS clause. Quite naturally, a machine set parameter (upper case) yields a given set. Likewise, a deferred set and an enumerated set defined in the SETS clause also yield given sets. Finally, the enumerated set elements are entered into the environment as one would expect.

The genuine type-checking of the machine is equivalent to the type-checking of a universal quantification applied to the scalar parameters of the machine and their constraints, then to a universal quantification of the constants and their properties, then to a universal quantification applied to the variables and their invariant, and then, finally, to the initialization and to the operations. Notice that we have separated the initialization U and the list of operations O with the conjunction operator as if they were predicates. In fact, since we are only type-checking, this slight abuse is of no consequence: as we know, the operator check distributes through conjunction (rule T1 in section 2.2).

It remains for us to define the type-checking of the operations. This is defined in the following table. The first rule corresponds to the obvious unwinding of a list of operations. The second rule corresponds to the type-checking of a single operation supposed to have one input and one output parameter (other cases with more or fewer parameters could be defined accordingly). Each input parameter must have a type defined in the pre-condition of the operation. This is the reason why the type-checking of the main substitution of the operation is performed under a universal quantification involving the pre-condition. As the output parameter is not typed a priori, it is entered into the environment as an output. The third rule corresponds to the case of a simple substitution whose left-hand side is an operation output parameter: it is then only required that the corresponding right-hand side expression be well typed (the type-checking "predicate" $\varnothing \equiv \text{type}\,(E)$ is just a trick used to simply express that the expression E is type-checkable).

Antecedents	Consequent
$\left\{ \begin{array}{l} ENV \;\vdash\; \text{check}\,(O) \\[2ex] ENV \;\vdash\; \text{check}\,(Q) \end{array} \right.$	$ENV \;\vdash\; \text{check}\,(O\,;Q)$
$\left\{ \begin{array}{l} u,O,w \quad \text{are all distinct} \\[1.5ex] u,O,w \setminus ENV \\[1.5ex] ENV, \text{output}\,(u) \\ \vdash \\ \text{check}\,(\forall w \cdot (P \;\Rightarrow\; S\,)) \end{array} \right.$	$ENV \;\vdash\; \text{check}\,(u \longleftarrow O(w) \;\widehat{=}\; P \mid S\,)$
$\left\{ \begin{array}{l} \text{output}\,(x) \quad \text{occurs in} \quad ENV \\[1.5ex] ENV \;\text{where output}\,(x) \\ \text{is replaced by } x \in \text{type}\,(E) \\ \vdash \\ \varnothing \equiv \text{type}\,(E\,) \end{array} \right.$	$ENV \;\vdash\; \text{check}\,(x := E\,)$

5.2.4. On the Constants

The (concrete) CONSTANTS are either scalar constants of a set, or total functions from a set (or a cartesian product of sets) to a set, or else subsets of a set. The sets in question are either enumerated sets, deferred sets (supposed to be independent of the machine formal parameters), or subsets of INT. On the other hand, the ABSTRACT_CONSTANTS can be of any type (supposed to be independent of the machine formal parameters).

5.2.5. Proof Obligations

In this section we present the axioms of Abstract Machines which, for historical reasons, are called "proof obligations". As for the type-checking in section 5.2.3, and to simplify matters, we shall only consider a particular Abstract Machine with two parameters. The first of these parameters, X, is supposed to be a set formal parameter, and the second one, x, is supposed to be a scalar formal parameter. We implicitly put together the abstract and concrete constants and variables in the two "clauses" (ABSTRACT_)CONSTANTS and (CONCRETE_)VARIABLES.

MACHINE
   $M(X,x)$
CONSTRAINTS
   C
SETS
   S ;
   $T = \{a, b\}$
(ABSTRACT_)CONSTANTS
   c
PROPERTIES
   P
(CONCRETE_)VARIABLES
   v
INVARIANT
   I
ASSERTIONS
   J
INITIALIZATION
   U
OPERATIONS
   $u \longleftarrow O(w) \;\; \widehat{=} \;\;$ PRE Q THEN V END ;
   ...

END

Before presenting the proof obligations, let us define the following two predicates
A and B which will become assumptions for our proof obligations to come. The
first one, A, states that the set machine parameter X is a non-empty subset of
INT. The second one, B, states that the deferred set S is a non-empty subset
of INT and that the enumerated set T is a non-empty subset of INT, consisting
exactly of the two distinct elements a and b.

By considering that all our given sets are subsets of INT, we simply "paint them
all in grey". At this point, and for the purpose of proving, that is our concern
with the proof obligations, there is no harm in doing so since, supposedly,
type-checking has already been done. Remember that INT is supposed to be
an interval from the integer minint to the natural number maxint; a certain
BASIC_CONSTANTS machine is defined in section 5.2.6 where such constants
are declared.

Abbreviation	Definition
A	$X \in \mathbb{P}_1(\text{INT})$
B	$S \in \mathbb{P}_1(\text{INT}) \;\wedge\; T \in \mathbb{P}_1(\text{INT}) \;\wedge\; T = \{a,b\} \;\wedge\; a \neq b$

We now describe our two proof obligations. The first one states that the initialization U establishes the invariant I. This is done under the two contextual
abbreviations A and B, the constraints C and the properties P.

$$A \;\wedge\; B \;\wedge\; C \;\wedge\; P \;\;\Rightarrow\;\; [U]I$$

The second proof obligation concerns the assertion J.

$$A \;\wedge\; B \;\wedge\; C \;\wedge\; P \;\wedge\; I \;\;\Rightarrow\;\; J$$

The third proof obligation states that the body V of the operation establishes
the invariant I. This is done under the two contextual abbreviations A and B,
the constraints C, the properties P, the invariant I, the assertion J and the
pre-condition Q of the operation.

$$A \;\wedge\; B \;\wedge\; C \;\wedge\; P \;\wedge\; I \;\wedge\; J \;\wedge\; Q \;\;\Rightarrow\;\; [V]I$$

Notice that the following proofs are not required:

- the existence of some machine scalar formal parameters satisfying their constraints,
- the existence of some concrete constants satisfying their properties,
- the existence of some variables satisfying their invariant,
- for each operation with input parameters, the existence of some input parameters satisfying their pre-conditions.

The reasons for the possible delays of the above proofs are the following:

- If, for a given machine, there are no scalar formal parameters satisfying the constraints, then we shall not be able to prove that any actualization of these parameters will ever satisfy these constraints and thus it will not be possible to instantiate the machine in question (section 7.4.3 and section 12.6.4).

- if there are no concrete constants satisfying their properties, then we shall not be able to prove that it is possible to give these concrete constants some values (section 12.6.4).

- if there are no variables satisfying their invariant, then we shall not be able to prove that a certain executable initialization indeed refines the corresponding more abstract initialization (section 12.6.4).

- if, for an operation, there are no input parameters satisfying their pre-conditions, then we shall not be able to prove, ever, that the operation is called within its pre-condition (section 7.4.3 and section 12.6.4).

In each of the above cases, we have replaced potential existence proofs, *to be performed as early as possible*, by constructive proofs, *to be performed as late as possible*, that is only when needed: such constructive proofs are well-known to be far easier than the former. The only existential proofs that remain to be done eventually are the proofs concerning the existence of the ABSTRACT-CONSTANTS (section 12.6.4).

5.2.6. About the Given Sets and the Pre-defined Constants

In section 5.2.3 on the type-checking of Abstract Machines, we have seen that the given sets of an abstract machine are the following:

- the machine set formal parameters,
- the deferred sets,
- the enumerated sets.

We wonder whether we have any other given sets at our disposal in an abstract machine. For instance, is $\mathbb{N}$ or $\mathbb{Z}$ also "given"? The answer is simple: the only other given set is BOOL which is equal to {true, false}. This means that we cannot use $\mathbb{N}$ or $\mathbb{Z}$ in an abstract machine *except* in the following one where the only pre-defined given set and constants are defined:

```
MACHINE

    BASIC_CONSTANTS

SETS

    BOOL = {false, true}

CONSTANTS

    minint, maxint, INT, NAT, NAT₁, CHAR

PROPERTIES

    minint ∈ ℤ    ∧
    maxint ∈ ℕ    ∧
    minint < 0    ∧
    maxint > 0    ∧
    INT = minint..maxint    ∧
    NAT = 0..maxint    ∧
    NAT₁ = 1..maxint    ∧
    INT₁ = minint..−1    ∧
    CHAR = 0..255

END
```

This machine is "seen" (section 12.2.2) implicitly by any other machine. This means that the defined enumerated set and the defined constants of this machine can be used freely in any other machine.

An important consequence of what we have just said is that *all the sets* we can ever manipulate in an abstract machine are *finite sets* (finite but unbounded since the value of minint and that of maxint are not known a priori). This is the reason why we can assume, in the proof obligation of an abstract machine (section 5.2.4), that the set formal parameters and the deferred sets are indeed finite sets.

This limitation about finite sets might seem too drastic. After all, this finiteness assumption might not be an indispensable requirement. In fact, provided we are never thinking of ever implementing an abstract machine, then, clearly, this limitation is not indispensable. If, however, we think that all our abstract machines are candidates for a future implementation, then this limitation makes sense. An abstract machine directly using the sets ℕ or ℤ or any other infinite set could not be implemented, since its eventual refinement needs some finiteness assumptions. In that case, we think that it is preferable to consider such limitations right from the beginning.

REFERENCE

[1] C.C. Morgan. *Programming from Specification* (Prentice Hall, 1990)

CHAPTER 6

Theory of Abstract Machines

THIS chapter is devoted to the study of various theoretical developments concerning Generalized Substitutions and Abstract Machines. Our ultimate goal is to construct some set-theoretic models for Abstract Machines and Generalized Substitutions. By doing so, we shall be able to conduct further developments of Abstract Machines (i.e. loop and refinement in chapters 9 and 11 respectively) on these models rather than on the notation itself. This will prove to be very convenient.

In section 6.1, we prove that any generalized substitution defined in terms of the basic constructs of the previous chapter can be put into a certain *normalized form*. An outcome of this result is that any proof involving a generalized substitution can be done by assuming, without any loss of generality, that the substitution in question is in normalized form.

In section 6.2, we prove two convenient properties of generalized substitutions: namely, that the establishment of a post-condition *distributes through conjunction* and that it is *monotonic under universal implication*. The first will have a clear practical impact whereas the second is useful for theoretical developments. These properties were named by E.W. Dijkstra the *Healthiness Conditions*.

In section 6.3, we study the problem of *termination* and that of *feasibility*. We give a simple characterization of these properties. We also explain how the Generalized Substitution Language has exactly the same expressive power as the *Before-after Predicates* as introduced in section 4.4.

Finally, in section 6.4, we shall present the *set-theoretic models* of abstract machines and generalized substitutions, that we mentioned earlier.

6.1. Normalized Form

In this section we show that each generalized substitution can be put into a certain *normalized form*. If x is the (list of) state variable(s) of an abstract machine, then any generalized substitution S working with that machine can be put into the following form, where P and Q are predicates and where x' is a variable distinct from x having no free occurrence in P. The predicate Q depends on x and x'.

$$S \;=\; P \mid @x' \cdot (Q \implies x := x')$$
$$\text{for some } P \text{ and } Q \text{ where } x' \setminus P$$

Theorem 6.1.1

The proof is by *structural induction* on all the generalized substitution constructs. More precisely, we first prove this result for the elementary substitution $x := E$ and for **skip**, and then we prove it for other substitutions under the relevant hypotheses. For instance, we shall prove it for $P \mid S$ under the assumption that it holds for S. Likewise, we shall prove it for $S \,[\!]\, T$ under the assumption that it holds for S and T.

The proof relies on a number of equivalence laws. All these laws are of the form $S = T$ where S and T are certain substitutions. Note that we have not yet defined what it means for two substitutions to be "equal". For the moment, it suffices to say that two substitutions are equal if and only if the establishment of any post-condition by one is equivalent to the establishment of the same post-condition by the other. The proofs of these algebraic laws are left as exercises for the reader.

Law	Left	Right
1	$x := E$	$@x' \cdot (x' = E \implies x := x')$ if $x' \setminus E$
2	S	$(x = x) \mid S$
3	$P \mid (Q \mid S)$	$(P \wedge Q) \mid S$
4	$(P \mid S) \,[\!]\, T$	$P \mid (S \,[\!]\, T)$
5	$S \,[\!]\, T$	$T \,[\!]\, S$
6	$P \implies (Q \implies S)$	$(P \wedge Q) \implies S$

Law	Left	Right
7	$P \implies (Q \mid S)$	$(P \implies Q) \mid (P \implies S)$
8	$(P \implies S) \, [\!] \, (Q \implies S)$	$(P \lor Q) \implies S$
9	$@z \cdot (P \mid S)$	$(\forall z \cdot P) \mid @z \cdot S$
10	$P \implies @z \cdot S$	$@z \cdot (P \implies S) \qquad \text{if} \quad z \setminus P$
11	$@z \cdot (P \implies S)$	$(\exists z \cdot P) \implies S \qquad \text{if} \quad z \setminus [S]R$ $\text{for any} \quad R \quad \text{s.t.} \quad z \setminus R$
12	$(@z \cdot S) \, [\!] \, (@z \cdot T)$	$@z \cdot (S \, [\!] \, T)$
13	$@z \cdot @u \cdot S$	$@u \cdot @z \cdot S$

We are now well equipped to prove the normalized form theorem.

Proof for Simple Substitution

$$x := E$$
$$=$$ \hfill Law 1
$$@\, x' \cdot (x' = E \implies x := x')$$
$$=$$ \hfill Law 2
$$(x = x) \mid @\, x' \cdot (x' = E \implies x := x')$$

***Proof for* skip**

$$\text{skip}$$
$$=$$
$$x := x$$
$$=$$ \hfill Law 1
$$@\, x' \cdot (x' = x \implies x := x')$$
$$=$$ \hfill Law 2
$$(x = x) \mid @\, x' \cdot (x' = x \implies x := x')$$

Proof for Pre-condition

$$A \mid (P \mid @\,x' \cdot (Q \implies x := x'))$$
$$=$$
Law 3
$$(A \wedge P) \mid @\,x' \cdot (Q \implies x := x')$$

Proof for Bounded Choice

$$(A \mid @\,x' \cdot (B \implies x := x')) \;[\!]\; (P \mid @\,x' \cdot (Q \implies x := x'))$$
$$=$$
Law 4
$$A \mid ((@\,x' \cdot (B \implies x := x') \;[\!]\; (P \mid @\,x' \cdot (Q \implies x := x')))$$
$$=$$
Law 5
$$A \mid ((P \mid @\,x' \cdot (Q \implies x := x')) \;[\!]\; @\,x' \cdot (B \implies x := x'))$$
$$=$$
Law 4
$$A \mid (P \mid (@\,x' \cdot (Q \implies x := x') \;[\!]\; @\,x' \cdot (B \implies x := x')))$$
$$=$$
Law 3
$$(A \wedge P) \mid (@\,x' \cdot (Q \implies x := x') \;[\!]\; @\,x' \cdot (B \implies x := x'))$$
$$=$$
Law 12
$$(A \wedge P) \mid @\,x' \cdot ((Q \implies x := x') \;[\!]\; (B \implies x := x'))$$
$$=$$
Law 8
$$(A \wedge P) \mid @\,x' \cdot ((Q \vee B) \implies x := x')$$

Proof for Guard (x' is supposed to be not free in A)

$$A \implies (P \mid @\,x' \cdot (Q \implies x := x'))$$
$$=$$
Law 7
$$(A \Rightarrow P) \mid (A \implies @\,x' \cdot (Q \implies x := x'))$$
$$=$$
Law 10
$$(A \Rightarrow P) \mid @\,x' \cdot (A \implies (Q \implies x := x'))$$
$$=$$
Law 6
$$(A \Rightarrow P) \mid @\,x' \cdot ((A \wedge Q) \implies x := x')$$

Proof for Unbounded Choice (z is supposed to be distinct from x and x')

$$@\,z \cdot (P \mid @\,x' \cdot (Q \implies x := x'))$$
$$=$$
Law 9
$$(\forall z \cdot P) \mid @\,z \cdot @\,x' \cdot (Q \implies x := x')$$
$$=$$
Law 13
$$(\forall z \cdot P) \mid @\,x' \cdot @\,z \cdot (Q \implies x := x')$$
$$=$$
Law 11
$$(\forall z \cdot P) \mid @\,x' \cdot ((\exists z \cdot Q) \implies x := x')$$

End of Proof

We notice the following property, which is valid for any generalized substitution in normalized form.

$$[P \mid @x' \cdot (Q \implies x := x')]\, R \quad \Leftrightarrow$$
$$P \wedge \forall x' \cdot (Q \Rightarrow [x := x']\, R)$$
Property 6.1.1

6.2. Two Useful Properties

In this section we intend to prove two general properties of generalized substitutions. Our first property states that the establishment of a post-condition by a substitution distributes through conjunction. More formally, given a generalized substitution S working with a variable x and two predicates A and B, we have

---

$$[S](A \wedge B) \;\Leftrightarrow\; [S]A \wedge [S]B \qquad\qquad \text{Property 6.2.1}$$

Proof

According to Theorem 6.1.1, the proof may be performed on the normalized form only. Consequently, we may assume the following:

$$S \;=\; (P \mid @x' \cdot (Q \implies x := x')) \qquad\qquad \text{Hypothesis 1}$$

The proof goes as follows:

$$[S](A \wedge B)$$
$$\Leftrightarrow \qquad\qquad\qquad\qquad\qquad\qquad\qquad \text{Hypothesis 1}$$
$$[P \mid @x' \cdot (Q \implies x := x')](A \wedge B)$$
$$\Leftrightarrow \qquad\qquad\qquad\qquad\qquad\qquad\qquad \text{Property 6.1.1}$$
$$P \wedge \forall x' \cdot (Q \implies [x := x'](A \wedge B))$$
$$\Leftrightarrow$$
$$P \wedge \forall x' \cdot (Q \implies ([x := x']A \wedge [x := x']B))$$
$$\Leftrightarrow$$
$$P \wedge \forall x' \cdot ((Q \implies [x := x']A) \wedge (Q \implies [x := x']B))$$
$$\Leftrightarrow$$
$$P \wedge \forall x' \cdot (Q \implies [x := x']A) \wedge P \wedge \forall x' \cdot (Q \implies [x := x']B)$$
$$\Leftrightarrow \qquad\qquad\qquad\qquad\qquad\qquad\qquad \text{Property 6.1.1}$$
$$[S]A \wedge [S]B$$

End of Proof

Our second property states that the establishment of a post-condition is *monotonic*. More formally, given a generalized substitution S working with a variable x and two predicates A and B, we have

---

$$\forall x \cdot (A \implies B) \;\Rightarrow\; ([S]A \implies [S]B) \qquad\qquad \text{Property 6.2.2}$$

Proof

According to Theorem 6.1.1, the proof may be performed on the normalized form only. Consequently, we may assume

$$S \;=\; (P \mid @x' \cdot (Q \implies x := x')) \qquad\qquad \text{Hypothesis 1}$$

We also assume

$$\forall x \cdot (A \;\Rightarrow\; B)$$

Hypothesis 2

and we have to prove

$$[S]A \;\Rightarrow\; [S]B$$

Goal 1

We may assume $[S]A$, that is, according to Hypothesis 1 and Property 6.1.1,

$$P$$
$$\forall x' \cdot (Q \;\Rightarrow\; [x := x']A)$$

Hypothesis 3
Hypothesis 4

and we have to prove $[S]B$, that is, again according to Hypothesis 1 and Property 6.1.1,

$$P$$
$$\forall x' \cdot (Q \;\Rightarrow\; [x := x']B)$$

Goal 2
Goal 3

As Goal 2 is exactly Hypothesis 3, it only remains for us to prove Goal 3. Since the variable x' is non-free in any of the pending hypotheses, we can remove the universal quantification. We assume

$$Q$$

Hypothesis 5

and we are left to prove

$$[x := x']B$$

Goal 4

According to Hypothesis 2, it is sufficient to prove $[x := x']A$, which is obvious according to Hypothesis 5 and Hypothesis 4.
End of Proof

Consequently, we have the following property, where S is a substitution and P and Q are predicates:

$$\forall x \cdot (P \;\Leftrightarrow\; Q) \;\Rightarrow\; ([S]P \;\Leftrightarrow\; [S]Q)$$

Property 6.2.3

We leave it as an exercise for the reader to prove the following, where S is a substitution and P and Q are predicates:

$$[S]P \;\wedge\; [S](P \;\Rightarrow\; Q) \;\Rightarrow\; [S]Q$$

Property 6.2.4

6.3. Termination, Feasibility and Before-after Predicate

We turn our attention now to problems dealing with the question of *termination* as envisaged in section 4.7 and the question of *feasibility* as envisaged in section 4.15. In this section we propose some simple formal definitions for these concepts. We shall also define rigorously the *before-after predicate* correponding to a generalized substitution.

6.3.1. Termination

Given a substitution S, we define the construct $\mathsf{trm}(S)$ to denote the predicate that holds when the substitution S "terminates". Rather than defining the predicate $\mathsf{trm}(S)$ directly, we reason about its negation $\mathsf{abt}(S)$ (pronounced "*abort* S"). Obviously, an aborting substitution is one that cannot establish anything. In other words, for any post-condition R, it is *not* the case that S establishes R. Formally

Syntax	Definition
$\mathsf{abt}(S)$	$\neg\,[S]R$ for any predicate R
$\mathsf{trm}(S)$	$\neg\,\mathsf{abt}(S)$

Clearly, such a second order definition is not very convenient in practice, so we simplify it as follows:

$\mathsf{abt}(S)\quad\Leftrightarrow\quad\neg\,[S]\,(x=x)$ Property 6.3.1

Proof

We first prove

$$\mathsf{abt}(S)\quad\Rightarrow\quad\neg\,[S]\,(x=x) \qquad\qquad \textbf{Goal 1}$$

We assume $\mathsf{abt}(S)$, that is

$$\neg\,[S]R\quad\text{for any predicate }R \qquad\qquad \textbf{Hypothesis 1}$$

and we have to prove $\neg\,[S]\,(x=x)$, which is obvious according to **Hypothesis 1**. We prove now

$$\neg\,[S]\,(x=x)\quad\Rightarrow\quad\neg\,[S]R\quad\text{for any predicate }R \qquad\qquad \textbf{Goal 2}$$

We assume

$$\neg\,[S]\,(x=x) \qquad\qquad \textbf{Hypothesis 2}$$

and we have to prove

$$\neg\,[S]R\quad\text{for any predicate }R \qquad\qquad \textbf{Goal 3}$$

Since we obviously have the following:

$$\forall x \cdot (R \;\Rightarrow\; x = x) \qquad \text{for any predicate } R \qquad\qquad \text{Derivation 1}$$

we deduce the following according to Property 6.2.2

$$[S]R \;\Rightarrow\; [S](x = x) \qquad \text{for any predicate } R \qquad\qquad \text{Derivation 2}$$

leading, by contraposition, to

$$\neg [S](x = x) \;\Rightarrow\; \neg [S]R \qquad \text{for any predicate } R \qquad\qquad \text{Derivation 3}$$

Goal 3 follows then according to Hypothesis 2.
End of Proof

We deduce immediately

$$\mathrm{trm}\,(S) \;\Leftrightarrow\; [S](x = x) \qquad\qquad\qquad\qquad \text{Property 6.3.2}$$

From the previous property, we can deduce (exercise) the following results showing the shape of $\mathrm{trm}\,(S)$ for our various generalized substitutions, for the normalized form and for some other substitutions:

$\mathrm{trm}\,(x := E)$		
$\mathrm{trm}\,(\mathsf{skip})$		
$\mathrm{trm}\,(P \mid S)$	$\Leftrightarrow$	$P \wedge \mathrm{trm}\,(S)$
$\mathrm{trm}\,(S \;[]\; T)$	$\Leftrightarrow$	$\mathrm{trm}\,(S) \wedge \mathrm{trm}\,(T)$
$\mathrm{trm}\,(P \Longrightarrow S)$	$\Leftrightarrow$	$P \Rightarrow \mathrm{trm}\,(S)$
$\mathrm{trm}\,(@z \cdot S)$	$\Leftrightarrow$	$\forall z \cdot \mathrm{trm}\,(S)$
$\mathrm{trm}\,(P \mid @x' \cdot (Q \Longrightarrow x := x'))$	$\Leftrightarrow$	P
$\mathrm{trm}\,(x :\in E)$		
$\mathrm{trm}\,(x : P)$		

6.3.2. Feasibility

The concept of *guard*, introduced in the section 4.15, has given us the possibility to specify *non-feasible* substitutions able to establish any post-condition. This clearly happens when the guard does not hold. Given a substitution S, we thus define the two constructs $\mathrm{mir}\,(S)$ and its negation $\mathrm{fis}\,(S)$ as follows:

Syntax	Definition
$mir(S)$	$[S]R$ for any predicate R
$fis(S)$	$\neg\, mir(S)$

Clearly, such a second order definition for $mir(S)$ is not very convenient in practice, so we simplify it to the following first order condition:

$$mir(S) \iff [S](x \neq x) \qquad\qquad \text{Property 6.3.3}$$

The proof of **Property 6.3.3**, very similar to that of **Property 6.3.1**, is left as an exercise to the reader. We have thus

---

$$fis(S) \iff \neg\,[S](x \neq x) \qquad\qquad \text{Property 6.3.4}$$

From the above definition and **Property 6.3.4**, we can deduce (exercise) the following results showing the shape of $fis(S)$ for our various generalized substitutions, for the normalized form and for some other substitutions:

$fis(x := E)$		
$fis(skip)$		
$fis(P \mid S)$	$\iff$	$P \implies fis(S)$
$fis(S \,[\!]\, T)$	$\iff$	$fis(S) \lor fis(T)$
$fis(P \implies S)$	$\iff$	$P \land fis(S)$
$fis(@z \cdot S)$	$\iff$	$\exists z \cdot fis(S)$

$$\mathsf{fis}\,(P \mid @x' \cdot (Q \implies x := x')) \qquad \Leftrightarrow \qquad P \implies \exists x' \cdot Q$$

$$\mathsf{fis}\,(x :\in E) \qquad \qquad \Leftrightarrow \qquad E \neq \varnothing$$

$$\mathsf{fis}\,(x : P) \qquad \qquad \Leftrightarrow \qquad \exists x' \cdot [x_0, x := x, x']\, P$$

The last but one result is very instructive. Clearly, the substitution $x :\in E$ which "assigns" to x any member of the set E is only feasible (that is, eventually implementable) if the set E is not empty. Otherwise, we are asking for the impossible. Likewise, in the last result, the substitution $x : P$ which "assigns" to x any value such that the predicate P holds is only feasible if the predicate P does hold for some after-value x' corresponding to the before-value x.

6.3.3. Before-after Predicate

In this section we study how we can do a systematic translation from a generalized substitution S to the corresponding before-after predicate introduced in section 4.4. Such a predicate will be denoted by $\mathsf{prd}_x(S)$. We shall then establish an identity on generalized substitutions. This identity will involve $\mathsf{trm}\,(S)$ and $\mathsf{prd}_x(S)$.

The reason why we have subscripted prd with the variable x in the construct $\mathsf{prd}_x(S)$ is that the definition of that predicate depends on the variable x of the abstract machine into which the substitution S is "plunged". So, we shall suppose in what follows (unless otherwise stated) that our generalized substitution S works with an abstract machine with the variable x. We shall also follow the classical convention that the after-value is denoted by priming the abstract machine variable. We suppose, of course, that the primed variable is a *fresh* variable. We have then the following definition

Syntax	Definition
$\mathsf{prd}_x(S)$	$\neg\,[S]\,(x' \neq x)$

Intuitively, the after-value x' is connected to the before-value x when it is not the case that S establishes that x and x' are distinct afterwards. In other words, x' is one (because of non-determinism) among the possible after-values. For example, we have

$$\mathsf{prd}_x((x := x + 1) \,[\!] \, (x := x - 1))$$

$$\Leftrightarrow$$

$$\neg \,[(x := x + 1) \,[\!] \, (x := x - 1)]\,(x' \neq x)$$

$$\Leftrightarrow$$

$$\neg\,((x' \neq x + 1) \,\wedge\, (x' \neq x - 1))$$

$$\Leftrightarrow$$

$$(x' = x + 1) \,\vee\, (x' = x - 1)$$

In the case where we place ourselves in a machine with two variables x and y, we have:

$$\mathsf{prd}_{x,y}\,((x := x + 1) \,[\!] \, (x := x - 1))$$

$$\Leftrightarrow$$

$$\neg\,[(x := x + 1) \,[\!] \, (x := x - 1)]\,(x',y' \neq x,y)$$

$$\Leftrightarrow$$

$$\neg\,((x',y' \neq x + 1, y) \,\wedge\, (x',y' \neq x - 1, y))$$

$$\Leftrightarrow$$

$$((x',y' = x + 1, y) \,\vee\, (x',y' = x - 1, y))$$

$$\Leftrightarrow$$

$$((x' = x + 1) \,\vee\, (x' = x - 1)) \,\wedge\, y' = y$$

As can be seen, the before-after predicate always depends on the variables of the machine within which it works. Here the variable y is not changed, since its after-value is the same as its before-value. This is clearly what we expect from a substitution which does not mention y at all. This illustrates one slight advantage of using generalized substitutions rather than before-after predicates. In the latter case, one always has to state explicitly that a variable is not modified. From the previous definition of prd_x, we can deduce (exercise) the following results showing the shape of $\mathsf{prd}_x(S)$ for our various generalized substitutions:

$$
\begin{array}{lcl}
\mathsf{prd}_x(x := E) & \Leftrightarrow & x' = E \\[2mm]
\mathsf{prd}_{x,y}\,(x := E) & \Leftrightarrow & x', y' = E, y \\[2mm]
\mathsf{prd}_x(\mathsf{skip}) & \Leftrightarrow & x' = x \\[2mm]
\mathsf{prd}_x(P \mid S) & \Leftrightarrow & P \Rightarrow \mathsf{prd}_x(S) \\[2mm]
\mathsf{prd}_x(S \,[\!] \, T) & \Leftrightarrow & \mathsf{prd}_x(S) \vee \mathsf{prd}_x(T) \\[2mm]
\mathsf{prd}_x(P \Longrightarrow S) & \Leftrightarrow & P \wedge \mathsf{prd}_x(S) \\[2mm]
\mathsf{prd}_x(@z \cdot S) & \Leftrightarrow & \exists z \cdot \mathsf{prd}_x(S) \quad \text{if } z \setminus x'
\end{array}
$$

$$\mathsf{prd}_x(@y \cdot T) \qquad\qquad\qquad \Leftrightarrow \quad \exists(y, y') \cdot \mathsf{prd}_{x,y}(T) \quad \text{if } y \setminus x' \qquad *$$

$$\mathsf{prd}_x(P \mid @x' \cdot (Q \implies x := x')) \quad \Leftrightarrow \quad P \implies Q$$

$$\mathsf{prd}_x(x :\in E) \qquad\qquad\qquad \Leftrightarrow \quad x' \in E$$

$$\mathsf{prd}_x(x : P) \qquad\qquad\qquad\quad \Leftrightarrow \quad [x_0, x := x, x']P$$

The case marked with an asterisk is rather peculiar. It corresponds to a sub-stitution T "modifying" both variables x and y (in the preceding case, the substitution S is supposed to "modify" x only, the variable z being just a "passive" parameter of the substitution S). As a hint for proving the asterisked case, put the substitution T into normalized form.

The proof concerning $\mathsf{prd}_x(P \mid @x' \cdot (Q \implies x := x'))$ must be done with some care. The reader must remember that the definition of $\mathsf{prd}_x(S)$ is $\neg[S](x \neq x')$. This means that there will be a clash of the external occurrence of x' in $(x \neq x')$ and the internal quantification introduced by $@x'$. The problem is easily solved by rewriting the statement as follows: $\mathsf{prd}_x(P \mid @x'' \cdot ([x' := x'']Q \implies x := x''))$.

We finally notice the following property, whose proof is left to the reader:

$$\mathsf{fis}(S) \quad \Leftrightarrow \quad \exists x' \cdot \mathsf{prd}_x(S) \qquad\qquad\qquad\qquad \text{Property 6.3.5}$$

This clearly indicates that a substitution is feasible (at x) if some after-value x' is reachable from the before-value x. We now prove the following equivalence which relates our previous constructs:

$$S \;=\; \mathsf{trm}(S) \mid @x' \cdot (\mathsf{prd}_x(S) \implies x := x') \qquad\qquad \text{Theorem 6.3.1}$$

Proof

As we have to prove the "equality" of two substitutions, it is sufficient to prove that any post-condition established by one is also established by the other. In other words, we prove the following, for any post-condition R:

$$[S]R \quad \Leftrightarrow \quad [\mathsf{trm}(S) \mid @x' \cdot (\mathsf{prd}_x(S) \implies x := x')]R \qquad \text{Goal 1}$$

According to Theorem 6.1.1, it is sufficient to perform the proof on the normal-ized form only. Consequently, we may assume

$$S = P \mid @x' \cdot (Q \implies x := x') \quad \text{where } x' \setminus P \qquad \text{Hypothesis 1}$$

The proof goes as follows:

$[S]R$

$\Leftrightarrow$ Hypothesis 1

$[P \mid @x' \cdot (Q \implies x := x')]R$

$\Leftrightarrow$

$P \wedge \forall x' \cdot (Q \Rightarrow [x := x']R)$

$\Leftrightarrow$ $x' \setminus P$

$P \wedge \forall x' \cdot ((P \Rightarrow Q) \Rightarrow [x := x']R)$

$\Leftrightarrow$

$P \wedge \forall x' \cdot (\mathrm{prd}_x(P \mid @x' \cdot (Q \implies x := x')) \Rightarrow [x := x']R)$

$\Leftrightarrow$ Hypothesis 1

$[\mathrm{trm}\,(S) \mid @x' \cdot (\mathrm{prd}_x(S) \longrightarrow x := x')]R$

End of Proof

A consequence of Theorem 6.3.1 is that both predicates $\mathrm{trm}\,(S)$ and $\mathrm{prd}_x(S)$ *characterize completely* the generalized substitution S supposed to work with an abstract machine with variable x. Note that we could equally well say that $\mathrm{trm}\,(S)$ and $\mathrm{trm}\,(S) \Rightarrow \mathrm{prd}_x(S)$ *characterize* the generalized substitution S. We are now ready to build the two set-theoretic models of abstract machines.

6.4. Set-Theoretic Models

6.4.1. First Model: a Set and a Relation

Given a non-empty set s, we consider a generalized substitution S working with the (list of) variable(s) x such that the membership of x in s is *invariant* under S. Formally

$$x \in s \wedge \mathrm{trm}\,(S) \Rightarrow [S]\,(x \in s)$$ Axiom 6.4.1

That is, we consider that all our substitutions work within the framework of an abstract machine whose (list of) variable(s) x has an invariant implying a predicate of the form $x \in s$. From here on, we shall always consider generalized substitutions that follow Axiom 6.4.1 and, in proofs, we shall always make implicit assumptions of the form $x \in s$.

To each such substitution S we associate a set $\mathrm{pre}\,(S)$, a binary relation $\mathrm{rel}\,(S)$ and a set $\mathrm{dom}\,(S)$ defined as follows:

Syntax	Definition
pre (S)	$\{x \mid x \in s \ \wedge \ \mathsf{trm}(S)\}$
rel (S)	$\{x, x' \mid x, x' \in s \times s \ \wedge \ \mathsf{prd}_x(S)\}$
dom (S)	$\{x \mid x \in s \ \wedge \ \mathsf{fis}(S)\}$

Intuitively, pre(S), the *pre-condition set*, corresponds to the set of points at which the pre-condition holds (where the substitution is meaningful), whereas rel(S) is a binary relation expressing the *dynamics* of the substitution since it relates the before-value to the corresponding after-value. And, finally, dom(S) is clearly the domain of the previous relation (remember **Property 6.3.5**). For instance, let s be the set $\mathbb{N}$, and S be the substitution

$$S \ = \ \text{PRE} \ x > 0 \ \text{THEN} \ x := x - 1 \ \text{END}$$

We have

$$
\begin{aligned}
\mathsf{pre}(S) \ &= \ \{x \mid x \in \mathbb{N} \wedge x > 0\} \\
&= \ \mathbb{N}_1
\end{aligned}
$$

$$
\begin{aligned}
\mathsf{rel}(S) \ &= \ \{x, x' \mid (x, x') \in \mathbb{N} \times \mathbb{N} \ \wedge \ \mathsf{prd}_x(x > 0 \mid x := x - 1)\} \\
&= \ \{x, x' \mid (x, x') \in \mathbb{N} \times \mathbb{N} \ \wedge \ (x > 0 \ \Rightarrow \ x' = x - 1)\} \\
&= \ \{x, x' \mid (x, x') \in \mathbb{N} \times \mathbb{N} \ \wedge \ (x = 0 \ \vee \ x' = x - 1)\} \\
&= \ \{0\} \times \mathbb{N} \ \cup \ \{x, x' \mid (x, x') \in \mathbb{N} \times \mathbb{N} \ \wedge \ x' = x - 1\}
\end{aligned}
$$

$$
\begin{aligned}
\mathsf{dom}(S) \ &= \ \{x \mid x \in \mathbb{N} \ \wedge \ \mathsf{fis}(x > 0 \mid x := x - 1)\} \\
&= \ \{x \mid x \in \mathbb{N}\} \\
&= \ \mathbb{N}
\end{aligned}
$$

Quite intuitively, the set pre(S) corresponds to the set of positive natural numbers as stipulated by the pre-condition, $x > 0$, of our substitution S. Contrary to intuition, however, the relation rel(S) is more than just the relation corresponding to the *active* part, $x := x - 1$, of the substitution S. As can be seen, we have the extra relation $\{0\} \times \mathbb{N}$ connecting the unique point, 0, lying outside pre(S) to every member of $\mathbb{N}$. We shall come back to this interesting phenomenon after the notational remark which follows.

Before proceeding, let us fix a point of notation. As there is no ambiguity concerning the set s, we shall use systematically in the remaining part of this chapter the following traditional notation to represent the set difference between s and one of its subsets p:

$$\overline{p} = s - p$$

From the definition of pre (S) and rel (S), we now derive two important properties. The first one expresses the fact that the relation obtained by linking every member of the complement of pre(S) to every member of s is included in rel(S). Formally

---

$$\overline{\text{pre}(S)} \times s \;\subseteq\; \text{rel}(S) \hspace{6cm} \text{Property 6.4.1}$$

Proof

We have to prove the following for all points x and x':

$$x \in s \,\wedge\, x \notin \text{pre}(S) \,\wedge\, x' \in s \;\Rightarrow\; (x,x') \in \text{rel}(S) \hspace{2cm} \text{Goal 1}$$

We assume the antecedents of that implication, that is equivalently after the definition of pre (S)

$$x \in s \hspace{6cm} \text{Hypothesis 1}$$
$$x' \in s \hspace{6cm} \text{Hypothesis 2}$$
$$\neg\, \text{trm}(S) \hspace{5.5cm} \text{Hypothesis 3}$$

and we have to prove

$$(x,x') \in \text{rel}(S) \hspace{6cm} \text{Goal 2}$$

that is equivalently after the definition of rel (S)

$$x \in s \hspace{6cm} \text{Goal 3}$$
$$x' \in s \hspace{6cm} \text{Goal 4}$$
$$\text{prd}_x(S) \hspace{5.8cm} \text{Goal 5}$$

Goal 3 and Goal 4 are exactly Hypothesis 1 and Hypothesis 2. We prove Goal 5 *by contradiction*. We thus assume $\neg\, \text{prd}_x(S)$, that is,

$$[S]\,(x \neq x') \hspace{5.5cm} \text{Hypothesis 4}$$

As we certainly have $\forall x \cdot (x \neq x' \;\Rightarrow\; x = x)$, then we deduce the following according to **Property 6.2.2**:

$$[S]\,(x \neq x') \;\Rightarrow\; [S]\,(x = x) \hspace{4cm} \text{Derivation 1}$$

Consequently and according to Hypothesis 4, we have $[S]\,(x = x)$, that is, equivalently, trm (S) according to **Property 6.3.2**, a fact contradicted by Hypothesis 3.

End of Proof

Our second property is a consequence of Theorem 6.3.1 which we re-state here:

$$S \;=\; \text{trm}(S) \,|\, @x' \cdot (\text{prd}_x(S) \;\Longrightarrow\; x := x')$$

From this, we obtain

$$S \;=\; x \in \mathsf{pre}\,(S) \mid @x' \cdot (\,(x,x') \in \mathsf{rel}\,(S) \implies x := x'\,) \qquad \text{Property 6.4.2}$$

We leave the proof of this property as an exercise for the reader. As a hint, you might first prove the following property and then use the definition of $\mathsf{rel}\,(S)$.

$$x \in s \;\wedge\; \mathsf{trm}\,(S) \;\wedge\; \mathsf{prd}_x(S) \;\Rightarrow\; x' \in s \qquad \text{Property 6.4.3}$$

Conversely, given a subset p of s and a binary relation r from s to s, let S be the following generalized substitution:

$$S \;=\; x \in p \mid @x' \cdot (\,(x,x') \in r \implies x := x'\,)$$

We obtain

$$\mathsf{pre}\,(S) \;=\; p$$

$$\mathsf{rel}\,(S) \;=\; (\overline{p} \times s) \cup r$$

This leads to the following property:

$$
\begin{array}{l}
p \subseteq s \\
r \in s \leftrightarrow s \\
\overline{p} \times s \subseteq r \\
S \;=\; x \in p \mid @x' \cdot (\,(x,x') \in r \implies x := x'\,) \\
\Rightarrow \\
\mathsf{pre}\,(S) \;=\; p \\
\mathsf{rel}\,(S) \;\;=\; r
\end{array}
\qquad \text{Property 6.4.4}
$$

In conclusion, it seems that to each statement involving a generalized substitution S, there corresponds a set-theoretic statement involving $\mathsf{pre}\,(S)$ and $\mathsf{rel}\,(S)$. Conversely, to each set-theoretic statement involving a set p and relation r such that $\overline{p} \times s$ is included in r, there corresponds a statement involving a certain generalized substitution. In what follows, we shall pursue this little investigation.

6.4.2. Second Model: Set Transformer

In this section we give a set-theoretic counterpart to predicates of the form $[S]\,(x \in q)$ where S is a generalized substitution obeying Axiom 6.4.1 and where q is a subset of s. More precisely, we have

$$\{x \mid x \in s \;\wedge\; [S]\,(x \in q)\} \;=\; \mathsf{pre}\,(S) \cap \overline{\mathsf{rel}\,(S)^{-1}[\overline{q}\,]} \qquad \text{Theorem 6.4.1}$$

Proof

$$\{x \mid x \in s \ \wedge \ [S](x \in q)\}$$
$$=$$
$$\{x \mid x \in s \ \wedge \ x \in \mathsf{pre}(S) \ \wedge \ \forall x' \cdot ((x,x') \in \mathsf{rel}(S) \ \Rightarrow \ x' \in q)\}$$
$$=$$
$$\{x \mid x \in s \ \wedge \ x \in \mathsf{pre}(S)\} \cap$$
$$\quad \{x \mid x \in s \ \wedge \ \forall x' \cdot ((x,x') \in \mathsf{rel}(S) \ \Rightarrow \ x' \in q)\}$$
$$=$$
$$\mathsf{pre}(S) \cap \{x \mid x \in s \ \wedge \ \neg \ \exists x' \cdot ((x,x') \in \mathsf{rel}(S) \ \wedge \ x' \notin q)\}$$
$$=$$
$$\mathsf{pre}(S) \cap \overline{\mathsf{rel}(S)^{-1}[\overline{q}]}$$

Property 6.4.2

End of Proof

When q is s, Theorem 6.4.1 reduces to the following statement which we could have obtained directly:

$$\{x \mid x \in s \ \wedge \ [S](x \in s)\} \ = \ \mathsf{pre}(S) \qquad\qquad \text{Property 6.4.5}$$

When q is distinct from s, Theorem 6.4.1 reduces (exercise) to the following:

$$\{x \mid x \in s \ \wedge \ [S](x \in q)\} \ = \ \overline{\mathsf{rel}(S)^{-1}[\overline{q}]} \qquad\qquad \text{Property 6.4.6}$$

From Theorem 6.4.1, we can prove the next two properties which link the present set-theoretic approach to the generalized substitution approach. More precisely, the two subsequent properties will allow us to conduct all our mathematical developments using sets and binary relations only (a situation which is quite comfortable for theoretical reasoning) and eventually to translate our practical results into the *generalized substitution notation* which we use in practice.

$$p \ \subseteq \ \mathsf{pre}(S) \cap \overline{\mathsf{rel}(S)^{-1}[\overline{q}]}$$
$$\Rightarrow$$
$$\forall x \cdot (x \in p \ \Rightarrow \ [S](x \in q))$$

Property 6.4.7

$$\forall x \cdot (x \in p \ \Rightarrow \ [S](x \in q))$$
$$\Rightarrow$$
$$p \ \subseteq \ \overline{\mathsf{rel}(S)^{-1}[\overline{q}]}$$

At this point, it might be useful to explain intuitively where the double negation present in $\overline{\mathsf{rel}(S)^{-1}[\overline{q}]}$ in the above property comes from and why we do not have just $\mathsf{rel}(S)^{-1}[q]$. A picture might be helpful:

dom(r) r ran(r)

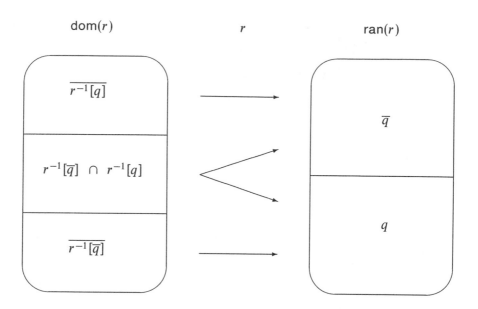

In this picture, one can "see" a relation r from its domain dom(r) to its range ran(r). The set ran(r) is supposed to contain *two* complementary sets q and $\overline{q}$. The set dom(r) thus contains *three* corresponding complementary sets:

- In the centre, is the set $r^{-1}[\overline{q}] \cap r^{-1}[q]$ containing those elements that are connected to *both* members of q and members of $\overline{q}$.

- At the top, is the set $\overline{r^{-1}[q]}$ whose elements are *not* in the inverse image of q: such elements are thus connected to members of $\overline{q}$ *only*.

- At the bottom, is the set $\overline{r^{-1}[\overline{q}]}$ whose elements are *not* in the inverse image of $\overline{q}$: such elements are thus connected to members of q *only*.

Note that the members of s that are *both* in $\overline{r^{-1}[q]}$ and in $\overline{r^{-1}[\overline{q}]}$ are not connected to any members of q nor to any members of $\overline{q}$: they are thus clearly not in the domain of r, as we expect.

As we know, the members of s satisfying the predicate $[S](x \in q)$ denote those elements of s establishing, through S, the predicate $x \in q$: these elements are clearly connected, through S, to members of q only, unless they also establish the predicate $x \notin q$, in which case they are members of the "miraculous" set $\overline{\text{dom}(\text{rel}(S))}$ and thus not connected at all. This is how the above picture "explains" why, in the first set-theoretic model that we have seen so far, such elements are exactly the members of the set $\overline{\text{rel}(S)^{-1}[\overline{q}]}$.

We give now a more formal status to what we have presented in this section. For this, we introduce the following definition, where S is a substitution working within an abstract machine with variable x:

Syntax	Definition
str (S)	$\lambda p \cdot (p \in \mathbb{P}(s) \mid \{ x \mid x \in s \wedge [S](x \in p) \})$

Notice that we have

$$\text{str}(S) \in \mathbb{P}(s) \to \mathbb{P}(s)$$

This is the reason why str (S) is called a set transformer. It enjoys the following interesting property (exercise) which is a direct set-theoretic translation of Theorem 6.3.1:

$x \in \text{str}(S)(p) \Leftrightarrow$
$\quad x \in \text{str}(S)(s) \wedge \forall x' \cdot (x' \in \overline{p} \Rightarrow x \in \text{str}(S)(\overline{\{x'\}}))$
          Property 6.4.8

Of course, str (S) is not independent of the previous constructs. Here are the obvious relationships (exercise) between them:

---

pre (S)	$=$	str $(S)(s)$
rel (S)	$\Leftrightarrow$	$\{ x, x' \mid (x, x') \in s \times s \wedge$
		$\qquad x \in \overline{\text{str}(S)(\overline{\{x'\}})} \}$
dom (S)	$=$	$\overline{\text{str}(S)(\varnothing)}$
str $(S)(p)$	$=$	pre $(S) \cap \overline{\text{rel}(S)^{-1}[\overline{p}]}$
rel $(S)^{-1}[p]$	$=$	$\overline{\text{str}(S)(\overline{p})}$ if $p \neq \varnothing$

Property 6.4.9

As can be seen, the two models we have presented in this and the previous section are equivalent since we can translate one into the other (see also exercises 9 and 10).

6.4.3. Set-theoretic Interpretations of the Constructs

In the following tables, we give the form of pre (S), rel (S) and str $(S)(p)$ for each basic construct of the generalized substitution notation. We first give the results for all the constructs but the last. In the following table, each generalized substitution is supposed to work with an abstract machine with variable x and invariant $x \in s$.

	pre ()	rel ()	str () (p)
$x := E$	s	$\lambda x \cdot (x \in s \mid E)$	$\{x \mid x \in s \land E \in p\}$
skip	s	$\text{id}(s)$	p
$P \mid S$	$\text{set}(P) \cap \text{pre}(S)$	$(\overline{\text{set}(P)} \times s) \cup \text{rel}(S)$	$\text{set}(P) \cap \text{str}(S)(p)$
$S \parallel T$	$\text{pre}(S) \cap \text{pre}(T)$	$\text{rel}(S) \cup \text{rel}(T)$	$\text{str}(S)(p) \cap \text{str}(T)(p)$
$P \Longrightarrow S$	$\overline{\text{set}(P)} \cup \text{pre}(S)$	$(\text{set}(P) \times s) \cap \text{rel}(S)$	$\overline{\text{set}(P)} \cup \text{str}(S)(p)$

where

$$\text{set}(P) = \{x \mid x \in s \land P\}$$

For the unbounded choice substitution, we have two cases to consider:

$$@z \cdot (z \in u \Longrightarrow S)$$

$$@y \cdot (y \in t \Longrightarrow T)$$

In the first case, the substitution S is supposed to work, as usual, within a machine with variable x. In the second case, the substitution T works with variables x and y supposed to be members of the sets s and t respectively. Next are the results for pre and rel:

	pre ()	rel ()
$@z \cdot (z \in u \Longrightarrow S)$	$\bigcap z \cdot (z \in u \mid \text{pre}(S))$	$\bigcup z \cdot (z \in u \mid \text{rel}(S))$
$@y \cdot (y \in t \Longrightarrow T)$	$\overline{\text{prj}_1(s,t)[\overline{\text{pre}(T)}]}$	$\text{prj}_1(s,t)^{-1} ; \text{rel}(T) ; \text{prj}_1(s,t)$

Next are the results for str:

	$\mathsf{str}\,()\,(p)$
$@z \cdot (z \in u \Longrightarrow S\,)$	$\bigcap z \cdot (z \in u \mid \mathsf{str}\,(S)(p))$
$@y \cdot (y \in t \Longrightarrow T\,)$	$\overline{\mathsf{prj}_1\,(s,t)[\,\mathsf{str}\,(T)(p \times t)\,]}$

The last result can be proved as follows:

$$\overline{\mathsf{prj}_1\,(s,t)(\overline{\mathsf{str}\,(T)(p \times t)})} \quad =$$

$$= \quad \overline{\mathsf{prj}_1\,(s,t)[\,\{\,x,y \mid (x,y) \in s \times t \ \wedge\ [T](x,y \in p \times t)\,\}\,]}$$

$$= \quad \overline{\mathsf{prj}_1\,(s,t)[\,\{\,x,y \mid (x,y) \in s \times t \ \wedge\ [T](x \in p)\,\}\,]}$$

$$= \quad \overline{\mathsf{prj}_1\,(s,t)[\,\{\,x,y \mid (x,y) \in s \times t \ \wedge\ \neg\,[T](x \in p)\,\}\,]}$$

$$= \quad \overline{\{\,x \mid x \in s \ \wedge\ \exists(x',y) \cdot ((x',y) \in s \times t \ \wedge\ \neg\,[T](x \in p) \ \wedge\ x' = x\,)\}}$$

$$= \quad \overline{\{\,x \mid x \in s \ \wedge\ \exists\,y \cdot (y \in t \ \wedge\ \neg\,[T](x \in p))\}}$$

$$= \quad \{\,x \mid x \in s \ \wedge\ \forall\,y \cdot (y \in t \ \Rightarrow\ [T](x \in p))\}$$

$$= \quad \{\,x \mid x \in s \ \wedge\ [@y \cdot (y \in t \Longrightarrow T)](x \in p\,)\}$$

$$= \quad \mathsf{str}\,(@y \cdot (y \in t \Longrightarrow T\,))(p)$$

We notice that this result is quite intuitive since, in the substitution $@y \cdot (y \in t \Longrightarrow T)$, the effect of the $@$ quantifier is to *hide* the second dimension with which the substitution T is supposed to work.

6.5. Exercises

1. Prove some of the laws of section 6.1.

2. Prove Property 6.2.4.

3. Prove the laws concerning the predicate $\mathsf{trm}\,(S)$ given in section 6.3.1.

4. Prove the laws concerning the predicate $\mathsf{fis}\,(S)$ given in section 6.3.2.

5. Prove the laws concerning the predicate $\mathrm{prd}_x(S)$ given in section 6.3.3.

6. Prove Property 6.3.5.

7. Prove Property 6.4.2.

8. Prove Property 6.4.8 and Property 6.4.9.

9. Consider a set s and a certain "set transformer" f:

$$f \in \mathbb{P}(s) \to \mathbb{P}(s)$$

such that f distributes over generalized intersection, that is, given $tt \in \mathbb{P}_1(\mathbb{P}(s))$:

$$f(\mathrm{inter}\,(tt)) \;=\; \mathrm{inter}\,(f\,[tt])$$

Prove that the right-hand side of the previous equality is well defined. In other words, prove that $f\,[tt]$ is not empty.
Prove that f is monotone, that is, given two subsets p and q of s:

$$p \subseteq q \;\Rightarrow\; f(p) \subseteq f(q)$$

Prove that it is possible to define a subset q of s and a binary relation r from s to s, such that, given a subset p of s, we have:

$$f(p) \;=\; q \cap \overline{r^{-1}[\bar{p}]}$$

Prove the following:

$$\bar{q} \times s \;\subseteq\; r$$

10. Conversely, consider a set s, a subset q of s and a binary relation r from s to s such that:

$$\bar{q} \times s \;\subseteq\; r$$

Let us define the "set transformer" f:

$$f \in \mathbb{P}(s) \to \mathbb{P}(s)$$

such that, given a subset p of s, we have:

$$f(p) \;=\; q \cap \overline{r^{-1}[\bar{p}]}$$

Prove that f distributes over generalized intersection, that is, given $tt \in \mathbb{P}_1(\mathbb{P}(s))$:

$$f(\mathrm{inter}\,(tt)) \;=\; \mathrm{inter}\,(f\,[tt])$$

Prove now that f can be decomposed (according to the previous exercise) into exactly the set q and the binary relation r. In other words, we have a one-to-one relationship between f and the pair (q,r).

11. Prove some of the set-theoretic interpretations of the basic generalized substitution given in the table of section 6.4.3.

12. Extend the table of section 6.4.3 with your guess for the shape of the construct dom (S) for the proposed generalized substitutions S. Prove your conjectures.

CHAPTER 7

Large Abstract Machines

THIS chapter is devoted to the problem of constructing large abstract machines. For doing this, we define a number of mechanisms allowing us to construct abstract machines in an *incremental fashion*. This chapter does not contain corresponding large examples: it will be the purpose of chapter 8. In the present chapter, we only concentrate on the informal then formal definitions of the new features.

We shall first introduce a new generalized substitution construct, the *multiple generalized substitution*, which will prove to be the basic ingredient allowing us to build large specifications (section 7.1).

We shall then enlarge the Abstract Machine Notation accordingly so that it will be possible to construct an abstract machine from smaller, already defined and *proved*, ones (section 7.2). Also in section 7.2, we shall enlarge the Generalized Substitution Language so that substitutions can themselves be subjected to substitutions.

We shall then further enlarge the Abstract Machine Notation, allowing us, this time, to construct abstract machines in an incremental and shared way (section 7.3).

Finally, we shall present the formal definition (syntax, type-checking and axioms) of the new constructs introduced in this chapter (section 7.4).

7.1. Multiple Generalized Substitution

In this section it is our intention to generalize the operator " $\|$ ". This construct was introduced at the end of section 4.12 as a mere "syntactic sugar" for multiple simple substitutions. We had the following syntactic extension:

307

Syntax	Definition
$x := E \quad \| \quad y := F$	$x, y := E, F$

The idea is now to give a formal meaning to the *multiple composition* of two *generalized substitutions* S and T (not only *simple* substitutions) supposed to work on two abstract machines M and N working with the respective, *distinct*, variables x and y.

7.1.1. Definition

Contrary to the other generalized substitution operators, we shall not present an axiom stating how a statement such as $[S \| T]R$ can be decomposed in terms of more elementary statements such as $[S]R$ and $[T]R$. We adopt another strategy consisting of defining the multiple composition of two substitutions S and T by defining both predicates $\mathrm{trm}(S \| T)$ and $\mathrm{prd}_{x,y}(S \| T)$. And we know, according to the remark made at the end of section 6.3.3, that this is sufficient to characterize a generalized substitution. More precisely, we have the following definitions, showing clearly that the operator $\|$ applied to two substitutions S and T (pronounced "S *with* T") consists in putting them together by conjoining their termination and their before-after predicates respectively:

$\mathrm{trm}(S \| T)$	$\mathrm{trm}(S) \wedge \mathrm{trm}(T)$
$\mathrm{prd}_{x,y}(S \| T)$	$\mathrm{prd}_x(S) \wedge \mathrm{prd}_y(T)$

7.1.2. Basic Properties

From the definitions of the previous section, we can immediately deduce the following equalities concerning the set-theoretic model of $S \| T$ (notice that we have subscripted the set-theoretic operators to avoid any ambiguity):

$$\mathrm{pre}_{x,y}(S \| T) \quad = \quad \mathrm{pre}_x(S) \times \mathrm{pre}_y(T)$$

$$\text{rel}_{x,y}(S \mid\mid T) \quad = \quad \text{rel}_x(S) \mid\mid \text{rel}_y(T)$$

$$\text{dom}_{x,y}(S \mid\mid T) \quad = \quad \text{dom}_x(S) \times \text{dom}_y(T)$$

From the definitions of the previous section, we can also deduce the following series of very intuitive equalities whose proofs can be conducted by proving the equivalences of the predicate $\text{trm}(X)$ and of the predicate $\text{prd}_x(X)$ or $\text{trm}(X) \Rightarrow \text{prd}_x(X)$ when X is replaced by the left- and right-hand side of each equality (such proofs are left as exercises to the reader):

$x := E \mid\mid y := F$	$=$	$x, y := E, F$
$S \mid\mid \text{skip}$	$=$	S
$S \mid\mid (P \mid T)$	$=$	$P \mid (S \mid\mid T)$
$S \mid\mid (T \parallel U)$	$=$	$(S \mid\mid T) \parallel (S \mid\mid U)$
$S \mid\mid (P \Longrightarrow T)$	$=$	$P \Longrightarrow (S \mid\mid T) \qquad$ if $\text{trm}(S)$ holds
$S \mid\mid (@z \cdot T)$	$=$	$@z \cdot (S \mid\mid T) \qquad$ if $z \setminus S$
$\text{skip} \mid\mid S$	$=$	S
$(P \mid T) \mid\mid S$	$=$	$P \mid (T \mid\mid S)$
$(T \parallel U) \mid\mid S$	$=$	$(T \mid\mid S) \parallel (U \mid\mid S)$
$(P \Longrightarrow T) \mid\mid S$	$=$	$P \Longrightarrow (T \mid\mid S) \qquad$ if $\text{trm}(S)$ holds
$(@z \cdot T) \mid\mid S$	$=$	$@z \cdot (T \mid\mid S) \qquad$ if $z \setminus S$
$(x :\in E) \mid\mid (y :\in F)$	$=$	$(x, y) :\in E \times F$
$(x : P) \mid\mid (y : Q)$	$=$	$(x, y) : (P \wedge Q) \qquad$ if $x \setminus Q \quad y \setminus P$

For the IF, SELECT, CASE and ANY constructs, we have the following:

$$S \; \| \;
\begin{array}{l}
\text{IF} \quad P \quad \text{THEN} \\
\quad T \\
\text{ELSE} \\
\quad U \\
\text{END}
\end{array}
\quad = \quad
\begin{array}{l}
\text{IF} \quad P \quad \text{THEN} \\
\quad S \; \| \; T \\
\text{ELSE} \\
\quad S \; \| \; U \\
\text{END}
\end{array}$$

$$S \; \| \;
\begin{array}{l}
\text{IF} \quad P \quad \text{THEN} \\
\quad T \\
\text{END}
\end{array}
\quad = \quad
\begin{array}{l}
\text{IF} \quad P \quad \text{THEN} \\
\quad S \; \| \; T \\
\text{ELSE} \\
\quad S \\
\text{END}
\end{array}$$

$$S \; \| \;
\begin{array}{l}
\text{SELECT} \quad P \quad \text{THEN} \\
\quad T \\
\ldots \\
\text{WHEN} \quad Q \quad \text{THEN} \\
\quad U \\
\text{ELSE} \\
\quad V \\
\text{END}
\end{array}
\quad = \quad
\begin{array}{l}
\text{SELECT} \quad P \quad \text{THEN} \\
\quad S \; \| \; T \\
\ldots \\
\text{WHEN} \quad Q \quad \text{THEN} \\
\quad S \; \| \; U \\
\text{ELSE} \\
\quad S \; \| \; V \\
\text{END}
\end{array}$$

$$S \; \| \;
\begin{array}{l}
\text{SELECT} \quad P \quad \text{THEN} \\
\quad T \\
\ldots \\
\text{WHEN} \quad Q \quad \text{THEN} \\
\quad U \\
\text{END}
\end{array}
\quad = \quad
\begin{array}{l}
\text{SELECT} \quad P \quad \text{THEN} \\
\quad S \; \| \; T \\
\ldots \\
\text{WHEN} \quad Q \quad \text{THEN} \\
\quad S \; \| \; U \\
\text{END}
\end{array}$$

if $\text{trm}(S)$ holds

$$S \; \| \;
\begin{array}{l}
\text{CASE} \quad E \quad \text{OF} \\
\quad \text{EITHER} \quad l \quad \text{THEN} \\
\qquad T \\
\quad \ldots \\
\quad \text{OR} \quad p \quad \text{THEN} \\
\qquad U \\
\quad \text{END} \\
\text{END}
\end{array}
\quad = \quad
\begin{array}{l}
\text{CASE} \quad E \quad \text{OF} \\
\quad \text{EITHER} \quad l \quad \text{THEN} \\
\qquad S \; \| \; T \\
\quad \ldots \\
\quad \text{OR} \quad p \quad \text{THEN} \\
\qquad S \; \| \; U \\
\quad \text{END} \\
\text{END}
\end{array}$$

$$
S \;\|\;
\begin{array}{l}
\text{CASE} \;\; E \;\; \text{OF} \\
\quad \text{EITHER} \;\; l \;\; \text{THEN} \\
\qquad T \\
\quad \cdots \\
\quad \text{OR} \;\; p \;\; \text{THEN} \\
\qquad U \\
\quad \text{ELSE} \\
\qquad V \\
\quad \text{END} \\
\text{END}
\end{array}
\quad = \quad
\begin{array}{l}
\text{CASE} \;\; E \;\; \text{OF} \\
\quad \text{EITHER} \;\; l \;\; \text{THEN} \\
\qquad S \;\|\; T \\
\quad \cdots \\
\quad \text{OR} \;\; p \;\; \text{THEN} \\
\qquad S \;\|\; U \\
\quad \text{ELSE} \\
\qquad S \;\|\; V \\
\quad \text{END} \\
\text{END}
\end{array}
$$

$$
S \;\|\;
\begin{array}{l}
\text{ANY} \;\; x \;\; \text{WHERE} \\
\quad P \\
\text{THEN} \\
\quad T \\
\text{END}
\end{array}
\quad = \quad
\begin{array}{l}
\text{ANY} \;\; x \;\; \text{WHERE} \\
\quad P \\
\text{ELSE} \\
\quad S \;\|\; T \\
\text{END}
\end{array}
$$

if $\mathrm{trm}\,(S)$ and $x \setminus [S]R$
for each R s.t. $x \setminus R$

Note that we have similar properties with the substitution S situated on the right-hand side of the $\|$ operator. The form of all these properties is enough to show that the $\|$ operator can be considered as a mere *syntactic device* that can always be eliminated.

7.1.3. The Main Result

The most important result about the multiple composition of substitutions is the following theorem: given two substitutions S and T working with *distinct* variables x and y respectively, and two predicates P and Q such that x is non-free in Q and y is non-free in P, then we can deduce $[S \;\|\; T]\,(P \wedge Q)$ from $[S]P$ and $[T]Q$, formally

---

$$[S]P \wedge [T]Q \;\Rightarrow\; [S \;\|\; T]\,(P \wedge Q)$$
$$\text{if} \;\; x \setminus Q \;\; \text{and} \;\; y \setminus P \qquad\qquad \text{Theorem 7.1.1}$$

Proof

We have the following side conditions:

$$x \setminus Q \qquad\qquad\qquad \text{Side Condition 1}$$
$$y \setminus P \qquad\qquad\qquad \text{Side Condition 2}$$

We may assume $[S]P \land [T]Q$, that is according to Theorem 6.3.1,

$$\mathrm{trm}\,(S) \qquad\qquad\qquad\qquad\qquad\qquad\qquad\text{Hypothesis 1}$$
$$\mathrm{trm}\,(T) \qquad\qquad\qquad\qquad\qquad\qquad\qquad\text{Hypothesis 2}$$
$$\forall x' \cdot (\,\mathrm{prd}_x(S)\ \Rightarrow\ [x := x']P\,) \qquad\qquad\text{Hypothesis 3}$$
$$\forall y' \cdot (\,\mathrm{prd}_y(T)\ \Rightarrow\ [y := y']Q\,) \qquad\qquad\text{Hypothesis 4}$$

and we have to prove the following statements according to the definitions of $\mathrm{trm}\,(S\ ||\ T)$ and $\mathrm{prd}_{x,y}\,(S\ ||\ T)$ given at the beginning of this section and, again, according to Theorem 6.3.1:

$$\mathrm{trm}\,(S) \qquad\qquad\qquad\qquad\qquad\qquad\qquad\text{Goal 1}$$
$$\mathrm{trm}\,(T) \qquad\qquad\qquad\qquad\qquad\qquad\qquad\text{Goal 2}$$
$$\forall\,(x',y') \cdot (\,\mathrm{prd}_x(S)\ \land\ \mathrm{prd}_y(T)\ \Rightarrow\ [x,y := x',y']\,(P\ \land\ Q))\quad\text{Goal 3}$$

To prove Goal 3, we may remove the quantification (since x' and y' are not free in the hypotheses). We assume

$$\mathrm{prd}_x(S) \qquad\qquad\qquad\qquad\qquad\qquad\qquad\text{Hypothesis 5}$$
$$\mathrm{prd}_y(T) \qquad\qquad\qquad\qquad\qquad\qquad\qquad\text{Hypothesis 6}$$

and we are left to prove

$$[x,y := x',y']\,(P\ \land\ Q) \qquad\qquad\qquad\qquad\text{Goal 4}$$

that is, equivalently, and according to the side conditions

$$[x := x']P \qquad\qquad\qquad\qquad\qquad\qquad\qquad\text{Goal 5}$$
$$[y := y']Q \qquad\qquad\qquad\qquad\qquad\qquad\qquad\text{Goal 6}$$

Goal 5 is obvious according to Hypothesis 5 and Hypothesis 3, and Goal 6 is obvious according to Hypothesis 6 and Hypothesis 4.
End of Proof

7.2. Incremental Specification

7.2.1. Informal Introduction

The theorem of the previous section is important because it constitutes the theoretical basis on which we can envisage *composing* the specifications of two (or more) abstract machines and thus, eventually, constructing abstract machine specifications in an *incremental way*. The purpose of this section is to present this feature.

Suppose we have two (or more) abstract machines M_1 and M_2 with *distinct* variables x_1 and x_2 and with invariants I_1 and I_2 respectively. Let $P_1\ |\ S_1$ and $P_2\ |\ S_2$ be two respective operations of these machines. We suppose that the following invariant preservation proof obligations have been fulfilled (section 5.2.5 of chapter 5) (to simplify matters without any loss of generality, we consider machines with no parameters, no sets, and no constants):

$$\forall x_1 \cdot (I_1 \ \land \ P_1 \ \ \Rightarrow \ \ [S_1]I_1)$$
$$\forall x_2 \cdot (I_2 \ \land \ P_2 \ \ \Rightarrow \ \ [S_2]I_2)$$

Consequently, and since the variables x_1 and x_2 are independent, we have

$$\forall(x_1, x_2) \cdot (I_1 \ \land \ I_2 \ \land \ P_1 \ \land \ P_2 \ \ \Rightarrow \ \ [S_1]I_1 \ \land \ [S_2]I_2)$$

As the variable x_2 is certainly non-free in I_1 and the variable x_1 is non-free in I_2, then we can apply Theorem 7.1.1, yielding eventually

$$\forall(x_1, x_2) \cdot (I_1 \ \land \ I_2 \ \land \ P_1 \ \land \ P_2 \ \ \Rightarrow \ \ [S_1 \ || \ S_2](I_1 \ \land \ I_2))$$

In other words, the operation

$$(P_1 \ \land \ P_2) \ | \ (S_1 \ || \ S_2)$$

preserves the invariant $I_1 \ \land \ I_2$. Also notice that each individual operation of one machine trivially preserves the invariant $I_1 \ \land \ I_2$. Finally, any combination of operations with other generalized substitution constructs also preserves the invariant $I_1 \ \land \ I_2$ (exercises).

This suggests a mechanism by which we could *include* a machine M_1 (or more than one) within a given machine M to obtain a new machine. This pre-supposes, of course, that the individual sets, constants and variables of M and M_1 are all *distinct*. The resulting machine is obtained by putting together the following clauses of M and M_1 as follows:

- the SETS clauses (by concatenation),
- the CONSTANTS clauses (by concatenation),
- the ABSTRACT_CONSTANTS clauses (by concatenation),
- the PROPERTIES clauses (by conjunction),
- the VARIABLES clauses (by concatenation),
- the CONCRETE_VARIABLES clauses (by concatenation),
- the INVARIANT clauses (by conjunction),
- the ASSERTION clauses (by conjunction),
- the INITIALIZATION clauses (by multiple composition).

Concerning the contents of the OPERATIONS clause, we could either *promote* unchanged certain operations of the included machine (this means that such operations become genuine operations of the including machine), or define new operations obtained by combining (with the multiple operator $||$ of the previous section) a certain *call* to an operation of M_1, (a certain *call* to an operation of another included machine, if any) and some generalized substitutions modifying the genuine variables of the including machine M. We could also combine the previous substitutions by means of any of the other generalized substitution constructs. In either case, and as already pointed out, the invariant I_1 of the included machine M_1 is preserved by these new operations provided this invariant has itself been already proved to be preserved by each operation of M_1. Only the additional invariant of M has to be proved to be preserved.

Notice that, within an operation of the including machine, *at most* one operation of a given included machine can be called. In section 7.2.3, we shall show what may happen if this limitation is not followed.

7.2.2. Operation Call

At the end of the previous section, we have used informally the notion of "call" of an operation of an included machine from within the operation of an including machine. The purpose of this section is to explain formally what such calls are.

A call to an operation has exactly the same shape as the header of that operation. The *formal* parameters of the operation are simply replaced by corresponding *actual* parameters. As a consequence, the syntax for an *Operation_Call* can be defined as follows:

Syntactic Category	Definition
Operation_Call	*Identifier* *Identifier* (*Expression_List*) *Variable_List* $\longleftarrow$ *Identifier* *Variable_List* $\longleftarrow$ *Identifier* (*Expression_List*)

For example, suppose we have the following operation, with formal parameters *report* and *value*, in a certain machine working with a variable *var*:

$$report \longleftarrow \text{change}(value) \; \mathrel{\widehat{=}}$$
$$\quad \text{PRE}$$
$$\qquad value \in \text{NAT}$$
$$\quad \text{THEN}$$
$$\qquad var, report := value, good$$
$$\quad \text{END}$$

A call of this operation might be the following:

$$rp \longleftarrow \text{change}(vv + 56)$$

As can be seen, the formal output parameter *report* has been replaced by the actual parameter *rp* and the formal input parameter *value* has been replaced by the actual parameter *vv* + 56. In fact, the call of an operation stands for the body of that operation with the occurrences of the formal parameters replaced by the corresponding actual parameters. In our example, the call $rp \longleftarrow \text{change}(vv + 56)$ thus stands for the following:

PRE
$$vv + 56 \in \mathsf{NAT}$$
THEN
$$var, rp := vv + 56, good$$
END

We have implicitly applied the substitution

$$report, value := rp, vv + 56$$

to the the body of our operation, that is to the substitution:

PRE
$$value \in \mathsf{NAT}$$
THEN
$$var, report := value, good$$
END

This raises the question of applying a substitution to a substitution. The remaining part of this section is devoted to introducing this concept formally. For this, we extend the syntax of *Substitution* already presented in section 5.1.1 as follows:

Syntactic Category	Definition
Substitution	*Variable* := *Expression* skip *Predicate* | *Substitution* *Substitution* [] *Substitution* *Predicate* $\Longrightarrow$ *Substitution* @*Variable* · *Substitution* *Substitution* || *Substitution* [*Variable* := *Expression*] *Substitution*

We have added a new form of substitution: the "substituted" substitution. This form consists of a simple (perhaps multiple) substitution applied to a substitution. We now give the formal rules allowing us to substitute in a substitution. These rules have the same shape as the rules SUB 1 to SUB 13 given in section 1.3.4, section 1.4 and section 1.5 for substituting in a predicate and the rules SUB 14 to SUB 20 given in section 2.1.1 for substituting in a set-theoretic expression. In the following table x, y and z are *Variables*, E and F are *Expressions*, P is a *Predicate*, and S and T are *Substitutions*:

	Substitution	Definition
SUB 21	$[x := E](y := F)$	$[x := E]y := [x := E]F$
SUB 22	$[x := E]\,\mathsf{skip}$	skip
SUB 23	$[x := E](P\mid S)$	$[x := E]P \mid [x := E]S$
SUB 24	$[x := E](S \mathbin{[\!]} T)$	$[x := E]S \mathbin{[\!]} [x := E]T$
SUB 25	$[x := E](P \implies S)$	$[x := E]P \implies [x := E]T$
SUB 26	$[x := E](@y \cdot S)$	$@z \cdot [x := E]S \quad y \setminus (x, E)$

Note: In SUB 21, the substitution $[x := E]\,y$, which is situated on the left-hand side of the operator ":=", must result in a *genuine variable*. In other words, the modified elementary variables of the (list of) variable(s) y can only be replaced *by other elementary variables* in such a way that the resulting substituted variable is indeed a *genuine* variable (that is, made of individual *distinct* elementary variables). In this way, after the substitution $x := E$ is performed on the substitution $y := F$, we obtain yet another substitution.

When applying the mechanism of substitution on a substitution for an operation call, this results in a very simple rule: the formal output parameter of an operation can only be actualized by *genuine* distinct variables. Such variables are either variables of the including machine or output parameters of an operation of the including machine. In our example, where the actualizing substitution was $report, value := rp, vv + 56$, rp must thus be such a variable.

7.2.3. The INCLUDES Clause

We now introduce a new clause into the Abstract Machine Notation, the INCLUDES clause, allowing us to include other machines in a given machine.

```
MACHINE
    M₁(X₁, x₁)
CONSTRAINTS
    C₁
    . . .
END
```

```
MACHINE
    M₂(X₂, x₂)
CONSTRAINTS
    C₂
    . . .
END
```

For instance, we may suppose that we have been given the two above machines M_1 and M_2 with formal parameters X_1, x_1 and X_2, x_2 respectively. The constants, sets, and variables of both machines are supposed to be *distinct*. We are also given a machine M with formal parameters X and x. The machine M INCLUDES both machines M_1 and M_2.

```
MACHINE
     M(X, x)
CONSTRAINTS
     C
SETS
     S ;
     T = {a, b}
(ABSTRACT_)CONSTANTS
     c
PROPERTIES
     P
INCLUDES
     M₁(N₁, n₁), M₂(N₂, n₂)
(CONCRETE_)VARIABLES
     v
INVARIANT
     I

     . . .
END
```

The constants, sets, and variables of M are supposed to be *distinct* from those of M_1 and M_2. As can be seen, the INCLUDES clause contains references to the two included machines M_1 and M_2. The formal parameters of M_1 and M_2 are actualized with N_1, n_1 and N_2, n_2 respectively. As we shall see in section 7.4.3, such "actual parameters" must obey the constraints C_1 and C_2 of M_1 and M_2 respectively. These actual parameters can be constructed from the formal parameters, the sets or the constants of machine M. This is indicated by the physical position of the INCLUDES clause.

The machine M has a so-called *gluing* invariant I which is supposed to depend not only on the variable x, local to machine M, but also on the variables x_1 and x_2 of the included machines M_1 and M_2. The operations of M may contain "calls" to the operations of M_1 and M_2.

It is worth mentioning that at most one operation of the included machine can be called from within an operation of the including machine. Otherwise we could break the invariant of the included machine. As an example suppose we have the following machine:

MACHINE

M_1

VARIABLES

v, w

INVARIANT

$v \in \mathsf{NAT}$ $\wedge$
$w \in \mathsf{NAT}$ $\wedge$
$v \leq w$

OPERATIONS

increment $\;\widehat{=}\;$ PRE $\;v < w\;$ THEN $\;v := v + 1\;$ END;

decrement $\;\widehat{=}\;$ PRE $\;v < w\;$ THEN $\;w := w - 1\;$ END

END

Suppose now that the above machine M_1 is included in another machine M. And suppose that, within M, we have the following operation with calls to increment and to decrement:

$$\text{PRE} \quad v < w \quad \text{THEN} \quad \text{increment} \quad || \quad \text{decrement} \quad \text{END}$$

Then clearly, this operation will result in a possible break of the invariant $v \leq w$ in the case where w is equal to $v + 1$. Although each of the individual pre-conditions holds, the combined effect of the two operations will result in v being equal to $w + 1$.

7.2.4. Visibility Rules

The *visibility* of the various objects of the included machines from within the various clauses of the including machine is best described by the following table. Each line corresponds to a specific category of objects of the included machines and each column corresponds to a specific clause of the including machine. A tick indicates that a certain category of objects of the included machines is indeed referenceable from within a certain clause of the including machine.

	PROPERTIES (of including)	INVARIANT (of including)	OPERATIONS (of including)
Parameters (of included)			
sets (of included)	√	√	√
constants (of included)	√	√	√
variables (of included)		√	read-only
operations (of included)			√

As you should have noticed, the formal *parameters* of the included machine cannot be referenced from within any clause of the including machine. The reason is that these parameters have been instantiated in the including machine.

The variables of the included machine are *not* referenceable in the left-hand side of a simple (or multiple) substitution (they are thus mentioned as "read-only"). Otherwise, as already stated, the invariant of the included machine could be broken.

These visibility rules clearly indicate that the INCLUDES mechanism is not an indispensable facility. In other words, any abstract machine containing an INCLUDES clause could have been defined equivalently without that clause.

7.2.5. Transitivity

The INCLUDES mechanism is *transitive*. This means that the inclusion of various machines in a machine M is automatically reflected in another machine N including M. In other words, in N, it is not necessary (and it is even forbidden) to include again the machines already included in M.

7.2.6. Machine Renaming

In some applications, it may happen that we would like to include two (or more) "identical" machines. In order to avoid an obvious clash, we have the possibility to rename a machine while including it. This is done simply by prefixing, in the INCLUDES clause, the name of the machine we want to rename with a certain identifier followed by a dot. This has the effect of renaming accordingly all the variables and operations of the machine concerned (notice that the sets and constants are not renamed). Notice that the renaming of a machine also renames the machines that are included within that machine: renaming is thus *transitive*.

7.2.7. The PROMOTES and the EXTENDS Clauses

We now introduce two more clauses: the PROMOTES and the EXTENDS clauses. In order to have a PROMOTES clause, the corresponding machine must already have an INCLUDES clause. The PROMOTES clause simply contains a list of certain operation names of the previously included machines. Such operations are then genuine operations of the including machine. As such, they need not be mentioned in the OPERATIONS clause of the including machine. The EXTENDS clause has exactly the same shape as an INCLUDES clause: it thus contains a list of actualized machine names. Such machines are supposed to be included and *all* their operations automatically promoted at the same time.

7.2.8. Example

As a rather trivial example, suppose we are given the following machine encapsulating a single scalar variable:

MACHINE

  $Scalar(VALUE)$

VARIABLES

  var

INVARIANT

  $var \in VALUE$

INITIALIZATION

  $var :\in VALUE$

```
    OPERATIONS

        chg (v)   ≙   PRE  v ∈ VALUE  THEN  var := v  END;

        v ⟵ val   ≙   BEGIN  v := var  END

    END
```

We now define the following machine obtained by coupling two renamed copies (prefixed with *xx.* and *yy.*) of the previous machine. As will be seen, we have used an EXTENDS clause so that both machines are included and their operations promoted automatically. Finally, we have added an extra operation for swapping the two variables.

```
    MACHINE

        TwoScalars(VALUE)

    EXTENDS

        xx.Scalar(VALUE), yy.Scalar(VALUE)

    OPERATIONS

        swap   ≙   BEGIN   xx.chg (yy.var) || yy.chg (xx.var)   END

    END
```

By expanding the calls *xx.*chg (*yy.var*) and *yy.*chg (*xx.var*) within swap, we obtain

$$
\text{PRE }\; yy.var \in VALUE \;\; \text{THEN}\;\; xx.var := yy.var \;\; \text{END} \;\; ||
$$
$$
\text{PRE }\; xx.var \in VALUE \;\; \text{THEN}\;\; yy.var := xx.var \;\; \text{END}
$$

that is, according to the properties presented in section 7.1.2 (notice that the || operator has disappeared)

$$
\begin{aligned}
&\text{PRE} \\
&\quad yy.var \in VALUE \quad \wedge \\
&\quad xx.var \in VALUE \\
&\text{THEN} \\
&\quad xx.var, yy.var := yy.var, xx.var \\
&\text{END}
\end{aligned}
$$

Since the machine *TwoScalars* has no invariant of its own, we only have to prove that the operation `swap` terminates under the conjunction of the invariants of the included machines. This yields the following, which holds trivially:

$$
\begin{array}{l}
xx.var \in VALUE \ \wedge \ yy.var \in VALUE \\
\Rightarrow \\
yy.var \in VALUE \ \wedge \ xx.var \in VALUE
\end{array}
$$

7.3. Incremental Specification and Sharing

7.3.1. Informal Introduction

Our intention, in this section, is to indicate how we can enlarge the facilities offered by the previous INCLUDES mechanism so that it is possible to *share* part of an abstract machine between several others in a read-only fashion. In order to explain this mechanism informally, we suppose that we have four machines related as follows:

$$
\begin{array}{ccc|c}
M_1 & M_2 & M_3 & \\
& & & \\
\nwarrow & \uparrow & \nearrow & \text{INCLUDES} \\
& M & &
\end{array}
$$

As we have seen in section 7.2.3, the main constraint concerning the three included machines M_1, M_2 and M_3 is that their variables are *distinct*. This is so because, in machine M, we would like to inherit the invariant properties of M_1, M_2 and M_3 without running any risk of conflict between them.

$$
\begin{array}{ccccc|c}
& \text{USES} & & \text{USES} & & \\
\hline
M_1 & \rightarrow & M_2 & \leftarrow & M_3 & \\
\nwarrow & & \uparrow & & \nearrow & \text{INCLUDES} \\
& & M & & &
\end{array}
$$

Sometimes, however, it is very useful to have the possibility in, say, both machines M_1 and M_3 to access some *static information* of M_2. In other words, we would like to factorize out M_2 so that both M_1 and M_3 can take advantage of this knowledge. This is done as shown in the above diagram. Each of machines M_1 and M_3 USES M_2.

One of the immediate problems raised by such a mechanism is that we do not want the text on M_2 to be included three times into that of M (twice, implicitly, through the inclusion of M_1 and M_3, and once explicitly). For this, the "usage" of M_2 in M_1 and M_3 is restricted to a *static* usage. In fact, the *entire text* of M_2, *excluding that of its operations*, is made available in M_1 and M_3. That is, the formal parameters (if any) of M_2 are concatenated to those of M_1 and M_3 respectively. Likewise, the various clauses of M_2 (except the operations clause) are put together with corresponding clauses of M_1 and M_3 respectively. This means that, in order to prove the invariant conservation of M_1 and M_3, we can assume the constraints, the properties and the invariant of M_2. Also note that, in the operations of M_1 and M_3, the variables of M_2 are referenceable (in a read-only fashion, of course).

In order to have an invariant property "gluing", say, M_1 and M_2, we have the possibility to reference the variables of M_2 from within the invariant of M_1. But, of course, we have to prove the preservation of such a gluing invariant since there is, a priori, no reason for that property to be kept invariant by the operations of M_1 or those of M_2. As this clearly cannot be proved in M_2 (which is "ignorant" of the fact that it is used by other machines), nor in machine M_1 which does not modify the variables of M_2, the only place where such a proof can be done is M, a machine which has full visibility of both M_1 and M_2. Such a proof is thus done when all machines are put together at the moment of their common inclusion in M.

7.3.2. The USES Clause

From a practical point of view, we introduce a new clause in Abstract Machine Notation: the USES clause. For instance, we may suppose that we are given a machine M_1 that USES a machine M_2 as shown:

MACHINE
$$M_1(X_1, x_1)$$
USES
$$M_2$$
. . .
END

MACHINE
$$M_2(X_2, x_2)$$
. . .
END

Notice that the reference to machine M_2, in the USES clause of machine M_1, is *not* actualized. As already explained in the previous section, the machine M_2 (including its formal parameters) is put together, clause by clause, with machine M_1. The machine M_1 thus appears to be parameterized, not only by its own parameters, but also by those of machine M_2 (which thus must be distinct from those of M_1).

When the machine M_1 is included in a machine M, then the machine M_2, that M_1 USES, must also be included in M. Moreover, any other machine that USES M_2 must be included in M together with M_2. In this way, the actualization of the formal parameters of M_2 is done only once, and in the same way, for each machine that USES M_2. That machine is thus indeed *shared* by all the machines that use it.

7.3.3. Visibility Rules

For the USES clause, we have visibility rules that are slightly different from those already presented in section 7.2.4 for the INCLUDES mechanism. The formal parameters of the used machine are visible. However, the operations of the used machines are not visible from within the operations of the using machine. As for the case of the INCLUDES mechanism, the variables of the used machine, although referenceable in the operation of the using machine, cannot appear in the left-hand side of a simple substitution (this is marked as read-only).

	PROPERTIES (of using)	INVARIANT (of using)	OPERATIONS (of using)
parameters (of used)		✓	✓
sets (of used)	✓	✓	✓
constants (of used)	✓	✓	✓
variables (of used)		✓	read-only

7.3.4. Transitivity

The USES mechanism is *not transitive*. This means that the use of a machine M_2 in a machine M_1 is *not* automatically reflected in the case that M_1 is itself used in another machine M_0. In other words, in M_0, it is necessary to use M_2 again eventhough it is already used in M_1.

The reason for the non-transitivity is that every machine M_1 using another machine M_2 *has always to be included eventually* in another machine M (section 7.3.2). Such an inclusion has to be done *together* with the machine M_2 used by M_1. And, of course, the used machine M_2 is only included once. This means that all the machines using M_2 have all to be included together in M. As a consequence, it is better to know directly which machines a given machine is using rather than to have to compute that fact by a transitive closure of the USES clause.

7.3.5. Machine Renaming

As for the case of the INCLUDES clause (section 7.2.4), machines referenced in a USES clause can be renamed. However, contrary to what happens for the included machines, renaming is not transitive for used machines. In other words, when a renamed machine USES another machine, the latter is not automatically renamed.

7.4. Formal Definition

7.4.1. Syntax

Here is the new syntax for *Machines*:

Machine	MACHINE
	Machine_Header
	CONSTRAINTS
	Predicate
	USES
	Id_List
	SETS
	Sets
	(ABSTRACT_) CONSTANTS
	Id_List
	PROPERTIES
	Predicate
	INCLUDES
	Machine_List
	PROMOTES
	Id_List
	EXTENDS
	Machine_List
	(CONCRETE_) VARIABLES
	Id_List
	INVARIANT
	Predicate

Machine (Cont'd)	ASSERTIONS *Predicate* DEFINITIONS *Predicate* INITIALIZATION *Substitution* OPERATIONS *Operations* END

We now present the syntax for a *Machine-call*:

Machine_List	*Machine_List, Machine_Call* *Machine_Call*
Machine_Call	*Identifier* *Identifier (Expression_List)*

We have to add the following to the clause dependencies already mentioned at section 5.2.1:

- a PROMOTES clause requires an INCLUDES clause.

7.4.2. Type-checking

Signatures of a Machine

Before presenting the type-checking rules for the extended *Machine* syntax defined in the previous section, we have to define the notion of a machine *signature*. Given a machine M_1, we denote its signature by $sig(M_1)$. This is, in a sense, a partial summary of the type-checking of M_1. More precisely, the signature of a machine M_1 is an environment made up of the following items:

- the scalar formal parameters of M_1, together with their type,
- the enumerated set members of M_1, together with their type,
- the constants of M_1, together with their type,
- the variables of M_1, together with their type,
- the signature of each operation of M_1.

All the above items, except the last one, can be found in the environment that is produced at the end of the (successful) type-checking session of M_1. The last item (the signature of an operation) requires some more explanations that will be given below.

Notice that the signature of a machine does *not contain* the given sets of that machine (set formal parameters, deferred sets and enumerated sets). When a signature is used in an environment, the given sets in question have thus to be declared explicitly. Sometimes, the signature will be instantiated. In this case, the given sets, corresponding to the formal parameters of the machine, will not be declared together with the signature. This is because the signature has then to be actualized: the formal parameters of the machine will thus disappear.

Signature of an Operation

The signature of an operation is a construct that corresponds exactly to the header of that operation with the parameters (if any) replaced by their respective types. For instance, given the following operation header: $x_1, x_2 \longleftarrow op(x_3, x_4)$, where each parameter x_i is supposed to be of type T_i, the signature of the operation op is then the following: $T_1, T_2 \longleftarrow op(T_3, T_4)$.

Type-checking a Machine with an INCLUDES Clause

We are now ready to present the type-checking rules for a machine that INCLUDES another one. Suppose we are given the following two machines M_1 and M_2 where M_1 includes M_2, with the set formal parameter X_2 actualized by N_2 and with the scalar formal parameter x_2 actualized by n_2. Before type-checking M_1, we suppose, of course, that M_2 has been successfully type-checked and that the signature, sig (M_2), of M_2 has thus been computed.

MACHINE
$M_1(X_1, x_1)$
CONSTRAINTS
C_1
(ABSTRACT_)CONSTANTS
c_1
PROPERTIES
P_1
INCLUDES
$M_2(N_2, n_2)$
SETS
S_1;
$T_1 = \{a_1, b_1\}$
(CONCRETE_)VARIABLES
v_1
INVARIANT
I_1

MACHINE
$M_2(X_2, x_2)$
CONSTRAINTS
C_2
SETS
S_2; $T_2 = \{a_2, b_2\}$
(ABSTRACT_)CONSTANTS
c_2
PROPERTIES
P_2
(CONCRETE_)VARIABLES
v_2
INVARIANT
I_2

```
┌─────────────────────┐        ┌─────────────────────┐
│  INITIALIZATION     │        │  INITIALIZATION     │
│      U₁             │        │      U₂             │
│  OPERATIONS         │        │  OPERATIONS         │
│      O₁             │        │      O₂             │
│  END                │        │  END                │
└─────────────────────┘        └─────────────────────┘
```

Here is the type-checking rule:

Antecedents	Consequent

$X_1, x_1, S_1, T_1, a_1, b_1, c_1, v_1,$
 $S_2, T_2, a_2, b_2, c_2, v_2$ are all distinct
 	
 Operation names of O_1 and O_2 are all distinct
 	
 $S_1, T_1, a_1, b_1, c_1, v_1 \setminus C_1$
 	
 $v_1 \setminus P_1$
 	
 given (X_1),
 given (S_1),
 given (T_1),
 $a_1 \in T_1,$
 $b_1 \in T_1$
 $\vdash$
 check $(\forall x_1 \cdot (C_1 \Rightarrow$
 $\qquad \forall c_1 \cdot (P_1 \Rightarrow [X_2, x_2 := N_2, n_2] C_2)))$
 	
 given (X_1),
 given (S_1),
 given (T_1),
 $a_1 \in T_1,$
 $b_1 \in T_1,$
 given (S_2),
 given (T_2),
 $[X_2, x_2 := N_2, n_2]$ sig (M_2)
 $\vdash$
 check $(\forall x_1 \cdot (C_1 \Rightarrow$
 $\qquad \forall c_1 \cdot (P_1 \Rightarrow \forall v_1 \cdot (I_1 \Rightarrow J_1 \wedge U_1 \wedge O_1))))$
	check (
	    MACHINE
	      $M_1(X_1, x_1)$
	    CONSTRAINTS
	      C_1
	    SETS
	      S_1 ;
	      $T_1 = \{a_1, b_1\}$
	    (ABSTRACT_)CONSTANTS
	      c_1
	    PROPERTIES
	      P_1
	    INCLUDES
	      $M_2(N_2, n_2)$
	    (CONCRETE_)VARIABLES
	      v_1
	    INVARIANT
	      I_1
	    ASSERTION
	      J_1
	    INITIALIZATION
	      U_1
	    OPERATIONS
	      O_1
	    END)

As can be seen, the type-checking rule is almost the same as the one already presented in section 5.2.3. The only difference are:

- some distinctness and freeness properties of the various objects of M_1 and of M_2,

- the correct type-checking of the actual parameters of M_2 (that is, N_2 and n_2), in the INCLUDES clause of M_1. This is done by verifying the correct type-checking of the constraints C_2 where the formal parameters X_2 and x_2 are replaced by N_2 and n_2,

- the enlargement of the environment of the type-checking of M_1 with the actualized signature of M_2. Notice that the given sets S_2 and T_2 of M_2 are declared in the environment. The given set X_2 need not be declared since it has been instantiated by N_2 in the signature of M_2.

Type-checking of an Operation Call

We now give the type-checking rule of an operation call. Such a call, as we know, may occur in an operation of a machine that includes another one. We only consider the case of an operation call with one output and one input parameter. Other cases (including the one with no parameter) can be deduced easily. Note that the signature of the operation has to occur in the environment. Next is the type-checking rule:

Antecedents	Consequent
$\begin{cases} S \longleftarrow op\,(T) \ \ \text{occurs in } ENV \\[2mm] ENV \ \vdash \ \text{check}\,(a \in S \ \wedge \ b \in T) \end{cases}$	$ENV \ \vdash \ \text{check}\,(a \longleftarrow op\,(b))$

Type-checking a Machine with a USES Clause

We now present the type-checking rules for a machine that USES another one. We suppose that we are given the following machines M_1 and M_2, where M_1 USES M_2:

```
MACHINE
  M₁(X₁, x₁)
CONSTRAINTS
  C₁
USES
  M₂
```

```
MACHINE
  M₂(X₂, x₂)
CONSTRAINTS
  C₂
```

<table>
<tr><td>

SETS
  S_1;
  $T_1 = \{a_1, b_1\}$
(ABSTRACT_)CONSTANTS
  c_1
PROPERTIES
  P_1
(CONCRETE_)VARIABLES
  v_1
INVARIANT
  I_1
ASSERTION
  J_1
INITIALIZATION
  U_1
OPERATIONS
  O_1
END

</td><td>

SETS
  S_2;
  $T_2 = \{a_2, b_2\}$
(ABSTRACT_)CONSTANTS
  c_2
PROPERTIES
  P_2
(CONCRETE_)VARIABLES
  v_2
INVARIANT
  I_2
ASSERTION
  J_2
INITIALIZATION
  U_2
OPERATIONS
  O_2
END

</td></tr>
</table>

Before type-checking M_1, we suppose, of course, that M_2 has been type-checked successfully and that the signature, $\mathrm{sig}\,(M_2)$, of M_2 has thus been computed. The type-checking rule is almost the same as the one already presented in section 5.2.3. The only differences are some distinctness and freeness properties of the various objects of M_1 and of M_2, and the enlargment of the environment of the type-checking of M_1 with the signature of M_2. Note that, this time, the signature is *not actualized*. As a consequence, the three given sets X_2, S_2 and T_2 of M_2 have to be declared in the environment together with the signature of M_2.

Antecedents	Consequent

$\begin{cases} X_1, x_1, S_1, T_1, a_1, b_1, c_1, v_1, \\ X_2, x_2, S_2, T_2, a_2, b_2, c_2, v_2 \quad \text{are all distinct} \\[2mm] \text{Operation names of } O_1 \text{ are all distinct} \\[2mm] S_1, T_1, a_1, b_1, c_1, v_1 \setminus C_1 \\[2mm] v_1 \setminus P_1 \end{cases}$	check (
	  MACHINE
	    $M_1(X_1, x_1)$
	  CONSTRAINTS
	    C_1
	  USES
	    M_2
	  SETS
	    S_1; $T_1 = \{a_1, b_1\}$

Antecedents (Cont'd)	Consequent (Cont'd)
$\begin{cases} \text{given}\,(X_2), \\ \text{given}\,(S_2), \\ \text{given}\,(T_2), \\ \text{sig}\,(M_2), \\ \text{given}\,(X_1), \\ \text{given}\,(S_1), \\ \text{given}\,(T_1), \\ a_1 \in T_1, \\ b_1 \in T_1 \\ \vdash \\ \text{check}\,(\forall\, x_1 \cdot (C_1 \;\Rightarrow\; \forall\, c_1 \cdot (P_1 \;\Rightarrow \\ \qquad \forall\, v_1 \cdot (I_1 \;\Rightarrow\; J_1 \,\wedge\, U_1 \,\wedge\, O_1)))) \end{cases}$	(ABSTRACT_)CONSTANTS c_1 PROPERTIES P_1 (CONCRETE_)VARIABLES v_1 INVARIANT I_1 ASSERTION J_1 INITIALIZATION U_1 OPERATIONS O_1 END)

7.4.3. Proof Obligations for the INCLUDES Clause

We are given the following machines M_1 and M such that M_1 INCLUDES M :

MACHINE
  $M_1(X_1, x_1)$
CONSTRAINTS
  C_1
SETS
  S_1 ;
  $T_1 = \{a_1, b_1\}$
(ABSTRACT_)CONSTANTS
  c_1
PROPERTIES
  P_1
INCLUDES
  $M(N, n)$
(CONCRETE_)VARIABLES
  v_1

MACHINE
  $M(X, x)$
CONSTRAINTS
  C
SETS
  S ;
  $T = \{a, b\}$
(ABSTRACT_)CONSTANTS
  c
PROPERTIES
  P
(CONCRETE_)VARIABLES
  v

```
INVARIANT
    I₁
ASSERTIONS
    J₁
INITIALIZATION
    U₁
OPERATIONS
    op₁(w₁)  ≙  PRE  Q₁  THEN  V₁  END;
    . . .
END
```

```
INVARIANT
    I
ASSERTIONS
    J
INITIALIZATION
    U
OPERATIONS
    . . .
END
```

Let us define the following abbreviations A_1, B_1, A and B as in section 5.2.5:

Abbreviation	Definition
A_1	$X_1 \in \mathbb{P}_1(\text{INT})$
B_1	$S_1 \in \mathbb{P}_1(\text{INT}) \wedge T_1 \in \mathbb{P}_1(\text{INT}) \wedge T_1 = \{a_1, b_1\} \wedge a_1 \neq b_1$
A	$X \in \mathbb{P}_1(\text{INT})$
B	$S \in \mathbb{P}_1(\text{INT}) \wedge T \in \mathbb{P}_1(\text{INT}) \wedge T = \{a, b\} \wedge a \neq b$

The first proof obligation of machine M_1 is to check that the machine M is correctly called in the INCLUDES clause of M_1. In other words, the constraints A and C of the formal parameters X and x of M must hold when X and x are actualized to N and n respectively. This proof is done under the proper assumptions of the formal constraints A_1 and C_1 of M_1, the abbreviation B_1 concerning the sets of M_1 and, finally, the properties P_1 of the constants of M_1. The reason for these assumptions is that the actual parameters N and n are possibly written in terms of the corresponding objects of M_1 (section 7.2.3).

$$
\overbrace{A_1 \ \wedge \ B_1 \ \wedge \ C_1 \ \wedge \ P_1}^{\text{Including}}
$$
$$
\Rightarrow
$$
$$
[X,x := N,n]\,\overbrace{(A \ \wedge \ C)}^{\text{Included}}
$$

The rôle of the next proof obligation is to guarantee that the initialization of the including machine M_1 establishes the invariant I_1 (we suppose, of course, that the proof obligations of the included machine M have already been proved and thus already guarantee the establishment and preservation of the invariant I).

$$
\overbrace{A_1 \ \wedge \ B_1 \ \wedge \ C_1 \ \wedge \ P_1}^{\text{Including}} \ \wedge
$$
$$
\overbrace{B \ \wedge \ P}^{\text{Included}}
$$
$$
\Rightarrow
$$
$$
\overbrace{[\,[X,x := N,n]U\,]\,[U_1]\,I_1}^{\text{Included}}
$$

The next proof obligation concerns the assertions of the including machine. Notice that, in the assumptions of this proof obligation, the invariant I and assertion J of the included machine M have been actualized. However, the property P of the included machine M has not been actualised since, by definition, the PROPERTIES clause of a machine is independent of its parameters (section 4.17).

$$
\overbrace{A_1 \ \wedge \ B_1 \ \wedge \ C_1 \ \wedge \ P_1 \ \wedge \ I_1}^{\text{Including}} \ \wedge
$$
$$
\overbrace{B \ \wedge \ P \ \wedge \ [X,x := N,n]\,(I \ \wedge \ J)}^{\text{Included}}
$$
$$
\Rightarrow
$$
$$
J_1
$$

Finally, we have the following proof obligation concerning the preservation of the invariant of the including machine.

$$
\overbrace{A_1 \ \wedge \ B_1 \ \wedge \ C_1 \ \wedge \ P_1 \ \wedge \ I_1 \ \wedge \ J_1 \ \wedge \ Q_1}^{\text{Including}} \ \wedge
$$

$$
\underbrace{B \ \wedge \ P \ \wedge \ [X,x := N,n]\,(I \ \wedge \ J)}_{\text{Included}}
$$

$$
\Rightarrow
$$

$$
[V_1]\,I_1
$$

We remind the reader that when the machine M_1 includes a machine M, itself using a machine M_2, in a such a way that some variables of M_2 are referenced in some part I' of the invariant of M, then I' has to be proved to be established and preserved in the proof obligation of M_1 which must *necessarily* also include M_2 besides M (end of section 7.3.1).

7.4.4. Proof Obligations for the USES Clause

MACHINE
   $M(X,x)$
CONSTRAINTS
   C
USES
   M_1
SETS
   S ;
   $T = \{a,b\}$
(ABSTRACT_)CONSTANTS
   c
PROPERTIES
   P
(CONCRETE_)VARIABLES
   v
INVARIANT
   $I \ \wedge \ I'$
ASSERTIONS
   J
INITIALIZATION
   U
OPERATIONS
   $op \ \ \widehat{=} \ \ $ PRE $\ Q \ $ THEN $\ V \ $ END ;
   . . .
END

MACHINE
   $M_1(X_1,x_1)$
CONSTRAINTS
   C_1
SETS
   S_1 ;
   $T_1 = \{a_1,b_1\}$
(ABSTRACT_)CONSTANTS
   c_1
PROPERTIES
   P_1
(CONCRETE_)VARIABLES
   v_1
INVARIANT
   I_1
ASSERTIONS
   J_1
INITIALIZATION
   U_1
OPERATIONS
   . . .
END

We are given the above machines M and M_1 such that M USES M_1. Notice that we have broken down the invariant of M into two parts. The first part, I, is supposed to be independent of the variables v_1 of M_1 whereas the second part, I', is not. Let us now define the following abbreviations A, B, A_1 and B_1 as in section 5.2.5:

Abbreviation	Definition
A	$X \in \mathbb{P}_1(\text{INT})$
B	$S \in \mathbb{P}_1(\text{INT}) \ \wedge \ T \in \mathbb{P}_1(\text{INT}) \ \wedge \ T = \{a,b\} \ \wedge \ a \neq b$
A_1	$X_1 \in \mathbb{P}_1(\text{INT})$
B_1	$S_1 \in \mathbb{P}_1(\text{INT}) \ \wedge \ T_1 \in \mathbb{P}_1(\text{INT}) \ \wedge \ T_1 = \{a_1,b_1\} \ \wedge \ a_1 \neq b_1$

These proof obligations are very close to those already given for a single machine in section 5.2.5. The only difference is that the machine M_1 (except its operations) is now put together with machine M. This yields the following, which is valid provided the side-condition $v_1 \setminus I$ holds. First the proof obligation for the initialization:

$$\overbrace{A_1 \ \wedge \ B_1 \ \wedge \ C_1 \ \wedge \ P_1}^{\text{Using}} \ \wedge$$
$$\underbrace{A \ \wedge \ B \ \wedge \ C \ \wedge \ P}_{\text{Used}}$$
$$\Rightarrow$$
$$[U]I$$

Then the proof obligation for the assertions:

$$
\underbrace{A_1 \ \wedge \ B_1 \ \wedge \ C_1 \ \wedge \ P_1 \ \wedge \ I_1 \ \wedge \ J_1}_{\text{Used}} \ \wedge \ \overset{\text{Using}}{}
$$

$$
\overbrace{A \ \wedge \ B \ \wedge \ C \ \wedge \ P \ \wedge \ I \ \wedge \ I'}
$$

$$
\Rightarrow
$$

$$
J
$$

And, finally, the proof obligation for the operation:

$$
\underbrace{A_1 \ \wedge \ B_1 \ \wedge \ C_1 \ \wedge \ P_1 \ \wedge \ I_1 \ \wedge \ J_1}_{\text{Used}} \ \wedge \ \overset{\text{Using}}{}
$$

$$
\overbrace{A \ \wedge \ B \ \wedge \ C \ \wedge \ P \ \wedge \ I \ \wedge \ I' \ \wedge \ J \ \wedge \ Q}
$$

$$
\Rightarrow
$$

$$
[V]I
$$

Notice that only part I of the invariant of M, which is not concerned with the variables v_1 of M_1, can be proved locally in M. The other part, I', will be proved in the machine within which M and M_1 have to be included simultaneously (end of section 7.3.1).

7.5. Exercises

1. Prove the equalities defining the set-theoretic model of the $||$ operator in section 7.1.2.

2. Prove some of the properties of the $||$ operator, as proposed in section 7.1.2.

3. Perform a hand type-checking of the example of section 7.2.8.

CHAPTER 8

Examples of Abstract Machines

In this chapter our intention is to present three large examples of abstract machines. In each of them, we would like to put the emphasis on a particular aspect of specifying.

The goal of the first example, the *Invoice System*, is to show how to build the technical specification of a data processing system in an incremental fashion. Another important aspect is that of defining how the errors can be trapped in a systematic way. Here, clearly, the intention is to build abstract machines whose operations are viewed as a "repertoire of instructions" for building further machines on top of them, and so on.

The second example (inspired by [1]) is a *Telephone Exchange System*. The goal here is to show how the concept of abstract machine can be used to model a system where "concurrent" activities take place. The machine we shall specify is intended to be an abstract model of the *entire activity* of a telephone exchange, where all the telephone conversations are handled simultaneously. Clearly, the mental image of the operations of such a machine does not correspond to "buttons" that can be pressed or to "instructions" that can be invoked. The idea is rather to consider that the operations are *events* that *may occur* for some reason. The pre-conditions of such operations are then viewed as the "firing conditions" of such events. In a first approximation, the "real" reason for the occurence of such events, once the firing conditions are met, are not our concern. Sometimes, it can be the consequence of physical events like someone lifting a telephone hand-set. Sometimes, it is rather a "spontaneous" decision of the system.

The third example, the *Lift Control System*, is apparently of the same flavour as the previous one. What makes it rather different from the previous one is that the informal requirement of this system contains dynamic constraints expressing "liveness" properties to be proved. For instance, we would like to prove that our model is such that no group of people may wait for ever at some floors for some lift to pick them up. We shall see that such properties could be stated in an "ad-hoc" fashion or, better, as properties that correspond to the concept of refinement as we shall study it in chapter 11.

8.1. An Invoice System

8.1.1. Informal Specification

Our intention is to specify a system capable of handling invoices for customers in a commercial environment. More precisely, the system has to manage the following entities: *client, product, invoice* and *line* (of invoice). Next is a brief description of each of them:

- A *client* is recorded in the system together with his *category* (he is either a *normal* client, a *dubious* client, or a *friend*) and also with his maximum *allowance*, which is a certain amount of money that cannot be exceeded in any invoice issued to that client. To each category of clients, there corresponds a certain *discount* applicable to the corresponding invoices.

- A *product* is recorded together with its *price*, its *status* (*available* or *sold out*), and its possible (if any) *substitute*, which is another product guaranteed not to be itself sold out.

- An *invoice* is first concerned with the *client* to whom it is issued. An invoice also has a discount represented by a certain *percentage* to be applied to the total of the invoice. Finally, an invoice is characterized by the maximum amount of money that is *allowed* to it. These two attributes of an invoice (*percentage* and amount *allowed*) are taken originally (that is, when the invoice is "created") from similar attributes of the client (*discount* and *allowance*).

- Each *line* of an invoice is concerned with a certain *article*, the *quantity* of that article and, finally, the *unit_cost* of that article. This last attribute of an invoice line is taken originally (that is, when the invoice line is "created") from the *price* attribute of the article.

The system should provide a number of operations for creating and modifying a client, for creating and modifying a product, for creating and destroying an invoice, and, finally, for adding a new line to an invoice. Next is a number of informally stated laws that the system should satisfy:

1. A sold out product cannot be made part of an invoice.

2. However, if there exists a substitute for such a sold out product, then the system must automatically replace, in the invoice, the product in question by its substitute.

3. No two distinct lines of the same invoice may correspond to the same article.

4. No invoice can be made for dubious clients.

5. The (discounted) total of an invoice must not be greater than the maximum amount of money allowed for that invoice.

6. Friend clients get a 20% discount, whereas other clients get no discount at all.

We might be interested in designing *good error reporting* for that system. For instance, there are various reasons why entering a new product in an invoice line could fail:

- the product might be sold out and there might be no corresponding substitute (laws 1 and 2),

- the product, or its substitute if needed, might not be present already in the invoice and there might be no more lines available in the system (laws 2 and 3),

- the maximum allowance (taking account of the discount) of the invoice would be reached by the introduction of the new product, or of its substitute if needed (laws 2, 5 and 6).

The strategy we shall follow to build the specification of this system is to progress gradually by defining various machines which we shall later put together. Roughly speaking, each machine encapsulates a specific set of objects of the system: client, product, and (in the same machine) invoice and line. In what follows, we describe each of these machines in turn.

8.1.2. The *Client* Machine

This machine encapsulates the clients. Two sets are defined: the first one, *CLIENT*, is a deferred set denoting all the possible (present and future) clients, and the second one, *CATEGORY*, denotes the various categories of clients.

```
MACHINE

    Client

SETS

    CLIENT ;
    CATEGORY = {friend, dubious, normal}
```

A constant, *discount*, denotes the function linking each category of clients to the corresponding percentage that will be applied to the total of their invoices. As can be seen, only *friend* clients get a 20% discount, in accordance with law 6 of the informal specification of section 8.1.1.

We have three variables, named *client*, *category* and *allowance*, denoting the set of clients "present" in the system, and the two attributes of each client.

CONSTANTS

   discount

PROPERTIES

   $discount \in CATEGORY \rightarrow (0 .. 100) \; \wedge$
   $discount = \{friend \mapsto 80, \; dubious \mapsto 100, \; normal \mapsto 100\}$

VARIABLES

   client, category, allowance

INVARIANT

   $client \subseteq CLIENT \quad \wedge$
   $category \in client \rightarrow CATEGORY \quad \wedge$
   $allowance \in client \rightarrow \text{NAT}$

INITIALIZATION

   $client, \; category, \; allowance := \varnothing, \; \varnothing, \; \varnothing$

The machine offers one operation (create_client) to create a client, and two operations (modify_category and modify_allowance) to modify the attributes of clients. In the operation create_client, the parameter a is supposed to be the allowance given initially to the newly created client. The initial category is supposed to be the *normal* category. Another operation (read_client) is supposed to get a client that is guaranteed to belong to the set *client*.

OPERATIONS

   $c \longleftarrow \text{create\_client}(a) \quad \hat{=}$
       PRE
           $a \in \text{NAT} \quad \wedge$
           $client \neq CLIENT$
       THEN
           . . .
       END ;

OPERATIONS (*Cont'd*)

$\quad$ modify_category(c, k) $\;\widehat{=}\;$ $\cdots$;

$\quad$ modify_allowance(c, a) $\;\widehat{=}\;$ $\cdots$;

$\quad$ $c \longleftarrow$ read_client $\;\widehat{=}$
$\qquad$ PRE $\;$ *client* $\neq \varnothing$ $\;$ THEN $\;$ $c :\in$ *client* $\;$ END

END

8.1.3. The *Product* Machine

Like the previous machine with the clients, the *Product* machine encapsulates the products and introduces their attributes. Two sets are defined: the first one, *PRODUCT*, is a deferred set denoting all the possible (present and future) products, and the second one, *STATUS*, denotes the two possible statuses of a product.

MACHINE

$\quad$ *Product*

SETS

$\quad$ $PRODUCT$;
$\quad$ $STATUS \;=\; \{available,\; sold\_out\}$

VARIABLES

$\quad$ *product*, *price*, *status*, *substitute*

INVARIANT

$\quad$ *product* $\subseteq PRODUCT \quad \wedge$
$\quad$ *price* $\in product \rightarrow$ NAT $\quad \wedge$
$\quad$ *status* $\in product \rightarrow STATUS \quad \wedge$
$\quad$ *substitute* $\in product \nrightarrow status^{-1}[\{available\}]$

We have four variables, *product*, *price*, *status*, *substitute*, denoting respectively the set of products "present" in the system and the three attributes of a product. Notice, from the invariant, that not all products have a substitute (the variable *substitute* is a partial function). Moreover, a substitute is guaranteed not to be a sold out product, as required in the informal specification. This is formalized by the fact that the range of the *substitute* function is included in the set of products whose *status* is *available*.

INITIALIZATION

    product, price, status, substitute := ∅, ∅, ∅, ∅

OPERATIONS

    $p \longleftarrow$ create_product (c) $\;\widehat{=}$
        PRE
            $c \in$ NAT $\quad \wedge$
            product $\neq PRODUCT$
        THEN
            . . .
        END ;

    modify_price (p,c) $\;=\;$ $\cdots$;

    make_unavailable (p) $\;\widehat{=}$
        PRE
            $p \in product$
        THEN
            $status(p) := sold\_out \;\; ||$
            $substitute := substitute \vartriangleright \{p\}$
        END ;

    assign_substitute (p,q) $\;\widehat{=}$
        PRE
            $p \in product \quad \wedge$
            $q \in product \quad \wedge$
            $status(q) = available$
        THEN
            $substitute(p) := q$
        END ;

    $p \longleftarrow$ read_product $\;\widehat{=}$
        PRE $\quad product \neq \emptyset \quad$ THEN $\quad p :\in product \quad$ END

END

An operation (create_product) is offered to create a product. The parameter *c* in this operation is supposed to denote the price of the product. The status of the new product is supposed to be *available*. There are other operations (modify_price, make_unavailable, assign_substitute) to modify the price of a product, to make a product unavailable and to assign a substitute to a product. A final operation (read_product) yields an existing product.

8.1.4. The *Invoice* Machine

The *Invoice* machine USES the *Client* machine and the *Product* machine because it needs to have access to some of the variables of these machines. Two sets are defined. The deferred set *INVOICE* denotes all the possible (present and future) invoices, and the deferred set *LINE* denotes all the possible (present and future) lines.

```
MACHINE

    Invoice

USES

    Client, Product

SETS

    INVOICE ;
    LINE
```

We have five variables that are concerned with the invoices: *invoice, customer, percentage, allowed, total*. And we have five variables that are concerned with the lines of invoices: *line, origin, article, quantity, unit_cost*.

```
VARIABLES

    invoice, customer, percentage, allowed, total,

    line, origin, article, quantity, unit_cost
```

The variables in the first series denote respectively the set of invoices "present" in the system and the four other attributes of an invoice. The last invariant concerned with the invoice expresses the fact that the *total* of an invoice must not exceed the maximum amount of money allowed to that invoice. This part of the invariant implements law 5 of our informal specification.

INVARIANT

$invoice \subseteq INVOICE \quad \wedge$
$customer \in invoice \rightarrow client \quad \wedge$
$percentage \in invoice \rightarrow (0..100) \quad \wedge$
$allowed \in invoice \rightarrow \mathsf{NAT} \quad \wedge$
$total \in invoice \rightarrow \mathsf{NAT} \quad \wedge$
$\mathsf{ran}\,(total \otimes allowed) \subseteq \mathsf{geq} \quad \wedge$

$line \subseteq LINE \quad \wedge$
$origin \in line \rightarrow invoice \quad \wedge$
$article \in line \rightarrow product \quad \wedge$
$quantity \in line \rightarrow \mathsf{NAT} \quad \wedge$
$unit\_cost \in line \rightarrow \mathsf{NAT} \quad \wedge$
$origin \otimes article \in line \rightarrowtail invoice \times product$

The variables in the second series denote respectively the set of lines "present" in the system and the four attributes of a line. The *origin* variable denotes the invoice within which each line occurs. The *article* variable denotes the product involved in the line. The *quantity* variable denotes the number of units of the product. Finally, the *unit_cost* variable denotes, within the invoice, the price of the product. As can be seen, we enforce, in the invariant, the fact that no two lines of the same invoice are concerned with the same product (law 3 of the informal specification). This is done by expressing that the direct product of the functions *origin* and *article* is a partial injection from the set *line* to the cartesian product *invoice* × *product*. As a result, we can get, *at most*, one line corresponding to a given invoice and a given product. Next is the initialization of the system:

INITIALIZATION

$invoice,\ customer,\ percentage,\ allowed,\ total := \varnothing,\ \varnothing,\ \varnothing,\ \varnothing,\ \varnothing \quad \|$

$line,\ origin,\ article,\ quantity,\ unit\_cost := \varnothing,\ \varnothing,\ \varnothing,\ \varnothing,\ \varnothing$

One operation (create_invoice_header) is offered to create an invoice for a given non-dubious client (law 4 of the informal specification). Of course, the newly created invoice has not yet got any lines in it; this is just an invoice header. It is related to a certain client and to the corresponding allowance and possible discount of that client. Notice that this transfer (of some of the client's data into the invoice) is done at the precise moment when the invoice is created.

As a result, any future change of these data, on the client's record, will not affect the eventual calculation of the invoice.

OPERATIONS

$i \longleftarrow$ create_invoice_header(c) $\;\widehat{=}\;$

    PRE

        $c \in client \;\wedge$
        $category(c) \neq dubious \;\wedge$
        $invoice \neq INVOICE$

    THEN

        ANY $\;j\;$ WHERE
            $j \in INVOICE - invoice$

        THEN

            $invoice := invoice \cup \{j\}\;\;\;||$
            $customer(j) := c\;\;\;||$
            $percentage(j) := discount(category(c))\;\;\;||$
            $allowed(j) := allowance(c)\;\;\;||$
            $i := j$

        END

    END ;

A second operation (remove_invoice_header) is offered in order to remove an invoice. This is because, in some cases, it might be necessary to remove an incomplete invoice whose final calculation would not be possible.

OPERATIONS $\quad$ (Cont'd)

remove_invoice_header(i) $\;\widehat{=}\;$

    PRE

        $i \in invoice$

    THEN

        $invoice := invoice - \{i\}\;\;\;||$
        $customer := \{i\} \triangleleft customer\;\;\;||$
        $percentage := \{i\} \triangleleft percentage\;\;\;||$
        $allowed := \{i\} \triangleleft allowed\;\;\;||$
        $total := \{i\} \triangleleft total$

    END ;

The next operation, $l \longleftarrow$ new_line, is for adding a line to an invoice when the (supposedly available) product does not already appear in another line of the same invoice.

OPERATIONS   *(Cont'd)*

$l \longleftarrow$ new_line(i, p) $\widehat{=}$

PRE

$i \in invoice$ $\wedge$

$p \in product$ $\wedge$

$status(p) = available$ $\wedge$

$(i, p) \notin \mathrm{ran}\,(origin \otimes article)$ $\wedge$

$line \neq LINE$

THEN

ANY m WHERE

$m \in LINE - line$

THEN

$line := line \cup \{m\}$ ||

$origin(m) := i$ ||

$article(m) := p$ ||

$quantity(m) := 0$ ||

$unit\_cost(m) := price(p)$ ||

$l := m$

END

END;

Notice that the line is created with the product and its current price but with a null quantity. Notice also that, in the pre-condition, the predicate expressing that the product is available corresponds to an implementation of law 1 of the informal specification. The operation the_line is to obtain the line of an available product which, this time, is supposed to appear already in a certain (unique) line of a certain invoice.

OPERATIONS   *(Cont'd)*

$l \longleftarrow$ the_line(i, p) $\widehat{=}$

PRE

$i \in invoice$ $\wedge$

$p \in product$ $\wedge$

$status(p) = available$ $\wedge$

$(i, p) \in \mathrm{ran}\,(origin \otimes article)$

THEN

$l := (origin \otimes article)^{-1}(i, p)$

END;

The operation increment_line is for incrementing a line, corresponding to an available product, with an extra quantity. It will be seen that the pre-condition prevents using that operation if the total of the invoice is at risk of exceeding the allowed limit.

OPERATIONS (*Cont'd*)

    increment_line(l, q) $\widehat{=}$
        PRE
            $l \in line$ $\wedge$
            $q \in \mathsf{NAT}$ $\wedge$
            $status(article(l)) = available$ $\wedge$
            $quantity(l) + q \in \mathsf{NAT}$ $\wedge$
            $total(i) + (q \times unit\_cost(l) \times percentage(i) / 100) \le allowed(i)$
        THEN
            $quantity(l) := quantity(l) + q$ $||$
            $total(i) := total(i) + (q \times unit\_cost(l) \times percentage(i) / 100)$
        END ;

A final operation, remove_all_lines, is offered to remove all the lines of an invoice:

OPERATIONS (*Cont'd*)

    remove_all_lines(i) $\widehat{=}$
        PRE
            $i \in invoice$
        THEN
            $line := line - lines(i)$ $||$
            $origin := lines(i) \triangleleft origin$ $||$
            $article := lines(i) \triangleleft article$ $||$
            $quantity := lines(i) \triangleleft quantity$ $||$
            $unit\_cost := lines(i) \triangleleft unit\_cost$
        END

    END

The operations defined in the present machine, as well as in the previous machines, constitute the basic "instruction repertoire" on which we are going to build the next layer of our system.

8.1.5. The *Invoice_System* Machine

The *Invoice_System* machine, is just the joining together of all the previous machines. We also add a number of operations, to help in defining good error reporting.

MACHINE

    Invoice_System

EXTENDS

    Client, *Product*, *Invoice*

OPERATIONS

    $b \longleftarrow$ some_client_exists $\;\widehat{=}\; \cdots\;$;

    $b \longleftarrow$ clients_not_saturated $\;\widehat{=}\; \cdots\;$;

    $b \longleftarrow$ client_not_dubious(c) $\;\widehat{=}\; \cdots\;$;

    $b \longleftarrow$ some_product_exists $\;\widehat{=}\; \cdots\;$;

    $b \longleftarrow$ products_not_saturated $\;\widehat{=}\; \cdots\;$;

    $b \longleftarrow$ product_available(p) $\;\widehat{=}\; \cdots\;$;

    $b \longleftarrow$ product_has_substitute(p) $\;\widehat{=}\; \cdots\;$;

    $b \longleftarrow$ invoices_not_saturated $\;\widehat{=}\; \cdots\;$;

    $b \longleftarrow$ new_product_in_invoice(i, p) $\;\widehat{=}\; \cdots\;$;

    $b \longleftarrow$ lines_not_saturated $\;\widehat{=}\; \cdots\;$;

    $b \longleftarrow$ quantity_not_exceeded_by_line(q, l) $\;\widehat{=}\; \cdots\;$;

    $b \longleftarrow$ total_not_exceeded_by_line_of_invoice(i, q, l) $\;\widehat{=}\; \cdots$

END

8.2. A Telephone Exchange

In this section we specify a telephone exchange. This is done according to the study made in [1]. The model is centred around a set of *subscribers* who may be engaged in telephone conversations through a network controlled by an exchange.

8.2.1. Informal specification

As the communication between two subscribers is not installed immediately, each subscriber navigates through a variety of statuses, which we study in detail in what follows.

Free Subscribers

To begin with, a subscriber might be *free* (for short, *fr*), meaning that he is not engaged in any telephone conversation or attempting to do so.

Unavailable Subscribers

We then consider the case of subscribers who are temporarily *unavailable* (for short *un*). As we shall see, subscribers may enter this status as a result of a *spontaneous* decision on the part of the exchange. This happens when a subscriber has been attempting to call another subscriber unsuccessfully for too long a period of time. We may also enter this status at the end of some conversation between two subscribers.

Initiators or Recipients

Non-free and non-unavailable subscribers are either *initiators* or *recipients* of telephone calls. These properties of subscribers will remain the same as long as they are engaged in telephone conversations. More precisely, an initiator is the only one able to terminate a telephone conversation. By contrast, a recipient hanging up just suspends the conversation, which may be resumed as soon as he again lifts his handset (unless, of course, the corresponding initiator has hung up in the meantime).

Attempting, Waiting or Speaking Initiators

An initiator may enter into various sub-states: he might be *attempting* to call somebody (for instance, he is in the process of dialling), or *waiting* for somebody to answer (this is the case when the connection has been established with a recipient whose telephone is ringing or who has taken the initiative to suspend an already engaged conversation), or finally *speaking* to somebody. The status of these three categories of initiators is represented conventionally by the acrnyms *ai*, *wi*, and *si*.

Waiting or Speaking Recipients

Likewise, a recipient might be *speaking*, or *waiting* (because his own telephone is ringing, or because he has suspended an already engaged telephone conversation). The status of these two categories of recipients is represented conventionally by the acronyms *wr* and *sr*. We can summarize these various statuses of a subscriber as follows:

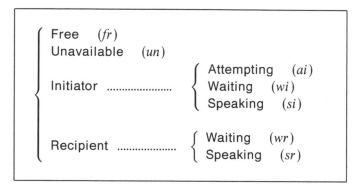

Our intention is to model the exchange *gradually*. As a first step, we do not want to deal with the question of dialling. Our main concern for the moment is rather to make clear the *protocol* by which people can engage or clear a telephone conversation. For doing so, we consider a number of operations (i.e.*events*) which might change the status of one or two subscribers.

There are various reasons why such events may occur. Sometimes, an event will be caused by a subscriber's action such as lifting the handset or hanging up. Sometimes, it will be just a "spontaneous" activity of the telephone exchange. Our coming specification is simply that of the semantics of these various events. Of course, the events will be specified together with a number of pre-conditions which indicate the way they can be fired. Next is an informal description of the events we shall consider to begin with.

Lift

The event Lift is caused by a free subscriber lifting his handset. He thus becomes an attempting initiator with status *ai*.

$$fr \quad \text{Lift} \quad ai$$

Connect

The event Connect is caused by a spontaneous activity of the exchange which, *somehow*, connects an attempting initiator to a free subscriber. These two subscribers become respectively a waiting initiator and a waiting recipient (whose telephone starts to ring). The way the exchange chooses the pair is "magic" for the moment. In the second phase of this model building, we shall consider the process by which an attempting initiator reveals his intentions.

$$ai, fr \quad \text{Connect} \quad wi, wr$$

MakeUn

The event MakeUn is also caused by a spontaneous activity of the exchange which decides to "punish" an attempting initiator who has seized a line for too long a period of time without succeeding in connecting to another subscriber. The initiator enters the status *un*. Notice that such an unavailable subscriber has certainly not yet hung up.

$$ai \quad \text{MakeUn} \quad un$$

Answer

The event Answer is caused by a waiting recipient lifting his handset: he might do so because his telephone is ringing or, spontaneously, after he has temporarily suspended an already engaged telephone conversation. This waiting recipient enters the status *sr* (speaking recipient) and the corresponding initiator enters the status *si* (speaking initiator).

$$wi, wr \quad \text{Answer} \quad si, sr$$

We now consider the various events by which a telephone conversation is cleared. Such events might be caused either by an initiator or by a recipient who hangs up.

ClearAttempt, ClearWait, ClearSpeak

In the case of an initiator, we have three possible events corresponding to the three possible statuses *ai*, *wi*, or *si*. These events are called respectively ClearAttempt, ClearWait, and ClearSpeak. In all three cases, the initiator re-enters the status *fr*. In the second and third cases, there exists a corresponding recipient who enters the status *fr* (if he is waiting) or *un* (if he is speaking).

$$ai \quad \text{ClearAttempt} \quad fr$$

$$wi, wr \quad \text{ClearWait} \quad fr, fr$$

$$si, sr \quad \text{ClearSpeak} \quad fr, un$$

Suspend

When a speaking recipient hangs up, the corresponding event is called Suspend because, as we have already indicated, the conversation is only suspended. In fact, both our recipient and his corresponding initiator enter a waiting status: that is, *wr* and *wi* respectively. As can be seen, we reach exactly the same situation as was the case after the *Connect* event, the only difference being that, this time, the recipient's telephone is not ringing.

$$si, sr \quad \text{Suspend} \quad wi, wr$$

ClearUn

The last event to consider is the one by which an unavailable subscriber hangs up: it is called ClearUn. The subscriber re-enters the status *fr*.

$$un \quad \text{ClearUn} \quad fr$$

Typical synchronizations of the previous events should be the following:

Lift $\leadsto$ ClearAttempt

Lift $\leadsto$ MakeUn $\leadsto$ ClearUn

Lift $\leadsto$ Connect $\leadsto$ ClearWait

Lift $\leadsto$ Connect $\leadsto$ Answer $\leadsto$ ClearSpeak $\leadsto$ ClearUn

Lift $\leadsto$ Connect $\leadsto$ Answer $\leadsto$ Suspend $\leadsto$ ClearWait

8.2.2. The *Simple_Exchange* Machine

We are now ready to define our first machine. We have a deferred set called *SUBSCRIBER* and an enumerated set called *STATUS*. The state is defined by two variables called respectively *status* and *caller*. The variable *status* denotes the possible *STATUS* of each *SUBSCRIBER*, as described previously. The variable *caller* denotes a function from subscribers to subscribers. Of course, this function is meaningful only for waiting or speaking recipients; and it is a *bijection* to waiting or speaking initiators respectively. More precisely, the domain restriction of that function to waiting recipients is a bijection to waiting initiators; and we have the same kind of bijection for speaking subscribers. This rule formalizes the fact that, in this telephone exchange, telephone conversations are between two subscribers only (that is, we have no conference call).

MACHINE

    Simple_Exchange

SETS

    SUBSCRIBER ;
    STATUS $= \{\, fr,\, un,\, ai,\, wi,\, si,\, wr,\, sr \,\}$

VARIABLES

    status, caller

INVARIANT

$status \in SUBSCRIBER \rightarrow STATUS$ ∧
$caller \in status^{-1}[\{wr, sr\}] \rightarrowtail status^{-1}[\{wi, si\}]$ ∧

$status^{-1}[\{wr\}] \lhd caller \in status^{-1}[\{wr\}] \rightarrowtail status^{-1}[\{wi\}]$ ∧
$status^{-1}[\{sr\}] \lhd caller \in status^{-1}[\{sr\}] \rightarrowtail status^{-1}[\{si\}]$

INITIALIZATION

$status, caller := SUBSCRIBER \times \{fr\}, \varnothing$

Next are the operations of the machine, as described previously:

OPERATIONS

Lift(*s*) $\widehat{=}$
    PRE
        $s \in status^{-1}[\{fr\}]$
    THEN
        $status(s) := ai$
    END ;

Connect(*s*, *t*) $\widehat{=}$
    PRE
        $s \in status^{-1}[\{ai\}]$ ∧
        $t \in status^{-1}[\{fr\}]$
    THEN
        $status := status \lhd\!\!\!- \{s \mapsto wi,\ t \mapsto wr\}$ ||
        $caller(t) := s$
    END ;

MakeUn(*s*) $\widehat{=}$
    PRE
        $s \in status^{-1}[\{ai\}]$
    THEN
        $status(s) := un$
    END ;

OPERATIONS   *(Cont'd)*

Answer(t) $\hat{=}$
    PRE
        $t \in status^{-1}[\{wr\}]$
    THEN
        $status := status \lessdot \{t \mapsto sr,\ caller(t) \mapsto si\}$
    END ;

ClearAttempt(s) $\hat{=}$
    PRE
        $s \in status^{-1}[\{ai\}]$
    THEN
        $status(s) := fr$
    END ;

ClearWait(s) $\hat{=}$
    PRE
        $s \in status^{-1}[\{wi\}]$
    THEN
        $status := status \lessdot \{s \mapsto fr,\ caller^{-1}(s) \mapsto fr\}$ $||$
        $caller := caller \rhd \{s\}$
    END ;

ClearSpeak(s) $\hat{=}$
    PRE
        $s \in status^{-1}[\{si\}]$
    THEN
        $status := status \lessdot \{s \mapsto fr,\ caller^{-1}(s) \mapsto un\}$ $||$
        $caller := caller \rhd \{s\}$
    END ;

Suspend(t) $\hat{=}$
    PRE
        $t \in status^{-1}[\{sr\}]$
    THEN
        $status := status \lessdot \{t \mapsto wr,\ caller(t) \mapsto wi\}$
    END ;

ClearUn(s) $\hat{=}$
    PRE $s \in status^{-1}[\{un\}]$ THEN $status(s) := fr$ END

END

8.2.3. The *Exchange* Machine

We now use the previous machine to build our final specification. We shall make precise the way an attempting initiator might be connected to a free subscriber. Each subscriber of the telephone exchange is assigned a unique telephone number which is a finite sequence of digits. Clearly, the dialling process is carried out step by step by each attempting initiator. We also know that after each dialling, we may end up in three possible situations: either the number we have dialled so far is indeed the telephone number of a certain subscriber, or it is definitely a bad number, or, finally, the number dialled so far might still become a genuine telephone number after more dialling.

We thus define an enumerated set that corresponds to the three possible statuses of each *sofar* dialled number: such a number could be *good*, *bad* or, say, *hopeful*. When the *sofar* dialled number is *good*, then there are obviously two cases to consider: either the corresponding subscriber is *free* or he is not *free* (engaged). In the former case, the attempting initiator becomes connectable.

We have a number of additional events which correspond to the various cases we have just envisaged. Next is a brief description of each of them:

LiftFree

The event LiftFree takes a *free* subscriber and extends the previous Lift event so that the new attempting initiator has an empty *sofar* dialled number.

Dial

In the event Dial, the *sofar* dialled number is *hopeful*.

WrongNumber

In the event WrongNumber, the *sofar* dialled number is *bad*.

Failure

In the event Failure, the *sofar* dialled number is *good* but the recipient is not *free*.

Success

In the last event, Success, the *sofar* dialled number is *good* and the recipient is indeed *free*. In fact, that event is exactly the Connect event of the previous machine: the new recipient being now determined (uniquely) by his telephone number.

Next are typical sequences that should be possible sequences of events:

$$\text{LiftFree} \rightsquigarrow \text{Dial} \rightsquigarrow \cdots \rightsquigarrow \text{Dial} \rightsquigarrow \text{WrongNumber}$$

$$\text{LiftFree} \rightsquigarrow \text{Dial} \rightsquigarrow \cdots \rightsquigarrow \text{Dial} \rightsquigarrow \text{Success}$$

$$\text{LiftFree} \rightsquigarrow \text{Dial} \rightsquigarrow \cdots \rightsquigarrow \text{Dial} \rightsquigarrow \text{Failure}$$

Next is our final machine:

MACHINE

    Exchange

INCLUDES

    Simple_Exchange

PROMOTES

    MakeUn, Answer, ClearAttempt, ClearWait, ClearSpeak,
    Suspend,
    ClearUn

SETS

    $NSTATUS = \{\, hopeful,\ bad,\ good \,\}$

CONSTANTS

    max_digit

PROPERTIES

    $max\_digit \in \mathsf{NAT}_1$

VARIABLES

    nstatus, subscriber, sofar

INVARIANT

    $nstatus \in \mathsf{seq}\,(0\,..\,max\_digit) \rightarrow NSTATUS \quad \wedge$
    $subscriber \in nstatus^{-1}[\{good\}] \rightarrowtail\!\!\!\rightarrow SUBSCRIBER \quad \wedge$
    $sofar \in SUBSCRIBER \rightarrow \mathsf{seq}\,(0\,..\,max\_digit)$

INITIALIZATION

    $nstatus :\in \mathsf{seq}\,(0\,..\,max\_digit) \rightarrow NSTATUS \quad ||$
    $subscriber :\in nstatus^{-1}[\{good\}] \rightarrowtail\!\!\!\rightarrow SUBSCRIBER \quad ||$
    $sofar := SUBSCRIBER \times \{[\,]\}$

OPERATIONS

  LiftFree(s) $\widehat{=}$
    PRE
      $s \in status^{-1}[\{fr\}]$
    THEN
      Lift(s) ||
      $sofar(s) := []$
    END ;

  Dial(s, d) $\widehat{=}$
    PRE
      $s \in status^{-1}[\{ai\}]$ $\wedge$
      $d \in 0..max\_digit$ $\wedge$
      $nstatus(sofar(s)) = hopeful$
    THEN
      $sofar(s) := sofar(s) \leftarrow d$
    END ;

  WrongNumber(s) $\widehat{=}$
    PRE
      $s \in status^{-1}[\{ai\}]$ $\wedge$
      $nstatus(sofar(s)) = bad$
    THEN
      skip
    END ;

  Failure(s) $\widehat{=}$
    PRE
      $s \in status^{-1}[\{ai\}]$ $\wedge$
      $nstatus(sofar(s)) = good$ $\wedge$
      $status(subscriber(sofar(s))) \neq fr$
    THEN
      skip
    END ;

  Success(s) $\widehat{=}$
    PRE
      $s \in status^{-1}[\{ai\}]$ $\wedge$
      $nstatus(sofar(s)) = good$ $\wedge$
      $status(subscriber(sofar(s))) = fr$
    THEN
      Connect(s, $subscriber(sofar(s))$)
    END

END

8.3. A Lift Control System

In this section, we study a problem that has been popular since 1984 when it was proposed by N. Davis as a case study for reacting systems. In the next section, we quote the problem statement, as it was presented originally.

8.3.1. Informal Specification

An *n* lift system is to be installed in a building with *m* floors. The lifts and the control mechanism are supplied by a manufacturer. The internal mechanisms of these are assumed (given) in this problem. Design the logic to move lifts between floors in the building according to the following rules:

1. Each lift has a set of buttons, one button for each floor. These illuminate when pressed and cause the lift to visit the corresponding floor. The illumination is cancelled when the corresponding floor is visited (i.e. stopped at) by the lift.

2. Each floor (except ground and top) has two buttons, one to request an up-lift and one to request a down-lift. These buttons illuminate when pressed. The buttons are cancelled when a lift visits the floor and is either travelling in the desired direction or visiting the floor with no requests outstanding. In the latter case, if both floor request buttons are illuminated, only one should be cancelled. The algorithm used to decide which to service should minimize the waiting time for both requests.

3. When a lift has no requests to service, it should remain at its final destination with its doors closed and await further requests (or model a 'holding' floor).

4. All requests for lifts from floors must be serviced eventually, with all floors given equal priority (can this be proved or demonstrated?).

5. All requests for floors within lifts must be serviced eventually, with floors being serviced sequentially in the direction of travel (can this be proved or demonstrated?).

6. Each lift has an emergency button which, when pressed, causes a warning to be sent to the site manager. The lift is then deemed 'out of service'. Each lift has a mechanism to cancel its 'out of service' status.

8.3.2. The *Lift* Machine

In the *Lift* machine that we propose as a model for the previous informal specification, we define two sets: *LIFT*, which is a deferred set, and the enumerated set *DIRECTION* (whose members are *up* and *dn*), indicating in which directions lifts (and passengers) are intended to travel. We also define two constants, *top* and *ground*, yielding the top and ground floors. And we define the set of *FLOOR* as the interval *ground .. top*.

MACHINE

   Lift

SETS

   LIFT ;
   $DIRECTION = \{up, dn\}$

CONSTANTS

   ground, *top*

PROPERTIES

   $ground \in \mathsf{NAT} \quad \wedge$
   $top \in \mathsf{NAT} \quad \wedge$
   $ground < top$

DEFINITIONS

   $FLOOR \mathrel{\widehat{=}} ground \mathbin{..} top$

VARIABLES

   moving, *floor*, *dir*, *in*, *out*

INVARIANT

   $moving \subseteq LIFT \quad \wedge$
   $floor \in LIFT \rightarrow FLOOR \quad \wedge$
   $dir \in LIFT \rightarrow DIRECTION \quad \wedge$
   $in \in FLOOR \leftrightarrow DIRECTION \quad \wedge$
   $out \in LIFT \leftrightarrow FLOOR \quad \wedge$
   $(ground \mapsto dn) \notin in \quad \wedge$
   $(top \mapsto up) \notin in \quad \wedge$
   $moving \triangleleft (out \cap floor) = \varnothing \quad \wedge$
   $in \cap \mathsf{ran}(moving \triangleleft (floor \otimes dir)) = \varnothing$

INITIALIZATION

   $in, out, moving := \varnothing, \varnothing, \varnothing \quad ||$
   $floor, dir := LIFT \times \{ground\}, LIFT \times \{up\}$

The system is formalized by means of five variables called *moving*, *floor*, *dir*, *in* and *out*, which we shall describe briefly in what follows. Each lift is obviously either stopped at some floor or moving between floors. We thus suppose that we have a variable, *moving*, which denotes the set of moving lifts. For each lift *l*, we have a corresponding floor, *floor*(*l*), which is supposed to be the floor at which *l* is stopped, if *l* is not moving, or the floor where lift *l* is about to arrive, if is moving. For each lift *l*, we have a direction, *dir*(*l*), supposed to be the direction in which *l* is travelling, if it is moving, or the direction in which *l* is "intended" to travel next, if it is not moving.

The variable *in* is a binary relation from *FLOOR* to *DIRECTION*. When the pair (f, d) belongs to *in*, this means that some people want to travel from floor f in direction d. Clearly, it should not be possible for people to travel down from the ground floor, nor to travel up from the top floor. We notice that dom(*in*) denotes the set of floors where people are waiting for some lift.

The variable *out* is a binary relation from *LIFT* to *FLOOR*. When the pair (l, f) belongs to *out*, this means that some people in lift *l* want to leave *l* at floor f. We notice that $out[\{l\}]$ denotes the set of floors at which people have asked lift *l* to stop.

Notice that the last but one invariant makes it impossible to ask, from a lift *l*, to have *l* stopping at a certain floor f if *l* is already stopped at f. Likewise, the last invariant makes it impossible to ask, from a floor f, for a lift *l* going in a certain direction d, in the case where there already exists a lift stopped at f and travelling in the direction d. These two invariants also express that the clients are effectively served when the conditions are met.

The operations of the machine correspond to "events" that can occur for various reasons.

```
OPERATIONS

    Request_Floor(l,f)  ≙
        PRE
            l ∈ LIFT   ∧
            f ∈ FLOOR   ∧
            ( l ∉ moving  ⇒  floor(l) ≠ f )
        THEN
            out := out ∪ {l ↦ f}
        END ;
```

OPERATIONS   (*Cont'd*)

Request_Lift(f, d) $\hat{=}$
  PRE

  $$f \in \textit{FLOOR} \quad \wedge$$
  $$d \in \textit{DIRECTION} \quad \wedge$$
  $$(f, d) \neq (\textit{ground}, \textit{dn}) \quad \wedge$$
  $$(f, d) \neq (\textit{top}, \textit{up}) \quad \wedge$$
  $$(f, d) \notin \mathsf{ran}\,(\textit{moving} \lhd (\textit{floor} \otimes \textit{dir}))$$

  THEN

  $$\textit{in} := \textit{in} \cup \{f \mapsto d\}$$

  END ;

The first two events we have considered are caused by specific actions of passengers pressing certain buttons either to request a lift from some floor (Request_Lift) or to request a floor from some lift (Request_Floor)

We now define some events by which it is decided (by the system) whether a moving lift, which is about to arrive at a certain floor, has to continue moving or if it has to stop at that floor. The key idea of the formalization we propose is first to define two predicates, named *attracted_up*(l) and *attracted_dn*(l), which are supposed to hold when a lift l (situated, or just arriving, at *floor*(l)) is attracted in the *up* direction or in the *dn* direction. Informally speaking, this is the case when *at least* one of the two conditions holds: some passengers travelling with lift l have expressed their intention to leave l at some floor ahead of *floor*(l) in the corresponding direction (for instance, for the *up* direction, this yields the fact that the set *out*$[\{l\}] \cap (\textit{floor}(l) + 1 .. \textit{top})$ is not empty), or some passengers are waiting for a lift at some floor ahead of *floor*(l) in the corresponding direction (for instance, for the *dn* direction, this yields the fact that the set dom$(\textit{in}) \cap (\textit{ground} .. \textit{floor}(l) - 1)$ is not empty).

DEFINITIONS

$$\textit{attracted\_up}(l) \quad \hat{=} \quad (\mathsf{dom}\,(\textit{in}) \cup \textit{out}\,[\{l\}]) \cap ((\textit{floor}(l) + 1) .. \textit{top}) \neq \varnothing ;$$

$$\textit{attracted\_dn}(l) \quad \hat{=} \quad (\mathsf{dom}\,(\textit{in}) \cup \textit{out}\,[\{l\}]) \cap (\textit{ground} .. (\textit{floor}(l) - 1)) \neq \varnothing ;$$

We are now ready to define two other predicates, which we call *can_continue_up*(l) and *can_continue_dn*(l). These predicates are supposed to hold when a moving lift l has no reason to stop at *floor*(l), where it is about to arrive. Obviously, this is when the following three conditions hold *simultaneously*: nobody wants to get out from l at *floor*(l) (that is, the pair $l \mapsto \textit{floor}(l)$ does not belong to *out*), and nobody wants to get in from *floor*(*l*) to travel in *dir*(*l*) (that is, the pair *floor*(*l*) ↦ *dir*(*l*) does not belong to *in*), and finally lift *l* is still attracted in the *dir*(*l*) direction (that is, either *attracted_up*(*l*) or *attracted_dn*(*l*) holds, depending upon the value of *dir*(*l*)).

When *can_continue_up*(*l*) does not hold, then, obviously, a lift travelling in the *up* direction must stop. By negating the previous conditions, this happens when *at least* one of the following three conditions holds: somebody wants to get out from *l* at *floor*(*l*), or somebody wants to get in at *floor*(*l*) to travel in *dir*(*l*), or else lift *l* is no longer attracted in the direction *dir*(*l*). Notice that, in case the third condition only holds, then lift *l* must indeed stop since *it has no reason to continue*. The above predicates can now be formally defined as follows:

DEFINITIONS   (*Cont'd*)

$$can\_continue\_up(l) \;\; \widehat{=} \;\; (l \mapsto floor(l)) \notin out \quad \land$$
$$(floor(l) \mapsto dir(l)) \notin in \quad \land$$
$$attracted\_up(l);$$

$$can\_continue\_dn(l) \;\; \widehat{=} \;\; (l \mapsto floor(l)) \notin out \quad \land$$
$$(floor(l) \mapsto dir(l)) \notin in \quad \land$$
$$attracted\_dn(l)$$

We can now define, in an obvious way, the events Continue_up, Continue_dn, Stop_up and Stop_dn:

OPERATIONS   (*Cont'd*)

Continue_up(*l*) $\widehat{=}$
   PRE
      $l \in moving \quad \land$
      $dir(l) = up \quad \land$
      $can\_continue\_up(l)$
   THEN
      $floor(l) := floor(l) + 1$
   END;

Continue_dn(*l*) $\widehat{=} \cdots;$

```
OPERATIONS     (Cont'd)

   Stop_up(l)  ≙
       PRE
              l ∈ moving    ∧
              dir(l) = up    ∧
              ¬ can_continue_up(l)
       THEN
              moving := moving − {l}    ||
              out := out − {l ↦ floor(l)}    ||
              in := in − {floor(l) ↦ dir(l)}
       END;

   Stop_dn(l)  ≙ ··· ;
```

Our last events have to do with the decision (by the system) for the departure of a lift from a floor in a certain direction (Depart_up and Depart_dn) or for the change of direction of a lift (Change_up_to_dn and Change_dn_to_up). The key idea here is that a lift gives the priority to continuing its travel in the direction it was travelling when it stopped at the floor. If the lift has no reason to travel in the same direction (that is, if it is no longer attracted in that direction), then it is free to change (if necessary) to the opposite direction. This results in the following events:

```
OPERATIONS     (Cont'd)

   Depart_up(l)  ≙
       PRE
              l ∈ LIFT − moving    ∧
              dir(l) = up    ∧
              attracted_up(l)
       THEN
              moving := moving ∪ {l}    ||
              floor(l) := floor(l) + 1
       END;

   Depart_dn(l)  ≙ ··· ;
```

OPERATIONS   (*Cont'd*)

Change_up_to_dn(*l*) $\widehat{=}$
 PRE
  $l \in LIFT - moving$ $\wedge$
  $dir(l) = up$ $\wedge$
  $\neg\, attracted\_up(l)$ $\wedge$
  $attracted\_dn(l)$
 THEN
  $in := in - \{floor(l) \mapsto dn\}$ $\|$
  $dir(l) := dn$
 END

Change_dn_to_up(*l*) $\widehat{=} \cdots$

END

8.3.3. Liveness Proof

Our intention is now to prove that the model defined in the previous section indeed implements requirements 4 and 5 of the informal specification. These requirements were that "all requests for lifts from floors must be serviced eventually" and that "all requests for floors within lifts must be serviced eventually". Generally speaking, such requirements are called "liveness" requirements: they correspond to properties that do not hold necessarily all the time, only from time to time, and, in any case, to properties that cannot be postponed indefinitely. In what follows, we shall develop a proof concerning the first of these requirements ("all requests for lifts from floors must be serviced eventually").

 In order to formalize rigorously what we want to prove, we define a notion of distance between two floors f and g, relative to two directions d and e. This is denoted by $dist(f, d, g, e)$. Informally speaking, such a distance denotes the maximum number of floors situated "in between" a floor f (at which lift travelling in direction d is supposed to be stopped or supposed to be arriving shortly) and a floor g (where somebody is supposed to have requested a lift to travel in direction e). Moreover, in this "maximum number of floors", each necessary change of direction is "counted" as an extra floor. For instance, suppose that we have the following figure: $f = 8, d = up, g = 3, e = up$. We have then:

$$
\begin{aligned}
dist(8, up, 3, up) &= (top - 8) + 1 + (top - ground) + 1 + (3 - ground) \\
&= 2 \times (top - ground) - 3
\end{aligned}
$$

That is, $(top - 8)$ corresponds to the lift going to the top floor from floor 8, 1 is for the necessary change of direction, $(top - ground)$ corresponds to the lift going down from top to bottom (it passes floor 3, but, unfortunately, it is going in the wrong direction), 1 is, again, for the change of direction, and, finally, $(3 - ground)$ corresponds to climbing up again to floor 3 (this time, in the right direction). The definition of $dist(f, d, g, e)$ is given in the following table:

Condition	d	e	$dist(f, d, g, e)$
$f > g$	up	up	$2 \times (top - ground) - f + g + 2$
		dn	$2 \times top - f - g + 1$
	dn	up	$f + g + 1 - 2 \times ground$
		dn	$f - g$
$f = g$	up	up	0
		dn	$2 \times top - f - g + 1$
	dn	up	$f + g + 1 - 2 \times ground$
		dn	0
$f < g$	up	up	$g - f$
		dn	$2 \times top - f - g + 1$
	dn	up	$f + g + 1 - 2 \times ground$
		dn	$2 \times (top - ground) - g + f + 2$

For a given lift l, we have then to prove that every event, except the first two, will decrease $dist(floor(l), dir(l), g, e)$, for each floor g and direction e such that $(g, e) \in in$. This is to be proved provided, of course, the operation concerned is called within its pre-condition and the invariant I of the *Lift* machine holds. For the operation Change_up_to_dn which replaces in by $in - \{floor(l) \mapsto dn\}$ and $dir(l)$ by dn, we must thus prove the following:

$$
\begin{aligned}
&I \\
&l \in LIFT - moving \\
&dir(l) = up \\
&\neg\, attracted\_up(l) \\
&attracted\_dn(l) \\
&\Rightarrow \\
&\quad \forall (g, e) \cdot ((g, e) \in in - \{floor(l) \mapsto dn\} \;\Rightarrow \\
&\qquad\qquad dist(floor(l), dn, g, e) < dist(floor(l), dir(l), g, e))
\end{aligned}
$$

If δ denotes the distance that holds before the operation takes place and δ' denotes the distance that holds just after the operation has taken place (if the pre-condition permits), then, in all relevant cases, it is easy to calculate that we have the following:

$$\delta - \delta' \;=\; 2 \times (top - floor(l)) + 1$$

For the operation Change_dn_to_up, we have (with similar notations):

$$\delta - \delta' \;=\; 2 \times (floor(l) - ground) + 1$$

Evidently, these quantities are always positive, hence the distance always decreases. Concerning the other relevant operations, we can calculate that the distance decreases by 1 in all cases.

8.3.4. Expressing Liveness Proof Obligations

In the previous section we have presented certain statements to be proved concerning all operations except the first two. In this section our intention is to show that such statements correspond *exactly* to the statements we shall obtain in chapter 11 for the proof obligations of refinement (the reader who has no previous knowledge of the theory of refinement presented in chapter 11 might skip this section, particularly the end of it). The idea is that the concerned operations have (up to their pre-conditions) a *common abstraction* corresponding to an operation that, *non-deterministically*, decreases the distances. For instance, here is the abstraction that would correspond to the operation Change_up_to_dn:

Change_up_to_dn(l) $\;\widehat{=}$
> PRE
>> $l \in LIFT - moving \quad \wedge$
>> $dir(l) = up \quad \wedge$
>> $\neg\,attracted\_up(l) \quad \wedge$
>> $attracted\_dn(l)$
> THEN
>> Decrease_Distances(l)
> END

The other abstractions are similar. It remains for us to define the operation Decrease_Distances:

Decrease_Distances(l) $\;\widehat{=}$
> PRE
>> $l \in LIFT$
> THEN
>> $moving, floor, dir, in, out \;:$
>> $$\left(\begin{array}{l} I \quad \wedge \\ in \subseteq in_0 \quad \wedge \\ out \subseteq out_0 \quad \wedge \\ \forall\,(g,e) \cdot ((g,e) \in in \;\Rightarrow \\ \quad dist\,(floor(l), dir(l), g, e) < dist\,(floor_0(l), dir_0(l), g, e)) \end{array} \right)$$
> END

In this operation, I stands for the invariant of the *Lift* machine. It will be seen that this specification is very "vague" (highly non-deterministic). The only thing it says is that it maintains the invariant while servicing some clients (this is expressed by $in \subseteq in_0$ and $out \subseteq out_0$) and while guaranteeing to decrease the distances between the lift l and the floors where requests have been made and are not yet serviced. Clearly, there are many ways to achieve that effect. This operation represents the most general (abstract) definition we can think of for the specification of the events governing the dynamic behaviour of the system: all such events must serve some clients while progressing towards servicing the others.

We shall see in chapter 11 that the fact that the operation Change_up_to_dn(l) refines Decrease_Distances(l), pre-conditioned by the pre-condition of the operation Change_up_to_dn(l), is expressed by the following refinement statement:

I
$l \in LIFT - moving$
$dir(l) = up$
$\neg \, attracted\_up(l)$
$attracted\_dn(l)$
$moving, \ldots, out = moving'', \ldots, out''$
$\Rightarrow$
$[[moving, \ldots, out := moving'', \ldots, out''] \, \mathsf{Change\_up\_to\_dn}\,(l)]$
   $\neg \, [\mathsf{Decrease\_Distances}(l)] \, \neg \, (moving, \ldots, out = moving'', \ldots, out'')$

We have

$\neg \, [\mathsf{Decrease\_Distances}(l)] \, \neg \, (moving, \ldots out = moving'', \ldots out'')$
$\Leftrightarrow$
$\exists \, (moving', \ldots, out') \cdot ($
$[moving, \ldots, out := moving', \ldots, out'] \, I \quad \wedge$
$in' \subseteq in \quad \wedge$
$out' \subseteq out \quad \wedge$
$\forall \, (g,e) \cdot ((g,e) \in in' \implies dist(floor'(l), dir'(l), g, e) < dist(floor(l), dir(l), g, e)) \wedge$
$moving', \ldots, out' = moving'', \ldots, out'')$
$\Leftrightarrow$
$[moving, \ldots, out := moving'', \ldots, out''] \, I \quad \wedge$
$in'' \subseteq in \quad \wedge$
$out'' \subseteq out \quad \wedge$
$\forall \, (g,e) \cdot ((g,e) \in in'' \implies dist(floor''(l), dir''(l), g, e) < dist(floor(l), dir(l), g, e))$

Thus we have

$[[moving, \ldots, out := moving'', \ldots, out''] \, \mathsf{Change\_up\_to\_dn}\,(l)]$
   $\neg \, [\mathsf{Decrease\_Distances}(l)] \, \neg \, (moving, \ldots, out = moving'', \ldots, out'')$
$\Leftrightarrow$
$[in'' := in'' - \{floor''(l) \mapsto dn\} \, || \, dir''(l) := dn] \, [moving, \ldots := moving'', \ldots] \, I \, \wedge$
$in'' - \{floor(l) \mapsto dn\} \subseteq in \wedge$
$out'' \subseteq out \quad \wedge$
$\forall \, (g,e) \cdot ((g,e) \in in'' - \{floor(l) \mapsto dn\} \implies$
                $dist(floor''(l), dn, g, e) < dist(floor(l), dir(l), g, e))$

Once the calculations have been carried out, we can deduce that our refinement statement is thus equivalent to the one we obtained at the end of previous section, namely:

$$I$$
$$l \in LIFT - moving$$
$$dir(l) = up$$
$$\neg\, attracted\_up(l)$$
$$attracted\_dn(l)$$
$$\Rightarrow$$
$$\forall\,(g,e) \cdot ((g,e) \in in - \{floor(l) \mapsto dn\} \;\Rightarrow$$
$$dist(floor(l), dn, g, e) < dist(floor(l), dir(l), g, e))$$

In other words, the fact that the operation Change_up_to_dn (l) decreases the distances can be expressed equivalently by the fact that Change_up_to_dn (l) is a *correct refinement* of the operation Decrease_Distances(l). That is, we do not have to have "special" proof obligations for "liveness proofs": they can all be expressed as mere refinement proof obligations.

The practical result provided by this example can be generalized. Our thesis is that all such *temporal properties* can be expressed in the form of highly non-deterministic abstractions to be refined by what used to be the "normal" specification of the problem. One has just to find a good model for the "distances".

8.4. Exercises

1. Specify all the operations of machine *Client* (8.1.2).

2. Generate all obligations of machine *Client* (8.1.2).

3. Prove all obligations generated in the previous exercise.

4. Generate and prove all obligations of machine *Product* (8.1.3).

5. Generate and prove all obligations of machine *Invoice* (8.1.4).

6. Generate and prove all obligations of machine *Simple_Exchange* (8.2.2).

7. Generate and prove all obligations of machine *Exchange* (8.2.3).

8. Modify both machines *Simple_Exchange* and *Exchange* to allow for "conference calls".

9. Generate and prove all the proof obligations of machine *Lift* (8.3.2).

10. Extend the concept of "distance" (section 8.3) so that this distance also

decreases for both operations Request_floor and Request_lift (hint: use a lexicographical distance).

11. Prove that the machine *Lift* of section 8.3.2 obeys requirement 5 of the informal specification of section 8.3.1 (Hint: introduce a notion of "distance" similar to that introduced in section 8.3.3).

REFERENCE

[1]   J. Woodcock and M. Loomes. *Software Engineering Mathematics* (Pitman, 1988).

PART THREE

Programming

CHAPTER 9

Sequencing and Loop

In chapter 4, we presented the concept of *abstract machines* together with a generalization of the notion of substitution. We also indicated how to use such *generalized substitutions* to express formally the specification of abstract machines.

In this chapter, we propose two more generalized substitution constructs: *sequencing* and *loop*. Such substitutions are *never* used in the specification of abstract machines. They might be used, however, for *refining* abstract machines, as will be explained in chapter 11.

The main part of this chapter is devoted to the mathematical study of loops. This development is based on the two set-theoretic models proposed in section 6.4. We remind the reader that these models constitute a *bridge* between the *logical* world of generalized substitutions and the *mathematical* world of set theory. It happens that, for doing our theoretical developments, the latter proves to be more suitable than the former.

The reason for doing the mathematical developments alluded above should be clear: despite its apparent simplicity, the *loop* concept is *not* a simple concept. It contains a number of hidden notions, to be studied first in order to derive, eventually, some convenient ways to construct and analyze loops in practice. So, clearly, our mathematical development is a way to understand loops both in depth as well as practically.

In the next chapter, we shall study a large number of examples dealing with sequencing and loops as introduced in this chapter; and in section 12.4, we shall study our last "programming" paradigm, namely recursion. We shall see how recursive operations can be defined as mere refinements of non-recursive abstractions.

9.1. Sequencing

9.1.1. Syntax

In developing programs from specifications, we inevitably encounter sooner or later the necessity of introducing some sort of sequencing. In imperative programming languages, sequencing is a very well-known construct, usually denoted by means of the operator ";".

Here, we would like to capture the same idea but still at the level of substitution. In other words, we would like to construct a substitution expressing that two component substitutions follow one another in a certain order. We also use the binary operator ";". As a result, we extend as follows the syntax of *Substitution* as already extended in section 7.2.2:

Syntactic Category	Definition
Substitution	. . .
	Substitution ; *Substitution*

9.1.2. Axiom

Given two substitutions S and T, and a predicate R, the predicate $[S ; T] R$ expresses the fact that $S ; T$ establishes R. Obviously, for that to hold, the substitution S, alone, should establish the fact that T establishes R. As a consequence, we extend as follows the axioms of generalized substitution, as presented in section 5.1.3:

Axiom
$[S ; T] R \iff [S] [T] R$

9.1.3. Basic Properties

From the above axiom, and after the definitions and properties given in section 6.3, we can deduce (exercise) the following:

$$\text{trm}(S;T) \quad \Leftrightarrow \quad (\text{trm}(S) \wedge \forall x' \cdot (\text{prd}_x(S) \Rightarrow [x := x'] \text{trm}(T)))$$

$$\text{prd}_x(S;T) \quad \Leftrightarrow \quad (\text{trm}(S) \Rightarrow \exists x'' \cdot ([x' := x''] \text{prd}_x(S) \wedge [x := x''] \text{prd}_x(T)))$$

$$\text{fis}(S;T) \quad \Leftrightarrow \quad (\text{trm}(S) \Rightarrow \exists x' \cdot (\text{prd}_x(S) \wedge [x := x'] \text{fis}(T)))$$

Likewise, we can deduce (exercise) the following from the definitions given in sections 6.4.1 and 6.4.2:

$\text{pre}(S;T)$	$\text{pre}(S) \cap \overline{\text{rel}(S)^{-1}[\overline{\text{pre}(T)}]}$
$\text{rel}(S;T)$	$\overline{\text{pre}(S)} \times s \;\cup\; \text{rel}(S); \text{rel}(T)$
$\text{dom}(S;T)$	$\overline{\text{pre}(S)} \;\cup\; \text{rel}(S)^{-1}[\text{dom}(T)]$
$\text{str}(S;T)(p)$	$\text{str}(S)(\text{str}(T)(p))$

From the previous axiom we can also deduce the following series of very intuitive laws whose proofs can be conducted by showing the equivalence of the establishment of the same post-condition by the left- and right-hand side of each equality (such proofs are left as exercises for the reader):

$$\text{skip}; S \qquad = \quad S$$

$$(P \mid S); T \qquad = \quad P \mid (S;T)$$

$$(P \implies S); T \qquad = \quad P \implies (S;T)$$

$$(S \,[\!]\, T); U \qquad = \quad (S;U) \,[\!]\, (T;U)$$

$$(@z \cdot S); T \qquad = \quad @z \cdot (S;T) \quad \text{if } z \text{ is non-free in } T$$

$$(S\,;T)\,;U \quad\quad = \quad S\,;(T\,;U)$$

$$S\,;\mathsf{skip} \quad\quad = \quad S$$

$$S\,;(P\mid T) \quad\quad = \quad [S]P\mid(S\,;T)$$

$$(x:=E)\,;(P\implies S) \quad = \quad [x:=E]P\implies(x:=E\,;S) \quad *$$

$$S\,;(T\,[\!]\,U) \quad\quad = \quad (S\,;T)\,[\!]\,(S\,;U)$$

$$S\,;@z\cdot T \quad\quad = \quad @z\cdot(S\,;T) \quad\text{if } z \text{ is non-free in } S$$

The above laws indicate that the sequencing operator *does not distribute symmetrically*. In particular, the equality with an asterisk would *not* hold in general with $x:=E$ replaced by an arbitrary substitution. This is due to non-determinism. From the above laws, we can deduce the following:

```
x := E ;                    IF   [x := E] P   THEN
IF   P    THEN                   x := E ;
     T                 =         T
ELSE                        ELSE
     U                           x := E ;
END                              U
                            END
```

```
x := E ;                    IF   [x := E] P   THEN
IF   P    THEN                   x := E ;
     T                 =         T
END                         ELSE
                                 x := E
                            END
```

```
IF   P    THEN              IF   P    THEN
     T                           T ;
ELSE                             S
     U                 =    ELSE
END ;                            U ;
S                                S
                            END
```

IF P THEN $\quad\quad\quad$ IF P THEN
$\quad\quad T$ $\quad\quad\quad\quad\quad\quad\quad T$;
$\quad\quad\quad\quad\quad\quad\quad\quad\quad$ = $\quad\quad\quad\quad S$
END ; $\quad\quad\quad\quad\quad\quad\quad\quad$ ELSE
S $\quad\quad\quad\quad\quad\quad\quad\quad\quad\quad S$
$\quad\quad\quad\quad\quad\quad\quad\quad\quad\quad\quad$ END

We have similar laws with the SELECT and CASE constructs.

Finally, we have the following property, which might be very interesting in practice. Given two substitutions S and T working with an abstract machine with variable x, and given predicates P and R, then if S establishes P and if P implies that T establishes R (for all x), then S ; T establishes R:

$[S]P \;\wedge\; \forall x \cdot (P \;\Rightarrow\; [T]R) \;\;\Rightarrow\;\; [S\,;T]R$ $\quad\quad\quad$ Property 9.1.1

This is a direct consequence of Property 6.2.2 concerning the monotonicity of generalized substitution. Notice that the universal quantification is fundamental.

9.2. Loop

9.2.1. Introduction

In imperative programming languages (this section has been prepared with the help of Guy Laffitte), loops are usually introduced by means of a construct looking more or less like this:

WHILE P DO S END

Informally, such a statement is interpreted as executing S if P holds (doing nothing if P does not hold) and then resuming execution of the loop. In other words, the previous statement can be expanded as shown by the following "equality":

$\quad\quad\quad\quad\quad\quad\quad\quad\quad$ IF P THEN
$\quad\quad\quad\quad\quad\quad\quad\quad\quad\quad\quad S$;
WHILE P DO S END $\quad$ = $\quad\quad$ WHILE P DO S END
$\quad\quad\quad\quad\quad\quad\quad\quad\quad$ END

In this section we would like to construct formally a loop substitution having a similar "behaviour". However, as for the conditional substitution, introduced in section 4.13, the present WHILE substitution is already too complicated. We would like first to capture the essence of looping, that is that of *repeating* a certain substitution, and only then to define the WHILE substitution in terms of that simplification.

We propose a substitution $T\hat{}$ which would be such that the following expansion holds:

$$T\hat{} \ = \ (T ; T\hat{}) \ [\!] \ \textsf{skip}$$

Supposing such a substitution is well-defined and formalized, then we could define the WHILE substitution, in terms of it, as follows:

Syntax	Definition
WHILE P DO S END	$(P \implies S)\hat{} ; (\neg P \implies \textsf{skip})$

It is then easy to prove the expansion of the WHILE substitution, as described at the beginning of this section, by using the expansion of $(P \implies S)\hat{}$. This can be done as follows, by using some of the basic properties of sequencing presented in section 9.1.3. For the sake of readability, we have replaced $P \implies S$ by U, and $\neg P \implies \textsf{skip}$ by V. This yields

> WHILE P DO S END
> $=$
> $U\hat{} ; V$
> $=$
> $(U ; U\hat{} \ [\!] \ \textsf{skip}) ; V$
> $=$
> $(U ; U\hat{} ; V) \ [\!] \ (\textsf{skip} ; V)$
> $=$
> $(P \implies (S ; U\hat{} ; V)) \ [\!] \ V$
> $=$
> $(P \implies (S ; \text{WHILE } P \text{ DO } S \text{ END})) \ [\!] \ (\neg P \implies \textsf{skip})$
> $=$
> IF P THEN
> $S ;$
>   WHILE P DO S END
> END

9.2.2. Definition

In order to define $T\hat{}$, we shall define its corresponding set-theoretic counterpart str$(T\hat{})$ (section 6.4.2). This means, as usual, that we suppose that our substitutions T and $T\hat{}$ are working within a certain machine with variable(s) x and invariant $x \in t$ for some set t. Starting from the previous expansion of $T\hat{}$, that is $\mathsf{skip} \ [] \ (T\,;T\hat{})$, and given a subset p of t, we have then (according to the results of section 6.4.2)

$$\mathsf{str}\,(T\hat{})(p) \;=\; p \,\cap\, \mathsf{str}\,(T)(\mathsf{str}\,(T\hat{})(p))$$

In other words, $\mathsf{str}\,(T\hat{})(p)$ appears to be a fixpoint. We can then define $\mathsf{str}\,(T\hat{})(p)$ as follows:

$$\boxed{\mathsf{str}\,(T\hat{})(p) \;=\; \mathsf{fix}\,(\lambda r \cdot (r \in \mathbb{P}(t) \mid p \,\cap\, \mathsf{str}\,(T)(r)))}$$

Notice that the fixpoint we have used in the above definition is indeed a fixpoint since $\mathsf{str}\,(T)$ is obviously a monotonic set function. We have no guarantee, however, that the new construct distributes over generalized intersection as is required for every construct of the generalized substitution language (section 6.2). In order to prove this, we need the following general theorem about set transformers:

$$\begin{array}{l}
g \in \mathbb{P}(t) \rightarrow \mathbb{P}(t) \\
f \;=\; \lambda p \cdot (p \in \mathbb{P}(t) \mid \lambda r \cdot (r \in \mathbb{P}(t) \mid p \cap g(r))) \\
\forall (a,b) \cdot (a \in \mathbb{P}(t) \;\wedge\; b \in \mathbb{P}(t) \;\;\Rightarrow \\
\quad g(a \cap b) \;=\; g(a) \cap g(b)) \\
\Rightarrow \\
\mathsf{fix}\,(f(p)) \;=\; \mathsf{fix}\,(g) \cap \mathsf{FIX}\,(f(p))
\end{array}$$

Theorem 9.2.1

Proof

We assume the following

$$f(p) \;=\; \lambda r \cdot (r \in \mathbb{P}(t) \mid p \cap g(r))$$ Hypothesis 1

Hypothesis 2

$$\forall (a,b) \cdot (a \in \mathbb{P}(t) \;\wedge\; b \in \mathbb{P}(t) \;\;\Rightarrow\;\; g(a \cap b) \;=\; g(a) \cap g(b))$$

and we have to prove

$$\mathsf{fix}\,(f(p)) \;=\; \mathsf{FIX}\,(f(p)) \cap \mathsf{fix}\,(g)$$ Goal 1

We first prove

$$\mathsf{fix}\,(f(p)) \;\subseteq\; \mathsf{FIX}\,(f(p)) \cap \mathsf{fix}\,(g)$$ Goal 2

In order to do this, it is obviously sufficient to prove the following, since we already have $\mathsf{fix}\,(f(p)) \subseteq \mathsf{FIX}\,(f(p))$:

$$\mathsf{fix}\,(f(p)) \;\subseteq\; \mathsf{fix}\,(g)$$ Goal 3

The form of this statement suggests applying Theorem 3.2.1. As a consequence, it is sufficient to prove the following:

$$f(p)(\mathsf{fix}\,(g)) \;\subseteq\; \mathsf{fix}\,(g)$$ Goal 4

That is, according to the definition of $f(p)$ (Hypothesis 1)

$$p \cap g(\text{fix}(g)) \subseteq \text{fix}(g) \qquad\qquad \text{Goal 5}$$

Since fix (g) is a fixpoint, we have to prove, equivalently, the following, which is obvious

$$p \cap \text{fix}(g) \subseteq \text{fix}(g) \qquad\qquad \text{Goal 6}$$

We now prove the reverse inclusion, that is

$$\text{FIX}(f(p)) \cap \text{fix}(g) \subseteq \text{fix}(f(p)) \qquad\qquad \text{Goal 7}$$

Defining a as fix $(f(p))$ and A as FIX $(f(p))$, this becomes, equivalently

$$\text{fix}(g) \subseteq a \cup \overline{A} \qquad\qquad \text{Goal 8}$$

For this, it is sufficient to prove the following (again applying Theorem 3.2.1):

$$g(a \cup \overline{A}) \subseteq a \cup \overline{A} \qquad\qquad \text{Goal 9}$$

which is equivalent to

$$g(a \cup \overline{A}) \cap A \subseteq a \qquad\qquad \text{Goal 10}$$

The proof of Goal 10 goes as follows:

$$g(a \cup \overline{A}) \cap A$$
$$=$$
$$g(a \cup \overline{A}) \cap f(p)(A)$$
$$=$$
$$g(a \cup \overline{A}) \cap p \cap g(A)$$
$$=$$
$$p \cap g(a \cup \overline{A}) \cap g(A)$$
$$=$$
$$p \cap g((a \cup \overline{A}) \cap A) \qquad\qquad \text{Hypothesis 2}$$
$$=$$
$$p \cap g(a \cap A)$$
$$=$$
$$p \cap g(a)$$
$$=$$
$$f(p)(a)$$
$$=$$
$$a$$

End of Proof

We now prove the following, showing the distribution over intersection:

$g \in \mathbb{P}(t) \rightarrow \mathbb{P}(t)$
$f = \lambda p \cdot (p \in \mathbb{P}(t) \mid \lambda r \cdot (r \in \mathbb{P}(t) \mid p \cap g(r)))$
$\forall (a,b) \cdot (a \in \mathbb{P}(t) \wedge b \in \mathbb{P}(t) \Rightarrow$
    $g(a \cap b) = g(a) \cap g(b))$

$\Rightarrow$

fix $(f(p \cap q)) =$ fix $(f(p)) \cap$ fix $(f(q))$

Theorem 9.2.2

Proof
We assume

$$f(p) = \lambda r \cdot (r \in \mathbb{P}(t) \mid p \cap g(r)) \qquad \text{Hypothesis 1}$$

$$f(q) = \lambda r \cdot (r \in \mathbb{P}(t) \mid q \cap g(r)) \qquad \text{Hypothesis 2}$$
Hypothesis 3

$$\forall (a,b) \cdot (a \in \mathbb{P}(t) \wedge b \in \mathbb{P}(t) \Rightarrow g(a \cap b) = g(a) \cap g(b))$$

and we have to prove

$$\text{fix}(f(p \cap q)) = \text{fix}(f(p)) \cap \text{fix}(f(q)) \qquad \text{Goal 1}$$

We prove the first inclusion, that is

$$\text{fix}(f(p \cap q)) \subseteq \text{fix}(f(p)) \cap \text{fix}(f(q)) \qquad \text{Goal 2}$$

According to Theorem 3.2.1, it is sufficient to prove

$$p \cap q \cap g(\text{fix}(f(p)) \cap \text{fix}(f(q))) \subseteq \text{fix}(f(p)) \cap \text{fix}(f(q)) \qquad \text{Goal 3}$$

that is, according to Hypothesis 3

$$p \cap q \cap g(\text{fix}(f(p))) \cap g(\text{fix}(f(q))) \subseteq \text{fix}(f(p)) \cap \text{fix}(f(q)) \quad \text{Goal 4}$$

which is obvious after the definitions of $f(p)$ and $f(q)$. We prove now the second inclusion:

$$\text{fix}(f(p)) \cap \text{fix}(f(q)) \subseteq \text{fix}(f(p \cap q)) \qquad \text{Goal 5}$$

According to Theorem 9.2.1, we can replace the right-hand side of this inclusion as follows:

$$\text{fix}(f(p)) \cap \text{fix}(f(q)) \subseteq \text{fix}(g) \cap \text{FIX}(f(p \cap q)) \qquad \text{Goal 6}$$

This leads to the following goals

$$\text{fix}(f(p)) \cap \text{fix}(f(q)) \subseteq \text{fix}(g) \qquad \text{Goal 7}$$

$$\text{fix}(f(p)) \cap \text{fix}(f(q)) \subseteq \text{FIX}(f(p \cap q)) \qquad \text{Goal 8}$$

Goal 7 is easily discharged according to Theorem 9.2.1. In order to prove Goal 8 it is sufficient to prove, according to Theorem 3.2.3,

$$\text{fix}(f(p)) \cap \text{fix}(f(q)) \subseteq p \cap q \cap g(\text{fix}(f(p)) \cap \text{fix}(f(q))) \qquad \text{Goal 9}$$

that is, according to Hypothesis 3

$$\mathsf{fix}\,(f(p)) \cap \mathsf{fix}\,(f(q)) \subseteq p \cap q \cap g(\mathsf{fix}\,(f(p))) \cap g(\mathsf{fix}\,(f(q)))\quad\text{Goal 10}$$

which is obvious after the definitions of $f(p)$ and $f(q)$.
End of Proof

It is easy to transpose the above result to $\mathsf{str}\,(T^\wedge)$. This yields the following property:

$p \in \mathbb{P}(t)$
$q \in \mathbb{P}(t)$
$\Rightarrow$ Property 9.2.1

$\mathsf{str}\,(T^\wedge)(p \cap q) = \mathsf{str}\,(T^\wedge)(p) \cap \mathsf{str}\,(T^\wedge)(q)$

The following more general result concerning generalized intersection is left as an exercise for the reader:

$tt \in \mathbb{P}_1(\mathbb{P}(t))$
$\Rightarrow$ Property 9.2.2

$\mathsf{str}\,(T^\wedge)(\mathsf{inter}\,(tt)) = \mathsf{inter}\,(\mathsf{str}\,(T^\wedge)[tt])$

9.2.3. Interpretation of Loop Termination

From the above definition of $\mathsf{str}\,(T^\wedge)$ (section 9.2.2), we can deduce immediately the value of $\mathsf{pre}\,(T^\wedge)$, since it is defined as $\mathsf{str}\,(T^\wedge)(t)$. We have:

$$\boxed{\mathsf{pre}\,(T^\wedge) = \mathsf{fix}\,(\mathsf{str}\,(T))}$$

We thus have:

$$\mathsf{pre}\,(T^\wedge) = \mathsf{str}\,(T)(\mathsf{pre}\,(T^\wedge))$$

and thus the following quite intuitive property:

$\mathsf{pre}\,(T^\wedge) \subseteq \mathsf{pre}\,(T)$ Property 9.2.3

In what follows, we shall give an intuitive interpretation of the equality $\mathsf{pre}\,(T^\wedge) = \mathsf{fix}\,(\mathsf{str}\,(T))$. For this, we shall first study the complement of $\mathsf{pre}\,(T^\wedge)$, that is the set from within which $T^\wedge$ does not terminate ("loops for ever"). We would like to understand, both formally and intuitively, what this means. We have

$$\overline{\mathsf{pre}\,(T^\wedge)} = \overline{\mathsf{fix}\,(\mathsf{str}\,(T))}$$

One can then prove (exercise 8) the following:

$$\overline{\mathsf{pre}\,(T\hat{\ })} \;=\; \mathsf{union}\,(\{\,p \mid p \in \mathbb{P}(t) \,\wedge\, p \subseteq \overline{\mathsf{str}\,(T)(\overline{p})}\,\})$$

that is, after Property 6.4.9,

$$\overline{\mathsf{pre}\,(T\hat{\ })} \;=\; \mathsf{union}\,(\{\,p \mid p \in \mathbb{P}(t) \,\wedge\, p \subseteq \mathsf{rel}\,(T)^{-1}[p]\,\}) \qquad (1)$$

The set $\overline{\mathsf{pre}\,(T\hat{\ })}$ is thus the union of all the subsets p of t such that $p \subseteq \mathsf{rel}\,(T)^{-1}[p]$ holds, namely

$$\forall x \cdot (x \in p \;\Rightarrow\; \exists y \cdot (y \in p \,\wedge\, (x,y) \in \mathsf{rel}\,(T)))$$

In other words, from *each* point x of p, one can always reach (with T) a certain point y which, again, is in p. That is, p is made of *cycles or infinite chains* of points related by T. Clearly, $T\hat{\ }$ will "loop for ever", if started from within p. More generally, $\overline{\mathsf{pre}\,(T\hat{\ })}$ is the *smallest* subset of t containing *all* such cycles or infinite chains.

Conversely, $\mathsf{pre}\,(T\hat{\ })$ is the *largest* subset of T where $\mathsf{rel}\,(T)$ has *no* cycles or infinite chains. If started from within $\mathsf{pre}\,(T\hat{\ })$, $T\hat{\ }$ will certainly terminate. The set $\mathsf{pre}\,(T\hat{\ })$ is then as follows (proof left to the reader):

$$\mathsf{pre}\,(T\hat{\ }) \;=\; \mathsf{inter}\,(\{\,p \mid p \in \mathbb{P}(t) \,\wedge\, \overline{\mathsf{rel}\,(T)^{-1}[\overline{p}]} \subseteq p\,\})$$

We thus have (since the previous condition is a fixpoint equation)

$$\overline{\mathsf{rel}\,(T)^{-1}[\overline{\mathsf{pre}\,(T\hat{\ })}]} \;=\; \mathsf{pre}\,(T\hat{\ })$$

thus we certainly have

$$\mathsf{rel}\,(T)^{-1}[\overline{\mathsf{pre}\,(T\hat{\ })}] \;\subseteq\; \overline{\mathsf{pre}\,(T\hat{\ })}$$

that is (exercise 11 of Chapter 2)

$$\mathsf{rel}\,(T)[\mathsf{pre}\,(T\hat{\ })] \;\subseteq\; \mathsf{pre}\,(T\hat{\ })$$

In other words, and as expected, $\mathsf{pre}\,(T\hat{\ })$ is *stable* under $\mathsf{rel}\,(T)$. That is

$$\mathsf{pre}\,(T\hat{\ }) \lhd \mathsf{rel}\,(T) \;\in\; \mathsf{pre}\,(T\hat{\ }) \leftrightarrow \mathsf{pre}\,(T\hat{\ })$$

Let p be a *non-empty* subset of $\mathsf{pre}\,(T\hat{\ })$. It is certainly not the case that the condition $p \subseteq \mathsf{rel}\,(T)^{-1}[p]$ holds since otherwise p would be included in $\overline{\mathsf{pre}\,(T\hat{\ })}$ (according to (1) above), which is impossible since, by definition, p is non-empty and included in $\mathsf{pre}\,(T\hat{\ })$. As a consequence, we have

$$\forall p \cdot (p \subseteq \mathsf{pre}\,(T\hat{\ }) \,\wedge\, p \subseteq r^{-1}[p] \;\Rightarrow\; p = \varnothing)$$

where r stands for $\mathsf{pre}\,(T\hat{\ }) \lhd \mathsf{rel}\,(T)$. The reader may have recognized one of the characteristic properties stating that the relation $\mathsf{pre}\,(T\hat{\ }) \lhd \mathsf{rel}\,(T)$ is a *well-founded* relation (section 3.11). We have thus proved the following:

$$\boxed{\;\mathsf{wfd}\,(\,\mathsf{pre}\,(T\hat{\ }) \lhd \mathsf{rel}\,(T)\,)\;}$$

We shall now prove that $\mathsf{pre}\,(T^\wedge)$ is the *largest* set that is stable under $\mathsf{rel}\,(T)$ and that is well-founded, formally:

$$\mathsf{rel}\,(T)[p] \subseteq p \;\wedge\; \mathsf{wfd}\,(p \lhd \mathsf{rel}\,(T)) \;\Rightarrow\; p \subseteq \mathsf{pre}\,(T^\wedge) \qquad \text{Property 9.2.4}$$

Proof

We assume

$$\mathsf{rel}\,(T)[p] \subseteq p \qquad\qquad \text{Hypothesis 1}$$

$$\mathsf{wfd}\,(p \lhd \mathsf{rel}\,(T)) \qquad\qquad \text{Hypothesis 2}$$

And we have to prove

$$p \subseteq \mathsf{pre}\,(T^\wedge) \qquad\qquad \text{Goal 1}$$

that is equivalently

$$p \cap \overline{\mathsf{pre}\,(T^\wedge)} = \varnothing \qquad\qquad \text{Goal 2}$$

According to Hypothesis 2 and the definition of well-foundedness as given in section 3.11.1, Goal 2 follows from the following:

$$p \cap \overline{\mathsf{pre}\,(T^\wedge)} \subseteq (p \lhd \mathsf{rel}\,(T))^{-1}[p \cap \overline{\mathsf{pre}\,(T^\wedge)}] \qquad\qquad \text{Goal 3}$$

that is equivalently

$$p \cap \overline{\mathsf{pre}\,(T^\wedge)} \subseteq p \cap \mathsf{rel}\,(T)^{-1}[p \cap \overline{\mathsf{pre}\,(T^\wedge)}] \qquad\qquad \text{Goal 4}$$

that is equivalently

$$p \cap \overline{\mathsf{pre}\,(T^\wedge)} \subseteq \mathsf{rel}\,(T)^{-1}[p \cap \overline{\mathsf{pre}\,(T^\wedge)}] \qquad\qquad \text{Goal 5}$$

From Hypothesis 1, we deduce immediately

$$\mathsf{rel}\,(T)[p \cap \overline{\mathsf{pre}\,(T^\wedge)}] \subseteq p \qquad\qquad \text{Derivation 1}$$

As a consequence, in order to prove Goal 5, it is sufficient to prove

$$p \cap \overline{\mathsf{pre}\,(T^\wedge)} \subseteq \mathsf{rel}\,(T)^{-1}[\mathsf{rel}\,(T)[p \cap \overline{\mathsf{pre}\,(T^\wedge)}] \cap \overline{\mathsf{pre}\,(T^\wedge)}] \quad \text{Goal 6}$$

As we have

$$\overline{\mathsf{pre}\,(T^\wedge)} = \mathsf{rel}\,(T)^{-1}[\overline{\mathsf{pre}\,(T^\wedge)}] \qquad\qquad \text{Derivation 2}$$

we deduce

$$p \cap \overline{\mathsf{pre}\,(T^\wedge)} \subseteq \mathsf{rel}\,(T)^{-1}[\overline{\mathsf{pre}\,(T^\wedge)}] \qquad\qquad \text{Derivation 3}$$

As a consequence, we have

$$p \cap \overline{\mathsf{pre}\,(T^\wedge)} \subseteq \mathsf{rel}\,(T)^{-1}[\mathsf{rel}\,(T)[p \cap \overline{\mathsf{pre}\,(T^\wedge)}] \cap \overline{\mathsf{pre}\,(T^\wedge)}] \;\cup$$
$$\mathsf{rel}\,(T)^{-1}[\mathsf{rel}\,(T)[p \cap \overline{\mathsf{pre}\,(T^\wedge)}] \cap \overline{\mathsf{pre}\,(T^\wedge)}] \qquad \text{Derivation 4}$$

Thus in order to prove Goal 6, it suffices to prove

$$p \cap \overline{\mathsf{pre}(T^\wedge)} \cap \overline{\mathsf{rel}(T)^{-1}[\mathsf{rel}(T)[p \cap \overline{\mathsf{pre}(T^\wedge)}] \cap \overline{\mathsf{pre}(T^\wedge)}]} = \varnothing \quad \text{Goal 7}$$

For this it is sufficient to prove

$$p \cap \overline{\mathsf{pre}(T^\wedge)} \cap \overline{\mathsf{rel}(T)^{-1}[\overline{\mathsf{rel}(T)[p \cap \overline{\mathsf{pre}(T^\wedge)}]}]} = \varnothing \quad \quad \text{Goal 8}$$

that is equivalently

$$\mathsf{rel}(T)^{-1}[\overline{\mathsf{rel}(T)[p \cap \overline{\mathsf{pre}(T^\wedge)}]}] \subseteq \overline{p \cap \overline{\mathsf{pre}(T^\wedge)}} \quad \quad \text{Goal 9}$$

which is obvious since it is equivalent to the following (exercise 11 of chapter 2):

$$\mathsf{rel}(T)[\overline{p \cap \overline{\mathsf{pre}(T^\wedge)}}] \subseteq \overline{\mathsf{rel}(T)[p \cap \overline{\mathsf{pre}(T^\wedge)}]} \quad \quad \text{Goal 10}$$

End of Proof

The above property can be given the following equivalent form that we shall use in the sequel:

$p \subseteq \mathsf{str}(T)(p)$
$\mathsf{wfd}(p \lhd \mathsf{rel}(T))$
$\Rightarrow$ Property 9.2.5
$p \subseteq \mathsf{pre}(T^\wedge)$.

9.2.4. Interpretation of the Before-after Relation of the Loop

In this section, we would like to calculate $\mathsf{rel}(T^\wedge)$ and understand it formally as well as intuitively. Starting from Property 6.4.9, we must have

$$(x, x') \in \mathsf{rel}(T^\wedge) \iff x \in \overline{\mathsf{str}(T^\wedge)(\overline{\{x'\}})}$$

Replacing the right-hand side by its definition (as given in section 9.2.2), one can then prove the following (with the help of exercise 8 of this chapter and Property 6.4.9):

$$(x, x') \in \mathsf{rel}(T^\wedge) \iff x \in \mathsf{FIX}(\lambda q \cdot (q \in \mathbb{P}(t) \mid \{x'\} \cup \mathsf{rel}(T)^{-1}[q]))$$

that is

$$(x, x') \in \mathsf{rel}(T^\wedge) \iff \exists q \cdot (q \in \mathbb{P}(t) \land x \in q \land (q \subseteq \{x'\} \cup \mathsf{rel}(T)^{-1}[q]))$$

By considering the binary relation r such that $r = q \times \{x'\}$, we can easily prove that the right-hand side implies the following:

$$\exists r \cdot (r \in t \leftrightarrow t \land (x, x') \in r \land (r \subseteq \mathsf{id}(t) \cup (\mathsf{rel}(T); r)))$$

Conversely, by considering the set q such that $q = r^{-1}[\{x'\}]$, the last condition implies the right-hand side. In other words, we have:

$$(x, x') \in \mathsf{rel}\,(T^\wedge) \quad \Leftrightarrow \quad (x, x') \in \mathsf{FIX}\,(\lambda r \cdot (r \in s \leftrightarrow s \mid \mathsf{id}\,(t) \cup (\mathsf{rel}\,(T) ; r)))$$

We thus have

$$\boxed{\mathsf{rel}\,(T^\wedge) \;=\; \mathsf{FIX}\,(\lambda r \cdot (r \in t \leftrightarrow t \mid \mathsf{id}\,(t) \cup (\mathsf{rel}\,(T) ; r)))}$$

This shows that $\mathsf{rel}\,(T^\wedge)$ is the *greatest* fixpoint of exactly the same function as the one that is used to define the transitive closure of $\mathsf{rel}\,(T)$ by a *least* fixpoint (the transitive closure is defined in section 3.5.10). In fact, we have more than that, since it is possible to prove the following theorem (with the help of exercises 9 and 10):

$$\mathsf{rel}\,(T^\wedge) \;=\; \overline{\mathsf{pre}\,(T^\wedge)} \times t \;\cup\; \mathsf{rel}\,(T)^* \qquad\qquad \text{Theorem 9.2.3}$$

We have what we expect. The cartesian product of the complement of the termination set with the entire set t is included in $\mathsf{rel}\,(T^\wedge)$ as required (recall Property 6.4.1). Moreover, the other part of $\mathsf{rel}\,(T^\wedge)$ is the classical transitive closure. It corresponds to the intuitive idea of applying $\mathsf{rel}\,(T)$ *repeatedly*.

By analogy with the transitive *closure*, the relation $\mathsf{rel}\,(T^\wedge)$ could be called the transitive *opening* of the relation $\mathsf{rel}\,(T)$. And, by extension, the substitution $T^\wedge$ could be called the opening of T.

9.2.5. Examples of Loop Termination

In this section we shall exhibit examples of substitutions S which are such that $S^\wedge$ always terminates. Let us consider first the following substitution S:

$$S \;=\; \mathsf{ANY}\;\; n' \;\; \mathsf{WHERE}\;\; n' \in \mathbb{N} \wedge n' < n \;\; \mathsf{THEN}\;\; n := n' \;\; \mathsf{END}$$

This substitution is supposed to work with an abstract machine with variable n and invariant $n \in \mathbb{N}$. We then have, for each subset p of $\mathbb{N}$,

$$\mathsf{str}\,(S)(p) \;=\; \{\,n \mid n \in \mathbb{N} \wedge [S]\,(n \in p)\,\}$$

that is

$$\mathsf{str}\,(S)(p) \;=\; \{\,n \mid n \in \mathbb{N} \wedge \forall n' \cdot (n' \in \mathbb{N} \wedge n' < n \;\Rightarrow\; n' \in p)\,\}$$

As a result, we have the following, for each subset p of $\mathbb{N}$ that is distinct from $\mathbb{N}$:

$$\mathsf{str}\,(S)(p) \;=\; 0\,..\,\mathsf{min}\,(\overline{p})$$

and also

$$\mathsf{str}\,(S)(\mathbb{N}) \;=\; \mathbb{N}$$

The only fixpoint (hence the least one) of $\mathsf{str}\,(S)$ is thus $\mathbb{N}$ and we have

$$\text{pre}\,(S\hat{\ }) = \mathbb{N}$$

The substitution $S\hat{\ }$ always terminates on $\mathbb{N}$.

As another example, let us consider now the following substitution S' working with a sequence of natural numbers s:

ANY s' WHERE $s' \in \text{seq}\,(\mathbb{N}) \land \text{size}\,(s') = \text{size}\,(s) \land s' \prec s$ THEN $s := s'$ END

As can be seen, the "after" value of s is lexicographically strictly smaller than its "before" value (lexicographical order on sequences of integers is defined in section 3.7.5). It can also be proved that the substitution $S'\hat{\ }$ always terminates on $\text{seq}\,(\mathbb{N})$.

9.2.6. The Invariant Theorem

In this section we prove the so-called Invariant Theorem. This theorem will allow us to perform useful practical reasoning on loops. The idea is to prove under which conditions the membership of a certain subset p of t is invariant under $T\hat{\ }$. In other words, we would like to have a method for proving a statement such as $p \subseteq \text{str}\,(T\hat{\ })(p)$.

After Theorem 9.2.1, we deduce immediately (with the same hypotheses and notations)

$$p \subseteq \text{FIX}\,(f(p)) \land p \subseteq \text{fix}\,(g) \;\Leftrightarrow\; p \subseteq \text{fix}\,(f(p))$$

But, according to Theorem 3.2.3, a sufficient condition for $p \subseteq \text{FIX}\,(f(p))$ to hold is $p \subseteq f(p)(p)$, that is $p \subseteq p \cap g(p)$, that is $p \subseteq g(p)$. We have thus proved the following theorem:

$g \in \mathbb{P}(t) \to \mathbb{P}(t)$
$f = \lambda p \cdot (p \in \mathbb{P}(t) \mid \lambda r \cdot (r \in \mathbb{P}(t) \mid p \cap g(r)))$
$\forall (a,b) \cdot (a \in \mathbb{P}(t) \land b \in \mathbb{P}(t) \;\Rightarrow$
  $g(a \cap b) = g(a) \cap g(b))$ Theorem 9.2.4

$\Rightarrow$

$p \subseteq g(p) \land p \subseteq \text{fix}\,(g) \;\Rightarrow\; p \subseteq \text{fix}\,(f(p))$

Transposing this result back to the substitution T, that is replacing $\text{fix}\,(f(p))$ by $\text{str}\,(T\hat{\ })(p)$, g by $\text{str}\,(T)$ (section 9.2.2) and thus $\text{fix}\,(g)$ by $\text{pre}\,(T\hat{\ })$ (section 9.2.3), we obtain the following:

$p \subseteq \text{str}\,(T)(p) \land p \subseteq \text{pre}\,(T\hat{\ }) \;\Rightarrow\; p \subseteq \text{str}\,(T\hat{\ })(p)$ Invariant Theorem

---

This theorem can be read "operationally" as follows: if a set p is invariant under T and if $T\hat{\ }$ *terminates* (when started in p), then p is also invariant under $T\hat{\ }$.

9.2.7. The Variant Theorem

In this section, we study the problem of the termination of $T^\wedge$. In other words, we would like to find some conditions which, together with the first antecedent of the Invariant Theorem, $p \subseteq \text{str}(T)(p)$, are sufficient to prove the second one, $p \subseteq \text{pre}(T^\wedge)$. That is, we would like to find some *conditions* such that the following holds:

$$p \subseteq \text{str}(T)(p)$$
$$\textit{conditions}$$
$$\Rightarrow$$
$$p \subseteq \text{pre}(T^\wedge)$$

By putting that statement (called the Variant Theorem) together with the previous Invariant Theorem, we obtain the following Variant and Invariant Theorem, which would certainly be easier to use than the Invariant Theorem alone (provided, of course, the *conditions* are simple):

$$p \subseteq \text{str}(T)(p)$$
$$\textit{conditions}$$
$$\Rightarrow$$
$$p \subseteq \text{str}(T^\wedge)(p)$$

Clearly, according to Property 9.2.5, the *condition* we are looking for might be the following:

$$\text{wfd}(p \lhd \text{rel}(T))$$

We remind the reader that in section 3.11.4, we proved (Theorem 3.11.1) that in order to ensure that a certain relation r' (from a certain set, say p, to itself) is well-founded it is sufficient to have an already well-founded relation r (from a certain set s to itself) and to exhibit a total relation v (from p to s) such that the following holds:

$$v^{-1} \,; r' \;\subseteq\; r \,; v^{-1}$$

The idea is thus to suppose that we have at our disposal a certain substitution S (working on a certain set s), such that $S^\wedge$ is *guaranteed* always to terminate on s, that is

$$\text{pre}(S^\wedge) = s$$

For instance, the substitution S presented in section 9.2.5, that is

$$S = \text{ANY } n' \text{ WHERE } n' \in \mathbb{N} \wedge n' < n \text{ THEN } n := n' \text{ END}$$

might be a good candidate (although certainly not the only one), since we have already proved (section 9.2.5) that $S^\wedge$ always terminates on $\mathbb{N}$. Putting the previous results within the present context means that we first have to exhibit a certain relation v typed as follows:

$$v \in p \leftrightarrow s \;\wedge\; \text{dom}(v) = p$$

For the relation $p \lhd \mathrm{rel}\,(T)$ to be well-founded, the relation v must then be such that the following holds:

$$v^{-1}; \mathrm{rel}\,(T) \;\subseteq\; \mathrm{rel}\,(S); v^{-1}$$

Notice that we have

$$\mathrm{pre}\,(S) \;=\; s$$

This is because $S\hat{}$ is supposed to always terminate on s ($\mathrm{pre}\,(S\hat{}) = s$), and because, according to Property 9.2.3, we have $\mathrm{pre}\,(S\dot{}) \subseteq \mathrm{pre}\,(S)$. As a consequence, we have

$$v^{-1}\,[\mathrm{pre}\,(S)] \;=\; p$$

since $v^{-1}\,[\mathrm{pre}\,(S)] = v^{-1}\,[s] = \mathrm{dom}\,(v) = p$. Notice also that we have:

$$p \;\subseteq\; \mathrm{pre}\,(T)$$

This results from the assumption $p \;\subseteq\; \mathrm{str}\,(T)(p)$. As a consequence, we have the following:

$$v^{-1}\,[\mathrm{pre}\,(S)] \;\subseteq\; \mathrm{pre}\,(T)$$

What is quite remarkable about the two previous boxed conditions is that *they correspond exactly to sufficient conditions for the refinement* of the substitution S by the substitution T. We shall establish this result in chapter 11 (Theorem 11.2.4). More precisely, we shall see in chapter 11 that refining a substitution S is the process by which we make it more precise (less non-deterministic) and by which we transform its variables so that they become easier to implement. The informal idea behind the notion of refinement is that the "external user" of S must not be aware that S has been replaced by one of its refinements T. In other words, the external behaviour of T must be the same as that of S. This is the reason why, intuitively, it is understandable that refinement can be helpful to prove termination. In other words, if $S\hat{}$ terminates, then $T\hat{}$ must terminate too because the external behaviour of S and T must be the same.

In chapter 11, the relation v is called the *abstraction* relation. Within the framework of this section, we shall call it the *variant* relation. The situation can be pictured as follows:

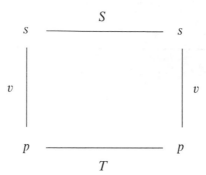

We shall also prove in chapter 11 that the two previous conditions are, in fact, equivalent to the following single one (Theorem 11.2.3):

$$\forall a \cdot (a \subseteq t \;\Rightarrow\; \mathrm{str}(S)(\,\overline{v\,[\overline{a}]}\,) \subseteq \overline{v\,[\,\overline{\mathrm{str}(T)(a)}\,]}\,)$$

In the previous condition the complements (indicated by overlining) have to be taken unambiguously either with respect to s, or with respect to t. In conclusion, we have now established the sufficient condition we were looking for at the beginning of this section.

By putting together the Invariant Theorem of the previous section and the Variant Theorem of this section, we obtain the following:

$p \subseteq \mathrm{str}(T)(p)$
$v \in p \leftrightarrow s$
$\mathrm{dom}(v) = p$
$\forall a \cdot (a \subseteq t \;\Rightarrow\; \mathrm{str}(S)(\,\overline{v\,[\overline{a}]}\,) \subseteq \overline{v\,[\,\overline{\mathrm{str}(T)(a)}\,]}\,)$ Variant and Invariant Th.
$\mathrm{pre}(S^{\wedge}) = s$
$\Rightarrow$
$p \subseteq \mathrm{str}(T^{\wedge})(p)$

9.2.8. Making the Variant and Invariant Theorem Practical

In this section our intention is to make the "Variant and Invariant" theorem more practical. The idea is to translate our theorem into the world of generalized substitutions. For this, we shall first systematically replace the condition $x \in p$ simply by I. We then consider each of the antecedents of the previous theorem in turn. The first antecedent, $p \subseteq \mathrm{str}(T)(p)$, becomes the following:

$$\forall x \cdot (I \;\Rightarrow\; [T]\,I\,)$$

The second antecedent, $v \in p \leftrightarrow s$, and the third antecedent, $\mathrm{dom}(v) = p$, can be translated by defining now v as a total function from p to s, by means of a certain expression V as follows:

$$v = \lambda x \cdot (I \mid V)$$

As a result, these two antecedents reduce to the condition $v \in p \to s$, which, itself, is a consequence of the following condition (according to Property 2.5.2):

$$\forall x \cdot (I \Rightarrow V \in s)$$

Moreover, as we shall see in section 11.2.6, the refinement condition corresponding to our fourth antecedent, that is

$$\forall a \cdot (a \subseteq t \Rightarrow \mathsf{str}(S)(\overline{v[\overline{a}]}) \subseteq \overline{v[\mathsf{str}(T)(a)]})$$

can be replaced by the following one, where n is a *fresh* variable that has no occurrences in S, T, I and V:

$$\forall (x, n) \cdot (I \wedge n = V \Rightarrow [T] \neg [S] \neg (I \wedge n = V))$$

Since I is supposed to be invariant under T, and since S does not depend on x, we have equivalently (exercise)

$$\forall (x, n) \cdot (I \wedge n = V \Rightarrow [T] \neg [S] \neg (n = V))$$

reducing to

$$\forall x \cdot (I \Rightarrow [n := V][T] \neg [S] \neg (n = V))$$

Finally, the consequent, $p \subseteq \mathsf{str}(T^\wedge)(p)$, of the theorem becomes

$$\forall x \cdot (I \Rightarrow [T^\wedge] I)$$

We finally obtain the following translation of our theorem:

$$\boxed{\begin{array}{l} \forall x \cdot (I \Rightarrow [T] I) \\ \forall x \cdot (I \Rightarrow V \in s) \\ \forall x \cdot (I \Rightarrow [n := V][T] \neg [S] \neg (n = V)) \\ \mathsf{pre}(S^\wedge) = s \\ \Rightarrow \\ \forall x \cdot (I \Rightarrow [T^\wedge] I) \end{array}}$$

Again, we insist that the variable n is *fresh*; it has no occurrences in S, T, I and V. It remains for us to eliminate the last antecedent, $\mathsf{pre}(S^\wedge) = s$, and to simplify the last but one. For this, we have to choose a certain generalized substitution S such that $S^\wedge$ is guaranteed to terminate. After the result of section 9.2.5, we can make the following choice:

$$S = \text{ANY } n' \text{ WHERE } n' \in \mathbb{N} \wedge n' < n \text{ THEN } n := n' \text{ END}$$

By making this choice, the set s becomes the set $\mathbb{N}$, and we can proceed with the translation of the last but one antecedent. We have

$$\neg\, [S]\, \neg\, (n = V)$$

$$\Leftrightarrow$$

$$\neg\, \forall\, n' \cdot (n' \in \mathbb{N} \,\wedge\, n' < n \;\Rightarrow\; [n := n']\, \neg\, (n = V))$$

$$\Leftrightarrow$$

$$\neg\, \forall\, n' \cdot (n' \in \mathbb{N} \,\wedge\, n' < n \;\Rightarrow\; \neg\, (n' = V))$$

$$\Leftrightarrow$$

$$\neg\, \forall\, n' \cdot (n' = V \;\Rightarrow\; \neg\, (n' \in \mathbb{N} \,\wedge\, n' < n))$$

$$\Leftrightarrow$$

$$\neg\, \neg\, (V \in \mathbb{N} \,\wedge\, V < n)$$

$$\Leftrightarrow$$

$$V \in \mathbb{N} \,\wedge\, V < n$$

The last condition reduces to $V < n$ since we have $I \;\Rightarrow\; V \in \mathbb{N}$ and also $I \;\Rightarrow\; [T]\, I$. The final translation of our theorem is thus the following:

$$\forall\, x \cdot (I \;\Rightarrow\; [T]\, I)$$
$$\forall\, x \cdot (I \;\Rightarrow\; V \in \mathbb{N})$$
$$\forall\, x \cdot (I \;\Rightarrow\; [n := V]\, [T]\, (V < n)) \qquad\qquad \text{Theorem 9.2.5}$$
$$\Rightarrow$$
$$\forall\, x \cdot (I \;\Rightarrow\; [T\hat{\ }]\, I)$$

In this theorem, the variant is a natural number and the well-founded relation is the classical "smaller than" relation. It is possible to envisage more elaborate variants. For instance, we know that the lexicographical order on natural number sequences of the same size is also a well-founded relation (section 3.7.5). As a consequence, we may rearrange the previous theorem as follows:

$$\forall\, x \cdot (I \;\Rightarrow\; [T]\, I)$$
$$\forall\, x \cdot (I \;\Rightarrow\; V \in \mathsf{seq}\,(\mathbb{N}))$$
$$\forall\, x \cdot (I \;\Rightarrow\; [s := V]\, [T]\, (V \prec s)) \qquad\qquad \text{Theorem 9.2.5'}$$
$$\Rightarrow$$
$$\forall\, x \cdot (I \;\Rightarrow\; [T\hat{\ }]\, I)$$

9.2.9. The Traditional Loop

In this section we shall translate the results of the previous section for the classical loop, which was defined as follows in section 9.2.1:

$$\text{WHILE } P \text{ DO } S \text{ END} \;=\; (P \implies S)\hat{\ }\,;(\neg\, P \implies \text{skip})$$

Our intention is to derive some classical laws *to be used in practice*. Before doing so, however, we shall calculate the str and pre constructs. We suppose that the substitution S works with variable x and invariant $x \in s$. We have then (with $\mathsf{set}\,(P)$ being equal to $\{x \mid x \in s \,\wedge\, P\}$)

str (WHILE P DO S END)(p)

$\Rightarrow$

str $((P \implies S)\hat{\ };(\neg P \implies \text{skip}))(p)$

$\Rightarrow$

str $((P \implies S)\hat{\ })(\text{set}(P) \cup p)$

$\Rightarrow$

fix $(\lambda q \cdot (q \in \mathbb{P}(s) \mid (\text{set}(P) \cup p) \cap (\overline{\text{set}(P)} \cup \text{str}(S)(q))))$

The last line is obtained according to the definition of str $(T\hat{\ })$ given in section 9.2.2. By replacing, in that definition, T by $P \implies S$ we use the set-theoretic interpretation of str $(P \implies S)$ given in section 6.4.3. We thus have the following properties:

Property 9.2.6

str (WHILE P DO S END)(p) =
$\quad$ fix $(\lambda q \cdot (q \in \mathbb{P}(s) \mid (\text{set}(P) \cup p) \cap (\overline{\text{set}(P)} \cup \text{str}(S)(q))))$

pre (WHILE P DO S END) = fix $(\lambda q \cdot (q \in \mathbb{P}(s) \mid \overline{\text{set}(P)} \cup \text{str}(S)(q)))$

We now prove the more practical results. We first prove the following:

$\forall x \cdot (I \wedge P \implies [S]I)$
$\forall x \cdot (I \implies V \in \mathbb{N})$
$\forall x \cdot (I \wedge P \implies [n := V][S](V < n))$ $\qquad$ Theorem 9.2.6
$\forall x \cdot (I \wedge \neg P \implies R)$
$\Rightarrow$
$\forall x \cdot (I \implies [\text{WHILE }P\text{ DO }S\text{ END}]R)$

Proof

We assume

$\qquad \forall x \cdot (I \wedge P \implies [S]I)$ $\qquad\qquad$ Hypothesis 1

$\qquad \forall x \cdot (I \implies V \in \mathbb{N})$ $\qquad\qquad$ Hypothesis 2

$\qquad \forall x \cdot (I \wedge P \implies [n := V][S](V < n))$ $\qquad\qquad$ Hypothesis 3

$\qquad \forall x \cdot (I \wedge \neg P \implies R)$ $\qquad\qquad$ Hypothesis 4

And we have to prove

$\qquad \forall x \cdot (I \implies [\text{WHILE }P\text{ DO }S\text{ END}]R)$ $\qquad\qquad$ Goal 1

From Hypothesis 4, we deduce

$$\forall x \cdot (I \;\Rightarrow\; (\neg P \;\Rightarrow\; R))$$

Derivation 1

that is

$$\forall x \cdot (I \;\Rightarrow\; [\neg P \;\Longrightarrow\; \text{skip}]\, R)$$

Derivation 2

Applying the monotonicity Property 6.2.2, we deduce

Derivation 3

$$\forall x \cdot ([(P \;\Longrightarrow\; S)\hat{\;}]\, I \;\Rightarrow\; [(P \;\Longrightarrow\; S)\hat{\;}]\,[\neg P \;\Longrightarrow\; \text{skip}]\, R)$$

that is

Derivation 4

$$\forall x \cdot ([(P \;\Longrightarrow\; S)\hat{\;}]\, I \;\Rightarrow\; [(P \;\Longrightarrow\; S)\hat{\;};(\neg P \;\Longrightarrow\; \text{skip})]\, R)$$

that is

$$\forall x \cdot ([(P \;\Longrightarrow\; S)\hat{\;}]\, I \;\Rightarrow\; [\text{WHILE } P \text{ DO } S \text{ END}]\, R) \qquad \text{Derivation 5}$$

From Hypothesis 1, Hypothesis 2, Hypothesis 3 and Theorem 9.2.5 (where T is replaced by $P \Longrightarrow S$), we deduce

$$\forall x \cdot (I \;\Rightarrow\; [(P \;\Longrightarrow\; S)\hat{\;}]\, I)$$

Derivation 6

Putting together Derivation 5 and Derivation 6, we obtain Goal 1.
End of Proof

As for Theorem 9.2.5, we can extend this theorem to take account of a more elaborate variant:

$$
\begin{array}{l}
\forall x \cdot (I \;\wedge\; P \;\;\Rightarrow\;\; [S]\, I) \\[2pt]
\forall x \cdot (I \;\;\Rightarrow\;\; V \in \text{seq}(\mathbb{N})) \\[2pt]
\forall x \cdot (I \;\wedge\; P \;\;\Rightarrow\;\; [s := V][S]\,(V \prec s)) \\[2pt]
\forall x \cdot (I \;\wedge\; \neg P \;\;\Rightarrow\;\; R) \\[2pt]
\Rightarrow \\[2pt]
\forall x \cdot (I \;\;\Rightarrow\;\; [\text{WHILE } P \text{ DO } S \text{ END}]\, R)
\end{array}
$$

Theorem 9.2.6'

In order to insist on the determination of the invariant and variant, we may write the loop as follows

$$\boxed{\quad \text{WHILE } P \text{ DO } S \text{ INVARIANT } I \text{ VARIANT } V \text{ END} \quad}$$

According to Theorem 9.2.6, we obtain, eventually:

$$I$$
$$\forall x \cdot (I \wedge P \;\;\Rightarrow\;\; [S]I\,)$$
$$\forall x \cdot (I \;\;\Rightarrow\;\; V \in \mathbb{N})$$
$$\forall x \cdot (I \wedge P \;\;\Rightarrow\;\; [n := V][S](V < n))$$ Theorem 9.2.7
$$\forall x \cdot (I \wedge \neg P \;\;\Rightarrow\;\; R\,)$$
$$\Leftrightarrow$$
$$[\text{WHILE } P \text{ DO } S \text{ INVARIANT } I \text{ VARIANT } V \text{ END}]\,R$$

When the variant is a sequence of natural numbers, we obtain the following:

$$I$$
$$\forall x \cdot (I \wedge P \;\;\Rightarrow\;\; [S]I\,)$$
$$\forall x \cdot (I \;\;\Rightarrow\;\; V \in \mathsf{seq}\,(\mathbb{N}))$$
$$\forall x \cdot (I \wedge P \;\;\Rightarrow\;\; [s := V][S](V \prec s))$$ Theorem 9.2.7'
$$\forall x \cdot (I \wedge \neg P \;\;\Rightarrow\;\; R\,)$$
$$\Leftrightarrow$$
$$[\text{WHILE } P \text{ DO } S \text{ INVARIANT } I \text{ VARIANT } V \text{ END}]\,R$$

Notice that in the statement of the last two theorems we have an equivalence operator (not an implication). This is due to the fact that this statement is also a "defining property" for the full construct:

$$\text{WHILE } P \text{ DO } S \text{ INVARIANT } I \text{ VARIANT } V \text{ END}$$

Notice that this defining property allows us to define the termination predicate as well as the before-after predicate of this compound construct (this has been suggested by Fernando Mejia). We have thus:

$$\mathrm{trm}\left(\begin{array}{c} \text{WHILE } P \text{ DO} \\ S \\ \text{INVARIANT} \\ I \\ \text{VARIANT} \\ V \\ \text{END} \end{array}\right) \;\;\Leftrightarrow\;\; \begin{array}{l} I \\ \forall x \cdot (I \wedge P \;\;\Rightarrow\;\; [S]I\,) \\ \forall x \cdot (I \;\;\Rightarrow\;\; V \in \mathbb{N}) \\ \forall x \cdot (I \wedge P \;\;\Rightarrow\;\; [n := V][S](V < n)) \end{array}$$

$$\mathrm{prd}_x \left(\begin{array}{c} \text{WHILE } P \text{ DO} \\ S \\ \text{INVARIANT} \\ I \\ \text{VARIANT} \\ V \\ \text{END} \end{array} \right) \quad \Leftrightarrow \quad [x := x']\,(I \ \wedge \ \neg P)$$

When the variant is more elaborate we have:

$$\mathrm{trm} \left(\begin{array}{c} \text{WHILE } P \text{ DO} \\ S \\ \text{INVARIANT} \\ I \\ \text{VARIANT} \\ V \\ \text{END} \end{array} \right) \quad \Leftrightarrow \quad \begin{array}{l} I \\ \forall x \cdot (I \ \wedge \ P \quad \Rightarrow \quad [S]I\,) \\ \forall x \cdot (I \quad \Rightarrow \quad V \in \mathsf{seq}\,(\mathbb{N})) \\ \forall x \cdot (I \ \wedge \ P \ \Rightarrow \ [s := V][S](V \prec s)) \end{array}$$

It might seem strange, at first glance, to have the predicates I and $\forall x \cdot (I \wedge P \Rightarrow [S]I\,)$ incorporated in the "termination" of the loop since such predicates are, apparently, not concerned with that problem. Here is an intuitive reason explaining why, after all, the presence of such predicates is not as strange as it might appear at first. In the present case, we have *extended* the loop definition with the extra assertions of the invariant I and of the variant V, which are thus, de facto, "first class" elements of the *meaning* of the loop. We could think of them being effectively "controlled" while the loop is "executed". And thus it makes sense to have them as part of the termination since, in case the corresponding assertions do not hold at some point during the "execution", then the loop should abort.

The before-after predicate is particularly illuminating. It shows what the loop is supposed to do, provided it terminates of course, namely to establish the post-condition $I \wedge \neg P$.

We shall also very frequently encounter practical cases where our problem is to prove that a substitution of the following form establishes a certain predicate R:

$$T \,; \text{WHILE } P \text{ DO } S \text{ INVARIANT } I \text{ VARIANT } V \text{ END}$$

Here, the substitution T is said to *initialize* the loop. We obviously have (according to the monotonicity Property 6.2.2)

$$\forall x \cdot (I \quad \Rightarrow \quad [\text{WHILE } P \text{ DO } S \text{ INVARIANT } I \text{ VARIANT } V \text{ END}]\,R)$$
$$\Rightarrow$$
$$[T]I \quad \Rightarrow \quad [T][\text{WHILE } P \text{ DO } S \text{ INVARIANT } I \text{ VARIANT } V \text{ END}]\,R$$

As a consequence, we have

$[T] I$
$\forall x \cdot (I \Rightarrow [\text{WHILE } P \text{ DO } S \text{ INVARIANT } I \text{ VARIANT } V \text{ END}] R)$
$\Rightarrow$
$[T ; \text{WHILE } P \text{ DO } S \text{ INVARIANT } I \text{ VARIANT } V \text{ END}] R$

Property 9.2.7

By putting together Property 9.2.5 and Theorem 9.2.7, we obtain eventually

---

Theorem 9.2.8

$[T] I$ (Initialization)
$\forall x \cdot (I \land P \Rightarrow [S] I)$ (Invariance)
$\forall x \cdot (I \Rightarrow V \in \mathbb{N})$ (Typing)
$\forall x \cdot (I \land P \Rightarrow [n := V][S](V < n))$ (Termination)
$\forall x \cdot (I \land \neg P \Rightarrow R)$ (Finalization)
$\Rightarrow$
$[T ; \text{WHILE } P \text{ DO } S \text{ INVARIANT } I \text{ VARIANT } V \text{ END}] R$

And when the variant is a sequence of natural numbers, we obtain the following:

Theorem 9.2.8'

$[T] I$ (Initialization)
$\forall x \cdot (I \land P \Rightarrow [S] I)$ (Invariance)
$\forall x \cdot (I \Rightarrow V \in \text{seq}(\mathbb{N}))$ (Typing)
$\forall x \cdot (I \land P \Rightarrow [s := V][S](V < s))$ (Termination)
$\forall x \cdot (I \land \neg P \Rightarrow R)$ (Finalization)
$\Leftrightarrow$
$[\text{WHILE } P \text{ DO } S \text{ INVARIANT } I \text{ VARIANT } V \text{ END}] R$

It should be noted that the introduction of the initializing substitution T does not change the requirement concerning the freshness of the variables n or s: in other words, no occurrences of n and s must be present in T.

In the remaining part of this section, we derive a number of other theorems that will allow us to transform a loop once we have used Theorem 9.2.8. The first of these theorems is to be used when one wants to add an extra invariant J.

$[T\,;\text{WHILE}\;\;P\;\;\text{DO}\;\;S\;\;\text{INVARIANT}\;\;I\;\;\text{VARIANT}\;\;V\;\;\text{END}]\,R$
$[T]\,J$
$\forall x \cdot (I \;\wedge\; P \;\wedge\; J \;\;\Rightarrow\;\; [S]\,J)$ Theorem 9.2.9
$\Rightarrow$
$[T\,;\text{WHILE}\;\;P\;\;\text{DO}\;\;S\;\;\text{INVARIANT}\;\;I \;\wedge\; J\;\;\text{VARIANT}\;\;V\;\;\text{END}]\,R$

The proof of this theorem is left as an exercise for the reader. Our next theorem is concerned with the modification of the guard.

$T\,;\text{WHILE}\;\;P\;\;\text{DO}\;\;S\;\;\text{INVARIANT}\;\;I\;\;\text{VARIANT}\;\;V\;\;\text{END}]\,R$
$\forall x \cdot (I \;\;\Rightarrow\;\; (P \;\;\Leftrightarrow\;\; H))$ Theorem 9.2.10
$\Rightarrow$
$T\,;\text{WHILE}\;\;H\;\;\text{DO}\;\;S\;\;\text{INVARIANT}\;\;I\;\;\text{VARIANT}\;\;V\;\;\text{END}]\,R$

The proof of this theorem is also left as an exercise for the reader. Our next theorem has to do with the addition of an extra (and fresh) variable y together with an extension B of the initialization of the loop and an extension A of the body of the loop. Of course, the substitutions A and B are not supposed to modify the main variable x of the loop.

$T\,;\text{WHILE}\;\;P\;\;\text{DO}\;\;S\;\;\text{INVARIANT}\;\;I\;\;\text{VARIANT}\;\;V\;\;\text{END}]\,R$
$\Rightarrow$ Theorem 9.2.11
$T\,;B\,;\;\text{WHILE}\;\;P\;\;\text{DO}\;\;S\,;A\;\;\text{INVARIANT}\;\;I\;\;\text{VARIANT}\;\;V\;\;\text{END}]\,R$

The proof of this theorem is straightforward since there are no occurrences of y appearing in T, P, S, I, V, and R.

9.3. Exercises

1. Prove the properties of section 9.1.3 concerning $\mathrm{trm}\,(S\,;T)$, $\mathrm{prd}_x(S\,;T)$ and $\mathrm{fis}\,(S\,;T)$.

2. Prove the properties of section 9.1.3 concerning $\mathrm{pre}\,(S\,;T)$, $\mathrm{rel}\,(S\,;T)$, $\mathrm{dom}\,(S\,;T)$ and $\mathrm{str}\,(S\,;T)$.

3. Prove the equality laws of section 9.1.3.

4. Prove the following, for any subset p of $\mathbb{N}$:

$$\mathsf{str}\,(\text{WHILE } x > 0 \text{ DO } x := x - 1 \text{ END})(p) \;=\; \begin{cases} \mathbb{N} & \text{if } 0 \in p \\[2mm] \varnothing & \text{otherwise} \end{cases}$$

5. Prove the following, for any subset p of $\mathbb{N}$:

$$\mathsf{str}\,(\text{WHILE } x = 0 \text{ DO skip END})(p) \;=\; p - \{0\}$$

6. Let S be the following substitution working with the variable x with invariant $x \in \mathbb{Z}$:

WHILE $x \neq 0$ DO
    IF $x < 0$ THEN $x :\in \mathbb{N}$ ELSE $x := x - 1$ END
END

We would like to construct the set transformer associated with S. For this we shall first prove a number of intermediate results.

(a) For any subset r of $\mathbb{Z}$, prove

$$\mathsf{str}\,(x :\in \mathbb{N})(r) \;=\; \begin{cases} \mathbb{Z} & \text{if } \mathbb{N} \subseteq r \\[2mm] \varnothing & \text{otherwise} \end{cases}$$

(b) For any subset r of $\mathbb{Z}$, prove (with succ extended to the negative members of $\mathbb{Z}$)

$$\mathsf{str}\,(x := x - 1)(r) \;=\; \mathsf{succ}[r]$$

(c) For any subset r of $\mathbb{Z}$, prove

$$\mathsf{str}\,(\text{IF } x < 0 \text{ THEN } x :\in \mathbb{N} \text{ ELSE } x := x - 1 \text{ END})(r)$$

$$=\; \begin{cases} (\mathbb{Z} - \mathbb{N}) \cup \mathsf{succ}[r] & \text{if } \mathbb{N} \subseteq r \\[2mm] \mathbb{N} \cap \mathsf{succ}\,[r] & \text{otherwise} \end{cases}$$

(d) From the previous questions, prove that $\mathsf{str}\,(S)(p)$ (for any subset p of $\mathbb{Z}$) is the least fixpoint of the following function f_p whose value $f_p(q)$ at any subset q of $\mathbb{Z}$ is as follows:

$$f_p(q) \;=\; \begin{cases} \mathbb{Z} & \text{if } 0 \in p \wedge \mathbb{N} \subseteq q \\[2mm] \{0\} \cup (\mathbb{N} \cap \mathsf{succ}\,[q]) & \text{if } 0 \in p \wedge \mathbb{N} \not\subseteq q \\[2mm] \mathbb{Z} - \{0\} & \text{if } 0 \notin p \wedge \mathbb{N} \subseteq q \\[2mm] \mathbb{N} \cap \mathsf{succ}\,[q] - \{0\} & \text{if } 0 \notin p \wedge \mathbb{N} \not\subseteq q \end{cases}$$

(e) From the previous question, prove the following:

$$\mathsf{str}\,(S)(p) \;=\; \begin{cases} \mathbb{Z} & \text{if } 0 \in p \\[2mm] \varnothing & \text{otherwise} \end{cases}$$

In other words S is the same as $x := 0$.

7. Let S be the following substitution working with the variable x with invariant $x \in \mathbb{Z}$:

$$
\begin{array}{l}
\text{WHILE } x \neq 0 \text{ DO} \\
\quad \text{IF } x < 0 \text{ THEN} \\
\qquad x : (x \in \mathbb{Z} \wedge x > x_0) \\
\quad \text{ELSE} \\
\qquad x := x - 1 \\
\quad \text{END} \\
\text{END}
\end{array}
$$

Prove that this substitution is the same as $x := 0$.

8. Given a set s and a function f from $\mathbb{P}(s)$ to itself, prove the following relationship:

$$\overline{\text{fix}\,(f)} \;=\; \text{FIX}\,(\text{dual}\,(f))$$

where $\text{dual}\,(f)$ is also a function from $\mathbb{P}(s)$ to itself, whose value at any subset p of s is the following:

$$\text{dual}\,(f)(p) \;=\; \overline{f(\overline{p})}$$

Deduce the following alternative result:

$$\overline{\text{FIX}\,(f)} \;=\; \text{fix}\,(\text{dual}\,(f))$$

9. Given a substitution S working with a machine with a variable x and invariant $x \in s$, prove that the set $\text{pre}\,(S^\wedge)$ obeys the following relationship:

$$\overline{\text{pre}\,(S^\wedge)} \;=\; \text{FIX}\,(\lambda p \cdot (p \in \mathbb{P}(s) \mid \text{rel}\,(S)^{-1}[p]))$$

Prove now the following relationship:

$$\overline{\text{pre}\,(S^\wedge)} \times s \;=\; \text{FIX}\,(\lambda t \cdot (t \in s \leftrightarrow s \mid \text{rel}\,(S); t))$$

10. We shall prove the theorem that is "dual" to Theorem 9.2.1. Given a set t, a subset p of t, a function g from $\mathbb{P}(t)$ to itself that distributes over set union, and a function $f(p)$ defined as follows:

$$f(p) \;=\; \lambda r \cdot (r \in \mathbb{P}(s) \mid p \cup g(r))$$

prove the following:

$$\text{FIX}\,(f(p)) \;=\; \text{FIX}\,(g) \;\cup\; \text{fix}\,(f(p))$$

11. Prove Property 9.2.2.

12. Given a set t, a subset p of t, a total relation v from p to s, a monotonic

set transformer f from $\mathbb{P}(s)$ to itself such that $\text{fix}(f) = s$, and a monotonic set transformer g from $\mathbb{P}(t)$ to itself, prove directly the following:

$$p \in \mathbb{P}(t)$$
$$v \in p \leftrightarrow s$$
$$\text{dom}(v) = p$$
$$\forall a \cdot (a \subseteq t \;\Rightarrow\; f(\overline{v[\overline{a}]}) \subseteq \overline{v[\overline{g(a)}]})$$
$$\text{fix}(f) = s$$
$$\Rightarrow$$
$$p \subseteq \text{fix}(g)$$

CHAPTER 10

Programming Examples

In the previous chapter, we presented the theory of the two basic programming constructs of imperative programming, namely sequencing and loops. This chapter is entirely devoted to the study of examples dealing with such constructs.

In section 10.1, we present a general paradigm for computing the minimum of a non-empty set of natural numbers. From that single example, we derive a large number of special cases. It seems that this search for a minimum could have been extended to other inductive structures. We have not tried to do so, however, in this book.

In the next three sections, we present general paradigms for computing recursive functions constructed on certain inductively defined sets, namely natural numbers (section 10.2), finite sequences (section 10.3), and finite trees (section 10.4). Again, from these schematic examples, we derive a large number of special cases.

The intention, with each of these examples, is *not* to present the most clever or efficient algorithm corresponding to a given problem. Rather, the aim is to show that each algorithm development could be performed as a coordinate activity, having strong connections with *other* algorithm developments. We try to *re-use*, as much as we can, material from previous developments. It is not claimed, of course, that this is always possible.

This chapter is an experiment in algorithm construction. In an initial section 10.0, we present a tentative methodology.

10.0. Methodology

10.0.1. Re-use of Previous Algorithms

Throughout this chapter, we follow a systematic methodology whose rôle is to enable us to take account of previous algorithm developments. This is explained in what follows.

All our algorithms will be developed in the form of "operations" of an *implicit* variable-free abstract machine. In other words, our algorithms will be self-contained. For instance, we might develop an algorithm, say alpha, with output paramater r and input parameter i. We shall present that algorithm as follows:

$$r \longleftarrow \text{alpha}(i) \;\; \mathrel{\widehat{=}}$$

PRE

$$P(i)$$

THEN

$$S(r,i)$$

END

where $P(i)$, the pre-condition, is a predicate depending on the input parameter i, and where $S(r,i)$ is a generalized substitution depending on the input parameter i and "assigning" the output parameter r. Together with such an algorithm, we shall also present and prove a certain property, which will always take the form of the establishment of a certain post-condition, usually of the form $r = f(i)$ (where f is a certain function), and this, of course, under the hypothesis of the pre-condition:

$$\forall i \cdot (P(i) \;\; \Rightarrow \;\; [r \longleftarrow \text{alpha}(i)]\,(r = f(i)))$$

This, in fact, stands for

$$\forall i \cdot (P(i) \;\; \Rightarrow \;\; [S(r,i)]\,(r = f(i))) \qquad\qquad (1)$$

Suppose now that we want to develop another algorithm, say beta, with output parameter s and input parameter j. Algorithm beta is supposed to establish a post-condition of the form $s = g(j)$ (where g is a certain function) under the pre-condition $Q(j)$. It might happen that we are able to establish a certain connection between this post-condition and the function f referenced in the post-condition of our previous algorithm alpha. For instance, we might have proved that the following holds:

$$\forall j \cdot (Q(j) \;\; \Rightarrow \;\; g(j) = f(E))$$

where E is a certain expression depending on j and supposed to be independent of r, i, and s. This statement can be extended as follows:

$$\forall j \cdot (Q(j) \;\; \Rightarrow \;\; \forall s \cdot (s = g(j) \;\; \Leftrightarrow \;\; s = f(E))) \qquad\qquad (2)$$

We might be tempted then to propose the following algorithm, with pre-condition $Q(j)$, and within which algorithm alpha is "called" with actual result s and actual input E:

$$
\begin{array}{|l|}
\hline
\\
s \longleftarrow \text{beta}(j) \ \ \hat{=} \\
\qquad \text{PRE} \\
\qquad\qquad Q(j) \\
\qquad \text{THEN} \\
\qquad\qquad s \longleftarrow \text{alpha}\,(E) \\
\qquad \text{END} \\
\\
\hline
\end{array}
$$

What we have then to prove is the following:

$$\forall j \cdot (Q(j) \;\Rightarrow\; [s \longleftarrow \text{alpha}\,(E)]\,(s = g(j)))$$

that is, equivalently (according to (2) and **Property 6.2.3**)

$$\forall j \cdot (Q(j) \;\Rightarrow\; [s \longleftarrow \text{alpha}\,(E)]\,(s = f(E)))$$

By expanding this "call", we obtain the following:

$$\forall j \cdot (Q(j) \;\Rightarrow\; [P(E)\,|\,S(s,E)]\,(s = f(E)))$$

that is

$$\boxed{\forall j \cdot (Q(j) \;\Rightarrow\; P(E) \wedge [S(s,E)]\,(s = f(E)))} \qquad (3)$$

This can be decomposed in the following two separate conjectures to be proved:

$$\forall j \cdot (Q(j) \;\Rightarrow\; P(E))$$

$$\forall j \cdot (Q(j) \;\Rightarrow\; [S(s,E)]\,(s = f(E)))$$

But, clearly, we have the following, as a special case of the already established property (1) of **alpha**:

$$P(E) \;\Rightarrow\; [S(s,E)]\,(s = f(E))$$

This has been obtained by replacing, in (1), the universally quantified variable i by E, and the output parameter r by s. As a consequence, the only property that it is necessary to prove, in order to establish (3), is clearly the following:

$$\boxed{\forall j \cdot (Q(j) \;\Rightarrow\; P(E))} \qquad (4)$$

This is indeed very intuitive. We have just to prove that algorithm **alpha** is "called", from **beta**, within its (instantiated) pre-condition. Now, provided (4) holds, we can rewrite our algorithm **beta** as the *in-line expansion* of the instantiated text of algorithm **alpha**, where the (now obsolete) pre-condition $P(E)$ has been removed. This yields the following:

$$s \longleftarrow \mathsf{beta}(j) \ \hat{=}$$

PRE

$$Q(j)$$

THEN

$$S(s, E)$$

END

and we have then

$$\forall j \cdot (Q(j) \ \Rightarrow \ [s \longleftarrow \mathsf{beta}(j)] \, (s = g(j)))$$

As can be seen, we are now in a situation allowing us to specialize our new algorithm beta, in very much the same way as we have done with algorithm alpha to obtain beta.

10.0.2. Loop Proof Rules

In order for this chapter to be self contained, we remind the reader of the loop proof rules we have established in chapter 9 under the names of Theorem 9.2.8 to Theorem 9.2.11. Hopefully, the methodology developed in the previous section will make it unnecessary to use these rules very often.

The first proof rule is the basic rule to be used in order to prove that an initialized loop (with invariant I and variant V) establishes a certain post-condition R:

LOOP 1	$[T]I$ $\forall x \cdot (I \ \wedge \ P \ \Rightarrow \ [S]I)$ $\forall x \cdot (I \ \Rightarrow \ V \in \mathbb{N})$ $\forall x \cdot (I \ \wedge \ P \ \Rightarrow \ [n := V][S](V < n))$ $\forall x \cdot (I \ \wedge \ \neg P \ \Rightarrow \ R)$ $\Leftrightarrow$ $[T\,;\,\text{WHILE } P \text{ DO } S \text{ INVARIANT } I \text{ VARIANT } V \text{ END}]R$

When the variant is a sequence of natural numbers instead of a simple natural number, we have the following:

LOOP 1′	$[T]I$ $\forall x \cdot (I \;\wedge\; P \quad\Rightarrow\quad [S]I\,)$ $\forall x \cdot (I \quad\Rightarrow\quad V \in \mathsf{seq}(\mathbb{N}))$ $\forall x \cdot (I \;\wedge\; P \quad\Rightarrow\quad [s := V][S](V \prec s))$ $\forall x \cdot (I \;\wedge\; \neg P \quad\Rightarrow\quad R\,)$ $\Leftrightarrow$ $[T\,; \text{WHILE } P \text{ DO } S \text{ INVARIANT } I \text{ VARIANT } V \text{ END}]R$

In this rule (as well as in subsequent rules), the variable x stands for the variable that is modified in the loop.

The second proof rule shows what is to be proved in order to add a new invariant to an already proved loop:

LOOP 2	$[T\,; \text{WHILE } P \text{ DO } S \text{ INVARIANT } I \text{ VARIANT } V \text{ END}]\, R$ $[T]J$ $\forall x \cdot (I \;\wedge\; P \;\wedge\; J \quad\Rightarrow\quad [S]J\,)$ $\Rightarrow$ $[T\,; \text{WHILE } P \text{ DO } S \text{ INVARIANT } I \;\wedge\; J \text{ VARIANT } V \text{ END}]\, R$

The third proof rule shows what is to be proved in order to replace the guard of an already proved loop.

LOOP 3	$[T\,; \text{WHILE } P \text{ DO } S \text{ INVARIANT } I \text{ VARIANT } V \text{ END}]\, R$ $\forall x \cdot (I \quad\Rightarrow\quad (P \;\Leftrightarrow\; H))$ $\Rightarrow$ $[T\,; \text{WHILE } H \text{ DO } S \text{ INVARIANT } I \text{ VARIANT } V \text{ END}]\, R$

Finally, the fourth proof rule shows what is to be proved in order to add (or remove) a fresh variable in the body of an already proved loop. Such a fresh variable is supposed to be initialized in the substitution B only, and it is supposed to be modified, in the body of the loop, in the substitution A only.

LOOP 4	$[T\,; \text{WHILE } P \text{ DO } S \text{ INVARIANT } I \text{ VARIANT } V \text{ END}]R$ $\Leftrightarrow$ $[T\,; B\,; \text{ WHILE } P \text{ DO } S\,; A \text{ INVARIANT } I \text{ VARIANT } V \text{ END}]R$

10.0.3. Sequencing Proof Rule

Finally, we remind the reader of the following proof rule for sequencing. This was established in the previous chapter under the name of **Property 9.1.1**:

$$\boxed{\text{SEQ} \quad [S]P \ \wedge \ \forall x \cdot (P \Rightarrow [T]R) \quad \Rightarrow \quad [S;T]R}$$

10.1. Unbounded Search

10.1.1. Introduction

Let c be a non-empty subset of $\mathbb{N}$. We would like to construct a substitution working with the variable r and establishing the following post-condition:

$$r = \min(c)$$

Before constructing our substitution, however, we recall the following properties (already presented in section 3.5.3) of the minimum of a non-empty set c of natural numbers: (1) $\min(c)$ is smaller than or equal to all members of c, and (2) $\min(c)$ is a member of c, formally:

$$\boxed{r \in c \ \Rightarrow \ r \geq \min(c)}$$

Condition 1

$$\boxed{\min(c) \in c}$$

Condition 2

From Condition 1, we deduce

$$r \in c \ \Rightarrow \ (r > \min(c) \ \vee \ r = \min(c))$$

that is

$$r \in c \ \Rightarrow \ (r \leq \min(c) \ \Rightarrow \ r = \min(c))$$

that is

$$(r \leq \min(c) \ \wedge \ r \in c) \ \Rightarrow \ r = \min(c)$$

that is (since c is a subset of $\mathbb{N}$)

$$\boxed{(r \in 0 \mathinner{..} \min(c) \ \wedge \ r \in c) \ \Rightarrow \ r = \min(c)}$$

Condition 3

This suggests the construction of a loop of the following form (where S is a substitution):

$$r := 0;$$
WHILE $r \notin c$ DO
$$S$$
INVARIANT
$$r \in 0 \,..\, \min(c)$$
VARIANT
$$\min(c) - r$$
END

This is so because, at the end of the loop (where the invariant still holds but the guard no longer holds), we have $r \in 0 \,..\, \min(c) \,\wedge\, r \in c$, a condition leading to the desired result, according to Condition 3. The body of the loop consists of increasing r. Here is the proposed algorithm:

$r \longleftarrow \text{MinSet}(c) \ \widehat{=}$
  PRE
  $$c \in \mathbb{P}_1(\mathbb{N})$$
  THEN
  $$r := 0;$$
  WHILE $r \notin c$ DO
  $$r := r + 1$$
  INVARIANT
  $$r \in 0 \,..\, \min(c)$$
  VARIANT
  $$\min(c) - r$$
  END
END

Algorithm 10.1.1

Our purpose is then to prove formally the following statement, expressing the fact that our proposed algorithm establishes that the condition $r = \min(c)$ holds:

$$c \in \mathbb{P}_1(\mathbb{N}) \ \Rightarrow\ [r \longleftarrow \text{MinSet}(c)]\,(r = \min(c))$$

As can be seen, this statement contains, quite naturally, the pre-condition of the algorithm as an explicit assumption. In what follows, to simplify matters, we shall systematically replace, in the statement of similar conjectures, the pre-condition of the algorithm by the abbreviation PRE. This is because the pre-condition can become quite heavy sometimes. This abuse of language will never result in any ambiguity, however, as PRE will always denote the pre-condition of the algorithm that is necessarily mentioned in the subsequent substitution. As a consequence, the statement to be proved reduces to the following:

PRE $\Rightarrow$ $[r \longleftarrow \text{MinSet}(c)]\,(r = \min(c))$ Property 10.1.1

Proof

We assume PRE, that is

$$c \in \mathbb{P}_1(\mathbb{N}) \qquad\qquad\qquad \text{Hypothesis 1}$$

The application of rule LOOP 1 then leads to the following lemmas to be proved:
Initialization Lemma: After performing the substitution, we have to prove the following, which is obvious:

$$0 \in 0\mathinner{\ldotp\ldotp}\min(c) \qquad\qquad\qquad \text{Goal 1}$$

Invariance Lemma: After performing the substitution, we have to prove the following:

$$(r \in 0\mathinner{\ldotp\ldotp}\min(c) \;\wedge\; r \notin c) \;\Rightarrow\; r+1 \in 0\mathinner{\ldotp\ldotp}\min(c) \qquad \text{Goal 2}$$

We assume

$$r \in 0\mathinner{\ldotp\ldotp}\min(c) \qquad\qquad\qquad \text{Hypothesis 2}$$
$$r \notin c \qquad\qquad\qquad \text{Hypothesis 3}$$

and we are left to prove

$$r+1 \in 0\mathinner{\ldotp\ldotp}\min(c) \qquad\qquad\qquad \text{Goal 3}$$

From Hypothesis 2, we obtain immediately

$$r+1 \in 0\mathinner{\ldotp\ldotp}\min(c)+1 \qquad\qquad\qquad \text{Derivation 1}$$

Hence, to prove Goal 3, it is sufficient to prove that $r+1$ is distinct from $\min(c)+1$. In other words, we have to prove that r is distinct from $\min(c)$. But this is obvious, since otherwise r would belong to c according to Condition 2, a fact contradicted by Hypothesis 3 (the guard of the loop). Notice that this is the first and only time we use Condition 2.

Typing Lemma: We have to prove the following, which is obvious:

$$r \in 0\mathinner{\ldotp\ldotp}\min(c) \;\Rightarrow\; \min(c)-r \in \mathbb{N} \qquad\qquad \text{Goal 4}$$

Termination Lemma: After performing the substitution, we have to prove the following which is obvious

$$r \in 0\mathinner{\ldotp\ldotp}\min(c) \;\wedge\; r \notin c \;\Rightarrow\; \min(c)-(r+1) < \min(c)-r \quad \text{Goal 5}$$

Finalization Lemma: We have to prove the following which is, again, obvious according to Condition 3:

$$r \in 0\mathinner{\ldotp\ldotp}\min(c) \;\wedge\; r \in c \;\Rightarrow\; r = \min(c) \qquad\qquad \text{Goal 6}$$

End of Proof

In the case where we have a natural number, say a, known to be less than or equal to $\min(c)$, we may start the iteration from a rather than from 0:

$$r \longleftarrow \text{MinSetMin}(c, a) \;\; \widehat{=}$$

PRE
$$c \in \mathbb{P}_1(\mathbb{N}) \quad \wedge$$
$$a \in 0 .. \min(c)$$
THEN
$$r := a;$$
WHILE $\quad r \notin c \quad$ DO
$$r := r + 1$$
INVARIANT
$$r \in a .. \min(c)$$
VARIANT
$$\min(c) - r$$
END
END

Algorithm 10.1.2

and we obviously have

PRE $\;\Rightarrow\; [r \longleftarrow \text{MinSetMin}(c, a)] \, (r = \min(c))$ Property 10.1.2

Remember that we have decided to systematically omit writing the pre-condition of the algorithm as an explicit assumption.

10.1.2. Comparing two Sequences

As a first application of the framework introduced in the previous section, let us construct a substitution whose rôle is to compare (for equality) two *non-empty* sequences s and t. These sequences are supposed to consist of positive natural numbers except for their last element, which must be the number 0. For instance, here are two such sequences:

$$s = [\, 4, 2, 6, 8, 0 \,]$$
$$t = [\, 4, 2, 6, 0 \,]$$

Formally, the conditions required on these sequences are the following:

$$
\begin{array}{|l|}
\hline
s \in \mathsf{seq}_1(\mathbb{N}) \\
t \in \mathsf{seq}_1(\mathbb{N}) \\
\mathsf{front}\,(s) \in \mathsf{seq}\,(\mathbb{N}_1) \\
\mathsf{front}\,(t) \in \mathsf{seq}\,(\mathbb{N}_1) \\
\mathsf{last}\,(s) = 0 \\
\mathsf{last}\,(t) = 0 \\
\hline
\end{array}
$$

Two such sequences are equal if and only if: (1) they have the same size, (2) their elements are identical on their common domain. Formally

$$
\begin{array}{|c|}
\hline
\\
\mathsf{size}\,(s) \;=\; \mathsf{size}\,(t) \\
\\
i \in 1\,..\,\mathsf{size}\,(s) \;\Rightarrow\; s\,(i) = t\,(i) \\
\\
\hline
\end{array}
$$

Condition 1

In order to compare these sequences, we propose to look for the smallest number n, common to the domains of both sequences, and such that either the quantity $s(n)$ is distinct from the quantity $t(n)$ or one of these two quantities is equal to 0. In other words, n is the minimum of the following set cc:

$$
\boxed{cc = \{\, m \mid m \in \mathsf{dom}(s) \cap \mathsf{dom}(t) \;\wedge\; (s(m) \neq t(m) \;\vee\; s(m) = 0 \;\vee\; t(m) = 0)\,\}}
$$

When this minimum, n, is such that the condition $s(n) = t(n)$ holds, then, as we shall explain in what follows, the two sequences are indeed equal. In fact, when the condition $s(n) = t(n)$ holds, then, by the definition of the set cc, we have $s(n) = 0 \;\vee\; t(n) = 0$, that is, in the present case, $s(n) = 0 \;\wedge\; t(n) = 0$ (since $s(n) = t(n)$). Consequently, n is the common size of the two sequences since the *last* element of such sequences is the only one that can be equal to 0. Moreover, since n is the *minimum* of cc, all numbers i in the interval $1\,..\,n-1$ are *not* members of cc. Thus, these numbers, which, however, certainly are members of the domains of both sequences, are such that the predicate $s(i) = t(i)$ holds. In other words, according to Condition 1, the two sequences are indeed equal.

To summarize at this point, we are looking for a substitution, $n \longleftarrow$ MinIndexSeq (s, t), establishing the post-condition $n = \min(cc)$.

According to Property 10.1.2, the substitution $n \longleftarrow$ MinSetMin$(cc, 1)$ seems to be able to do the job. We thus propose the following:

$$
\begin{array}{l}
n \longleftarrow \mathsf{MinIndexSeq}\,(s,t) \;\;\widehat{=} \\
\quad \textsc{PRE} \\
\qquad s \in \mathsf{seq}_1(\mathbb{N}) \quad \wedge \\
\qquad t \in \mathsf{seq}_1(\mathbb{N}) \quad \wedge \\
\qquad \mathsf{front}\,(s) \in \mathsf{seq}\,(\mathbb{N}_1) \quad \wedge \\
\qquad \mathsf{front}\,(t) \in \mathsf{seq}\,(\mathbb{N}_1) \quad \wedge \\
\qquad \mathsf{last}\,(s) = 0 \quad \wedge \\
\qquad \mathsf{last}\,(t) = 0 \\
\quad \textsc{THEN} \\
\qquad n \longleftarrow \mathsf{MinSetMin}(cc,1) \\
\quad \textsc{END}
\end{array}
$$

and we would like to prove

$$
\mathsf{PRE} \;\Rightarrow\; [\,n \longleftarrow \mathsf{MinIndexSeq}(s,t)\,]\,(r = \min(cc))
$$

According to what has been proved in section 10.0.1, we have then just to prove that the pre-condition of MinIndexSeq implies the instantiated pre-condition of MinSetMin, formally

$$
\begin{array}{l}
s \in \mathsf{seq}_1(\mathbb{N}) \;\wedge \\
t \in \mathsf{seq}_1(\mathbb{N}) \;\wedge \\
\mathsf{front}\,(s) \in \mathsf{seq}\,(\mathbb{N}_1) \;\wedge \\
\mathsf{front}\,(t) \in \mathsf{seq}\,(\mathbb{N}_1) \;\wedge \\
\mathsf{last}\,(s) = 0 \;\wedge \\
\mathsf{last}\,(t) = 0 \\
\Rightarrow \\
cc \in \mathbb{P}_1(\mathbb{N}) \\
1 \in 0\,.\,.\,\min\,(cc)
\end{array}
$$

We notice, first, that cc clearly is *not empty* (remember, the sequences are not empty, by definition). We also notice that the smallest element in the domain of any non-empty sequence is 1. As a consequence, we have indeed $1 \in 0\,.\,.\,\min(cc)$. In other words, both pre-conditions of the substitution MinSetMin are fulfilled by our actual parameters cc and 1. According to the results of section 10.0, we thus obtain the following, by expanding $n \longleftarrow \mathsf{MinSetMin}(cc,1)$ within $\mathsf{MinIndexSeq}\,(s,t)$:

$$n \longleftarrow \text{MinIndexSeq}(s,t) \quad \hat{=}$$

PRE

$\ldots$

THEN

$\quad n := 1\,;$

WHILE $\quad n \notin cc \quad$ DO

$\quad\quad n := n + 1$

INVARIANT

$\quad\quad n \in 1\,..\,\min(cc)$

VARIANT

$\quad\quad \min(cc) - n$

END

END

Algorithm 10.1.3

We can then apply rule LOOP 3 for modifying the guard, yielding the following new guard (obtained by expanding the condition $n \notin cc$):

$$n \in \text{dom}(s) \cap \text{dom}(t) \;\Rightarrow\; (s(n) = t(n) \;\wedge\; s(n) \neq 0 \;\wedge\; t(n) \neq 0)$$

As, obviously, the extra invariant $n \in \text{dom}(s) \cap \text{dom}(t)$ holds, we can apply rule LOOP 2 for adding an extra invariant and then, again, rule LOOP 3 for changing the guard, yielding the following substitution:

$$n \longleftarrow \text{MinIndexSeq}(s,t) \quad \hat{=}$$

PRE

$\ldots$

THEN

$\quad n := 1\,;$

WHILE $\quad s(n) = t(n) \,\wedge\, s(n) \neq 0 \,\wedge\, t(n) \neq 0 \quad$ DO

$\quad\quad n := n + 1$

INVARIANT

$\quad\quad n \in 1\,..\,\min(cc) \quad \wedge$

$\quad\quad n \in \text{dom}(s) \cap \text{dom}(t)$

VARIANT

$\quad\quad \min(cc) - n$

END

END

Algorithm 10.1.4

We then have

$$\text{PRE} \;\Rightarrow\; [n \longleftarrow \mathsf{MinIndexSeq}(s,t)]\,(n = \min(cc)) \qquad \text{Property 10.1.3}$$

---

where, again

$$cc \;=\; \{m \mid m \in (\mathrm{dom}(s) \cap \mathrm{dom}(t)) \;\wedge\; (s(m) \neq t(m) \;\vee\; s(m) = 0 \;\vee\; t(m) = 0)\}$$

We then define the following substitution:

$$
\begin{aligned}
b \longleftarrow&\; \mathsf{EqualSeq}\,(s,t) \;\;\widehat{=} \\
&\text{PRE} \\
&\quad\quad s \in \mathsf{seq}_1(\mathbb{N}) \quad \wedge \\
&\quad\quad t \in \mathsf{seq}_1(\mathbb{N}) \quad \wedge \\
&\quad\quad \mathsf{front}\,(s) \in \mathsf{seq}\,(\mathbb{N}_1) \quad \wedge \\
&\quad\quad \mathsf{front}\,(t) \in \mathsf{seq}\,(\mathbb{N}_1) \quad \wedge \\
&\quad\quad \mathsf{last}\,(s) = 0 \quad \wedge \\
&\quad\quad \mathsf{last}\,(t) = 0 \\
&\text{THEN} \\
&\quad\quad \text{VAR} \quad n \quad \text{IN} \\
&\quad\quad\quad n \longleftarrow \mathsf{MinIndexSeq}\,(s,t); \\
&\quad\quad\quad b := \mathsf{bool}(s(n) = t\,(n)) \\
&\quad\quad \text{END} \\
&\text{END}
\end{aligned}
$$

Algorithm 10.1.5

and we can formally prove the following (exercise):

$$\text{PRE} \;\Rightarrow\; [b \longleftarrow \mathsf{EqualSeq}\,(s,t)]\,(b = \mathsf{true} \;\Leftrightarrow\; s = t) \qquad \text{Property 10.1.4}$$

Hint: according to rule **SEQ** and **Property 10.1.3**, it suffices to prove the following:

$$\forall n \cdot (n = \min(cc) \;\Rightarrow\; (s(n) = t\,(n) \;\Leftrightarrow\; s = t\,))$$

The following substitution tests whether a sequence is a *prefix* of another one:

$b \longleftarrow \mathsf{IsPrefix}\,(s,t) \;\;\widehat{=}$

     PRE

         $s \in \mathsf{seq_1}(\mathbb{N}) \quad \wedge$
         $t \in \mathsf{seq_1}(\mathbb{N}) \quad \wedge$
         $\mathsf{front}\,(s) \in \mathsf{seq}\,(\mathbb{N}_1) \quad \wedge$
         $\mathsf{front}\,(t) \in \mathsf{seq}\,(\mathbb{N}_1) \quad \wedge$
         $\mathsf{last}\,(s) = 0 \quad \wedge$
         $\mathsf{last}\,(t) = 0$

     THEN

         VAR n IN

            $n \longleftarrow \mathsf{MinIndexSeq}\,(s,t)\,;$
            $b := \mathsf{bool}(s(n) = 0)$

         END

     END

Algorithm 10.1.6

and we can prove formally the following (exercise):

$\mathsf{PRE} \;\Rightarrow\; [b \longleftarrow \mathsf{IsPrefix}\,(s,t)]$
         $(b = \mathsf{true} \;\Leftrightarrow\; \mathsf{front}\,(s) \subseteq \mathsf{front}\,(t))$ Property 10.1.5

Hint: again, it is sufficient to prove the following:

$$\forall n \cdot (n = \min\,(cc) \;\Rightarrow\; (s(n) = 0 \;\Leftrightarrow\; \mathsf{front}\,(s) \subseteq \mathsf{front}\,(t)))$$

10.1.3. Computing the Natural Number Inverse of a Function

As another application of the framework introduced in section 10.1.1, we would like to construct now two substitutions able to "compute" the value of the *natural number inverse* of a *monotonic* natural number function, and this, either *by excess* or *by defect*. More precisely, we suppose that we have been given a natural number function f obeying the following conditions:

$$f \in \mathbb{N} \to \mathbb{N}$$

$$m \in \mathbb{N} \;\Rightarrow\; f(m) < f(m+1)$$

From the second condition, we can deduce (proof by induction on n) the following:

$$m \in \mathbb{N} \;\wedge\; n \in \mathbb{N} \;\wedge\; m < n \;\Rightarrow\; f(m) < f(n)$$

From this condition, we deduce that, when a natural number m is distinct from a natural number n (that is, when one of $m < n$ or $n < m$ holds), then $f(m)$

is distinct from $f(n)$. As a consequence, the function f is *injective*. Thus, given a natural number p, there exists *at most* one natural number r such that $f(r)$ is equal to p. The number r is called the *inverse* of p under f. However, the function f is not necessarily *surjective*, so that, given a number p, such a number r does not always exist. In order to *totalize* the inversion process, we may apply two distinct strategies: either we take an inverse *by excess* or an inverse *by defect*. Here are examples of the two natural number inverses of the square function at the point 14:

$$\lfloor \sqrt{14} \rfloor = 3$$

$$\lceil \sqrt{14} \rceil = 4$$

These results follow from double inequality

$$3^2 < 14 < 4^2$$

The inverse "by excess"

In the "by excess" case, we take, for the inverse of f at p, the smallest natural number r such that p is smaller than or equal to $f(r)$. In other words, we take the minimum of the following set e:

$$e = \{n \mid n \in \mathbb{N} \ \wedge \ p \leq f(n)\}$$

In fact, the minimum r is such that the following equivalent condition holds:

$$r = 0 \ \Rightarrow \ p \leq f(0)$$

$$r > 0 \ \Rightarrow \ f(r-1) < p \leq f(r)$$

Condition E

The inverse "by defect"

In the "by defect" case, we take, for the inverse of f at p, the smallest natural number r such that p is (strictly) smaller than $f(r+1)$. In other words, we take the minimum of the following set d:

$$d = \{n \mid n \in \mathbb{N} \ \wedge \ p < f(n+1)\}$$

In fact, the minimum r is such that the following equivalent condition holds:

$$r = 0 \quad \Rightarrow \quad p < f(1)$$

$$r > 0 \quad \Rightarrow \quad f(r) \le p < f(r+1)$$

Condition D

We notice that Condition D is not as "pure" as Condition E. When p is (strictly) smaller than $f(0)$, the value of the inverse by defect of p is 0, and this despite the fact that 0 is clearly a "by excess" inverse. This is because, we want the inversion process to yield a natural number. Of course, this does not cause any harm when $f(0)$ is exactly equal to 0, since, in that case, the natural number p cannot be (strictly) smaller than $f(0)$. This is what we have for the multiplication by a number and for the squaring function. Consequently, we have no pathological case for natural number division or for natural number square root. But this is not the case for the exponentiation function. For instance, as we know (section 3.5.7), the logarithm by defect in the base b (where b is greater than 1) of 0 is 0, and this despite the fact that the value of b^0 is 1, a number that is clearly "in excess" with regard to 0.

We now define the substitution $r \longleftarrow \mathsf{InvExc}\,(f,p)$ by means of the substitution $r \longleftarrow \mathsf{MinSet}\,(e)$ as defined by Algorithm 10.1.1.

$r \longleftarrow \mathsf{InvExc}(f,p) \quad \widehat{=}$
> PRE
>> $f \in \mathbb{N} \to \mathbb{N} \quad \wedge$
>> $\forall m \cdot (m \in \mathbb{N} \;\Rightarrow\; f(m) < f(m+1)) \quad \wedge$
>> $p \in \mathbb{N}$
> THEN
>> $r \longleftarrow \mathsf{MinSet}\,(e)$
> END

Since, clearly, the set e is non-empty (this is because the function f is monotonic), then the pre-condition of InvExc implies the instantiated pre-condition of MinSet. As a consequence, and according to Property 10.1.1, we have

---

Property 10.1.6

$\mathsf{PRE} \;\Rightarrow\; [r \longleftarrow \mathsf{InvExc}(f,p)]$
$\qquad\qquad (r = 0 \;\Rightarrow\; p \le f(0)) \quad \wedge \quad (r > 0 \;\Rightarrow\; f(r-1) < p \le f(r))$

We can thus expand in-line the instantiated text of Algorithm 10.1.1 (where the pre-condition is removed), yielding

$r \longleftarrow \mathsf{InvExc}(f, p) \ \widehat{=}$

    PRE

        $f \in \mathbb{N} \to \mathbb{N} \quad \wedge$
        $\forall m \cdot (m \in \mathbb{N} \ \Rightarrow \ f(m) < f(m + 1)) \quad \wedge$
        $p \in \mathbb{N}$

    THEN

        $r := 0;$
        WHILE $\quad r \notin \{n \mid n \in \mathbb{N} \ \wedge \ p \le f(n)\} \quad$ DO
          $r := r + 1$
        INVARIANT
          $r \in 0 .. \min(\{n \mid n \in \mathbb{N} \ \wedge \ p \le f(n)\})$
        VARIANT
          $\min(\{n \mid n \in \mathbb{N} \ \wedge \ p \le f(n)\}) - r$
        END

    END

By applying the rule **LOOP 3**, we can easily change the guard, yielding the following final algorithm:

$r \longleftarrow \mathsf{InvExc}(f, p) \ \widehat{=}$

    PRE

        $f \in \mathbb{N} \to \mathbb{N} \quad \wedge$
        $\forall m \cdot (m \in \mathbb{N} \ \Rightarrow \ f(m) < f(m + 1)) \quad \wedge$
        $p \in \mathbb{N}$

    THEN

        $r := 0;$
        WHILE $\quad f(r) < p \quad$ DO
          $r := r + 1$
        INVARIANT
          $r \in 0 .. \min(\{n \mid n \in \mathbb{N} \ \wedge \ p \le f(n)\})$
        VARIANT
          $\min(\{n \mid n \in \mathbb{N} \ \wedge \ p \le f(n)\}) - r$
        END

    END

Algorithm 10.1.7

Likewise, we obtain the following:

$$r \longleftarrow \mathsf{InvDef}(f,p) \;\; \widehat{=}$$

PRE

$$f \in \mathbb{N} \to \mathbb{N} \quad \wedge$$
$$\forall m \cdot (m \in \mathbb{N} \;\Rightarrow\; f(m) < f(m+1)) \quad \wedge$$
$$p \in \mathbb{N}$$

THEN

$$r := 0;$$

WHILE $f(r+1) \leq p$ DO

$$r := r+1$$

INVARIANT

$$r \in 0 \mathinner{\ldotp\ldotp} \min(\{n \mid n \in \mathbb{N} \wedge p < f(n+1)\})$$

VARIANT

$$\min(\{n \mid n \in \mathbb{N} \wedge p < f(n+1)\}) - r$$

END

END

Algorithm 10.1.8

together with

Property 10.1.7

$$\mathsf{PRE} \;\Rightarrow\; [r \longleftarrow \mathsf{InvDef}(f,p)]$$
$$(r = 0 \;\Rightarrow\; p < f(1)) \quad \wedge \quad (r > 0 \;\Rightarrow\; f(r) \leq p < f(r+1))$$

10.1.4. Natural Number Division

As an application of the scheme presented in the previous section, we shall construct, in this section, a substitution computing the natural number division of two natural numbers. Given a *positive* natural number b, we remind the reader (section 3.5.7) that $\mathsf{mult}(b)$ is the obviously monotonic function from $\mathbb{N}$ to itself which "multiplies by b" (when b is equal to 0, $\mathsf{mult}(b)$ is *not monotonic*, it is just a constant function with value 0). This function can then be "natural number inverted" by the following algorithm:

$$q \longleftarrow \mathsf{Div}(a,b) \;\; \widehat{=}$$

PRE

$$a \in \mathbb{N} \quad \wedge$$
$$b \in \mathbb{N}_1$$

THEN

$$q \longleftarrow \mathsf{InvDef}(\mathsf{mult}(b), a)$$

END

This algorithm clearly computes the natural number division of a by b, which is equal, by definition (section 3.5.7), to the following:

$$a/b \;=\; \min\left(\{n \mid n \in \mathbb{N} \;\wedge\; a < b \times (n+1)\}\right)$$

After Algorithm 10.1.8, and since the call is clearly done within the pre-condition, we then have the following (since $\mathsf{mult}(b)(q+1)$ is equal to $b \times (q+1)$):

$$
\begin{aligned}
&q \longleftarrow \mathsf{Div}(a,b) \;\; \widehat{=} \\
&\quad \text{PRE} \\
&\qquad\quad a \in \mathbb{N} \quad \wedge \\
&\qquad\quad b \in \mathbb{N}_1 \\
&\quad \text{THEN} \\
&\qquad\quad q := 0; \\
&\qquad \text{WHILE}\quad b \times (q+1) \le a \quad \text{DO} \\
&\qquad\qquad q := q+1 \\
&\qquad \text{INVARIANT} \\
&\qquad\qquad q \in 0\mathinner{.\,.}a/b \\
&\qquad \text{VARIANT} \\
&\qquad\qquad a/b - q \\
&\qquad \text{END} \\
&\quad \text{END}
\end{aligned}
$$

Algorithm 10.1.9

And, according to **Property 10.1.7**, we have

$$\text{PRE} \;\Rightarrow\; [\,q \longleftarrow \mathsf{Div}(a,b)\,]\,(q = 0 \;\Rightarrow\; a < b) \wedge (q > 0 \;\Rightarrow\; b \times q \le a < b \times (q+1))$$

As the post-condition can be simplified to $0 \le a - b \times q < b$, we have equivalently

---

$$\text{PRE} \;\Rightarrow\; [\,q \longleftarrow \mathsf{Div}(a,b)\,]\,(0 \le a - b \times q < b) \qquad\qquad \text{Property 10.1.8}$$

Note that the remainder, $a - (b \times q)$, of this division has indeed the well-known property. Notice again that the minimum we are computing corresponds exactly to the definition given in section 3.5.7. So that, we have indeed

---

$$\text{PRE} \;\Rightarrow\; [\,q \longleftarrow \mathsf{Div}(a,b)\,]\,(q = a/b) \qquad\qquad\qquad \text{Property 10.1.9}$$

10.1.5. The Special Case of Recursive Functions

Going back to our original substitution $r \longleftarrow \mathsf{InvDef}(f, p)$, as given by Algorithm 10.1.8, we can see that the expression $f(r+1)$ appears in the guard of this loop. In what follows, we would like to improve the calculation of this expression a little.

We suppose we are given a natural number a and a total function g from $\mathbb{N}$ to $\mathbb{N}$, formally

$$a \in \mathbb{N}$$

$$g \in \mathbb{N} \to \mathbb{N}$$

We suppose now that the function f can be defined *recursively* (section 3.5.6) as follows, for each natural number r:

$$\begin{cases} f(0) = a \\ f(r+1) = g(f(r)) \end{cases}$$

Then, an obvious slight improvement of the previous loop consists of computing $f(r+1)$ gradually from an already known value of $f(r)$. This leads to the following algorithm, obtained from InvDef by adding an extra fresh variable, k, initialized to $g(a)$ and modified in the body of the loop by the statement $k := g(k)$:

$$
\begin{array}{l}
r \longleftarrow \mathsf{RecInvDef}(g, a, p) \quad \widehat{=} \\
\quad \text{PRE} \\
\qquad g \in \mathbb{N} \to \mathbb{N} \quad \wedge \\
\qquad a \in \mathbb{N} \quad \wedge \\
\qquad \forall m \cdot (m \in \mathbb{N} \;\Rightarrow\; m < g(m)) \quad \wedge \\
\qquad p \in \mathbb{N} \\
\quad \text{THEN} \\
\qquad \text{VAR} \quad k \quad \text{IN} \\
\qquad\quad r, k := 0, g(a); \\
\qquad\quad \text{WHILE} \quad f(r+1) \leq p \quad \text{DO} \\
\qquad\qquad r, k := r+1, g(k) \\
\qquad\quad \text{INVARIANT} \\
\qquad\qquad \cdots \\
\qquad\quad \text{END} \\
\qquad \text{END} \\
\quad \text{END}
\end{array}
$$

We can now prove that the condition $k = f(r+1)$ is an extra invariant of this loop. We can then replace the guard $f(r+1) \leq p$ by $k \leq p$:

$$r \longleftarrow \text{RecInvDef}(g, a, p) \quad \hat{=}$$
PRE
  . . .
THEN
  VAR k IN
    $r, k := 0, g(a);$
    WHILE $k \le p$ DO
      $r, k := r + 1, g(k)$
    INVARIANT
      . . .
    END
  END
END

Algorithm 10.1.10

By a similar exercise, we can derive the following substitution for the "by excess" case (here the extra invariant $k = f(r)$ should hold):

$$r \longleftarrow \text{RecInvExc}(g, a, p) \quad \hat{=}$$
PRE
  . . .
THEN
  VAR k IN
    $r, k := 0, a;$
    WHILE $k < p$ DO
      $r, k := r + 1, g(k)$
    INVARIANT
      . . .
    END
  END
END

Algorithm 10.1.11

For instance, the function mult(b) of our previous example is defined recursively as follows (section 3.5.7):

$$\begin{cases} \text{mult}(b)(0) = 0 \\ \text{mult}(b)(n + 1) = \text{plus}(b)(\text{mult}(b)(n)) \end{cases}$$

where the function plus (b) has been defined, again, in section 3.5.7. As a consequence, mult (b) can be "natural number inverted" by the substitution

$$q \longleftarrow \mathsf{RecInvDef}(\mathsf{plus}(b), 0, a)$$

and we can redefine the substitution $q \longleftarrow \mathsf{Div}(a, b)$ as follows according to Algorithm 10.1.10 (bearing in mind that $\mathsf{plus}\,(b)(k)$ is equal to $k + b$):

$$q \longleftarrow \mathsf{Div}(a, b) \quad \widehat{=}$$

PRE
$$a \in \mathbb{N} \quad \wedge$$
$$b \in \mathbb{N}_1$$

THEN
    VAR k IN
$$q, k := 0, b\,;$$
      WHILE $k \leq a$ DO
$$q, k := q + 1, k + b$$
      INVARIANT
$$r \in 0 .. a/b \quad \wedge$$
$$k = b \times (q + 1)$$
      VARIANT
$$a/b - q$$
      END
    END
END

Algorithm 10.1.12

10.1.6. Logarithm in a Given Base

As another example, we remind the reader of the function exp (section 3.5.7) which yields "the nth power of x", that is

$$\mathsf{exp}\,(x)(n) = x^n$$

When x is greater than 1, this function is monotonic (when x is either 0 or 1, it is a function with constant value x, except for 0^0 which is equal, by definition, to 1). The function $\mathsf{exp}(x)$ was defined recursively as follows:

$$\begin{cases} \mathsf{exp}(x)(0) & = \quad 1 \\ \mathsf{exp}(x)(n + 1) & = \quad \mathsf{mult}(x)(\mathsf{exp}(x)(n)) \end{cases}$$

Hence, its "natural number inverse", computed by the substitution $l \longleftarrow \mathsf{Log}\,(x, y)$, is equal to $l \longleftarrow \mathsf{RecInvDef}(\mathsf{mult}(x), 1, y)$ yielding, according to Algorithm 10.1.10 (since $\mathsf{mult}\,(x)(k)$ is equal to $k \times x$)

$$l \longleftarrow \mathsf{Log}\,(x,y) \ \ \widehat{=}$$

    PRE

$$x \in \mathbb{N} \quad \wedge$$
$$x > 1 \ \wedge$$
$$y \in \mathbb{N}$$

    THEN

        VAR k IN

$$l,k \ := 0,x\,;$$

            WHILE $k \le y$ DO

$$l,k \ := l+1, k \times x$$

            INVARIANT

$$l \in 0\,..\,\log_x(y) \quad \wedge$$
$$k = x^{l+1}$$

            VARIANT

$$\log_x(y) - l$$

            END

        END

    END

Algorithm 10.1.13

Applying Property 10.1.7, this substitution is then such that

---

Property 10.1.10

$$\mathsf{PRE} \ \Rightarrow \ [l \longleftarrow \mathsf{Log}\,(x,y)]$$
$$(l = 0 \ \Rightarrow \ y < x) \ \wedge \ (l > 0 \ \Rightarrow \ x^l \le y < x^{l+1})$$

Notice that the minimum we are computing corresponds exactly to the definition given in section 3.5.7. So that we have indeed

---

$$\mathsf{PRE} \ \Rightarrow \ [l \longleftarrow \mathsf{Log}\,(x,y)]\,(l = \log_x(y))$$ Property 10.1.11

10.1.7. Integer Square Root

As a last example of the scheme developed in section 10.1.3, consider the following squaring function which is indeed monotonic:

$$\mathsf{square} = \lambda\, n.(n \in \mathbb{N} \mid n^2)$$

In order to compute the natural number inverse of this function (with the substitution $r \longleftarrow \mathsf{Sqrt}\,(p)$), the best thing we can do is to use our general framework, that is, in this case, the substitution $r \longleftarrow \mathsf{InvDef}(\mathsf{square}, p)$. This is so because, apparently, the function **square** cannot be defined recursively. This yields the following according to Algorithm 10.1.8:

$r \longleftarrow \mathsf{Sqrt}(p) \quad \hat{=}$

  PRE

      $p \in \mathbb{N}$

  THEN

      $r := 0;$

    WHILE $(r+1)^2 \leq p$ DO

      $r := r + 1$

  INVARIANT

      $r \in 0 \, .. \, \min(\{n \mid n \in \mathbb{N} \ \wedge \ p < (n+1)^2\})$

  VARIANT

      $\min(\{n \mid n \in \mathbb{N} \ \wedge \ p < (n+1)^2\}) - r$

  END

END

Algorithm 10.1.14

and we have, according to Property 10.1.7

    PRE $\Rightarrow$ $[r \longleftarrow \mathsf{Sqrt}(p)]\,((r = 0 \ \Rightarrow \ p < 1) \ \wedge \ (r > 0 \ \Rightarrow \ r^2 \leq p < (r+1)^2))$

As the post-condititon can be simplified to $r^2 \leq p < (r+1)^2$, we obtain

---

    PRE $\Rightarrow$ $[r \longleftarrow \mathsf{Sqrt}(p)]\,(r^2 \leq p < (r+1)^2)$ Property 10.1.12

However, the expansion of the square of $r + 1$, that is $r^2 + (2r + 1)$, suggests looking for a recursive function f yielding *simultaneously* r^2 and $2r + 1$, that is:

$$f(r) = (r^2, \ 2r + 1)$$

We have indeed (exercise):

$$\begin{cases} f(0) = (0, 1) \\[2mm] f(r+1) = g(f(r)) \end{cases}$$

$$\text{where} \quad g(a, b) = (a + b, b + 2)$$

As a consequence, using the substitution RecInvDef (as defined by Algorithm 10.1.10) and introducing two extra variables instead of one, we obtain the following substitution since, obviously, $g(0,1)$ is equal to the pair $(1,3)$. Also notice that in the invariant, the pair (a,b), being equal to $f(r+1)$ (according to Algorithm 10.1.10), is thus equal to the pair $((r+1)^2, \ 2r+3)$

$$r \longleftarrow \mathsf{Sqrt}\,(p) \quad \hat{=}$$

PRE

$$p \in \mathbb{N}$$

THEN

VAR a, b IN

$$r, a, b := 0, 1, 3\,;$$

WHILE $a \le p$ DO

$$r, a, b := r + 1,\; a + b,\; b + 2$$

INVARIANT

$$r \in 0 \,..\, \min(\{n \mid n \in \mathbb{N} \;\wedge\; p < (n + 1)^2\}) \quad \wedge$$
$$a = (r + 1)^2 \quad \wedge$$
$$b = 2r + 3$$

VARIANT

$$\min\,(\{n \mid n \in \mathbb{N} \;\wedge\; p < (n + 1)^2\}) - r$$

END

END

END

Algorithm 10.1.15

10.2. Bounded Search

10.2.1. Introduction

In this section we have exactly the same goal as in section 10.1.1, namely that of constructing a substitution computing the minimum of a non-empty set c of natural numbers. But this time we assume that we have more information at our disposal:

1. We are given two natural numbers, a and b, such that, somehow, we know that $\min(c)$ belongs to the interval $a..b$. This is why our search is said to be "bounded".

2. We have a way to, somehow, *easily* compare $\min(c)$ with any member of the interval $a..b$.

With this in mind, we would like then to construct a substitution, named $r \longleftarrow \mathsf{BoundedMinSearch}\,(a, b, c)$, establishing the post-condition $r = \min(c)$. The idea underlying this construction is to reduce the difference between two natural numbers r and k, both belonging to the interval $a..b$, and such that $\min(c)$ belongs to the interval $r..k$. This suggests the construction of a loop of the following form (where S is a substitution):

$$r, k := a, b;$$
$$\text{WHILE} \quad r \neq k \quad \text{DO}$$
$$S$$
INVARIANT
$$r \in a \mathinner{..} b \quad \wedge$$
$$k \in a \mathinner{..} b \quad \wedge$$
$$\min(c) \in r \mathinner{..} k$$
VARIANT
$$k - r$$
END

Clearly, at the end of the loop, where the guard does not hold any more, the condition $r = k$ holds and, according to the invariant (which still holds), we have then $\min(c) \in r \mathinner{..} r$, so that the value of r is indeed equal to $\min(c)$. We now have to make explicit the body S of the loop. We propose the following:

$$\text{ANY} \quad m \quad \text{WHERE}$$
$$m \in (r + 1) \mathinner{..} k$$
THEN
$$\text{IF} \quad \min(c) < m \quad \text{THEN}$$
$$k := m - 1$$
ELSE
$$r := m$$
END
END

The idea is to choose *any* number m situated within the interval $(r + 1) \mathinner{..} k$. Notice that such a number m always exists. This is so because, within the loop, the predicate $r + 1 \leq k$ always holds. This is a consequence of the facts that $r \leq k$ holds according to the invariant and $r \neq k$ holds according to the guard. We then compare $\min(c)$ and m, and we take either the "new" k to be $m - 1$ (when $\min(c) < m$), or the "new" r to be m (when $m \leq \min(c)$). So that, in either case, the invariant is indeed preserved and the variant indeed decreases. Formally, this is a consequence of the following lemmas:

$$r \in a\mathbin{..}b \qquad\qquad r \in a\mathbin{..}b$$
$$k \in a\mathbin{..}b \qquad\qquad k \in a\mathbin{..}b$$
$$l \in r\mathbin{..}k \qquad\qquad\; l \in r\mathbin{..}k$$
$$m \in (r+1)\mathbin{..}k \qquad m \in (r+1)\mathbin{..}k$$
$$l < m \qquad\qquad\quad m \le l$$
$$\Rightarrow \qquad\qquad\qquad \Rightarrow$$
$$m-1 \in a\mathbin{..}b \qquad\; m \in a\mathbin{..}b$$
$$l \in r\mathbin{..}m-1 \qquad\; l \in m\mathbin{..}k$$
$$m-1-r < k-r \qquad k-m < k-r$$

We thus propose the following substitution:

$r \longleftarrow$ BoundedMinSearch$(a,b,c) \ \hat{=}$

    PRE

        $a \in \mathbb{N} \quad \wedge$
        $b \in \mathbb{N} \quad \wedge$
        $c \in \mathbb{P}_1(\mathbb{N}) \quad \wedge$
        $\min(c) \in a\mathbin{..}b$

    THEN

        VAR k IN

          $r,k := a,b \,;$

          WHILE $r \ne k$ DO

            ANY m WHERE

              $m \in (r+1)\mathbin{..}k$

            THEN

              IF $\min(c) < m$ THEN

                $k := m-1$

              ELSE

                $r := m$

              END

            END

          INVARIANT

            $r \in a\mathbin{..}b \;\; \wedge$
            $k \in a\mathbin{..}b \;\; \wedge$
            $\min(c) \in r\mathbin{..}k$

          VARIANT

            $k-r$

          END

        END

    END

Algorithm 10.2.1

We can then prove the following property (exercise):

$$\text{PRE} \;\Rightarrow\; [r \longleftarrow \text{BoundedMinSearch}(a,b,c)] \; (r = \min(c))$$

The problem, of course, is now to find cases where a comparison of the form $\min(c) < m$, which occurs in the substitution $r \longleftarrow \text{BoundedMinSearch}(a,b,c)$, is easily implementable independently of $\min(c)$. This is what we are going to investigate in sections 10.2.2 and 10.2.3.

10.2.2. Linear Search

In the previous section we developed an algorithm made of a loop whose body was of the following non-deterministic form

```
ANY   m   WHERE
    m ∈ (r + 1) .. k
THEN
    IF   min(c) < m   THEN
        k := m − 1
    ELSE
        r := m
    END
END
```

In this section we are looking for a (first) way to make that substitution more deterministic. We also want the comparision of $\min(c)$ with m to be made independently of $\min(c)$. This non-deterministic substitution is replaced by a completely deterministic one, obtained by "choosing" a particular value for m within the interval $(r + 1) .. k$. In fact, we simply choose m to be $r + 1$. The condition $\min(c) < m$ is then equivalent to $\min(c) < r + 1$, that is $\min(c) \le r$, that is $\min(c) = r$ (since the condition $r \le \min(c)$ already holds, according to the invariant of the loop). Finally, this equality between r and $\min(c)$ reduces equivalently to $r \in c$ (since, again, we have $r \le \min(c)$). We shall thus replace the previous substitution by the following one:

```
IF   r ∈ c   THEN
    k := r
ELSE
    r := r + 1
END
```

Notice that our *choice* for m obeys the condition of the ANY clause since we obviously have $r + 1 \in (r + 1) .. k$. In section 11.1.4, we shall justify formally our right to replace the body of a loop by a less non-deterministic substitution. Consequently, we can now define the following substitution, as a *special case* (less non-deterministic) of the substitution $r \longleftarrow$ BoundedMinSearch (a, b, c):

$r \longleftarrow$ LinearMinSearch $(a, b, c) \;\widehat{=}$

    PRE

        $a \in \mathbb{N} \quad \wedge$
        $b \in \mathbb{N} \quad \wedge$
        $c \in \mathbb{P}_1(\mathbb{N}) \quad \wedge$
        $min(c) \in a \mathinner{\ldotp\ldotp} b$

    THEN

        VAR $\;k\;$ IN

            $r, k := a, b\,;$

            WHILE $\;r \neq k\;$ DO

                IF $\;r \in c\;$ THEN $\;k := r\;$ ELSE $\;r := r + 1\;$ END

            INVARIANT

                $r \in a \mathinner{\ldotp\ldotp} b \quad \wedge$
                $k \in a \mathinner{\ldotp\ldotp} b \quad \wedge$
                $min(c) \in r \mathinner{\ldotp\ldotp} k$

            VARIANT

                $k - r$

            END

        END

    END

Algorithm 10.2.2

Notice also how the loop is left either *from the middle*, with a result r strictly smaller than b, or else *naturally*, with a result that is exactly b.

Since the substitution $r \longleftarrow$ LinearMinSearch (a, b, c) is *less non-deterministic* than the substitution $r \longleftarrow$ BoundedMinSearch (a, b, c), we can replace the latter by the former in Property 10.2.1 (again, all this is justified in section 11.1.4), yielding:

    PRE $\;\Rightarrow\; [r \longleftarrow$ LinearMinSearch$(a, b, c)] \; (r = min(c))$ Property 10.2.2

10.2.3. Linear Search in an Array

As an application of the framework presented in the previous section, our purpose is to present, in this section, a number of algorithms for doing various searches in an "array". Such a data structure is just a function whose domain is a non-empty interval. More precisely, let a and b be two natural numbers, let s

be a non-empty "array" built on a certain set t and with bounds a and b, and let e be a subset of t. Formally

$$
\begin{aligned}
&a \in \mathbb{N} \\
&b \in \mathbb{N} \\
&a \leq b \\
&s \in (a \mathinner{\ldotp\ldotp} b) \to t \\
&e \subseteq t
\end{aligned}
$$

We would like to construct a substitution, $r \longleftarrow$ SearchSetInArray(a, b, s, e), with the above pre-condition. This substitution is intended to compute the smallest index r of s such that $s(r)$ belongs to the set e, and, in case such an index does not exist, the special value $b + 1$ must be returned. We can call our previous substitution $r \longleftarrow$ LinearMinSearch(a, b, c), defined by Algorithm 10.2.2, replacing b by $b + 1$, and the set c by the inverse image of e under s augmented with the *special* element $b + 1$, that is $c = s^{-1}[e] \cup \{b + 1\}$.

It is easy to establish that the substitution LinearMinSearch $(a, b+1, s^{-1}[e] \cup \{b + 1\})$ is called within its pre-condition and we can expand it in-line within SearchSetInArray. Notice that the condition $r \in c$, appearing in LinearMinSearch, becomes equivalently $s(r) \in e \lor r = b + 1$. But inside the loop, we clearly have $r \neq b + 1$ (since $r < k$). Hence, the condition reduces simply to $s(r) \in e$. We thus have:

$r \longleftarrow$ SearchSetInArray$(a, b, s, e) \ \ \widehat{=}$

    PRE

       . . .

       $e \subseteq t$

    THEN

       VAR k IN

          $r, k := a, b + 1;$

          WHILE $r \neq k$ DO

              IF $s(r) \in e$ THEN $k := r$ ELSE $r := r + 1$ END

          INVARIANT

            . . .

          VARIANT

            $k - r$

          END

       END

    END

Algorithm 10.2.3

And we have

PRE $\Rightarrow$ $[r \longleftarrow \text{SearchSetInArray}(a, b, s, e)]$
$$(r = \min(s^{-1}[e] \cup \{b+1\}))$$

Property 10.2.3

For instance, by replacing, in the above algorithm, the set e by the singleton $\{v\}$, where v is supposed to be a member of t, we obtain the following substitution for searching for the value v:

$r \longleftarrow \text{SearchValueInArray}(a, b, s, v) \ \ \hat{=}$

    PRE

       $\cdots$

       $v \in t$

    THEN

       VAR $\ k \ $ IN

          $r, k := a, b + 1;$

          WHILE $\ r \neq k \ $ DO

              IF $\ s(r) = v \ $ THEN $\ k := r \ $ ELSE $\ r := r + 1 \ $ END

          INVARIANT

              $\cdots$

          VARIANT

              $k - r$

          END

       END

    END

Algorithm 10.2.4

We have then

PRE $\Rightarrow$ $[r \longleftarrow \text{SearchValueInArray}(a, b, s, v)]$
$$(r = \min(s^{-1}[\{v\}] \cup \{b+1\}))$$

Property 10.2.4

10.2.4. Linear Search in a Matrix

In this section we generalize what we have done in the previous section, for one-dimensional arrays, to arrays of dimension two or more. The idea is to have exactly *the same loop structure* as previously. This is achieved by transforming our multi-dimensional array into a one-dimensional one. More precisely, we suppose that we have been given a matrix *mat* (built on a set t) which is such that

$$mat \in (0..(c-1)) \times (0..(d-1)) \to t$$

where c and d are supposed to be two *positive* natural numbers. In order to linearize our matrix *mat*, we compose it with a bijection called $\mathsf{linearize}\,(c,d)$ such that

$$\mathsf{linearize}\,(c,d) \;\in\; (0\,..\,(c \times d) - 1) \;\rightarrowtail\; (0\,..\,(c-1)) \times (0\,..\,(d-1))$$

and where we have, for all r in $0\,..\,((c \times d) - 1)$:

$$\mathsf{linearize}\,(c,d)(r) \;=\; (r \bmod c, r/c)$$

So that we have

$$\mathit{mat}\,(\mathsf{linearize}\,(c,d)(r)) \;=\; \mathit{mat}\,(r \bmod c, r/c)$$

For example, this leads to the following algorithm:

$r \longleftarrow \mathsf{SearchValueInMatrix}\,(c,d,\mathit{mat},v) \;\;\widehat{=}$

    PRE

        $c \in \mathbb{N}_1 \quad \wedge$

        $d \in \mathbb{N}_1 \quad \wedge$

        $\mathit{mat} \in (0\,..\,(c-1)) \times (0\,..\,(d-1)) \rightarrow t \quad \wedge$

        $v \in t$

    THEN

        VAR $\;k\;$ IN

            $r,k \;:=\; 0, c \times d\;;$

            WHILE $\;r \neq k\;$ DO

                IF $\;\mathit{mat}\,(r \bmod c, r/c) = v\;$ THEN

                    $k := r$

                ELSE

                    $r := r + 1$

                END

            INVARIANT

                $r \in 0\,..\,c \times d \quad \wedge$

                $k \in 0\,..\,c \times d \quad \wedge$

                $\min((\mathit{mat} \circ \mathsf{linearize}(c,d))^{-1}[\{v\}] \;\cup\; \{c \times d\}) \in r\,..\,k$

            VARIANT

                $k - r$

        END

        END

    END

Algorithm 10.2.5

which is equal to

$$r \longleftarrow \mathsf{SearchValueInArray}\,(0,\ c \times d - 1,\ \mathit{mat} \circ \mathsf{linearize}\,(c,d), v)$$

Note that the condition $0 \le c \times d - 1$ holds (since both c and d are supposed to be positive) and also that the function $mat \circ \mathsf{linearize}\,(c,d)$ is indeed a function from $0\,..\,c \times d - 1$ to t (since $\mathsf{linearize}\,(c,d)$ is a bijection). Hence, the algorithm SearchValueInArray is called within its pre-condition, and it can thus be expanded in-line, yielding

---

Property 10.2.5

$$\mathsf{PRE} \;\Rightarrow\; [\,r \longleftarrow \mathsf{SearchValueInMatrix}(c,d,mat,v)\,]$$
$$(r = \min((mat \circ \mathsf{linearize}(c,d))^{-1}[\{v\}] \;\cup\; \{c \times d\}))$$

The linearization technique used in this section for a two-dimensional array could easily be generalized to more dimensions. Again, the interesting aspect of such algorithms is that we leave the loop "from the middle", as soon as the result is found.

10.2.5. Binary Search

In section 10.2.1, we developed an algorithm made of a loop whose body was of the following non-deterministic form:

$$
\begin{aligned}
&\text{ANY} \quad m \quad \text{WHERE} \\
&\qquad m \in (r+1)\,..\,k \\
&\text{THEN} \\
&\qquad \text{IF} \quad \min(c) < m \quad \text{THEN} \\
&\qquad\qquad k := m - 1 \\
&\qquad \text{ELSE} \\
&\qquad\qquad r := m \\
&\qquad \text{END} \\
&\text{END}
\end{aligned}
$$

In this section we are looking for a (second) way to make that substitution more deterministic. We also want the comparison of $\min(c)$ with m to be made independently of $\min(c)$. In fact, there exists a typical case where the test can be evaluated easily without referring to $\min(c)$. This is when the set c is *monotonic*, formally

$$\forall n \cdot (n \in c \;\Rightarrow\; n+1 \in c)$$

Because then we have

$$m-1 \in c \;\Leftrightarrow\; \min(c) < m$$

Notice that the proof of the first implication,

$$m-1 \in c \;\Rightarrow\; \min(c) < m$$

does not require the monotonicity property of the set c (it simply follows from the basic property of min and from the fact that $m - 1$ is indeed a natural number). Whereas the second implication,

$$\min(c) < m \quad \Rightarrow \quad m - 1 \in c$$

does not hold in general (here, we definitely need the monotonicity property). As a consequence, the substitution $r \longleftarrow$ BoundedMinSearch (a, b, c) becomes

$r \longleftarrow$ BoundedMonMinSearch$(a, b, c) \;\; \widehat{=}$

    PRE

        $a \in \mathbb{N} \quad \wedge$

        $b \in \mathbb{N} \quad \wedge$

        $c \in \mathbb{P}_1(\mathbb{N}) \quad \wedge$

        $\min(c) \in a\mathbin{..}b \quad \wedge$

        $\forall n \cdot (n \in c \;\Rightarrow\; n + 1 \in c)$

    THEN

        VAR k IN

        $r, k := a, b\,;$

          WHILE $r \neq k$ DO

            ANY m WHERE

                $m \in (r + 1)\mathbin{..}k$

            THEN

               IF $m - 1 \in c$ THEN

                  $k := m - 1$

               ELSE

                  $r := m$

               END

            END

          INVARIANT

            $r \in a\mathbin{..}b \quad \wedge$

            $k \in a\mathbin{..}b \quad \wedge$

            $\min(c) \in r\mathbin{..}k$

          VARIANT

            $k - r$

          END

        END

    END

Algorithm 10.2.6

In section 11.1.4 we shall justify formally our right to replace the body of a loop by a less non-deterministic substitution. Consequently, we feel free now to choose m to be the *middle* point, $(r + 1 + k)/2$, of the interval $(r + 1)\mathbin{..}k$. That middle point, certainly, is a member of the interval $(r+1)..k$. We finally obtain the following substitution, named $r \longleftarrow$ BinMinSearch (a, b, c):

```
r ⟵ BinMinSearch(a, b, c)  ≙
    PRE
        . . .
    THEN
        VAR  k  IN
            r, k := a, b ;
            WHILE  r ≠ k  DO
                LET  m  BE
                    m = (r + 1 + k)/2
                IN
                    IF  m − 1 ∈ c  THEN
                        k := m − 1
                    ELSE
                        r := m
                    END
            END
        INVARIANT
            . . .
        END
    END
END
```

Algorithm 10.2.7

And, then, the following holds:

PRE $\Rightarrow$ $[r \longleftarrow$ BinMinSearch$(a, b, c)]$ $(r = \min(c))$ Property 10.2.6

In order to use this substitution, we should look now for problems where the set c is monotonic. This is what we intend to do in the two subsequent sections.

10.2.6. Monotonic Functions Revisited

In section 10.1.3, we developed two substitutions for computing the natural number inverse (either by excess or by defect) of a *monotonic* natural number function f at some point p. These substitutions computed the minimum of two sets e and d respectively. Since the function f is monotonic, *then so are these sets*. As a consequence, the substitution BinMinSearch, defined as Algorithm 10.2.7 in the previous section, is a good candidate for computing the minimum of these sets (provided, of course, we are able to find two numbers a and b such that $\min(e) \in a \mathrel{..} b$ and $\min(d) \in a \mathrel{..} b$, respectively).

For instance, here is a substitution calculating the natural number inverse by defect. Notice that the condition $m - 1 \in \{n \mid n \in \mathbb{N} \wedge p < f(n + 1)\}$, which occurs in the substitution $r \longleftarrow \mathsf{BinMinSearch}(a, b, d)$, becomes, equivalently, $p < f(m)$. As a result, we obtain

---

$r \longleftarrow \mathsf{BinInvDef}(f, a, b, p) \;\; \widehat{=}$

  PRE

  $\quad f \in \mathbb{N} \to \mathbb{N} \quad \wedge$
  $\quad \forall m \cdot (m \in \mathbb{N} \;\Rightarrow\; f(m) < f(m+1)) \quad \wedge$
  $\quad a \in \mathbb{N} \quad \wedge$
  $\quad b \in \mathbb{N} \quad \wedge$
  $\quad p \in \mathbb{N} \quad \wedge$
  $\quad \min(\{n \mid n \in \mathbb{N} \wedge p < f(n+1)\}) \in a \mathrel{..} b$

  THEN

  $\quad$ VAR $\quad k \quad$ IN

  $\qquad r, k := a, b \,;$

  $\qquad$ WHILE $\quad r \neq k \quad$ DO

  $\qquad\quad$ LET $\quad m \quad$ BE

  $\qquad\qquad m = (r + 1 + k)/2$

  $\qquad\quad$ IN

  $\qquad\qquad$ IF $\quad p < f(m) \quad$ THEN

  $\qquad\qquad\quad k := m - 1$

  $\qquad\qquad$ ELSE

  $\qquad\qquad\quad r := m$

  $\qquad\qquad$ END

  $\qquad\quad$ END

  $\qquad$ INVARIANT

  $\qquad\quad$ . . .

  $\qquad$ END

  $\quad$ END

  END

Algorithm 10.2.8

And we have the following:

$\mathsf{PRE} \;\Rightarrow\; [r \longleftarrow \mathsf{BinInvDef}(f, p)]$
$\qquad (r = 0 \;\Rightarrow\; p < f(1)) \quad \wedge \quad (r > 0 \;\Rightarrow\; f(r) \le p < f(r+1))$

In the "by excess" case, we propose the following substitution. Notice that the condition $m - 1 \in \{n \mid n \in \mathbb{N} \ \wedge \ p \le f(n)\}$, which occurs in the substitution BinMinSearch (a, b, e), becomes, equivalently, $p \le f(m-1)$ since, again, we have $m - 1 \in \mathbb{N}$. As a result, we obtain

$$r \longleftarrow \text{BinInvExc}(f, a, b, p) \ \ \widehat{=}$$
PRE
$$\ldots$$
THEN
VAR $\ k \ $ IN
$$r, k := a, b \, ;$$
WHILE $\ r \ne k \ $ DO
LET $\ m \ $ BE
$$m = (r + 1 + k)/2$$
IN
IF $\ p \le f(m - 1) \ $ THEN
$$k := m - 1$$
ELSE
$$r := m$$
END
END
INVARIANT
$$\ldots$$
END
END
END

Algorithm 10.2.9

And we have the following:

Property 10.2.8

PRE $\ \Rightarrow \ [r \longleftarrow \text{BinInvExc}(f, p)]$
$\qquad (r = 0 \ \Rightarrow \ p \le f(0)) \ \wedge \ (r > 0 \ \Rightarrow \ f(r-1) < p \le f(r))$

Our intention is now to reconstruct, using this approach, the algorithms for computing the natural number division, logarithm and square root which have already been developed in sections 10.1.4, 10.1.6 and 10.1.7 respectively. We call these new algorithms BinDiv, BinLog and BinSqrt respectively.

In order to construct, eventually, a substitution yielding the natural number inverse of a function f at p, our remaining problem, however, is to compute two numbers a and b such that the following holds (this is required by the pre-condition of substitution BinInvDef):

$$\min(\{n \mid n \in \mathbb{N} \ \wedge \ p < f(n+1)\}) \in a \mathinner{.\,.} b$$

In what follows, we shall do so case by case. For instance, with division we have

$$a \in \mathbb{N} \,\wedge\, b \in \mathbb{N}_1 \,\Rightarrow\, a/b \in 0..a$$

and also

$$a \in \mathbb{N} \,\wedge\, b \in \mathbb{N}_1 \,\Rightarrow\, \min(\{n \mid n \in \mathbb{N} \,\wedge\, a < b \times (n+1)\}) \,=\, a/b$$

We, thus, certainly have

$$a \in \mathbb{N} \,\wedge\, b \in \mathbb{N}_1 \,\Rightarrow\, \min(\{n \mid n \in \mathbb{N} \,\wedge\, a < b \times (n+1)\}) \in 0..a$$

As a consequence, we can define the substitution $q \longleftarrow \mathrm{BinDiv}(a, b)$ to be equal to $q \longleftarrow \mathrm{BinInvDef}(\mathrm{mult}(b), 0, a, a)$, that is, according to Algorithm 10.2.8,

$$
\begin{aligned}
&r \longleftarrow \mathrm{BinDiv}(a, b) \,\,\widehat{=} \\
&\quad \text{PRE} \\
&\qquad a \in \mathbb{N} \quad \wedge \\
&\qquad b \in \mathbb{N}_1 \\
&\quad \text{THEN} \\
&\qquad \text{VAR} \quad k \quad \text{IN} \\
&\qquad\quad r, k := 0, a\,; \\
&\qquad\quad \text{WHILE} \quad r \neq k \quad \text{DO} \\
&\qquad\qquad \text{LET} \quad m \quad \text{BE} \\
&\qquad\qquad\quad m = (r + 1 + k)/2 \\
&\qquad\qquad \text{IN} \\
&\qquad\qquad\quad \text{IF} \quad a < b \times m \quad \text{THEN} \\
&\qquad\qquad\qquad k := m - 1 \\
&\qquad\qquad\quad \text{ELSE} \\
&\qquad\qquad\qquad r := m \\
&\qquad\qquad\quad \text{END} \\
&\qquad\qquad \text{END} \\
&\qquad\quad \text{INVARIANT} \\
&\qquad\qquad r \in 0..a \quad \wedge \\
&\qquad\qquad k \in 0..a \quad \wedge \\
&\qquad\qquad a/b \in r..k \\
&\qquad\quad \text{VARIANT} \\
&\qquad\qquad k - r \\
&\qquad\quad \text{END} \\
&\qquad \text{END} \\
&\quad \text{END}
\end{aligned}
$$

Algorithm 10.2.10

For the logarithm in a given base, we have

$$\min(\{n \mid n \in \mathbb{N} \,\wedge\, y < x^{n+1}\}) \,=\, \log_x(y)$$

and also

$$x \in \mathbb{N} \ \wedge \ x > 1 \ \wedge \ y \in \mathbb{N} \ \Rightarrow \ \log_x(y) \in 0..y$$

As a consequence, we can define the substitution $n \longleftarrow \mathsf{BinLog}(x, y)$ to be equal to $q \longleftarrow \mathsf{BinInvDef}(\exp(x), 0, y, y)$, that is, according to Algorithm 10.2.8,

$$
\begin{aligned}
&r \longleftarrow \mathsf{BinLog}(x, y) \ \ \widehat{=} \\
&\quad \textsc{PRE} \\
&\qquad x \in \mathbb{N} \quad \wedge \\
&\qquad x > 1 \quad \wedge \\
&\qquad y \in \mathbb{N} \\
&\quad \textsc{THEN} \\
&\qquad \textsc{VAR} \quad k \quad \textsc{IN} \\
&\qquad\quad r, k := 0, y \ ; \\
&\qquad\quad \textsc{WHILE} \quad r \neq k \quad \textsc{DO} \\
&\qquad\qquad \textsc{LET} \quad m \quad \textsc{BE} \\
&\qquad\qquad\quad m = (r + 1 + k)/2 \\
&\qquad\qquad \textsc{IN} \\
&\qquad\qquad\quad \textsc{IF} \quad y < x^m \quad \textsc{THEN} \\
&\qquad\qquad\qquad k := m - 1 \\
&\qquad\qquad\quad \textsc{ELSE} \\
&\qquad\qquad\qquad r := m \\
&\qquad\qquad\quad \textsc{END} \\
&\qquad\qquad \textsc{END} \\
&\qquad\quad \textsc{INVARIANT} \\
&\qquad\qquad r \in 0..y \quad \wedge \\
&\qquad\qquad k \in 0..y \quad \wedge \\
&\qquad\qquad \log_x(y) \in r..k \\
&\qquad\quad \textsc{VARIANT} \\
&\qquad\qquad k - r \\
&\qquad\quad \textsc{END} \\
&\qquad \textsc{END} \\
&\quad \textsc{END}
\end{aligned}
$$

Algorithm 10.2.11

For the integer square root, we have

$$x \in \mathbb{N} \ \Rightarrow \ \min(\{n \mid n \in \mathbb{N} \ \wedge \ x < (n + 1)^2\}) \in 0..x$$

since we obviously have

$$x \in \mathbb{N} \ \Rightarrow \ x < (x + 1)^2$$

As a consequence, we can define the substitution $n \longleftarrow \mathsf{BinSqrt}(x)$ to be equal to $q \longleftarrow \mathsf{BinInvDef}(\mathsf{square}, 0, x, x)$, that is, according to Algorithm 10.2.8,

$r \longleftarrow \mathsf{BinSqrt}(x) \quad \hat{=}$
   PRE
      $x \in \mathbb{N}$
   THEN
      VAR k IN
         $r, k := 0, x$;
         WHILE $r \neq k$ DO
            LET m BE
               $m = (r + 1 + k)/2$
            IN
               IF $x < m^2$ THEN
                  $k := m - 1$
               ELSE
                  $r := m$
               END
            END
         INVARIANT
            $r \in 0 .. x$ $\wedge$
            $k \in 0 .. x$ $\wedge$
            $\min \{ n \mid n \in \mathbb{N} \wedge x < (n+1)^2 \} \in r .. k$
         VARIANT
            $k - r$
         END
      END
   END

Algorithm 10.2.12

10.2.7. Binary Search in an Array

In this section we investigate how to reconstruct the classical binary search in a *non-decreasing* natural number "array" of a natural number argument p. The array is simply a function, s say, whose domain is finite and of the form $a .. b$, where a and b are two *positive* natural numbers such that $a \leq b$. In order to eventually obtain *monotonic* sets (as required by algorithm BinMinSearch of section 10.2.5) we can always extend s so as to become a *non-decreasing* and *unbounded* function f, depending on p, and defined as follows:

$$f = s \ \cup \ \lambda n \cdot (n \in \mathbb{N} \wedge n > b \mid s(b) + p + n)$$

Our intention is to have, as usual, two substitutions computing, respectively, the natural number inverse of f *by excess* or *by defect*.

$r \longleftarrow \mathsf{BinarySearchInArrayExc}(a, b, s, p) \ \hat{=}$

PRE

$a \in \mathbb{N} \quad \wedge$
$b \in \mathbb{N} \quad \wedge$
$a \leq b \quad \wedge$
$s \in (a \mathbin{..} b) \to \mathbb{N} \quad \wedge$
$\forall m \cdot (m \in a \mathbin{..} b - 1 \ \Rightarrow \ s(m) \leq s(m+1)) \quad \wedge$
$p \in \mathbb{N}$

THEN

VAR k IN

$r, k := a, b + 1 \, ;$

WHILE $r \neq k$ DO

LET m BE

$m = (r + 1 + k)/2$

IN

IF $p \leq s(m - 1)$ THEN

$k := m - 1$

ELSE

$r := m$

END

END

INVARIANT

$r \in a \mathbin{..} b + 1 \quad \wedge$
$k \in a \mathbin{..} b + 1 \quad \wedge$
$\min(e) \in r \mathbin{..} k$

VARIANT

$k - r$

END

END

END

Algorithm 10.2.13

In other words, two substitutions computing the minimum of the following sets e and d (section 10.1.3) which, obviously, are *monotonic*:

$$e = \{n \mid n \in \mathbb{N} \ \wedge \ n \geq a \ \wedge \ p \leq f(n)\}$$
$$d = \{n \mid n \in \mathbb{N} \ \wedge \ n \geq a - 1 \ \wedge \ p < f(n+1)\}$$

Notice that we make the set d start at $a - 1$. This is only used in the "by defect" case, in order to be able to compare effectively p with $f(a)$ (and not with $f(a + 1)$). Clearly, the sets e and d are monotonic. In order to be able to use BinMinSearch (Algorithm 10.2.7), however, we have also to find bounds for the minima of these two sets. We propose the following:

$$\min(e) \in a\,..\,(b+1)$$
$$\min(d) \in (a-1)\,..\,b$$

We have $b+1 \in e$ since $p \le f(b+1)$ (in fact, by definition of f, we have $p < f(b+1)$). hence, we have $\min(e) \le b+1$. We certainly have $a \le \min(e)$. We have $b \in d$ since, as we have just seen, we have $p < f(b+1)$. Hence, we have $\min(d) \le b$. Finally, we certainly have $a-1 \le \min(d)$.

The minimum, r, of e can then be computed by the substitution $r \longleftarrow \mathrm{BinMinSearch}\,(a, b+1, e)$ (Algorithm 10.2.7). The minimum r of e is such that the following holds:

$$r = a \quad \Rightarrow \quad p \le f(a)$$
$$r > a \quad \Rightarrow \quad f(r-1) < p \le f(r)$$

After the definition of f in terms of s, this relationship becomes

$$r = a \qquad\qquad \Rightarrow \quad p \le s(a)$$
$$r \in (a+1)\,..\,b \quad \Rightarrow \quad s(r-1) < p \le s(r)$$
$$r = b+1 \qquad\quad \Rightarrow \quad s(b) < p$$

As a result, we have the following:

PRE $\Rightarrow$ $[r \longleftarrow \mathrm{BinarySearchInArrayExc}(a, b, s, p)]$

$$r = a \qquad\qquad \Rightarrow \quad p \le s(a)$$
$$r \in (a+1)\,..\,b \quad \Rightarrow \quad s(r-1) < p \le s(r)$$
$$r = b+1 \qquad\quad \Rightarrow \quad s(b) < p$$

Property 10.2.9

The minimum r of d can then be computed by the substitution $r \longleftarrow \mathrm{BinMinSearch}\,(a-1, b, d)$ as described in Algorithm 10.2.7. This minimum is such that the following holds:

$$r = a-1 \quad \Rightarrow \quad p < f(a)$$
$$r \ge a \qquad\ \Rightarrow \quad f(r) \le p < f(r+1)$$

After the definition of f in terms of s, this relationship becomes the following:

$$r = a-1 \qquad\qquad \Rightarrow \quad p < s(a)$$
$$r \in a\,..\,(b-1) \quad \Rightarrow \quad s(r) \le p < s(r+1)$$
$$r = b \qquad\qquad\quad \Rightarrow \quad s(b) \le p$$

As a result, we have the following:

PRE $\Rightarrow$ $[r \longleftarrow \mathrm{BinarySearchInArrayDef}(a, b, s, p)]$

$$r = a-1 \qquad\qquad \Rightarrow \quad p < s(a)$$
$$r \in a\,..\,(b-1) \quad \Rightarrow \quad s(r) \le p < s(r+1)$$
$$r = b \qquad\qquad\quad \Rightarrow \quad s(b) \le p$$

Property 10.2.10

And here is the corresponding algorithm:

$$r \longleftarrow \text{BinarySearchInArrayDef}(a, b, s, p) \ \hat{=}$$

PRE
$$a \in \mathbb{N} \quad \wedge$$
$$b \in \mathbb{N} \quad \wedge$$
$$a \leq b \quad \wedge$$
$$s \in (a \mathinner{..} b) \to \mathbb{N} \quad \wedge$$
$$\forall m \cdot (m \in a \mathinner{..} b - 1 \ \Rightarrow \ s(m) \leq s(m+1)) \quad \wedge$$
$$p \in \mathbb{N}$$

THEN
    VAR k IN
$$r, k := a - 1, b \,;$$
      WHILE $r \neq k$ DO
        LET m BE
$$m = (r + 1 + k)/2$$
        IN
          IF $p < s(m)$ THEN
$$k := m - 1$$
          ELSE
$$r := m$$
          END
        END
      INVARIANT
$$r \in a \mathinner{..} b + 1 \quad \wedge$$
$$k \in a \mathinner{..} b + 1 \quad \wedge$$
$$\min(d) \in r \mathinner{..} k$$
      VARIANT
$$k - r$$
      END
    END
  END

Algorithm 10.2.14

In order to emphasize the difference between the two above algorithms, let us show their results on the following array s (defined on the interval $1 \mathinner{..} 6$):

m	1	2	3	4	5	6
$s(m)$	4	4	4	6	6	6

Next are various values of $\min(e)$ and $\min(d)$ corresponding to various values of p:

p	3	4	5	6	7
min (e)	1	1	4	4	7
min (d)	0	3	3	6	6

10.3. Natural Number

In this section we envisage the systematic construction of loop substitutions computing the value of natural number functions defined *recursively*.

10.3.1. Basic Scheme

As we know from section 3.5.6, given a set s, an element a of s, and a function g from s to s, formally

$$a \in s$$

$$g \in s \to s$$

then the following conditions, valid for all natural numbers n

$$\begin{cases} f(0) = a \\ f(n+1) = g(f(n)) \end{cases}$$

allow us to define recursively a total function f from $\mathbb{N}$ to s. We would like to construct a loop substitution $r \longleftarrow \mathsf{RecNat}(a, g, n)$ computing the value of f at n. We propose the following definition:

$$
\begin{array}{l}
r \longleftarrow \mathsf{RecNat}(a, g, n) \ \ \widehat{=} \\
\quad \text{PRE} \\
\qquad a \in s \quad \wedge \\
\qquad g \in s \rightarrow s \quad \wedge \\
\qquad n \in \mathbb{N} \\
\quad \text{THEN} \\
\qquad \text{VAR} \ \ k \ \ \text{IN} \\
\qquad\quad r, k := a, \ 0; \\
\qquad\quad \text{WHILE} \ \ k < n \ \ \text{DO} \\
\qquad\qquad r, k := g(r), \ k + 1 \\
\qquad\quad \text{INVARIANT} \\
\qquad\qquad k \in 0..n \quad \wedge \\
\qquad\qquad r = f(k) \\
\qquad\quad \text{VARIANT} \\
\qquad\qquad n - k \\
\qquad\quad \text{END} \\
\qquad \text{END} \\
\quad \text{END}
\end{array}
$$

Algorithm 10.3.1

We leave the proof of the following property as an exercise for the reader.

PRE $\Rightarrow$ $[r \longleftarrow \mathsf{RecNat}(a, g, n)] \ (r = f(n))$ Property 10.3.1

10.3.2. Natural Number Exponentiation

As a first application of the scheme developed in the previous section, we recall
the recursive definition of the function $\exp(x)$ given in section 3.5.7:

$$
\begin{cases}
\exp(x)(0) & = \ 1 \\
\exp(x)(n + 1) & = \ \mathsf{mult}(x)(\exp(x)(n))
\end{cases}
$$

We thus define a substitution $r \longleftarrow \mathsf{Pow}(x, n)$ calculating $\exp(x)(n)$ by means
of the substitution $r \longleftarrow \mathsf{RecNat}(1, \mathsf{mult}(x), n)$ as follows :

$r \longleftarrow \mathsf{Pow}(x, n) \;\; \widehat{=}$
    PRE
        $x \in \mathbb{N} \quad \wedge$
        $n \in \mathbb{N}$
    THEN
        VAR $\;k\;$ IN
            $r, k := 1, 0;$
            WHILE $\;k < n\;$ DO
                $r, k := x \times r, \; k + 1$
            INVARIANT
                $k \in 0..n \quad \wedge$
                $r = x^k$
            VARIANT
                $n - k$
            END
        END
    END

Algorithm 10.3.2

yielding

PRE $\quad \Rightarrow \quad [r \longleftarrow \exp(x, n)] \, (r = x^n)$ Property 10.3.2

10.3.3. Extending the Basic Scheme

The basic scheme presented in section 10.3.1 is limited in that it only allows us to compute a recursive function f whose value at $n + 1$ has the form $g(f(n))$. Sometimes, the recurrence relation "defining" f is more complicated. More precisely, given a set s, an element a of s, and a function g from $s \times \mathbb{N}$ to s, formally

$$a \in s$$

$$g \in s \times \mathbb{N} \to s$$

we would like to construct a function specified by the following properties valid for all natural numbers n:

$$\begin{cases} f(0) = a \\ f(n + 1) = g(f(n), n) \end{cases}$$

Obviously, this recurrence relation does not obey the general form (section 3.5.6) that allows one to say that there exists a total function f from $\mathbb{N}$ to s following that specification. However, we can define recursively (and, this time, rigorously) the following function ff from $\mathbb{N}$ to $s \times \mathbb{N}$:

$$\begin{cases} ff(0) = (a,0) \\ ff(n+1) = h(ff(n)) \end{cases}$$

where, for all x in s and y in $\mathbb{N}$, we have

$$h(x,y) = (g(x,y), y+1)$$

Now, we define f as follows:

$$f = ff \,; \mathsf{prj}_1(s, \mathbb{N})$$

And we can prove, eventually, the following by induction on n (hint: first prove that, for all n in $\mathbb{N}$, we have $ff(n) = (x,n)$ for some x in s):

$$\begin{cases} f(0) = a \\ f(n+1) = g(f(n), n) \end{cases}$$

We have indeed found the desired function. From this, we can easily construct a substitution computing f, by first constructing one computing ff (called $x, y \longleftarrow$ ComputeFf) by means of $x, y \longleftarrow$ RecNat(a, h, n) as defined by Algorithm 10.3.1, that is

---

$x, y \longleftarrow$ ComputeFf$(a, g, n) \;\; \widehat{=}$

   PRE

      $a \in s \quad \wedge$

      $g \in s \times \mathbb{N} \to s \quad \wedge$

      $n \in \mathbb{N}$

   THEN

      VAR k IN

         $x, y, k := a, 0, 0;$

         WHILE $k < n$ DO

            $x, y, k := g(x, y), y + 1, k + 1$

         INVARIANT

            $k \in 0..n \quad \wedge$

            $x, y = ff(k)$

         VARIANT

            $n - k$

         END

      END

   END

Algorithm 10.3.3

As we have the extra invariant $k = y$, we can remove y, yielding the following:

$$
\begin{array}{l}
x \longleftarrow \mathsf{ExtendedRecNat}(a,g,n) \;\;\widehat{=}\\[4pt]
\quad \text{PRE}\\
\qquad a \in s \quad \wedge\\
\qquad g \in s \times \mathbb{N} \to s \quad \wedge\\
\qquad n \in \mathbb{N}\\
\quad \text{THEN}\\
\qquad \text{VAR}\;\; k \;\; \text{IN}\\
\qquad\quad x,k := a,0;\\
\qquad\quad \text{WHILE}\;\; k < n \;\; \text{DO}\\
\qquad\qquad x,k := g\,(x,k), k+1\\
\qquad\quad \text{INVARIANT}\\
\qquad\qquad k \in 0..n \quad \wedge\\
\qquad\qquad x = f(k)\\
\qquad\quad \text{VARIANT}\\
\qquad\qquad n - k\\
\qquad\quad \text{END}\\
\qquad \text{END}\\
\quad \text{END}
\end{array}
$$

Algorithm 10.3.4

And we thus have

$$
\text{PRE} \quad \Rightarrow \quad [\,x \longleftarrow \mathsf{ExtendedRecNat}(a,g,n)\,]\,(x = f(n)) \qquad \text{Property 10.3.3}
$$

10.3.4. Summing a Sequence

Letting t be an *infinite* sequence of natural numbers (in other words, a function from $\mathbb{N}$ to $\mathbb{N}$), the summation, $\mathsf{sig}\,(t)(n)$ of its first $n+1$ elements obeys the following obvious relationship:

$$
\begin{cases}
\mathsf{sig}\,(t)(0) & = \; 0\\[6pt]
\mathsf{sig}\,(t)(n+1) & = \; \mathsf{sig}\,(t)(n) + t(n)
\end{cases}
$$

As a consequence, we define the substitution $x \longleftarrow \mathsf{Sigma}\,(t,n)$ by means of $x \longleftarrow \mathsf{ExtendedRecNat}\,(0, \lambda(a,b)\cdot(a,b \in \mathbb{N} \times \mathbb{N} \mid a + t(b)), n)$. This yields:

$$x \longleftarrow \text{Sigma}\,(t,n) \ \hat{=}$$

PRE
$$t \in \mathbb{N} \to \mathbb{N} \quad \wedge$$
$$n \in \mathbb{N}$$

THEN
VAR k IN
$$x,k := 0,0;$$
WHILE $k < n$ DO
$$x,k := x + t(k), k + 1$$
INVARIANT
$$k \in 0\,..\,n \quad \wedge$$
$$x,k = \text{sig}\,(k), k$$
VARIANT
$$n - k$$
END
END
END

Algorithm 10.3.5

10.3.5. Shifting a Sub-sequence

As another example of using the extended scheme of section 10.3.3, we would like to construct a substitution able to *right shift* part of an "array" s (constructed on a set v, with bounds a and b). More precisely, we shall define a function shift$(a,b,v,j)(n)$ such that

$$\text{shift}\,(a,b,v,j) \ \in \ \mathbb{N} \to ((a\,..\,b) \to v)$$

whose value at n is another array, similar to s, but with the sub-sequence finishing at index j and of length n right-shifted. We suppose, of course, that j is a member of $a\,..\,b - 1$ and that n belongs to the interval $0\,..\,j - a + 1$ (so that the beginning of the sub-sequence, at index $j - n + 1$, is indeed greater then or equal to the initial index, a, of s). For instance, given the following sequence of length 7 (that is, an array with lower bound a equal to 1 and upper bound b equal to 7), together with j equal to 4 and n equal to 3:

$$s = [1,\underline{2,3,4},5,6,7]$$
$$\uparrow \quad \uparrow$$
$$j - n + 1 \quad j$$

we have

$$\text{shift}\,(1,7,s,4)(3) = [1,2,\underline{2,3,4},6,7]$$

The part of s that has been shifted (the sub-sequence $[2,3,4]$) corresponds to the restriction of s to the interval $2\,..\,4$, that is $(j - n + 1)\,..\,j$. As shifting consists of composing s with the predecessor function pred, we have the following formal definition:

$$
\begin{array}{l}
a \in \mathbb{N} \\
b \in \mathbb{N} \\
a < b \\
s \in a \mathrel{..} b \to v \\
j \in a \mathrel{..} b - 1 \\
n \in 0 \mathrel{..} (j + 1 - a) \\
\Rightarrow \\
\mathsf{shift}(a, b, s, j)(n) \;=\; s \mathbin{\lhd\!\!\!+} (\mathsf{pred} \mathbin{;} ((j - n + 1) \mathrel{..} j) \lhd s)
\end{array}
$$

For instance, in the case of our example, we have

$$
\begin{array}{lcl}
j - n + 1 & = & 2 \\
(2 \mathrel{..} 4) \lhd s & = & \{2 \mapsto 2,\; 3 \mapsto 3,\; 4 \mapsto 4\} \\
\mathsf{pred} \mathbin{;} (2 \mathrel{..} 4) \lhd s & = & \{3 \mapsto 2,\; 4 \mapsto 3,\; 5 \mapsto 4\} \\
s \mathbin{\lhd\!\!\!+} (\mathsf{pred} \mathbin{;} (2 \mathrel{..} 4) \lhd s) & = & [1, 2, 2, 3, 4, 6, 7]
\end{array}
$$

From this definition, we can deduce the following:

$$\mathsf{shift}(a, b, s, j)(n + 1)$$
$$=$$
$$s \mathbin{\lhd\!\!\!+} (\mathsf{pred} \mathbin{;} (j - n \mathrel{..} j) \lhd s)$$
$$=$$
$$s \mathbin{\lhd\!\!\!+} (\mathsf{pred} \mathbin{;} ((j - n + 1 \mathrel{..} j) \cup \{j - n\}) \lhd s)$$
$$=$$
$$s \mathbin{\lhd\!\!\!+} ((\mathsf{pred} \mathbin{;} (j - n + 1 \mathrel{..} j) \lhd s) \cup (\mathsf{pred} \mathbin{;} \{j - n\} \lhd s))$$
$$=$$
$$s \mathbin{\lhd\!\!\!+} ((\mathsf{pred} \mathbin{;} (j - n + 1 \mathrel{..} j) \lhd s) \cup \{j - n + 1 \mapsto s(j - n)\})$$
$$= \qquad\qquad\qquad \text{since } j - n + 1 \notin \mathsf{pred}^{-1}[j - n + 1 \mathrel{..} j]$$
$$s \mathbin{\lhd\!\!\!+} ((\mathsf{pred} \mathbin{;} (j - n + 1 \mathrel{..} j) \lhd s) \mathbin{\lhd\!\!\!+} \{j - n + 1 \mapsto s(j - n)\})$$
$$=$$
$$\mathsf{shift}(a, b, s, j)(n) \mathbin{\lhd\!\!\!+} \{j - n + 1 \mapsto s(j - n)\}$$

As we also obviously have $\mathsf{shift}(a, b, s, j)(0) = s$, we can write

$$
\left\{
\begin{array}{l}
\mathsf{shift}(a, b, s, j)(0) \;=\; s \\
\\
\mathsf{shift}(a, b, s, j)(n + 1) \;=\; \mathsf{shift}(a, b, s, j)(n) \mathbin{\lhd\!\!\!+} \{j - n + 1 \mapsto s(j - n)\}
\end{array}
\right.
$$

We know, from the previous section, that this relationship defines a function computable by means of our extended scheme. As a consequence, we define a substitution $t \longleftarrow \mathsf{Move}\,(a, b, s, j, n)$ by means of $\mathsf{ExtendedRecNat}\,(s, g(j, n), n)$ as defined by Algorithm 10.3.4, where

$$g(j, n) \in ((a \mathrel{..} b) \to v) \times \mathbb{N} \to ((a \mathrel{..} b) \to v)$$

and with

$$g(j,n)(t,k) \;=\; t \Leftarrow \{j-n+1 \mapsto t(j-k)\}$$

We have then

$t \longleftarrow \mathsf{Move}(a,b,s,j,n) \;\; \widehat{=}$

    PRE

        $a \in \mathbb{N} \;\; \wedge$

        $b \in \mathbb{N} \;\; \wedge$

        $a < b \;\; \wedge$

        $s \in (a \mathbin{..} b) \to v \;\; \wedge$

        $j \in a \mathbin{..} b - 1 \;\; \wedge$

        $n \in 0 \mathbin{..} (j - a + 1)$

    THEN

        VAR k IN

            $t, k := s,\; 0;$

            WHILE $k < n$ DO

                $t, k := t \Leftarrow \{j - k + 1 \mapsto t(j - k)\},\; k + 1$

            INVARIANT

                $k \in 0 \mathbin{..} n \;\; \wedge$

                $t = \mathsf{shift}(a, b, s, j)(k)$

            VARIANT

                $n - k$

        END

    END

  END

Algorithm 10.3.6

and we have then

PRE $\Rightarrow$ $[t \longleftarrow \mathsf{Move}(a,b,s,j,n)]\;(t = \mathsf{shift}(a,b,s,j,n))$ Property 10.3.4

10.3.6. Insertion into a Sorted Array

As an application of the previous example, we now develop an algorithm for inserting an element into a sorted array. More precisely, let s be a sorted array of natural numbers with bounds a and b, formally

$$a \in \mathbb{N}$$
$$b \in \mathbb{N}$$
$$a \leq b$$
$$s \in (a \mathbin{..} b) \to \mathbb{N}$$
$$\forall n \cdot (n \in a \mathbin{..} (b - 1) \;\; \Rightarrow \;\; s(n) \leq s(n + 1))$$

The obvious ideas underlying the algorithm are: (1) to find out the place where to insert the element, (2) to move rightwards the elements of the array from this place, and (3) to insert the new element in its due place. Formally, we define the following function ins:

$$\text{ins}(a,b,s,x) \;=\; \text{shift}(a,b,s \leftarrow x,b)(b+1-r)\triangleleft\!\!+\!\{r \mapsto x\}$$

where shift has been defined in the previous section, and where r is the index where we have to insert the element x. That index is obviously such that

$$
\begin{aligned}
r &= a & &\Rightarrow & x &\le s(a) \\
r &\in a+1\mathinner{\ldotp\ldotp}b & &\Rightarrow & s(r-1) &< x \le s(r) \\
r &= b+1 & &\Rightarrow & s(b) &< x
\end{aligned}
$$

Looking at Property 10.2.9 shows that we can compute r by means of the substitution $r \longleftarrow \text{BinarySearchInArrayExc}\,(a,b,s,x)$ as defined by Algorithm 10.2.13. Hence, we can construct the following substitution $t \longleftarrow \text{Insert}\,(a,b,s,x)$, forming our *by excess* insertion:

$t \longleftarrow \text{Insert}(a,b,s,x) \;\; \hat{=}$

    PRE

        $a \in \mathbb{N}$ $\wedge$

        $b \in \mathbb{N}$ $\wedge$

        $a \le b$ $\wedge$

        $s \in (a\mathinner{\ldotp\ldotp}b) \to \mathbb{N}$ $\wedge$

        $\forall n \cdot (n \in a\mathinner{\ldotp\ldotp}(b-1) \;\Rightarrow\; s(n) \le s(n+1))$ $\wedge$

        $x \in \mathbb{N}$

    THEN

        VAR r IN

            $r \longleftarrow \text{BinarySearchInArrayExc}(a,b,s,x)$;

            $t \longleftarrow \text{Move}(a,b,s \leftarrow x,b,b+1-r)$;

            $t(r) := x$

        END

    END

Algorithm 10.3.7

and we have

$[t \longleftarrow \text{Insert}(a,b,s,x)]\,(t = \text{ins}(a,b,s,x))$ Property 10.3.5

We can also use a *by defect* insertion which, by the way, is more economical than the previous *by excess* version since it uses fewer moves. The index where we have to insert the new element is *one more* than the following value r, which is such that

$$r = a - 1 \qquad \Rightarrow \quad x < s(a)$$
$$r \in a \mathbin{..} b - 1 \quad \Rightarrow \quad s(r) \le x < s(r+1)$$
$$r = b \qquad\qquad \Rightarrow \quad s(b) \le x$$

This yields the following alternative definition for the substitution Insert:

$t \longleftarrow \mathsf{Insert}(a, b, s, x) \;\;\widehat{=}$

    PRE

        $a \in \mathbb{N}_1 \quad \wedge$

        $b \in \mathbb{N} \quad \wedge$

        $a \le b \quad \wedge$

        $s \in (a \mathbin{..} b) \to \mathbb{N} \quad \wedge$

        $\forall n \cdot (n \in a \mathbin{..} (b-1) \;\Rightarrow\; s(n) \le s(n+1)) \quad \wedge$

        $x \in \mathbb{N}$

    THEN

        VAR r IN

            $r \longleftarrow \mathsf{BinarySearchInArrayDef}(a, b, s, x);$

            $t \longleftarrow \mathsf{Move}(a, b, s \leftarrow x, b, b - r);$

            $t(r+1) := x$

        END

    END

Algorithm 10.3.8

10.4. Sequences

10.4.1. Introduction

As for natural numbers, a function can be defined recursively on sequences (section 3.7.1) provided we give its value at the empty sequence and at the sequence $s \leftarrow x$ in terms of x and s. More precisely, given two sets u and v, an element a of v, and a total function g from $v \times u$ to v, we can define recursively a total function f from $\mathsf{seq}(u)$ to v as follows:

$$\begin{cases} f([\,]) = a \\[2mm] f(s \leftarrow x) = g(f(s), x) \end{cases}$$

We would like to construct a substitution, named $r \longleftarrow \mathsf{RightRecSeq}(a, g, s)$, computing the value of the function f at s. We propose the following definition:

$r \longleftarrow$ RightRecSeq(a, g, s) $\;\widehat{=}$

PRE

$\quad a \in v \quad \wedge$

$\quad g \in v \times u \to v \quad \wedge$

$\quad s \in \text{seq}(u)$

THEN

$\quad$ VAR $\;\; k \;\;$ IN

$\quad\quad r, k := a, \; 1 \;;$

$\quad\quad$ WHILE $\;\; k \leq \text{size}(s) \;\;$ DO

$\quad\quad\quad r, k := g(r, s(k)), \; k + 1$

$\quad\quad$ INVARIANT

$\quad\quad\quad k \in 1 \mathinner{\ldotp\ldotp} \text{size}(s) + 1 \quad \wedge$

$\quad\quad\quad r = f(s \uparrow (k - 1))$

$\quad\quad$ VARIANT

$\quad\quad\quad \text{size}(s) + 1 - k$

$\quad\quad$ END

$\quad$ END

END

Algorithm 10.4.1

We leave the proof of the following property as an exercise for the reader:

PRE $\;\Rightarrow\; [r \longleftarrow$ RightRecSeq$(a, g, s)] \, (r = f(s))$ $\qquad$ Property 10.4.1

The recursive function f can also be defined the other way around. In that case, we use an element a of v and total function h from $u \times v$ to v, as follows:

$$\begin{cases} f([\,]) = a \\ f(x \to s) = h(x, f(s)) \end{cases}$$

We then define the following substitution:

$$
\begin{array}{l}
r \longleftarrow \text{LeftRecSeq}(a,h,s) \;\; \widehat{=} \\
\qquad \text{PRE} \\
\qquad\qquad a \in v \quad \wedge \\
\qquad\qquad h \in u \times v \to v \quad \wedge \\
\qquad\qquad s \in \text{seq}\,(u) \\
\qquad \text{THEN} \\
\qquad\qquad \text{VAR} \quad k \quad \text{IN} \\
\qquad\qquad\qquad r,k := a,\ \text{size}(s); \\
\qquad\qquad\qquad \text{WHILE} \quad k > 0 \quad \text{DO} \\
\qquad\qquad\qquad\qquad r,k := h(s\,(k),r),\ k-1 \\
\qquad\qquad\qquad \text{INVARIANT} \\
\qquad\qquad\qquad\qquad k \in 0\,..\,\text{size}(s) \quad \wedge \\
\qquad\qquad\qquad\qquad r = f(s \downarrow k) \\
\qquad\qquad\qquad \text{VARIANT} \\
\qquad\qquad\qquad\qquad k \\
\qquad\qquad\qquad \text{END} \\
\qquad\qquad \text{END} \\
\qquad \text{END}
\end{array}
$$

Algorithm 10.4.2

Again, we leave the proof of the following property as an exercise for the reader:

$$ \text{PRE} \;\Rightarrow\; [\,r \longleftarrow \text{LeftRecSeq}(a,h,s)\,]\,(r = f(s)) \qquad \text{Property 10.4.2} $$

Sometimes, recursive functions on sequences are only defined for *non-empty* sequences. This means that the recursion "starts" at a singleton sequence. More precisely, given a function l from u to v and, as before, a function g or a function h, we define functions by right or left recursion on non-empty sequences as follows:

$$
\begin{cases}
f([x]) \;=\; l(x) \\[2mm]
f(s \leftarrow x) = g(f(s),x)
\end{cases}
$$

and also

$$
\begin{cases}
f([x]) \;=\; l(x) \\[2mm]
f(x \to s) = h(x,f(s))
\end{cases}
$$

This leads to the following algorithms which are obtained after obvious slight modifications of the two previous ones:

$$
\begin{array}{l}
r \longleftarrow \mathsf{LeftRecSeq1}(l,h,s) \; \widehat{=} \\
\quad \text{PRE} \\
\qquad l \in u \to v \quad \wedge \\
\qquad h \in u \times v \to v \quad \wedge \\
\qquad s \in \mathsf{seq}_1(u) \\
\quad \text{THEN} \\
\qquad \text{VAR} \quad k \quad \text{IN} \\
\qquad\quad r,k := l(\mathsf{last}(s)), \; \mathsf{size}(s) - 1 \, ; \\
\qquad\quad \text{WHILE} \quad k > 0 \quad \text{DO} \\
\qquad\qquad r,k := h(s(k),r), \; k - 1 \\
\qquad\quad \text{INVARIANT} \\
\qquad\qquad k \in 0 \, .. \, (\mathsf{size}(s) - 1) \quad \wedge \\
\qquad\qquad r = f(s \downarrow k) \\
\qquad\quad \text{VARIANT} \\
\qquad\qquad k \\
\qquad\quad \text{END} \\
\qquad \text{END} \\
\quad \text{END}
\end{array}
$$

Algorithm 10.4.3

We have a similar algorithm for right recursion.

10.4.2. Accumulating the Elements of a Sequence

In this section we develop a schematic algorithm by which an associative binary operator can be "accumulated" on the elements of a sequence. Let the symbol $\odot$ denote an associative binary operator applicable to the elements of a set u and delivering results again in u. We define a corresponding function prod as follows:

$$
\mathsf{prod} = \lambda(m,n) \cdot (m,n \in u \times u \mid m \odot n)
$$

We also suppose that the operator $\odot$ has a *unit*, denoted by the symbol $\bot$. We have then

$$
m \odot \bot = m
$$

$$
\bot \odot m = m
$$

We now define recursively the following function right_accum_prod:

$$
\left\{
\begin{array}{l}
\mathsf{right\_accum\_prod}(\,[\,]\,) = \bot \\[2ex]
\mathsf{right\_accum\_prod}(s \leftarrow x) = \mathsf{right\_accum\_prod}(s) \odot x
\end{array}
\right.
$$

We construct a substitution $r \longleftarrow$ RightAccumSeq(s) computing the accumulated *product* with $\odot$ of the elements of a sequence. It is equal to $r \longleftarrow$ RightRecSeq $(\bot, \mathrm{prod}, s)$

$r \longleftarrow$ RightAccumSeq$(s) \quad \widehat{=}$
    PRE
        $s \in \mathsf{seq}(u)$
    THEN
       VAR k IN
          $r, k := \bot,\ 1;$
           WHILE $k \leq \mathsf{size}(s)$ DO
             $r, k := r \odot s(k),\ k + 1$
           INVARIANT
             $k \in 1\,..\,\mathsf{size}(s) + 1$ $\wedge$
             $r = \mathsf{right\_accum\_prod}(s \uparrow (k - 1))$
           VARIANT
             $\mathsf{size}(s) + 1 - k$
          END
       END
    END

Algorithm 10.4.4

And we have

Property 10.4.3

$\mathsf{PRE} \quad \Rightarrow \quad [r \longleftarrow \mathsf{RightAccumSeq}(s)]\,(r = \mathsf{right\_accum\_prod}(s))$

By using the other scheme, we would have obtained a similar algorithm. By instantiating, in the previous schematic algorithms, the set u to $\mathbb{N}$, the operator $\odot$ to $\times$, and the unit element $\bot$ to 1, we obtain algorithms computing the product of the elements of a natural number sequence. By further instantiating the parameter s to be the sequence $\mathsf{id}\,(1\,..\,n)$, we obtain an algorithm computing $n!$. This yields the following, since $s(k)$ is k and $\mathsf{size}\,(s)$ is n:

```
r ⟵ RightFact(n)  ≙
    PRE
        n ∈ ℕ
    THEN
        VAR  k   IN
            r, k := 1, 1 ;
            WHILE  k ≤ n   DO
                r, k := r × k,  k + 1
            INVARIANT
                k ∈ 1 .. n + 1   ∧
                r = (k − 1) !
            VARIANT
                n + 1 − k
            END
        END
    END
```

Algorithm 10.4.5

By using the other scheme, we would have obtained:

```
r ⟵ LeftFact(n)  ≙
    PRE
        n ∈ ℕ
    THEN
        VAR  k   IN
            r, k := 1,  n ;
            WHILE  k > 0   DO
                r, k := k × r,  k − 1
            INVARIANT
                k ∈ 0 .. n   ∧
                r = n! / k !
            VARIANT
                k
            END
        END
    END
```

Algorithm 10.4.6

10.4.3. Decoding the Based Representation of a Number

As another example, the following function, called num_b, yields the value of a natural number given its representation in a numerical system with base b (where b is a natural number greater than or equal to 2). Such a representation takes the form of a non-empty sequence belonging to the set $seq_1 (0 .. (b-1))$. It can be defined recursively as follows

$$\begin{cases} num_b([\,]) = 0 \\ \\ num_b(s \leftarrow n) = n + b \times num_b(s) \end{cases}$$

We can then define the substitution $r \longleftarrow ValNum(b, s)$ transforming the representation s of a natural number with base b into that very number. This is done by means of the substitution RightRecSeq developed as Algorithm 10.4.1 in section 10.4.1, yielding

$r \longleftarrow ValNum(b, s)\ \ \widehat{=}$

    PRE

        $b \in \mathbb{N}_1\ \ \wedge$
        $s \in seq_1 (0 .. b - 1)$

    THEN

        VAR k IN

          $r, k := 0,\ 1\ ;$

          WHILE $k \le size(s)$ DO

            $r, k := s(k) + b \times r,\ k + 1$

          INVARIANT

            $k \in 2 .. size(s) + 1\ \ \ \wedge$
            $r = num_b(s \uparrow (k - 1))$

          VARIANT

            $size(s) + 1 - k$

          END

        END

    END

Algorithm 10.4.7

And we have

PRE $\Rightarrow$ $[r \longleftarrow ValNum(b, s)]\ (r = num_b(s))$ Property 10.4.4

10.4.4. Transforming a Natural Number into its Based Representation

In this section we construct a substitution which is the *reverse* of the one constructed in the previous section: we transform a natural number into its based representation. Let's first give the recursive definitions of two functions called $\mathsf{decsucc}_b$ and denum_b.

The first one, $\mathsf{decsucc}_b$, is a function which transforms the representation, in base b, of a number n, into the representation of $n+1$ in the same base. You can see how the possible carry is moved towards the beginning of the representation:

$$\left\{ \begin{array}{lll} \mathsf{decsucc}_b([\,]) & = & [1] \\[2mm] \mathsf{decsucc}_b(s \leftarrow x) & = & \left\{ \begin{array}{ll} s \leftarrow (x+1) & \text{if } x < b-1 \\ \mathsf{decsucc}_b(s) \leftarrow 0 & \text{otherwise} \end{array} \right. \end{array} \right.$$

For example, we have

$$\begin{array}{lll} \mathsf{decsucc}_{10}([9,9]) & = & \mathsf{decsucc}_{10}([9]) \leftarrow 0 \\ & = & \mathsf{decsucc}_{10}([\,]) \leftarrow 0 \leftarrow 0 \\ & = & [1] \leftarrow 0 \leftarrow 0 \\ & = & [1,0,0] \end{array}$$

The second function, denum_b, transforms a number into its base representation:

$$\left\{ \begin{array}{lll} \mathsf{denum}_b(0) & = & [0] \\[3mm] \mathsf{denum}_b(n+1) & = & \mathsf{decsucc}_b(\mathsf{denum}_b(n)) \end{array} \right.$$

We can then prove the following by (sequence) induction on s:

$\mathsf{num}_b(\mathsf{decsucc}_b(s)) = \mathsf{num}_b(s) + 1$ Property 10.4.5

---

and then also the following by (natural number) induction on n:

$\mathsf{num}_b(\mathsf{denum}_b(n)) = n$ Property 10.4.6

We can also prove the following two properties (also by induction on n):

$\mathsf{last}(\mathsf{denum}_b(n)) = n \bmod b$ Property 10.4.7

---

and (hint: use Property 10.4.5)

$\mathsf{num}_b(\mathsf{front}(\mathsf{denum}_b(n))) = n/b$ Property 10.4.8

We would like to construct a substitution $s \longleftarrow$ Encode(b, n) establishing the post-condition $s =$ denum$_b(n)$. For this, we first define the following trivial cop operation:

$$\begin{cases} \text{cop}([x]) & = & [x] \\ \text{cop}(x \to s) & = & x \to \text{cop}(s) \end{cases}$$

which we implement with the following substitution $s \longleftarrow$ Copy(t) by means of the substitution LeftRecSeq1 (that is, Algorithm 10.4.3) as follows:

$s \longleftarrow$ Copy(t) $\;\widehat{=}$
    PRE
        $t \in$ seq$_1(v)$
    THEN
        VAR k IN
            $s, k := [\,\text{last}(t)\,],\ \text{size}(t) - 1$;
            WHILE $k > 0$ DO
                $s, k := t(k) \to s,\ k - 1$
            INVARIANT
                $k \in 0\,..\,(\text{size}(s) - 1)\quad \wedge$
                $s = t \downarrow k$
            VARIANT
                k
            END
        END
    END

The substitution $s \longleftarrow$ Encode(b, n) can then be defined as follows:

$s \longleftarrow$ Encode(b, n) $\;\widehat{=}$
    PRE
        $b \in \mathbb{N}_1$
        $n \in \mathbb{N}$
    THEN
        $s \longleftarrow$ Copy(denum$_b(n)$)
    END

Algorithm 10.4.8

We now proceed by transforming this substitution. First, we expand Copy, yielding

$s \longleftarrow \text{Encode}\,(b,n) \;\; \widehat{=}$
    PRE
        $b \in \mathbb{N}_1 \quad \wedge$
        $n \in \mathbb{N}$
    THEN
        VAR k IN
            $s,k \;:=\; [\,\text{last}\,(\text{denum}_b(n))\,], \; \text{size}(\text{denum}_b(n)) - 1\,;$
            WHILE $k > 0$ DO
                $s,k \;:=\; \text{denum}_b(n)(k) \rightarrow s,\; k - 1$
            INVARIANT
                $k \in 0\,..\,(\text{size}(s) - 1) \quad \wedge$
                $s = \text{denum}_b(n) \downarrow k$
            VARIANT
                k
            END
        END
    END

Then we introduce the extra variable m with initialization $m := n/b$ and a corresponding extension of the loop body with substitution $m := m/b$. We can then prove that we have the extra invariant (hint: use Property 10.4.8)

$$m \in 0\,..\,n/b$$
$$k = \text{size}\,(\text{denum}_b(m \times b)) - 1$$
$$m = \text{num}_b(\text{denum}_b(n) \uparrow k)$$

This yields the following:

$s \longleftarrow \text{Encode}\,(b,n) \;\; \widehat{=}$
    PRE
        $b \in \mathbb{N}_1 \; \wedge$
        $n \in \mathbb{N}$
    THEN
        VAR k,m IN
            $s,k,m \;:=\; [\,n \bmod b\,], \; \text{size}(\text{denum}_b(n)) - 1, \; n/b\,;$
            WHILE $m > 0$ DO
                $s,k,m \;:=\; (m \bmod b) \rightarrow s,\; k - 1,\; m/b$
            INVARIANT
                $\ldots$
            END
        END
    END

We have replaced, in the initialization, the expression $\text{last}\,(\text{denum}_b(n))$ by

$n \bmod b$ (hint: use Property 10.4.7). Also we have replaced, in the body of the loop, the expression $\text{denum}_b(n)(k)$ by $m \bmod b$ (hint: again, use Property 10.4.7). Finally the guard, $k > 0$, of the loop has been replaced equivalently by $m > 0$. We can now remove the variable k, yielding our final substitution:

$s \longleftarrow \text{Encode}(b, n) \;\; \widehat{=}$

> PRE
>> $n \in \mathbb{N}$
> THEN
>> VAR $\quad m \quad$ IN
>>> $s, m := [\, n \bmod b \,], \, n/b \, ;$
>>> WHILE $\quad m > 0 \quad$ DO
>>>> $s, m := (m \bmod b) \rightarrow s, \, m/b$
>>> INVARIANT
>>>> $m \in 0 \, .. \, n/b \quad \wedge$
>>>> $s = \text{denum}_b(n) \downarrow (\text{size}(\text{denum}_b(m \times b)) - 1)$
>>> VARIANT
>>>> $\text{size}(\text{denum}_b(m \times b)) - 1$
>>> END
>> END
> END

Algorithm 10.4.9

10.4.5. Fast Binary Operation Computations

In this section our aim is to transform the previous algorithm in order to construct other algorithms performing the (fast) computation of certain *binary operations*.

Let the symbol $\odot$ denote a binary operation whose right-hand side parameter is a natural number and whose left-hand side parameter belongs to a set which is the same as the result of the binary operation. Examples of such operations are: natural number multiplication, natural number exponentiation, square matrix exponentiation and function iterate. Given a natural number n, we would like to compute the value of $x \odot n$. For this, we use the binary representation, $\text{denum}_2(n)$, of n as defined in section 10.4.4:

$$n = 2^{p-1} \times d_p + \cdots + 2^{i-1} \times d_i + \cdots + 2^0 \times d_1$$

where

$$[d_p, \ldots, d_i, \ldots, d_1] = \text{denum}_2(n)$$

And we have then

$$x \odot n = x \odot (2^{p-1} \times d_p + \cdots + 2^{i-1} \times d_i + \cdots + 2^0 \times d_1)$$

As a first property of the operator $\odot$, we suppose that it "almost" distributes through natural number addition by transforming the natural number addition operator $+$ into a certain binary operator $\oplus$, namely

$$x \odot (a + b) = (x \odot a) \oplus (x \odot b)$$

Rule 1

This yields the following:

$$x \odot n = x \odot (2^{p-1} \times d_p) \oplus \cdots \oplus x \odot (2^{i-1} \times d_i) \oplus \cdots \oplus x \odot (2^0 \times d_1)$$

As a second property of the operator $\odot$, we suppose that it is "almost" associative by transforming $\times$ into the operator $\odot$ itself, that is

$$x \odot (a \times b) = x \odot a \odot b$$

Rule 2

This yields the following:

$$x \odot n = (x \odot 2^{p-1} \odot d_p) \oplus \cdots \oplus (x \odot 2^{i-1} \odot d_i) \oplus \cdots \oplus (x \odot 2^0 \odot d_1)$$

We suppose finally that 1 is a unit for the operator $\odot$, that is

$$x \odot 1 = x$$

Rule 3

Defining now a_i to be equal to $x \odot 2^{i-1}$, we easily obtain the following rewriting rules using Rule 2 and Rule 3:

$$\begin{cases} a_1 & = x \\ a_{i+1} & = a_i \odot 2 \end{cases}$$

We have then the following which gives us an informal clue as how to construct an algorithm computing $x \odot n$:

$$x \odot n = (a_p \odot d_p) \oplus \cdots \oplus (a_i \odot d_i) \oplus \cdots \oplus (a_1 \odot d_1)$$

Let us now rewrite Algorithm 10.4.9 of the previous section by specializing it to base 2:

$$s \longleftarrow \text{EncodeBinary}\,(n) \ \ \widehat{=}$$
> PRE
> > $n \in \mathbb{N}$
>
> THEN
> > VAR m IN
> > > $s, m := [n \bmod 2], n/2 \,;$
> > > WHILE $m > 0$ DO
> > > > $s, m := (m \bmod 2) \to s, \ m/2$
> > >
> > > INVARIANT
> > > > $m \in 0 \,.. \, n/2$ $\wedge$
> > > > $s = \text{denum}_2(n) \downarrow (\text{size}\,(\text{denum}_2(m \times 2)) - 1)$
> > >
> > > VARIANT
> > > > $\text{size}\,(\text{denum}_2(m \times 2)) - 1$
> > >
> > > END
> >
> > END
>
> END

We can transform this algorithm by adding an extra input parameter x and an extra ouptut parameter r whose final value is intended to be $x \odot n$. We also add an extra local variable c, together with an extra invariant.

$$r, s \longleftarrow \text{ComputeEncodeBinary}\,(x, n) \ \ \widehat{=}$$
> PRE
> > $n \in \mathbb{N}$
>
> THEN
> > VAR c, m IN
> > > $r, c, s, m := x \odot (n \bmod 2), \ x, \ [n \bmod 2], \ n/2 \,;$
> > > WHILE $m > 0$ DO
> > > > $r, c, s, m := (c \odot 2 \odot (m \bmod 2)) \oplus r, \ c \odot 2, \ (m \bmod 2) \to s, \ m/2$
> > >
> > > INVARIANT
> > > > $m \in 0 \,.. \, n/2$ $\wedge$
> > > > $s = \text{denum}_2(n) \downarrow (\text{size}\,(\text{denum}_2(m \times 2)) - 1)$ $\wedge$
> > > > $c = x \odot 2^{\text{size}\,(s) - 1}$ $\wedge$
> > > > $r = (a_{\text{size}\,(s)} \odot d_{\text{size}\,(s)}) \oplus \cdots \oplus (a_1 \odot d_1)$
> > >
> > > VARIANT
> > > > $\text{size}\,(\text{denum}_2(m \times 2)) - 1$
> > >
> > > END
> >
> > END
>
> END

It will be seen that the final result for r (that is $x \odot n$) is indeed reached since we know that the final value of s is precisely the binary representation, $\text{denum}_2(n)$, of n. We can throw away the output parameter s, yielding the following algorithm:

$r \longleftarrow \text{ComputeBinary}(x,n) \;\;\widehat{=}\;$
    PRE
        $n \in \mathbb{N}$
    THEN
        VAR c, m IN
            $r,c,m := x \odot (n \bmod 2),\; x, n/2\,;$
            WHILE $m > 0$ DO
                $r,c,m := (c \odot 2 \odot (m \bmod 2)) \oplus r,\; c \odot 2,\; m/2$
            INVARIANT
                $m \in 0..n/2\;\;\;\wedge$
                $c = x \odot 2^{\,\text{size}(s)-1}\;\;\;\wedge$
                $r = (a_{\,\text{size}(s)} \odot d_{\,\text{size}(s)}) \;\oplus\; \cdots \;\oplus\; (a_1 \odot d_1)$
            VARIANT
                $\text{size}(\text{denum}_2(m \times 2)) - 1$
            END
        END
    END

where s is the quantity $\text{denum}_2(n) \downarrow (\text{size}(\text{denum}_2(m \times 2)) - 1)$. As applications of the previous *generic* algorithm, we can confirm that it holds for the following instantiations of x, $\odot$ and $\oplus$:

x	$\odot$	$\oplus$
Natural Number	*Multiplication*	*Addition*
Natural Number	*Exponentiation*	*Multiplication*
Square Matrix	*Exponentiation*	*Multiplication*
Binary Relation	*Iterate*	*Composition*

As an example, we now construct an algorithm performing (fast) exponentiation:

$r \longleftarrow \text{FastExponentiation}\,(x, n) \;\; \widehat{=}$

    PRE

        $x \in \mathbb{N} \quad \wedge$

        $n \in \mathbb{N}$

    THEN

        VAR c, m IN

            $r, c, m := x^n \bmod 2,\; x,\, n/2;$

            WHILE $m > 0$ DO

                $r, c, m := r \times (c^2)^m \bmod 2,\; c^2,\, m/2$

            INVARIANT

                $\ldots$

            VARIANT

                $\ldots$

            END

        END

    END

Algorithm 10.4.10

And we have

PRE $\;\Rightarrow\;$ $[r \longleftarrow \text{FastExponentiation}\,(x, n)]\,(r = x^n)$ Property 10.4.9

10.4.6. Left and Right Recursion

In section 10.4.1, we presented two general algorithms for computing functions defined recursively on finite sequences: one for functions defined by *right* recursion and the other for functions defined by *left* recursion.

In this section we propose to reconcile these two aspects of sequence recursion by considering functions defined by left and right recursion *simultaneously*. More precisely, let u and v be two sets. We are given five functions g, g_1, g_2, g_3 and g_4 such that:

$$g \in u \to v$$
$$g_1 \in u \times v \to v$$
$$g_2 \in v \times u \to v$$
$$g_3 \in u \times v \times u \to v$$
$$g_4 \in u \times v \times u \to v$$

A function f is defined by left and right recursion once we have some rewriting rules of the following forms, where x and y are members of u, s is a member of $\mathsf{seq}(u)$, and $C_1(x, y)$, $C_2(x, y)$, $C_3(x, y)$ and $C_4(x, y)$ are four predicates:

$$
\left\{
\begin{array}{ll}
f([\,]) & = a \\
f([x\,]) & = g(x) \\
f(x \rightarrow s \leftarrow y) & = \left\{
\begin{array}{ll}
g_1(x, f(s \leftarrow y)) & \text{if } C_1(x, y) \\
g_2(f(x \rightarrow s), y) & \text{if } C_2(x, y) \\
g_3(x, f(s), y) & \text{if } C_3(x, y) \\
g_4(y, f(s), x) & \text{if } C_4(x, y)
\end{array}
\right.
\end{array}
\right.
$$

Notice that, in practical instantiations of these generic rewriting rules, we might have fewer cases. Our only requirement is that the various conditions are mutually disjoint and do not leave room for extra conditions. Such rules are sufficient to define a total function f from $\mathsf{seq}(u)$ to v. In fact, the previous scheme is an instance of the recursive technique developed in section 3.11.3 on well-founded relations. In the present case, the well founded relation is the relation that holds between two sequences s_1 and s_2 when the size of s_1 is strictly greater than that of s_2.

As examples of the above generic rewriting rules, we now present various instantiations. Our first example deals with the reversing of a sequence.

$$
\left\{
\begin{array}{ll}
\mathsf{revlr}([\,]) & = [\,] \\
\mathsf{revlr}([x\,]) & = [x\,] \\
\mathsf{revlr}(x \rightarrow s \leftarrow y) & = y \rightarrow \mathsf{revlr}(s) \leftarrow x
\end{array}
\right.
$$

Second, we present an example dealing with the partitioning of a sequence according to a certain natural number n.

$$
\left\{
\begin{array}{ll}
\mathsf{partlr}(n)([\,]) & = [\,] \\
\mathsf{partlr}(n)([x\,]) & = [x\,] \\
\mathsf{partlr}(n)(x \rightarrow s \leftarrow y) & = \left\{
\begin{array}{ll}
x \rightarrow \mathsf{partlr}(n)(s \leftarrow y) & \text{if } x \leq n \text{ and } y \leq n \\
\mathsf{partlr}(n)(x \rightarrow s) \leftarrow y & \text{if } n < x \text{ and } n < y \\
y \rightarrow \mathsf{partlr}(n)(s) \leftarrow x & \text{if } n < x \text{ and } y \leq n \\
x \rightarrow \mathsf{partlr}(n)(s) \leftarrow y & \text{if } x \leq n \text{ and } n < y
\end{array}
\right.
\end{array}
\right.
$$

The final sequence is supposed to be a permutation of the original one (supposed itself to be a sequence of natural numbers) rearranged in such a way that we first find all the elements whose values are smaller than or equal to n and then all the remaining elements of the original sequence.

As you can see, these examples (revlr and partlr) are very similar in that they only differ in the number of cases and, of course, the rewriting conditions. In fact, they are both special cases of the following rewriting rules:

$$
\begin{cases}
f([\,]) & = & [\,] \\
f([x]) & = & [x] \\
f(x \rightarrow s \leftarrow y) & = &
\begin{cases}
x \rightarrow f(s \leftarrow y) & \text{if } C_1(x,y) \\
f(x \rightarrow s) \leftarrow y & \text{if } C_2(x,y) \\
x \rightarrow f(s) \leftarrow y & \text{if } C_3(x,y) \\
y \rightarrow f(s) \leftarrow x & \text{if } C_4(x,y)
\end{cases}
\end{cases}
$$

We now propose the following algorithm:

$t \longleftarrow \mathsf{LeftRightRec}(s) \;\; \widehat{=}$
    PRE
        $s \in \mathsf{seq}(u)$
    THEN
        VAR i,j IN
           $i,j,t := 1,\ \mathsf{size}(s),\ s\,;$
           WHILE $i < j$ DO
               SELECT $C_1(s(i), s(j))$ THEN
                  $i := i + 1$
               WHEN $C_2(s(i), s(j))$ THEN
                  $j := j - 1$
               WHEN $C_3(s(i), s(j))$ THEN
                  $i,j := i + 1,\ j - 1$
               WHEN $C_4(s(i), s(j))$ THEN
                  $t := t \Lleftarrow \{i \mapsto t(j),\ j \mapsto t(i)\}\,;$
                  $i,j := i + 1,\ j - 1$
               END
           INVARIANT
              $t \in \mathsf{seq}(u)$ $\wedge$
              $i \in 1 .. \mathsf{size}(s)$ $\wedge$
              $j \in 1 .. \mathsf{size}(s)$ $\wedge$
              $i \leq j + 1$ $\wedge$
              $\mathsf{size}(s) = \mathsf{size}(t)$ $\wedge$
              $f(s) = (t \uparrow i - 1) \frown f(t \uparrow j \downarrow i - 1) \frown (t \downarrow j)$
           VARIANT
              $j + 1 - i$
           END
        END
    END

Algorithm 10.4.11

We would like this algorithm to establish the following:

PRE $\Rightarrow$ $[t \longleftarrow \mathsf{LeftRightRec}(s)]\,(t = f(s))$ Property 10.4.10

The proof is straightforward although a bit tedious.

We now study our second example: the partitioning of a sequence. This leads to the following classical algorithm doing the "in place" partitioning:

$t \longleftarrow \mathsf{LeftRightPart}(n,s) \;\;\widehat{=}$

    PRE

        $n \in \mathbb{N} \quad \wedge$

        $s \in \mathsf{seq}\,(\mathbb{N})$

    THEN

        VAR $\;\; i,j \;\;$ IN

            $i,j,t := 1,\; \mathsf{size}\,(s),\; s\;;$

            WHILE $\;\; i < j \;\;$ DO

                SELECT $\;\; (s(i) \le n) \;\; \wedge \;\; (s(j) \le n) \;\;$ THEN

                    $i := i + 1$

                WHEN $\;\; (n < s(i)) \;\; \wedge \;\; (n < s(j)) \;\;$ THEN

                    $j := j - 1$

                WHEN $\;\; (n < s(i)) \;\; \wedge \;\; (s(j) \le n) \;\;$ THEN

                    $t := t \lhd\!\!+ \{i \mapsto t(j),\, j \mapsto t(i)\}\;;$

                    $i,\, j := i + 1,\, j - 1$

                WHEN $\;\; (s(i) \le n) \;\; \wedge \;\; (n < s(j)) \;\;$ THEN

                    $i,\, j := i + 1,\, j - 1$

                END

            INVARIANT

                $\ldots$

            VARIANT

                $j + 1 - i$

            END

        END

    END

Algorithm 10.4.12

And we have

PRE $\Rightarrow$ $[t \longleftarrow \mathsf{LeftRightPart}(s)]\,(t = \mathsf{partlr}(s))$ Property 10.4.11

Notice that we may end up either with $i = j$ or with $i = j + 1$.

We can also use the generic algorithm to derive the following reversing substitution. The corresponding classical algorithm doing the "in place" reversing follows immediately.

$t \longleftarrow \mathsf{LeftRightRevlr}(s) \;\; \widehat{=}$

    PRE

        $s \in \mathsf{seq}(u)$

    THEN

        VAR i,j IN

            $i,j,t := 1, \mathsf{size}(s), s\,;$

            WHILE $i < j$ DO

                $t := t \lessdot \{i \mapsto t(j), j \mapsto t(i)\}\,;$

                $i,j := i + 1, j - 1$

            INVARIANT

                $\ldots$

            VARIANT

                $j + 1 - i$

            END

        END

    END

Algorithm 10.4.13

And we have

PRE $\Rightarrow$ $[t \longleftarrow \mathsf{LeftRightRevlr}(s)]\,(t = \mathsf{revlr}(s))$ Property 10.4.12

Notice again that we may end up either with $i = j$ or with $i = j + 1$.

10.4.7. Filters

Within this section (prepared with the help of Rosemary Docherty), we consider a function, say f, transforming an element of a certain set u into a sequence of elements of u:

$$f \in u \to \mathsf{seq}(u)$$

Composing such a function with a certain sequence s belonging to $\mathsf{seq}(u)$

$$s \in \mathsf{seq}(u)$$

yields a sequence of sequences

$$(f \circ s) \in \mathsf{seq}(\mathsf{seq}(u))$$

Once flattened, this sequence of sequences produces a simple sequence of elements of u. This flattening is performed by means of the generalized concatenation operator, conc, which was defined in section 3.7.3.

$$\text{conc}\,(f \circ s) \in \text{seq}\,(u)$$

This process is called a "filter", because we may consider that the input sequence s has been filtered into the output sequence $\text{conc}\,(f \circ s)$. This can be formalised by means of the following function:

$$\text{filter} \in (u \to \text{seq}\,(u)) \to (\text{seq}\,(u) \to \text{seq}\,(u))$$

which is thus defined as follows:

$$\boxed{\text{filter}\,(f)(s) = \text{conc}\,(f \circ s)}$$

For instance, given the following function f:

$$f = \lambda x \cdot (x \in \mathbb{N} \mid [x,x])$$

we have

$$\text{filter}\,(f)(\,[1,2,3]\,)$$
$$=$$
$$\text{conc}\,(f \circ [1,2,3]\,)$$
$$=$$
$$\text{conc}\,(\,[f(1),f(2),f(3)]\,)$$
$$=$$
$$\text{conc}\,(\,[\,[1,1],\ [2,2],\ [3,3]\,]\,)$$
$$=$$
$$[1,1,2,2,3,3]$$

From the above definition, we deduce immediately the following property:

$$\text{filter}\,(f)(s \frown t) = \text{filter}\,(f)(s) \frown \text{filter}\,(f)(t) \qquad \text{Property 10.4.13}$$

We also deduce the following two recursive definitions:

$$\boxed{\begin{aligned}
\text{filter}\,(f)(\,[\,]\,) &= [\,] \\
\text{filter}\,(f)(x \to s) &= f(x) \frown \text{filter}\,(f)(s) \\
\text{filter}\,(f)(s \leftarrow x) &= \text{filter}\,(f)(s) \frown f(x)
\end{aligned}}$$

As a consequence and thanks to the substitution RightRecSeq given by Algorithm 10.4.1, we can define the following substitution computing a filter:

$$
\begin{array}{l}
r \longleftarrow \mathsf{EvalFilter}\,(f,s) \;\; \widehat{=} \\
\quad \text{PRE} \\
\qquad f \in u \to \mathsf{seq}\,(u)) \quad \wedge \\
\qquad s \in \mathsf{seq}\,(u) \\
\quad \text{THEN} \\
\qquad \text{VAR} \quad k \quad \text{IN} \\
\qquad\quad r,k \,:=\, [\,]\,,\ 1\,; \\
\qquad\quad \text{WHILE} \quad k \le \mathsf{size}\,(s) \quad \text{DO} \\
\qquad\qquad r,k \,:=\, r \mathbin{\frown} f(s(k)),\ k+1 \\
\qquad\quad \text{INVARIANT} \\
\qquad\qquad k \in 1\mathinner{\ldotp\ldotp}\mathsf{size}(s)+1 \quad \wedge \\
\qquad\qquad r = \mathsf{filter}\,(s \uparrow (k-1)) \\
\qquad\quad \text{VARIANT} \\
\qquad\qquad \mathsf{size}(s)+1-k \\
\qquad\quad \text{END} \\
\qquad \text{END} \\
\quad \text{END}
\end{array}
$$

Algorithm 10.4.14

Clearly, once a sequence has been passed through a filter, it can be filtered again through another filter, and so on, through the various elements of a finite sequence of filters. If we consider just the initial input together with the final output, such sequences could equally well be considered as the input and output of a *single* filter, which we call a "filter-pipe". In fact, a filter-pipe is just the composition of a sequence of filters. The following fpipe function evaluates a filter-pipe:

$$
\mathsf{fpipe} \in \mathsf{seq}\,(u \to \mathsf{seq}\,(u)) \to (\mathsf{seq}\,(u) \to \mathsf{seq}\,(u))
$$

It is defined by composing together the filters of the sequence of filters:

$$
\mathsf{fpipe}\,(sf) = \mathsf{comp}\,(\mathsf{filter} \circ sf)
$$

where comp is the *generalized composition* operator defined in section 3.7.3. For instance, consider the following functions f, g, and h:

$$
\begin{aligned}
f &= \lambda x \cdot (x \in \mathbb{N} \mid [x,x]) \\
g &= \lambda x \cdot (x \in \mathbb{N} \mid [x+1]) \\
h &= \lambda x \cdot (x \in \mathbb{N} \mid [x]) \mathbin{\lhd\!\!\!-} \{3 \mapsto [\,]\}
\end{aligned}
$$

Notice that the last function, h, generates a singleton sequence corresponding to its input, unless the input is the number 3, in which case the output is the empty sequence. We have then

$$\text{fpipe} ([f, g, h]) ([1, 2, 3])$$
$$=$$
$$\text{comp} (\text{filter} \circ [f, g, h])([1, 2, 3])$$
$$=$$
$$\text{comp} ([\text{filter} (f), \text{filter} (g), \text{filter} (h)]) ([1, 2, 3])$$
$$=$$
$$(\text{filter} (h) \circ \text{filter} (g) \circ \text{filter} (f)) ([1, 2, 3])$$
$$=$$
$$(\text{filter} (h) \circ \text{filter} (g)) ([1, 1, 2, 2, 3, 3])$$
$$=$$
$$\text{filter} (h) ([2, 2, 3, 3, 4, 4])$$
$$=$$
$$[2, 2, 4, 4]$$

Again, we could have defined a *single* filter acting as this filter-pipe and thus transforming the sequence $[1, 2, 3]$ directly into the sequence $[2, 2, 4, 4]$. Our thesis, however, is that such a definition might be too complicated. We believe that a better approach consists of defining the three filters independently, and then having a *unique mechanism* allowing us to monitor them. In the remaining part of this section, our intention is to construct an algorithm able to *compute* a filter-pipe from its component filters.

From the previous definition, we deduce immediately the following property:

$$\text{fpipe} (sf \frown sg) = \text{fpipe} (sg) \circ \text{fpipe} (sf) \qquad \text{Property 10.4.14}$$

---

and also

$$\text{fpipe} ([f]) = \text{filter} (f) \qquad \text{Property 10.4.15}$$

We also deduce easily the following recursive definitions:

$$\text{fpipe} ([]) = \text{id} (\text{seq} (u))$$
$$\text{fpipe} (sf \leftarrow f) = \text{filter} (f) \circ \text{fpipe} (sf)$$
$$\text{fpipe} (f \rightarrow sf) = \text{fpipe} (sf) \circ \text{filter} (f)$$

Our next step consists of associating, with each component filter of a filter-pipe, a corresponding *input* sequence, as shown in the following picture

The idea we have in mind is that the output sequence of a filter f (output produced by the first element of the input sequence associated with f) will be appended to the input sequence of the filter g situated next to f in the filter-pipe. For this, we define a function seqFpipe which is given, as arguments, a filter-pipe and a sequence of sequences (of the *same size* as the filter-pipe), and which will produce a corresponding output sequence. Formally

$$\text{seqFpipe} \in \text{seq}(u \to \text{seq}(u)) \times \text{seq}(\text{seq}(u)) \twoheadrightarrow \text{seq}(u)$$

The function seqFpipe is defined recursively on both sequences *simultaneously* as follows:

---

seqFpipe $([\,],[\,]) = [\,]$
seqFpipe $(sf \leftarrow f, \; ss \leftarrow s) = \text{filter}(f)(s) \frown \text{filter}(f)(\text{seqFpipe}(sf, ss))$

For instance, taking the same example functions f, g and h as before, we have

seqFpipe $([f, g, h], [[1, 2], [2, 3], [4, 5]])$
$=$
　filter $(h)([4, 5]) \frown$ filter $(h)(\text{seqFpipe}([f, g], [[1, 2], [2, 3]]))$
$=$
　$[4, 5] \frown$ filter $(h)(\text{filter}(g)([2, 3]) \frown$ filter $(g)(\text{seqFpipe}([f], [[1, 2]])))$
$=$
　$[4, 5] \frown$ filter $(h)([3, 4] \frown$ filter $(g)(\text{filter}(f)([1, 2])))$
$=$
　$[4, 5] \frown$ filter $(h)([3, 4]) \frown$ filter $(h)(\text{filter}(g)(\text{filter}(f)([1, 2])))$
$=$
　$[4, 5] \frown [4] \frown$ filter $(h)(\text{filter}(g)([1, 1, 2, 2]))$
$=$
　$[4, 5, 4] \frown$ filter $(h)([2, 2, 3, 3])$
$=$
　$[4, 5, 4] \frown [2, 2]$
$=$
　$[4, 5, 4, 2, 2]$

From the above definition, we deduce the following properties:

Property 10.4.16

seqFpipe $(sf \frown sg, \; ss \frown tt) = \text{seqFpipe}(sg, tt) \frown \text{fpipe}(sg)(\text{seqFpipe}(sf, ss))$

Proof
　The proof is by (simultaneous) induction on sg and tt.
　Base Case: We have to prove

　　　seqFpipe $(sf \frown [\,], \; ss \frown [\,]) =$
　　　　seqFpipe $([\,],[\,]) \frown \text{fpipe}([\,])(\text{seqFpipe}(sf, ss))$

The proof goes as follows:

$$\mathsf{seqFpipe}\,(\,[\,],[\,]\,)\,{}^\frown\mathsf{fpipe}\,(\,[\,]\,)(\mathsf{seqFpipe}\,(sf,ss))$$
$$=\qquad\qquad\qquad\qquad\qquad\text{Definition of seqFpipe}$$
$$\mathsf{fpipe}\,(\,[\,]\,)(\mathsf{seqFpipe}\,(sf,ss))$$
$$=\qquad\qquad\qquad\qquad\qquad\text{Recursive definition of fpipe}$$
$$\mathsf{seqFpipe}\,(sf,ss)$$
$$=$$
$$\mathsf{seqFpipe}\,(sf\,{}^\frown[\,],\ ss\,{}^\frown[\,]\,)$$

Step Case: We assume

$$\mathsf{seqFpipe}\,(sf\,{}^\frown sg,\ ss\,{}^\frown tt)\,=\qquad\qquad\qquad\text{Hypothesis}$$
$$\mathsf{seqFpipe}\,(sg,tt)\,{}^\frown\mathsf{fpipe}\,(sg)(\mathsf{seqFpipe}\,(sf,ss))$$

And we have to prove

$$\mathsf{seqFpipe}\,(sf\,{}^\frown sg\leftarrow g,\ ss\,{}^\frown tt\leftarrow t)\,=$$
$$\mathsf{seqFpipe}\,(sg\leftarrow g,\ tt\leftarrow t)\,{}^\frown\mathsf{fpipe}\,(sg\leftarrow g)(\mathsf{seqFpipe}\,(sf,ss))$$

The proof goes as follows:

$$\mathsf{seqFpipe}\,(sf\,{}^\frown sg\leftarrow g,\ ss\,{}^\frown tt\leftarrow t)$$
$$=\qquad\qquad\qquad\qquad\qquad\text{Definition of seqFpipe}$$
$$\mathsf{filter}\,(g)(t)\,{}^\frown\mathsf{filter}\,(g)(\mathsf{seqFpipe}\,(sf\,{}^\frown sg,\ ss\,{}^\frown tt)$$
$$=\qquad\qquad\qquad\qquad\qquad\text{Hypothesis}$$
$$\mathsf{filter}\,(g)(t)\,{}^\frown\mathsf{filter}\,(g)(\mathsf{seqFpipe}\,(sg,tt)\,{}^\frown$$
$$\qquad\mathsf{fpipe}\,(sg)(\mathsf{seqFpipe}\,(sf,ss)))$$
$$=\qquad\qquad\qquad\qquad\qquad\text{Property 10.4.13}$$
$$\mathsf{filter}\,(g)(t)\,{}^\frown\mathsf{filter}\,(g)(\mathsf{seqFpipe}\,(sg,tt))\,{}^\frown$$
$$\qquad\mathsf{filter}\,(g)(\mathsf{fpipe}\,(sg)(\mathsf{seqFpipe}\,(sf,ss)))$$
$$=\qquad\qquad\qquad\qquad\qquad\text{Definition of seqFpipe}$$
$$\mathsf{seqFpipe}\,(sg\leftarrow g,\ tt\leftarrow t)\,{}^\frown$$
$$\qquad\mathsf{filter}\,(g)(\mathsf{fpipe}\,(sg)(\mathsf{seqFpipe}\,(sf,ss)))$$
$$=\qquad\qquad\qquad\qquad\qquad\text{Recursive definition of fpipe}$$
$$\mathsf{seqFpipe}\,(sg\leftarrow g,\ tt\leftarrow t)\,{}^\frown\mathsf{fpipe}\,(sg\leftarrow g)(\mathsf{seqFpipe}\,(sf,ss))$$

End of Proof

We also have

$$\mathsf{seqFpipe}\,([f],\ [s])=\mathsf{filter}\,(f)(s)\qquad\qquad\qquad\text{Property 10.4.17}$$

Our next property shows how our intuitive intention is formally realized. More precisely, it shows how the first filter, f, of two consecutive filters f and g "passes" to the second one, g, the result of filtering the *first* element of its input sequence (supposed to be non-empty). In other words, the resulting sequence is concatenated to the end of the input sequence associated with g. More formally, we have:

$$\text{seqFpipe} \left([f, g], [x \to s, t] \right) =$$
$$\text{seqFpipe} \left([f, g], [s, t \cap f(x)] \right)$$

Property 10.4.18

Proof

The proof of this property goes as follows:

$\text{seqFpipe} \left([f, g], [x \to s, t] \right)$
$=$ Property 10.4.16
$\text{seqFpipe} \left([g], [t] \right) \cap \text{fpipe} \left([g] \right) \left(\text{seqFpipe} \left([f], [x \to s] \right) \right)$
$=$ Property 10.4.17
$\text{filter} (g)(t) \cap \text{fpipe} \left([g] \right) \left(\text{filter} (f)(x \to s) \right)$
$=$ Property 10.4.15
$\text{filter} (g)(t) \cap \text{filter} (g) \left(\text{filter} (f)(x \to s) \right)$
$=$ Recursive definition of filter
$\text{filter} (g)(t) \cap \text{filter} (g) \left(f(x) \cap \text{filter} (f)(s) \right)$
$=$ Property 10.4.13
$\text{filter} (g)(t \cap f(x) \cap \text{filter} (f)(s))$
$=$ Property 10.4.13
$\text{filter} (g)(t \cap f(x)) \cap \text{filter} (g) \left(\text{filter} (f)(s) \right)$
$=$ Property 10.4.15
$\text{filter} (g)(t \cap f(x)) \cap \text{fpipe} \left([g] \right) \left(\text{filter} (f)(s) \right)$
$=$ Property 10.4.17
$\text{seqFpipe} \left([g], [t \cap f(x)] \right) \cap \text{fpipe} \left([g] \right) \left(\text{seqFpipe} \left([f], [s] \right) \right)$
$=$ Property 10.4.16
$\text{seqFpipe} \left([f, g], [s, t \cap f(x)] \right)$

End of Proof

The previous property can be generalized. We still consider two consecutive filters f and g as before but, this time, these elements are supposed to be embedded in a larger filter-pipe. The result is essentially the same: the filter f passes to g the computation of the first element of its input sequence to be appended to the input sequence of g. And this is done while the other filters remain inactive. We leave the proof of this property as an exercise for the reader.

$$\text{seqFpipe} \left(sf \cap [f, g] \cap sg, ss \cap [x \to s, t] \cap tt \right)$$
$$=$$ Property 10.4.19
$$\text{seqFpipe} \left(sf \cap [f, g] \cap sg, ss \cap [s, t \cap f(x)] \cap tt \right)$$

Next is another form of Property 10.4.19:

$k \in \mathsf{dom}\,(ss)$
$ss(k) \neq [\,]$
$\Rightarrow$ **Property 10.4.20**
$\mathsf{seqFpipe}\,(sf,\ ss) =$
    $\mathsf{seqFpipe}\,(sf,\ ss \lhd\!\!\!+ \{\, k \mapsto \mathsf{tail}\,(ss(k)),\ (k+1) \mapsto sf(k)(\mathsf{first}\,(ss(k)))\,\})$

Finally, we consider the case of the last filter of a pipe. This corresponds to the following property, whose proof is left to the reader.

Property 10.4.21
$\mathsf{seqFpipe}\,(sf \leftarrow f,\ ss \leftarrow (x \rightarrow s)) \ = \ f(x) \,\frown\, \mathsf{seqFpipe}\,(sf \leftarrow f,\ ss \leftarrow s)$

Next is another form of **Property 10.4.21**:

$k = \mathsf{size}\,(ss)$
$k \neq 0$
$ss(k) \neq [\,]$ **Property 10.4.22**
$\Rightarrow$
$\mathsf{seqFpipe}\,(sf,\ ss) =$
    $sf(k)(\mathsf{first}\,(ss(k))) \,\frown\, \mathsf{seqFpipe}\,(sf,\ ss \lhd\!\!\!+ \{\, k \mapsto \mathsf{tail}\,(ss(k))\,\})$

Property 10.4.20 and **Property 10.4.22** form the theoretical basis on which our forthcoming algorithm is constructed. We notice that a sequence of filters whose input sequences are all empty, is itself empty. This can be formalized in the following property:

$\mathsf{seqFpipe}\,(sf,\ \mathsf{dom}\,(sf) \times \{[\,]\}) = [\,]$ **Property 10.4.23**

This can be proved by induction on sf. Our final property expresses the fact that a non-empty filter-pipe may be computed by a **seqFpipe** initialized with empty sequences, except for the first one.

Property 10.4.24
$\mathsf{fpipe}\,(f \rightarrow sf)(s) = \mathsf{seqFpipe}\,(f \rightarrow sf,\ s \rightarrow \mathsf{dom}\,(sf) \times \{[\,]\})$

This initial situation can be represented pictorially as follows:

All this leads to the following substitution:

$r \longleftarrow \text{EvalFpipe}(sf, s) \ \widehat{=}$
  PRE
    $sf \in \text{seq}_1(u \to \text{seq}(u)) \quad \wedge$
    $s \in \text{seq}(u)$
  THEN
    VAR ss, k IN
      $r, ss, k := [], \ s \to (1 .. \text{size}(sf) - 1) \times \{[]\}, \ 1;$
      WHILE $k > 0$ DO
        IF $ss(k) = []$ THEN
          $k := k - 1$
        ELSIF $k < \text{size}(ss)$ THEN
          $ss := ss \Leftarrow \{ k \mapsto \text{tail}(ss(k)), \ (k+1) \mapsto sf(k)(\text{first}(ss(k))) \};$
          $k := k + 1$
        ELSE
          $r := r \frown sf(k)(\text{first}(ss(k)));$
          $ss(k) := \text{tail}(ss(k))$
        END
      INVARIANT
        $r \in \text{seq}(u) \quad \wedge$
        $ss \in \text{seq}(\text{seq}(u)) \quad \wedge$
        $\text{size}(ss) = \text{size}(sf) \quad \wedge$
        $k \in 0 .. \text{size}(ss) \quad \wedge$
        $r \frown \text{seqFpipe}(sf, ss) = \text{fpipe}(sf)(s) \quad \wedge$
        $\text{ran}(ss \downarrow k) = \{[]\}$
      VARIANT
        $(\text{size}; ss)$
      END
    END
  END

Algorithm 10.4.15

Notice that the variant is a sequence of natural numbers. We leave the proof of the following as an exercise for the reader:

PRE $\Rightarrow$ $[r \longleftarrow \text{EvalFpipe}(sf, s)](r = \text{fpipe}(sf)(s))$ Property 10.4.25

Proof of Property 10.4.24

The proof of this property goes as follows:

$$\mathsf{seqFpipe}\,(f \to sf,\ s \to \mathrm{dom}\,(sf) \times \{[]\})$$

$$=\qquad\qquad\qquad\qquad\qquad\qquad\qquad \text{Property 10.4.16}$$

$$\mathsf{seqFpipe}\,(sf,\ \mathrm{dom}\,(sf) \times \{[]\}) \frown \mathsf{fpipe}\,(sf)(\mathsf{seqFpipe}\,([f],\ [s]))$$

$$=\qquad\qquad\qquad\qquad\qquad\qquad\qquad \text{Property 10.4.23}$$

$$\mathsf{fpipe}\,(sf)(\mathsf{seqFpipe}\,([f],\ [s]))$$

$$=\qquad\qquad\qquad\qquad\qquad\qquad\qquad \text{Property 10.4.17}$$

$$\mathsf{fpipe}\,(sf)(\mathsf{filter}\,(f)(s))$$

$$=\qquad\qquad\qquad\qquad\qquad\qquad \text{Recursive definition of fpipe}$$

$$\mathsf{fpipe}\,(f \to sf)(s)$$

End of Proof

10.5. Trees

In this section, we develop various examples dealing with the processing of binary trees as defined in section 3.10. Such trees are good candidates to formalize the kinds of mathematical formulae we encounter in this book. In what follows, we shall develop an algorithm to parse such formulae. The next sections introduce the notion of formulae (section 10.5.1), the transformation of a binary tree into a formula (section 10.5.2), the transformation of a binary tree into a Polish string (section 10.5.3), and finally, the direct transformation of a formula into a Polish string (section 10.5.4).

We shall first suppose that our formulae are built by means of a set TOK. Moreover, we suppose that this set can be *partitioned* into three sets called ATM, OPR and BRK. For example, we might have

$$TOK = \{+,\ -,\ *,\ /,\ \mathrm{a},\ \mathrm{b},\ \mathrm{c},\ \mathrm{d},\ \mathrm{e},\ (,\ )\}$$

$$OPR = \{+,\ -,\ *,\ /\}$$

$$ATM = \{\mathrm{a},\ \mathrm{b},\ \mathrm{c},\ \mathrm{d},\ \mathrm{e}\}$$

$$BRK = \{(,\ )\}$$

In this example, we have used a typewriter font to represent the members of the set TOK. In fact, this is just for convenience. These symbols are supposed to denote "painted" representations of distinct natural numbers.

From an abstract point of view, a formula is just a member of the set $\mathrm{bin}\,(OPR \cup ATM)$ of labelled binary trees built on the set $OPR \cup ATM$. We remind the reader that the set $\mathrm{bin}\,(s)$ of labelled binary trees built on a set s has been defined in section 3.10. Here, we have the special extra restriction that the leaves of such binary trees are labelled by elements belonging to the set ATM, whereas the internal nodes are labelled by elements belonging to the set OPR.

The set of such special binary trees will be denoted by ftree throughout this section. Each element of such a set is either a *singleton* tree, say $\langle a \rangle$, where a is an element of the set *ATM*, or a *genuine* tree, say $\langle f, o, g \rangle$, where o is an element of the set *OPR* and where f and g are themselves elements of the set ftree. For instance, the following is a member of the set ftree:

$$\langle \langle \langle a \rangle, -, \langle b \rangle \rangle, +, \langle \langle c \rangle, *, \langle \langle d \rangle, -, \langle e \rangle \rangle \rangle \rangle$$

10.5.1. The Notion of Formula

In order to *present* elements of ftree, it is traditional to transform them into readable (and writable) *flat sequences* called *formulae*. To achieve this, one uses certain conventions whose rôle is to enhance readability without losing the underlying tree structure. For instance, we could agree that elements of the sets *ATM* and *OPR* are printed as such. Moreover, we may decide to use parentheses to isolate sub-formulae. By using these conventions on the example of the previous section, we obtain the following:

$$[(, a, -, b,), +, (, c, *, (, d, -, e,),),)]$$

In order to enhance the readability of such sequence formulae, we shall adopt the convention, throughout this section, of removing the external square brackets and the internal commas separating the elements of these sequences. This yields the following:

$$(\quad a \quad - \quad b \quad) \quad + \quad (\quad c \quad * \quad (\quad d \quad - \quad e \quad) \quad)$$

Clearly, such a formula contains too many brackets. In order to remove some of them, we may adopt some further conventions: we may agree that operators *associate to the left* so that *implicit* parentheses always surround the left most part of sub-formulae. For instance, following this convention, a formula such as a+b-c+d-e stands for (((a+b)-c)+d)-e. On our previous example, we obtain:

$$a \quad - \quad b \quad + \quad (\quad c \quad * \quad (\quad d \quad - \quad e \quad) \quad)$$

A notion of *operator precedence* has been introduced in order to remove more brackets. More precisely, to each member of the set *OPR*, we associate a natural number called its *priority*. The higher the priority, the higher the *power of attraction* of the corresponding operator. For instance, we might assign the following priorities to our example operators:

operator	+	−	*	/
priority	1	1	2	2

Then the formula `a+b*c` stands for `a+(b*c)`: this is so because the left asssociation convention is overridden by the fact that the priority of `*` is greater than that of `+`. In other words, the operator `*` attracts more strongly than the operator `+` does. In our previous example, the application of the priority rule leads to the following final formula:

$$a \quad - \quad b \quad + \quad c \quad * \quad (\quad d \quad - \quad e \quad)$$

We now define the priorities in the form of a certain function prit:

$$\text{prit} \in TOK \rightarrow \mathbb{N}$$

The function prit has the following properties stating that the priorities of brackets are smaller than those of operators, which are themselves smaller than those of atoms.

$$\forall (b,o) \cdot (b \in BRK \ \wedge \ o \in OPR \ \Rightarrow \ \text{prit}(b) < \text{prit}(o))$$

$$\forall (o,a) \cdot (o \in OPR \ \wedge \ a \in ATM \ \Rightarrow \ \text{prit}(o) < \text{prit}(a))$$

For later convenience, we now extend this notion of priority, defined so far for elements of the set TOK, to members of the set ftree. This can be done by means of the following obvious recursive definition of a function called prif:

$$\begin{cases} \text{prif}(\langle a \rangle) & = & \text{prit}(a) \\ \text{prif}(\langle f,o,g \rangle) & = & \text{prit}(o) \end{cases}$$

10.5.2. Transforming a Tree into a Formula

We are now ready to define a function gen transforming an element of ftree into a formula, that is a certain sequence of elements of the set TOK, formally

$$\text{gen} \in \text{ftree} \rightarrow \text{seq}(TOK)$$

Here is the recusive definition of gen:

$$
\begin{cases}
\text{gen}(\langle a \rangle) \quad = \quad [a] \\[2ex]
\text{gen}(\langle f, o, g \rangle) \quad = \quad
\begin{cases}
[(]\,{}^\frown \text{gen}(f)\,{}^\frown [)]\,{}^\frown [o]\,{}^\frown \text{gen}(g) & \text{if } P \wedge Q \\
[(]\,{}^\frown \text{gen}(f)\,{}^\frown [)]\,{}^\frown [o]\,{}^\frown [(]\,{}^\frown \text{gen}(g)\,{}^\frown [)] & \text{if } P \wedge \neg Q \\
\text{gen}(f)\,{}^\frown [o]\,{}^\frown \text{gen}(g) & \text{if } \neg P \wedge Q \\
\text{gen}(f)\,{}^\frown [o]\,{}^\frown [(]\,{}^\frown \text{gen}(g)\,{}^\frown [)] & \text{if } \neg P \wedge \neg Q
\end{cases}
\end{cases}
$$

where

$$
\begin{cases}
P \;\hat{=}\; \text{prif}(f) < \text{prit}(o) \\[1ex]
Q \;\hat{=}\; \text{prit}(o) < \text{prif}(g)
\end{cases}
$$

As an example, we now compute the following:

$$\text{gen}(\langle \langle \langle a \rangle, -, \langle b \rangle \rangle, +, \langle \langle c \rangle, *, \langle \langle d \rangle, -, \langle e \rangle \rangle \rangle \rangle)$$

=

$$\text{gen}(\langle \langle a \rangle, -, \langle b \rangle \rangle)\,{}^\frown [+]\,{}^\frown \text{gen}(\langle \langle c \rangle, *, \langle \langle d \rangle, -, \langle e \rangle \rangle \rangle)$$

=

$$[a]\,{}^\frown [-]\,{}^\frown [b]\,{}^\frown [+]\,{}^\frown \text{gen}(\langle \langle c \rangle, *, \langle \langle d \rangle, -, \langle e \rangle \rangle \rangle)$$

=

$$[a]\,{}^\frown [-]\,{}^\frown [b]\,{}^\frown [+]\,{}^\frown [c]\,{}^\frown [*]\,{}^\frown [(]\,{}^\frown \text{gen}(\langle \langle d \rangle, -, \langle e \rangle \rangle)\,{}^\frown [)]$$

=

$$[a]\,{}^\frown [-]\,{}^\frown [b]\,{}^\frown [+]\,{}^\frown [c]\,{}^\frown [*]\,{}^\frown [(]\,{}^\frown [d]\,{}^\frown [-]\,{}^\frown [e]\,{}^\frown [)]$$

=

$$a \quad - \quad b \quad + \quad c \quad * \quad (\quad d \quad - \quad e \quad)$$

We now have to prove what we claim informally, namely that the conventions adopted to remove brackets in formulae *do not destroy their underlying tree structure*. This can be formalized by the fact that the function gen is indeed *injective*. For proving this property, we need the following lemma which is left as an exercise for the reader:

$$\text{gen}(f) = s\,{}^\frown [o]\,{}^\frown t \;\Rightarrow\; \text{prif}(f) \leq \text{prit}(o) \qquad \text{Property 10.5.1}$$

---

where s and t are members of ran (gen) or are sequences of the form $[(]\,{}^\frown u\,{}^\frown [)]$, where u is a member of ran (gen). We now prove our main property, namely

---

$$\text{gen} \in \text{ftree} \rightarrowtail \text{seq}(TOK) \qquad \text{Property 10.5.2}$$

Proof

We can re-phrase the statement to be proved as follows:

$$\forall f \cdot (f \in \mathsf{ftree} \;\Rightarrow\; \forall h \cdot (h \in \mathsf{ftree} \;\wedge\; \mathsf{gen}(f) = \mathsf{gen}(h) \;\Rightarrow\; f = h\,))$$

The proof is by induction on f. As the base case is obvious, we shall proceed directly with the induction step. We assume

$f \in \mathsf{ftree}$	Hypothesis 1
$\forall h \cdot (h \in \mathsf{ftree} \;\wedge\; \mathsf{gen}(f) = \mathsf{gen}(h) \;\Rightarrow\; f = h\,))$	
$g \in \mathsf{ftree}$	
$\forall h \cdot (h \in \mathsf{ftree} \;\wedge\; \mathsf{gen}(g) = \mathsf{gen}(h) \;\Rightarrow\; g = h\,))$	
$o \in OPR$	

And we have to prove

$$\forall h \cdot (h \in \mathsf{ftree} \;\wedge\; \mathsf{gen}(\langle f, o, g\rangle) = \mathsf{gen}(h) \;\Rightarrow\; \langle f, o, g\rangle = h\,)) \quad \text{Goal 1}$$

Obviously, this result holds when h is a singleton ftree (since in that case, we clearly have $\langle f, o, g\rangle) \neq \mathsf{gen}(h)$), so that we can suppose that h is of the form $\langle f', o', g'\rangle$. We assume then the following:

$f' \in \mathsf{ftree}$	Hypothesis 2
$g' \in \mathsf{ftree}$	
$o' \in OPR$	
$\mathsf{gen}(\langle f, o, g\rangle) = \mathsf{gen}(\langle f', o', g'\rangle)$	

and we are left to prove

$$\langle f, o, g\rangle = \langle f', o', g'\rangle \qquad\qquad \text{Goal 2}$$

The proof proceeds by contradiction. In other words, we suppose

$$\langle f, o, g\rangle) \;\neq\; \langle f', o', g'\rangle \qquad\qquad \text{Hypothesis 3}$$

and we try to derive a contradiction. The proof now proceeds by cases corresponding to the various cases encountered in the definition of gen. We have first

$$\mathsf{prif}(f) < \mathsf{prit}(o) \;\wedge\; \mathsf{prit}(o) < \mathsf{prif}(g) \qquad\qquad \text{case 1}$$

From Hypothesis 2, Case 1 and the definition of gen, we can then deduce the following:

$$[(] \,\frown\, \mathsf{gen}(f) \,\frown\, [)] \,\frown\, [o] \,\frown\, \mathsf{gen}(g) \;=\; \mathsf{gen}(\langle f', o', g'\rangle) \;\; \text{Derivation 1}$$

Suppose now that $\mathsf{gen}(f')$ is equal to $\mathsf{gen}(f)$ then $\mathsf{gen}(\langle f', o', g'\rangle)$ must necessarily start with $[(] \,\frown\, \mathsf{gen}(f') \,\frown\, [)]$, thus necessarily $o = o'$ and then $\mathsf{gen}(g') = \mathsf{gen}(g)$. From Hypothesis 1, we would then have $f = f'$ and $g = g'$ and thus $\langle f, o, g\rangle = \langle f', o', g'\rangle$, contradicting Hypothesis 3. Thus we have necessarily

Derivation 2

$$\mathsf{gen}(\langle f', o', g'\rangle) \;=\; [(] \,\frown\, \mathsf{gen}(f) \,\frown\, [)] \,\frown\, [o] \,\frown\, s \,\frown\, [o'] \,\frown\, t$$

where s and t are non-empty sequences. And thus, according to the definition of gen, we have

$$\text{prit}(o') \le \text{prif}(f') \qquad\qquad \text{Derivation 3}$$

Moreover, from Derivation 1 and Derivation 2, we then deduce:

$$\text{gen}(f') = [(] \frown \text{gen}(f) \frown [)] \frown [o] \frown s \qquad \text{Derivation 4}$$

and also

$$\text{gen}(g) = s \frown [o'] \frown t \qquad\qquad \text{Derivation 5}$$

From Derivation 4 and Property 10.5.1, we deduce

$$\text{prif}(f') \le \text{prit}(o) \qquad\qquad \text{Derivation 6}$$

Likewise, from Derivation 5 and Property 10.5.1, we deduce

$$\text{prif}(g) \le \text{prit}(o') \qquad\qquad \text{Derivation 7}$$

Putting together Derivation 3 and Derivation 6 and also Case 1 and Derivation 7, we now obtain the following, which is an obvious contradiction:

$$\text{prit}(o') \le \text{prit}(o) \ \land \ \text{prit}(o) < \text{prit}(o') \qquad \text{Derivation 8}$$

By studying the other cases, we would obtain similar contradictions.
End of Proof

In what follows, the set ran(gen) is called formula.

10.5.3. Transforming a Tree into a Polish String

In order to process an element of ftree, an interesting and economical technique consists of flattening it in a way which is very similar to what we have just done with the function gen. Here, however, the problem is not so much that of reading or writing formulae; rather it is that of storing and transforming them. A form which meets these requirements is obtained by flattening our ftree into the corresponding *postfixed* sequence. Throughout this section, the set of such postfixed sequences is abbreviated as polish. We remind the reader of the definition of the function post (already defined in section 3.10.4):

$$\begin{cases} \text{post}(\langle a \rangle) & = \ [a] \\ \text{post}(\langle f, o, g \rangle) & = \ \text{post}(f) \frown \text{post}(g) \leftarrow o \end{cases}$$

For instance, in our example, where we had the following member, f, of ftree:

$$f = \langle\langle\langle a \rangle, -, \langle b \rangle\rangle, +, \langle\langle c \rangle, *, \langle\langle d \rangle, -, \langle e \rangle\rangle\rangle\rangle$$

we obtain the following postfixed form which is a member of polish

$$\text{post}(f) = \text{a} \quad \text{b} \quad - \quad \text{c} \quad \text{d} \quad \text{e} \quad - \quad * \quad +$$

We also obtained the following which is a member of formula:

$$\text{gen}\,(f) \;=\; a \;-\; b \;+\; c \;*\; (\quad d \;-\; e \quad)$$

10.5.4. Transforming a Formula into a Polish String

The final problem that we want to address now is that of the construction of an algorithm *directly transforming* a formula, such as gen (f), into a polish such as post (f). This transformation is called the *parsing* of gen (f). Clearly, the function gen^{-1} ; post will do the job. Our strategy will be the following: we shall first propose a series of *rewriting rules*, then we shall prove that these rules define a function which will eventually parse a formula, and finally we shall construct our algorithm. Our rewriting rules define transformations for constructs of the form parse (t,s) where t and s are such that the following holds:

$$t \in \text{seq}\,(OPR \cup \{(\}) $$
$$s \in \text{seq}\,(TOK) $$

In the rule, we also use variables l and r which are such that

$$l \in OPR \cup \{(\} $$
$$r \in TOK $$

Here are the rules:

$$
\left\{
\begin{array}{llll}
\text{parse}\,(\,[\,],\; s) & = \; [\,] & & (1) \\[2mm]
\text{parse}\,(t,\; [\,]) & = \; [\,] & & (2) \\[2mm]
\text{parse}\,(t \leftarrow l,\; r \rightarrow s) & = &
\left\{
\begin{array}{ll}
r \rightarrow \text{parse}\,(t \leftarrow l,\; s) & \text{if} \quad r \in ATM \qquad (3) \\
\text{parse}\,(t \leftarrow l \leftarrow r,\; s) & \text{if} \quad r = (\qquad\qquad (4) \\
\text{parse}\,(t,s) & \text{if} \quad l = (\quad \text{and} \quad r =) \quad (5) \\
\text{parse}\,(t \leftarrow l \leftarrow r,\; s) & \text{if} \quad \text{prit}\,(l) < \text{prit}\,(r) \quad (6) \\
l \rightarrow \text{parse}\,(t,\; r \rightarrow s) & \text{otherwise} \qquad\qquad\quad (7)
\end{array}
\right.
\end{array}
\right.
$$

Notice that these rules constitute an instance of the general recursive scheme defined in section 3.11.3 on well-founded sets. Here the well-founded set is the one formed by a pair of sequences t, s, and the corresponding well-founded relation is the relation r between such pairs such that the following holds:

$$(t_1, s_1) \mapsto (t_2, s_2) \in r \quad \Leftrightarrow \quad 2 \times \text{size}\,(s_1) + \text{size}\,(t_1) \;>\; 2 \times \text{size}\,(s_2) + \text{size}\,(t_2)$$

Next is an example of applying the above rewriting rules:

```
parse( (   ,   a - b + c * ( d - e ) ) )
=                                                          case 3
a    ⌒   parse( (   ,    - b + c * ( d - e ) ) )
=                                                          case 6
a    ⌒   parse( ( -   ,   b + c * ( d - e ) ) )
=                                                          case 3
a  b   ⌒   parse( ( -   ,   + c * ( d - e ) ) )
=                                                          case 7
a  b  -   ⌒   parse( (   ,   + c * ( d - e ) ) )
=                                                          case 6
a  b  -   ⌒   parse( ( +   ,   c * ( d - e ) ) )
=                                                          case 3
a  b  - c   ⌒   parse( ( +   ,   * ( d - e ) ) )
=                                                          case 6
a  b  - c   ⌒   parse( ( + *   ,   ( d - e ) ) )
=                                                          case 4
a  b  - c   ⌒   parse( ( + * (   ,   d - e ) ) )
=                                                          case 3
a  b  - c  d   ⌒   parse( ( + * (   ,   - e ) ) )
=                                                          case 6
a  b  - c  d   ⌒   parse( ( + * ( -   ,   e ) ) )
=                                                          case 3
a  b  - c  d  e   ⌒   parse( ( + * ( -   ,   ) ) )
=                                                          case 7
a  b  - c  d  e  -   ⌒   parse( ( + * (   ,   ) ) )
=                                                          case 5
a  b  - c  d  e  -   ⌒   parse( ( + *   ,   ) )
=                                                          case 7
a  b  - c  d  e  - *   ⌒   parse( ( +   ,   ) )
=                                                          case 7
a  b  - c  d  e  - * +   ⌒   parse( (   ,   ) )
=                                                          case 5
a  b  - c  d  e  - * +   ⌒   parse( []   ,   [] )
=
a  b  - c  d  e  - * +
```

Our intention is to prove the following property for all tree f belonging to ftree:

$parse([( ], \ gen(f) \leftarrow)) = post(f)$ Property 10.5.3

In order to do so, we shall use the following alternative definition of gen which is clearly equivalent to the one given in section 10.5.2. This definition makes use of two extra abbreviations called gen_1 and gen_2

$$
\begin{cases}
gen(\langle a \rangle) & = \quad [a] \\
gen(\langle f, o, g \rangle) & = \quad gen_1(f, o) \frown [o] \frown gen_2(o, g)
\end{cases}
$$

where

$$
\begin{cases}
gen_1(f, o) & = \quad \begin{cases} [(] \frown gen(f) \frown [)] & \text{if } prif(f) < prit(o) \\ gen(f) & \text{otherwise} \end{cases} \\
\\
gen_2(o, g) & = \quad \begin{cases} gen(g) & \text{if } prit(o) < prif(g) \\ [(] \frown gen(g) \frown [)] & \text{otherwise} \end{cases}
\end{cases}
$$

Given the following definition:

$$
\begin{aligned}
HYP(f) \quad \hat{=} \quad & t \in seq\,(OPR \cup \{(\}) \\
& l \in OPR \cup \{(\} \\
& r \in TOK \\
& s \in seq\,(TOK) \\
& prit\,(l) < prif\,(f) \\
& prit\,(r) \le prif\,(f)
\end{aligned}
$$

Property 10.5.3 is an immediate consequence of the following more general property of members of ftree:

$f \in$ ftree

$\Rightarrow$

$\forall\,(t, l, r, s) \cdot (HYP(f) \;\Rightarrow$ Property 10.5.4

   $parse\,(t \leftarrow l,\; gen\,(f) \frown (r \rightarrow s)) \;=\; post\,(f) \frown parse\,(t \leftarrow l,\; r \rightarrow s)\,)$

Proof

The proof of this property is by induction on the ftree f, and relies on two lemmas, named **Lemma 1** and **Lemma 2**, that we shall prove just after the present proof.

Base Case: We have to prove the following for any *ATM* a:

$$
\begin{aligned}
\forall\,(t, l, r, s) \cdot (HYP(\langle a \rangle) \;\Rightarrow \qquad & \text{Goal 1} \\
parse\,(t \leftarrow l,\; gen\,(\langle a \rangle) \frown (r \rightarrow s)) = & \\
post\,(\langle a \rangle) \frown parse\,(t \leftarrow l,\; r \rightarrow s)\,) &
\end{aligned}
$$

We prove directly the following, which is obviously the same as the consequent of our previous goal according to the definitions of gen and post:

$$\mathsf{parse}\,(t \leftarrow l,\ [a] \frown (r \rightarrow s)) = [a] \frown \mathsf{parse}\,(t \leftarrow l,\ r \rightarrow s)\quad\text{Goal 2}$$

That is

$$\mathsf{parse}\,(t \leftarrow l,\ a \rightarrow r \rightarrow s) = [a] \frown \mathsf{parse}\,(t \leftarrow l,\ r \rightarrow s)\quad\text{Goal 3}$$

We then obtain the following obvious goal according to the definition of parse (case 3):

$$a \rightarrow \mathsf{parse}\,(t \leftarrow l,\ r \rightarrow s) = [a] \frown \mathsf{parse}\,(t \leftarrow l,\ r \rightarrow s)\quad\text{Goal 4}$$

Step Case: We assume the following:

$$f \in \mathsf{ftree}$$
$$g \in \mathsf{ftree}\qquad\qquad\qquad\qquad\qquad\qquad\qquad\text{Hypothesis 1}$$
$$o \in OPR$$

$$\forall\,(t,l,r,s)\cdot(HYP(f)\ \Rightarrow$$
$$\quad\mathsf{parse}\,(t \leftarrow l,\ \mathsf{gen}\,(f) \frown (r \rightarrow s)) =\qquad\qquad\text{Hypothesis 2}$$
$$\quad\mathsf{post}\,(f) \frown \mathsf{parse}\,(t \leftarrow l,\ r \rightarrow s)\ )$$

$$\forall\,(t,l,r,s)\cdot(HYP(g)\ \Rightarrow$$
$$\quad\mathsf{parse}\,(t \leftarrow l,\ \mathsf{gen}\,(g) \frown (r \rightarrow s)) =\qquad\qquad\text{Hypothesis 3}$$
$$\quad\mathsf{post}\,(g) \frown \mathsf{parse}\,(t \leftarrow l,\ r \rightarrow s)\ )$$

and we have to prove the following:

$$\forall\,(t,l,r,s)\cdot(HYP(\langle f,o,g\rangle)\ \Rightarrow$$
$$\quad\mathsf{parse}\,(t \leftarrow l,\ \mathsf{gen}\,(\langle f,o,g\rangle) \frown (r \rightarrow s)) =\qquad\text{Goal 5}$$
$$\quad\mathsf{post}\,(\langle f,o,g\rangle) \frown \mathsf{parse}\,(t \leftarrow l,\ r \rightarrow s)\ )$$

We may remove the universal quantification, so that we now assume $HYP(\langle f,o,g\rangle)$, that is:

$$t \in \mathsf{seq}\,(OPR \cup \{\langle\rangle)$$
$$l \in OPR \cup \{\langle\}$$
$$r \in TOK\qquad\qquad\qquad\qquad\qquad\qquad\qquad\text{Hypothesis 4}$$
$$s \in \mathsf{seq}\,(TOK)$$
$$\mathsf{prit}\,(l) < \mathsf{prit}\,(o)$$
$$\mathsf{prit}\,(r) \le \mathsf{prit}\,(o)$$

and we have to prove

$$\mathsf{parse}\,(t \leftarrow l,\ \mathsf{gen}\,(\langle f,o,g\rangle) \frown (r \rightarrow s))$$
$$=\qquad\qquad\qquad\qquad\qquad\qquad\qquad\qquad\text{Goal 6}$$
$$\mathsf{post}\,(\langle f,o,g\rangle) \frown \mathsf{parse}\,(t \leftarrow l,\ r \rightarrow s)$$

After the definitions of gen and post, we are left to prove

$$\text{parse}\,(t \leftarrow l, \ \text{gen}_1(f,o) \frown [o] \frown \text{gen}_2(o,g) \frown (r \to s))$$
$$=$$
$$(\text{post}\,(f) \frown \text{post}\,(g) \leftarrow o) \frown \text{parse}\,(t \leftarrow l, \ r \to s)$$

Goal 7

The proof goes as follows:

$$\text{parse}\,(t \leftarrow l, \ \text{gen}_1(f,o) \frown [o] \frown \text{gen}_2(o,g) \frown (r \to s))$$
$$=$$

Lemma 1

$$\text{post}\,(f) \frown \text{parse}\,(t \leftarrow l, \ o \to \text{gen}_2(o,g) \frown (r \to s))$$
$$=$$

parse (case 6)

$$\text{post}\,(f) \frown \text{parse}\,(t \leftarrow l \leftarrow o, \ \text{gen}_2(o,g) \frown (r \to s))$$
$$=$$

Lemma 2

$$\text{post}\,(f) \frown \text{post}\,(g) \frown \text{parse}\,(t \leftarrow l \leftarrow o, \ r \to s)$$
$$=$$

parse (case 7)

$$(\text{post}\,(f) \frown \text{post}\,(g) \leftarrow o) \frown \text{parse}\,(t \leftarrow l, \ r \to s)$$

End of Proof

We finally prove our two pending lemmas.

$f \in$ ftree

$\forall\, (t,l,r,s) \cdot (HYP(f) \ \Rightarrow$
$\quad \text{parse}\,(t \leftarrow l, \ \text{gen}\,(f) \frown (r \to s)) = \text{post}\,(f) \frown \text{parse}\,(t \leftarrow l, \ r \to s)\,)$

$o \in OPR$

$t \in \text{seq}\,(OPR \cup \{(\})$

$l \in OPR \cup \{(\}$

$s \in \text{seq}\,(TOK)$

$\text{prit}\,(l) < \text{prit}\,(o)$

Lemma 1

$\Rightarrow$

$\text{parse}\,(t \leftarrow l, \ \text{gen}_1(f,o) \frown [o] \frown s) = \text{post}\,(f) \frown \text{parse}\,(t \leftarrow l, \ o \to s)$

Proof of Lemma 1: We assume

$$\forall\, (t,l,r,s) \cdot (HYP(f) \ \Rightarrow$$
$$\text{parse}\,(t \leftarrow l, \ \text{gen}\,(f) \frown (r \to s)) =$$
$$\text{post}\,(f) \frown \text{parse}\,(t \leftarrow l, \ r \to s)\,)$$

Hypothesis 1

and also

$f \in$ ftree
$o \in OPR$
$t \in \text{seq}\,(OPR \cup \{(\})$
$l \in OPR \cup \{(\}$
$s \in \text{seq}\,(TOK)$
$\text{prit}\,(l) < \text{prit}\,(o)$

Hypothesis 2

We have to prove

$$\text{parse}\,(t \leftarrow l, \ \text{gen}_1(f,o) \frown [\,o\,] \frown s)$$
$$=$$
$$\text{post}\,(f) \frown \text{parse}\,(t \leftarrow l, \ o \rightarrow s)$$

Goal 1

The proof proceeds by cases

Case 1: $\text{prif}\,(f) < \text{prit}\,(o)$. The proof goes as follows:

$$\text{parse}\,(t \leftarrow l, \ \text{gen}_1(f,o) \frown [\,o\,] \frown s)$$
$$=$$
gen$_1$
$$\text{parse}\,(t \leftarrow l, \ (\ \rightarrow \text{gen}\,(f) \leftarrow) \frown [\,o\,] \frown s)$$
$$=$$
parse (case 4)
$$\text{parse}\,(t \leftarrow l \leftarrow (, \ \text{gen}\,(f) \leftarrow) \frown [\,o\,] \frown s)$$
$$=$$
Hypothesis 1
$$\text{post}\,(f) \frown \text{parse}\,(t \leftarrow l \leftarrow (, \ ) \rightarrow o \rightarrow s)$$
$$=$$
parse (case 5)
$$\text{post}\,(f) \frown \text{parse}\,(t \leftarrow l, \ o \rightarrow s)$$

Case 2: $\text{prit}\,(o) \le \text{prif}\,(f)$. The proof goes as follows:

$$\text{parse}\,(t \leftarrow l, \ \text{gen}_1(f,o) \frown [\,o\,] \frown s)$$
$$=$$
gen$_1$
$$\text{parse}\,(t \leftarrow l, \ \text{gen}\,(f) \frown [\,o\,] \frown s)$$
$$=$$
Case 2, Hypothesis 2, Hypothesis 1
$$\text{post}\,(f) \frown \text{parse}\,(t \leftarrow l, \ o \rightarrow s)$$

End of Proof

Lemma 2

$g \in \text{ftree}$
$\forall\,(t,l,r,s) \cdot (HYP(g) \ \Rightarrow$
    $\text{parse}\,(t \leftarrow l, \ \text{gen}\,(g) \frown (r \rightarrow s)) = \text{post}\,(g) \frown \text{parse}\,(t \leftarrow l, \ r \rightarrow s)\,)$
$o \in OPR$
$t \in \text{seq}\,(OPR \cup \{(\}) \qquad\qquad\qquad\qquad$ Lemma 1
$r \in TOK$
$s \in \text{seq}\,(TOK)$
$\text{prit}\,(r) \le \text{prit}\,(o)$
$\Rightarrow$
$\text{parse}\,(t \leftarrow o, \ \text{gen}_2(o,g) \frown (r \rightarrow s)) = \text{post}\,(g) \frown \text{parse}\,(t \leftarrow o, \ r \rightarrow s)$

Proof of Lemma 2: We assume

$$\forall\,(t,l,r,s) \cdot (HYP(g) \ \Rightarrow$$
$$\text{parse}\,(t \leftarrow l, \ \text{gen}\,(g) \frown (r \rightarrow s)) =$$
Hypothesis 1
$$\text{post}\,(g) \frown \text{parse}\,(t \leftarrow l, \ r \rightarrow s)\,)$$

and also

$$g \in \text{ftree}$$
$$o \in OPR$$
$$t \in \text{seq}\,(OPR \cup \{(\})$$ Hypothesis 2
$$r \in TOK$$
$$s \in \text{seq}\,(TOK)$$
$$\text{prit}\,(r) \le \text{prit}\,(o)$$

We have to prove

$$\text{parse}\,(t \leftarrow o, \ \ \text{gen}_2(o,g) \frown (r \to s))$$
$$=$$ Goal 1
$$\text{post}\,(g) \frown \text{parse}\,(t \leftarrow o, \ \ r \to s)$$

The proof proceeds by cases

Case 1: $\text{prif}\,(g) \le \text{prit}\,(o)$. The proof goes as follows:

$$\text{parse}\,(t \leftarrow o, \ \ \text{gen}_2(o,g) \frown (r \to s))$$
$$=$$ gen_2
$$\text{parse}\,(t \leftarrow o, \ \ (\ \to \text{gen}\,(g) \leftarrow) \frown (r \to s))$$
$$=$$ parse (case 4)
$$\text{parse}\,(t \leftarrow o \leftarrow (, \ \text{gen}\,(g) \leftarrow) \frown (r \to s))$$
$$=$$ Hypothesis 1
$$\text{post}\,(g) \frown \text{parse}\,(t \leftarrow o \leftarrow (, \ ) \to r \to s)$$
$$=$$ parse (case 5)
$$\text{post}\,(g) \frown \text{parse}\,(t \leftarrow o, \ \ r \to s)$$

Case 2: $\text{prit}\,(o) < \text{prif}\,(g)$. The proof goes as follows:

$$\text{parse}\,(t \leftarrow o, \ \ \text{gen}_2(o,g) \frown (r \to s))$$
$$=$$ gen_2
$$\text{parse}\,(t \leftarrow o, \ \ \text{gen}\,(g) \frown (r \to s))$$
$$=$$ Case 2, Hypothesis 2, Hypothesis 1
$$\text{post}\,(g) \frown \text{parse}\,(t \leftarrow o, \ \ r \to s)$$

End of Proof

It remains for us to construct the final parsing algorithm. This is easily done as follows, by mimicking the behaviour of the rewriting rules:

$o \longleftarrow \mathsf{Parser}\,(i) \;\; \widehat{=}$
   PRE
      $i \in \mathsf{formula}$
   THEN
      VAR t, s IN
         $o, t, s := [], [\,(\,], i \leftarrow)\,;$
         WHILE $s \neq [] \wedge t \neq []$ DO
            LET v, l, r, u BE
               $v, l, r, u = \mathsf{front}\,(t),\, \mathsf{last}\,(t),\, \mathsf{first}\,(s),\, \mathsf{tail}\,(s)$.
            IN
               IF $r \in ATM$ THEN
                  $o, s := o \leftarrow r,\, u$
               ELSIF $r = ($ THEN
                  $t, s := t \leftarrow r,\, u$
               ELSIF $l = (\;\wedge\; r =)$ THEN
                  $t, s := v,\, u$
               ELSIF $\mathsf{prit}\,(l) < \mathsf{prit}\,(r)$ THEN
                  $t, s := t \leftarrow r,\, u$
               ELSE
                  $o, t := o \leftarrow l,\, v$
               END
            END
         INVARIANT
            $o \in \mathsf{seq}\,(ATM \,\cup\, OPR)\;\;\wedge$
            $t \in \mathsf{seq}\,(TOK - \{\,)\,\})\;\;\wedge$
            $s \in \mathsf{seq}\,(TOK)\;\;\wedge$
            $o \,^\frown \mathsf{parse}\,(t, s) \;=\; \mathsf{post}\,(\mathsf{gen}^{-1}\,(i))$
         VARIANT
            $[\,\mathsf{size}\,(s), \mathsf{size}\,(t)\,]$
         END
      END
   END

Algorithm 10.5.1

Notice that the variant is a sequence. We can then prove the following property:

$\mathsf{PRE} \;\Rightarrow\; [\,o \longleftarrow \mathsf{Parser}\,(i)\,]\,(o = \mathsf{post}\,(\mathsf{gen}^{-1}\,(i)))$ Property 10.5.5

10.6. Exercises

1. Modify Algorithm 10.2.5 defining the operation SearchValueInMatrix by introducing two variables handling $r \bmod c$ and r/c (Hint: Make use of the approprite LOOP rules of section 10.0.2.)

2. In Algorithm 10.2.4 defining the operation SearchValueInArray, the index r is iterated from a to b. You are asked to have now the index i starting at any value i situated within the interval $a \ .. \ b$ and progressing by zig-zaging systematically on the left and on the right of i, and so forth. In this way the found index is one that is closest to i (Hint: Define a "zig-zag" function and compose it with the domain $a \ .. \ b$ of the array.)

3. Given a sequence s of integers, construct an algorithm to compute the sum of the elements of the segment of s where that sum is maximal. This problem was proposed by E.W. Dijkstra in [1]. A segment of a sequence s is a subsequence of the form $s \downarrow i \uparrow j$ where i and j are elements of $0 \ .. \ \text{size}(s)$ such that $i \leq j$. (Hint: Define a recursive function on sequences of integers defining the sum in question in terms of the sum of the element of the suffix whose sum is maximal. Then define both these concepts in the *same* recursive function. Then you can use Algorithm 10.4.1 defining the operation RightRecSeq.)

4. The problem is to construct an algorithm to determine a certain candidate b (chosen among a set C of candidates) which *may* be the one having won the absolute majority in a ballot. This problem was proposed by R.C. Backhouse in [2]. The ballot is defined by a sequence s belonging to $\text{seq}(C)$. The size of s corresponds to the number of people who participated in the ballot. The candidate b we would like to determine is only a potential absolute majority winner. This means that the *other* candidates x have not obtained the absolute majority. In other words, for such candidates, we have: $2 \times \text{vote}(x)(s) \leq \text{size}(s)$, where $\text{vote}(x)(s)$ is the number of votes won by candidate x in the ballot s. It is thus possible to express the problem as that of finding a member b of C and a natural number e such that the following holds:

$$2 \times \text{vote}(x)(s) \leq \text{size}(s) - e \quad \text{if} \quad x \neq b$$
$$2 \times \text{vote}(x)(s) \leq \text{size}(s) + e \quad \text{if} \quad x = b$$

(a) Define recursively the function $\text{vote}(x)$.
(b) Define recursively a function state computing simultaneously b and e.
(c) Use Algorithm 10.4.1 defining the operation RightRecSeq to construct your algorithm.

5. Generalize the concept of "filter" (section 10.4.7) in order to define that of "finite automaton". A finite automaton is a filter with memory. Like a filter, an automaton produces a sequence in reaction to an input element. But, this time,

the sequence that is produced also depends on the "state" of the automaton. And the state in question is also modified by an input element.

(a) Define recursively a function of an input sequence producing simultaneously a new state and an output sequence (one thus needs an initial state that is part of the definition of the automaton besides its "input-state" function and its "input-output" function).

(b) Construct an algorithm for evaluating an automaton on an input sequence.

(c) Develop the construction of an algorithm for "piping" a finite sequence of automata. Hint: Follow closely the development carried out in section 10.4.7 for filters.

6. In this exercise, we place ourselves within the context of section 10.5 on trees. We first enlarge the notation by defining the arity of each token as being equal to 0 for an element of *ATM* and to 2 for an element of *OPR*, that is:

$$\text{arity} = ATM \times \{0\} \cup OPR \times \{2\}$$

(a) Given an element f of the set ftree, prove by binary tree induction on f that the following holds:

$$\text{size}(\text{post}(f)) = 1 + \sum i \cdot (i \in \text{dom}(\text{post}(f)) \mid \text{arity}(\text{post}(f)(i)))$$

(b) Given an element f of the set ftree, prove by binary tree induction on f that the following holds for each n in $\text{dom}(\text{post}(f))$:

$$\text{size}(\text{post}(f) \downarrow n) <$$
$$1 + \sum i \cdot (i \in \text{dom}(\text{post}(f) \downarrow n) \mid \text{arity}(\text{post}(f)(i)))$$

(c) Using the results established in (a) and (b), prove that the function post is injective. That is, prove the following by binary tree induction on the ftree f:

$$\forall h \cdot (h \in \text{ftree} \wedge \text{post}(f) = \text{post}(h) \Rightarrow f = h)$$

(d) Given an element f of the set ftree, a sequence s of the form $u \frown \text{post}(f) \frown v$, and a number k that is supposed to be equal to $\text{size}(u \frown \text{post}(f))$, prove the following:

$$\text{size}(\text{post}(f)) = \min(\{n \mid n \in 1..k \wedge$$
$$n = 1 + \sum i \cdot (i \in 1..n \mid \text{arity}(s(k+1-i)))\})$$

Then construct an algorithm for computing $\text{size}(\text{post}(f))$ given s and k.

REFERENCES

[1] E.W. Dijkstra and W.H.J. Feijen. *A Method of Programming* (Addison-Wesley, 1988)

[2] R.C. Backhouse. *Program Construction and Verification* (Prentice Hall, 1986)

PART FOUR

Refinement

CHAPTER 11

Refinement

In the second part of this book, we introduced a notation for modelling the dynamic behaviour of software systems. This notation is an extension of E.W. Dijkstra's language of *guarded commands* [1]. Also inherited from Dijkstra was our use of the predicate transformer technique to formally define each construct of the notation.

Here, we address the problem of refinement. Refinement is a technique used to transform the "abstract" model of a software system (its specification) into another mathematical model that is more "concrete" (its refinement). This second model can be more concrete in two ways: first, it can contain more detail of the original informal specification and, second, it can be closer to an implementation. In the next chapter we shall study, by means of two large examples, these practical aspects of refinement.

Refinement has been studied intensively for many years ([2], [3], [4], [5], [6], [7], [8], and [9]) in various forms. The presentation given here is inspired by [5].

In section 11.1, we deal with generalized substitution refinement. Then, in section 11.2, we make precise what we mean by the refinement of one abstract machine by another. Finally, in section 11.3, we summarize all the formal definitions dealing with refinement (this is the equivalent of what we have done for abstract machines in chapter 5 and in section 7.4).

11.1. Refinement of Generalized Substitutions

11.1.1. Informal Approach

Roughly speaking, a substitution S (working within the context of a certain abstract machine M) is said to be *refined* by a substitution T, if T can be used in place of S without the "user" of the machine noticing it. In practice, this means that all our expectations about S will be fulfilled by T. If this is the case, then T is said to be a *refinement* of S, and S an *abstraction* of T. For instance,

501

suppose we are given the following two substitutions S and T working with an abstract machine with variable x:

$$S \;\;\widehat{=}\;\; x := 0 \;\|\; x := x - 1$$

$$T \;\;\widehat{=}\;\; x := x - 1$$

We claim that S is refined by T. In fact, all our expectations about S and T are of the general form $[S]R$ and $[T]R$, where R is a predicate depending upon the variables of the machine M (R might be the invariant of M). For instance, in the present case, we have

$$[S]R \;\;\Leftrightarrow\;\; [x := 0]R \;\wedge\; [x := x - 1]R$$

$$[T]R \;\;\Leftrightarrow\;\; [x := x - 1]R$$

If the predicate $[S]R$ holds, then, by definition, S establishes the predicate R. But, in this case, we also obviously have $[T]R$, so T establishes R too. Consequently, if we place ourselves in a situation where $[S]R$ holds, then using T in place of S does not make any difference (at least as far as establishing the predicate R is concerned); since this is obviously the case whatever the predicate R, then T refines S.

We have just seen an example of refinement in which the refinement T is *less non-deterministic* than the abstraction S. There exists another typical case of refinement: this is one in which the refinement has a *weaker pre-condition* than that of the abstraction. Next is an example.

$$S \;\;\widehat{=}\;\; x > 5 \;|\; x := x - 1$$

$$T \;\;\widehat{=}\;\; x > 0 \;|\; x := x - 1$$

For any predicate R we have

$$[S]R \;\;\Leftrightarrow\;\; x > 5 \;\wedge\; [x := x - 1]R$$

$$[T]R \;\;\Leftrightarrow\;\; x > 0 \;\wedge\; [x := x - 1]R$$

Clearly, $[S]R$ implies $[T]R$. In other words, if, once again, we place ourselves in a situation where $[S]R$ holds then $[T]R$ holds too: thus, T refines S. Here is a final example where we have both cases occurring at the same time:

$$S \;\;\widehat{=}\;\; x > 5 \;|\; (x := x - 1 \;\|\; x := 0)$$

$$T \;\;\widehat{=}\;\; x > 0 \;|\; x := x - 1$$

For any predicate R, we have:

$$[S]R \;\;\Leftrightarrow\;\; x > 5 \;\wedge\; [x := x - 1]R \;\wedge\; [x := 0]R$$

$$[T]R \;\;\Leftrightarrow\;\; x > 0 \;\wedge\; [x := x - 1]R$$

Obviously, and once again, $[S]R$ implies $[T]R$: thus T refines S. As you can see, here the refinement T "does less" but, at the same time, may "do more" than the abstraction S: T "does less" in that it is less non-deterministic than S, and this, within the termination conditions of S. But T also "does more" in that it might terminate if started in situations where S would not have terminated. The fact that T "does more" in this case is no problem since we use T "as if it were S" (within the termination conditions of S). Consequently, we will never notice that T may do things that S is unable to do itself: we are merely using a refinement which is too sophisticated with respect to the corresponding abstraction.

11.1.2. Definition

After the previous informal introduction, the formal definition of refinement should be quite clear. Given two generalized substitutions S and T working with the same abstract machine M (with variable x and invariant $x \in s$ for some set s), S is said to be refined by T when, for any subset a of s, the value of the set transformer $\mathrm{str}(S)$ at a is included in that of $\mathrm{str}(T)$ at the same set a. The construct $S \sqsubseteq T$ (pronounced "S is refined by T") is thus defined as follows:

Syntax	Definition
$S \sqsubseteq T$	$\forall a \cdot (a \subseteq s \;\Rightarrow\; \mathrm{str}(S)(a) \subseteq \mathrm{str}(T)(a))$

We remind the reader that the construct str has been defined in section 6.4.2. After the various results of **Property 6.4.9**, it can be shown that we have the alternative equivalent definition:

$$S \sqsubseteq T \;\Leftrightarrow\; \mathrm{pre}(S) \subseteq \mathrm{pre}(T) \;\wedge\; \mathrm{rel}(T) \subseteq \mathrm{rel}(S) \qquad \text{Property 11.1.1}$$

This property establishes the necessary link between our formal definition and the informal presentation of the previous section: we clearly see the weakening of the pre-condition and the decreasing of non-determinism.

11.1.3. Equality of Generalized Substitution

We now define *equality* between substitutions as equalities between the values of the corresponding set transformers, formally:

Syntax	Definition
$S = T$	$\text{str}(S) = \text{str}(T)$

From the previous definitions, we deduce immediately that refinement is *reflexive*, *transitive* and *anti-symmetric*. Refinement is thus a *partial order* on substitutions. Formally:

$$S \sqsubseteq S$$

$$S \sqsubseteq T \wedge T \sqsubseteq U \;\Rightarrow\; S \sqsubseteq U$$

$$S \sqsubseteq T \wedge T \sqsubseteq S \;\Rightarrow\; S = T$$

11.1.4. Monotonicity

An important aspect of the above definitions is that each basic construct of the generalized substitution notation, as defined in chapters 4 and 9, is *monotonic* with respect to refinement. This is expressed formally by the seven laws given below.

Notice that in all cases, except in the fifth one dealing with the multiple substitution operator $||$, the substitutions S, T, U, and V are all supposed to work within the framework of the same abstract machine. In the fifth case, U and V are working with one machine while S and T are working with another one.

$$S \sqsubseteq T \quad\Rightarrow\quad (P \,|\, S) \sqsubseteq (P \,|\, T)$$

$$(U \sqsubseteq V) \wedge (S \sqsubseteq T) \quad\Rightarrow\quad (U \,[\!]\, S) \sqsubseteq (V \,[\!]\, T)$$

$$S \sqsubseteq T \quad\Rightarrow\quad (P \Longrightarrow S) \sqsubseteq (P \Longrightarrow T)$$

$$\forall z \cdot (S \sqsubseteq T) \quad\Rightarrow\quad @z \cdot S \sqsubseteq @z \cdot T$$

$$(U \sqsubseteq V) \wedge (S \sqsubseteq T) \quad\Rightarrow\quad (U \,||\, S) \sqsubseteq (V \,||\, T)$$

$$(U \sqsubseteq V) \wedge (S \sqsubseteq T) \quad\Rightarrow\quad (U \,;\, S) \sqsubseteq (V \,;\, T)$$

$$S \sqsubseteq T \quad\Rightarrow\quad S\hat{\;} \sqsubseteq T\hat{\;}$$

We leave the proofs of the first six laws as exercises for the reader and concentrate here on the last one (hint: for the law concerning the multiple operator ||, use Property 11.1.1, which will allow you to use the basic properties of the multiple operator as described in section 7.1.2).

Proof of Monotonicity of the Opening Operator

We assume

$$S \sqsubseteq T \qquad\qquad \text{Hypothesis 1}$$

which is equivalent to the following:

$$\forall a \cdot (a \subseteq s \;\Rightarrow\; \text{str}(S)(a) \subseteq \text{str}(T)(a)) \qquad\qquad \text{Derivation 1}$$

And we have to prove $S\hat{} \sqsubseteq T\hat{}$, that is

$$\forall a \cdot (a \subseteq s \;\Rightarrow\; \text{str}(S\hat{})(a) \subseteq \text{str}(T\hat{})(a)) \qquad\qquad \text{Goal 1}$$

We remove universal quantification and assume

$$a \subseteq s \qquad\qquad \text{Hypothesis 2}$$

And we have to prove

$$\text{str}(S\hat{})(a) \subseteq \text{str}(T\hat{})(a) \qquad\qquad \text{Goal 2}$$

that is, according to the definition of $\text{str}(S\hat{})$ (section 9.2.1):

$$\text{fix}(f) \subseteq \text{fix}(g) \qquad\qquad \text{Goal 3}$$

where

$$f \;=\; \lambda q \cdot (q \in \mathbb{P}(s) \mid a \cap \text{str}(S)(q)) \qquad\qquad \text{Definition 1}$$

$$g \;=\; \lambda q \cdot (q \in \mathbb{P}(s) \mid a \cap \text{str}(T)(q)) \qquad\qquad \text{Definition 2}$$

It is then sufficient to prove (according to Theorem 3.2.1)

$$f(\text{fix}(g)) \subseteq \text{fix}(g) \qquad\qquad \text{Goal 4}$$

That is, according to Definition 1,

$$a \cap \text{str}(S)(\text{fix}(g)) \subseteq \text{fix}(g) \qquad\qquad \text{Goal 5}$$

According to Hypothesis 2 and Derivation 1, it is then sufficient to prove

$$a \cap \text{str}(T)(\text{fix}(g)) \subseteq \text{fix}(g) \qquad\qquad \text{Goal 6}$$

which is obvious according to Definition 2.

End of Proof

A consequence of the above monotonicity properties is that the refinement of some part of a substitution induces the refinement of the whole. In chapter 10, we have used this fact in section 10.2.2 and also in section 10.2.5.

11.1.5. Refining a Generalized Assignment

In this section we give a simplified version of refinement, which is valid when the substitution to be refined has the following form:

$$P \mid (x : Q)$$

where P and Q are predicates depending on the variable x only, and where P and Q each imply $x \in s$ for some set s. Notice that, in general, the predicate Q may also depend on the before-value x_0, but this is not the case in this section. We shall then draw some consequences of the result we shall obtain.

We remind the reader that the construct $x : Q$ is a shorthand for the "assignment" to x of any value such that the predicate Q holds. Its formal definition, which follows, was given in section 5.1.1:

$$x : Q \;=\; @x \cdot ([x := x']Q \implies x := y)$$

where x' is a fresh variable. Consequently, given a subset r of s, we have

$$\mathrm{str}(P \mid (x : Q))(r)$$
$$=$$
$$\{ x \mid x \in s \,\wedge\, P \,\wedge\, \forall x' \cdot ([x := x']Q \;\Rightarrow\; x' \in r) \}$$
$$=$$
$$\{ x \mid x \in s \,\wedge\, P \,\wedge\, \forall x \cdot (Q \;\Rightarrow\; x \in r) \}$$
$$=$$
$$\{ x \mid x \in s \,\wedge\, P \,\wedge\, (\mathrm{set}(Q) \subseteq r) \}$$

where

$$\mathrm{set}(Q) \;=\; \{ x \mid x \in s \,\wedge\, Q \}$$

Hence we have

$$P \mid (x : Q) \sqsubseteq T$$
$$\Leftrightarrow$$
$$\forall r \cdot (r \subseteq s \;\Rightarrow\; \{ x \mid x \in s \,\wedge\, P \,\wedge\, (\mathrm{set}(Q) \subseteq r) \} \subseteq \mathrm{str}(T)(r))$$
$$\Leftrightarrow$$
$$\forall r \cdot (r \subseteq s \;\Rightarrow\; \forall x \cdot (x \in s \,\wedge\, P \,\wedge\, (\mathrm{set}(Q) \subseteq r) \;\Rightarrow\; x \in \mathrm{str}(T)(r)))$$
$$\Leftrightarrow$$
$$\forall x \cdot (P \;\Rightarrow\; \forall r \cdot (r \subseteq s \,\wedge\, (\mathrm{set}(Q) \subseteq r) \;\Rightarrow\; x \in \mathrm{str}(T)(r)))$$
$$\Leftrightarrow$$
$$\forall x \cdot (P \;\Rightarrow\; x \in \mathrm{str}(T)(\mathrm{set}(Q)))$$
$$\Leftrightarrow$$
$$\forall x \cdot (P \;\Rightarrow\; [T]Q)$$

The last but one step is due to the fact that $\mathrm{str}(T)$ is monotone with respect to set inclusion. We thus have proved the following property:

| $(P \mid (x : Q)) \sqsubseteq T \;\Leftrightarrow\; \forall x \cdot (P \;\Rightarrow\; [T]Q)$ | Property 11.1.2 |

Interpretation of Proof Obligation

The previous property gives us a possible interpretation for the proof obligation of an operation of the form $P \mid S$, supposed to work with a machine with variable x and invariant I. We claimed, at the end of section 4.7, that the proof obligation was

$$\forall x \cdot (I \wedge P \quad \Rightarrow \quad [S]I)$$

This statement can be re-interpreted as saying that the substitution S refines the substitution $(I \wedge P) \mid (x : I)$ (the most non-deterministic substitution re-establishing the invariant I), that is:

$$(I \wedge P) \mid (x : I) \sqsubseteq S$$

According to Property 11.1.2, this is equivalent to:

$$\forall x \cdot (I \wedge P \quad \Rightarrow \quad [S]I)$$

Justification of Practice of Chapter 10

When, in Property 11.1.2, the predicate Q is simplified to the statement

$$x = E$$

where E is a set-theoretic expression *supposed to contain no occurrence of* x, then we have

$$(x := E) \quad = \quad (x : (x = E))$$

Consequently, we have

$$(P \mid x := E) \sqsubseteq T \quad \Leftrightarrow \quad \forall x \cdot (P \quad \Rightarrow \quad [T](x = E)) \qquad \text{Property 11.1.3}$$

We remind the reader that, in chapter 10, we proved many theorems of a form corresponding to the right-hand side of this statement. This simply means that we were refining abstractions having the form of simple substitutions.

11.2. Refinement of Abstract Machines

11.2.1. Informal Approach

In this section we define informally what we mean by the refinement of one abstract machine by another. For this, we shall use a little example consisting of two abstract machines. Our first machine has a unique state variable, y, denoting a set of natural numbers. It offers two operations named enter and $m \longleftarrow$ maximum. The former allows its user to enter a new number into the set y, while the latter provides the maximum of y (when this is meaningful).

MACHINE

    Little_Example_1

VARIABLES

    y

INVARIANT

    $y \in \mathbb{F}(\text{NAT}_1)$

INITIALIZATION

    $y := \varnothing$

OPERATIONS

    $\text{enter}(n)\ \ \widehat{=}$
        PRE $n \in \text{NAT}_1$ THEN $y := y \cup \{n\}$ END ;

    $m \longleftarrow \text{maximum}\ \ \widehat{=}$
        PRE $y \neq \varnothing$ THEN $m := \text{max}(y)$ END

END

Consider now the following machine:

MACHINE

    Little_Example_2

VARIABLES

    z

INVARIANT

    $z \in \text{NAT}$

INITIALIZATION

  $z := 0$

OPERATIONS

  enter(n) $\widehat{=}$
    PRE $n \in \text{NAT}_1$ THEN $z := \max(\{z, n\})$ END;

  $m \longleftarrow$ maximum $\widehat{=}$
    PRE $z \neq 0$ THEN $m := z$ END

END

As can be seen, this second machine resembles the previous one. In particular it offers operations "similar" to the operations of the first one: same names, same input parameters (if any), same result parameters (if any). These two machines are said to have the *same signature*.

However, they are definitely distinct machines: in particular, their state variables are quite different in nature. In fact, *we have lost information*, in that the entire set, denoted by the variable y of the first machine, is now "reduced" to the "maximum so far", denoted by the variable z of the second machine. Nevertheless, by considering them more closely, we have the vague impression that "they behave in a similar way": in other words, that any use of one yields the same result as the other.

Informally speaking, the reason why this loss of information does no harm is that the state of the first machine *is too rich* with regard to the operations the machine offers. In other words, that richness (the set structure of the variable y) is only needed for a *convenient, and easy to understand, specification* of the machine. The set y appears to record some kind of "history" of the past behaviour of the machine. But clearly, that history is not necessary to define the maximum operation, provided we record the maximum in question when the operation enter is called. While we could have presented the second machine directly as "the" specification, it would not have been immediately clear what it was supposed to do: the "real" specification would have been missing and, worse, it would have been impossible to express it formally. On the other hand, the second machine is closer to a final implementation, since the "fixed length data structure" of z is, clearly, simpler than the "variable length data structure" of y.

In conclusion, both machines are equally formal, and both are equally needed, but for quite different reasons. The first is made for human readers to *understand* what the problem is. The second describes the model of a possible computation, as prescribed by the first. But, of course, we need to be sure that the second behaves in a similar way to the first. More precisely, the human reader of the first machine is required to keep believing that the possible computation, as described by the second machine, is the one defined by the first machine. The human reader should continue to reason in an *abstract* world, whereas the computation is done in a more *concrete* world. In what follows, we shall make more precise this notion of "similar" behaviour between the abstract and the concrete.

For this, we consider an "external" substitution capable of being "implemented" on each of these two machines. The "external" substitution in question is any generalized substitution (built on the basic notations presented in chapter 4 and 9) that *does not contain any explicit reference to the state variables of each machine*, only "calls" to their common operations. This requirement is called the *Hiding Principle*: it forces the state variables of an abstract machine to be hidden within it. Here is such an "external" substitution called prog:

$$
\begin{aligned}
\text{prog} \;\widehat{=}\; & \text{enter}(5)\,; \\
& \text{enter}(3)\,; \\
& x_1 \longleftarrow \text{maximum}\,; \\
& \text{enter}(2)\,; \\
& \text{enter}(6)\,; \\
& x_2 \longleftarrow \text{maximum}
\end{aligned}
$$

By two "implementations" of prog on each of the two machines, we mean two generalized substitutions T and U, obtained by initializing the two machines and then by replacing, in prog, the parameterized calls of the operations of the machines by their respective definitions in each of them respectively. This yields the following for T, supposed to be "implemented" on *Little_Example_1*:

$$
\begin{aligned}
T \;\widehat{=}\; & y := \varnothing\,; \\
& \text{PRE } 5 \in \text{NAT} \quad \text{THEN} \quad y := y \cup \{5\} \quad \text{END}\,; \\
& \text{PRE } 3 \in \text{NAT} \quad \text{THEN} \quad y := y \cup \{3\} \quad \text{END}\,; \\
& \text{PRE } y \neq \varnothing \quad \text{THEN} \quad x_1 := \max(y) \quad \text{END}\,; \\
& \text{PRE } 2 \in \text{NAT} \quad \text{THEN} \quad y := y \cup \{2\} \quad \text{END}\,; \\
& \text{PRE } 6 \in \text{NAT} \quad \text{THEN} \quad y := y \cup \{6\} \quad \text{END}\,; \\
& \text{PRE } y \neq \varnothing \quad \text{THEN} \quad x_2 := \max(y) \quad \text{END}
\end{aligned}
$$

and for U, supposed to be "implemented" on *Little_Example_2*, we have:

$$
\begin{aligned}
U \;\widehat{=}\; & z := 0\,; \\
& \text{PRE } 5 \in \text{NAT} \quad \text{THEN} \quad z := \max(\{z,\, 5\}) \quad \text{END}\,; \\
& \text{PRE } 3 \in \text{NAT} \quad \text{THEN} \quad z := \max(\{z,\, 3\}) \quad \text{END}\,; \\
& \text{PRE } z \neq 0 \quad \text{THEN} \quad x_1 := z \quad \text{END}\,; \\
& \text{PRE } 2 \in \text{NAT} \quad \text{THEN} \quad z := \max(\{z,\, 2\}) \quad \text{END}\,; \\
& \text{PRE } 6 \in \text{NAT} \quad \text{THEN} \quad z := \max(\{z,\, 6\}) \quad \text{END}\,; \\
& \text{PRE } z \neq 0 \quad \text{THEN} \quad x_2 := z \quad \text{END}
\end{aligned}
$$

As our "external" substitution prog, *does not directly use* the internal variables y and z of the two machines, we obtain two substitutions working with variables

x_1, x_2 and y for T and x_1, x_2 and z for U. After reducing these two substitutions, we obtain, apparently, the *same* values 5 and 6 for the two external variables x_1 and x_2. More formally, we can prove the following:

$$[T]\,(x_1, x_2 = 5, 6)$$

$$[U]\,(x_1, x_2 = 5, 6)$$

According to Property 11.1.3, this means that, whatever reduction of the "external" substitution we consider, it refines the substitution

$$x_1, x_2 := 5, 6$$

But we seem to have more: namely that, provided we are interested in these two variables x_1 and x_2 only, then our reductions and the substitution $x_1, x_2 := 5, 6$ are identical. As experience shows, it also seems that this nice interchangeability property holds for *any external substitution*, like prog, implemented on both machines. In what follows, we would like to make all this a little more precise.

Technically, however, we certainly cannot directly *compare* our two substitutions T and U because *they do not work with the same variable space*; although the two spaces they work with obviously overlap. Therefore, in order to formally compare our two substitutions, we have to consider their effect *on their common variables only* (in our case x_1 and x_2). This can be achieved in a very simple manner by *hiding* the other (internal) variables so that the resulting substitutions work on the *same* space. We have then just to prove the following:

$$@y \cdot T \;=\; @z \cdot U$$

Notice that in our example we have an *equality* relationship between the two. But, more generally, we could have had a generalized substitution *refinement* relationship, as described in section 11.1. This would yield the following:

$$@y \cdot T \;\sqsubseteq\; @z \cdot U$$

In summary, to the two orthogonal phenomena at work in the refinement of generalized substitutions, as described in section 11.1.1 (namely, decreasing the non-determinism and weakening the pre-condition), the refinement of the abstract machine adds a third phenomenon: that of *changing the variable space*.

11.2.2. Formal Definition

More generally, we consider two abstract machines M and N with the same signature. The variables, named respectively y and z, of these two machines must be *distinct*. Moreover, these variables are supposed to be members of sets b and c respectively.

The first abstract machine, M, is said to be refined by the second one, N, if *each* "external" substitution, working with its own variable x supposed to be a member of a set a, and "implemented" on M and N in the form of the two respective substitutions T and U, is such that the following holds:

$$@y \cdot (y \in b \implies T) \sqsubseteq @z \cdot (z \in c \implies U)$$

Notice that T and U contain the initialization of machines M and N respectively. In the above definition, we have added guards to the definitions we reached at the end of the previous section. This does not change the definition at all (since the guards are supposed to be invariant); it is just a technicality allowing us to type the quantified variables y and z. By extending the operator $\sqsubseteq$ to abstract machines, we obtain the following definition:

Syntax	Definition
$M \sqsubseteq N$	$@y \cdot (y \in b \implies T) \sqsubseteq @z \cdot (z \in c \implies U)$

for each "external" substitution working with its own variable x belonging to a set a and "implemented" on machines M and N in the form of the two substitutions T and U respectively.

Notice that this definition immediately implies the *transitivity* of abstract machine refinement. Also notice that this definition is quite general and complex in that it contains an *informal* universal quantification over each "external" substitution. In subsequent sections, we shall manage to remove this quantification.

After the definition of refinement, as given in section 11.1.2, and after the set-theoretic interpretation of the quantifier @, as given at the end of section 6.4.3, the previous definition can be transformed into the following equivalent one:

$M \sqsubseteq N$ Theorem 11.2.1

$\Leftrightarrow$

$$\forall p \cdot (p \subseteq a \implies \mathsf{PRJ}_1(a,b)(\mathsf{str}(T)(p \times b)) \subseteq \mathsf{PRJ}_1(a,c)(\mathsf{str}(U)(p \times c)))$$

---

where

$$\mathsf{PRJ}_1(s,t)(r) = \overline{\mathsf{prj}_1(s,t)[\overline{r}]}$$

11.2.3. Sufficient Conditions

The definition of abstract machine refinement, as proposed in the previous section, is not very helpful in practice because it is far too general. This is the reason why we introduce, in this section, a *sufficient* refinement condition leading to laws that will prove to be quite easy to use in practice.

The principle of this sufficient condition relies on the existence of a *total* binary relation v linking the *concrete* set c of machine N (with variable z and invariant $z \in c$) and the *abstract* set b of machine M (with variable y and invariant $y \in b$). Formally:

$$v \in c \leftrightarrow b \;\wedge\; \mathsf{dom}(v) = c$$

As in the previous sections, we suppose that the "external" substitution, which may be "implemented" on the machine M or N, has its own variable x, supposed to be a member of the set a. As a consequence, we extend the relation v by means of the function $\mathsf{id}(a)$, so as to obtain a new relation, w, working with the sets $a \times c$ and $a \times b$. Formally

$$w \;=\; \mathsf{id}(a) \;||\; v$$

We thus have

$$w \;\in\; (a \times c) \leftrightarrow (a \times b)$$

We now consider a "substitution" W, such that the value at r (where r is a subset of $a \times c$) of the corresponding set transformer $\mathsf{str}(W)$ is given by

$$\mathsf{str}(W)(r) \;=\; \overline{w\,[\overline{r}\,]}$$

Notice that W is not exactly a "substitution" since it does not work with the same before and after sets. We have just introduced this abuse of language in order to be able to give a very simple form to the sufficient refinement condition.

All this can be represented pictorially in the following diagram, where it can be seen that substitution T works with the "external" set a and with the set b of machine M, whereas substitution U works with the "external" set a and with the set c of machine N :

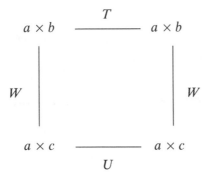

With this in mind, the proposed sufficient condition is the following:

$$\boxed{\; T \,;\, W \;\sqsubseteq\; W \,;\, U \;}$$

As can be seen, this condition reduces to a simple substitution refinement, as presented in section 11.1.2, when the "substitution" W reduces to skip (this implies that the sets b and c are identical and that the relation v is the identity relation). This special case is very intuitive as no change of variable occurs.

According to the definition of $\mathsf{str}(W)(r)$ that we have just provided (that is,

$\overline{w\,[\overline{r}]}$), the above condition can be translated immediately into our set-theoretic model as follows:

$$\forall r \cdot (r \subseteq (a \times c) \;\Rightarrow\; \mathsf{str}(T)(\overline{w\,[\overline{r}]}) \;\subseteq\; \overline{w\,[\mathsf{str}(U)(r)]}\,)$$

The Refinement Condition

It remains for us to prove that this condition is indeed sufficient to obtain abstract machine refinement. In other words, we have to prove the following:

$$
\begin{aligned}
&v \in c \leftrightarrow b \\
&\mathsf{dom}(v) = c \\
&w = (\mathsf{id}(a) \;||\; v) \\
&\forall r \cdot (r \subseteq (a \times c) \;\Rightarrow\; \mathsf{str}(T)(\overline{w\,[\overline{r}]}) \;\subseteq\; \overline{w\,[\mathsf{str}(U)(r)]}\,) \\
&\Rightarrow \\
&M \sqsubseteq N
\end{aligned}
\qquad \text{Theorem 11.2.2}
$$

for each "external" substitution "implemented" on the machines M and N in the form of the two substitutions T and U respectively. In the following proof, we use two properties, Property 11.2.1 and Property 11.2.2, that we shall prove immediately after this one.

Proof

We assume

$$\forall r \cdot (r \subseteq (a \times c) \;\Rightarrow\; \mathsf{str}(T)(\overline{w\,[\overline{r}]})) \;\subseteq\; \overline{w\,[\mathsf{str}(U)(r)]}\,) \quad \text{Hypothesis 1}$$

And we have to prove $M \sqsubseteq N$, that is (according to Theorem 11.2.1):

Goal 1

$$\forall p \cdot (p \subseteq a \;\Rightarrow\; \mathsf{PRJ}_1(a,b)(\mathsf{str}\,(T)(p \times b)) \subseteq \mathsf{PRJ}_1(a,c)(\mathsf{str}\,(U)(p \times c)))$$

We thus assume

$$p \subseteq a \qquad\qquad\qquad \text{Hypothesis 2}$$

And we are left to prove

$$\mathsf{PRJ}_1(a,b)(\mathsf{str}\,(T)(p \times b)) \subseteq \mathsf{PRJ}_1(a,c)(\mathsf{str}\,(U)(p \times c)) \qquad \text{Goal 2}$$

The proof goes as follows:

$$
\begin{aligned}
&\mathsf{PRJ}_1(a,b)(\mathsf{str}\,(T)(p \times b)) \\
&\subseteq && \text{Property 11.2.1} \\
&\mathsf{PRJ}_1(a,b)(\mathsf{str}\,(T)(\overline{w\,[\overline{p \times c}]})) \\
&\subseteq && \text{Hypotheses 1,2} \\
&\mathsf{PRJ}_1(a,b)(\overline{w\,[\mathsf{str}(U)(p \times c)]}) \\
&\subseteq && \text{Property 11.2.2} \\
&\mathsf{PRJ}_1(a,c)(\mathsf{str}\,(U)(p \times c))
\end{aligned}
$$

End of Proof

It remains for us to prove **Property 11.2.1** and **Property 11.2.2** that we used in the previous proof. Here is the first one:

$$p \subseteq a$$
$$v \in c \leftrightarrow b$$
$$w = (\text{id}(a) \mid\mid v)$$ Property 11.2.1
$$\Rightarrow$$
$$p \times b \subseteq \overline{w[\overline{p \times c}]}$$

Proof

The proof goes as follows:

$$p \times b$$
$$\subseteq$$
$$(p \times b) \cup (\overline{p} \times \overline{v[c]})$$
$$=$$
$$\overline{\overline{p} \times v[c]}$$
$$=$$
$$\overline{(\text{id}(a) \mid\mid v)[\overline{p} \times c]}$$
$$=$$
$$\overline{w[\overline{p \times c}]}$$

End of Proof

Here is the second property to be proved. Notice that the hypothesis of the *totality* of the relation v (that is $\text{dom}(v) = c$) plays an indispensable rôle in this proof.

$$r \subseteq a \times c$$
$$v \in c \leftrightarrow b$$
$$\text{dom}(v) = c$$ Property 11.2.2
$$w = (\text{id}(a) \mid\mid v)$$
$$\Rightarrow$$
$$\text{PRJ}_1(a,b)(\overline{w[\overline{r}]}) = \text{PRJ}_1(a,c)(r)$$

Proof

We assume

$$v \in c \leftrightarrow b$$ Hypothesis 1
$$\text{dom}(v) = c$$ Hypothesis 2

and we have to prove

$$\text{PRJ}_1(a,b)(\overline{w[\overline{r}]}) = \text{PRJ}_1(a,c)(r)$$ Goal 1

We can translate Hypothesis 2 (using Hypothesis 1) into the following condition:

$$\forall z \cdot (z \in c \;\Rightarrow\; \exists y \cdot (y \in b \,\wedge\, (z,y) \in v))$$
Derivation 1

Goal 1 can be transformed equivalently into the following, which should hold for all x:

$$x \in \mathsf{PRJ}_1(a,b)(\overline{w\,[\overline{r}]}) \;\Leftrightarrow\; x \in \mathsf{PRJ}_1(a,c)(r)$$
Goal 2

The proof of the last goal goes as follows:

$x \in \mathsf{PRJ}_1(a,b)(\overline{w\,[\overline{r}]})$
$\Leftrightarrow$
$x \in \overline{\mathsf{prj}_1(a,b)[w\,[\overline{r}]]}$
$\Leftrightarrow$
$x \in a \,\wedge\, \neg\exists(x',y)\cdot((x',y) \in w\,[\overline{r}] \,\wedge\, x = x')$
$\Leftrightarrow$
$x \in a \,\wedge\, \neg\exists y \cdot(y \in b \,\wedge\, (x,y) \in w\,[\overline{r}])$
$\Leftrightarrow$
$x \in a \,\wedge\, \forall y \cdot(y \in b \;\Rightarrow\; (x,y) \in \overline{w\,[\overline{r}]})$
$\Leftrightarrow$
$x \in a \,\wedge\, \forall y \cdot(y \in b \;\Rightarrow\; \neg\exists(x',z)\cdot((x',z) \in \overline{r} \,\wedge\, x = x' \,\wedge\, (z,y) \in v))$
$\Leftrightarrow$
$x \in a \,\wedge\, \forall y \cdot(y \in b \;\Rightarrow\; \neg\exists z \cdot(z \in c \,\wedge\, (x,z) \in \overline{r} \,\wedge\, (z,y) \in v))$
$\Leftrightarrow$
$x \in a \,\wedge\, \forall y \cdot(y \in b \;\Rightarrow\; \forall z \cdot(z \in c \,\wedge\, (z,y) \in v \;\Rightarrow\; (x,z) \in r))$
$\Leftrightarrow$
$x \in a \,\wedge\, \forall z \cdot(z \in c \;\Rightarrow\; \forall y \cdot(y \in b \,\wedge\, (z,y) \in v \;\Rightarrow\; (x,z) \in r))$
$\Leftrightarrow$
$x \in a \,\wedge\, \forall z \cdot(z \in c \,\wedge\, \exists y \cdot(y \in b \,\wedge\, (z,y) \in v) \;\Rightarrow\; (x,z) \in r)$
$\Leftrightarrow$
Derivation 1

$x \in a \,\wedge\, \forall z \cdot(z \in c \;\Rightarrow\; (x,z) \in r)$
$\Leftrightarrow$
$x \in a \,\wedge\, \neg\exists z \cdot(z \in c \,\wedge\, (x,z) \in \overline{r})$
$\Leftrightarrow$
$x \in a \,\wedge\, \neg\exists(x',z)\cdot((x',z) \in \overline{r} \,\wedge\, x' = x)$
$\Leftrightarrow$
$x \in \overline{\mathsf{prj}_1(a,c)[\overline{r}]}$
$\Leftrightarrow$
$x \in \mathsf{PRJ}_1(a,c)(r)$

End of Proof

11.2.4. Monotonicity

In the previous section we exhibited some sufficient conditions for abstract machine refinement (Theorem 11.2.2). These conditions were supposed to be easy to use in practice. In fact, these conditions are still not very convenient because they have to be proved for each "external" substitution implemented on machines M and N in the form of the two substitutions T and U respectively. In this section our intention is to remove this informal universal quantification.

More precisely, we now show that such proofs have to be made for the *corresponding basic operations of the machines only*. Should these proofs be performed successfully, then they can be *extended automatically to each "external" substitution* envisaged previously. This is so because the sufficient condition of the previous section is actually *monotonic* under the various constructs of our generalized substitution notation (as presented in chapters 4 and 9). The purpose of this section is therefore to prove the monotonicity of our sufficient condition.

We use exactly the same notations as in the previous section, namely:

- A substitution T working with the "external" variable x, belonging to a set a, and with the variable y of machine M, belonging to a set b.

- A substitution U, working with the "external" variable x, belonging to the set a, and with the variable z of machine N, belonging to a set c.

- A total relation v from c to b, as in the previous section. This relation is extended to the relation w that is equal to $\mathsf{id}(a) \parallel v$.

- A "substitution" W which is such that $\mathsf{str}(W)(r) = \overline{w\,[\overline{r}]}$.

Let us now define the following construct expressing that substitution T is refined by substitution U under the "change of variable" W. Formally

Syntax	Definition
$T \sqsubseteq_W U$	$T\,;W \sqsubseteq W\,;U$

We have then the following monotonicity properties:

$$S \sqsubseteq_W T \qquad\qquad \Rightarrow \qquad (P \mid S) \sqsubseteq_W (P \mid T)$$

$$(U \sqsubseteq_W V) \wedge (S \sqsubseteq_W T) \qquad \Rightarrow \qquad (U [] S) \sqsubseteq_W (V [] T)$$

$$S \sqsubseteq_W T \qquad\qquad \Rightarrow \qquad (P \Longrightarrow S) \sqsubseteq_W (P \Longrightarrow T)$$

$$\forall t \cdot (S \sqsubseteq_W T) \qquad\qquad \Rightarrow \qquad @t \cdot S \sqsubseteq_W @t \cdot T$$

$$(U \sqsubseteq_W V) \wedge (S \sqsubseteq_W T) \qquad \Rightarrow \qquad (U \,;S) \sqsubseteq_W (V \,;T)$$

$$S \sqsubseteq_W T \qquad\qquad \Rightarrow \qquad S\hat{\ } \sqsubseteq_W T\hat{\ }$$

Notice that the predicate P in the first and third statements is a predicate *involving x only* (neither y nor z): this is because our "external" substitutions are *not* supposed to access the "internal" variables of the machines (Hiding Principle).

Also notice that, for the moment, we have not mentioned any monotonicity property concerning the multiple operator ||. It will be done and proved at the end of this section only.

In what follows, we prove the monotonicity of the opening operator. We leave the other proofs as exercises for the reader:

Proof of the Monotonicity of the Opening Operator

We assume

$$S \sqsubseteq_W T \qquad\qquad\qquad\qquad \text{Hypothesis 1}$$

which is equivalent to the following (according to the Refinement Condition of section 11.2.3):

$$\forall r \cdot (r \subseteq (a \times c) \;\Rightarrow\; \mathrm{str}(S)(\overline{w \, [\overline{r}]}) \subseteq \overline{w \, [\overline{\mathrm{str}(T)(r)}]}) \qquad \text{Derivation 1}$$

And we have to prove $S\hat{\ } \sqsubseteq T\hat{\ }$, that is

$$\forall r \cdot (r \subseteq (a \times c) \;\Rightarrow\; \mathrm{str}(S\hat{\ })(\overline{w \, [\overline{r}]}) \subseteq \overline{w \, [\overline{\mathrm{str}(T\hat{\ })(r)}]}) \qquad \text{Goal 1}$$

We remove universal quantification and assume

$$r \subseteq (a \times c) \qquad\qquad\qquad\qquad \text{Hypothesis 2}$$

And we have to prove

$$\mathrm{str}(S\hat{\ })(\overline{w \, [\overline{r}]}) \subseteq \overline{w \, [\overline{\mathrm{str}(T\hat{\ })(r)}]}$$

that is (according to the definition of $\mathrm{str}(S\hat{\ })$ given in section 9.2.1):

$$\mathrm{fix}(f) \subseteq \overline{w \, [\overline{\mathrm{str}(T\hat{\ })(r)}]} \qquad\qquad \text{Goal 3}$$

where

$$f \;=\; \lambda q \cdot (q \in \mathbb{P}(a \times b) \mid \overline{w \, [\overline{r}]} \cap \mathrm{str}(S)(q)) \qquad \text{Definition 1}$$

It is then sufficient to prove (according to Theorem 3.2.1)

$$f(\overline{w\,[\mathsf{str}(T^{\wedge})(r)]}) \;\subseteq\; \overline{w\,[\mathsf{str}(T^{\wedge})(r)]} \qquad\qquad \text{Goal 4}$$

That is, according to Definition 1,

$$\overline{w\,[\bar{r}]} \cap \mathsf{str}(S\,)(\overline{w\,[\mathsf{str}(T^{\wedge})(r)]}) \;\subseteq\; \overline{w\,[\mathsf{str}(T^{\wedge})(r)]} \qquad\qquad \text{Goal 5}$$

According to Hypothesis 2 and Derivation 1, it is then sufficient to prove

$$\overline{w\,[\bar{r}]} \cap \overline{w\,[\mathsf{str}(T)(\mathsf{str}(T^{\wedge})(r))]} \;\subseteq\; \overline{w\,[\mathsf{str}(T^{\wedge})(r)]} \qquad\qquad \text{Goal 6}$$

That is

$$\overline{w\,[r \cap \mathsf{str}(T)(\mathsf{str}(T^{\wedge})(r))]} \;\subseteq\; \overline{w\,[\mathsf{str}(T^{\wedge})(r)]} \qquad\qquad \text{Goal 7}$$

which is obvious according to the fixpoint definition of $\mathsf{str}(T^{\wedge})(r)$ as given in section 9.2.1.

End of Proof

A consequence of the monotonicity properties exhibited in this section is that we can now restate **Theorem 11.2.2** showing the sufficient conditions for abstract machine refinement. This takes the form of the following theorem:

$$
\begin{aligned}
&v \in c \leftrightarrow b \\
&\mathrm{dom}(v) = c \\
&\forall q \cdot (q \subseteq c \;\Rightarrow\; \mathsf{str}(T)(\overline{v\,[\bar{q}]}) \subseteq \overline{v\,[\mathsf{str}(U)(q)]}\,) \qquad\qquad \text{Theorem 11.2.3} \\
&\Rightarrow \\
&M \sqsubseteq N
\end{aligned}
$$

---

for each *corresponding* operation T and U of the machines M and N respectively.

You may have noticed the difference between **Theorem 11.2.3** and **Theorem 11.2.2**. We use the relation v only (its extension w to "external" variables has obviously become pointless) and the *informal quantification* is now performed over the various corresponding operations of both machines.

An Alternative Equivalent Formulation of the Refinement Condition

The previous statement of the refinement condition is expressed in tems of the construct str. In the remaining part of this section, we shall present an alternative formulation of this condition involving the other two constructs pre and rel. For doing this, we first instantiate the subset q with c. This yields the following:

$$\mathsf{str}\,(T)(b) \;\subseteq\; \overline{v\,[\mathsf{str}\,(U\,)(c)]}$$

that is (according to **Property 6.4.9**):

$$\mathsf{pre}\,(T) \;\subseteq\; \overline{v\,[\mathsf{pre}\,(U\,)]}$$

that is (according to exercise 11 of chapter 2)

$$v^{-1}[\mathsf{pre}\,(T)] \;\subseteq\; \mathsf{pre}\,(U)$$

By now instantiating q with $\overline{\{z'\}}$ for each element z' of c, we obtain

$$\forall z' \cdot (z' \in c \;\Rightarrow\; \mathsf{str}(T)(\overline{v\,[\{z'\}]}) \;\subseteq\; \overline{v\,[\mathsf{str}(U)(\overline{\{z'\}})]})$$

that is (according to Property 6.4.9)

$$\forall z' \cdot (z' \in c \;\Rightarrow\; \overline{\mathsf{rel}(T)^{-1}[v\,[\{z'\}]]} \;\subseteq\; \overline{v\,[\mathsf{rel}(U)^{-1}[\{z'\}]]})$$

that is (by contraposition)

$$\forall z' \cdot (z' \in c \;\Rightarrow\; v\,[\mathsf{rel}(U)^{-1}[\{z'\}]] \;\subseteq\; \mathsf{rel}(T)^{-1}[v\,[\{z'\}]])$$

that is

$$\mathsf{rel}(U)^{-1}\,;v \;\subseteq\; v\,;\mathsf{rel}(T)^{-1}$$

which is

$$v^{-1}\,;\mathsf{rel}(U) \;\subseteq\; \mathsf{rel}(T)\,;v^{-1}$$

Conversely, it can be proved that the refinement conditions involving the constructs pre and rel, together imply the refinement condition involving the construct str. By putting together these conditions, we obtain an alternative formulation of Theorem 11.2.3, in terms of the constructs pre and rel.

$v \in c \leftrightarrow b$
$\mathsf{dom}(v) = c$
$v^{-1}[\mathsf{pre}\,(T)] \;\subseteq\; \mathsf{pre}\,(U)$
$v^{-1}\,;\mathsf{rel}(U) \;\subseteq\; \mathsf{rel}(T)\,;v^{-1}$
$\Rightarrow$
$M \sqsubseteq N$

Theorem 11.2.4

It is interesting to compare these alternative conditions of refinement with those presented in Property 11.1.1 for the refinement of generalized substitution. As already noticed, we can see that the former reduces to the latter when v is the identity relation.

Monotonicity of the Multiple Operator ||

Equipped with the above alternative formulation of the refinement condition, we are now in a position to state and establish the monotonicity of the multiple operator, namely

$$(A \sqsubseteq_V B) \wedge (S \sqsubseteq_W T) \quad \Rightarrow \quad (A \mid\mid S) \sqsubseteq_{V \mid\mid W} (B \mid\mid T)$$

As can be seen, we suppose that the substitutions A and S are refined independently by means of V and W respectively, yielding B and T. The law then says that the multiple composition $A \mid\mid S$ is refined by means of the multiple composition of $V \mid\mid W$, yielding the multiple composition $B \mid\mid T$.

Proof

We assume

$$A \sqsubseteq_V B \qquad\qquad \text{Hypothesis 1}$$

$$S \sqsubseteq_W T \qquad\qquad \text{Hypothesis 2}$$

That is, using the alternative formulation:

$$v^{-1}[\mathsf{pre}\,(A)] \subseteq \mathsf{pre}\,(B) \qquad\qquad \text{Derivation 1}$$

$$v^{-1}; \mathsf{rel}(B) \subseteq \mathsf{rel}(A); v^{-1} \qquad\qquad \text{Derivation 2}$$

$$w^{-1}[\mathsf{pre}\,(S)] \subseteq \mathsf{pre}\,(T) \qquad\qquad \text{Derivation 3}$$

$$w^{-1}; \mathsf{rel}(T) \subseteq \mathsf{rel}(S); w^{-1} \qquad\qquad \text{Derivation 4}$$

And we have to prove

$$(A \mid\mid S) \sqsubseteq_{V \mid\mid W} (B \mid\mid T) \qquad\qquad \text{Goal 1}$$

That is, using the alternative formulation,

$$(v \mid\mid w)^{-1}[\mathsf{pre}\,(A \mid\mid S)] \subseteq \mathsf{pre}\,(B \mid\mid T) \qquad\qquad \text{Goal 2}$$

$$(v \mid\mid w)^{-1}; \mathsf{rel}(B \mid\mid T) \subseteq \mathsf{rel}(A \mid\mid S); (v \mid\mid w)^{-1} \qquad \text{Goal 3}$$

That is (according to the basic properties of section 7.1.2),

$$(v \mid\mid w)^{-1}[\mathsf{pre}\,(A) \times \mathsf{pre}\,(S)] \subseteq \mathsf{pre}\,(B) \times \mathsf{pre}\,(T) \qquad\qquad \text{Goal 4}$$

$$(v \mid\mid w)^{-1}; (\mathsf{rel}(B) \mid\mid \mathsf{rel}(T)) \subseteq (\mathsf{rel}(A) \mid\mid \mathsf{rel}(S)); (v \mid\mid w)^{-1} \quad \text{Goal 5}$$

That is (according to a law relating the inverse of a relation and the parallel product at section 2.6.4)

$$(v^{-1} \mid\mid w^{-1})[\mathsf{pre}\,(A) \times \mathsf{pre}\,(S)] \subseteq \mathsf{pre}\,(B) \times \mathsf{pre}\,(T) \qquad\qquad \text{Goal 6}$$

$$\qquad\qquad \text{Goal 7}$$

$$(v^{-1} \mid\mid w^{-1}); (\mathsf{rel}(B) \mid\mid \mathsf{rel}(T)) \subseteq (\mathsf{rel}(A) \mid\mid \mathsf{rel}(S)); (v^{-1} \mid\mid w^{-1})$$

That is (according to two laws relating the image of a relation and the parallel product and also the composition of relations and the parallel product at section

2.6.4)

$$v^{-1}[\text{pre}(A)] \times w^{-1}[\text{pre}(S)] \subseteq \text{pre}(B) \times \text{pre}(T) \qquad \text{Goal 8}$$

$$\text{Goal 9}$$

$$(v^{-1}\,;\text{rel}(B)) \mid\mid (w^{-1}\,;\text{rel}(T)) \subseteq (\text{rel}(A)\,;v^{-1}) \mid\mid (\text{rel}(S)\,;w^{-1})$$

These goals are easily discharged according to the previous Derivations, the monotonicity of the cartesian product (section 2.1.3) and the monotonicity of the parallel product (section 2.6.2).

End of Proof

11.2.5. Example Revisited

In this section we show how we define refinements in practice. For this, we come back to our previous example of section 11.2.1, which we reproduce here:

MACHINE

    Little_Example_1

VARIABLES

    y

INVARIANT

    $y \in \mathbb{F}(\text{NAT}_1)$

INITIALIZATION

    $y := \varnothing$

OPERATIONS

    enter(n) $\;\widehat{=}$
        PRE $n \in \text{NAT}_1$ THEN $y := y \cup \{n\}$ END;

    $m \longleftarrow$ maximum$\;\widehat{=}$
        PRE $y \neq \varnothing$ THEN $m := \text{max}(y)$ END

END

From here on, we do not define another machine as in section 11.2.1. Rather, we *propose a refinement* as shown in what follows:

REFINEMENT

    Little_Example_2

REFINES

    Little_Example_1

VARIABLES

    z

INVARIANT

    $z = \max(y \cup \{0\})$

INITIALIZATION

    $z := 0$

OPERATIONS

    $\text{enter}(n) \;\widehat{=}$
        PRE $n \in \text{NAT}_1$ THEN $z := \max(\{z, n\})$ END;

    $m \longleftarrow \text{maximum} \;\widehat{=}$
        PRE $z \neq 0$ THEN $m := z$ END

END

As can be seen, the keyword MACHINE has been replaced by the new keyword REFINEMENT: this is to indicate that what has been written is *not* an abstract machine. It is, rather, a refinement of the machine whose name is written within the clause REFINES. This refinement is defined by means of a change of variable, as described in the corresponding INVARIANT clause. There follow a number of operations *claiming* to refine those of the original abstract machine. The idea is that this refinement can be used, together with the corresponding machine, to produce a *new machine* claiming to refine the first one.

11.2.6. The Final Touch

In this section our intention is to give practical laws to prove abstract machine refinement. More precisely, our intention is, eventually, to transform the antecedents of Theorem 11.2.3. They will be replaced by conditions working on generalized substitutions only (not with the str constructs).

As we have seen in the previous section, a refinement is thus a sort of *differential* to be "added" to a given machine M, in order to build (at least, in principle) a new machine N, supposed to refine M.

More abstractly, what is shown in the following figure is how a schematic machine and a corresponding refinement can be *combined syntactically* to form, in principle, a new machine (note that we have omitted, on purpose, the clause REFINES).

MACHINE	REFINEMENT	MACHINE
M	N	N
VARIABLES	VARIABLES	VARIABLES
y	z	z
INVARIANT	INVARIANT	INVARIANT
I	J	$\exists y \cdot (I \wedge J)$
INITIALIZATION	INITIALIZATION	INITIALIZATION
B	C	C
OPERATIONS	OPERATIONS	OPERATIONS
$T \mathrel{\widehat{=}}$	$U \mathrel{\widehat{=}}$	$U \mathrel{\widehat{=}}$
PRE	PRE	PRE
P	Q	$Q \wedge$ $\exists y \cdot (I \wedge J \wedge P)$
THEN	THEN	THEN
K	L	L
END	END	END
END	END	END

In practice, we shall *never* write down the machine N explicitly, since it can always be *produced mechanically* from machine M and refinement N. Machine N is just written here to make precise what the proof obligations are. Next is the proof obligation of machine M concerning operation T (section 5.2.5). We suppose, of course, that this condition has already been proved:

$$\forall y \cdot (I \ \wedge \ P \ \Rightarrow \ [K]I \,) \qquad \text{(Condition 1)}$$

We remind the reader that the above proof obligation of machine M amounts to proving that the invariant I is preserved by the operation T. The proof obligation for operation U of machine N, considered alone, can easily be reduced to the following. This one, of course, remains to be proved:

$$\forall (y, z) \cdot (I \ \wedge \ J \ \wedge \ P \ \wedge \ Q \ \Rightarrow \ [L] \exists y \cdot (I \ \wedge \ J \,)) \qquad \text{(Condition 2)}$$

In the remaining part of this section, we are going to translate the various antecedents of Theorem 11.2.3. In order to do so, we have to establish some correspondence between the notations used in section 11.2.4 and those used in this section. In section 11.2.4, we used the letter b to denote the *abstract* set of machine M, which is here $\{y \mid I\}$. We used the letter c to denote the *concrete* set of machine N, which is here $\{z \mid \exists y \cdot (I \ \wedge \ J \,)\}$. And, finally, we used the letter v to denote a certain binary relation between c and b, which we choose here to be $\{z, y \mid I \ \wedge \ J \,\}$. We thus have the following correspondence:

b	$\{y \mid I\}$
c	$\{z \mid \exists y \cdot (I \ \wedge \ J \,)\}$
v	$\{z, y \mid I \ \wedge \ J \,\}$

Notice that we obviously have

$$v \in c \leftrightarrow b \ \ \wedge \ \ \mathrm{dom}(v) = c$$

As already indicated, our refinement proof obligations are dictated by the antecedents of Theorem 11.2.3, which we write again here.

$$
\begin{aligned}
&v \in c \leftrightarrow b \\
&\mathrm{dom}(v) = c \\
&\forall q \cdot (q \subseteq c \ \Rightarrow \ \mathrm{str}(T)(\overline{v\,[\overline{q}]}) \ \subseteq \ \overline{v\,[\overline{\mathrm{str}(U)(q)}]}\,) \\
&\Rightarrow \\
&M \ \sqsubseteq \ N
\end{aligned}
$$

Since, as we have just seen, the first two antecedents already hold, our refinement proof obligation thus corresponds to the last antecedent of Theorem 11.2.3, that is

$$\forall q \cdot (q \subseteq c \;\Rightarrow\; \mathsf{str}(T)(\overline{v\,[\overline{q}]}) \;\subseteq\; \overline{v\,[\overline{\mathsf{str}(U\,)(q)]}}) \qquad \text{(Condition 3)}$$

Our claim is that this condition is implied by the following:

$$\forall (z, y) \cdot (I \;\wedge\; J \;\wedge\; P \;\Rightarrow\; [U]\,\neg\,[K]\,\neg\,J\,) \qquad \text{(Condition 4)}$$

We shall thus prove

$$\text{Condition 4} \quad \Rightarrow \quad \text{Condition 3}$$

Before proving this implication, however, we have to prove that the condition $z \in c$ (that is $\exists y \cdot (I \;\wedge\; J\,)$) is indeed invariant under the operation U of machine N (this is Condition 2), since otherwise the construct $\mathsf{str}\,(U)$ would not make sense. We remind the reader that the definition of the set-theoretic models in section 6.4 (hence the definition of a construct such as $\mathsf{str}\,(U)$) requires that the generalized substitution U is working within a machine having an invariant of the form of a set membership. Notice that we already know that the condition $y \in b$ (that is I) is invariant under operation T of machine M (this is Condition 1). Hence the construct $\mathsf{str}\,(T)$ does make sense. We shall then prove the following:

$$\text{Condition 1} \;\wedge\; \text{Condition 4} \quad \Rightarrow \quad \text{Condition 2}$$

For this, we first prove the following property:

Condition 1
$\Rightarrow$ Property 11.2.3
$\forall y \cdot (I \;\wedge\; P \;\Rightarrow\; \forall z \cdot (\neg\,[K]\,\neg\,J \;\Rightarrow\; \exists y \cdot (I \;\wedge\; J\,)))$

Proof

We assume Condition 1, that is

$$\forall y \cdot (I \;\wedge\; P \;\Rightarrow\; [K]\,I\,) \qquad\qquad \text{Hypothesis 1}$$

and we have to prove

$$\forall y \cdot (I \;\wedge\; P \;\Rightarrow\; \forall z \cdot (\neg\,[K]\,\neg\,J \;\Rightarrow\; \exists y \cdot (I \;\wedge\; J\,))) \qquad \text{Goal 1}$$

We assume

$$I \;\wedge\; P \qquad\qquad \text{Hypothesis 2}$$

and we are left to prove

$$\forall z \cdot (\neg\,[K]\,\neg\,J \;\Rightarrow\; \exists y \cdot (I \;\wedge\; J\,)) \qquad \text{Goal 2}$$

that is, by contraposition

$$\forall z \cdot (\forall y \cdot (I \Rightarrow \neg J) \Rightarrow [K] \neg J) \qquad \text{Goal 3}$$

We assume then

$$\forall y \cdot (I \Rightarrow \neg J) \qquad \text{Hypothesis 3}$$

And we have to prove eventually

$$[K] \neg J \qquad \text{Goal 4}$$

But, from Hypothesis 2 and Hypothesis 1, we deduce

$$[K] I \qquad \text{Derivation 1}$$

Goal 4 follows then from Hypothesis 3, Derivation 1, and the monotonicity of substitution (this is Property 6.2.2).
End of Proof

We prove now our second property:

Condition 1 $\wedge$ Condition 4 $\Rightarrow$ Condition 2 $\qquad$ **Property 11.2.4**

Proof
We assume Condition 1 and Condition 4, that is

$$\forall y \cdot (I \wedge P \Rightarrow [K] I) \qquad \text{Hypothesis 1}$$

$$\forall (z, y) \cdot (I \wedge J \wedge P \Rightarrow [U] \neg [K] \neg J) \qquad \text{Hypothesis 2}$$

And we have to prove Condition 2, that is

$$\forall (y, z) \cdot (I \wedge J \wedge P \wedge Q \Rightarrow [L] \exists y \cdot (I \wedge J)) \qquad \text{Goal 1}$$

We assume then

$$I \wedge J \wedge P \wedge Q \qquad \text{Hypothesis 3}$$

and we have to prove

$$[L] \exists y \cdot (I \wedge J) \qquad \text{Goal 2}$$

From Hypothesis 1 and Property 11.2.3, we deduce

$$\forall y \cdot (I \wedge P \Rightarrow \forall z \cdot (\neg [K] \neg J \Rightarrow \exists y \cdot (I \wedge J))) \qquad \text{Derivation 1}$$

From Derivation 1 and Hypothesis 3, we deduce then

$$\forall z \cdot (\neg [K] \neg J \Rightarrow \exists y \cdot (I \wedge J)) \qquad \text{Derivation 2}$$

And from Hypothesis 2 and Hypothesis 3, we deduce

$$[U] \neg [K] \neg J \qquad \text{Derivation 3}$$

From Derivation 2, Derivation 3, and the monotonicity of substitution (Property 6.2.2), we deduce

$$[U]\,\exists\,y\cdot(I\,\wedge\,J\,)\qquad\qquad\text{Derivation 4}$$

But we have, by definition,

$$U\;=\;Q\,\wedge\,\exists\,y\cdot(I\,\wedge\,J\,\wedge\,P\,)\mid L$$

Thus Goal 2 follows immediately from Derivation 4.
End of Proof

We notice that the pre-condition Q of the refinement plays no rôle in this proof. We shall now prove our main property:

Condition 4 $\Rightarrow$ Condition 3   Property 11.2.5

Proof

We assume Condition 4, that is

$$\forall\,(z,y)\cdot(I\,\wedge\,J\,\wedge\,P\;\Rightarrow\;[U]\,\neg\,[K]\,\neg\,J\,)\qquad\text{Hypothesis 1}$$

And we have to prove Condition 3, that is

$$\forall\,q\cdot(q\subseteq c\;\Rightarrow\;\mathrm{str}(T)(\overline{v\,[\overline{q}]})\subseteq\overline{v\,[\overline{\mathrm{str}(U)(q)}]}\,)\qquad\text{Goal 1}$$

We assume then

$$q\subseteq c\qquad\qquad\text{Hypothesis 2}$$

and we have to prove

$$\mathrm{str}(T)(\overline{v\,[\overline{q}]})\subseteq\overline{v\,[\overline{\mathrm{str}(U)(q)}]}\qquad\text{Goal 2}$$

that is

$$\forall\,y\cdot(y\in\mathrm{str}(T)(\overline{v\,[\overline{q}]})\;\Rightarrow\;y\in\overline{v\,[\overline{\mathrm{str}(U)(q)}]}\,)\qquad\text{Goal 3}$$

We thus assume

$$y\in\mathrm{str}(T)(\overline{v\,[\overline{q}]})\qquad\qquad\text{Hypothesis 3}$$

from which we deduce immediately $y\in b\,\wedge\,\mathrm{str}(T)(y\in b)$, that is

$$I\,\wedge\,P\qquad\qquad\text{Derivation 1}$$

and we have to prove

$$y\in\overline{v\,[\overline{\mathrm{str}(U)(q)}]}\qquad\qquad\text{Goal 4}$$

From Hypothesis 3 we also deduce (according to Property 6.4.8)

$$y\in\mathrm{str}(T)(b)\,\wedge\,\forall\,y'\cdot(\,y'\in v\,[\overline{q}]\;\Rightarrow\;y\in\mathrm{str}(T)(\overline{\{y'\}})\,)\qquad\text{Derivation 2}$$

that is

$$y \in \mathsf{str}(T)(b) \;\wedge\; \forall\, y' \cdot ($$
$$\exists\, z \cdot (z \in \overline{q} \;\wedge\; (z, y') \in v) \;\Rightarrow\; y \in \mathsf{str}(T)(\overline{\{y'\}}))$$

Derivation 3

that is

$$y \in \mathsf{str}(T)(b) \;\wedge\; \forall\, y' \cdot \forall\, z \cdot ($$
$$z \in \overline{q} \;\wedge\; (z, y') \in v \;\Rightarrow\; y \in \mathsf{str}(T)(\overline{\{y'\}}))$$

Derivation 4

that is

$$\forall\, z \cdot (z \in \overline{q} \;\Rightarrow$$
$$(y \in \mathsf{str}(T)(b) \;\wedge\; \forall\, y' \cdot (y' \in v[\{z\}] \;\Rightarrow\; y \in \mathsf{str}(T)(\overline{\{y'\}}))))$$

Derivation 5

that is, according to **Property 6.4.8**,

$$\forall\, z \cdot (z \in \overline{q} \;\Rightarrow\; y \in \mathsf{str}(T)(\overline{v[\{z\}]}))$$

Derivation 6

that is, according to the definition of $\mathsf{str}(T)$ given in section 6.4.2,

$$\forall\, z \cdot (z \in \overline{q} \;\Rightarrow\; y \in b \;\wedge\; [T](y \in \overline{v[\{z\}]}))$$

Derivation 7

We have then the following (since $y \in \overline{v[\{z\}]} \;\Rightarrow\; \neg J$ and since T is $P \mid K$):

$$\forall\, z \cdot (z \in \overline{q} \;\Rightarrow\; I \;\wedge\; P \;\wedge\; [K]\neg J)$$

Derivation 8

that is (after **Derivation 1**)

$$\forall\, z \cdot (z \in \overline{q} \;\Rightarrow\; [K]\neg J)$$

Derivation 9

that is, by contraposition,

$$\forall\, z \cdot (\neg [K]\neg J \;\Rightarrow\; z \in q)$$

Derivation 10

Now **Goal 4** is equivalent to

$$y \in b \;\wedge\; \neg\, \exists\, z \cdot (z \notin \mathsf{str}(U)(q) \;\wedge\; z, y \in v)$$

Goal 5

The sub-goal $y \in b$, that is I, is discharged by **Derivation 1**. The second sub-goal is equivalent to the following (according to the definition of $\mathsf{str}(U)$ given in section 6.4.2):

$$\forall\, z \cdot (z \in c \;\wedge\; \neg [U](z \in q) \;\Rightarrow\; \neg(I \;\wedge\; J))$$

Goal 6

that is, by contraposition (and since $z \in c$, that is $\exists\, z \cdot (I \;\wedge\; J)$, is implied $I \;\wedge\; J$),

$$\forall\, z \cdot (I \;\wedge\; J \;\Rightarrow\; [U](z \in q))$$

We assume then

$$I \;\wedge\; J$$

and we are left to prove

$$[U](z \in q)$$

But from Derivation 1, Hypothesis 4, and Hypothesis 1, we deduce

$$[U] \neg [K] \neg J \qquad\qquad \text{Derivation 11}$$

Goal 8 then follows from Derivation 10, Derivation 11, and the monotonicity of substitution (Property 6.2.2).

End of Proof

We have so far studied the refinement of an abstract machine operation. We obtain, clearly, a similar although simpler result in the case of the initialization of an abstract machine. To summarize, the proof obligations concerning an abstract machine (1 and 2) and its refinement (3 and 4) can now be stated in their final forms:

$[B]I$	(Obligation 1)
$\forall y \cdot (I \wedge P \Rightarrow [K]I)$	(Obligation 2)
$[C] \neg [B] \neg J$	(Obligation 3)
$\forall (y,z) \cdot (I \wedge J \wedge P \Rightarrow Q \wedge [L] \neg [K] \neg J)$	(Obligation 4)

When the abstract machine operation corresponding to substitution T and its refinement U has a *result*, say r, then Obligation 4 has to be transformed as follows:

$$\forall (y,z) \cdot (I \wedge J \wedge P \Rightarrow Q \wedge [[r := r']L] \neg [K] \neg (J \wedge r = r'))$$

11.2.7. An Intuitive Explanation of the Refinement Condition

After the very formal developments done in the previous sections, it is worth trying to understand intuitively the results that we have obtained. The next figure will support our intuitive understanding. In order to simplify matters, we consider Obligation 4 without the universal quantification:

$$I \wedge J \wedge P \Rightarrow Q \wedge [L] \neg [K] \neg J$$

We remind the reader that I is the invariant of an abstract machine working with variable y, and, similarly, J is the change of variable of a refinement of that machine. This refinement works with variable z. Thus J relates the abstract variable y and the concrete variable z. Moreover, K is the "active part" of an abstract operation with pre-condition P, whereas L is the active part of the corresponding concrete operation with pre-condition Q.

The above formal statement expresses the sufficient condition to be proved in order to ensure that $P \mid K$ is refined by $Q \mid L$. It can be read as follows: under the invariant I, the pre-condition P, and the change of variable J, which connects an abstract point y to a concrete point z, we have to prove that the pre-condition Q holds, and that the refined operation L (started at z) establishes that it is not the case that the abstract operation K (started at y) establishes $\neg J$.

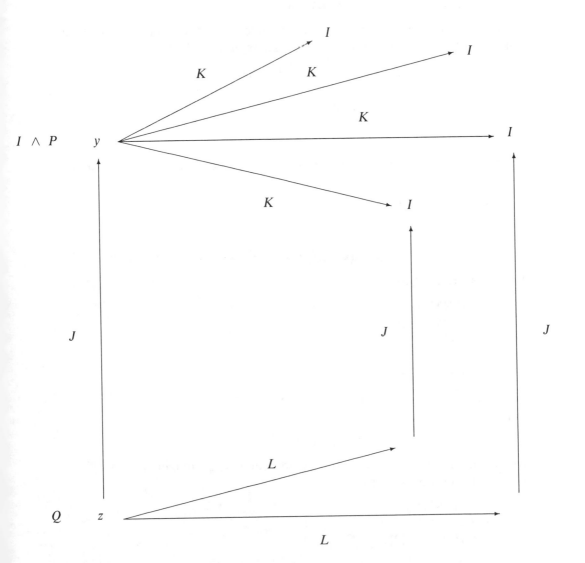

In other words, *all* possible "computations" of the refined operation L (started within its pre-condition Q, at the concrete point z) end up in concrete points, connected (through J) to abstract points, which are, themselves, the final points of *some* "computations" of the abstract operation K, supposed to have started at the abstract point y within its pre-condition P. Notice that it is not necessarily the case that all abstract computations of K have a concrete counterpart in L (this is due to the decreasing of non-determinism). On the other hand, it is demanded that *not all* abstract computations have *no* concrete counterpart: some must have one, that is some must be refined.

11.2.8. Application to the Little Example

We now re-consider the little example presented in sections 11.2.1 and 11.2.5. Obligation 3 about initialization can be discharged as follows:

$$[z := 0] \neg [y := \varnothing] \neg (z = \max(y \cup \{0\}))$$

$$\Leftrightarrow$$

$$[z := 0] (z = \max(\varnothing \cup \{0\}))$$

$$\Leftrightarrow$$

$$0 = 0$$

Obligation 4 applied to operation enter yields, after obvious simplifications,

$$y \in \mathbb{F}(\mathsf{NAT}_1)$$
$$z = \max(y \cup \{0\})$$
$$n \in \mathsf{NAT}_1$$
$$\Rightarrow$$
$$n \in \mathsf{NAT}_1 \ \wedge \ [z := \max(\{z, n\})] \neg [y := y \cup \{n\}] \neg (z = \max(y \cup \{0\}))$$

That is, equivalently,

$$y \in \mathbb{F}(\mathsf{NAT}_1)$$
$$z = \max(y \cup \{0\})$$
$$n \in \mathsf{NAT}_1$$
$$\Rightarrow$$
$$\max(\{z, n\}) = \max(y \cup \{n\} \cup \{0\})$$

which is obvious since we have the following general law (provided s is not empty)

$$\max(s \cup \{x\}) = \max(\{\max(s), x\})$$

We now discharge Obligation 4 for the operation $m \longleftarrow$ maximum. This yields, after obvious simplifications,

$$y \in \mathbb{F}(\mathsf{NAT}_1)$$
$$y \neq \varnothing$$
$$z = \max(y \cup \{0\})$$
$$\Rightarrow$$
$$z \neq 0 \ \wedge \ [m' := z] \neg [m := \max(y)] \neg (z = \max(y \cup \{0\}) \ \wedge \ m = m')$$

After more simplifications, we obtain the obvious statement

$$
y \in \mathbb{F}(\text{NAT}_1)
$$
$$
y \neq \varnothing
$$
$$
z = \max(y)
$$
$$
\Rightarrow
$$
$$
z \neq 0 \ \wedge \ z = \max(y)
$$

11.3. Formal Definition

11.3.1. Syntax

In this section we present the syntax of *Refinements*. As can be seen, a *Refinement* has a syntactic structure that is very close to that of a *Machine*. The REFINES clause refers either to a (list of) machine(s) or to another (more abstract) (list of) refinement(s) (the reason for having a *list* in the REFINES clause is explained in section 12.3 on multiple refinement). Notice that the list of formal parameters of the machine it comes from must be repeated in a refinement. Also notice that a refinement, like a machine, may have sets, concrete variables, (abstract) constants and properties. A refinement may also include one or several machines and it has, with respect to these machines, the same visibility rules as the one that were presented for machines in section 7.2.4.

Syntactic Category	Definition

Refinement	REFINEMENT
	   Machine_Header
	REFINES
	   Id_List
	SETS
	   Sets
	CONSTANTS
	   Id_List
	ABSTRACT_CONSTANTS
	   Id_List
	PROPERTIES
	   Predicate

Syntactic Category	Definition
Refinement (Cont'd)	INCLUDES 　　*Machine_List* PROMOTES 　　*Id_List* EXTENDS 　　*Machine_List* VARIABLES 　　*Id_List* CONCRETE_VARIABLES 　　*Id_List* INVARIANT 　　*Predicate* ASSERTIONS 　　*Predicate* DEFINITIONS 　　*Definitions* INITIALIZATION 　　*Substitution* OPERATIONS 　　*Operations* END

11.3.2. Type-checking

We now give the rule for type-checking refinements. For doing this, we consider a machine M_1 and a list of refinements $M_2, \ldots, M_n$. Also notice that the refinement M_n is supposed to include a machine M defined formally in the same way as M_1 (without the subscript 1).

```
MACHINE
  M₁(X₁, x₁)
CONSTRAINTS
  C₁
SETS
  S₁ ;
  T₁ = {a₁, b₁}
(ABSTRACT_)CONSTANTS
  c₁
```

. . .

```
REFINEMENT
  Mₙ(X₁, x₁)
REFINES
  Mₙ₋₁
SETS
  Sₙ ;
  Tₙ = {aₙ, bₙ}
(ABSTRACT_)CONSTANTS
  cₙ
```

```
          PROPERTIES                              PROPERTIES
           P₁                                      Pₙ
          (CONCRETE_)VARIABLES                    INCLUDES
           v₁                                      M (N , n)
          INVARIANT                               (CONCRETE_)VARIABLES
           I₁                                       vₙ
          ASSERTIONS              ...             INVARIANT
           J₁                                      Iₙ
          INITIALIZATION                          ASSERTIONS
           U₁                                      Jₙ
          OPERATIONS                              INITIALIZATION
           O₁                                      Uₙ
          END                                     OPERATIONS
                                                   Oₙ
                                                  END
```

Here is the type-checking rule:

Antecedents	Consequent
$O_n, O, M_i, X_1, x_1, S_i, T_i, a_i, b_i, c_n, v_n,$ X, S, T, a, b, c, v are all distinct U_n and O_n do not contain occurences of variables in v_i that are not in v_n $\mathsf{given}(X_1),\ \mathsf{given}(S_1),\ \mathsf{given}(T_1),$ $a_1 \in T_1,\ b_1 \in T_1,\ \mathsf{sig}\,(M_1),$ $\cdots$ $\mathsf{given}\,(S_{n-1}),\ \mathsf{given}\,(T_{n-1}),\ \mathsf{sig}\,(M_{n-1}),$ $\mathsf{given}\,(S_n),\ \mathsf{given}\,(T_n),$ $a_n \in T_n,\ b_n \in T_n$ $\vdash$ $\mathsf{check}\,(\forall\, x_1 \cdot (C_1\ \Rightarrow$ $\qquad\qquad \forall\, c_n \cdot (P_n\ \Rightarrow\ [X, x := N, n]\, C)))$	$\mathsf{check}\,($ REFINEMENT $\quad M_n(X_1, x_1)$ REFINES $\quad M_{n-1}$ SETS $\quad S_n\,;$ $\quad T_n = \{a_n, b_n\}$ (ABSTRACT_)CONSTANTS $\quad c_n$ PROPERTIES $\quad P_n$ INCLUDES $\quad M (N , n)$ (CONCRETE_)VARIABLES $\quad v_n$

Antecedents (Cont'd)	Consequent (Cont'd)
$\left\{ \begin{array}{l} \text{given}(X_1), \ \text{given}(S_1), \ \text{given}(T_1), \ \text{sig}(M_1), \\ \cdots \\ \text{given}(S_{n-1}), \ \text{given}(T_{n-1}), \ \text{sig}(M_{n-1}) \\ \text{given}(S_n), \ \text{given}(T_n), \ a_n \in T_n, \ b_n \in T_n, \\ \text{given}(S), \ \text{given}(T), \\ [X, x := N, n] \, \text{sig}(M) \\ \vdash \\ \text{check}(\forall v_n \cdot (I_n \ \Rightarrow \ J_n \ \wedge \ U_n \ \wedge \ O_n)) \end{array} \right.$	INVARIANT I_n ASSERTIONS J_n INITIALIZATION U_n OPERATIONS O_n END)

In the above rule, the list of variables v_n of refinement M_n and the list of variables v_{n-1} of refinement (or machine) M_{n-1} may *overlap*. Each variable, say x, that is present in both lists is supposed to be *implicitly* re-defined as, say, x_{n-1} in v_{n-1} and x_n in v_n. Moreover, we suppose that we have the *implicit* change of variable $x_{n-1} = x_n$. Such a case, which is very frequent in practice, corresponds to a refinement where we are interested in genuinely refining certain variables only. When a variable disappears, at some point in a refinement, it cannot reappear further down in subsequent refinements. Of course, the CONCRETE_VARIABLES remain present as soon as they appear in the development since, by definition, they are never refined.

The INVARIANT clause of refinement M_n may contain occurrences of variables of both lists v_n and v_{n-1} since, by definition, it contains the *change of variable* between the two. However, it cannot contain other variables of other machines or refinements that are not present in v_n and v_{n-1}.

The initialization U_n and the operations O_n of refinement M_n may only contain occurrences of variables of v_n. Any variable that is a member of a list v_i (where $i < n$), but not a member of the list v_n, is disallowed in the initialization U_n and in the operations O_n.

What we have just said of the variables is applicable, by analogy, to the constants. The CONSTANTS are of the same nature as the CONCRETE_VARIABLES, the ABSTRACT_CONSTANTS are of the same nature as the VARIABLES, and the PROPERTIES are of the same nature as the INVARIANT. As a consequence, the CONSTANTS are always present, whereas any member of the list of ABSTRACT_CONSTANTS may disappear and will thus never reappear in a subsequent refinement. We shall see in section 12.1.3 that in the last refinement (called an IMPLEMENTATION), no ABSTRACT_CONSTANTS are allowed: each such constant either disappears completely (probably in an operation) or must be implemented eventually by some concrete constants.

Finally, we shall see that in an IMPLEMENTATION the concrete constants are given a final value in a special clause called the VALUES clause (section 12.1.7).

The above type-checking rule is a generalization of that of a machine containing an INCLUDES clause (section 7.4.2). The type-checking of the initialization and of the operations is done under the control of the signatures (section 7.4.2) of the initial machine and of those of the previous refinements. Notice that the signature of M_i (for i in $1 .. n - 1$) is preceded by the declarations of its given sets S_i and T_i.

The presence of signatures for $M_2, ..., M_{n-1}$ raises the question of the exact definition of the signature of a refinement. In fact, the signature of a refinement is defined in exactly the same way as was the signature of a machine (section 7.4.2), except, of course, that it does not contain the signature of the operations. These are defined, once and for all, in the signature of the original machine M_1. As a consequence, we have to add an extra rule to the rules defining the type-checking of an operation (section 5.2.3). This is because when we are type-checking an operation of a refinement, we already know (from the signature of the original machine) what the signature of the operation is.

Antecedents	Consequent
$\begin{cases} S \longleftarrow O\,(T) \quad \text{occurs in} \quad ENV \\[1em] ENV, \\ u \in S, \\ w \in T \\ \vdash \\ \text{check}\,(P \wedge U\,) \end{cases}$	$ENV \;\vdash\; \text{check}\,(u \longleftarrow O(w) \;\;\widehat{=}\;\; P \mid U\,)$

11.3.3. Proof Obligations

In this section we make precise the proof obligations of refinement. Suppose we have the following machine and the following ultimate refinement (intermediate refinements have exactly the same structure):

```
+--------------------------------------+
|                                      |
|  MACHINE                             |
|    M₁(X₁, x₁)                         |
|  CONSTRAINTS                         |
|    C₁                                 |
|  SETS                                |
|    S₁ ;                              |
|    T₁ = {a₁, b₁}                      |
|  (ABSTRACT_)CONSTANTS                |
|    c₁                                 |
|  PROPERTIES                          |
|    P₁                                 |
|  (CONCRETE_)VARIABLES                |
|    v₁                                 |
|  INVARIANT                           |
|    I₁                                 |
|  ASSERTIONS                          |
|    J₁                                 |
|  INITIALIZATION                      |
|    U₁                                 |
|  OPERATIONS                          |
|    u₁ ⟵ op₁(w₁)  ≙                    |
|      PRE                             |
|        Q₁                            |
|      THEN                            |
|        V₁                            |
|      END ;                           |
|        . . .                         |
|  END                                 |
|                                      |
+--------------------------------------+
```

```
+--------------------------------------+
|                                      |
|  REFINEMENT                          |
|    Mₙ(X₁, x₁)                         |
|  REFINES                             |
|    Mₙ₋₁                               |
|  SETS                                |
|    Sₙ ;                              |
|    Tₙ = {aₙ, bₙ}                      |
|  (ABSTRACT_)CONSTANTS                |
|    cₙ                                 |
|  PROPERTIES                          |
|    Pₙ                                 |
|  INCLUDES                            |
|    M(N, n)                           |
|  (CONCRETE_)VARIABLES                |
|    vₙ                                 |
|  INVARIANT                           |
|    Iₙ                                 |
|  ASSERTIONS                          |
|    Jₙ                                 |
|  INITIALIZATION                      |
|    Uₙ                                 |
|  OPERATIONS                          |
|    u₁ ⟵ op₁(w₁)  ≙                    |
|      PRE                             |
|        Qₙ                            |
|      THEN                            |
|        Vₙ                            |
|      END ;                           |
|        . . .                         |
|  END                                 |
|                                      |
+--------------------------------------+
```

The refinement M_n is supposed to include a certain machine M with the same formal structure as that of M_1 (without the subscript 1). Before presenting the proof obligations, let us define (as in sections 5.2.5 and 7.4.3) the following predicates A_1, B_i (for i in $1 .. n$), A and B. The first one, A_1, states that the set machine parameter X_1 is a non-empty subset of INT, the second one, B_i, states that the deferred set S_i (for i in $1 .. n$) is a non-empty subset of INT and that the enumerated set T_i (for i in $1 .. n$) is a non-empty subset of INT, consisting exactly of the two distinct elements a_i and b_i :

Abbreviation	Definition
A_1	$X_1 \in \mathbb{P}_1(\mathsf{INT})$
B_i for i in $1 .. n$	$S_i \in \mathbb{P}_1(\mathsf{INT}) \ \wedge \ T_i \in \mathbb{P}_1(\mathsf{INT}) \ \wedge \ T_i = \{a_i, b_i\} \ \wedge \ a_i \neq b_i$
A	$X \in \mathbb{P}_1(\mathsf{INT})$
B	$S \in \mathbb{P}_1(\mathsf{INT}) \ \wedge \ T \in \mathbb{P}_1(\mathsf{INT}) \ \wedge \ T = \{a, b\} \ \wedge \ a \neq b$

The first proof obligation of refinement M_n states that the included machine M is correctly called in the INCLUDES clause of M_n. In other words, the constraints A and C of the formal parameters X and x of M must hold when X and x are actualized to N and n respectively. This proof is done under the proper assumptions of the formal constraints A_1 and C_1 of M_1, the abbreviations B_i concerning the sets of M_i (for i in $1 .. n$) and, finally, the properties P_i of the constants of M_i (for i in $1 .. n$). The reason for these assumptions is that the actual parameters N and n are possibly written in terms of the corresponding objects of $M_1, \ldots, M_n$.

$$
\begin{array}{l}
\overbrace{A_1 \ \wedge \ B_1 \ \wedge \ \cdots \ \wedge \ B_n \ \wedge \ C_1 \ \wedge \ P_1 \ \wedge \ \cdots \ \wedge \ P_n}^{\textstyle \text{Including}} \\
\Rightarrow \\
[X, x := N, n] \, \overbrace{(A \ \wedge \ C)}^{\textstyle \text{Included}}
\end{array}
$$

The next proof obligation concerns the assertions of the refinement. Notice that, in the assumptions of this proof obligation, the invariant I and assertion J of the included machine M have been actualized. However, the property P of the included machine M has not been actualized since, by definition, the PROPERTIES clause of a machine is independent of its parameters (section 4.17).

$$\overbrace{A_1 \ \wedge \ B_1 \ \wedge \ \cdots \ \wedge \ B_n \ \wedge \ C_1 \ \wedge \ P_1 \ \wedge \ \cdots \ \wedge \ P_n}^{\text{Including}} \ \wedge$$

$$\overbrace{I_1 \ \wedge \ \cdots \ \wedge \ I_n \ \wedge \ J_1 \ \wedge \ \cdots \ \wedge \ J_{n-1}}^{\text{Including}} \ \wedge$$

$$\overbrace{B \ \wedge \ P \ \wedge \ [X, x := N, n] (I \ \wedge \ J)}^{\text{Included}}$$

$$\Rightarrow$$

$$J_n$$

The rôle of the next proof obligation is to guarantee that the initialization of the refinement M_n refines the initialization of the abstraction M_{n-1} (section 11.2.6).

$$\overbrace{A_1 \ \wedge \ B_1 \ \wedge \ \cdots \ \wedge \ B_n \ \wedge \ C_1 \ \wedge \ P_1 \ \wedge \ \cdots \ \wedge \ P_n}^{\text{Including}} \ \wedge$$

$$\overbrace{B \ \wedge \ P}^{\text{Included}}$$

$$\Rightarrow$$

$$\overbrace{[[X, x := N, n]U \ ; \ U_n] \neg [U_{n-1}] \neg I_n}^{\text{Included}}$$

The last proof obligation states that the operation refines the corresponding operation of the previous level (section 11.2.6).

$$\overbrace{A_1 \ \wedge \ B_1 \ \wedge \ \cdots \ \wedge \ B_n \ \wedge \ C_1 \ \wedge \ P_1 \ \wedge \ \cdots \ \wedge \ P_n}^{\text{Including}} \ \wedge$$

$$\overbrace{I_1 \ \wedge \ \cdots \ \wedge \ I_n \ \wedge \ J_1 \ \wedge \ \cdots \ \wedge \ J_n \ \wedge \ Q_1 \cdots \ \wedge \ Q_{n-1}}^{\text{Including}} \ \wedge$$

$$\overbrace{B \ \wedge \ P \ \wedge \ [X, x := N, n] (I \ \wedge \ J)}^{\text{Included}}$$

$$\Rightarrow$$

$$Q_n \ \wedge \ [[u_1 := u_1'] V_n] \neg [V_{n-1}] \neg (I_n \ \wedge \ u_1 = u_1')$$

Notice that the intermediate pre-conditions $Q_2, \ldots, Q_{n-1}$ can be assumed, since they must have been proved as a consequence of the proofs of the intermediate refinements M_2 to M_{n-1}.

11.4. Exercises

1. Prove that the machine M_1 is correct and that the refinement M_2 refines M_1.

MACHINE

M_1

VARIABLES

x

INVARIANT

$x \in 0..20$

INITIALIZATION

$x := 10$

OPERATIONS

opr $\widehat{=}$
　　PRE
　　　　$x + 2 \leq 20$ $\wedge$
　　　　$x - 2 \geq 0$
　　THEN
　　　　CHOICE
　　　　　　$x := x + 2$
　　　　OR
　　　　　　$x := x - 2$
　　　　END
　　END

END

REFINEMENT

M_2

REFINES

M_1

VARIABLES

y

INVARIANT

　　$y \in 0..10$ $\wedge$
　　$x = 2 \times y$

INITIALIZATION

　　$y := 5$

OPERATIONS

　　opr_1 $\widehat{=}$
　　　　BEGIN
　　　　　　$y := y + 1$
　　　　END

END

2. Prove that the following machine is correct:

MACHINE

    M_1

VARIABLES

    table_1

INVARIANT

    $table\_1 \in (1 .. 10) \to (0 .. 20)$

INITIALIZATION

    $table\_1 :\in (1 .. 10) \to (0 .. 20)$

OPERATIONS

    opr $\widehat{=}$ BEGIN $table\_1 := (table\_1 ; \mathrm{div}(2))$ END

END

Consider the following refinement:

REFINEMENT

    M_2

REFINES

    M_1

VARIABLES

    table_2

INVARIANT

    $table\_2 = table\_1$

INITIALIZATION

$$table\_2 := (1 .. 10) \times \{20\}$$

OPERATIONS

opr $\hat{=}$
    VAR i IN
      $i := 1$;
      WHILE $i \le 10$ DO
        $table\_2(i) := table\_2(i)/2$;
        $i := i + 1$
      INVARIANT
        ?
      VARIANT
        ?
      END
    END

END

Propose an invariant and a variant for the loop (hint: the invariant may contain the abstract variable $table\_1$). Prove that this refinement indeed refines the previous machine.

3. We consider the set of sequences built on the cartesian product of the sets $\{0, 1\}$ and $\mathbb{N}$

$$\mathsf{seq}(\{0, 1\} \times \mathbb{N})$$

For instance, the following sequence, ss, belongs to that set:

$$ss = [(0,3), (0,2), (0,4), (1,3), (0,2), (1,2)]$$

(a) Define recursively the two functions h and k such that

$$\mathsf{h} \in \mathsf{seq}(\{0, 1\} \times \mathbb{N}) \to \mathsf{seq}(\mathbb{N})$$
$$\mathsf{k} \in \mathsf{seq}(\{0, 1\} \times \mathbb{N}) \to \mathsf{seq}(\mathbb{N})$$

and whose definitions are the following. The values of these two functions, applied to a sequence ss, are the two sequences constructed from the second elements of the pairs forming the sequence ss, whose order is kept, and whose first element is equal to 0 or 1 respectively. For instance, we have:

$$\mathsf{h}(ss) = [3, 2, 4, 2]$$
$$\mathsf{k}(ss) = [3, 2]$$

(b) Consider the following abstract machine where the two functions defined previously are used:

MACHINE

Q_1

VARIABLES

ss

INVARIANT

$ss \in \text{seq}(\{0, 1\} \times \mathbb{N})$ $\quad \wedge$
$k(ss) \subseteq h(ss)$

INITIALIZATION

$ss \in []$

OPERATIONS

write(x) $\;\;\widehat{=}$
    PRE
        $x \in \mathbb{N}$
    THEN
        $ss := ss \leftarrow (0, x)$
    END ;

$x \longleftarrow$ read $\;\;\widehat{=}$
    PRE
        $k(ss) \subset h(ss)$
    THEN
        LET $\;y\;$ BE
            $y = h(ss)(\text{size}(k(ss)) + 1)$
        IN
            $ss := ss \leftarrow (1, y)$ $\quad ||$
            $x := y$
        END
    END

END

What is the value of *ss* after the initialization followed by the calls:

$$
\begin{aligned}
&\text{write}(3);\\
&\text{write}(2);\\
&\text{write}(4);\\
&a \longleftarrow \text{read};\\
&\text{write}(2);\\
&a \longleftarrow \text{read}
\end{aligned}
$$

What interpretation can you give of the variable ss?, of the invariant $k(ss) \subseteq h(ss)$?, and of the pre-condition $k(ss) \subset h(ss)$? Prove that this machine is correct.

(c) Refine the previous machine. This will be done by introducing two variables hh and kk, related to ss as follows:

$$
\begin{aligned}
hh &= h(ss)\\
kk &= k(ss)
\end{aligned}
$$

What information is lost in this refinement? Prove that the refinement is correct.

(d) Refine the previous refinement. You are asked to provide a new change of variable whose effect is to lose more information.

4. We are given a set s and a total and transitive relation r from s to itself

$$
\begin{aligned}
&r \in s \leftrightarrow s\\
&\mathrm{dom}\,(r) = s\\
&r \circ r \subseteq r
\end{aligned}
$$

and the following machine where the above set and relation s and r are used:

```
MACHINE
    M_1
VARIABLES
    m
INVARIANT
    m ∈ s
INITIALIZATION
    m :∈ s
OPERATIONS
    op ≙ BEGIN  m :∈ r[{m}]  END
END
```

Prove that the following refinement indeed refines this machine:

REFINEMENT

M_2

REFINES

M_1

VARIABLES

m'

INVARIANT

$m' = m$

INITIALIZATION

$m' :\in s$

OPERATIONS

op $\;\widehat{=}$
    VAR x IN
        $m' :\in r[\{m'\}]\,;$
        $x :\in \mathbb{N}\,;$
        WHILE $x > 0 \land P$ DO
            $m' :\in r[\{m'\}]\,;$
            $x := x - 1$
        INVARIANT
            ?
        VARIANT
            ?
        END
    END

END

The predicate P in the loop is supposed to be a predicate of the variable m'. (Hint: The loop invariant may contain the abstract variable m).

Use what you have just proved to justify that the specification of the writing on a disk that may either write effectively on the disk (success), or not write at all on the disk (failure), might be refined by the same operation repeated a certain number of times (unless it succeeds).

5. Consider a generalized substitution S of the form:

$$S = (P \Longrightarrow S_1) \; [] \; (\neg P \Longrightarrow S_2)$$

Suppose that this substitution is refined by a certain substitution T under the change of variable J.
a) Show that the refining predicate

$$[T] \neg [S] \neg J$$

is equivalent to the following predicate (bear in mind that the variables of T are necessarily distinct from those of S):

$$(P \Rightarrow [T] \neg [S_1] \neg J) \quad \wedge \quad (\neg P \Rightarrow [T] \neg [S_2] \neg J)$$

In other words, it is effectively trying to "couple" the concrete computation T with every disjoint abstract computation (notice that S_1 and S_2 might be non-deterministic).
b) More generally, if S is of the form:

$$S = (P_1 \Longrightarrow S_1) \; [] \; \cdots \; [] \; (P_n \Longrightarrow S_n)$$

with

$$P_1 \vee \cdots \vee P_n$$

and

$$\neg (P_i \wedge P_j) \quad \text{for all} \quad i \neq j$$

show that the refining predicate $[T] \neg [S] \neg J$ is equivalent to:

$$(P_1 \Rightarrow [T] \neg [S_1] \neg J) \quad \wedge \quad \cdots \quad \wedge \quad (P_n \Rightarrow [T] \neg [S_n] \neg J)$$

(c) We now apply the above results to the refinement of a non-deterministic finite automaton defined by the following abstract machine:

MACHINE

   Automaton_1

VARIABLES

   s

INVARIANT

   $s \in \{0, 1, 2\}$

INITIALIZATION

   $s := 0$

OPERATIONS

   $y \longleftarrow$ action $(x) \quad \widehat{=}$
     PRE
       $x \in \{0, 1\}$
     THEN
       SELECT $\quad s = 0 \ \wedge \ x = 0 \quad$ THEN
         $y :\in \{0, 1\}$
       WHEN $\quad s = 0 \ \wedge \ x = 1 \quad$ THEN
         $y, s := 0, 1$
       WHEN $\quad s = 1 \ \wedge \ x = 0 \quad$ THEN
         $y, s := 0, 2$
       WHEN $\quad s = 1 \ \wedge \ x = 1 \quad$ THEN
         $y, s := 0, 0$
       WHEN $\quad s = 2 \ \wedge \ x = 0 \quad$ THEN
         $y, s := 1, 1$
       WHEN $\quad s = 2 \ \wedge \ x = 1 \quad$ THEN
         $y, s := 0, 0$
       END
     END

END

We propose the following incomplete refinement defining a deterministic automaton:

REFINEMENT

    Automaton_2

REFINES

    Automaton_1

VARIABLES

    s'

INVARIANT

    $s' \in \{1, 2\} \;\land\; ?$

INITIALIZATION

    $s' := 1$

OPERATIONS

    $y \longleftarrow \text{action}\,(x) \;\;\widehat{=}$
        SELECT $s' = 1 \;\land\; x = 0$ THEN
          $y, s' := 0, 2$
        WHEN $s' = 1 \;\land\; x = 1$ THEN
          $y := 0$
        WHEN $s' = 2 \;\land\; x = 0$ THEN
          $y, s' := 1, 1$
        WHEN $s' = 2 \;\land\; x = 1$ THEN
          $y, s' := 0, 1$
        END

END

Complete the change of variable and prove that this refinement refines its abstraction.

6. Given the following machine M and the following refinement R

```
MACHINE
   M
VARIABLES
   x
INVARIANT
   x ∈ ℕ
INITIALIZATION
   x := 0
OPERATIONS
   op  ≙  BEGIN   x := 4   END
END
```

```
REFINEMENT
   R
REFINES
   M
VARIABLES
   y
INVARIANT
   y ∈ ℕ
INITIALIZATION
   y := 10
OPERATIONS
   op  ≙  BEGIN   y := 7   END
END
```

Prove that R indeed refines M. Justify this rather strange result.

REFERENCES

[1] E.W. Dijkstra. *A Discipline of Programming* (Prentice Hall, 1976)

[2] R. Milner. *An Algebraic Definition of Simulation Between Programs* (Stanford University, 1971)

[3] C.A.R. Hoare. *Proof of Correctness of Data Representation* (Acta 1, 1972)

[4] R.-J.R. Back. *On the Correctness of Refinement Steps in Program Development* (University of Helsinki, 1978)

[5] J. He, C.A.R. Hoare and J.W. Sanders. *Data Refinement Refined* (Oxford University, 1985)

[6] C.B. Jones. *Systematic Software Development Using VDM* (Prentice Hall, 1986)

[7] J.M. Morris. *A Theoretical Basis for Stepwise Refinement* (Science of Computer Programming, 9(3) 1987)

[8] C.C. Morgan, K.A. Robinson, and P.H.B. Gardiner. *On the Refinement Calculus* (Oxford University, 1988)

[9] C.C. Morgan. *Programming from Specification* (Prentice Hall, 1990)

CHAPTER 12

Constructing Large Software Systems

IN this chapter we explain how to construct large software systems as layers of *modules*. The idea is that the mathematical *model* of an abstract machine is refined several times until the final refinement is directly executable on a computer. Such a final refinement may *import* other machines (other models) on which it is eventually implemented. For that reason, it is called an *implementation*. All this is explained in section 12.1. In section 12.2, we show how a given module can be shared by others, provided they only use the former in a passive fashion. In section 12.3, we introduce the notion of multiple refinement. In section 12.4, we touch briefly on loop invariants in order to make precise what kind of variables they may contain. In section 12.5, we show how abstract operations can be implemented by *recursive* operations. Finally, section 12.6 contains the formal definition of the previous material.

This chapter only contains small examples. In the next chapter we shall illustrate the material presented in this chapter with some more elaborate examples.

12.1. Implementing a Refinement

12.1.1. Introduction

In this section we present informally the technique by which we can use the specification of an abstract machine to *implement* the final refinement of another (or the same) one. In order to introduce this notion gradually, let us reconsider the example of the previous chapter. We had the following specification:

MACHINE

 Little_Example_1

VARIABLES

 y

INVARIANT

 $y \in \mathbb{F}(\text{NAT}_1)$

INITIALIZATION

 $y := \varnothing$

OPERATIONS

 $\text{enter}(n) \;\; \widehat{=}$
  PRE $n \in \text{NAT}_1$ THEN $y := y \cup \{n\}$ END;

 $m \longleftarrow \text{maximum} \;\; \widehat{=}$
  PRE $y \neq \varnothing$ THEN $m := \max(y)$ END

END

Then, we had the following refinement:

REFINEMENT

 Little_Example_2

REFINES

 Little_Example_1

VARIABLES

 z

INVARIANT

$$z = \max(y \cup \{0\})$$

INITIALIZATION

$$z := 0$$

OPERATIONS

enter(n) $\widehat{=}$
    PRE $n \in \mathsf{NAT}_1$ THEN $z := \max(\{z, n\})$ END;

$m \longleftarrow$ maximum $\widehat{=}$
    PRE $z \neq 0$ THEN $m := z$ END

END

We now propose the following refinement, which refines the previous one:

REFINEMENT

    Little_Example_3

REFINES

    Little_Example_2

VARIABLES

    z'

INVARIANT

    $z' = z$

INITIALIZATION

    $z' := 0$

```
OPERATIONS

    enter(n) ≙
        IF   n ≥ z'   THEN   z' := n   END;

    m ⟵ maximum ≙
        BEGIN   m := z'   END

END
```

As can be seen, the operation enter now provides an "implementation" of the max operator that was present in the previous refinement. Also, in the operation maximum, the pre-condition has disappeared.

Our purpose is to show how such a refinement could be defined as a mere "user" of another simpler abstract machine, which we present now, and which could be, supposedly, available "off the shelf":

```
MACHINE

    Scalar(initval)

CONSTRAINTS

    initval ∈ NAT

VARIABLES

    z'

INVARIANT

    z' ∈ NAT

INITIALIZATION

    z' := initval
```

```
OPERATIONS

    modify(v)  ≙
        PRE   v ∈ NAT   THEN   z' := v   END ;

    v ⟵ value  ≙
        BEGIN   v := z'   END

END
```

This machine is parameterized with the initializing value. We now propose to rewrite our previous refinement as follows:

```
IMPLEMENTATION

    Little_Example_3

REFINES

    Little_Example_2

IMPORTS

    Scalar(0)

INVARIANT

    z' = z

OPERATIONS

    enter(n)  ≙
        VAR   v   IN
            v ⟵ value ;
            IF   n ≥ v   THEN   modify(n)   END
        END ;

    m ⟵ maximum  ≙
        BEGIN   m ⟵ value   END

END
```

The last refinement is now called an IMPLEMENTATION. This is to indicate that it is the *ultimate* refinement of our original abstract machine. We have a new clause, IMPORTS, invoking the previously defined *Scalar* machine together with the actual parameter 0. The rôle of the IMPORTS clause is to put the imported machine(s) within the *scope* of our implementation. It will also be seen that the VARIABLES clause has disappeared. The variable z' is now *entirely hidden* in the abstract machine *Scalar*. Moreover, that variable must not appear explicitly in the operations. In fact, the operations essentially consist of "calls" to the operations offered by the *imported machine*. Clearly, the operations of this refinement obey the *Hiding Principle*. The only place where the variable z' may appear is the invariant linking the "abstract" variable z and the "concrete" variable z'.

12.1.2. The Practice of Importation

From a practical point of view, the refinement proofs should be done after the following steps have been performed:

1. instantiating the imported machine with the *actual parameter* as provided in the IMPORTS clause,

2. incorporating the *variables* of the instantiated imported machine, so that they become the genuine variables of our implementation,

3. conjoining the *invariant* of the instantiated imported machine with that of the implementation,

4. composing (with the sequencing operator) the *initialization* of the instantiated imported machine with the initialization (if any) of the implementation,

5. performing the text expansion of the *operation-calls* of the operations of the instantiated imported machine within the operations of the implementation. Of course, such text expansions are done after the proper substitution of the actual parameters to the formal parameters is performed within the bodies of the called operations. This is done in exactly the same way as explained in section 7.2.2.

As soon as these steps are accomplished (probably with the help of some automatic tool), then we are in a *normal* refinement situation, so that we can proceed by using the general proof obligations of section 11.3.3. For instance, after *expanding* the various *calls* to the operations of the *Scalar* machine found in our last refinement of the operation enter(n), we obtain the following:

$$\text{enter}(n) \;\widehat{=}$$

```
VAR   v   IN
    BEGIN   v := z'   END;
    IF   n ≥ v   THEN
        PRE   n ∈ NAT   THEN   z' := n   END
    END
END
```

The proof obligation of section 11.3.3 applied to this operation yields the following:

$$y \in \mathbb{F}(\mathsf{NAT}_1)$$
$$z = \mathsf{max}(y \cup \{0\})$$
$$z' = z$$
$$z' \in \mathsf{NAT}$$
$$n \in \mathsf{NAT}$$
$$\Rightarrow$$
$$[\mathsf{enter}(n)] \neg [z := \mathsf{max}(\{z,n\})] \neg (z' = z)$$

Notice how we *accumulate* the invariant and the changes of variables: this is because we refine a refinement, which in turn refines our original specification. Performing the innermost substitution yields the following:

$$y \in \mathbb{F}(\mathsf{NAT}_1)$$
$$z = \mathsf{max}(y \cup \{0\})$$
$$z' = z$$
$$z' \in \mathsf{NAT}$$
$$n \in \mathsf{NAT}$$
$$\Rightarrow$$
$$[\mathsf{enter}(n)] (z' = \mathsf{max}(\{z,n\}))$$

We now expand the body of the operation enter, yielding the following:

$$y \in \mathbb{F}(\mathsf{NAT}_1)$$
$$z = \mathsf{max}(y \cup \{0\})$$
$$z' = z$$
$$z' \in \mathsf{NAT}$$
$$n \in \mathsf{NAT}$$
$$\Rightarrow$$

```
[VAR   v   IN
      BEGIN    v := z'   END;
      IF   n ≥ v   THEN
            PRE   n ∈ NAT   THEN   z' := n   END
      END
END] (z' = max({z,n}))
```

That is

$$y \in \mathbb{F}(\text{NAT}_1)$$
$$z = \max(y \cup \{0\})$$
$$z' = z$$
$$z' \in \text{NAT}$$
$$n \in \text{NAT}$$
$$\Rightarrow$$
$$\forall v \cdot ($$

[BEGIN $v := z'$ END;

IF $n \geq v$ THEN

PRE $n \in \text{NAT}$ THEN $z' := n$ END

END] $(z' = \max(\{z, n\})))$

Since v is non-free in the antecedents, we obtain

$$y \in \mathbb{F}(\text{NAT}_1)$$
$$z = \max(y \cup \{0\})$$
$$z' = z$$
$$z' \in \text{NAT}$$
$$n \in \text{NAT}$$
$$\Rightarrow$$

[BEGIN $v := z'$ END;

IF $n \geq v$ THEN

PRE $n \in \text{NAT}$ THEN $z' := n$ END

END] $(z' = \max(\{z, n\}))$

That is (by expanding the conditional substitution)

$$y \in \mathbb{F}(\text{NAT}_1)$$
$$z = \max(y \cup \{0\})$$
$$z' = z$$
$$z' \in \text{NAT}$$
$$n \in \text{NAT}$$
$$\Rightarrow$$

[BEGIN $v := z'$ END;

IF $n \geq v$ THEN

PRE $n \in \text{NAT}$ THEN $z' := n$ END

ELSE

skip

END] $(z' = \max(\{z, n\}))$

Performing the conditional substitution yields

$$y \in \mathbb{F}(\text{NAT}_1)$$
$$z = \max(y \cup \{0\})$$
$$z' = z$$
$$z' \in \text{NAT}$$
$$n \in \text{NAT}$$
$$\Rightarrow$$
$$[v := z']$$
$$(n \geq v \;\; \Rightarrow \;\; (n \in \text{NAT} \;\wedge\; n = \max(\{z, n\}))) \quad\wedge$$
$$\neg\,(n \geq v) \;\; \Rightarrow \;\; z' = \max(\{z, n\}))$$

After performing the remaining substitution and doing some simplifications, we obtain the following (notice that we prove that the operation modify was indeed called *within its pre-condition* $n \in$ NAT):

$$y \in \mathbb{F}(\text{NAT}_1)$$
$$z = \max(y \cup \{0\})$$
$$z' = z$$
$$z' \in \text{NAT}$$
$$n \in \text{NAT}$$
$$\Rightarrow$$
$$n \geq z' \;\; \Rightarrow \;\; n = \max(\{z, n\})$$
$$n < z' \;\; \Rightarrow \;\; z' = \max(\{z, n\})$$

This yields the following to be proved which is obvious:

$$y \in \mathbb{F}(\text{NAT}_1)$$
$$z = \max(y \cup \{0\})$$
$$n \in \text{NAT}$$
$$\Rightarrow$$
$$n \geq z \;\; \Rightarrow \;\; n = \max(\{z, n\})$$
$$n < z \;\; \Rightarrow \;\; z = \max(\{z, n\})$$

An important consequence of what we have done in this section is that we do not need to *further* refine our *Little_Example_3* implementation. This is because any refinement of the *Scalar* machine will *automatically* refine *Little_Example_3*. This is due to the fact that refinement is *monotonic* on all our generalized substitution constructs, as proved in section 11.2.4.

In this section we have presented the concept of *implementing* the refinement of an abstract machine on the specification of another one. It is definitely a fundamental concept, since it allows us to design our system as *layers* of modules with well-defined relationships. It also shows the possibility of *re-using* already specified abstract machines.

12.1.3. The IMPLEMENTATION Construct

An IMPLEMENTATION refines either a MACHINE or a REFINEMENT. But an IMPLEMENTATION cannot be further refined. This has the following important consequences:

An IMPLEMENTATION has no abstract VARIABLES of its own. An IMPLEMENTATION gets its abstract VARIABLES, indirectly, through one or more abstract machines that it IMPORTS (section 12.1.4). Such variables are accessed and modified through the operations of the imported machines. These variables can of course be related to more abstract variables of the machine or refinement that the implementation is supposed to refine: this is done, as usual, in the INVARIANT clause of the implementation.

An IMPLEMENTATION may have some CONCRETE_VARIABLES (section 4.21). All the concrete variables that have been defined in the previous abstractions (machine or refinements) of an implementation must be present either in the implementation itself or as CONCRETE_VARIABLES of the machines that the implementation IMPORTS (section 12.1.3). In the former case, such concrete variables can be accessed or modified directly in the implementation. In the latter case, such variables can be accessed directly in the implementation, but they cannot be modified directly this must be performed by means of operations of the imported machines. If a CONCRETE_VARIABLE is introduced into the implementation, it is of course typed and possibly further constrainted and related to other more abstract variables in the INVARIANT clause.

An IMPLEMENTATION has no ABSTRACT_CONSTANTS (section 4.21) of its own. An IMPLEMENTATION gets its abstract constants, indirectly, through one or more abstract machines that it IMPORTS (section 12.1.4). Such abstract constants are accessed through operations of the imported machines. Such imported abstract constants can of course be related to more abstract constants in the PROPERTIES clause, as can be done in a refinement.

An IMPLEMENTATION may have some concrete CONSTANTS. All the concrete constants that have been defined in the previous abstractions (machine or refinements) of an implementation must be present either in the implementation itself or as concrete CONSTANTS of the machines that that implementation IMPORTS. In the former case, the values of such concrete constants are defined in a special clause of the implementation, called the VALUES clause (section 12.1.7). In all cases, such concrete constants can be accessed directly in the implementation. If a concrete CONSTANT is introduced into the implementation, it is of course typed and possibly further constrainted and related to other more abstract constants in the PROPERTIES clause.

All the deferred SETS that have been declared in the various abstractions (machine or refinement) of an IMPLEMENTATION must be given a concrete value in that implementation. This is done in the VALUES clause (section 12.1.7) that we have already mentioned.

The operations of an IMPLEMENTATION must be "implementable". Such limitations will be made more precise in section 12.1.10.

The enumerated or deferred SETS, the concrete CONSTANTS and the CONCRETE_-VARIABLES of a machine imported in an IMPLEMENTATION are fully visible from within that implementation (the visibility rules will be made more precise in section 12.1.5).

Note that an enumerated set declared in an imported machine of an implementation can also be an enumerated set declared within that implementation itself or within one of its abstractions, or else within a machine seen from that implementation. This is possible, of course, provided the set in question *has exactly the same members disposed in the same order in its various declarations.*

12.1.4. The IMPORTS Clause

The IMPORTS clause of an implementation contains the list of the (possibly renamed) imported machines. When such an imported machine is parameterized, some actual parameters are provided that must indeed obey the CONSTRAINTS of the imported machine.

We remind the reader that the formal parameters of an abstract machine (section 4.8) may be of two possible kinds: they can be either set parameters or scalar parameters. When a parameterized abstract machine M is imported into an implementation M_n refining ultimately an abstract machine M_1, we have to provide instantiations for the formal parameters of M. Such instantiations are restricted to the following.

- For a scalar formal parameter of the imported machine M, the corresponding actual parameter can be:

  - a scalar formal parameter of M_1,

  - a member of an enumerated set declared in one of $M_1, \ldots, M_n$,

  - a concrete constant or an enumerated set member of a "seen" machine (section 12.2)

  - an arithmetic expression formed by means of numeric formal parameters of M_1, of numeric concrete constants declared in one of $M_1, \ldots, M_n$, and of literal numeric values. The allowed arithmetic operators are $+$, $-$, $*$, $/$, exponentiation, mod, succ and pred.

- For a set formal parameter of the imported machine M, the corresponding actual parameter can be:

  - a set formal parameter of M_1,

  - a deferred or enumerated set declared in one of $M_1, \ldots, M_n$, or in a "seen" machine (section 12.2),

  - a non-empty interval whose bounds are numeric scalars similar to those allowed for defining a numeric scalar actual parameter.

12.1.5. Visibility Rules

The *visibility* of the various objects of the imported machines from within the various clauses of an implementation is best described by the following table. Each line corresponds to a specific category of objects of the imported machines and each column corresponds to a specific clause of the implementation. A tick indicates that a certain category of objects of the imported machines is referenceable from within a certain clause of the implementation.

	VALUES (impl.)	PROPERTIES (impl.)	INVARIANT (impl.)	OPERATIONS (impl.)
parameters (of imported)				
sets (of imported)	√	√	√	√
constants (of imported)	√	√	√	√
abstract_constants (of imported)		√	√	in loop invariant only
concrete_variables (of imported)			√	√
variables (of imported)			√	in loop invariant only
operations (of imported)				√

As can be seen, the formal parameters of an imported machine are not visible in an implementation. This is normal since they have just been instantiated. In the VALUES clause (section 12.1.7) of an implementation the sets and concrete constants of the imported machine are fully visible. In the PROPERTIES clause of an implementation, the sets and (abstract or concrete) constants of the imported machine are visible. In the INVARIANT clause of an implementation, the sets, the (abstract or concrete) constants and the (abstract or concrete) variables of the imported machine are visible: in this way, one can express the linkage between the variables of the imported machine and the variables of the construct (machine or refinement) refined by the implementation. Note, finally, that the variables and abstract constants of the imported machine are not visible from within the OPERATIONS of an implementation (Hiding Principle) except in a loop invariant (section 12.3).

The VALUES clause of an implementation cannot contain any reference to the formal parameters of the top machine of which that implementation is the final refinement.

12.1.6. Machine Renaming

As for the INCLUDES clause (section 7.2.6), machines referenced in a IMPORTS clause can be renamed (remember that in a renamed machine, the sets and constants are not renamed). Notice that the renaming of a machine also renames the machines that are imported within the ultimate implementation of that machine: renaming is thus *transitive* across the entire development of a machine.

12.1.7. The VALUES Clause

The VALUES clause contains the final concrete values of some of the concrete constants and deferred sets that have been declared in the various abstractions (machine or refinements) of our implementation. Each of the remaining non-locally valued concrete constants or deferred sets must be declared in one of the machines imported or "seen" (section 12.2) from the implementation.

Next are the rules that concern the locally valued concrete constants or deferred sets. We suppose that we are given an implementation M_n, which finally refines a certain machine M_1, together with the intermediate refinements $M_2, \ldots, M_{n-1}$. Moreover, M_n is supposed to import a certain machine M.

Values of the Visible Constants

A concrete constant that has been declared in one of $M_1, \ldots, M_n$ may eventually receive a value in the VALUES clause of the implementation M_n. Such a value takes the form of an equality whose left-hand part is the constant in question, and whose right-hand part may be:

- a concrete constant of the machine M imported by M_n or of any machine "seen" (section 12.2) by M_n,

- an enumerated set member of an enumerated set declared in one of $M_1, \ldots, M_n$, or in a machine "seen" (section 12.2) by M_n,

- an arithmetic expression formed by means of numeric concrete constants of the imported machine M or of any machine "seen" (section 12.2) by M_n, and of literal numeric values (the allowed arithmetic operators are $+$, $-$, $*$, $/$, exponentiation, mod, succ and pred),

- a total function defined in extension with values that are scalars defined in one of the three previous ways,

- a total function defined as the identity function on some interval with constant scalar bounds defined as above.

- a set that is visible from the imported machine M or from a machine that is "seen" (section 12.2) from M_n,

- an interval defined by means of two arithmetic expressions as defined above.

A concrete constant declared in one of $M_1, \ldots, M_n$ cannot be valued by means of any scalar formal parameter of M_1 or by means of any other concrete constant declared in one of $M_1, \ldots, M_n$. Except in the case of enumerated set members, a concrete constant is thus always valued by means of literal constants or by means of concrete constants coming "from the bottom" (from the imported machine M) or from a "seen" machine (section 12.2). This is to avoid circular definitions. For example, the situation where a concrete constant s, is declared in one of $M_1, \ldots, M_n$, and valued by means of a concrete constant u of M, itself valued implicitly by s, is simply not possible. This would only have been possible provided s had been passed as an actual parameter replacing the formal parameter t of the imported machine M (this is possible as is explained in section 12.1.4), and provided the concrete constant u of M had been explicitly valued in the implementation of M by means of the scalar formal parameter t of M, which is impossible: the circular chain is thus broken.

In the case where a concrete constant s, declared in one of $M_1, \ldots, M_n$, is also declared as a concrete constant in the imported machine M or in any machine "seen" (section 12.2) from M_n, the value of s is *not* given in the VALUES clause of the implementation M_n. It is supposed to be given eventually in the implementation of the machine M or in that of the "seen" machine (either in the VALUES clause of that implementation or in a deeper implementation).

Values of the Deferred Sets

A deferred set that has been declared in one of $M_1, \ldots, M_n$ may eventually receive a value in the VALUES clause of the implememtation M_n. Such a value takes the form of an equality whose left-hand part is the deferred set in question, and whose right-hand part may be:

- a deferred set of the machine M imported by M_n or of any machine "seen" (section 12.2) by M_n,

- a non-empty interval whose limits are numeric scalars similar to those allowed for defining the value of a numeric concrete constant.

As for the concrete constants, a deferred set declared in one of $M_1, \ldots, M_n$ cannot be valued by means of any set or scalar formal parameter of M_1 nor by means of any other deferred set declared in one of $M_1, \ldots, M_n$. A deferred set is thus always valued by means of literal constants or by means of concrete objects coming "from the bottom" (from the imported machine M) or from a "seen" machine (section 12.2). This is to avoid circular definitions. For example, the situation where a deferred set S is declared in one of $M_1, \ldots, M_n$, and valued by means of a deferred set U of M, itself valued implicitly by S, is simply not possible. This would only have been possible provided S had been passed as an actual parameter replacing the formal parameter T of the imported machine M (this is possible as is explained in section 12.1.4), and provided the deferred set U of M had been explicitly valued in the implementation of M by means of the formal parameter T of M, which is impossible: again, the circular chain is thus broken.

In the case where a deferred set S, declared in one of $M_1, \ldots, M_n$, is also declared as a deferred set in the imported machine M or in any machine "seen" (section 12.2) from M_n, then the value of S is *not* given in the VALUES clause of the implementation M_n. It is supposed to be given eventually in the implementation of the machine M or in that of the "seen" machine (either in the VALUES clause of that implementation or in a deeper implementation).

12.1.8. Comparing the IMPORTS and the INCLUDES Clauses

It is important to clarify the distinction between the INCLUDES clause used in an abstract machine specification (section 7.2.3) and the IMPORTS clause used in an abstract machine implementation (section 12.1.4). Including one machine in another, is a mechanism used to construct a large *specification* text. Importing one machine in the implementation of another, is a mechanism by which we construct our *final software system*. Clearly, the same machine could be first included and later imported, but this is not a necessity. The composition of a specification from smaller machines and the decomposition of an implementation into various machines do not necessarily obey the same laws.

The difference between the two clauses concerning the visibility rules is worth mentioning too (section 4.2.5 and section 12.1.5). The variables of an included machine are partly visible (read-only) to the OPERATIONS clause of the including machine (semi-hiding), whereas the abstract variables of an imported machine are invisible (full hiding) to the OPERATIONS of an importing implementation. This is the only difference between the two visibility rules.

12.1.9. The PROMOTES and EXTENDS Clauses

A PROMOTES clause in an implementation contains a list of certain operation names of some of the imported machines of the implementation. Such a promoted operation is called automatically by the operation bearing the same name of the implementation. As such, it need not be mentioned in the OPERATIONS clause of the implementation. The EXTENDS clause is like an IMPORTS clause followed by a PROMOTES of all its operations.

Notice that, although both have the same name, there are no possibilities of confusion between the PROMOTES and EXTENDS clauses of a machine (section 7.2.7) and the PROMOTES and EXTENDS clauses of an implementation. This is so because a machine cannot import another machine, and an implementation cannot include another machine.

12.1.10. Concrete Constants and Concrete Variables Revisited

In an implementation, the only remaining constants and variables are the concrete ones. Such objects can be used in any operation of the implementation. As the operations of an implementation are subjected to a direct translation into a classical programming language, it is clearly very important that such constants or variables are implementable. This is the reason why every such objects must be of one the following types only (sections 4.17 and 4.21): a single scalar set, T; a total function from a scalar set to a scalar set, $A \rightarrow T$; a total function from the cartesian product of scalar sets to a scalar set, $A \times \ldots \times B \rightarrow T$; a subset of a scalar set (notice that such subsets are constants only (not variables) and are not implemented). In the translation into a simple programming language, such constants or variables will be translated, as we expect, into simple scalars or arrays.

12.1.11. Allowed Constructs in an Implementation

Since an implementation constitutes the ultimate refinement of an original abstract machine, the remaining (necessarily concrete) variables and constants, and also the operations of an implementation, must be translatable into a programming language and be executable by a computer. The rôle of this section is to show how such computability is ensured.

Syntactic Category	Definition
Statement	skip *Assignment_Statement* *Call_Statement* *Sequencing_Statement* *Local_Statement* *While_Statement* *If_Statement* *Case_Statement*

Each operation of an implementation contains a limited number of possible *Substitutions*. In what follows, we make precise what these *Substitutions* are. We shall also make precise which computable *Expressions* and *Predicates* are allowed and how. For defining these limited *Substitutions*, *Expressions* and *Predicates*, we introduce three special syntactic categories called *Statements*, *Terms*, and *Conditions*. Of course, *Statements* are genuine *Substitutions*, *Terms* are genuine *Expressions* and *Conditions* are genuine *Predicates*. We have only used these new syntactic categories in order to emphasize the fact that we now have "executable" *Substitutions* and "evaluable" *Expressions* and *Predicates*. The above syntax defined these allowed *Statements*.

Note that what is presented in this section corresponds to a minimal kernel that is easily translatable into any imperative programming language. It is by no means the only possibility. In particular, we have not allowed the multiple operator "||" to be kept. Clearly, this would have been possible since, as we know, that operator is monotonic with respect to refinement (section 11.2.4).

As we have said, *Statements* have a dual interpretation. They can be interpreted as genuine *Substitutions*, that is as predicate transformers. Alternatively, they can be given the operational interpretation of classical programming language constructs. The rôle of any translator from the "*Statement* language" to a classical imperative programming language is thus to find, in that programming language, a construct corresponding to each *Statement*. Each of the *Statements* is now redefined syntactically. We first define the *Assignment_Statement* and the *Call_Statement* as being *Protected* or *Unprotected*. The reason for this protection, as we shall see, is that the classical arithmetic operators *have now become partial*.

Syntactic Category	Definition
Assignment_Statement	*Protected_Assignment* *Unprotected_Assignment*
Call_Statement	*Protected_Call* *Unprotected_Call*

The *Unprotected_Assignment* is defined as follows:

Syntactic Category	Definition
Unprotected_Assignment	*Identifier_List* := *Term_List* *Identifier*(*Term_List*) := *Term* *Identifier* := bool(*Condition*) *Identifier*(*Term_List*) := bool(*Condition*)

The first alternative corresponds to the multiple simple substitution, which we have kept at this level although such a concept is rarely present (if not totally missing) in classical imperative programming languages. The identifiers of the *Identifier_List* are supposed to be distinct identifiers corresponding either to scalar concrete variables, to local variables (as introduced by the construct VAR), or to output parameters. The second alternative corresponds to the case of a function concrete variable. In the third and fourth alternatives, we have kept the bool operator (first introduced in section 4.18) that transforms a predicate into a boolean expression. Normally the operator bool is associated with a *Predicate*. Here we have a *Condition*: this is because the syntactic category *Predicate* also has got a computable version named *Condition* that we shall make precise below. The *Unprotected_Call* is now defined as follows:

Syntactic Category	Definition
Unprotected_Call	*Identifier_List* ⟵ *Identifier* (*Term_List*) *Identifier_List* ⟵ *Identifier* *Identifier* (*Term_List*) *Identifier*

The last two previous syntactic definitions immediately raise the question of the exact definition of *Terms*. Like *Statements* (denoting the operational counterpart of *Substitutions*), *Terms* are the operational counterpart of *Expressions*. This means that *Terms* also have a dual interpretation: either they are set-theoretic expressions or they are programming expressions that can be translated as such into a programming language and then "evaluated" by a computer. As a consequence, the problem of the correct evaluation of such expressions raises a very serious question that cannot be avoided. Next is the syntactic definitions of *Terms*:

Syntactic Category	Definition
Term	*Simple_Term* *Function_Constant_Identifier* (*Term_List*) *Function_Variable_Identifier* (*Term_List*) *Term* + *Term* *Term* − *Term* *Term* × *Term* *Term* / *Term*

Since *Terms* are subjected to a possible translation into a programming language, and even to a possible evaluation by a computer, the presence of arithmetic subexpressions in a *Term* must be treated with care. The exact meaning of each of the various arithmetic operators is questionable. What is already certain is that this meaning is different from those of its mathematical counterpart (although denoted by means of the same symbol). Before addressing that problem, however, let us first define *Simple_Terms* in an obvious way as follows:

Syntactic Category	Definition
Simple_Term	*Scalar_Variable_Identifier* *Operation_Input_Formal_Parameter* *Operation_Output_Formal_Parameter* *Simple_Constant*

And we now define *Simple_Constants* as follows:

Syntactic Category	Definition
Simple_Constant	*Enumerated_Set_Element_Identifier* *Scalar_Constant_Identifier* *Numeric_Literal*

In order to take account of the inherent partialness of the arithmetic operators that one may encounter in an arithmetic *Term*, we require that each *Assignement_Statement* or *Call_Statement* containing numeric sub-expressions is necessarily *Protected*. This means that a (local) pre-condition must be prefixed to the corresponding *Unprotected* assignment or call. We thus have the following:

Syntactic Category	Definition
Protected_Assignment	PRE *Predicate* THEN *Unprotected_Assignment* END
Protected_Call	PRE *Predicate* THEN *Unprotected_Call* END

The rôle of the pre-condition is to ensure that a proof can be performed guaranteeing that the arithmetic terms are well-defined. The pre-condition can be constructed in a systematic fashion by first collecting all the individual arithmetic sub-expressions E that can be found in the *Unprotected_Assignment* or in the *Unprotected_Call*, and then by forming predicates of the form "$E \in$ INT". We remind the reader that the set INT is equal to the interval minint .. maxint. It is supposed to correspond to the interval where the arithmetic operators of our *Terms* are to be meaningful. Finally, all such predicates are conjoined to form the pre-condition. For example, consider the following *Unprotected_Assignment*:

$$a := b + c \times d$$

The various arithmetic sub-expressions of the right-hand side of this unprotected assignment statement are $b, c, d, c \times d$ and $b + c \times d$. The corresponding protected assignment is thus the following:

PRE
$$b \in \text{INT} \quad \wedge$$
$$c \in \text{INT} \quad \wedge$$
$$d \in \text{INT} \quad \wedge$$
$$c \times d \in \text{INT} \quad \wedge$$
$$b + c \times d \in \text{INT}$$
THEN
$$a := b + c \times d$$
END

Note that the transformation of an unprotected assignment or an unprotected call into a protected one can be done *automatically* by a very simple program. We shall suppose that we have such a program at our disposal so that, in what follows, we shall always write unprotected assignements or unprotected calls.

The remaining constructs of our simple "implementation" language have obvious corresponding counterparts in any imperative programming language. This will allow us to have an easy translation of the operations of an implementation into procedures (or macro-instructions) of any classical programming language.

Syntactic Category	Definition
Sequencing_Statement	*Statement* ; *Statement*
Local_Statement	VAR *Identifier_List* IN *Statement* END
While_Statement	WHILE *Condition* DO *Statement* END

Syntactic Category	Definition
If_Statement	*Normal_If* *Small_If* *Normal_Elsif* *Small_Elsif*
Case_Statement	*Normal_Case* *Small_Case*

Next is the *Normal_If*:

Syntactic Category	Definition

Normal_If	IF *Condition* THEN
	    Statement
	ELSE
	    Statement
	END

Then the *Small_If*

Syntactic Category	Definition
Small_If	IF *Condition* THEN *Statement* END

Next is the *Normal_Elsif*

Syntactic Category	Definition

Normal_Elsif	IF *Condition* THEN
	   Statement
	ELSIF
	   Statement
	ELSIF
	   . . .
	ELSE
	   Statement
	END

Then the *Small_Elsif*

Syntactic Category	Definition

Small_Elsif	IF *Condition* THEN
	   Statement
	ELSIF
	   Statement
	ELSIF
	   . . .
	END

Next is the *Normal_Case*:

Syntactic Category	Definition

Normal_Case	CASE *Simple_Term* OF
	   EITHER *Constant_List* THEN
	      Statement
	   OR *Constant_List* THEN
	      Statement
	   OR *Constant_List* THEN
	      . . .
	
	   ELSE
	      Statement
	   END
	END

And then the *Small_Case*:

Syntactic Category	Definition

Small_Case	CASE *Simple_Term* OF
	   EITHER *Constant_List* THEN
	      Statement
	   OR *Constant_List* THEN
	      Statement
	   OR *Constant_List* THEN
	      . . .
	   END
	END

It remains for us to define *Conditions*. It will be seen that *Conditions* do not contain *Terms*, only *Simple_Terms*; hence, *Conditions* are not to be *Protected*. In fact, it would have been difficult to do so, in particular for the *Conditions* involved in the *While_Statements*. Notice, of course, that arithmetic comparisons between *Simple_Terms* are only possible for numeric *Simple_Terms* (as usual, the syntax is slightly lax, but this is checked by type-checking).

Syntactic Category	Definition
Condition	$Simple\_Term = Simple\_Term$ $Simple\_Term \neq Simple\_Term$ $Simple\_Term < Simple\_Term$ $Simple\_Term \leq Simple\_Term$ $Simple\_Term > Simple\_Term$ $Simple\_Term \geq Simple\_Term$ $Condition \wedge Condition$ $Condition \vee Condition$ $\neg \ Condition$

12.2. Sharing

In section 7.3, we have already introduced the concept of sharing at the specification stage (this was done practically through the USES clause). In this section we introduce the same idea of sharing, but, this time, at the implementation stage (this mechanism has been suggested by Fernando Mejia).

12.2.1. Introduction

In order to introduce gradually the idea of sharing at the implementation stage, consider the following development of a certain machine M_0 which is refined twice and then implemented on three machines M_1, M_2 and M_3:

$$M_0$$

$$\uparrow \qquad \text{REFINES}$$

$$R_0$$

$$\uparrow \qquad \text{REFINES}$$

$$I_0$$

$$\swarrow \quad \downarrow \quad \searrow \qquad \text{IMPORTS}$$

$$M_1 \qquad M_2 \qquad M_3$$

We now extend this diagram downwards. We suppose, to simplify matters, that we only have a single refinement step between each machine and its final implementation. We might have then have the following three *independent* developments for M_1, M_2 and M_3.

M_1	M_2	M_3	
$\uparrow$	$\uparrow$	$\uparrow$	REFINES
I_1	I_2	I_3	
$\swarrow$ $\searrow$		$\downarrow$	IMPORTS
M_4 M_5		M_6	
$\uparrow$ $\uparrow$		$\uparrow$	REFINES
I_4 I_5		I_6	

Putting together these *independent* developments and that of the previous diagram, and removing the intermediate refinement steps, we obtain the following diagram:

$$
\begin{array}{ccc}
 & M_0 & & \text{REFINES} \\
 & \uparrow & & \\
 & I_0 & & \\
\swarrow & \downarrow & \searrow & \text{IMPORTS} \\
M_1 & M_2 & M_3 & \\
\uparrow & \uparrow & \uparrow & \text{REFINES} \\
I_1 & I_2 & I_3 & \\
\swarrow \quad \searrow & & \downarrow & \text{IMPORTS} \\
M_4 \quad M_5 & & M_6 & \\
\uparrow \quad \uparrow & & \uparrow & \text{REFINES} \\
I_4 \quad I_5 & & I_6 &
\end{array}
$$

By now omitting the REFINES arrow, we obtain the following showing each machine-implementation (model-module) pair organized as a tree structure:

$$
\begin{array}{ccc}
 & \begin{array}{c} M_0 \\ I_0 \end{array} & & \\
\swarrow & \downarrow & \searrow & \text{IMPORTS} \\
\begin{array}{c} M_1 \\ I_1 \end{array} & \begin{array}{c} M_2 \\ I_2 \end{array} & \begin{array}{c} M_3 \\ I_3 \end{array} & \\
\swarrow \quad \searrow & & \downarrow & \text{IMPORTS} \\
\begin{array}{cc} M_4 & M_5 \\ I_4 & I_5 \end{array} & & \begin{array}{c} M_6 \\ I_6 \end{array} &
\end{array}
$$

By removing the implementations from this diagram, we obtain the organization of our software system from the point of view of its specification.

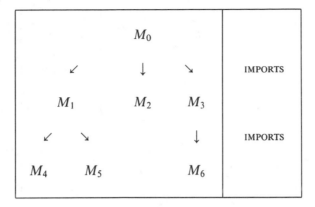

And by omitting the machines, we obtain the organization of our software system from the point of view of its final implementation:

```
                        I₀

              ↙          ↓          ↘              IMPORTS

           I₁          I₂          I₃

          ↙     ↘                    ↓              IMPORTS

        I₄      I₅                  I₆
```

Clearly, such a structure corresponds to the way software systems might be organized in practice, that is as *layers of independent modules* with well-defined interfaces. Such structures, however, are sometimes inefficient in that no *direct* connection between two modules of the tree is possible. In the above diagram, such connections can only be established *indirectly* through the common ancestors of the two modules concerned. In other words, it might be advisable to have the possibility of establishing *short-circuits* between modules.

Such direct connections are not dangerous, as far as the overall consistency of the system is concerned, *provided* these short-circuits only correspond to *inquiries* from one module to the encapsulated data of another. A classical example is one where the imodule receiving the inquiry is *variable-free* as is typically the case for a Mathematical Library. Of course, this is not the most general case. We might sometimes need to share machines having genuine variables. For instance, it might be interesting to establish such a connection between modules I_1 and I_2 and also between modules I_3 and I_2 of our previous diagram. This is indicated in the following diagram by the two horizontal arrows pointing to module I_2:

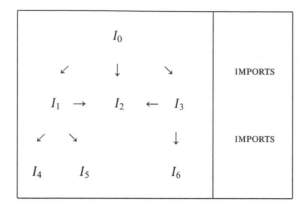

We would say that each of the modules I_1 and I_3 SEES the module I_2. And, again, the only possible connections are the invocations from within I_1 and I_3 of *inquiry* operations of I_2. Such operations are guaranteed not to modify the encapsulated data of I_2.

Our problem is now to reflect such connections at the upper stages of the developments of I_1, I_2 and I_3. In other words, we would like to know what the form of such short-circuit connections is, at the level of the corresponding machine specifications. The idea is to have the machines M_1 and M_3 already connected to machine M_2 as follows

	SEES		SEES	
M_1	$\rightarrow$	M_2	$\leftarrow$	M_3

The constraints on the seeing machines with regard to the seen machine should be clear: the variables of M_2 can be referenced (read-only, of course) from within any operation of M_1 or M_3. This agrees with the fact that, at the future implementation stage, only inquiry operations will be allowed.

However, the variables of M_2 cannot be referenced from within the invariants of M_1 or M_3 because we want M_2 to be *independent* of M_1 and M_3. We do not want M_2 to be aware of the fact that it is seen by other machines. In particular, we do not want to have to re-prove M_2, as would happen if some extra constraints concerning the variables of M_2 were to appear in the invariants of M_1 or M_3. Again, this agrees with the fact that that mechanism of shared use of the inquiry services of M_2 is just an optimization (a short-circuit). As a consequence, there is no reason for M_2 to "pay" anything for that (however, if, in the future, the need for the variables of a seen machine to be possibly referenced in the invariant of a seeing construct appears, then it could be allowed since it does not raise any special problem except, apparently, that of re-proving the seen machine).

Proceeding down the development of machine M_1 or M_3, we have to continue to see M_2 as indicated in the following diagram:

	SEES		SEES		
M_1	$\rightarrow$	M_2	$\leftarrow$	M_3	
$\uparrow$				$\uparrow$	REFINES
R_1	$\rightarrow$	M_2	$\leftarrow$	R_3	
$\uparrow$				$\uparrow$	REFINES
I_1	$\rightarrow$	M_2	$\leftarrow$	I_3	

The constraints put on R_1, I_1, R_3, I_3 with regard to the seen machine M_2 are of the same nature as those put previously on M_1 and M_3 with regard to M_2, except that, now, the variables of M_2 are not referenceable from within the operations of I_1 and I_3 (except when they are CONCRETE_VARIABLES of course). This is because we do not know how M_2 will be refined. The (abstract) variables of M_2 may have no existence in its final implementation and, consequently, they cannot be referenced from outside (again, this is full hiding). In fact, and as expected, the only connections from I_1 and I_3 to M_2 have to be made through the available *inquiry* operations offered by M_2. And eventually, we shall also have that sort of connection between I_1 and I_3 and the final implementation I_2 of M_2. Remember, this is what we were aiming at from the beginning!

12.2.2. The SEES Clause

As shown in the previous section, a SEES clause can be found in either a machine, a refinement or an implementation. The same machine can be referenced in several SEES clauses. A machine that is seen should be imported (only once) somewhere in the development. When a parameterized machine is mentioned in a SEES clause, the parameters of the machine are not instantiated. This is because the parameters are, in fact, instantiated in the unique IMPORTS clause corresponding to the machine. Notice that although a "seen" machine can contain an INCLUDES clause, it cannot contain a USES clause.

12.2.3. Visibility Rules

The *visibility* of the various objects of a "seen" machine from within the various clauses of a "seeing" construct (machine, refinement or implementation) is described in the following tables. Each line corresponds to a specific category of objects of the seen machine and each column corresponds to a specific clause of the seeing construct. A tick indicates that a certain category of objects of the seen machine is referenceable from within a certain clause of the seeing construct.

	INCL (of mach.)	PROP (of mach.)	INV (of mach.)	OPER (of mach.)
parameters (of seen)				
sets (of seen)	√	√	√	√
concrete constants (of seen)	√	√	√	√
abstract constants (of seen)	√	√	√	√
concrete variables (of seen)				read-only
abstract variables (of seen)				read-only
operations (of seen)				

The first of these tables describes the situation for a seeing machine. The formal parameters of the seen machine are not visible. This is because we have no

way to know how they will be instantiated by the implementation importing
the corresponding machine. As expected, the sets and (concrete or abstract)
constants of the seeing machine are fully visible. The (concrete or abstract)
variables are not visible from within the invariant (we do want to have to
re-prove the seen machine). The (concrete or abstract) variables are only visible
from within the operations of the seeing machine (in a read-only fashion, of
course).

	INCL (of ref.)	PROP (of ref.)	INV (of ref.)	OPER (of ref.)
parameters (of seen)				
concrete constants (of seen)	√	√	√	√
abstract constants (of seen)	√	√	√	√
concrete variables (of seen)				read-only
abstract variables (of seen)				read-only
operations (of seen)				inquiry

In the case of a seeing refinement, the situation evolves a little in that the inquiry
operations are now visible from the operations of the refinement (the abstract
variables and constants of the seen machine being still visible).

	PROP (of impl.)	VAL (of impl.)	INV (of impl.)	OPER (of impl.)
parameters (of seen)				
sets (of seen)	√	√	√	√
concrete constants (of seen)	√	√	√	√
abstract constants (of seen)	√			in loop invariant
concrete variables (of seen)				read-only
abstract variables (of seen)				in loop invariant
operations (of seen)				inquiry

In the last case, corresponding to an implementation, the abstract variables are not visible any more from within the operations of the seeing construct. Only *inquiry* operations (as for the previous case, refinement) are visible from the operations of the implementation. The abstract constants are still visible from within the PROPERTIES clause but not from within the VALUES clause that has been added in this case. As we shall see in section 12.3, the *abstract* constants or variables can be referenced from within a loop invariant.

12.2.4. Transitivity and Circularity

The SEES clause *is not transitive* across the hierarchy of refinements. In other words, the fact that a machine M SEES a machine N does not mean that a refinement (or an implementation) M' refining M SEES N automatically. This must be repeated in a SEES clause of M'. The reason is one of readability. It would be hard to remember in M' all the machines that M SEES. In this way, M' is self contained. As a consequence, once a machine N is seen by a machine M or by a refinement R, N has to be seen explicitly by every refinement (or implementation) refining M or R. But, conversely, a machine N, seen by a refinement (or an implementation), need not be necessarily seen by its abstraction.

It is not possible to have "cycles" of SEES clauses. In other words, it is not possible for a machine M to see a machine N, seeing ..., seeing M itself. Likewise, it is not possible for a machine, a refinement or an implementation to see a machine that is one of its ancestors (or descendants) through a chain of IMPORTS clauses. In other words, if a machine M is refined by R, ..., and is then implemented by M' which itself IMPORTS a machine N, then neither R, M', N, nor any of its refinements, implementation and subsequent importations, can see M. Note finally that a seen machine cannot contain a USES clause, although it can contain an INCLUDES clause.

12.2.5. Machine Renaming

As for the USES clause (section 7.3.5), machines referenced in a SEES clause can be renamed. As for the used machines, renaming is not transitive for seen machines. In other words, when a renamed machine SEES another machine, the latter is not automatically renamed.

However, consider an implementation I that is renamed as $P.I$ via a certain abstract machine M that is renamed as $P.M$. It should be noted that M is not necessarily the direct abstraction of I. It is quite possible that the abstraction of I, say H, is imported by the implementation of M or one of its descendants, etc. Suppose that the implementation I SEES a certain machine N, possibly renamed as $P.N$ as a consequence of the *same* renaming as the one that has renamed M as $P.M$. In this case, what $P.I$ SEES is $P.N$, *not* N.

12.2.6. Comparing the USES and the SEES Clauses

It is worth comparing the USES and the SEES clauses. These two clauses are concerned with sharing, but from completely different points of view. In the case of the USES clause, the sharing concerns a certain piece of *formal text* that is common to several specifications. In a sense, the very fact that a shared text has been incorporated is forgotten in the final specification, which must include all the machines using the same one simultaneously. In the case of the SEES clause, the intended sharing, concerns certain implementations (modules) that will be present in the final executing code: the shared code will remain visible (as a module) in the final implementation.

This has some consequences for the visibility rules. As can be seen from the previous section, whatever the seeing construct, no variable of a seen machine can be referenced in the INVARIANT clause of a seeing construct. This is one of the main differences between the SEES clause and the USES clause (section 7.3.3), for which this was indeed possible. Also remember that, in the case of the USES clause, no operation of a used machine could ever be called from within an operation of a using machine (again, section 7.3.3). Here, in the case of the SEES clause, *inquiry* operations of a seen machine can be called from within an operation of a seeing refinement or of a seeing implementation. Finally, in the case of the USES clause, the formal parameters of the used machine are fully visible from within the using machine, because the used machine and the using machine have to be included, eventually, simultaneously in another machine. This is not the case for the SEES clause, where the formal parameters are *never* visible, because there is no reason for the various machines seeing a given machine to be imported simultaneously with that seen machine.

12.3. Loops Revisited

In this short section, we make precise the rules for the visibility of variables and constants in loop invariants. This could not be done before, since we have only now introduced all the necessary notions.

Clearly, a loop invariant can contain references to the concrete variables and constants of the implementation where it is situated.

A loop invariant can also contain references to the concrete and abstract constants and variables of the machines it IMPORTS or of the machines it SEES.

Finally, it can contain references to the variables or constants of the abstraction it refines. If such variables are also present in the implementation, a renaming must occur in order to make a clear distinction between a reference to the occurrence of the variable in the implementation and to that of the variable in the abstraction: by convention, the latter is subscripted with a 0.

12.4. Multiple Refinement and Implementation

Multiple refinement of abstract machines is a technique by which a single refinement may refine several abstractions simultaneously. This does not constitute a new concept, it is rather a technique that could be used at the end of a development in order to optimize the overall architecture. For instance, suppose that we have a development corresponding to the following diagram:

$$M_0$$
$$I_0$$

↙   ↓   ↘   IMPORTS

M_1 M_2 M_3
I_1 I_2 I_3

↙   ↘   ↓   IMPORTS

M_4 M_5 M_6
I_4 I_5 I_6

It might happen that the machines M_5 and M_6 are easily implementable on a *single* machine. For instance, both machines may be dealing with some kind of memory management which, clearly, could be implemented on a single machine M_{56} (later implemented by I_{56}) provided, of course, that the data of the machines *do not interfere*. This would correspond to the following schema:

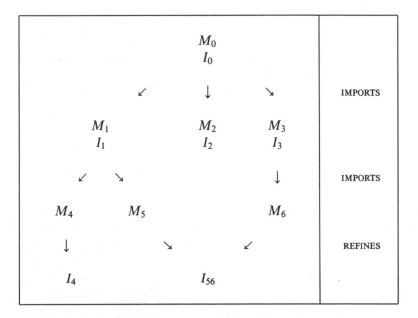

This idea could be exploited at any level in a development. Let us present it in a small example corresponding to the following simple machines:

```
MACHINE

    M_x

VARIABLES

    x

INVARIANT

    x ∈ 0..9

INITIALIZATION

    x := 0

OPERATIONS

    modify_x(n)  ≘
        PRE
            n ∈ 0..9
        THEN
            x := n
        END ;

    n ⟵ value_x  ≘
        BEGIN
            n := x
        END

END
```

```
MACHINE

    M_y

VARIABLES

    y

INVARIANT

    y ∈ 0..9

INITIALIZATION

    y := 0

OPERATIONS

    modify_y(n)  ≘
        PRE
            n ∈ 0..9
        THEN
            y := n
        END ;

    n ⟵ value_y  ≘
        BEGIN
            n := y
        END

END
```

We now refine *both* these machines with a *single* refinement at once. We propose the following refinement where the only slight difference from a normal one is that the REFINES clause now contains a *list* of abstractions.

REFINEMENT

   M_xy

REFINES

   M_x, M_y

VARIABLES

   xy

INVARIANT

   $xy = 10 \times x + y$

INITIALIZATION

   $xy := 0$

OPERATIONS

     modify_x(n) $\widehat{=}$ BEGIN $xy := 10 \times n + (xy \bmod 10)$ END;

     $n \longleftarrow$ value_x $\widehat{=}$ BEGIN $n := xy/10$ END

     modify_y(n) $\widehat{=}$ BEGIN $xy := (xy/10) + n$ END;

     $n \longleftarrow$ value_y $\widehat{=}$ BEGIN $n := xy \bmod 10$ END

END

As can be seen, the two abstract variables x and y are now coupled to form the single variable xy. And the coupling invariant $xy = 10 \times x + y$ performs a double change of variables while keeping the abstract variables *fully independent*.

12.5. Recursively Defined Operations

Recursion is a very classical concept offered by many programming languages. One might wonder whether this concept could be integrated, in one way or another, into the language of generalized substitutions and abstract machines. The purpose of this section is to show how (and when) this can be done.

As for sequencing and loop in the context of generalized substitutions (chapter 9), recursively defined operations are *not* allowed in a specification or a refinement. This is because recursion (in the context of abstract machine operations) is not a specification concept but a programming concept: a recursively defined operation deals with the eventual *computation* of a more abstract, *non-recursive*, specification. Recursive operations will thus *always* be introduced in the last phase of a development (IMPLEMENTATION). This might be done for two reasons: first, in order to refine an already specified abstraction, and second, in order to provide a formal text to be translated, as such, into a certain target programming language supposed to offer recursion as a possible computational paradigm.

It is worth recalling, however, that we have already introduced a notion of recursion in chapter 3 (in sections 3.5.6, 3.5.7, 3.7.1, 3.7.3, 3.8.4, 3.8.5, 3.9.4, 3.9.5, 3.10.3, 3.10.4 and 3.11.3) where we were dealing with the construction of mathematical objects. The concept of recursion, as introduced in chapter 3, was certainly not introduced as a *refinement* technique (still less as a computational technique); it was rather introduced as a *mathematical* technique that allowed us to *define* some total functions on inductively defined sets. In other words, the recursion concept introduced in chapter 3 and the one introduced in this chapter are clearly *distinct* concepts although, as will become clear, they obviously have some common flavour.

12.5.1. Introduction

The approach we are going to take is similar to the one we have already followed for loops (section 9.2). We shall first define recursive operations within the set-theoretic model of set transformers and then we shall transport our results into the world of generalized substitutions and abstract machines.

For a given generalized substitution S, supposed to work with a variable belonging to a certain set s, the set transformer $\mathsf{str}(S)$ is, as we know, a function from $\mathbb{P}(s)$ to itself (section 6.4.2). If the substitution S is parameterized with a parameter belonging to a certain set t, then the corresponding set transformer becomes a function of the following type:

$$\mathsf{str}(S) \in t \rightarrow (\mathbb{P}(s) \rightarrow \mathbb{P}(s))$$

When a set t is inductively defined, we know (according to the various developments presented in chapter 3) that it is possible to define a total function on t recursively. It is thus clearly possible to apply this technique to define the function corresponding to a parameterized set transformer. For example, let the above sets s and t both be equal to the set $\mathbb{N}$. We can then define recursively a function f of type

$$f \in \mathbb{N} \rightarrow (\mathbb{P}(\mathbb{N}) \rightarrow \mathbb{P}(\mathbb{N}))$$

as follows:

$$f(n) \;=\; \begin{cases} \mathsf{str}\,(r := 1) & \text{if} \quad n = 0 \\[2mm] f(n-1) \;\circ\; \mathsf{str}\,(r := r \times n) & \text{otherwise} \end{cases}$$

We shall then prove that $f(n)$ is exactly the set transformer corresponding to the generalized substitution $r := n!$. But we first remind the reader that $n!$, the factorial of n, is the product of the first n positive natural numbers. In other words, we have

$$n! \;=\; \mathsf{prod}\,(\mathsf{id}\,(1..n))$$

From this definition, we can easily deduce the following:

$$\begin{cases} 0! & = & 1 \\ (n+1)! & = & n! \times (n+1) \end{cases}$$

We now prove the following:

$$\forall n \cdot (n \in \mathbb{N} \;\Rightarrow\; f(n) = \mathsf{str}\,(r := n!))$$ Property 12.5.1

Proof: The proof is by induction on n.
Base Step: We have to prove the following which is obvious

$$f(0) \;=\; \mathsf{str}\,(r := 0\,!)$$ Goal 1

noindent**Induction Step**: We assume

$$n \in \mathbb{N}$$ Hypothesis 1

$$f(n) \;=\; \mathsf{str}\,(r := n!)$$ Hypothesis 2

and we have to prove

$$f(n+1) \;=\; \mathsf{str}\,(r := (n+1)\,!)$$ Goal 2

The proof goes as follows:

$$f(n+1)$$
$$=$$ Recursive definition of f
$$f(n) \;\circ\; \mathsf{str}\,(r := r \times (n+1))$$
$$=$$ Hypothesis 2
$$\mathsf{str}\,(r := n!) \;\circ\; \mathsf{str}\,(r := r \times (n+1))$$
$$=$$
$$\mathsf{str}\,(r := n!;\; r := r \times (n+1))$$
$$=$$
$$\mathsf{str}\,(r := n! \times (n+1))$$
$$=$$ Property of $n!$
$$\mathsf{str}\,(r := (n+1)\,!)$$

End of Proof

By supposing now that $f(n)$ is the set transformer of a certain operation called $r \longleftarrow \text{fact}(n)$, we are led to the following:

$$\text{str}(r \longleftarrow \text{fact}(n)) \ \hat{=} \ \begin{cases} \text{str}(r := 1) & \text{if} \quad n = 0 \\ \text{str}(r \longleftarrow \text{fact}(n-1)) \circ \text{str}(r := r \times n) & \text{otherwise} \end{cases}$$

that is

$$\text{str}(r \longleftarrow \text{fact}(n)) \ \hat{=} \ \begin{cases} \text{str}(r := 1) & \text{if} \quad n = 0 \\ \text{str}(r \longleftarrow \text{fact}(n-1); \ r := r \times n) & \text{otherwise} \end{cases}$$

that is

$$\text{str}(r \longleftarrow \text{fact}(n)) \ \hat{=} \ \text{str} \left(\begin{array}{l} \text{IF} \quad n = 0 \quad \text{THEN} \\ \qquad r := 1 \\ \text{ELSE} \\ \qquad r \longleftarrow \text{fact}(n-1); \\ \qquad r := r \times n \\ \text{END} \end{array} \right)$$

By removing the "str" operator on both sides, we obtain the following recursive operation:

$$\boxed{\begin{array}{l} r \longleftarrow \text{fact}(n) \quad \hat{=} \\ \text{IF} \quad n = 0 \quad \text{THEN} \\ \qquad r := 1 \\ \text{ELSE} \\ \qquad r \longleftarrow \text{fact}(n-1); \\ \qquad r := r \times n \\ \text{END} \end{array}}$$

What we have just shown is that the previous recursive implementation constitutes a correct refinement of the following specification:

$$\boxed{\begin{array}{l} r \longleftarrow \text{fact}(n) \quad \hat{=} \\ \text{PRE} \\ \qquad n \in \mathbb{N} \\ \text{THEN} \\ \qquad r := n! \\ \text{END} \end{array}}$$

Similar recursive implementations can be provided in this way for specifications dealing with other inductively defined sets such as sequences, trees and so on.

12.5.2. Syntax

In practice, and as for loops (section 9.2.9), we shall see that the termination of the recursive operation requires a certain "variant". This is an expression that is defined in terms of the input parameters of the recursive operation, and that we shall have to prove that it decreases at each recursive call. In order to define this variant, we propose to extend as follows the syntax for *Operation_Declaration*, as defined in section 5.2.1:

Syntactic Category	Definition
Operation_Declaration	*Operation_Header* $\;\hat{=}\;$ *Substitution* *Operation_Header* $\;\hat{=}\;$ REC *Expression* THEN *Substitution* END

The *Expression* situated in between the REC and THEN keywords is supposed to denote the variant. In our previous example, this yields the following:

$$r \longleftarrow \mathsf{fact}(n) \quad \hat{=}$$
$$\text{REC} \quad n \quad \text{THEN}$$
$$\text{IF} \quad n = 0 \quad \text{THEN}$$
$$r := 1$$
$$\text{ELSE}$$
$$r \longleftarrow \mathsf{fact}(n-1);$$
$$r := r \times n$$
$$\text{END}$$
$$\text{END}$$

12.5.3. Proof Rule

In this section, our intention is to propose a rule to be applied in practice to prove that a recursive operation indeed refines its (non-recursive) abstraction. We suppose that we have an abstraction defined by the following, necessarily *non-recursive*, operation:

$$\mathsf{op}(x) \quad \hat{=} \quad \text{PRE} \quad P \quad \text{THEN} \quad S \quad \text{END}$$

and a corresponding concrete recursive implementation that is defined as follows:

$$\mathsf{op}(x) \quad \hat{=} \quad \text{REC} \quad V \quad \text{THEN} \quad T \quad \text{END}$$

The idea is that the recursive calls to op that one may find within T are *not* genuine calls to the implemented operation itself (which is meaningless), but calls to the operation of an (implicit) importation of the machine we are just implementing. So, quite naturally (and as explained in section 12.1.2), the proof that our implemented operation indeed refines its abstraction necessitates the replacement in T of the recursive calls to op by the in-line instantiated expansions *of the abstract operation itself* : by doing this we *remove the recursion* from our implementation.

Of course, we also have to prove that the parameter of the operation indeed belongs to a well-founded set and that each of the recursive calls has an actual parameter that is "smaller" than the formal parameter of the operation itself: for this, it suffices to prove that the variant "decreases". We remind the reader that, in a loop, the variant is either a natural number or a sequence of natural numbers; in what follows, we shall adopt the same kind of variants for recursive implementations.

As a consequence, in order to prove that our implementation refines its abstraction, we shall use *almost exactly* the same rule as the one presented at the end of section 11.2.6. The only difference is that the recursive implementation op (x) is replaced by the following non-recursive operation op$'(x)$:

$$\text{op}'(x) \;\;\widehat{=}\;\; \text{VAR}\quad v\quad \text{IN}$$
$$v := V\,;$$
$$T'$$
$$\text{END}$$

Here v is supposed to be a *fresh* variable used to "store" the value of the variant when entering the operation, and T' is obtained from T by replacing each recursive call of the form op (F) by the following, if the variant is a natural number:

$$[x := F] \;\text{PRE}\;\; V < v \;\wedge\; P \;\text{THEN}\; S \;\text{END}$$

or by the following if the variant is a sequence of natural numbers:

$$[x := F] \;\text{PRE}\;\; V \prec v \;\wedge\; P \;\text{THEN}\; S \;\text{END}$$

As can be seen, the pre-condition P of the abstraction is extended with a predicate expressing that the variant "decreases".

Recursive operations and loops are clearly very close to each other. We have already seen that, in both cases, we have a variant. We might wonder whether there exists a "recursive" equivalent to the loop invariant. The answer is simple: this is just the abstraction itself (together with its pre-condition, of course).

In our previous example, this replacement yields the following operation, *which is not recursive any more*:

$$
\begin{array}{l}
r \longleftarrow \mathsf{fact'}\,(n) \quad \widehat{=} \\
\quad \text{VAR} \quad v \quad \text{IN} \\
\qquad v := n\,; \\
\qquad \text{IF} \quad n = 0 \quad \text{THEN} \\
\qquad\quad r := 1 \\
\qquad \text{ELSE} \\
\qquad\quad \text{PRE} \\
\qquad\qquad n - 1 < v \quad \wedge \\
\qquad\qquad n - 1 \in \mathbb{N} \\
\qquad\quad \text{THEN} \\
\qquad\qquad r := (n - 1)\,! \\
\qquad\quad \text{END}\,; \\
\qquad\quad r := r \times n \\
\qquad \text{END} \\
\quad \text{END}
\end{array}
$$

Proving that this new implementation refines its abstraction yields the following statements to be proved (after some simplifications):

$$
n \in \mathbb{N} \quad \Rightarrow \quad [\,[r := r']\,(r \longleftarrow \mathsf{fact'}\,(n))\,] \neg [r := n\,!\,] \neg (r = r')
$$

that is

$$
n \in \mathbb{N} \quad \Rightarrow \quad [\,[r := r']\,(r \longleftarrow \mathsf{fact'}\,(n))\,]\,(n\,! = r')
$$

yielding (after some simplifications) the following two obvious predicates:

$$
n \in \mathbb{N} \wedge n = 0 \quad \Rightarrow \quad n\,! = 1
$$

$$
\begin{array}{rl}
n \in \mathbb{N} \wedge n \neq 0 \quad \Rightarrow \quad & n - 1 < n \quad \wedge \\
& n - 1 \in \mathbb{N} \quad \wedge \\
& n\,! \;=\; (n - 1)\,! \times n
\end{array}
$$

What is interesting (and not so surprising) is that we obtain statements that are very close to the ones we obtained in the course of the proof (by induction) of Property 12.5.1 above.

12.6. Formal Definition

12.6.1. Syntax of an IMPLEMENTATION

Syntactic Category	Definition
Implementation	IMPLEMENTATION 　*Machine_Header* REFINES 　*Id_List* SETS 　*Sets* CONSTANTS 　*Id_List* PROPERTIES 　*Predicate* VALUES 　*Predicate* IMPORTS 　*Machine_List* PROMOTES 　*Id_List* EXTENDS 　*Machine_List* CONCRETE_VARIABLES 　*Id_List* INVARIANT 　*Predicate* ASSERTIONS 　*Predicate* DEFINITIONS 　*Definitions* INITIALIZATION 　*Substitution* OPERATIONS 　*Operations* END

As can be seen, the syntax of an implementation is very close to that of a refinement (section 11.3.1). We have no ABSTRACT_CONSTANTS any more, nor have we (abstract) VARIABLES. The possible INCLUDES clause is replaced by a possible IMPORTS clause. Moreover, we have an extra VALUES clause.

12.6.2. Type-checking with an IMPORTS Clause

As for the type-checking of a refinement in section 11.3.2, we consider a machine M_1 and a list of successive refinements or implementation from M_2 to M_n. This time, the last construct M_n is an implementation supposed to import a certain machine M. Also note that in M_n, the deferred sets and the constants of M_1 to M_n are given values.

```
                              IMPLEMENTATION
                                M_n(X_1, x_1)
                              REFINES
 MACHINE                        M_{n-1}                      MACHINE
   M_1(X_1, x_1)              SETS                              M(X, x)
 CONSTRAINTS                    S_n ;                        CONSTRAINTS
   C_1                          T_n = {a_n, b_n}               C
 SETS                         CONSTANTS                      SETS
   S_1 ;                        c_n                            S ;
   T_1 = {a_1, b_1}           PROPERTIES                       T = {a, b}
 (ABSTRACT_)CONSTANTS           P_n                          (ABSTRACT_)CONSTANTS
   c_1                        IMPORTS                          c
 PROPERTIES                     M(A, a)                      PROPERTIES
   P_1                ...     VALUES                           P
 (CONCRETE_)VARIABLES           S_1 = E_1  ∧  S_2 = E_2 ···  (CONCRETE_)VARIABLES
   v_1                          c_1 = d_1  ∧  c_2 = d_2 ···    v
 INVARIANT                    CONCRETE_VARIABLES             INVARIANT
   I_1                          v_n                            I
 ASSERTIONS                   INVARIANT                      ASSERTIONS
   J_1                          I_n                            J
 INITIALIZATION               ASSERTIONS                     INITIALIZATION
   U_1                          J_n                            U
 OPERATIONS                   INITIALIZATION                 OPERATIONS
   O_1                          U_n                            O
 END                          OPERATIONS                     END
                                O_n
                              END
```

The problem of type-checking an implementation is slightly different from that of type-checking a refinement (section 11.3.2). This is because, here, we are at the border between two separate type systems: the type system of the sequence of constructs M_1 to M_n, with the given sets X_1, S_i and T_i (for i in $1 .. n$), and the type system of the imported machine M with the given sets X, S and T. This has the following consequences:

1. The deferred set S_i of contruct M_i (for i in $1..n$) is no longer a given set, so it now has type $\mathbb{P}(\text{super}(E_i))$. This takes account of the VALUES clause $S_i = E_i$.

2. The set formal parameter X of the imported machine M is, again, no longer a given set, so it now has type $\mathbb{P}(\text{super}(A))$. This takes account of the fact that the formal parameter X is instantiated by A.

Antecedent	Consequent
$v \setminus X_1, x_1, S_i, T_i, a_i, b_i, E_i, d_i, U_n, O_n$ $v_n \setminus E_j, d_j$ for all i, j in $1..n$ $\text{given}(X_1),$ $S_1 \in \mathbb{P}(\text{super}(E_1)),$ $\text{given}(T_1),$ $\text{sig}(M_1),$ $\cdots$ $S_i \in \mathbb{P}(\text{super}(E_i)),$ $\text{given}(T_i),$ $\text{sig}(M_i),$ $\cdots$ $S_n \in \mathbb{P}(\text{super}(E_n)),$ $\text{given}(T_n),$ $X \in \mathbb{P}(\text{super}(A)),$ $\text{given}(S),$ $\text{given}(T),$ $\text{sig}(M)$ $\vdash$ $\text{check}((x = a) \quad \wedge$ $\quad (c_1 = d_1) \wedge \cdots \wedge (c_n = d_n) \wedge$ $\quad (I_n \Rightarrow J_n \wedge U_n \wedge O_n))$	check (IMPLEMENTATION $M_n(X_1, x_1)$ REFINES M_{n-1} SETS $S_n;$ $T_n = \{a_n, b_n\}$ CONSTANTS c_n PROPERTIES P_n IMPORTS $M(A, a)$ VALUES $S_1 = E_1 \wedge \cdots \wedge S_n = E_n \quad \wedge$ $c_1 = d_1 \wedge \cdots \wedge c_n = d_n$ CONCRETE_VARIABLES v_n INVARIANT I_n ASSERTIONS J_n INITIALIZATION U_n OPERATIONS O_n END)

12.6.3. Type-checking with a SEES Clause

The type-checking of a certain construct (machine, refinement or implementation) that contains a SEES clause is just a direct extension of the rule of type-checking to be used for that construct (section 5.2.3, sections 7.4.2, section 11.3.2, and section 12.6.2).

In fact, the signature of the seen machine is just put systematically into the various environments. This is done, however, *without* the given sets corresponding to the formal parameters of the seen machine. In this way, any attempt to access such sets in the type-checking leads to a type-checking failure. Of course, it is required that the formal parameters of the seen machine are independent of those of the seeing construct.

12.6.4. Proof Obligations of an IMPLEMENTATION

The implemetation M_n is supposed to import a certain machine M with the same formal structure as that of M_1 (without the subscripted 1).

MACHINE
  $M_1(X_1, x_1)$
CONSTRAINTS
  C_1
SETS
  S_1 ;
  $T_1 = \{a_1, b_1\}$
CONSTANTS
  c_1
ABSTRACT_CONSTANTS
  c_1'
PROPERTIES
  P_1
(CONCRETE_)VARIABLES
  v_1
INVARIANT
  I_1
ASSERTIONS
  J_1
INITIALIZATION
  U_1

. . .

IMPLEMENTATION
  $M_n(X_1, x_1)$
REFINES
  M_{n-1}
SETS
  S_n ;
  $T_n = \{a_n, b_n\}$
CONSTANTS
  c_n
PROPERTIES
  P_n
IMPORTS
  $M(N, n)$
VALUES
  $S_1 = E_1 \;\wedge\; S_i = E_i \cdots \;\wedge$
  $c_1 = d_1 \;\wedge\; c_i = d_i \cdots$
CONCRETE_VARIABLES
  v_n
INVARIANT
  I_n
ASSERTIONS
  J_n
INITIALIZATION
  U_n

```
┌─────────────────────────────┐          ┌─────────────────────────────┐
│                             │          │                             │
│   OPERATIONS                │          │   OPERATIONS                │
│     u₁ ⟵ op₁(w₁)  ≙        │          │     u₁ ⟵ op₁(w₁)  ≙        │
│        PRE                  │          │        PRE                  │
│         Q₁                  │          │         Qₙ                  │
│        THEN                 │   . . .  │        THEN                 │
│         V₁                  │          │         Vₙ                  │
│        END ;                │          │        END ;                │
│         . . .               │          │         . . .               │
│                             │          │                             │
│   END                       │          │   END                       │
│                             │          │                             │
└─────────────────────────────┘          └─────────────────────────────┘
```

Before presenting the proof obligations, let us define (as in sections 5.2.5 and 7.4.3) the following predicates A_1, B_i (for i in $1 .. n$), A and B. The first one, A_1, states that the set machine parameter X_1 is a non-empty subset of INT. The second one, B_i, states that the deferred set S_i (for i in $1 .. n$) is a non-empty subset of INT and that the enumerated set T_i (for i in $1 .. n$) is a non-empty subset of INT consisting exactly of the two distinct elements a_i and b_i:

Abbreviation	Definition
A_1	$X_1 \in \mathbb{P}_1(\text{INT})$
B_i for i in $1 .. n$	$S_i \in \mathbb{P}_1(\text{INT}) \ \wedge \ T_i \in \mathbb{P}_1(\text{INT}) \ \wedge \ T_i = \{a_i, b_i\} \ \wedge \ a_i \neq b_i$
A	$X \in \mathbb{P}_1(\text{INT})$
B	$S \in \mathbb{P}_1(\text{INT}) \ \wedge \ T \in \mathbb{P}_1(\text{INT}) \ \wedge \ T = \{a, b\} \ \wedge \ a \neq b$

Our first proof obligation concerns the constraints A and C of the imported machine M, which must be obeyed by the actual parameters N and n. Note that this proof obligation is exactly the same as the one we had for the case of a machine inclusion (section 7.4.3):

$$\overbrace{A_1 \; \wedge \; B_1 \; \wedge \; \cdots \; \wedge \; B_n \; \wedge \; C_1 \; \wedge \; P_1 \; \wedge \; \cdots \; \wedge \; P_n}^{\text{Importing}}$$
$$\Rightarrow$$
$$[X, x := N, n] (\overbrace{A \; \wedge \; C}^{\text{Imported}})$$

The next proof obligation concerns the assertions of the implementation. Notice that, in the assumptions of this proof obligation, the invariant I and assertion J of the imported machine M have been actualized. However, the property P of the imported machine M has not been actualized since, by definition, the PROPERTIES clause of a machine is independent of its parameters (section 4.17).

$$\overbrace{A_1 \; \wedge \; B_1 \; \wedge \; \cdots \; \wedge \; B_n \; \wedge \; C_1 \; \wedge \; P_1 \; \wedge \; \cdots \; \wedge \; P_n}^{\text{Importing}} \; \wedge$$
$$\overbrace{I_1 \; \wedge \; \cdots \; \wedge \; I_n \; \wedge \; J_1 \; \wedge \; \cdots \; \wedge \; J_{n-1}}^{\text{Importing}} \; \wedge$$
$$\overbrace{B \; \wedge \; P \; \wedge \; [X, x := N, n] (I \; \wedge \; J)}^{\text{Imported}}$$
$$\Rightarrow$$
$$J_n$$

The next proof obligation concerns the VALUES given in M_n to the deferred sets and to the concrete constants introduced step by step during the development from M_1 to M_n. It also concerns the existence of the abstract constants introduced during that development. As we know (section 12.1.7), the values of the abstract constants are defined *solely* in terms of those parts of the imported machine M that are visible and that are not subjected to an instantiation; namely the SETS and the PROPERTIES clauses of M. This is the reason why, in the forthcoming proof obligation, we have the predicates B and P as hypotheses (such predicates yields the properties of the sets and constants of the imported machine M). The proof obligation then states that there exists some abstract constants obeying the various properties $P_1, \ldots, P_n$ as transformed by the substitution defined in the VALUES clause.

$$\overbrace{B \; \wedge \; P}^{\text{Imported}}$$
$$\Rightarrow$$
$$\exists (c'_1, \ldots, c'_{n-1}) \cdot [S_1, c_1, \ldots, S_n, c_n := E_1, d_1, \ldots, E_n, d_n] (\overbrace{P_1 \; \wedge \; \ldots \; \wedge \; P_n}^{\text{Importing}})$$

The next proof obligation concerns the refinement of the initialization. As can be seen, the initialization U_n (if any) of the implementation is appended to the (instantiated) initialization of the imported machines. The initialization U_n consists of calls to operations of the imported machine M.

$$
\overbrace{A_1 \wedge B_1 \wedge \ldots \wedge B_n \wedge C_1 \wedge P_1 \wedge \ldots \wedge P_n}^{\text{Importing}} \wedge
$$
$$
\overbrace{B \wedge P}^{\text{Imported}}
$$
$$
\Rightarrow
$$
$$
\overbrace{[[X,x := N,n]U}^{\text{Imported}} \; ; \; U_n] \neg [U_{n-1}] \neg I_n
$$

The last proof obligation concerns the refinement of an operation:

$$
\overbrace{A_1 \wedge B_1 \wedge \ldots \wedge B_n \wedge C_1 \wedge P_1 \wedge \ldots \wedge P_n}^{\text{Importing}} \wedge
$$
$$
\overbrace{I_1 \wedge \ldots \wedge I_n \wedge J_1 \wedge \ldots \wedge J_n \wedge Q_1 \ldots \wedge Q_{n-1}}^{\text{Importing}} \wedge
$$
$$
\overbrace{B \wedge P \wedge [X,x := N,n](I \wedge J)}^{\text{Imported}}
$$
$$
\Rightarrow
$$
$$
Q_n \wedge [[u_1 := u_1'] V_n] \neg [V_{n-1}] \neg (I_n \wedge u_1 = u_1')
$$

Note that the instantiated invariant and assertion $[X,x := N,n](I \wedge J)$ of the imported machine M is an antecedent of the proof obligation of the operation of the implementation. However, this invariant is not present in the right-hand side of this proof obligation since it is supposed to have already been proved to be preserved in machine M. There is also no risk of such a proof being corrupted since the operations of the implementation *never* modify the variables (even the concrete ones) of the imported machines directly (only through the operations of the imported machines). Also remember that, before doing our proof, the body V_1 of the implemented operation is transformed by the in-line expansion of the calls to the operations of the imported machines.

It is interesting to compare the last two proof obligations with the corresponding ones for the INCLUDES clause (section 7.4.3): the assumptions are almost excactly the same (in the present case, we have all the invariant I_2 to I_n). These proof obligations are also very close to the corresponding ones given for refinement (section 11.3.3).

12.6.5. Proof Obligation for a SEES Clause

The proof obligation of a certain construct (machine, refinement or implementation) that contains a SEES clause, is just a direct extension of the proof obligations to be used for that construct (section 5.2.4, sections 7.4.3 and 7.4.4, section 11.3.3, and section 12.3.3). In fact, the SETS, PROPERTIES and INVARIANT clauses of the seen machine are all assumed in the proofs. Remember that the formal parameters of the seen machine are not visible.

CHAPTER 13

Examples of Refinements

THIS last chapter contains several examples of program developments. The first one is a complete development from specification down to implementation (section 13.2). Before presenting that example, however, we propose the specification (section 13.1) of a number of elementary abstract machines representing the necessary interface to some basic data structures. Then, we briefly present some ideas concerning the construction of a library of useful machines (section 13.3). In section 13.4, we present the development of a simple reactive system, where the emphasis is put on the methodology.

13.1. A Library of Basic Machines

In this section we propose a number of *BASIC* abstract machines. Such machines are supposed to contain the specification of "hardware" on which other machines will eventually be implemented. As a consequence, none of these basic machines are refined and, a fortiori, implemented; they are just given. Corresponding codes, in various programming languages, might be available. These machines are the following:

- *BASIC_CONSTANTS*
- *BASIC_IO*
- *BASIC_BOOL*
- *BASIC_enum*
- *BASIC_FILE_VAR*

The first machine contains the definition of a number of pre-defined constants. In the second machine, we specify some input-output operations for integers, booleans, characters and strings. The third machine contains some constants for encoding booleans. The fourth machine is a "generic" machine that constitutes a general model for an enumerated set machine. In the last machine, a file variable is encapsulated and a number of operations on it are offered.

13.1.1. The *BASIC_CONSTANTS* Machine

We remind the reader of the following *BASIC_CONSTANTS* machine that was already presented in section 5.2.6. This machine is implicitly seen by any machine, refinement or implementation.

MACHINE

    BASIC_CONSTANTS

SETS

    BOOL = {false, true}

CONSTANTS

    minint, maxint, INT, NAT, INT_1, NAT_1, CHAR

PROPERTIES

    $minint \in \mathbb{Z}$ $\wedge$
    $maxint \in \mathbb{N}$ $\wedge$
    $minint < 0$ $\wedge$
    $maxint > 0$ $\wedge$
    $INT = minint .. maxint$ $\wedge$
    $NAT = 0 .. maxint$ $\wedge$
    $NAT_1 = 1 .. maxint$ $\wedge$
    $INT_1 = minint .. -1$ $\wedge$
    $CHAR = 0 .. 255$

END

13.1.2. The *BASIC_IO* Machine

The proposed machine of this section contains a sample of *elementary* input-output operations to be used to establish communications with a user terminal. More elaborate input-output operations, like the one proposed by the C programming language, could be specified in the same way. The parameter of the last operation is a sequence of CHAR that is understood to be a *literal* sequence of characters.

MACHINE

   BASIC_IO

OPERATIONS

   $n \longleftarrow$ INTERVAL_READ (a, b) $\,\widehat{=}\,$
     PRE
       $a \in$ INT $\wedge$ $b \in$ INT $\wedge$ $a \leq b$
     THEN
       $n :\in a \mathbin{..} b$
     END ;

   INT_WRITE (n) $\,\widehat{=}\,$
     PRE $n \in$ INT   THEN skip   END ;

   $b \longleftarrow$ BOOL_READ $\,\widehat{=}\,$
     BEGIN $b :\in$ BOOL   END ;

   BOOL_WRITE (b) $\,\widehat{=}\,$
     PRE $b \in$ BOOL   THEN skip   END ;

   $b \longleftarrow$ CHAR_READ $\,\widehat{=}\,$
     BEGIN $b :\in$ CHAR   END ;

   CHAR_WRITE (b) $\,\widehat{=}\,$
     PRE $b \in$ CHAR   THEN skip   END ;

   STRING_WRITE (s) $\,\widehat{=}\,$
     PRE $s \in$ seq $($CHAR$)$ THEN skip   END

END

13.1.3. The *BASIC_BOOL* Machine

This variable-free machine provides two (visible) constants which are bijections from the set BOOL to the set $\{0, 1\}$ and vice-versa. This is useful for encoding or decoding the set BOOL.

```
MACHINE

    BASIC_BOOL

CONSTANTS

    code_BOOL, decode_BOOL

PROPERTIES
```

$$code\_BOOL \in \mathsf{BOOL} \rightarrowtail \{0,1\} \quad \wedge$$
$$decode\_BOOL = code\_BOOL^{-1}$$

```
END
```

13.1.4. The *BASIC_enum* Machine for Enumerated Sets

In this section we present a general machine yielding operations working on an enumerated set. The machine we present is a general model that should be adapted to each specific enumerated set. Such an adaptation could be done by a small utility program.

```
MACHINE

    BASIC_enum

SETS
```

$$enum = \{\cdots\}$$

```
CONSTANTS

    code_enum, decode_enum

PROPERTIES
```

$$code\_enum \in enum \rightarrowtail \{0, 1, \cdots\} \quad \wedge$$
$$decode\_enum = code\_enum^{-1}$$

```
OPERATIONS

    r ⟵ enum_READ  ≙  BEGIN  r :∈ enum  END ;

    enum_WRITE (i)  ≙  PRE  i ∈ enum  THEN  skip  END

END
```

As can be seen, this (model) machine contains a declaration of the enumerated set. It provides operations for reading and writing elements of the set. It also contains two (visible) constants, which are bijections from the enumerated set to a finite (and supposedly dense) subset of the set of natural numbers and vice-versa. Such constants can be used to encode or decode the enumerated set explicitly.

13.1.5. The *BASIC_FILE_VAR* Machine

This machine encapsulates a file variable considered to be a sequence built on a certain set of "record values", which is the set of total functions from a certain set, *INDEX*, to another one, *VALUE*. These two sets are formal parameters of the machine. The sequence size is limited to a certain value, *max_rec*, which is a scalar parameter of the machine. The machine also encapsulates a buffer, which is a single "record value". It provides operations for moving a record value from the file to the buffer and vice-versa. It also provides operations to modify or to access the buffer, to create a new record in the file, to reset the file and, finally, an operation yielding the size of the file. Of course, this machine is very elementary. We have just tried to present the simplest file machine we could think of in order to develop our subsequent example. A more sophisticated machine modelling an entire file system could be developed.

```
MACHINE

    BASIC_FILE_VAR (max_rec, INDEX, VALUE)

CONSTRAINTS

    max_rec ∈ NAT₁

VARIABLES

    file_vrb
```

CONCRETE_VARIABLES

   buf_vrb

INVARIANT

   $buf\_vrb \in INDEX \rightarrow VALUE \quad \wedge$
   $file\_vrb \in \mathsf{seq}(INDEX \rightarrow VALUE) \quad \wedge$
   $\mathsf{size}(file\_vrb) < max\_rec$

INITIALIZATION

   $buf\_vrb :\in INDEX \rightarrow VALUE \quad ||$
   $file\_vrb := []$

OPERATIONS

   READ_FILE$(i) \quad \widehat{=}$
       PRE $i \in \mathsf{dom}(file\_vrb)$ THEN $buf\_vrb := file\_vrb(i)$ END;

   WRITE_FILE$(i) \quad \widehat{=}$
       PRE $i \in \mathsf{dom}(file\_vrb)$ THEN $file\_vrb(i) := buf\_vrb$ END;

   NEW_RECORD$(v) \quad \widehat{=}$
       PRE
           $v \in VALUE \quad \wedge$
           $\mathsf{size}(file\_vrb) \neq max\_rec$
       THEN
           $file\_vrb := file\_vrb \leftarrow (INDEX \times \{v\})$
       END;

   $v \longleftarrow$ SIZE_FILE $\quad \widehat{=}$ BEGIN $v := \mathsf{size}(file\_vrb)$ END;

   RESET_FILE $\quad \widehat{=}$ BEGIN $file\_vrb := []$ END

END

13.2. Case Study: Data-base System

This section contains a complete development of the simple data-base already presented in chapter 4 (the final version of it is in section 4.19). In what follows, we present a general outline of this development. This presentation is made from the bottom up. That is, we start by specifying the file on which our data-base will eventually reside, and finish by specifying the external interface. Alternatively, we could have chosen to present things from the top down.

We first present a machine for handling a file (section 13.2.1). It is called the *FILE* machine, and it provides operations for the *direct* access and modification of our file. This machine is implemented on a *FILE_BUFFER* machine, which, as its name indicates, contains a file and a buffer. This second machine is itself implemented on a certain *FILE_ACCESS* machine, whose rôle is to optimize the movement of data between the file and the buffer. Finally, this last machine is implemented by using the *BASIC_FILE_VAR* machine of section 13.1.5. In the following diagram, each simple arrow stands for the "IMPORTS" relationship.

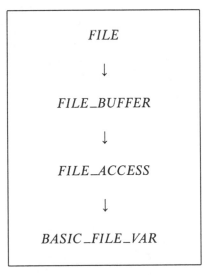

We then specifiy various machines for handling *objects* (section 13.2.2). First, the *TOTAL_OBJECT* machine handling objects defined in the form of *total* functions. This machine is implemented on the *FILE* machine mentioned in the previous paragraph. Second, the *PARTIAL_OBJECT* machine handling objects defined in the form of *partial* functions. This second machine is then implemented on the above *TOTAL_OBJECT* machine.

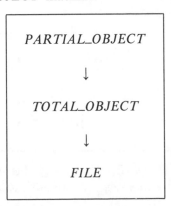

We then develop the data-base (section 13.2.3). Our first specification is that of the *DATA_BASE* machine itself. It is then implemented on the above *PARTIAL_OBJECT* machine and it SEES a number of *BASIC* machines. In the next and subsequent diagrams, a double arrow indicates a SEES relationship.

DATA_BASE   ⇒   BASIC_IO
                                   BASIC_SEX
         ↓   BASIC_STATUS

PARTIAL_OBJECT

We then develop a number of interfaces (section 13.2.4) built on the top of the previous *DATA_BASE* machine. Our first specification is that of a *QUERY* machine whose rôle is to "query" the external user, by asking him to enter some data into the data-base. Such data are checked by the *QUERY* machine, whose implementation possibly delivers a number of error messages. The *QUERY* machine SEES the *DATA_BASE* machine and a number of *BASIC* machines.

QUERY   ⇒   DATA_BASE

      ⇓

BASIC_IO
BASIC_SEX
BASIC_STATUS

Our second specification is that of the *INNER_INTERFACE* machine. It corresponds to the main actions to be performed on the data-base. Such actions are now completely protected: that is, all the operations of the *DATA_BASE* machine are guaranteed to be called within their pre-conditions. The *INNER_INTERFACE* machine is thus implemented on the *DATA_BASE* machine and on the above *QUERY* machine.

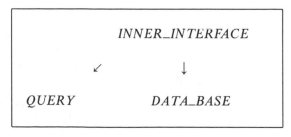

INNER_INTERFACE

      ↙   ↓

QUERY   DATA_BASE

Finally, we have the *MAIN_INTERFACE*. The rôle of this machine is to give the external user the ability to enter "commands" to activate the system. This machine is then implemented on the above *INNER_INTERFACE* machine and on a number of *BASIC* machines.

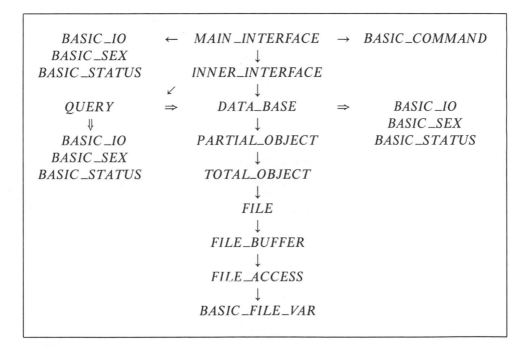

By putting together all the previous diagrams, we obtain the following complete picture of the architecture of our system:

13.2.1. Machines for Files

The FILE Machine

The machine proposed in this section encapsulates a *file*, considered to be a finite sequence (of "record values") of maximum size *max_rec*. A "record value" is a total function from a certain set, *FIELD*, to another one, *VALUE*.

MACHINE

   $FILE(max\_rec, FIELD, VALUE)$

CONSTRAINTS

   $max\_rec \in \mathsf{NAT}_1$

VARIABLES

   file

INVARIANT

   $file \in \mathsf{seq}(FIELD \rightarrow VALUE)$ $\wedge$
   $\mathsf{size}(file) \leq max\_rec$

INITIALIZATION

   $file := []$

OPERATIONS

   $v \longleftarrow \mathsf{val\_file}(o, i)$ $\widehat{=}$
       PRE
           $o \in \mathsf{dom}(file)$ $\wedge$
           $i \in FIELD$
       THEN
           $v := file(o)(i)$
       END ;

   $\mathsf{mod\_file}(o, i, v)$ $\widehat{=}$
       PRE
           $o \in \mathsf{dom}(file)$ $\wedge$
           $i \in FIELD$ $\wedge$
           $v \in VALUE$
       THEN
           $file(o)(i) := v$
       END ;

The machine offers operations for modifying or accessing the value of a particular field of a certain record in the file, for enlarging the file, and a final operation returning the value of the file size.

OPERATIONS   (Cont'd)

$o \longleftarrow$ create_record $(v) \quad \widehat{=}$
  PRE
  $\quad v \in VALUE \quad \wedge$
  $\quad$ size $(file) < max\_rec$
  THEN
  $\quad\quad file := file \longleftarrow (INDEX \times \{v\}) \quad ||$
  $\quad\quad o := $ size $(file) + 1$
  END ;

$v \longleftarrow$ size_file $\quad \widehat{=}$
  BEGIN
  $\quad\quad v := $ size $(file)$
  END

END

The FILE_BUFFER Machine

In order to refine in a realistic way the above specification of our *FILE* machine, we introduce a so-called buffer, which is the part of the file that is supposed to reside in the core for further processing. Consequently, all changes or accesses to the file are made through the buffer. Thus we now have two variables instead of one. These variables are called *bfile* and *buffer* and they obey the following invariant showing that the domain of *buffer* is included in that of *bfile*:

$$bfile \in \mathsf{seq}(FIELD \rightarrow VALUE)$$

$$buffer \in \mathsf{dom}(bfile) \rightarrowtail (FIELD \rightarrow VALUE)$$

Our change of variable is then clearly the following:

$$file = bfile \lhd\!\!- buffer$$

As can be seen, the (abstract) *file* is equal to the (concrete) *bfile* overridden by the *buffer*. The variables *buffer* and *bfile* are encapsulated in a new machine called the *FILE_BUFFER* machine which is as follows:

MACHINE

    FILE_BUFFER(*max_rec*, *FIELD*, *VALUE*)

CONSTRAINTS

    $max\_rec \in \mathsf{NAT_1}$

VARIABLES

    buffer, *bfile*

INVARIANT

    $bfile \in \mathsf{seq}\,(FIELD \rightarrow VALUE) \quad \wedge$
    $buffer \in \mathsf{dom}\,(bfile) \rightarrowtail (FIELD \rightarrow VALUE)$

INITIALIZATION

    $sfile,\ buffer := [\,],\ \varnothing$

OPERATIONS

    $o \longleftarrow \mathsf{create\_record}\,(v) \quad \widehat{=}$
      PRE
        $v \in VALUE \quad \wedge$
        $\mathsf{size}\,(bfile) \neq max\_rec$
      THEN
        $bfile := bfile \leftarrow (INDEX \times \{v\}) \quad \|$
        $o := \mathsf{size}\,(bfile) + 1$
      END ;

    $\mathsf{load\_buffer}\,(o) \quad \widehat{=}$
      PRE
        $o \in \mathsf{dom}\,(bfile) \quad \wedge$
        $o \notin \mathsf{dom}\,(buffer)$
      THEN
        $bfile := bfile \lhd\!\!\!- buffer \quad \|$
        $buffer := \{\, o \mapsto bfile(o) \,\}$
      END ;

    $v \longleftarrow \mathsf{size\_file} \quad \widehat{=}$
      BEGIN $v := \mathsf{size}\,(bfile)$ END ;

OPERATIONS   (Cont'd)

$v \longleftarrow$ not_in_buffer (o) $\widehat{=}$
  PRE
    $o \in 1 .. \, \mathsf{size}(\mathit{bfile})$
  THEN
    $v := \mathsf{bool}(o \notin \mathsf{dom}(\mathit{buffer}))$
  END ;

mod_buffer (o, i, v) $\widehat{=}$
  PRE
    $o \in \mathsf{dom}(\mathit{buffer}) \; \wedge$
    $i \in \mathit{FIELD} \; \wedge$
    $v \in \mathit{VALUE}$
  THEN
    $\mathit{buffer}(o)(i) := v$
  END ;

$v \longleftarrow$ val_buffer (o, i) $\widehat{=}$
  PRE
    $o \in \mathsf{dom}(\mathit{buffer}) \; \wedge$
    $i \in \mathit{FIELD}$
  THEN
    $v := \mathit{buffer}(o)(i)$
  END

END

We are now ready to implement the *FILE* machine on the *FILE_BUFFER* machine.

IMPLEMENTATION

  $FILE\_1(max\_rec, \; FIELD, \; VALUE)$

REFINES

  $FILE$

IMPORTS

   $FILE\_BUFFER(max\_rec,\ FIELD,\ VALUE)$

PROMOTES

   create_record, size_file

INVARIANT

   $file\ =\ bfile \Leftaffect buffer$

OPERATIONS

   mod_file $(o, i, v)\ \ \widehat{=}$
       VAR *test* IN
           test ⟵ not_in_buffer (o);
           IF *test* = true THEN
               load_buffer (o)
           END;
           mod_buffer (o, i, v)
       END;

   v ⟵ val_file $(o, i)\ \ \widehat{=}$
       VAR *test* IN
           test ⟵ not_in_buffer (o);
           IF *test* = true THEN
               load_buffer (o)
           END;
           v ⟵ val_buffer (o, i)
       END

END

The FILE_ACCESS Machine

In order to refine the above *FILE_BUFFER* machine, we wish to optimize the movement of data between the *bfile* situated on the disk and the *buffer* situated in the core. Our intention is to have data written back on the *bfile*, but only when they have been modified in the *buffer*. For doing so, we introduce an extra (visible) boolean variable, *updated*, which guarantees, when it is false, that the *buffer* has not been changed (it is then indeed included in the *bfile*). When *updated* is true, it means that the *buffer* has been "touched". Its value might be left unchanged but we do not know. In any case, when *updated* is true, the *buffer* is not empty. The other variables are the same as before. As a consequence, our change of variable will clearly be the following:

$$
\begin{array}{l}
updated \in BOOL \\
updated = \mathsf{false} \quad \Rightarrow \quad buffer \subseteq bfile \\
updated = \mathsf{true} \quad \Rightarrow \quad buffer \neq \varnothing
\end{array}
$$

As in the previous section, we define a new machine, called the *FILE_ACCESS* machine. This machine will be imported by our future implementation of the *FILE_BUFFER* machine. The *FILE_ACCESS* machine offers specific operations to move a record from the *bfile* to the *buffer*, to copy the *buffer* on to the *bfile*, and to return the value of *updated*. The other operations handling the contents of the *buffer* are as for the *FILE_BUFFER* machine. Next is our machine:

MACHINE

    FILE_ACCESS (*max_rec*, *FIELD*, *VALUE*)

CONSTRAINTS

    $max\_rec \in \mathsf{NAT}_1$

VARIABLES

    bfile, *buffer*, *updated*

VISIBLE_VARIABLES

    updated

INVARIANT

    $bfile \in \mathsf{seq}\,(FIELD \rightarrow VALUE) \quad \wedge$
    $buffer \in \mathsf{dom}\,(bfile) \rightarrowtail (FIELD \rightarrow VALUE) \quad \wedge$
    $updated \in BOOL \quad \wedge$
    $updated = \mathsf{false} \quad \Rightarrow \quad buffer \subseteq bfile \quad \wedge$
    $updated = \mathsf{true} \quad \Rightarrow \quad buffer \neq \varnothing$

INITIALIZATION

    bfile, *buffer*, *updated*, := [], ∅, false

OPERATIONS

    get_record (*o*) ≙
        PRE
            o ∈ dom (*bfile*)
        THEN
            buffer := { *o* ↦ *bfile*(*o*) } ||
            updated := false
        END ;

    put_buffer ≙
        PRE
            updated = true
        THEN
            bfile := *bfile* ⧏ *buffer*
        END ;

    o ⟵ create_record (*v*) ≙
        PRE
            v ∈ *VALUE* ∧
            size (*bfile*) ≠ *max_rec*
        THEN
            bfile := *bfile* ← (*INDEX* × {*v*}) ||
            o := size (*bfile*) + 1
        END ;

    v ⟵ not_in_buffer (*o*) ≙
        PRE
            o ∈ 1 .. size (*bfile*)
        THEN
            v := bool (*o* ∉ dom (*buffer*))
        END ;

    mod_buffer (*o*, *i*, *v*) ≙
        PRE
            o ∈ dom (*buffer*) ∧
            i ∈ *FIELD* ∧
            v ∈ *VALUE*
        THEN
            buffer(*o*)(*i*) := *v* ||
            updated := true
        END ;

```
OPERATIONS   (Cont'd)

    v ⟵ val_buffer (o, i)  ≙
        PRE
            o ∈ dom (buffer) ∧
            i ∈ FIELD
        THEN
            v := buffer(o)(i)
        END ;

    v ⟵ size_file  ≙
        BEGIN
            v := size (bfile)
        END


END
```

We implement the *FILE_BUFFER* machine by importing the *FILE_ACCESS* machine. For the moment, we only implement the operation for loading the buffer. The other operations are directly promoted from the *FILE_ACCESS* machine.

```
IMPLEMENTATION

    FILE_BUFFER_1(max_rec, FIELD, VALUE)

REFINES

    FILE_BUFFER

IMPORTS

    FILE_ACCESS (max_rec, FIELD, VALUE)

PROMOTES

    create_record, not_in_buffer, mod_buffer,
    val_buffer, size_file
```

```
OPERATIONS

    load_buffer (o)   ≙
        BEGIN
            IF   updated = true   THEN
                    put_buffer
            END ;
            get_record (o)
        END


END
```

It remains for us to implement the *FILE_ACCESS* machine. For doing so, our idea is to replace the variable *buffer* by two concrete variables called *name* and *record*. We can do so, in fact, because *buffer* is a function with at most one pair. As we know, the domain of *buffer* is included in that of *bfile*. So, when *buffer* is not empty, the variable *name*, denoting the unique element of this domain, must be in the set $1..\text{size}\,(bfile)$. Also we choose to have the variable *name* equal to 0 when *buffer* is empty. The variable *record* denotes a total function from *FIELD* to *VALUE*. Next is our refinement.

```
REFINEMENT

    FILE_ACCESS_1(max_rec, FIELD, VALUE)

REFINES

    FILE_ACCESS

VARIABLES

    bfile

VISIBLE_VARIABLES

    updated, name, record
```

INITIALIZATION

    bfile, *updated*, *name* := [], false, 0 ||
    record :∈ *FIELD* → *VALUE*

INVARIANT

    name ∈ 0 .. size (*bfile*)   ∧
    record ∈ *FIELD* → *VALUE*   ∧
    buffer = {0} ◁ { *name* ↦ *record* }

OPERATIONS

    get_record (*o*) ≙
      BEGIN   *name*, *record*, *updated* := *o*, *bfile*(*o*), false   END;

    put_buffer ≙
      BEGIN   *bfile*(*name*) := *record*   END;

    o ⟵ create_record (*v*) ≙
      BEGIN
          bfile := *bfile* ← (*INDEX* × {*v*}) ||
          o := size (*bfile*) + 1
      END;

    mod_buffer (*o*, *i*, *v*) ≙
      BEGIN
          record(*i*) := *v* ||
          updated := true
      END;

    v ⟵ not_in_buffer (*o*) ≙ BEGIN   *v* := bool (*name* ≠ *o*)   END;

    v ⟵ size_file ≙ BEGIN   *v* := size (*bfile*)   END

END

We finally implement *FILE_ACCESS*_1 by importing *BASIC_FILE_VAR*.

IMPLEMENTATION

$FILE\_ACCESS\_2(max\_rec,\ FIELD,\ VALUE)$

REFINES

$FILE\_ACCESS\_1$

IMPORTS

$BASIC\_FILE\_VAR(max\_rec,\ FIELD,\ VALUE)$

VISIBLE_VARIABLES

updated, *name*

INVARIANT

$bfile = file\_vrb$ $\land$
$record = buf\_vrb$

INITIALIZATION

$updated := \mathsf{false}\,;$
$name := 0$

OPERATIONS

get_record (o) $\widehat{=}$
  BEGIN
    $name := o\,;$
    READ_FILE $(name)\,;$
    $updated := \mathsf{false}$
  END ;

put_buffer $\widehat{=}$
  BEGIN
    WRITE_FILE $(name)$
  END ;

OPERATIONS   (Cont'd)

$o \longleftarrow$ create_record(v) $\widehat{=}$
  BEGIN
      NEW_RECORD(v);
      $o \longleftarrow$ SIZE_FILE
  END;

mod_buffer(o, i, v) $\widehat{=}$
  BEGIN
      STR_BUFFER(i, v);
      updated := true
  END;

$v \longleftarrow$ not_in_buffer(o) $\widehat{=}$
  BEGIN
      $v :=$ bool$(o \neq name)$
  END;

$v \longleftarrow$ size_file $\widehat{=}$
  BEGIN
      $v \longleftarrow$ SIZE_FILE
  END

END

13.2.2. Machines for Objects

The TOTAL_OBJECT Machine

In this section our intention is to specify, and subsequently refine, a machine encapsulating a data-base of dynamic objects described by means of a number of *total* functions. The machine can handle at most *max_obj* objects, where *max_obj* is a scalar parameter of the machine. The number of objects created so far, at a given moment in the data-base, is denoted by a certain variable called *object*. As we cannot remove an object once created, we can name each object present in the data-base by using a number in the interval $1 .. object$ which we call *OBJECT*. When a new object is created (if possible), it is given the name *object* $+ 1$.

Objects are represented by means of various total functions from the set *OBJECT* to a certain set called *VALUE*. Each such total function corresponds to a member of a certain set called *FIELD*. As a consequence, these total functions are collectively represented by a variable *total_field* such that the following holds:

$$total\_field \; \in \; FIELD \rightarrow (OBJECT \rightarrow VALUE)$$

MACHINE

  $TOTAL\_OBJECT(max\_obj, \; FIELD, \; VALUE)$

CONSTRAINTS

  $max\_obj \in \mathsf{NAT}_1$

VARIABLES

  $total\_object, \; total\_field$

DEFINITIONS

  $OBJECT \; \widehat{=} \; 1 \mathbin{..} total\_object$

INVARIANT

  $total\_object \; \in \; 0 \mathbin{..} max\_obj \quad \wedge$
  $total\_field \; \in \; FIELD \rightarrow (OBJECT \rightarrow VALUE)$

INITIALIZATION

  $total\_object, \; total\_field \; := \; 0, \; FIELD \times \{\varnothing\}$

OPERATIONS

  $o \longleftarrow \mathsf{create\_total\_object}(v) \quad \widehat{=}$
    PRE
      $v \in VALUE \quad \wedge$
      $total\_object \neq max\_obj$
    THEN
      $total\_object := total\_object + 1 \quad ||$
      $total\_field := \lambda i \cdot (i \in FIELD \;|$
          $total\_field(i) \cup \{ (total\_object + 1) \mapsto v \}) \quad ||$
      $o := total\_object + 1$
    END;

Notice that the sets *FIELD* and *VALUE* are set formal parameters of the machine. The machine offers operations for creating a new object (with any values for the fields), and for modifying or accessing the fields of an object. Finally, we have an operation returning the number of already created objects.

OPERATIONS   (Cont'd)

mod_field (i, o, v) $\widehat{=}$
  PRE
       $i \in FIELD$ $\wedge$
       $o \in OBJECT$ $\wedge$
       $v \in VALUE$
  THEN
       $total\_field(i)(o) := v$
  END ;

$v \longleftarrow$ val_field (i, o) $\widehat{=}$
  PRE
       $i \in FIELD$ $\wedge$
       $o \in OBJECT$
  THEN
       $v := total\_field(i)(o)$
  END ;

$v \longleftarrow$ nbr_object $\widehat{=}$
       BEGIN $v := total\_object$ END

END

We now implement the *TOTAL_OBJECT* machine on the *FILE* machine of the previous section. The idea is to "transpose" the *total_field* function of our machine into the *file* sequence of the *FILE* machine. In fact, juxtaposing the *total_field* function and the *file* sequence, considered to be a total function with domain given by the interval $1 \mathbin{..} \mathsf{size}\,(file)$, we obtain:

$$total\_field \ \in \ FIELD \ \to \ ((1 \mathbin{..} total\_object) \to VALUE)$$

$$file \ \in \ (1 \mathbin{..} \mathsf{size}\,(file)) \to (FIELD \to VALUE)$$

By equating *total_object* and $\mathsf{size}\,(file)$, and transposing one into the other, we obtain the following obvious change of variable between the two:

$$file \ = \ \lambda o \cdot (o \in OBJECT \mid \lambda i \cdot (i \in FIELD \mid total\_field(i)(o)))$$

Next is our refinement:

IMPLEMENTATION

   $TOTAL\_OBJECT\_1(max\_obj,\ FIELD,\ VALUE)$

REFINES

   $TOTAL\_OBJECT$

IMPORTS

   $FILE(max\_obj,\ FIELD,\ VALUE)$

INVARIANT

   $file\ =\ \lambda o \cdot (o \in OBJECT\ |\ \lambda i \cdot (i \in FIELD\ |\ total\_field(i)(o)))$

OPERATIONS

   $o \longleftarrow$ create_total_object$(v)\ \ \hat{=}\ $ BEGIN $o \longleftarrow$ create_record$(v)\ $ END ;

   mod_field$(i, o, v)\ \ \hat{=}\ $ BEGIN   mod_file$(o,\ i,\ v)\ $ END ;

   $v \longleftarrow$ val_field$(i, o)\ \ \hat{=}\ $ BEGIN $v \longleftarrow$ val_file$(o,\ i)\ $ END ;

   $v \longleftarrow$ nbr_object $\ \hat{=}\ $ BEGIN $v \longleftarrow$ size_file   END

END

The *PARTIAL_OBJECT* Machine

We now present the specification, and the subsequent refinement, of a machine encapsulating a data-base of objects, described, this time, by means of *partial* functions. This machine, very similar to the one presented in the previous section, offers various operations to create an object and to modify or access an object's field (when that makes sense). It also offers two new operations due to the partialness of the fields: an operation to test whether an object's field is indeed defined and an operation to "remove" the field of an object. Notice that the range of possible "values" is now defined by the explicit interval *min_val* .. *max_val* where *min_val* and *max_val* are members of NAT (with *min_val* strictly smaller than maxint).

MACHINE

$PARTIAL\_OBJECT(max\_obj, max\_field, min\_val, max\_val)$

CONSTRAINTS

$max\_obj \in \text{NAT}_1 \quad \wedge$
$max\_field \in \text{NAT}_1 \quad \wedge$
$min\_val \in \text{NAT} \quad \wedge$
$max\_val \in \text{NAT} \quad \wedge$
$max\_val < \text{maxint}$

VARIABLES

$partial\_object, partial\_field$

DEFINITIONS

$FIELD \; \hat{=} \; 1 .. max\_field \;;$
$OBJECT \; \hat{=} \; 1 .. partial\_object \;;$
$VALUE \; \hat{=} \; min\_val .. max\_val$

INVARIANT

$partial\_object \in 0 .. max\_obj \quad \wedge$
$partial\_field \in FIELD \rightarrow (OBJECT \nrightarrow VALUE)$

INITIALIZATION

$partial\_object := 0 \quad ||$
$partial\_field := \varnothing$

OPERATIONS

$o \longleftarrow \text{create\_partial\_object} \; \hat{=}$
    PRE
        $partial\_object \neq max\_obj$
    THEN
        $partial\_object := partial\_object + 1 \quad ||$
        $o := partial\_object + 1$
    END ;

OPERATIONS   (Cont'd)

mod_field (i, o, v) $\widehat{=}$
> PRE
>> $i \in FIELD$ $\wedge$
>> $o \in OBJECT$ $\wedge$
>> $v \in VALUE$
> THEN
>> $partial\_field(i)(o) := v$
> END ;

rem_field (i, o) $\widehat{=}$
> PRE
>> $i \in FIELD$ $\wedge$
>> $o \in OBJECT$
> THEN
>> $partial\_field(i) := \{o\} \lhd partial\_field(i)$
> END ;

$v \longleftarrow$ def_field (i, o) $\widehat{=}$
> PRE
>> $i \in FIELD$ $\wedge$
>> $o \in OBJECT$
> THEN
>> $v := \mathrm{bool}\,(o \in \mathrm{dom}\,(partial\_field(i)))$
> END ;

$v \longleftarrow$ val_field (i, o) $\widehat{=}$
> PRE
>> $i \in FIELD$ $\wedge$
>> $o \in \mathrm{dom}\,(partial\_field(i))$
> THEN
>> $v := partial\_field(i)(o)$
> END ;

$v \longleftarrow$ nbr_object $\widehat{=}$ BEGIN $v := partial\_object$ END

END

Our intention is now to implement our *PARTIAL_OBJECT* machine on the *TOTAL_OBJECT* machine defined earlier in this section. The problem, of course, is then to transform the partial functions of the *PARTIAL_OBJECT* machine into the total functions of the *TOTAL_OBJECT* machine. The idea is to encode, in a special way, the fact that a field is not defined. There are various ways to do this. For example, we could have decided to use a (total) boolean function telling us, for each object and each field, whether the field in question is indeed defined. But, in our case, as the *max_val* parameter of the *PARTIAL_OBJECT* machine is guaranteed to be strictly smaller than maxint (remember the CONSTRAINTS clause of that machine), we can use maxint, as a "special" value, to encode the fact that the corresponding field is not defined for a specific object. Our implementation thus IMPORTS the *TOTAL_OBJECT* machine by instantiating its *VALUE* parameter with the interval *min_val*..maxint. So the change of variable between the two machines is then obviously the following:

$$\forall i \cdot (i \in FIELD \;\Rightarrow\; partial\_field(i) = total\_field(i) \rhd \{\, \mathsf{maxint} \,\})$$

Next is our implementation:

IMPLEMENTATION

    *PARTIAL_OBJECT_*1(*max_obj*, *max_field*, *min_val*, *max_val*)

REFINES

    PARTIAL_OBJECT

IMPORTS

    TOTAL_OBJECT(*max_obj*, 1..*max_field*, *min_val*.. maxint)

PROMOTES

    mod_field, val_field, nbr_object

INVARIANT

    partial_object = *total_object* ∧
    $\forall i \cdot (i \in (1..max\_field) \;\Rightarrow\; partial\_field(i) = total\_field(i) \rhd \{\, \mathsf{maxint} \,\})$

OPERATIONS

    $o \longleftarrow$ create_partial_object $\;\widehat{=}$
        BEGIN
            $o \longleftarrow$ create_total_object (maxint)
        END ;

```
┌─────────────────────────────────────────────────┐
│                                                  │
│   OPERATIONS   (Cont'd)                          │
│                                                  │
│      rem_field (i, o)   ≙                         │
│         BEGIN                                     │
│            mod_field (i, o, maxint)              │
│         END ;                                     │
│                                                  │
│      v ⟵ def_field (i, o)   ≙                     │
│         VAR   w   IN                              │
│            w ⟵ val_field (i, o);                  │
│            v := bool (w ≠ maxint)                │
│         END                                       │
│                                                  │
│                                                  │
│   END                                            │
│                                                  │
└─────────────────────────────────────────────────┘
```

Notice how we have ensured that each field of a newly created object is indeed undefined (has a value equal to maxint).

13.2.3. A Data-base

The DATA_BASE Machine

In this section we present the specification of the simple data-base of persons already studied in chapter 4. Before doing so, however, we show the two special machines *BASIC_SEX* and *BASIC_STATUS* that define operations for the correponding enumerated sets. A general model for such machines has been presented in section 13.1.4. Next is the *BASIC_SEX* machine.

```
┌─────────────────────────────────────────┐
│                                          │
│   MACHINE                                │
│                                          │
│      BASIC_SEX                           │
│                                          │
│   SETS                                   │
│                                          │
│      SEX = {man, woman}                  │
│                                          │
│   CONSTANTS                              │
│                                          │
│      code_SEX , decode_SEX               │
│                                          │
└─────────────────────────────────────────┘
```

PROPERTIES

$code\_SEX \in SEX \rightarrowtail \{0, 1\} \quad \land$
$decode\_SEX = code\_SEX^{-1}$

OPERATIONS

$r \longleftarrow$ SEX_READ $\;\widehat{=}\;$ BEGIN $\;r :\in SEX\;$ END;

SEX_WRITE $(i) \;\widehat{=}\;$ PRE $\;i \in SEX\;$ THEN skip END

END

The machine *BASIC_STATUS* is very similar to the previous one. We are now ready to present, once again, the *DATA_BASE* machine:

MACHINE

$DATA\_BASE$

SETS

$PERSON$

SEES

$BASIC\_SEX, BASIC\_STATUS$

CONSTANTS

max_pers

PROPERTIES

$max\_pers = \mathsf{card}\,(PERSON)$

VARIABLES

person, sex, status, mother, husband, wife

DEFINITIONS

$MAN \ \hat{=} \ sex^{-1}[\{man\}]$;
$WOMAN \ \hat{=} \ sex^{-1}[\{woman\}]$;
$LIVING \ \hat{=} \ status^{-1}[\{living\}]$;
$DEAD \ \hat{=} \ status^{-1}[\{dead\}]$;
$MARRIED \ \hat{=} \ \mathsf{dom}\,(husband \cup wife)$;
$SINGLE \ \hat{=} \ person - MARRIED$;
$ANGEL \ \hat{=} \ PERSON - person$

INVARIANT

$person \ \subseteq \ PERSON \quad \wedge$
$sex \ \in \ person \rightarrow SEX \quad \wedge$
$status \ \in \ person \rightarrow STATUS \quad \wedge$
$mother \ \in \ person \rightarrowtail (MARRIED \cap WOMAN) \quad \wedge$
$husband \ \in \ WOMAN \rightarrowtail MAN \quad \wedge$
$wife \ = \ husband^{-1}$

INITIALIZATION

$person \ := \ \varnothing \quad ||$
$sex \ := \ \varnothing \quad ||$
$status \ := \ \varnothing \quad ||$
$mother \ := \ \varnothing \quad ||$
$husband \ := \ \varnothing \quad ||$
$wife \ := \ \varnothing$

OPERATIONS

death $(p) \quad \hat{=}$
    PRE $\quad p \in LIVING \quad$ THEN $\quad status(p) := dead \quad$ END ;

marriage $(bride, groom) \quad \hat{=}$
    PRE
        $bride \in SINGLE \cap WOMAN \quad \wedge$
        $groom \in SINGLE \cap MAN$
    THEN
        $husband(bride) := groom \quad ||$
        $wife(groom) := bride$
    END ;

OPERATIONS

$baby \longleftarrow \text{first\_human}(s) \quad \widehat{=}$
    PRE
        $ANGEL \neq \varnothing \quad \wedge$
        $s \in SEX$
    THEN
        ANY *angel* WHERE
           $angel \in ANGEL$
        THEN
           $person := person \cup \{angel\} \quad ||$
           $status(angel) := living \quad ||$
           $sex(angel) := s \quad ||$
           $baby := angel$
        END
    END ;

$baby \longleftarrow \text{new\_born}(s,m) \quad \widehat{=}$
    PRE
        $ANGEL \neq \varnothing \quad \wedge$
        $s \in SEX \quad \wedge$
        $m \in MARRIED \cap WOMAN$
    THEN
        ANY *angel* WHERE
           $angel \in ANGEL$
        THEN
           $person := person \cup \{angel\} \quad ||$
           $status(angel) := living \quad ||$
           $sex(angel) := s \quad ||$
           $mother(angel) := m \quad ||$
           $baby := angel$
        END
    END ;

$report \longleftarrow \text{not\_saturated} \quad \widehat{=}$
    BEGIN $report := \text{bool}(ANGEL \neq \varnothing) \quad$ END ;

$report \longleftarrow \text{is\_present}(p) \quad \widehat{=}$
    PRE $p \in PERSON \quad$ THEN $report := \text{bool}(p \in person) \quad$ END ;

$report \longleftarrow \text{is\_living}(p) \quad \widehat{=}$
    PRE $p \in person \quad$ THEN $report := \text{bool}(p \in LIVING) \quad$ END ;

$report \longleftarrow \text{is\_woman}(p) \quad \widehat{=}$
    PRE $p \in person \quad$ THEN $report := \text{bool}(p \in WOMAN) \quad$ END ;

OPERATIONS (Cont'd)

   report ⟵ is_married (p) $\hat{=}$
      PRE $p \in person$ THEN *report* := bool $(p \in MARRIED)$ END;

   report ⟵ has_mother (p) $\hat{=}$
      PRE $p \in person$ THEN *report* := bool $(p \in$ dom $(mother))$ END;

   v ⟵ val_status (p) $\hat{=}$
      PRE $p \in person$ THEN $v := status(p)$ END;

   v ⟵ val_sex (p) $\hat{=}$
      PRE $p \in person$ THEN $v := sex(p)$ END;

   v ⟵ val_spouse (p) $\hat{=}$
      PRE $p \in MARRIED$ THEN $v := (husband \cup wife)(p)$ END;

   v ⟵ val_mother (p) $\hat{=}$
      PRE $p \in$ dom $(mother)$ THEN $v := (mother)(p)$ END;

   p ⟵ PERSON_read $\hat{=}$ BEGIN $p :\in PERSON$ END;

   PERSON_write (p) $\hat{=}$
      PRE $p \in PERSON$ THEN skip END

END

For refining this *DATA_BASE*, we IMPORT the *PARTIAL_OBJECT* machine. The *PARTIAL_OBJECT* machine will be instantiated as follows. The first formal parameter, *max_obj*, is instantiated to 10000, meaning that the *DATA_BASE* cannot handle more than that number of persons. The second parameter, *max_field*, is instantiated to 4. This corresponds to the 4 "attributes" of a person, namely *sex*, *status*, *mother* and *spouse*. The third and fourth parameters, *min_val* and *max_val*, are respectively instantiated to 0 and 10000. In this way, the 4 fields of the *PARTIAL_OBJECT* machine could contain elements of the interval 1 .. 10000 (corresponding to the possible persons) and elements of the interval 0 .. 1 (corresponding to the coding intervals of the enumerated sets *SEX* and *STATUS*). The interval 0 .. 1 is the range of both bijections *code_SEX* and *code_STATUS* that allow us to transform elements of the corresponding enumerated sets into numbers. Next is our implementation:

IMPLEMENTATION

DATA_BASE_1

REFINES

DATA_BASE

IMPORTS

PARTIAL_OBJECT(10000, 4, 0 , 10000)

SEES

BASIC_IO , *BASIC_SEX* , *BASIC_STATUS*

VALUES

$PERSON = 1 .. 10000;$
$max\_pers = 10000$

INVARIANT

$person = 1 .. object \quad \wedge$
$partial\_field(1) = (sex \; ; code\_SEX) \quad \wedge$
$partial\_field(2) = (status \; ; code\_STATUS) \quad \wedge$
$partial\_field(3) = mother \quad \wedge$
$partial\_field(4) = husband \cup wife$

OPERATIONS

death $(p) \quad \hat{=}$
   BEGIN
      mod_field $(2, p, code\_STATUS(dead))$
   END ;

marriage $(bride, groom) \quad \hat{=}$
   BEGIN
      mod_field $(4, bride, groom);$
      mod_field $(4, groom, bride)$
   END ;

OPERATIONS   (Cont'd)

$baby \longleftarrow$ first_human $(s) \quad \widehat{=}$
    BEGIN
        $baby \longleftarrow$ create_partial_object;
        mod_field $(1, baby, code\_SEX(s))$;
        mod_field $(2, baby, code\_STATUS(living))$
    END;

$report \longleftarrow$ not_saturated $\quad \widehat{=}$
    VAR n IN
        $n \longleftarrow$ nbr_object;
        $report := $ bool $(n \neq max\_pers)$
    END;

$baby \longleftarrow$ new_born $(s, m) \quad \widehat{=}$
    BEGIN
        $baby \longleftarrow$ create_partial_object;
        mod_field $(1, baby, code\_SEX(s))$;
        mod_field $(2, baby, code\_STATUS(living))$;
        mod_field $(3, baby, m)$
    END;

$report \longleftarrow$ is_present $(p) \quad \widehat{=}$
    VAR n IN
        $n \longleftarrow$ nbr_object;
        $report := $ bool $(p \leq n)$
    END;

$report \longleftarrow$ is_living $(p) \quad \widehat{=}$
    VAR s IN
        $s \longleftarrow$ val_field $(2, p)$;
        $report := $ bool $(s = code\_STATUS(living))$
    END;

$report \longleftarrow$ is_woman $(p) \quad \widehat{=}$
    VAR s IN
        $s \longleftarrow$ val_field $(1, p)$;
        $report := $ bool $(s = code\_SEX(woman))$
    END;

$report \longleftarrow$ is_married $(p) \quad \widehat{=}$
    BEGIN $report \longleftarrow$ def_field $(4, p)$ END;

OPERATIONS (Cont'd)

$report \longleftarrow$ has_mother (p) $\;\widehat{=}$
  BEGIN $report \longleftarrow$ def_field $(3, p)$ END;

$v \longleftarrow$ val_status (p) $\;\widehat{=}$
  VAR S IN
    $s \longleftarrow$ val_field $(2, p)$;
    $v := decode\_STATUS(s)$
  END;

$v \longleftarrow$ val_sex (p) $\;\widehat{=}$
  VAR S IN
    $s \longleftarrow$ val_field $(1, p)$;
    $v := decode\_SEX(s)$
  END;

$v \longleftarrow$ val_spouse (p) $\;\widehat{=}$
  BEGIN $v \longleftarrow$ val_field $(4, p)$ END;

$v \longleftarrow$ val_mother (p) $\;\widehat{=}$
  BEGIN $v \longleftarrow$ val_field $(3, p)$ END;

$p \longleftarrow$ PERSON_read $\;\widehat{=}$
  BEGIN $p \longleftarrow$ INTERVAL_READ $(1, max\_pers)$ END;

PERSON_write (p) $\;\widehat{=}$
  BEGIN INT_WRITE (p) END

END

13.2.4. Interfaces

The QUERY Machine

The rôle of the *QUERY* machine is to encapsulate completely the communication between an external user and the data-base. It offers a number of operations delivering output parameters whose intended rôle is to serve as input parameters for the operations death, marriage, new_born and first_human of the *DATA_BASE* machine. Such output parameters must therefore obey the pre-conditions of these operations. As this will not always be possible (in case the user enters wrong values), each operation of the *QUERY* machine provides an extra boolean output parameter. When such a parameter has the value true then the other output parameters are *guaranteed* to obey the pre-condition of the corresponding operation. Next is the *QUERY* machine which SEES the *DATA_BASE* machine. Notice the high degree of non-determinacy.

MACHINE

   QUERY

SEES

   DATA_BASE, *BASIC_SEX*, *BASIC_STATUS*

OPERATIONS

   $p, b \longleftarrow$ get_new_dead_person $\;\widehat{=}$
     CHOICE
       $p :\in LIVING$ $\|$
       $b :=$ true
     OR
       $p :\in PERSON$ $\|$
       $b :=$ false
     END ;

   $s, b \longleftarrow$ get_sex_of_new $\;\widehat{=}$
     BEGIN
       $s :\in SEX$ $\|$
       $b :=$ bool$(ANGEL \neq \varnothing)$
     END ;

   get_and_print_person $\;\widehat{=}$ skip ;

   $m, w, b \longleftarrow$ get_new_couple $\;\widehat{=}$
     CHOICE
       $m :\in SINGLE \cap MAN$ $\|$
       $w :\in SINGLE \cap WOMAN$ $\|$
       $b :=$ true
     OR
       $m :\in PERSON$ $\|$
       $w :\in PERSON$ $\|$
       $b :=$ false
     END ;

OPERATIONS   (Cont'd)

$\quad s, w, b \longleftarrow$ get_sex_and_mother $\;\widehat{=}$
$\qquad$ CHOICE
$\qquad\quad s :\in SEX \quad ||$
$\qquad\quad w :\in MARRIED \cap WOMAN \quad ||$
$\qquad\quad b := \mathsf{bool}\,(ANGEL \neq \varnothing)$
$\qquad$ OR
$\qquad\quad s :\in SEX \quad ||$
$\qquad\quad w :\in PERSON \quad ||$
$\qquad\quad b := \mathsf{false}$
$\qquad$ END

END

Next is the implementation of the above machine:

IMPLEMENTATION
$\quad QUERY\_1$
REFINES
$\quad QUERY$
SEES
$\quad DATA\_BASE,\ BASIC\_IO,\ BASIC\_SEX,\ BASIC\_STATUS$
OPERATIONS

$\quad p, b \longleftarrow$ get_new_dead_person $\;\widehat{=}$
$\qquad$ BEGIN
$\qquad\quad$ STRING_WRITE ("Mother Id: ");
$\qquad\quad p \longleftarrow$ PERSON_read;
$\qquad\quad b \longleftarrow$ is_present (p);
$\qquad\quad$ IF $\;b = \mathsf{false}\;$ THEN
$\qquad\qquad$ STRING_WRITE ("Person does not exist\n")
$\qquad\quad$ ELSE
$\qquad\qquad b \longleftarrow$ is_living (p);
$\qquad\qquad$ IF $\;b = \mathsf{false}\;$ THEN
$\qquad\qquad\quad$ STRING_WRITE ("Person must be alive\n")
$\qquad\qquad$ END
$\qquad\quad$ END
$\qquad$ END;

OPERATIONS   (Cont'd)

$s, b \longleftarrow$ get_sex_of_new $\;\widehat{=}$
   BEGIN
      STRING_WRITE ("Sex: ");
      $s \longleftarrow$ SEX_READ;
      $b \longleftarrow$ not_saturated;
      IF $b =$ false   THEN
         STRING_WRITE ("System full\n");
      END
   END ;

$s, w, b \longleftarrow$ get_sex_and_mother $\;\widehat{=}$
BEGIN
   STRING_WRITE ("Sex: ");
   $s \longleftarrow$ SEX_READ;
   STRING_WRITE ("Mother Id: ");
   $w \longleftarrow$ PERSON_read;
   $b \longleftarrow$ is_present (w);
   IF $b =$ false   THEN
      STRING_WRITE ("Person does not exist\n")
   ELSE
      $b \longleftarrow$ is_woman (w);
      IF $b =$ false   THEN
         STRING_WRITE ("Person must be a woman\n")
      ELSE
         $b \longleftarrow$ is_married (w);
         IF $b =$ false   THEN
            STRING_WRITE ("Person must be married\n")
         ELSE
            $b \longleftarrow$ not_saturated;
            IF $b =$ false   THEN
               STRING_WRITE ("System full\n");
            END
         END
      END
   END
END ;

```
OPERATIONS  (Cont'd)

    m, w, b ⟵ get_new_couple  ≙
        VAR  pm, pw, bm, bms, bw, bws  IN
            b := true;
            STRING_WRITE ("Man Id: ");
            m ⟵ PERSON_read;
            STRING_WRITE ("Woman Id: ");
            w ⟵ PERSON_read;
            pm ⟵ is_present (m);
            pw ⟵ is_present (w);
            IF  pm = false  THEN
                b := false;
                STRING_WRITE ("First person does not exist\n")
            END;
            IF  pw = false  THEN
                b := false;
                STRING_WRITE ("Second person does not exist\n")
            END;
            IF  b = true  THEN
                bm ⟵ is_woman (m);
                bms ⟵ is_married (m);
                bw ⟵ is_woman (w);
                bws ⟵ is_married (w);
                IF  bm = true  THEN
                    b := false;
                    STRING_WRITE ("First person must be a man\n")
                END;
                IF  bms = true  THEN
                    b := false;
                    STRING_WRITE ("First person must not be married\n")
                END;
                IF  bw = false  THEN
                    b := false;
                    STRING_WRITE ("Second person must be a woman\n")
                END;
                IF  bws = true  THEN
                    b := false;
                    STRING_WRITE ("Second person must not be married\n")
                END
            END
        END;
```

OPERATIONS   (Cont'd)

    get_and_print_person $\hat{=}$
       VAR p, b, v, u, w, tt IN
         STRING_WRITE (`"Person Id: "`);
         $p \longleftarrow$ PERSON_read;
         $b \longleftarrow$ is_present (p);
         IF $b =$ false   THEN
            STRING_WRITE (`"Person does not exist\n"`)
         ELSE
            STRING_WRITE (`"\n Person: "`);
            PERSON_write (p);
            STRING_WRITE (`"\n Sex: "`);
            $v \longleftarrow$ val_sex (p);
            SEX_WRITE (v);
            STRING_WRITE (`"\n Status: "`);
            $u \longleftarrow$ val_status (p);
            STATUS_WRITE (u);
            $b \longleftarrow$ has_mother (p);
            IF $b =$ true   THEN
               STRING_WRITE (`"\n Mother: "`);
               $w \longleftarrow$ val_mother (p);
               PERSON_write (w)
            END;
            $b \longleftarrow$ is_married (p);
            IF $b =$ true   THEN
               STRING_WRITE (`"\n Spouse: "`);
               $tt \longleftarrow$ val_spouse (p);
               PERSON_write (tt)
            END
         END
       END

  END

The *INNER_INTERFACE* Machine

The variable-free *INNER_INTERFACE* machine offers five operations called death_operation, marriage_operation, first_operation, birth_operation and print_operation. The implementations of the first four operations will correspond to "safe" versions of the corresponding operations of the *DATA_BASE* machine. At the present specification level, however, they are just specified as skip. Although very weak, these specifications must nevertheless be implemented by operations that "terminate". Next is the *INNER_INTERFACE* machine:

```
MACHINE

    INNER_INTERFACE

OPERATIONS

    death_operation  ≙  skip;

    marriage_operation  ≙  skip;

    first_operation  ≙  skip;

    birth_operation  ≙  skip;

    print_operation  ≙  skip

END
```

We now implement the *INNER_INTERFACE* machine in a straightforward way, by importing the *DATA_BASE* machine and the *QUERY* machine:

```
IMPLEMENTATION

    INNER_INTERFACE_1

REFINES

    INNER_INTERFACE

IMPORTS

    DATA_BASE, QUERY

OPERATIONS

    death_operation  ≙
        VAR  p, b  IN
            p, b  ⟵  get_new_dead_person;
            IF  b = true  THEN
                death (p)
            END
        END ;
```

```
OPERATIONS
    marriage_operation  ≙
        VAR   w, m, b   IN
            m, w, b  ⟵  get_new_couple ;
            IF   b = true   THEN
                marriage (w, m)
            END
        END ;

    first_operation  ≙
        VAR   s, b, p   IN
            s, b  ⟵  get_sex_of_new ;
            IF   b = true   THEN
                p  ⟵  first_human (s)
            END
        END ;

    birth_operation  ≙
        VAR   w, s, b, p   IN
            s, w, b  ⟵  get_sex_and_mother ;
            IF   b = true   THEN
                p  ⟵  new_born (s, w)
            END
        END

    print_operation  ≙
        BEGIN   get_and_print_person   END

END
```

The final machine, the *MAIN_INTERFACE* machine, is also variable-free. It has a single operation, main, specified, again, as skip:

```
MACHINE

    MAIN_INTERFACE

OPERATIONS

    main  ≙  skip

END
```

We now implement the *MAIN_INTERFACE* machine. This is done by importing the *INNER_INTERFACE* and also the following *BASIC_COMMAND* machine, which is a special case of the general machine already presented in section 13.1.4 for enumerated sets.

MACHINE

    BASIC_COMMAND

SETS

    $COMMAND = \{\, new,\ birth,\ marriage,\ death,\ print,\ quit \,\}$

CONSTANTS

    $code\_COMMAND,\ decode\_COMMAND$

PROPERTIES

    $code\_COMMAND \in COMMAND \rightarrowtail\!\!\!\rightarrow \{0, 1, 2, 3, 4, 5\} \quad \wedge$
    $decode\_COMMAND = code\_COMMAND^{-1}$

OPERATIONS

    $r \longleftarrow$ COMMAND_READ $\;\widehat{=}$
      BEGIN
        $r :\in COMMAND$
      END **;**

    COMMAND_WRITE $(i) \;\widehat{=}$
      PRE
        $i \in COMMAND$
      THEN
        skip
      END

END

The implementation of main contains the "main loop" of our system. Notice that we have a local variable, x, initialized to maxint and decremented within the loop. In this way, we can prove that our implementation of main indeed terminates and thus refines skip.

IMPLEMENTATION

    *MAIN_INTERFACE*_1

REFINES

    MAIN_INTERFACE

IMPORTS

    INNER_INTERFACE,
    BASIC_COMMAND,
    BASIC_SEX,
    BASIC_STATUS,
    BASIC_IO

OPERATIONS

```
main  ≙
    VAR  c, x  IN
        c ⟵ COMMAND_READ ;
        x := maxint ;
        WHILE  (c ≠ quit) ∧ (x ≠ 0)  DO
            CASE  c  OF
                EITHER  new  THEN
                    first_operation
                OR  birth  THEN
                    birth_operation
                OR  marriage  THEN
                    marriage_operation
                OR  death  THEN
                    death_operation
                OR  print  THEN
                    print_operation
                END
            END ;
            c ⟵ COMMAND_READ ;
            x := x − 1
        INVARIANT
            x ∈ NAT
        VARIANT
            x
        END
    END
```

END

13.3. A Library of Useful Abstract Machines

In this section our intention is to give some directions on how to build, from the bottom up, a library of useful machines. Machines in this library will ultimately be implemented on the *BASIC* machines of section 13.1. The library is organized as follows. First, we build an *ARITHMETIC* machine containing a series of operations for calculating (fast) exponentiation, logarithms (by defect and by excess), square root, etc. Such operations are realized by means of the algorithms developed in chapter 10. Then we build a series of machines encapsulating some simple data-struture variables: these are the *ARRAY_VAR* machine, the *SEQUENCE_VAR* machine and the *SET_VAR* machine. Finally, we define a series of machines handling dynamic collections of variables: these are the *ARRAY_COLLECTION*, the *SEQUENCE_COLLECTION*, the *SET_COLLECTION* and the *TREE_VAR* machines.

13.3.1. The *ARRAY_VAR* Machine

This machine encapsulates a single array (that is a total function from one finite set to another). It contains operations for swapping two elements, for searching an element according to various criteria, for shifting consecutive elements in various ways, for filling the array with a specific element, etc. It can be extended with operations to reverse the array and to sort it in various ways.

13.3.2. The *SEQUENCE_VAR* Machine

This machine encapsulates a single finite sequence. It is quite similar to the previous one (on which it is implemented). Besides those of that machine, it has some specific operations for acquiring the size of the sequence, and for extending and shrinking the sequence in various ways. The maximum size of the sequence could be a parameter of the machine. Alternatively, this can be left undefined at the specification level. In the latter case, some of the operations should provide a boolean result telling whether they have been successful or not.

13.3.3. The *SET_VAR* Machine

This machine encapsulates a single finite set. It offers elementary operations for acquiring the cardinal of the set, for adding or removing an element, for testing for the presence of an element (according to certain criteria), and for resetting the set. Besides the set variable, the specification contains another variable which is a permutation of the set. This allows one to easily define an external iteration on the set. The permutation is supposed to be non-deterministically reordered by each operation modifying the set. This machine is implemented on the previous one, and like the previous one, we might have different ways of handling the problem of the maximum size of the set.

13.3.4. The *ARRAY_COLLECTION* Machine

This machine handles a dynamic collection of fixed-size arrays. We have the ability to create a new array in the collection or to remove an already created array from the collection.

This machine inherits the operations of the *ARRAY_VAR* machine (although with an extra parameter defining which array is concerned). It may also have operations dealing with two or more arrays in various ways (comparison, element-by-element product or sum, etc.).

As we have supposed that the sizes of all the dynamic arrays are the same, it is easy to implement that machine on the *ARRAY_VAR* machine.

13.3.5. The *SEQUENCE_COLLECTION* Machine

The rôle of this machine is to record dynamic sequences. Operations are offered to create a new (empty) sequence and to remove a sequence. This machine inherits the operations of the *SEQUENCE_VAR* machine (although with an extra parameter defining which sequence is concerned). It may also have operations dealing with two or more sequences in various ways (comparison, element by element product or sum, concatenation, overriding, etc.).

As an implementation, the sequences are simply stored in a sequence of sequences of a certain size corresponding to the overall number, *max_obj* (a parameter of the machine), of sequences (be they dead or live). At the beginning, all *max_obj* sequences are considered dead. We also suppose that the "memory" has a limited size. This means that the sum of the sizes of all the live sequences is smaller than or equal to a certain value, *maxmem* (a dead sequence is supposed to be empty).

Next are some suggestions for implementing the previous machine on a simpler one, *SIMPLE_SEQUENCE_COLLECTION*, which offers parts of the operations of the previous one. This simpler machine, like the previous one, also handles a sequence of sequences, say *tt*. But, this time, its size is only smaller than or equal to *max_obj* because this machine is not concerned with the dead sequences. It has however the same limitation concerning the memory size *maxmem*.

We can then proceed with the implementation of the machine *SEQUENCE_COLLECTION*. It is done on the machines *SIMPLE_SEQ-UENCE_COLLECTION* and *SEQUENCE_VAR*. The latter encapsulates a single sequence containing those dead sequences that are included in the domain of *tt*. The other dead sequences are, implicitly, those sequences that are not members of the domain of *tt*.

Then we refine the *SIMPLE_SEQUENCE_COLLECTION* machine. We can do so by considering that each sequence of the collection is associated with another sequence, called its "gap". When a sequence is made smaller, the corresponding gap is augmented accordingly. Conversely, when a sequence is made bigger, a certain non-empty gap is made smaller in order to acquire some room. Moreover, we suppose that we have an extra "dummy" sequence (therefore a "dummy" gap too) situated at the end of the sequence of sequences. Thanks to this dummy sequence, the sum of the sizes of the sequences and of their gaps is now exactly equal to *maxmem*. Finally, a new variable (yet another sequence), *siz*, contains the sum of the size of the sequences of *tt*. The technical choice we suggest for refining the previous refinement is to implement it on a flat memory, *mem*, which is a sequence of size *maxmem*. The various sequences composing the sequence of sequences *tt* and their gaps are disposed, next to each other, on *mem* as shown in the following figure:

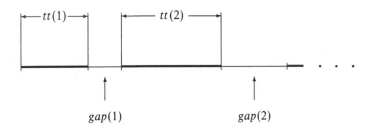

In order to be able to access each individual sequence $tt(i)$, we introduce three extra variables called *adr*, *len* and *gap*. The variable *adr* denotes a sequence of size $n + 1$ where n is the size of the original sequence of sequences *tt*. The variable *len* denotes a sequence of size n handling the sizes of the individual sequences of *tt*. Finally, the variable *gap* denotes a sequence of size n handling the sizes of the various gaps. All this can be summarized in the following figure:

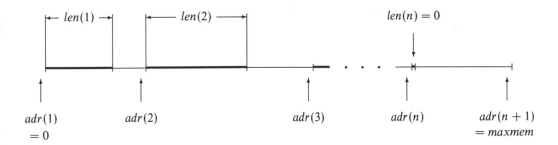

The expression $adr(i)$ (for i in $1..n$) denotes the address of *mem* preceeding that where the sequence $tt(i)$ starts (note that, quite naturally, $adr(1)$ is equal to 0). The nth sequence stored in *mem* is the dummy sequence of size 0. Finally, $adr(n + 1)$ is exactly equal to *maxmem* which, itself, is equal to the last address of the memory *mem*. Obviously, the following relation must hold in order for the various sequences to be able to be stored in the memory:

$$\forall i \cdot (i \in 1..n \;\Rightarrow\; adr(i) + len(i) + gap(i) \;=\; adr(i+1))$$

13.3.6. The *SET_COLLECTION* Machine

In this section we present a *SET_COLLECTION* machine whose rôle is to record finite sets. The machine has a number of limitations: the number of sets is equal to *max_obj* and the sum of the cardinals of these sets must not exceed *maxmem*. Among these *max_obj* sets, some of them are considered to be "dead". By construction, the dead sets are empty. Operations are offered to create a set (a dead one is then chosen non-deterministically), to remove a set (which thus becomes dead again, and also empty), and to perform various classical operations on sets. The sets are simply "stored" in a sequence of sets of size *max_obj*.

The *SET_COLLECTION* machine can be implemented in a straightforward fashion on the above *SEQUENCE_COLLECTION* machine.

13.3.7. The *TREE_VAR* Machine

In this section we present a tree machine whose rôle is to record a finite tree. The number of nodes of the tree is limited to *maxnode*. Operations are offered to perform various classical operations on the tree.

MACHINE

   TREE_VAR(*VALUE*, *initval*, *maxnode*)

CONSTRAINTS

   $initval \in VALUE \quad \wedge$
   $maxnode \in \mathsf{NAT}_1$

DEFINITIONS

   $NODE \;\widehat{=}\; (1..maxnode)$

VARIABLES

   tr, nd

INVARIANT

   $tr \in \mathsf{tree}(VALUE) \quad \wedge$
   $nd \in \mathsf{dom}(tr) \rightarrowtail NODE$

INITIALIZATION

$$tr := \{ [ ] \mapsto initval \}$$

OPERATIONS

$n \longleftarrow$ SIZE_TREE $\;\widehat{=}\;$
  BEGIN $n := \mathsf{card}\,(\mathsf{dom}\,(tr))$ END ;

$n \longleftarrow$ ROOT_TREE $\;\widehat{=}\;$
  BEGIN $n := nd([ ])$ END ;

$v \longleftarrow$ VAL_TREE (n) $\;\widehat{=}\;$
  PRE
   $n \in \mathsf{ran}\,(nd)$
  THEN
   $v := tr(nd^{-1}(n))$
  END ;

STR_TREE (n, v) $\;\widehat{=}\;$
  PRE
   $n \in \mathsf{ran}\,(nd)$ $\wedge$
   $v \in VALUE$
  THEN
   $tr(nd^{-1}(n)) := v$
  END ;

$m \longleftarrow$ SON_TREE (n, i) $\;\widehat{=}\;$
  PRE
   $n \in \mathsf{ran}\,(nd)$ $\wedge$
   $i \in 1\,..\,\mathsf{arity}\,(tr)(nd^{-1}(n))$
  THEN
   $m := \mathsf{son}\,(tr)(nd^{-1}(n))(i)$
  END ;

$m \longleftarrow$ FATHER_TREE (n) $\;\widehat{=}\;$
  PRE
   $n \in \mathsf{ran}\,(nd)$ $\wedge$
   $nd^{-1}(n) \neq [ ]$
  THEN
   $m := \mathsf{father}\,(tr)(nd^{-1}(n))$
  END ;

OPERATIONS   (Cont'd)

$r \longleftarrow$ RANK_TREE (n) $\widehat{=}$
   PRE
       $n \in \mathrm{ran}\,(nd) \quad \wedge$
       $nd^{-1}(n) \neq [\,]$
   THEN
       $r := \mathrm{rank}\,(tr)(nd^{-1}(n))$
   END ;

$a \longleftarrow$ ARITY_TREE (n) $\widehat{=}$
   PRE
       $n \in \mathrm{ran}\,(nd)$
   THEN
       $a := \mathrm{arity}\,(tr)(nd^{-1}(n))$
   END ;

PSH_TREE (n,v) $\widehat{=}$
   PRE
       $n \in \mathrm{ran}\,(nd) \quad \wedge$
       $v \in VALUE \quad \wedge$
       $NODE - \mathrm{ran}\,(nd) \neq \varnothing$
   THEN
       ANY m WHERE
           $m \in NODE - \mathrm{ran}\,(nd)$
       THEN
           $tr(nd^{-1}(n) \leftarrow (\mathrm{arity}\,(tr)(nd^{-1}(n)) + 1)) := v \ ||$
           $nd(m) := nd^{-1}(n) \leftarrow (\mathrm{arity}\,(tr)(nd^{-1}(n)) + 1)$
       END
   END ;

POP_TREE (n) $\widehat{=}$
   PRE
       $n \in \mathrm{ran}\,(nd) \quad \wedge$
       $\mathrm{arity}\,(tr,n) \neq 0 \quad \wedge$
       $\mathrm{arity}\,(tr, \mathrm{son}\,(tr)(n)(\mathrm{arity}\,(tr,n))) = 0$
   THEN
       $tr := \{nd^{-1}(n) \leftarrow (\mathrm{arity}\,(tr)(nd^{-1}(n)))\} \vartriangleleft tr \ ||$
       $nd := \{nd^{-1}(n) \leftarrow (\mathrm{arity}\,(tr)(nd^{-1}(n)))\} \vartriangleleft nd$
   END

END

The operation PSH_TREE (n, v) appends a new singleton sub-tree labelled with v to the sequence of son sub-trees of node n. The operation POP_TREE (n) removes the last sub-tree (supposed to exist) from the sequence of sub-trees of node n. Next is a straightforward refinement of the previous machine.

REFINEMENT
   $TREE\_VAR\_1(VALUE, initval, maxnode)$
REFINES
   $TREE\_VAR$
VARIABLES
   $node, root, val, sons, father, rank$
INVARIANT
   $node \in \mathbb{P}(NODE)$ ∧
   $root \in NODE$ ∧
   $val \in node \to VALUE$ ∧
   $sons \in node \to \text{seq}(node)$ ∧
   $father \in (node - \{root\}) \to node$ ∧
   $rank \in (node - \{root\}) \to \text{NAT1}$ ∧
   $node = \text{ran}(nd)$ ∧
   $root = nd([])$ ∧
   $val = (nd^{-1}; tr)$ ∧
   $sons = (nd^{-1}; \text{son}(tr); \text{cmp}(nd))$ ∧
   $father = (nd^{-1}; \text{father}(tr))$ ∧
   $rank = (nd^{-1}; \text{rank}(tr))$
INITIALIZATION
   ANY m WHERE
      $m \in NODE$
   THEN
      $node := \{m\}$ ||
      $root := m$ ||
      $val := \{m \mapsto initval\}$ ||
      $sons := \{m \mapsto []\}$ ||
      $father := \varnothing$ ||
      $rank := \varnothing$
   END
OPERATIONS

   $n \longleftarrow$ SIZE_TREE $\cong$
      BEGIN $n := \text{card}(node)$ END;

   $n \longleftarrow$ ROOT_TREE $\cong$
      BEGIN $n := root$ END;

OPERATIONS

$v \longleftarrow$ VAL_TREE (n) $\widehat{=}$
BEGIN $v := val(n)$ END;

STR_TREE (n, v) $\widehat{=}$
BEGIN $val(n) := v$ END;

$m \longleftarrow$ SON_TREE (n, i) $\widehat{=}$
BEGIN $m := sons(n)(i)$ END;

$m \longleftarrow$ FATHER_TREE (n) $\widehat{=}$
BEGIN $m := father(n)$ END;

$r \longleftarrow$ RANK_TREE (n) $\widehat{=}$
BEGIN $r := rank(n)$ END;

$a \longleftarrow$ ARITY_TREE (n) $\widehat{=}$
BEGIN $a := \text{size}(sons(n))$ END;

PSH_TREE (n, v) $\widehat{=}$
ANY m WHERE
$\quad m \in NODE - node$
THEN
$\quad node := node \cup \{m\}$ ||
$\quad val(m) := v$ ||
$\quad sons := sons \mathbin{\lhd\mkern-9mu-} \{ n \mapsto (sons(n) \leftarrow m), \, m \mapsto [\,] \}$ ||
$\quad father(m) := n$ ||
$\quad rank(m) := \text{size}(sons(n)) + 1$
END;

POP_TREE (n) $\widehat{=}$
LET m BE
$\quad m = \text{last}(sons(n))$
IN
$\quad node := node - \{m\}$ ||
$\quad val := \{m\} \mathbin{\lhd\mkern-9mu-} val$ ||
$\quad sons := \{m\} \mathbin{\lhd\mkern-9mu-} sons \mathbin{\lhd\mkern-9mu-} \{ n \mapsto \text{front}(sons(n)) \}$ ||
$\quad father := \{m\} \mathbin{\lhd\mkern-9mu-} father$ ||
$\quad rank := \{m\} \mathbin{\lhd\mkern-9mu-} rank$
END

END

We leave it to the reader to implement the previous refinement by means of the *ARRAY_COLLECTION* machine and the *SEQUENCE_COLLECTION* machine.

13.4. Case Study: Boiler Control System

13.4.1. Introduction

The problem that we address in this case study is to design a system capable of controlling the water level in a steam boiler. The correct behaviour of such a system is very important because a boiler can be seriously damaged if its water level is either too low or too high.

The function of the system is thus to maintain the water level in the boiler between two pre-defined thresholds. Besides this main function, the system must also maintain safety by shutting the boiler down in extreme cases. Finally, the system must be able to withstand some failures, by continuing to operate while part of the equipment is malfunctioning, until it is repaired.

The informal specification to come is a simplification of a specification [1] written by J.C. Bauer for the Institute of Risk Research of the University of Waterloo (Ontario) (it has been passed to me by the Institut de Protection et de Sûreté Nucléaire, which I would like to thank).

The main goal of this case study is to make explicit the *methodology* that is used while analyzing and constructing the system.

Here is a summary of the contents of this study. Section 13.4.2 will contain the Informal Specification of the system as it could have been produced by the "client". Sections 13.4.3 and 13.4.4 are called respectively System Analysis and System Synthesis. Both these sections constitute a *very important pre-requisite* to the next one. In the System Analysis section, we make the informal specification more precise by rephrasing it in a more formal setting: the model of the system is thus sketched step by step through a number of definitions of its main variables and constants, and through a number of equations establishing their relationships. In the System Synthesis section, the idea is to study the previous equations in order to establish a typology of the variables (input, output, persistent, local) and also an "order of abstraction". This is done as a means to prepare some systematic rationale for the future design.

Section 13.4.5 contains the Formal Specification and Design of the system. In that section, we explore an approach in which specifying and designing are not clearly separated as is usually recommended. The idea is to make a "non-flat" specification using the technique of refinement as a means of introducing the *details of the specifications of the problem* step by step. This departs, in a sense, from the well-known classical use of refinement, which is often understood as a means of introducing only the *details of implementation of the problem* step by step. In section 13.4.6, a summary of the architecture is presented. Finally, in section 13.4.7, we investigate the very frequent practical situation where a change in the specification occurs after the solution of the problem has been finalized.

13.4.2. Informal Specification

Physical Environment

As far as our problem is concerned, the boiler can be abstracted to a certain reservoir, the boiler itself, within which water can be poured through a pump, and out of which steam can exit in order to activate an engine. Besides this basic "hardware", we have a number of sensors whose rôle is to measure relevant data: the water level, the rate of outgoing steam, the rate of incoming water. The physical environment thus consists of the following devices:

- the boiler,

- the water level measuring equipment,

- the outgoing steam rate measuring equipment,

- the pump, together with an incoming water rate measuring equipment,

- the message transmission system,

- the terminal,

- the computer.

Simplified Behaviour of the System

The computer program that controls the boiler is to work on a "cycle" basis. Each such cycle can be *viewed* as consisting of three successive phases:

- In the first phase, a number of messages are received from the physical environment through the tramsmission system: among other things, such messages can contain information on the water level in the boiler, on the rate of outgoing steam and on the rate of incoming water (throughput of the pump).

- In the second phase, these messages are analyzed and a number of decisions are taken. In fact, the program controls the system in the following way: if the water level in the boiler is *too high*, the program decides to close the pump. Conversely, if it is *too low*, the program decides to open the pump. Otherwise (when the water level is neither too low nor too high), the program does nothing (that is, does not change the present status of the pump). Notice, finally, that when the water level is *far too high* or *far too low*, the program decides to shut the system down.

- In the third phase, a number of messages are transmitted back to the physical environment through the transmission system: among other things, such messages contain the order to open or close the pump.

Measurement of incoming water rate and outgoing steam rate

Notice that, a priori, the only necessary measurement is that of the water level. This is because the decision to open or close the pump only depends on the comparison of the water level measurement with pre-defined thresholds (too low or too high). As we have already remarked however, the outgoing steam rate and the incoming water rate are also measured and sent to the program. This is for two reasons:

- At the end of each cycle, such measurements, together with the order sent to the pump, allow us to calculate the next *expected* value of the water level.

- At the beginning of each cycle, the *raw* water level value, as received in the incoming message, is compared with the expected water level value, as calculated at the previous cycle. This may allow us to detect, in case there is a serious discrepancy between the two, that the water level measurement equipment has failed. The raw level is thus *adjusted* (replaced by the calculated value), so that the "mission" of the system can continue until the water level measurement equipment is repaired.

Equipment Failure

Of course, the introduction of extra measurements also introduces the possibility that the corresponding pieces of equipment may themselves fail. More precisely, the following pieces of equipment can be broken:

- the water level measuring equipment,

- the outgoing steam rate measuring equipment,

- the incoming water rate measuring equipment (the pump).

The decision whether part of the equipment has failed is determined by the program by comparing the incoming *raw* measurement with a *calculated* expected measurement based on the dynamics of the system. When a part is considered broken by the program, the following sequence of actions is supposed to take place between the program and the physical environment:

- The program sends a certain "failure" message to the physical environment.

- An operator is supposed to read this message and repair the faulty equipment.

- When the repair is completed, the operator is supposed to send a certain "repair" message to the program.

- In between these two (failure and repair) messages, the program considers that the equipment in question is broken and thus *ignores* the corresponding information. It replaces the missing information by an *estimatate* based on the calculated dynamics of the physical system.

System Shutdown

In some special circumstances to follow, the program may decide to shut the system down:

- The water level is *far too low* or *far too high.*

- The water level measuring equipment and the steam rate measuring equipment are *simultaneously* broken.

- The transmission system is suspect. This is decided by the program according to a number of criteria, which depend on the equipment:

  - From the point of view of the water level measuring equipment, the transmission system is considered broken when either the value of the raw water level is greater than the maximum capacity of the boiler or when the water level equipment repair message is received while the corresponding equipment has not been detected as broken (aberrant repair message).

  - From the point of view of the steam rate measuring equipment, the transmission system is considered broken when either the value of the raw steam rate is greater than a pre-defined maximum steam rate or when the steam rate equipment repair message is received while the corresponding equipment has not been detected as broken (aberrant repair message).

  - From the point of view of the water rate measuring equipment, the transmission system is considered broken when the water rate equipment repair message is received while the corresponding equipment has not been detected as broken (aberrant repair message).

Messages

Here is a list of the messages that the system may receive at each cycle:

IncomingMessage	Comment
Pump_State(b)	b is open or closed
Water_Level(n)	n is a number (this message must always be present)
Steam_Rate(n)	n is a number (this message must always be present)

IncomingMessage
Pump_Repaired
Water_Level_Repaired
Steam_Rate_Repaired

Here is a list of the messages that the system may send at each cycle:

OutgoingMessage	Comment
Open_Pump	should not be contradictory with next message
Close_Pump	should not be contradictory with previous message
Pump_Failed	
Water_Level_Failed	
Steam_Rate_Failed	
System_Shut_Down	

Notice that it must not be possible to send contradictory pump messages (to close and to open the pump simultaneously).

Constants and Units

In order to simplify matters, the main unit will be the *litre*. The water level is characterized by a number of constants, which are the following:

Constant	Unit	Comment
Maximum Capacity	litre	Boiler volume
Upper Safety Limit	litre	Beyond this limit, shut down
Lower Safety Limit	litre	Below this limit, shut down
Upper Functioning Limit	litre	Beyond this limit, closing pump
Lower Functioning Limit	litre	Below this limit, opening pump

The steam rate is characterized by the following constants. Such constants will be useful to determine the calculated dynamics of the system:

Constant	Unit
Maximum Steam Rate	litre/sec
Maximum Positive Steam Rate Gradient	litre/sec/sec
Maximum Negative Steam Rate Gradient	litre/sec/sec

The pump is characterized by the following constant:

Constant	Unit
Pump Rate	litre/sec

13.4.3. System Analysis

In this section our intention is to make more precise the various technical elements we have only introduced informally in the previous sections.

Water Level

In what follows, we shall adopt the following naming conventions for the constants and variables that deal with the water level:

Acronym	Expansion	Comment
leh	level extremal high	Maximum Capacity
lsh	level safety high	Upper Safety Limit
lsl	level safety low	Lower Safety Limit
lfh	level function high	Upper Functioning Limit
lfl	level function low	Lower Functioning Limit
lr	level raw	Level as delivered in the message

As we shall see, the variable that corresponds to the water level, as delivered in the incoming message, might be corrupted if the corresponding equipment is broken. In that case, this raw value is adjusted and replaced by an *interval* of "measured" values calculated at the previous cycle (for the sake of simplicity, in the case where the equipment is not considered to be broken, we nevertheless have such "measured" values, which are then both identical to the raw value). Notice that the equipment is considered broken if the raw value does not lie within the interval of the values calculated at the previous cycle. The precise way in which these values are calculated is defined below. All this corresponds to the following extra state variables:

Acronym	Expansion	Comment
lmh	level measured high	Upper adjusted level (for this cycle)
lml	level measured low	Lower adjusted level (for this cycle)
lch	level calculated high	Upper calculated level (for next cycle)
lcl	level calculated low	Lower calculated level (for next cycle)

Outgoing Steam Rate

Likewise, we shall adopt the following naming conventions for the constants and variables that deal with the steam rate:

Acronym	Expansion	Comment
seh	steam extremal high	Maximum Steam Rate
sdi	steam delta increase	Maximum Positive Steam Rate Gradient
sdd	steam delta decrease	Maximum Negative Steam Rate Gradient
sr	steam raw	Steam rate as delivered in the message

As for the water level, the variable that corresponds to the steam rate, as delivered in the incoming message, might be corrupted if the corresponding equipment is broken. In that case, the raw value is replaced by an *interval* of "measured" values, which has been calculated at the previous cycle. The precise way in which these values are calculated is defined below. All this corresponds to the following extra state variables:

Acronym	Expansion	Comment
smh	steam measured high	Upper adjusted steam rate (for this cycle)
sml	steam measured low	Lower adjusted steam rate (for this cycle)
sch	steam calculated high	Upper calculated steam rate (for next cycle)
scl	steam calculated low	Lower calculated steam rate (for next cycle)

Incoming Water Rate

Finally, we have the following names for the constant water nominal rate and for the variable that denotes the water rate:

Acronym	Expansion	Comment
wnr	water nominal rate	Pump rate
wr	water raw	Water rate as delivered in the message

As previously, the variable that corresponds to the water rate, as delivered in the incoming message, might be corrupted if the pump is broken. In that case, the raw value is replaced by an *interval* of "measured" values, which has been calculated at the previous cycle. That interval of values will also be used to validate the incoming raw value. The precise way in which these values are calculated is defined below. All this corresponds to the following extra state variables:

Acronym	Expansion	Comment
wmh	water measured high	Upper adjusted water rate (for this cycle)
wml	water measured low	Lower adjusted water rate (for this cycle)
wch	water calculated high	Upper calculated water rate (for next cycle)
wcl	water calculated low	Lower calculated water rate (for next cycle)

Function and Safety

The rôle of the program is to ensure the normal function of the system while maintaining its safety. This can be summarized in the following three laws. The first two are the function laws, and the third is the safety law:

Level Too Low
⇔
Pump Opening

Level Too High
⇔
Pump Closing

Level Safe ∧
Equipments Safe
⇔
Boiler Ok

In order to formalize the above laws, we shall introduce the following extra boolean variables:

Acronym	Expansion
pop	pump opening (message)
pcl	pump closing (message)

Acronym	Expansion
bok	boiler (is) OK (message)
lvs	level safe
eqs	equipment safe

Notice that, for the pump order not to be contradictory, we must have the following constraint making it impossible to open and close the pump at the same time:

$$pop = \text{true} \quad \Rightarrow \quad pcl = \text{false}$$

The third law can then be made more formal as follows:

Variable	Translation
bok	$\text{bool}(\,lvs = \text{true} \;\wedge\; eqs = \text{true}\,)$

It remains for us to formalize the above predicates in terms of the proposed constants and variables of the system. The values of the boolean variables *pop* and *pcl* can be calculated by comparing the interval $lml \mathrel{..} lmh$ of measured values with the pre-defined threshold interval $lfl \mathrel{..} lfh$. Since the *low* values are, by construction, smaller than or equal to the *high* values, we have, a priori, 6 possible cases as follows:

Case	RelativePositions				Decision
1	*lml*	*lmh*	*lfl*	*lfh*	Opening pump
2	*lml*	*lfl*	*lmh*	*lfh*	Opening pump
3	*lml*	*lfl*	*lfh*	*lmh*	?
4	*lfl*	*lml*	*lmh*	*lfh*	Do nothing
5	*lfl*	*lml*	*lfh*	*lmh*	Closing pump
6	*lfl*	*lfh*	*lml*	*lmh*	Closing pump

As can be seen, in case 3, the interval of "measured" levels, *lml* .. *lmh*, includes that of the two thresholds *lfl* .. *lfh*. In other words, in that case, the two measured values depart too much from each other. Since we have no reason to either open or close the pump, we have then no choice but to decide to "Do nothing" as in case 4. Consequently, we have the following translations:

Variable	Translation
pop	bool (*lml* < *lfl* ∧ *lmh* ≤ *lfh*)
pcl	.bool (*lml* ≥ *lfl* ∧ *lmh* > *lfh*)

Notice that the condition *pop* = true ⇒ *pcl* = false is indeed satisfied. For the safety law, we have the following translation for the safe level:

Variable	Translation
lvs	bool (*lml* ∈ *lsl* .. *lsh* ∧ *lcl* ∈ *lsl* .. *lsh*)

In other words, we consider that the levels are safe (so that shut-down is not required) when the measured levels (for the present cycle) and the calculated values (for the next cycle) are all situated inside the safety levels.

Equipment Failure

In order to formally translate the "Equipment safe" informal predicate denoted by the predicate *eqs* = true, we need a few more state variables. We might first have some boolean state variables recording the status of the various parts of the equipment:

Acronym	Expansion	Comment
lok	level OK	Water level measuring equipment status
sok	steam OK	Steam rate measuring equipment status
wok	water pump OK	Water pump status
tok	transmission OK	Transmission status

We consider that the equipment is safe (so that shut-down is not required) when the transmission system is safe and when at least one of the two measuring devices is safe. Formally:

Variable	Translation
eqs	bool (*tok* = true ∧ (*lok* = true ∨ *sok* = true))

It remains for us to formalize the precise conditions under which the program can decide that some part of the equipment is safe, and also the conditions under which we have to transmit equipment failure messages. In order to formalize this, we shall need more *boolean* variables recording the fact that certain incoming messages are present, and the fact that certain outgoing messages are necessary. These are the following for the incoming messages:

Acronym	Expansion	Comment
lim	level information message	Presence of a water level message
lrm	level repair message	Presence of a level repair message
sim	steam information message	Presence of a steam rate message
srm	steam repair message	Presence of a steam repair message
wim	water information message	Presence of a water rate message
wrm	water repair message	Presence of a water repair message

And we have the following for the outgoing messages:

Acronym	Expansion	Comment
lfm	level failure message	Necessity of a water level failure message
sfm	steam failure message	Necessity of a steam failure message
wfm	water failure message	Necessity of a water failure message

For the water level, steam rate or pump measuring equipment, we have the following conditions asserting safety:

Variable	Translation
lok	bool (*lr* $\in$ *lcl* .. *lch* $\wedge$ (*lok* $=$ true $\vee$ *lrm* $=$ true))
sok	bool (*sr* $\in$ *scl* .. *sch* $\wedge$ (*sok* $=$ true $\vee$ *srm* $=$ true))
wok	bool (*wr* $\in$ *wcl* .. *wch* $\wedge$ (*wok* $=$ true $\vee$ *wrm* $=$ true))

In other words, the level measuring equipment is considered safe if the incoming level message conveys a value *lr* that is inside the possible range of values calculated during the previous cycle, always provided that the water level measuring equipment was not considered broken at the previous cycle (*lok* $=$ true), unless it has just been declared repaired in a corresponding repair message at the present cycle (*lrm* $=$ true). That last piece of clause formalizes the fact that a broken equipment remains broken until a corresponding repair message is received. We have similar conditions for the steam rate measuring equipment and for the pump.

We now define the formal conditions for the necessity of some failure messages for the measuring equipment:

Variable	Translation
lfm	bool (*lr* $\notin$ *lcl* .. *lch* $\wedge$ (*lok* $=$ true $\vee$ *lrm* $=$ true))
sfm	bool (*sr* $\notin$ *scl* .. *sch* $\wedge$ (*sok* $=$ true $\vee$ *srm* $=$ true))
wfm	bool (*wr* $\notin$ *wcl* .. *wch* $\wedge$ (*wok* $=$ true $\vee$ *wrm* $=$ true))

In other words, a level failure message is necessary if the incoming level message conveys a value that is not inside the possible range of values calculated during the previous cycle (the equipment is thus not safe), always provided that the water level measuring equipment was not considered broken at the previous cycle, unless it has just been declared repaired in a corresponding repair message. This second clause formalizes the fact that, once a failure message has been sent, we do not want to send additional messages until a corresponding repair message is received. We have similar conditions for the steam rate measuring equipment and for the pump.

The failure of the transmission system can be formalized as follows:

Variable	Translation
tok	$\mathsf{bool}\,(\,ltk = \mathsf{true} \;\land\; stk = \mathsf{true} \;\land\; wtk = \mathsf{true}\,)$

The three boolean variables *ltk*, *stk*, and *wtk* are supposed to denote the "contribution" of the various devices to the transmission system. In other words, we have several ways, depending on the equipment (water level, steam or pump), to detect whether the transmission system is safe or not. We thus have the following definitions:

Variable	Translation
ltk	$\mathsf{bool}\,(\,lim = \mathsf{true} \;\land\; lr \le leh \;\land\; (lok = \mathsf{false} \;\lor\; lrm = \mathsf{false}\,))$
stk	$\mathsf{bool}\,(\,sim = \mathsf{true} \;\land\; sr \le seh \;\land\; (sok = \mathsf{false} \;\lor\; srm = \mathsf{false}\,))$
wtk	$\mathsf{bool}\,(\,wok = \mathsf{false} \;\lor\; wrm = \mathsf{false}\,)$

For instance, we consider that the transmission system is safe (from the point of view of the water level equipment) when the water level message is present, the transmitted raw level is smaller than or equal to the maximum capacity of the boiler, and either we have no level repair message or the water level equipment is broken. The last clause formalizes the fact that a level repair message appearing while the level measuring equipment is safe is considered to be a transmission failure (aberrant message). We have similar conditions for the steam rate information and for the pump.

System Dynamics

The dynamics of the system expresses how the (adjusted) measured values are determined at each cycle in terms of the previous calculated values. Likewise, it is expressed how the next calculated values are determined in terms of the present measured values.

(a) Measured values

The water level measured values are both equal to the raw value in case the water level measuring equipment is not determined to be broken in the present cycle and provided a level message has been received, otherwise they are equal to the previous calculated values. We have similar equalities for the other measured variables:

Variable	Translation
lml, lmh	$\begin{cases} lr, lr & \text{if } lok = \text{true} \land lim = \text{true} \\ lcl, lch & \text{otherwise} \end{cases}$
sml, smh	$\begin{cases} sr, sr & \text{if } sok = \text{true} \land sim = \text{true} \\ scl, sch & \text{otherwise} \end{cases}$
wml, wmh	$\begin{cases} wr, wr & \text{if } wok = \text{true} \land wim = \text{true} \\ wcl, wch & \text{otherwise} \end{cases}$

(b) Calculated values

The calculated values of the water level (for the next cycle) are simply defined from the three first terms of the series expansion, taking account of the steam rate and its extreme gradients (note that dt denotes the cycle time):

Variable	Translation
lcl	$lml - smh \times dt - \frac{sdi \times dt^2}{2} + wml \times dt$
lch	$lmh - sml \times dt + \frac{sdd \times dt^2}{2} + wmh \times dt$

The calculated values of the steam rate are defined from the two first terms of the series expansion, taking account of the extreme gradients of the steam rate:

Variable	Translation
scl	$sml - sdd \times dt$
sch	$smh + sdi \times dt$

Finally, the calculated values of the water rate are as follows:

Variable	Translation
wcl	$\begin{cases} 0 & \text{if } wok = \text{false } \lor pcl = \text{true } \lor (pop = \text{false } \land wml = 0) \\ wnr & \text{otherwise} \end{cases}$
wch	$\begin{cases} wnr & \text{if } wok = \text{false } \lor pop = \text{true } \lor (pcl = \text{false } \land wmh = wnr) \\ 0 & \text{otherwise} \end{cases}$

In other words, the calculated *low* incoming water rate (for the present cycle) is 0 if and only if either (1) the pump was considered broken at the previous cycle (since, in that case, we have *no information* and thus estimate that the *worst minimal* throughput is 0), or (2) when the order to close the pump was given at the previous cycle (the calculated throughput must then be 0) or (3) the order to open the pump was not given at the previous cycle and the measured low value of the throughput at the previous cycle was already 0 (in that case, it must then so remain in the absence of any order).

We have a similar rationale for the calculated *high* incoming water rate (for the present cycle). It is equal to the nominal pump rate *wnr* if and only if either (1) the pump was considered broken at the previous cycle (since, in that case, we have *no information* and thus estimate that the *worst maximal* throughput is *wnr*) or (2) when the order to open the pump was given at the previous cycle (the calculated throughput must then be *wnr*) or (3) the order to close the pump was not given at the previous cycle and the measured high value of the throughput at the previous cycle was already *wnr* (in that case, it must then so remain in the absence of any order).

13.4.4. System Synthesis

Before engaging in the proper formal specification and design of the system in the next section, we would like to prepare the future architecture by studying the relationship that holds between the variables we have determined in the previous sections. This can be summarized in certain tables with two columns: the left column contains the left-hand part of the "equations" we have determined in the previous sections, while the right-hand columns contain the corresponding dynamic definitions.

In order to emphasize with precision what the right-hand column values are, that is those values of the variables determined either at the previous cycle or at the present cycle, we subscript the former with a 0, and we prime the latter. And the lines of each table are ordered systematically according to the following constraints (which anticipate the possibility of finding some sequential program for implementing what is expressed in these tables):

If a *primed variable* appearing in the right column of a certain current line in a table also appears in the left column of a certain line of the same table, then that line is necessarily situated above the current line.

The variables *subscripted with* 0 are all, of course, situated in the right columns. When such a variable appears in a certain line, it also appears primed either in the left column of the same line or in some lines situated below the current line.

Our first table concerns the most "abstract" variables:

bok'	$\mathsf{bool}\,(\,lvs' = \mathsf{true}\ \wedge\ eqs' = \mathsf{true}\,)$
pop'	$\mathsf{bool}\,(\,lmh' \leq lfh\ \wedge\ lml' < lfl\,)$
pcl'	$\mathsf{bool}\,(\,lmh' > lfh\ \wedge\ lml' \geq lfl\,)$
lvs'	$\mathsf{bool}\,(\,lml' \geq lsl\ \wedge\ lmh' \leq lsh\ \wedge\ lcl' \geq lsl\ \wedge\ lch' \leq lsh\,)$

The next table is concerned with the water level:

ltk'	$\mathsf{bool}\,(\,lim' = \mathsf{true}\ \wedge\ lr' \leq leh\ \wedge\ (lok_0 = \mathsf{false}\ \vee\ lrm' = \mathsf{false}\,))$
lfm'	$\mathsf{bool}\,(\,lr' \notin lcl_0 \mathbin{..} lch_0\ \wedge\ (lok_0 = \mathsf{true}\ \vee\ lrm' = \mathsf{true}\,))$
lok'	$\mathsf{bool}\,(\,lr' \in lcl_0 \mathbin{..} lch_0\ \wedge\ (lok_0 = \mathsf{true}\ \vee\ lrm' = \mathsf{true}\,))$
lml', lmh'	$\begin{cases} lr', lr' & \text{if } lok' = \mathsf{true}\ \wedge\ lim' = \mathsf{true} \\ lcl_0, lch_0 & \text{otherwise} \end{cases}$
lcl'	$lml' - smh' \times dt - \frac{sdi \times dt^2}{2} + wml'$
lch'	$lmh' - sml' \times dt + \frac{sdd \times dt^2}{2} + wmh'$
eqs'	$\begin{aligned}\mathsf{bool}\,(\,ltk' = \mathsf{true}\ &\wedge\ stk' = \mathsf{true}\ \wedge\ wtk' = \mathsf{true}\ \wedge \\ (\,lok' = \mathsf{true}\ &\vee\ sok' = \mathsf{true}\,))\end{aligned}$

Now comes the table concerned with the steam measurement equipment:

stk'	$\mathsf{bool}\,(\,sim' = \mathsf{true}\ \wedge\ sr' \leq seh\ \wedge\ (sok_0 = \mathsf{false}\ \vee\ srm' = \mathsf{false}\,))$
sfm'	$\mathsf{bool}\,(\,sr' \notin scl_0 \mathbin{..} sch_0\ \wedge\ (sok_0 = \mathsf{true}\ \vee\ srm' = \mathsf{true}\,))$
sok'	$\mathsf{bool}\,(\,sr' \in scl' \mathbin{..} sch'\ \wedge\ (sok_0 = \mathsf{true}\ \vee\ srm' = \mathsf{true}\,))$
sml', smh'	$\begin{cases} sr', sr' & \text{if } sok' = \mathsf{true}\ \wedge\ sim' = \mathsf{true} \\ scl_0, sch_0 & \text{otherwise} \end{cases}$
scl', sch'	$sml' - sdd \times dt,\ smh' + sdi \times dt$

Finally, we have the table concerned with the pump:

wcl'	$\begin{cases} 0 & \text{if} \quad \begin{aligned} & wok_0 = \text{false} \quad \vee \quad pcl_0 = \text{true} \quad \vee \\ & (pop_0 = \text{false} \quad \wedge \quad wml_0 = 0) \end{aligned} \\ wnr & \text{otherwise} \end{cases}$
wch'	$\begin{cases} wnr & \text{if} \quad \begin{aligned} & wok_0 = \text{false} \quad \vee \quad pop_0 = \text{true} \quad \vee \\ & (pcl_0 = \text{false} \quad \wedge \quad wmh_0 = wnr) \end{aligned} \\ 0 & \text{otherwise} \end{cases}$
wtk'	$\text{bool}(wok_0 = \text{false} \quad \vee \quad wrm' = \text{false})$
wfm'	$\text{bool}(wr' \notin wcl'..wch' \quad \wedge \quad (wok_0 = \text{true} \quad \vee \quad wrm' = \text{true}))$
wok'	$\text{bool}(wr' \in wcl'..wch' \quad \wedge \quad (wok_0 = \text{true} \quad \vee \quad wrm' = \text{true}))$
wml', wmh'	$\begin{cases} wr', wr' & \text{if} \quad wok' = \text{true} \quad \wedge \quad wim' = \text{true} \\ wcl', wch' & \text{otherwise} \end{cases}$

Notice that, contrary to what has been done previously for the water level and steam variables, here the calculated values are determined from certain values determined at the *previous* cycle. Likewise the measured values are defined in terms of the calculated values determined at the *same* cycle: this is because the calculated values depend on the pump orders (pcl_0 and pop_0) of the previous cycle (technically, it would have been a little more difficult to use the pump orders determined at the same cycle).

By carefully studying the previous tables, we can determine the following kinds of objects:

- The outputs: this corresponds to primed identifiers that are present in the left columns but not in the right ones. We have 4 of them:

$$bok, \ lfm, \ sfm, \ wfm$$

- The persistent variables: this corresponds to identifiers that are present in the left columns and also in the right columns where they are subscripted with a 0 (and perhaps also primed). We have 11 of them:

$$pop, \ pcl, \ lcl, \ lch, \ lok, \ scl, \ sch, \ sok, \ wml, \ wmh, \ wok$$

- The internal variables: this corresponds to identifiers that are present in the left columns and also in the right columns, where they appear primed only. We have 11 of them:

$$lvs, \ eqs, \ ltk, \ lml, \ lmh, \ stk, \ sml, \ smh, \ wtk, \ wcl, \ wch$$

- The inputs: this corresponds to identifiers that are not present in the left columns, only in the right columns, where they appear primed only. We have 8 of them:

$$lim, \ lr, \ lrm, \ sim, \ sr, \ srm, \ wr, \ wrm$$

- The constants: this corresponds to identifiers that are only present in the right columns, where they appear plain. We have 10 of them:

$$leh, \ lsl, \ lsh, \ lfl, \ lfh, \ seh, \ sdi, \ sdd, \ wnr, \ dt$$

In all, we have 44 different objects. Notice that we have, more or less, what is expected intuitively: the inputs correspond exactly to the incoming messages, the outputs correspond to some of the outgoing messages (*pop* and *pcl* are missing), and finally, the persistent variables correspond to the state of each sensor (level, steam, and pump). We only have a *slight irregularity* in that the pump outgoing messages (*pop* and *pcl*) are also persistent variables: this is because we need their previous values in order to calculate the pump calculated value.

13.4.5. Formal Specification and Design

What is already clear, from the analysis and synthesis presented in the previous sections, is that the structure of the "data" of this problem is almost non-existent (boolean or integers). Likewise, the structure of the "algorithms" is elementary (simple arithmetic calculations). In spite of that, what makes this problem an interesting one, even a challenging one, is the complexity of the relationships holding between the variables. This is also what makes this problem quite representative of what might be encountered in practice.

Our purpose in the forthcoming construction is thus to make clear the way we are going to approach the problem via a certain methodology designed to meet that challenge: in other words, we would like develop our architecture in such a way as to control systematically the problem of the complexity of the relationships between the variables. Moreover, we would like to be sure that the proposed architecture can "resist" modifications of the external specifications that might be imposed by the client (a very frequently encountered situation in practice): in the next section, we shall propose such modifications.

The formal model that we shall present in this section corresponds to the specification and design of only *one cycle* of the execution of the system. The main idea of our formal approach is to construct our model by working *backwards*. In other words, we shall start from what we would like to achieve at the end of a cycle, namely the generation of a number of outgoing messages to be sent to the outside environement in order to control the boiler. We shall then refine this first, very abstract and non-deterministic, specification by formalizing the way the messages in question are elaborated step by step, thus taking account of more details in the problem. In doing so, we shall be guided by the system synthesis performed in the previous section. You will notice that, in applying this methodology, we proceed by establishing, more or less simultaneously, the specification of some parts of the system as well as the design of others. Again, this is accomplished by working *against the flow of control* that will eventually take place during the execution of a cycle. Notice that, in order to simplify the presentation of the forthcoming machines, we omit to write their INITIALIZATIONS.

The Cycle_A Machine

In our first machine, only a single operation is specified, which generates non-deterministically the main outgoing messages in the form of a number of boolean variables:

MACHINE

    *Cycle_A_*1

VISIBLE_VARIABLES

    pop, pcl, bok

INVARIANT

    pop, pcl, bok $\in$ BOOL $\times$ BOOL $\times$ BOOL

OPERATIONS

    main_A $\widehat{=}$
        BEGIN *pop, pcl, bok* $:\in$ BOOL $\times$ BOOL $\times$ BOOL END

END

As can be seen, we have taken a low profile as far as the invariant and the abstract operation of this machine are concerned. We shall adopt this style throughout: in other words, the invariants will all be typing invariants and the abstract operations will all be operations maintaining these typing invariants in a non-deterministic way. The "intelligence" of the problem will be put into the operations only. The main reason for adopting this style is one of space.

    Clearly, a different style where the various invariants were richer, perhaps straightforward copies of the tables of previous sections, could have been adopted. Likewise, the abstract operations could have been defined as maintaining these richer invariants. By doing so, of course, one would have had to prove that the concrete operations indeed implement the abstract ones, thus validating these operations. We encourage the reader to try this second style.

Implementation of the Cycle_A Machine on the Cycle_B and Service_A Machines

The idea of the proposed implementation is to break down the main_A operation of the *Cycle_A* machine into two pieces. The first piece, called main_B, will very much resemble the main_A operation. It will just assign, in a non-deterministic way, the same kind of variable as main_A does, except that the variable *bok* will be replaced by the two variables *evs* and *eqs*. The second piece, called shut_down_test, corresponds to the translation of the *bok* variable in terms of the two boolean variables *evs* and *eqs* as proposed in section 13.4.3.

Notice that the operation main_B will be the *only* operation of a certain new machine *Cycle_B*. As a consequence, we will be able to use, in order to decompose main_B, the same approach as we have just used here to decompose main_A. This is the reason why the operation shut_down_test is put in a separate machine that could be refined independently of *Cycle_B* and that sees the machine *Cycle_B*. Here is our implementation:

```
IMPLEMENTATION

    Cycle_A_2

REFINES

    Cycle_A_1

IMPORTS

    Cycle_B_1, Service_A_1

OPERATIONS

    main_A  ≘
        BEGIN
            main_B;
            shut_down_test
        END

END
```

This can be pictured in the following diagram where single arrows, such as ↗ and ↖, denote the IMPORTS relationship, while a double arrow, such as ⟸, denotes a SEES relationship:

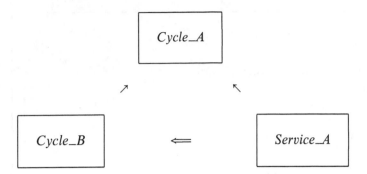

The *Cycle_B* machine is now defined in a straightforward way:

```
MACHINE

    Cycle_B_1

VISIBLE_VARIABLES

    pop, pcl, lvs, eqs

INVARIANT

    pop, pcl ∈ BOOL × BOOL    ∧
    lvs, eqs ∈ BOOL × BOOL

OPERATIONS

    main_B  ≙
        BEGIN
            pop, pcl :∈  BOOL × BOOL    ||
            lvs, eqs :∈  BOOL × BOOL
        END

END
```

And we have the following *Service_A* machine, which we shall not refine further:

MACHINE

   Service_A_1

SEES

   Cycle_B_1

VISIBLE_VARIABLES

   bok

INVARIANT

   bok ∈ BOOL

OPERATIONS

   shut_down_test ≙
      BEGIN
         bok := bool (*lvs* = true ∧ *eqs* = true)
      END

END

Notice how the substitution defining *bok* is a straightforward copy of the first line of the first table of section 13.4.4.

Implementation of the Cycle_B Machine on the Cycle_L and Service_B Machines

We apply exactly the same technique as in the previous section: the operation main_B is decomposed into the three operations main_L, functional_level_test, and level_safe_test. The last two are defined within a certain machine *Service_B*, whereas the first is, again, the unique non-deterministic operation of a certain machine *Cycle_L*. Here is the implementation:

IMPLEMENTATION

    Cycle_B_2

REFINES

    Cycle_B_1

IMPORTS

    Cycle_L_1, Service_B_1

OPERATIONS

    main_B $\widehat{=}$
        BEGIN
            main_L;
            functional_level_test;
            level_safe_test
        END

END

The structure of this implementation can be pictured in the following diagram:

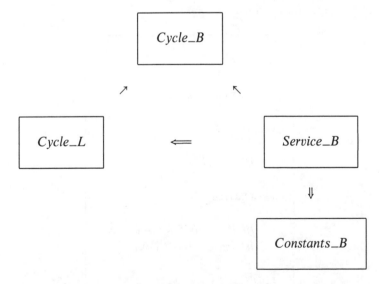

The *Cycle_L* machine is now defined in a straightforward way:

MACHINE

    Cycle_L_1

VISIBLE_VARIABLES

    lml, lmh, lcl, lch, eqs

INVARIANT

    $lml, lmh, lcl, lch \in \text{NAT} \times \text{NAT} \times \text{NAT} \times \text{NAT} \quad \wedge$
    $eqs \in \text{BOOL}$

OPERATIONS

    main_L $\;\widehat{=}\;$
      BEGIN
        $lml, lmh :\in \text{NAT} \times \text{NAT} \quad ||$
        $lcl, lch :\in \text{NAT} \times \text{NAT} \quad ||$
        $eqs :\in \text{BOOL}$
      END

END

Before presenting the machine *Service_B_1*, we need to define some of the constants in a separate machine:

MACHINE

    Constants_L_1

CONSTANTS

    lfl, lfh, lsl, lsh

PROPERTIES

    $lfl, lfh \in \text{NAT} \times \text{NAT} \quad \wedge$
    $lsl, lsh \in \text{NAT} \times \text{NAT}$

END

In the next machine, *Service_B_1*, you can recognize the contents of the second table of section 13.4.4:

MACHINE

    Service_B_1

SEES

    Constants_L_1, Cycle_L_1

VISIBLE_VARIABLES

    pop, pcl, lvs

INVARIANT

    $pop, pcl, lvs \in \mathsf{BOOL} \times \mathsf{BOOL} \times \mathsf{BOOL}$

OPERATIONS

    functional_level_test $\;\widehat{=}$
        BEGIN
            $pop := \mathsf{bool}\,(\; lmh \leq lfh \quad \wedge \quad lml < lfl\;) \quad ||$
            $pcl := \mathsf{bool}\,(\; lmh > lfh \quad \wedge \quad lml \geq lfl\;)$
        END ;

    level_safe_test $\;\widehat{=}$
        BEGIN
            $lvs := \mathsf{bool}\,(\; lml \geq lsl \quad \wedge \quad lmh \leq lsh \quad \wedge$
                      $lcl \geq lsl \quad \wedge \quad lch \leq lsh\;)$
        END

END

Implementation of the Cycle_L Machine on the Cycle_S, Cycle_W and Service_L_1 Machines

In this implementation, we import the machines *Cycle_S* (the "steam" machine), *Cycle_W* (the "water pump" machine) and a certain *Service_L* machine. This corresponds to the following diagram:

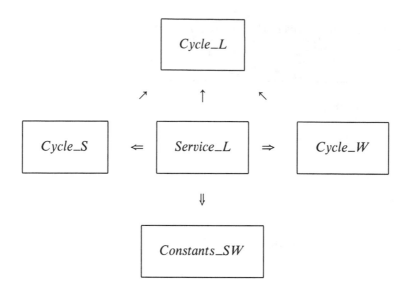

```
IMPLEMENTATION

    Cycle_L_2

REFINES

    Cycle_L_1

IMPORTS

    Cycle_S_1, Service_L_1, Cycle_W_1

OPERATIONS

    main_L  ≙
        BEGIN
            main_S;
            main_W;
            read_level;
            level_test;
            adjust_level;
            calculate_next_level;
            equipment_test
        END

END
```

Next is the specification of the *Cycle_S_1* machine:

```
MACHINE

    Cycle_S_1

VISIBLE_VARIABLES

    sml, smh, stk, sok

INVARIANT

        sml, smh ∈ NAT × NAT    ∧
        stk, sok ∈ BOOL × BOOL

OPERATIONS

    main_S  ≙
        BEGIN
            sml, smh :∈ NAT × NAT    ||
            stk, sok :∈ BOOL × BOOL
        END

END
```

Then the specification of the *Cycle_W_1* machine is given by

```
MACHINE

    Cycle_W_1

VISIBLE_VARIABLES

    wml, wmh, wtk

INVARIANT

        wml, wmh ∈ NAT × NAT    ∧
        wtk ∈ BOOL
```

OPERATIONS

$\quad$ main_W $\;\widehat{=}$
$\qquad$ BEGIN
$\qquad\quad$ $wml, wmh, wtk \;:\in\; \text{NAT} \times \text{NAT} \times \text{BOOL}$
$\qquad$ END

END

Before proceeding, we need to define a few more constants:

MACHINE

$\quad$ *Constants_SW_1*

CONSTANTS

$\quad$ $seh, sdi, sdd, leh, wnr, dt$

PROPERTIES

$\quad$ $seh, sdi, sdd, leh, wnr, dt \in \text{NAT} \times \text{NAT} \times \text{NAT} \times \text{NAT} \times \text{NAT} \times \text{NAT}$

END

We now define the *Service_L_1* machine:

MACHINE

$\quad$ *Service_L_1*

SEES

$\quad$ *Cycle_W_1, Cycle_S_1, Constants_SW_1*

VISIBLE_VARIABLES

$\quad$ $lim, lrm, lr, lml, lmh, lcl, lch, lfm, lok, ltk, eqs$

INVARIANT

$lim, lrm, lr \in$ BOOL $\times$ BOOL $\times$ NAT $\quad \wedge$
$lml, lmh, lcl, lch \in$ NAT $\times$ NAT $\times$ NAT $\times$ NAT $\quad \wedge$
$lfm, lok, ltk, eqs \in$ BOOL $\times$ BOOL $\times$ BOOL $\times$ BOOL

OPERATIONS

read_level $\;\widehat{=}$
   BEGIN
      $lim, lrm, lr \;:\in\;$ BOOL $\times$ BOOL $\times$ NAT
   END ;

level_test $\;\widehat{=}$
   BEGIN
      $ltk :=$ bool $(\,lim =$ true $\wedge \; lr \le leh \quad \wedge$
               $(\,lok =$ false $\vee \; lrm =$ false $)\,)$ ||
      $lfm :=$ bool $(\,lr \notin lcl \mathrel{..} lch \quad \wedge$
                $(\,lok =$ true $\vee \; lrm =$ true $)\,)$ ||
      $lok :=$ bool $(\,lr \in lcl \mathrel{..} lch \quad \wedge$
                 $(\,lok =$ true $\vee \; lrm =$ true $)\,)$
   END ;

adjust_level $\;\widehat{=}$
   IF $\quad lok =$ true $\wedge \; lim =$ true $\quad$ THEN
      $lml, lmh \;:= lr, lr$
   ELSE
      $lml, lmh \;:= lcl, lch$
   END ;

calculate_next_level $\;\widehat{=}$
   LET $\quad x, y \quad$ BE
      $x \; = \; lml - smh \times dt - (sdi \times dt \times dt)/2 + wml \quad \wedge$
      $y \; = \; lmh - sml \times dt + (sdd \times dt \times dt)/2 + wmh$
   IN
      $lcl \;:= \; \min(\{\max(\{x, 0\}), maxint\}) \quad$ ||
      $lch \;:= \; \min(\{\max(\{y, 0\}), maxint\})$
   END ;

equipment_test $\;\widehat{=}$
   BEGIN
      $eqs :=$ bool $(\,ltk =$ true $\wedge \; stk =$ true $\wedge \; wtk =$ true $\quad \wedge$
               $(\,lok =$ true $\vee \; sok =$ true $)\,)$
   END

END

Implementation of the Cycle_S Machine on the Service_S Machine

The *Cycle_S* machine is now implemented according to this diagram:

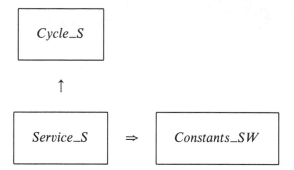

Here is our implementation:

```
IMPLEMENTATION

    Cycle_S_2

REFINES

    Cycle_S_1

IMPORTS

    Service_S_1

OPERATIONS

    main_S  ≙
        BEGIN
            read_steam;
            steam_test;
            adjust_steam;
            calculate_next_steam
        END

END
```

Next is the specification of the *Service_S_1* machine:

MACHINE

   Service_S_1

SEES

   Constants_SW_1

VISIBLE_VARIABLES

   sim, *srm*, *sr*,
   sml, *smh*, *scl*, *sch*, *sfm*, *sok*, *stk*

INVARIANT

   $sim, srm, sr \in$ BOOL $\times$ BOOL $\times$ NAT $\wedge$
   $sml, smh, scl, sch \in$ NAT $\times$ NAT $\times$ NAT $\times$ NAT $\wedge$
   $sfm, sok, stk \in$ BOOL $\times$ BOOL $\times$ BOOL

OPERATIONS

   read_steam $\widehat{=}$
      BEGIN
        $sim, srm, sr :\in$ BOOL $\times$ BOOL $\times$ NAT
      END ;

   steam_test $\widehat{=}$
      BEGIN
        $stk :=$ bool $(sim =$ true $\wedge\ sr \leq seh\ \wedge$
                      $(sok =$ false $\vee\ srm =$ false $))$ $||$
        $sfm :=$ bool $(sr \notin scl .. sch\ \wedge$
                      $(sok =$ true $\vee\ srm =$ true $))$ $||$
        $sok :=$ bool $(sr \in scl .. sch\ \wedge$
                      $(sok =$ true $\vee\ srm =$ true $))$
      END ;

   adjust_steam $\widehat{=}$
      IF $sok =$ true $\wedge\ sim =$ true   THEN
        $sml, smh := sr, sr$
      ELSE
        $sml, smh := scl, sch$
      END ;

OPERATIONS   (Cont'd)

calculate_next_steam $\widehat{=}$
  LET x, y BE
    $x \ = \ sml - sdd \times dt$ $\wedge$
    $y \ = \ smh + sdi \times dt$
  IN
    $scl := \min(\{\max(\{x, 0\}), maxint\})$ ||
    $sch := \min(\{\max(\{y, 0\}), maxint\})$
  END

END

Implementation of the Cycle_W Machine on the Service_W Machine

Next we implement the *Cycle_W* machine. This corresponds to the following diagram:

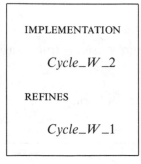

Here is our implementation:

IMPLEMENTATION

Cycle_W_2

REFINES

Cycle_W_1

```
IMPORTS

    Service_W_1

OPERATIONS

    main_W  ≙
        BEGIN
            read_water;
            calculate_previous_water;
            water_test;
            adjust_water
        END

END
```

Next is the specification of the *Service_W_1* machine:

```
MACHINE

    Service_W_1

SEES

    Constants_SW_1

VISIBLE_VARIABLES

    wim, wrm, wr, pop_0, pcl_0
    wml, wmh, wcl, wch, wfm, wok, wtk

INVARIANT

    wim, wrm, wr ∈ BOOL × BOOL × NAT    ∧
    pop_0, pcl_0 ∈ NAT × NAT    ∧
    wml, wmh, wcl, wch ∈ NAT × NAT × NAT × NAT    ∧
    wfm, wok, wtk ∈ BOOL × BOOL × BOOL
```

OPERATIONS

read_water $\widehat{=}$
    BEGIN
        $wim, wrm, wr, pop_0, pcl_0 :\in$ BOOL $\times$ BOOL $\times$ NAT $\times$ NAT $\times$ NAT
    END ;

calculate_previous_water $\widehat{=}$
    BEGIN
        IF $wok =$ false $\vee$ $pcl_0 =$ true $\vee$
            $(pop_0 =$ false $\wedge$ $wml = 0)$ THEN
            $wcl := 0$
        ELSE
            $wcl := wnr$
        END $||$
        IF $wok =$ false $\vee$ $pop_0 =$ true $\vee$
            $(pcl_0 =$ false $\wedge$ $wmh = wnr)$ THEN
            $wch := wnr$
        ELSE
            $wch := wnr$
        END
    END ;

water_test $\widehat{=}$
    BEGIN
        $wtk :=$ bool $(wok =$ false $\vee$ $wrm =$ false $)$ $||$
        $wfm :=$ bool $(wr \notin wcl .. wch \wedge$
                $(wok =$ true $\vee$ $wrm =$ true $))$ $||$
        $wok :=$ bool $(wr \in wcl .. wch \wedge$
                $(wok =$ true $\vee$ $wrm =$ true $))$
    END ;

adjust_water $\widehat{=}$
    IF $wok =$ true $\wedge$ $wim =$ true   THEN
        $wml, wmh := wr, wr$
    ELSE
        $wml, wmh := wcl, wch$
    END

END

As you may have noticed, the value of the *previous* messages *pop* and *pcl* (which we call here pcl_0 and pop_0) are supposed to be read from the external environment (in fact they are re-entered into the system from one cycle to the other): in this way the circuit is cut.

13.4.6. Final Architecture

By putting together the various machines we have developed so far, we obtain the following diagram representing the complete architecture of the system.

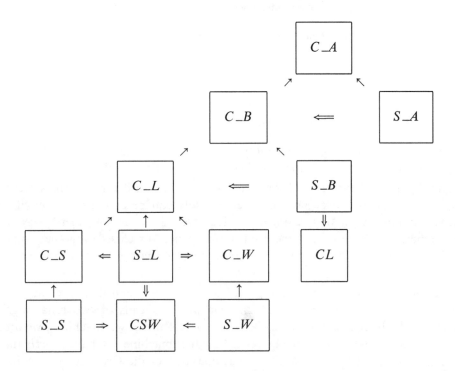

It is worth mentioning that this architecture is only a "design architecture". It is quite possible to have the various "main" operations translated into code by means of an in-line expansion of their contents. As a result, the final code will be just a patch-work of the various abstractions, all flattened into a single efficient program such as the following:

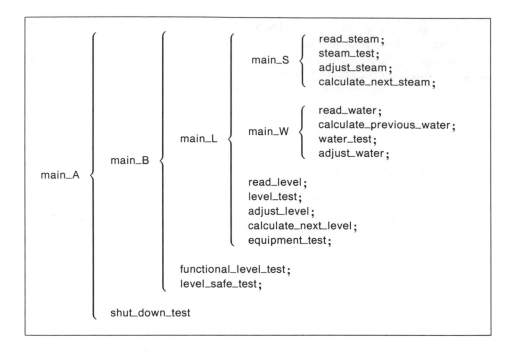

13.4.7. Modifying the Initial Specification

In this section we investigate the ability of the previous formal design to "resist" siginificant modifications of the initial specification of the problem.

The change we have in mind is concerned with the "hardware" of the system. The "client" might think that the system's safety can be enhanced by having, say, two pumps rather than a single one. However, the behaviour of the system is to remain the same in that the pumps are opened (or closed) together when the water level is too high (or too low). In a sense, we have a kind of refinement of the pumps.

The idea is to try to modify the previous architecture as little as we can. We are going to duplicate the *Cycle_W_*1 machine by means of two renamings, say *P*1.*Cycle_W_*1 and *P*2.*Cycle_W_*1. In front of these two machines, we are going to have an extra level called *Cycle_X_*1: that machine will have *exactly* the same specification as the *Cycle_W_*1 machine. In fact the *Cycle_X_*1 machine will now replace the *Cycle_W_*1 in the importation made in implementation *Cycle_L_*2, which is thus modified as follows (in main_L the only change consists in replacing the call to main_W by a call to main_X):

IMPLEMENTATION

　　Cycle_L_2

REFINES

　　Cycle_L_1

IMPORTS

　　Cycle_S_1, Service_L_1, Cycle_X_1

OPERATIONS

　　main_L $\hat{=}$

　　　　BEGIN

　　　　　　main_S;
　　　　　　main_X;
　　　　　　read_level;
　　　　　　level_test;
　　　　　　adjust_level;
　　　　　　calculate_next_level;
　　　　　　equipment_test

　　　　END

END

The *Service_L_1* machine is very slightly modified: it now sees *Cycle_X_1* instead of *Cycle_W_1*. As already stated, the machine *Cycle_X_1* is a simple copy of *Cycle_W_1*:

MACHINE
　　Cycle_X_1
INCLUDES
　　Cycle_W_1
OPERATIONS
　　main_X $\hat{=}$ main_W
END

The machine *Cycle_X_1* is now implemented by importing the two renamed machines *P1.Cycle_W_1* and *P2.Cycle_W_1* as well as the machine *Service_X_1*:

```
IMPLEMENTATION

    Cycle_X_2

REFINES

    Cycle_X_1

IMPORTS

    P1.Cycle_W_1, P2.Cycle_W_1, Service_X_1

OPERATIONS

    main_X  ≙
        BEGIN
            P1.main_W;
            P2.main_W;
            synthesis_water
        END

END
```

Next is the specification of *Service_X_1* making the "synthesis" of the two renamed machines *P1.Cycle_W_1* and *P2.Cycle_W_1*:

```
MACHINE

    Service_X_1

SEES

    P1.Cycle_W_1, P2.Cycle_W_1

CONCRETE_VARIABLES

    wml, wmh, wtk

INVARIANT

    wml, wmh, wtk ∈ NAT × NAT × BOOL
```

```
OPERATIONS

    synthesis_water  ≙
        BEGIN
            wml := P1.wml + P2.wml    ||
            wmh := P1.wmh + P2.wmh    ||
            wtk := bool(P1.wtk ∧ P2.wtk)
        END

END
```

Notice that the refinement of the machine *Cycle_W* is not modified. Next is the new "flat" structure of the system:

The reader is encouraged to further modify the system by having several water level sensors and steam rate sensors both monitored by some kind of majority vote decision procedures.

REFERENCE

[1] J.C. Bauer. *Specification for a Software Program for a Boiler Water Content Monitor and Control System.* (Institute of Risk Research, University of Waterloo, Ontario, Canada 1993)

Appendices

Summary of Notations

A.1. Propositional Calculus (§1.2)

Conjunction	$P \wedge Q$
Implication	$P \Rightarrow Q$
Negation	$\neg P$
Disjunction	$P \vee Q$
Equivalence	$P \Leftrightarrow Q$

A.2. Predicate Calculus (§1.3)

Universal quantification	$\forall\, x \cdot P$
Substitution	$[\, x := E\,]\, P$
Existential quantification	$\exists\, x \cdot P$

A.3. Equality and Ordered Pairs (§1.4, §1.5)

Equality	$E \;=\; F$
Ordered pair	E, F $E \mapsto F$

A.4. Basic and Derived Set Constructs (§2.1, §2.3)

Membership	$x \in s$
Cartesian product	$s \times t$
Set of subsets of a set	$\mathbb{P}(s)$

Set defined in comprehension	$\{ x \mid x \in s \ \wedge \ P \}$
Inclusion of one set in another	$a \subseteq b$
Union of two sets	$a \cup b$
Intersection of two sets	$a \cap b$
Difference of two sets	$a - b$
Set defined in extension	$\{ x, \ y, \ z \}$
Empty set	$\varnothing$
Set of non-empty subsets of a set	$\mathbb{P}_1 (s)$

A.5. Binary Relations (§2.4)

Set of binary relations	$s \leftrightarrow t$
Inverse of a relation	r^{-1}
Domain of a relation	$\mathrm{dom} (r)$
Range of a relation	$\mathrm{ran} (r)$

Composition of two relations	$p \,;q$ $q \circ p$
Identity relation	$\text{id}\,(s)$
Domain restriction of a relation by a set	$u \lhd r$
Range restriction of a relation by a set	$r \rhd v$
Domain subtraction of a relation by a set	$u \vartriangleleft\!\!\!\!- r$
Range subtraction of a relation by a set	$r \,{-}\!\!\!\!\vartriangleright v$
Image of a set under a relation	$r\,[w]$
Overriding of a relation by another	$q \lessdot\!\!\!- r$
Direct product of two relations	$f \otimes g$
First projection function	$\text{prj}_1\,(s,t)$
Second projection function	$\text{prj}_2\,(s,t)$
Parallel product of two relations	$p \parallel q$

A.6. Functions (§2.5)

Application of a function	$f(x)$
Functional abstraction	$\lambda x \cdot (x \in s \mid E)$ $\lambda x \cdot (x \in s \land P \mid E)$
Set of partial functions	$s \nrightarrow t$
Set of total functions	$s \rightarrow t$
Set of partial injections	$s \rightarrowtail\!\!\!\!\!\rightarrow t$
Set of total injections	$s \rightarrowtail t$
Set of partial surjections	$s \twoheadrightarrow t$
Set of total surjections	$s \twoheadrightarrow t$
Set of partial bijections	$s \rightarrowtail\!\!\!\twoheadrightarrow t$
Set of total bijections	$s \rightarrowtail\!\!\!\twoheadrightarrow t$

A.7. Generalized Intersection and Union (§3.1)

Intersection of a non-empty set of sets	inter (s)
Union of a set of sets	union (s)
Intersection of set expressions indexed by a non-empty set	$\bigcap x \cdot (x \in s \mid E)$ $\bigcap x \cdot (x \in s \land P \mid E)$
Union of set expressions indexed by a set	$\bigcup x \cdot (x \in s \mid E)$ $\bigcup x \cdot (x \in s \land P \mid E)$

A.8. Finiteness (§3.3, §3.4)

Set of finite subsets of a set	$\mathbb{F}(s)$
Set of finite non-empty subsets of a set	$\mathbb{F}_1(s)$
Finite set predicate	finite (s)
Infinite set predicate	infinite (s)

A.9. **Natural Numbers** (§3.5)

Set of natural numbers	$\mathbb{N}$
Successor function	succ
Predecessor function	pred
Less than or equal operator	$n \leq m$
Less than operator	$n < m$
Greater than or equal operator	$n \geq m$
Greater than operator	$n > m$
Greater than or equal relation	geq
Greater than relation	gtr
Less than or equal relation	leq
Less than relation	lss
Minimum of a non-empty set	$\min(s)$
Maximum of a finite non-empty set	$\max(s)$

Addition unary function	plus (m)
Multiplication unary function	mult (m)
Exponentiation unary function	exp (m)
Subtraction unary function	minus (m)
Division unary function	div (m)
Remainder unary function	rem (m)
Relational iteration	iter (r)
Adder	$m + n$
Multiplier	$m \times n$
Exponentiator	m^{n}
Subtractor	$m - n$
Divisor	m/n
Modulo	$m \bmod n$
Logarithm by excess	$\mathrm{LOG}_{m}(n)$
Logarithm by defect	$\log_{m}(n)$

nth Iterate of a relation	r^n
Transitive and reflexive closure of a relation	r^*
Transitive closure of a relation	r^+
Cardinal of a finite set	$\mathrm{card}\,(s)$

A.10. Integers (§3.6)

Set of integers	$\mathbb{Z}$
Set of negative integers	$\mathbb{Z}_1$
Successor	succ
Predecessor	pred
Less than or equal operator	$n \leq m$
Less than operator	$n < m$
Greater than or equal operator	$n \geq m$
Greater than operator	$n > m$

Unary minus function	uminus (m)
Greater than or equal relation	geq
Greater than relation	gtr
Less than or equal relation	leq
Less than relation	lss
Minimum of a set	min (s)
Maximum of a set	max (s)
Addition unary function	plus (m)
Multiplication unary function	mult (m)
Subtraction unary function	minus (m)
Division unary function	div (m)
Adder	$m + n$
Multiplier	$m \times n$
Subtractor	$m - n$
Divisor	m / n

A.11. Finite Sequences (§3.7)

Set of sequences	$\mathsf{seq}\,(s)$
Empty sequence	$[\,]$
Set of non-empty sequences	$\mathsf{seq}_1\,(s)$
Prefixing an element to a sequence	$x \rightarrow t$
Set of injective sequences	$\mathsf{iseq}\,(s)$
Set of permutations of a finite set	$\mathsf{perm}\,(s)$
Interval of integers	$a \mathbin{..} b$
Length of a sequence	$\mathsf{size}\,(s)$
Concatenation of two sequences	$s \mathbin{^\frown} t$
Appending an element to a sequence	$t \leftarrow y$
Reversing a sequence	$\mathsf{rev}\,(t)$
Generalized concatenation of a sequence of sequences	$\mathsf{conc}\,(t)$
Sum of the elements of a sequence of integers	$\mathsf{sum}\,(t)$
Composition of the elements of a sequence of relations	$\mathsf{comp}\,(t)$

Product of the elements of a sequence of integers	prod (t)
Sequence defined in extension	$[a, b, c]$
Keeping the n first elements of a sequence	$t \uparrow n$
Removing the n first elements of a sequence	$t \downarrow n$
First element of a sequence	first (t)
Last element of a sequence	last (t)
Sequence minus first element	tail (t)
Sequence minus last element	front (t)
Catenation (with a sequence) on a sequence	cat (t)
Composition (with a function) on a sequence	cmp (t)
Sorting a sequence of integers	sort (s)
Sorting a finite set of integers	sortset (s)
Squashing a finite function of integers	squash (f)
Lexicographical orders on integer sequences	$s \leq t$ $s < t$

Sum of the elements of a finite integer function	sumf (f)
Product of the elements of a finite integer function	prodf (f)
Sum of integer expressions indexed by a finite set	$\sum x \cdot (x \in s \mid E)$ $\sum x \cdot (x \in s \wedge P \mid E)$
Product of integer expressions indexed by a finite set	$\prod x \cdot (x \in s \mid E)$ $\prod x \cdot (x \in s \wedge P \mid E)$

A.12. Finite Trees (§3.8, §3.9, §3.10)

Set of trees	tree (s)
Tree constructor	cons (x, st)
Top of a tree	top (t)
Sons of a tree	sons (t)
Pre-ordering of a tree	pre (t)
Size of a tree	sizet (t)

Post-ordering of a tree	$\text{post}(t)$
Mirror image of a tree	$\text{mirror}(t)$
Rank of a node	$\text{rank}(t)(n)$
Father of a node	$\text{father}(t)(n)$
Ranked node son of a node	$\text{son}(t)(n)(i)$
Sub-tree of a node	$\text{subt}(t)(n)$
Arity of a node	$\text{arity}(t)(n)$
Set of binary trees	$\text{bin}(s)$
Singleton binary tree	$\langle x \rangle$
Binary tree constructor	$\langle l, x, r \rangle$
Left sub-tree	$\text{left}(t)$
Right sub-tree	$\text{right}(t)$
Infix ordering	$\text{infix}(t)$

Syntax

B.1. Predicate (§1.2.1, §1.3.1, §2.1.1)

Syntactic Category	Definition
Predicate	*Predicate* ∧ *Predicate* *Predicate* ⇒ *Predicate* ¬ *Predicate* ∀ *Variable* · *Predicate* [*Substitution*] *Predicate* *Expression* = *Expression* *Expression* ∈ *Set*

B.2. **Expression** (§1.3.1, §2.1.1)

Syntactic Category	Definition
Expression	*Variable* [*Variable* := *Expression*] *Expression* *Expression*, *Expression* choice (*Set*) *Set*
Variable	*Identifier* *Variable*, *Variable*
Set	*Set* × *Set* $\mathbb{P}$ (*Set*) { *Variable* | *Predicate* } BIG

B.3. **Substitution** (§5.1.1, §7.2.2, §9.1.1, §9.2.1)

Syntactic Category	Definition
Substitution	*Variable* := *Expression* skip *Predicate* | *Substitution* *Substitution* [] *Substitution* *Predicate* $\implies$ *Substitution* @ *Variable* · *Substitution* *Substitution* || *Substitution* *Substitution* ; *Substitution* *Substitution*^ [*Variable* := *Expression*] *Substitution*

B.4. Machine (§5.2.1, §7.4.1)

Syntactic Category	Definition

Machine	MACHINE
	   Machine_Header
	CONSTRAINTS
	   Predicate
	USES
	   Id_List
	SETS
	   Sets
	CONSTANTS
	   Id_List
	ABSTRACT_CONSTANTS
	   Id_List
	PROPERTIES
	   Predicate
	INCLUDES
	   Machine_List
	PROMOTES
	   Id_List
	EXTENDS
	   Machine_List
	VARIABLES
	   Id_List
	CONCRETE_VARIABLES
	   Id_List
	INVARIANT
	   Predicate
	ASSERTIONS
	   Predicate
	DEFINITIONS
	   Definitions
	INITIALIZATION
	   Substitution
	OPERATIONS
	   Operations
	END

Machine_Header	*Identifier* *Identifier* (*Id_List*)

Syntactic Category	Definition
Sets	*Sets* ; *Set_Declaration* *Set_Declaration*
Set_Declaration	*Identifier* *Identifier* = {*Id_List*}
Machine_List	*Machine_List* , *Machine_Call* *Machine_Call*
Machine_Call	*Identifier* *Identifier* (*Expression_List*)
Definitions	*Definitions* ; *Definition_Declaration* *Definition_Declaration*
Definition_Declaration	*Identifier* $\widehat{=}$ *Formal_Text* *Identifier* (*Id_List*) $\widehat{=}$ *Formal_Text*
Operations	*Operations* ; *Operation_Declaration* *Operation_Declaration*
Operation_Declaration	*Operation_Header* $\widehat{=}$ *Substitution*
Operation_Header	*Id_List* ⟵ *Identifier* (*Id_List*) *Identifier* (*Id_List*) *Id_List* ⟵ *Identifier* *Identifier*
Id_List	*Id_List* , *Identifier* *Identifier*
Expression_List	*Expression_List* , *Expression* *Expression*

B.5. Refinement (§11.3.1)

Syntactic Category	Definition

Refinement	REFINEMENT
	    Machine_Header
	REFINES
	    Id_List
	SETS
	    Sets
	CONSTANTS
	    Id_List
	ABSTRACT_CONSTANTS
	    Id_List
	PROPERTIES
	    Predicate
	INCLUDES
	    Machine_List
	PROMOTES
	    Id_List
	EXTENDS
	    Machine_List
	VARIABLES
	    Id_List
	CONCRETE_VARIABLES
	    Id_List
	INVARIANT
	    Predicate
	ASSERTIONS
	    Predicate
	DEFINITIONS
	    Definitions
	INITIALIZATION
	    Substitution
	OPERATIONS
	    Operations
	END

B.6. Implementation (§12.6.1)

Syntactic Category	Definition
Implementation	IMPLEMENTATION 　*Machine_Header* REFINES 　*Id_List* SETS 　*Sets* CONSTANTS 　*Id_List* PROPERTIES 　*Predicate* VALUES 　*Predicate* IMPORTS 　*Machine_List* PROMOTES 　*Id_List* EXTENDS 　*Machine_List* CONCRETE_VARIABLES 　*Id_List* INVARIANT 　*Predicate* ASSERTIONS 　*Predicate* DEFINITIONS 　*Definitions* INITIALIZATION 　*Substitution* OPERATIONS 　*Operations* END
Operation_Declaration	*Operation_Header*　$\widehat{=}$　*Substitution* *Operation_Header*　$\widehat{=}$　REC *Expression* THEN 　　　　*Substitution* 　　　　END

B.7. Statement (§12.1.11)

Syntactic Category	Definition
Statement	skip *Assignment_Statement* *Call_Statement* *Sequencing_Statement* *Local_Statement* *While_Statement* *If_Statement* *Case_Statement*
Assignment_Statement	*Protected_Assignment* *Unprotected_Assignment*
Call_Statement	*Protected_Call* *Unprotected_Call*
Unprotected_Assignment	*Identifier_List* := *Term_List* *Identifier*(*Term_List*) := *Term* *Identifier* := bool(*Condition*) *Identifier*(*Term_List*) := bool(*Condition*)
Unprotected_Call	*Identifier_List* ⟵ *Identifier*(*Term_List*) *Identifier_List* ⟵ *Identifier* *Identifier*(*Term_List*) *Identifier*
Protected_Assignment	PRE *Predicate* THEN *Unprotected_Assignment* END
Protected_Call	PRE *Predicate* THEN *Unprotected_Call* END

Syntactic Category	Definition
Term	*Simple_Term* *Function_Constant_Identifier* (*Term_List*) *Function_Variable_Identifier* (*Term_List*) *Term* + *Term* *Term* − *Term* *Term* × *Term* *Term* / *Term*
Simple_Term	*Scalar_Variable_Identifier* *Operation_Input_Formal_Parameter* *Operation_Output_Formal_Parameter* *Simple_Constant*
Simple_Constant	*Enumerated_Set_Element_Identifier* *Scalar_Constant_Identifier* *Numeric_Literal*
Sequencing_Statement	*Statement* ; *Statement*
Local_Statement	VAR *Identifier_List* IN *Statement* END
While_Statement	WHILE *Condition* DO *Statement* END
If_Statement	*Normal_If* *Small_If* *Normal_Elsif* *Small_Elsif*
Case_Statement	*Normal_Case* *Small_Case*

Syntactic Category	Definition

Normal_If	IF *Condition* THEN
	    Statement
	ELSE
	    Statement
	END

Small_If	IF *Condition* THEN *Statement* END

Normal_Elsif	IF *Condition* THEN
	    Statement
	ELSIF
	    Statement
	ELSIF
	    . . .
	ELSE
	    Statement
	END

Small_Elsif	IF *Condition* THEN
	    Statement
	ELSIF
	    Statement
	ELSIF
	    . . .
	END

Syntactic Category	Definition

Normal_Case	CASE *Simple_Term* OF
	    EITHER *Constant_List* THEN
	        Statement
	    OR *Constant_List* THEN
	        Statement
	    OR *Constant_List* THEN
	        . . .
	    ELSE
	        Statement
	    END
	END

Small_Case	CASE *Simple_Term* OF
	    EITHER *Constant_List* THEN
	        Statement
	    OR *Constant_List* THEN
	        Statement
	    OR *Constant_List* THEN
	        . . .
	    END
	END

Condition	$Simple\_Term = Simple\_Term$ $Simple\_Term \neq Simple\_Term$ $Simple\_Term < Simple\_Term$ $Simple\_Term \leq Simple\_Term$ $Simple\_Term > Simple\_Term$ $Simple\_Term \geq Simple\_Term$ $Condition \wedge Condition$ $Condition \vee Condition$ $\neg \, Condition$

Definitions

C.1. Logic Definitions (§1.2.5, §1.3.8, §1.5)

Syntax	Definition
$P \vee Q$	$\neg P \Rightarrow Q$
$P \Leftrightarrow Q$	$(P \Rightarrow Q) \wedge (Q \Rightarrow P)$
$\exists x \cdot P$	$\neg \forall x \cdot \neg P$
$E \mapsto F$	E, F

C.2. Basic Set-theoretic Definitions (§2.1, §2.3)

Syntax	Definition	Condition
$s \subseteq t$	$s \in \mathbb{P}(t)$	
$s \subset t$	$s \subseteq t \ \wedge \ s \neq t$	
$u \cup v$	$\{ x \mid x \in s \ \wedge \ (x \in u \ \vee \ x \in v) \}$	$u \subseteq s \ \wedge \ v \subseteq s$
$u \cap v$	$\{ x \mid x \in s \ \wedge \ (x \in u \ \wedge \ x \in v) \}$	$u \subseteq s \ \wedge \ v \subseteq s$
$u - v$	$\{ x \mid x \in s \ \wedge \ (x \in u \ \wedge \ x \notin v) \}$	$u \subseteq s \ \wedge \ v \subseteq s$
$\{E\}$	$\{ x \mid x \in s \ \wedge \ x = E \}$	$E \in s \quad x \setminus (s, E)$
$\{L, E\}$	$\{L\} \cup \{E\}$	$\{L\} \subseteq s \ \wedge \ E \in s$
$\varnothing$	$\mathsf{BIG} - \mathsf{BIG}$	
$\mathbb{P}_1(s)$	$\mathbb{P}(s) - \{\varnothing\}$	

C.3. Binary Relation Definitions (§2.4)

Syntax	Definition	Condition
$s \leftrightarrow t$	$\mathbb{P}(s \times t)$	
r^{-1}	$\{ y, x \mid (y, x) \in t \times s \ \wedge \ (x, y) \in r \}$	$r \in s \leftrightarrow t$
$\mathrm{dom}(r)$	$\{ x \mid x \in s \ \wedge \ \exists y \cdot (y \in t \ \wedge \ (x, y) \in r) \}$	$r \in s \leftrightarrow t$
$\mathrm{ran}(r)$	$\mathrm{dom}(r^{-1})$	$r \in s \leftrightarrow t$

Syntax	Definition	Condition
$q \,;\, r$	$\{\, x,z \mid (x,z) \in s \times u \ \wedge$ $\qquad\qquad \exists y \cdot (y \in t \ \wedge \ (x,y) \in q \ \wedge \ (y,z) \in r)\,\}$	$q \in s \leftrightarrow t$ $r \in t \leftrightarrow u$
$r \circ q$	$q \,;\, r$	$q \in s \leftrightarrow t$ $r \in t \leftrightarrow u$
$\mathrm{id}(s)$	$\{\, x,y \mid (x,y) \in s \times s \ \wedge \ x = y \,\}$	
$u \vartriangleleft r$	$\mathrm{id}(u)\,;\, r$	$r \in s \leftrightarrow t$ $u \subseteq s$
$r \vartriangleright v$	$r \,;\, \mathrm{id}(v)$	$r \in s \leftrightarrow t$ $v \subseteq t$
$u \vartriangleleft\!\!\!- r$	$(\mathrm{dom}(r) - u) \vartriangleleft r$	$r \in s \leftrightarrow t$ $u \subseteq s$
$r \vartriangleright\!\!\!- v$	$r \vartriangleright (\mathrm{ran}(r) - v)$	$r \in s \leftrightarrow t$ $v \subseteq t$
$r[w]$	$\mathrm{ran}(w \vartriangleleft r)$	$r \in s \leftrightarrow t$ $w \subseteq s$
$q \ll\!\!+ r$	$(\mathrm{dom}(r) \vartriangleleft\!\!\!- q) \cup r$	$q \in s \leftrightarrow t$ $r \in s \leftrightarrow t$
$f \otimes g$	$\{\, x,(y,z) \mid (x,(y,z)) \in s \times (u \times v) \ \wedge$ $\qquad\qquad (x,y) \in f \ \wedge \ (x,z) \in g\}$	$f \in s \leftrightarrow u$ $g \in s \leftrightarrow v$
$\mathrm{prj}_1(s,t)$	$\{\, x,y,z \mid (x,y,z) \in s \times t \times s \ \wedge \ z = x \,\}$	
$\mathrm{prj}_2(s,t)$	$\{\, x,y,z \mid (x,y,z) \in s \times t \times t \ \wedge \ z = y \,\}$	
$h \parallel k$	$\{\, (x,y),(z,w) \mid ((x,y),(z,w)) \in (s \times t) \times (u \times v) \ \wedge$ $\qquad\qquad (x,z) \in h \ \wedge \ (y,w) \in k \,\}$	$h \in s \leftrightarrow u$ $k \in t \leftrightarrow v$

C.4. Function Definitions (§2.5)

Syntax	Definition	Condition
$s \nrightarrow t$	$\{\, r \mid r \in s \leftrightarrow t \;\wedge\; (r^{-1};r) \subseteq \mathrm{id}\,(t)\,\}$	
$s \rightarrow t$	$\{\, f \mid f \in s \nrightarrow t \;\wedge\; \mathrm{dom}\,(f) = s \,\}$	
$s \nrightarrowtail t$	$\{\, f \mid f \in s \nrightarrow t \;\wedge\; f^{-1} \in t \nrightarrow s \,\}$	
$s \rightarrowtail t$	$s \nrightarrowtail t \;\cap\; s \rightarrow t$	
$s \twoheadrightarrow t$	$\{\, f \mid f \in s \nrightarrow t \;\wedge\; \mathrm{ran}\,(f) = t \,\}$	
$s \twoheadrightarrow t$	$s \twoheadrightarrow t \;\cap\; s \rightarrow t$	
$s \nrightarrowtail\!\!\!\twoheadrightarrow t$	$s \nrightarrowtail t \;\cap\; s \twoheadrightarrow t$	
$s \rightarrowtail\!\!\!\twoheadrightarrow t$	$s \rightarrowtail t \;\cap\; s \twoheadrightarrow t$	
$\lambda x \cdot (x \in s \mid E)$	$\{\, x, y \mid (x,y) \in s \times t \;\wedge\; y = E \,\}$	$\forall x \cdot (x \in s \;\Rightarrow\; E \in t)$
$\lambda x \cdot (x \in s \;\wedge\; P \mid E)$	$\{\, x, y \mid (x,y) \in s \times t \;\wedge\; P \;\wedge\; y = E \,\}$	$\forall x \cdot (x \in s \;\wedge\; P \;\Rightarrow\; E \in t)$
$f(E)$	$\mathrm{choice}\,(f[\{E\}])$	$f \in s \nrightarrow t$ $E \in \mathrm{dom}\,(f)$

C.5. Fixpoint Definitions (§3.1, §3.2.2)

Syntax	Definition	Condition
$\mathrm{inter}\,(u)$	$\{\, x \mid x \in s \;\wedge\; \forall y \cdot (y \in u \;\Rightarrow\; x \in y)\,\}$	$u \in \mathbb{P}_1(\mathbb{P}(s))$
$\bigcap x \cdot (x \in s \mid E)$	$\{\, y \mid y \in t \;\wedge\; \forall x \cdot (x \in s \;\Rightarrow\; y \in E)\,\}$	$\forall x \cdot (x \in s \;\Rightarrow\; E \subseteq t)$

Syntax	Definition	Condition
$\bigcap x \cdot (x \in s \;\wedge\; P \mid E)$	$\{\, y \mid y \in t \;\wedge\; \forall x \cdot (x \in s \;\wedge\; P \;\Rightarrow\; y \in E)\,\}$	$\forall x \cdot (x \in s \;\wedge\; P \;\Rightarrow\; E \subseteq t)$
union (u)	$\{\, x \mid x \in s \;\wedge\; \exists y \cdot (y \in u \;\wedge\; x \in y)\,\}$	$u \in \mathbb{P}(\mathbb{P}(s))$
$\bigcup x \cdot (x \in s \mid E)$	$\{\, y \mid y \in t \;\wedge\; \exists x \cdot (x \in s \;\wedge\; y \in E)\,\}$	$\forall x \cdot (x \in s \;\Rightarrow\; E \subseteq t)$
$\bigcup x \cdot (x \in s \;\wedge\; P \mid E)$	$\{\, y \mid y \in t \;\wedge\; \exists x \cdot (x \in s \;\wedge\; P \;\wedge\; y \in E)\,\}$	$\forall x \cdot (x \in s \;\wedge\; P \;\Rightarrow\; E \subseteq t)$
fix (f)	inter $(\{\, x \mid x \in \mathbb{P}(s) \;\wedge\; f(x) \subseteq x\,\})$	$f \in \mathbb{P}(s) \to \mathbb{P}(s)$
FIX (f)	union $(\{\, x \mid x \in \mathbb{P}(s) \;\wedge\; x \subseteq f(x)\,\})$	$f \in \mathbb{P}(s) \to \mathbb{P}(s)$

C.6. Finiteness Definitions (§3.4)

Syntax	Definition
add (s)	$\lambda (u, x) \cdot ((u, x) \in s \times \mathbb{P}(s) \mid \{u\} \cup x)$
genfin (s)	$\lambda z \cdot (z \in \mathbb{P}(\mathbb{P}(s)) \mid \{\varnothing\} \cup \text{add}\,(s)[s \times z])$
$\mathbb{F}(s)$	fix (genfin (s))
$\mathbb{F}_1(s)$	$\mathbb{F}(s) - \{\varnothing\}$
finite (s)	$s \in \mathbb{F}(s)$
infinite (s)	$\neg$ finite (s)

C.7. Natural Number Definitions (§3.5)

Syntax	Definition	Condition
0	BIG − BIG	
succ	$\lambda n \cdot (n \in \mathbb{F}(\text{BIG}) \mid$ $\{\text{choice}(\text{BIG} - n)\} \cup n)$	
genat	$\lambda s \cdot (s \in \mathbb{P}(\mathbb{F}(\text{BIG})) \mid \{0\} \cup \text{succ}[s])$	
$\mathbb{N}$	fix (genat)	
1	succ (0)	
$\mathbb{N}_1$	$\mathbb{N} - \{0\}$	
pred	$\text{succ}^{-1} \rhd \mathbb{N}$	
$n \leq m$	$n \subseteq m$	$m \in \mathbb{N} \wedge n \in \mathbb{N}$
$n < m$	$n \neq m \wedge n \leq m$	$m \in \mathbb{N} \wedge n \in \mathbb{N}$
$n \geq m$	$m \leq n$	$m \in \mathbb{N} \wedge n \in \mathbb{N}$
$n > m$	$m < n$	$m \in \mathbb{N} \wedge n \in \mathbb{N}$
geq	$\{m, n \mid (m, n) \in \mathbb{N} \times \mathbb{N} \wedge m \leq n\}$	
gtr	$\{m, n \mid (m, n) \in \mathbb{N} \times \mathbb{N} \wedge m < n\}$	
leq	$\{m, n \mid (m, n) \in \mathbb{N} \times \mathbb{N} \wedge m \geq n\}$	
lss	$\{m, n \mid (m, n) \in \mathbb{N} \times \mathbb{N} \wedge m > n\}$	
$\min(s)$	inter(s)	$s \in \mathbb{P}_1(\mathbb{N})$
$\max(s)$	union(s)	$s \subset \mathbb{F}_1(\mathbb{N})$

Syntax	Definition	Condition
plus $(m)(0)$ plus $(m)($succ $(n))$	m succ $($plus $(m)(n))$	$m \in \mathbb{N} \,\wedge\, n \in \mathbb{N}$
mult $(m)(0)$ mult $(m)($succ $(n))$	0 plus $(m)($mult $(m)(n))$	$m \in \mathbb{N} \,\wedge\, n \in \mathbb{N}$
exp $(m)(0)$ exp $(m)($succ $(n))$	1 mult $(m)($exp $(m)(n))$	$m \in \mathbb{N} \,\wedge\, n \in \mathbb{N}$
iter $(r)(0)$ iter $(r)($succ $(n))$	id (s) $r \,;$ iter $(r)(n)$	$r \in s \leftrightarrow s$ $n \in \mathbb{N}$
$m + n$	plus $(m)(n)$	$m \in \mathbb{N} \,\wedge\, n \in \mathbb{N}$
$m \times n$	mult $(m)(n)$	$m \in \mathbb{N} \,\wedge\, n \in \mathbb{N}$
m^n	exp $(m)(n)$	$m \in \mathbb{N} \,\wedge\, n \in \mathbb{N}$
$n - m$	plus $(m)^{-1}(n)$	$m \in \mathbb{N} \,\wedge\, n \in \mathbb{N} \,\wedge\, m \le n$
n / m	$\min(\{\, x \mid x \in \mathbb{N} \,\wedge\, n < m \times \text{succ}(x)\,\})$	$n \in \mathbb{N} \,\wedge\, m \in \mathbb{N}_1$
$n \ \text{mod}\ m$	$n - m \times (n/m)$	$n \in \mathbb{N} \,\wedge\, m \in \mathbb{N}_1$
minus (m)	$\lambda\, n \cdot (n \in 0 .. m \mid m - n)$	$m \in \mathbb{N}$
div (m)	$\lambda\, n \cdot (n \in \mathbb{N}_1 \mid m/n)$	$m \in \mathbb{N}$
rem (m)	$\lambda\, n \cdot (n \in \mathbb{N}_1 \mid m \ \text{mod}\ n)$	$m \in \mathbb{N}$
$\log_m(n)$	$\min(\{\, x \mid x \in \mathbb{N} \,\wedge\, n < m^{\text{succ}(x)}\,\})$	$n \in \mathbb{N} \,\wedge\, m \in \mathbb{N} \,\wedge\, m > 1$
$\text{LOG}_m(n)$	$\min(\{\, x \mid x \in \mathbb{N} \,\wedge\, n \le m^x\,\})$	$n \in \mathbb{N} \,\wedge\, m \in \mathbb{N} \,\wedge\, m > 1$
r^n	iter $(r)(n)$	$r \in s \leftrightarrow s \,\wedge\, n \in \mathbb{N}$
card (t)	$\min(\{n \mid n \in \mathbb{N} \,\wedge\, t \in \text{genfin}(s)^n(\{\varnothing\})\})$	$t \in \mathbb{F}(s)$

Syntax	Definition	Condition
genr (r)	$\lambda h \cdot (h \in \mathbb{P}(s \times s) \mid \mathrm{id}(s) \cup (r\,;h))$	$r \in s \leftrightarrow s$
r^*	$\mathrm{fix}(\mathrm{genr}(s))$	$r \in s \leftrightarrow s$
genrp (r)	$\lambda h \cdot (h \in \mathbb{P}(s \times s) \mid r \cup (r\,;h))$	$r \in s \leftrightarrow s$
r^+	$\mathrm{fix}(\mathrm{genrp}(s))$	$r \in s \leftrightarrow s$

C.8. Integer Extensions (§3.6)

Syntax	Definition	Condition
uminus	$\lambda n \cdot (n \in \mathbb{Z} \mid -n)$	
$-(-n)$	n	$n \in \mathbb{N}$
$\mathrm{succ}(-n)$	$-\mathrm{pred}(n)$	$n \in \mathbb{N}$
$\mathrm{pred}(-n)$	$-\mathrm{succ}(n)$	$n \in \mathbb{N}$
$(-n) \leq m$	$0 \leq m$	$n \in \mathbb{N} \wedge m \subset \mathbb{N}$
$n \leq (-m)$	$n = 0 \wedge m = 0$	$n \in \mathbb{N} \wedge m \in \mathbb{N}$
$(-n) \leq (-m)$	$m \leq n$	$n \in \mathbb{N} \wedge m \in \mathbb{N}$
$(-m) + n$	$n - m$	$n \in \mathbb{N} \wedge m \in \mathbb{N}$
$m + (-n)$	$m - n$	$n \in \mathbb{N} \wedge m \in \mathbb{N}$

Syntax	Definition	Condition
$(-m) + (-n)$	$-(m + n)$	$n \in \mathbb{N} \wedge m \in \mathbb{N}$
$(-m) \times n$	$-(m \times n)$	$n \in \mathbb{N} \wedge m \in \mathbb{N}$
$m \times (-n)$	$-(m \times n)$	$n \in \mathbb{N} \wedge m \in \mathbb{N}$
$(-m) \times (-n)$	$m \times n$	$n \in \mathbb{N} \wedge m \in \mathbb{N}$
$(-m) - n$	$-(m + n)$	$n \in \mathbb{N} \wedge m \in \mathbb{N}$
$m - (-n)$	$m + n$	$n \in \mathbb{N} \wedge m \in \mathbb{N}$
$(-m) - (-n)$	$n - m$	$n \in \mathbb{N} \wedge m \in \mathbb{N}$
$m - n$	$-(n - m)$	$n \in \mathbb{N} \wedge m \in \mathbb{N} \wedge n > m$
$(-n)/m$	$-(n/m)$	$n \in \mathbb{N} \wedge m \in \mathbb{N}_1$
$n/(-m)$	$-(n/m)$	$n \in \mathbb{N} \wedge m \in \mathbb{N}_1$
$(-n)/(-m)$	n/m	$n \in \mathbb{N} \wedge m \in \mathbb{N}_1$
$\text{plus}\,(m)(n)$	$m + n$	$n \in \mathbb{Z} \wedge m \in \mathbb{Z}$
$\text{mult}\,(m)(n)$	$m \times n$	$n \in \mathbb{Z} \wedge m \in \mathbb{Z}$
$\text{minus}\,(m)(n)$	$m - n$	$n \in \mathbb{Z} \wedge m \in \mathbb{Z}$
$\text{div}\,(m)(n)$	m/n	$n \in \mathbb{Z} - \{0\} \wedge m \in \mathbb{Z}$
$\min(s)$	$-\max(\text{uminus}\,[s \cap \mathbb{Z}_1])$	$s \in \mathbb{P}_1(\mathbb{Z}) \wedge (s \cap \mathbb{Z}_1) \in \mathbb{F}(\mathbb{Z}_1)$ $s \cap \mathbb{Z}_1 \neq \varnothing$
$\max(s)$	$-\min(\text{uminus}\,[s])$	$s \in \mathbb{P}_1(\mathbb{Z}) \wedge (s \cap \mathbb{N}) \in \mathbb{F}(\mathbb{N})$

C.9. Finite Sequence Definitions (§3.7)

Syntax	Definition	Condition
$x \to f$	$\{1 \mapsto x\} \cup (\mathsf{pred};f)$	$x \in s \ \wedge\ f \in \mathbb{N}_1 \nrightarrow s$
$\mathsf{insert}(s)$	$\lambda(x,t) \cdot ((x,t) \in s \times (\mathbb{N}_1 \nrightarrow s) \mid x \to t)$	
$\mathsf{genseq}(s)$	$\lambda z \cdot (z \in \mathbb{P}(\mathbb{N}_1 \nrightarrow s) \mid \{[]\} \ \cup$ $\qquad\qquad \mathsf{insert}(s)[s \times z])$	
$\mathsf{seq}(s)$	$\mathsf{fix}(\mathsf{genseq}(s))$	
$\mathsf{seq}_1(s)$	$\mathsf{seq}(s) - \{[]\}$	
$\mathsf{iseq}(s)$	$\mathsf{seq}(s) \cap (\mathbb{N}_1 \rightarrowtail s)$	
$\mathsf{perm}(s)$	$\mathsf{iseq}(s) \cap (\mathbb{N}_1 \twoheadrightarrow s)$	$\mathsf{finite}(s)$
$m \mathinner{..} n$	$\{p \mid p \in \mathbb{N} \ \wedge\ m \le p \ \wedge\ p \le n\}$	$m \in \mathbb{N} \ \wedge\ n \in \mathbb{N}$
$\mathsf{size}([])$ $\mathsf{size}(x \to t)$	0 $\mathsf{size}(t) + 1$	$x \in s \ \wedge\ t \in \mathsf{seq}(s)$
$[] \mathbin{\frown} u$ $(x \to t) \mathbin{\frown} u$	u $x \to (t \mathbin{\frown} u)$	$u \in \mathsf{seq}(s)$ $x \in s \ \wedge\ t \in \mathsf{seq}(s)$
$[] \leftarrow y$ $(x \to t) \leftarrow y$	$y \to []$ $x \to (t \leftarrow y)$	$y \in s$ $x \in s \ \wedge\ t \in \mathsf{seq}(s)$
$\mathsf{rev}([])$ $\mathsf{rev}(x \to t)$	$[]$ $\mathsf{rev}(t) \leftarrow x$	$x \in s \ \wedge\ t \in \mathsf{seq}(s)$
$\mathsf{conc}([])$ $\mathsf{conc}(x \to t)$	$[]$ $x \mathbin{\frown} \mathsf{conc}(t)$	$x \in \mathsf{seq}(s)$ $t \in \mathsf{seq}(\mathsf{seq}(s))$
$\mathsf{sum}([])$ $\mathsf{sum}(x \to t)$	0 $x + \mathsf{sum}(t)$	$x \in \mathbb{N} \ \wedge\ t \in \mathsf{seq}(\mathbb{Z})$

Syntax	Definition	Condition
$\mathsf{prod}\,([\,])$ $\mathsf{prod}\,(x \to t)$	1 $x \times \mathsf{prod}\,(t)$	$x \in \mathbb{N} \;\wedge\; t \in \mathsf{seq}\,(\mathbb{Z})$
$\mathsf{comp}\,([\,])$ $\mathsf{comp}\,(r \to t)$	$\mathsf{id}\,(s)$ $r \,;\mathsf{comp}\,(t)$	$r \in s \leftrightarrow s$ $t \in \mathsf{seq}\,(s \leftrightarrow s)$
$\mathsf{sumf}\,(f)$	$\mathsf{sum}\,(\mathsf{choice}\,(\mathsf{perm}\,(\mathsf{dom}\,(f)))\,;f)$	$f \in s \nrightarrow \mathbb{Z} \;\wedge\; \mathsf{finite}\,(f)$
$\mathsf{prodf}\,(f)$	$\mathsf{prod}\,(\mathsf{choice}\,(\mathsf{perm}\,(\mathsf{dom}\,(f)))\,;f)$	$f \in s \nrightarrow \mathbb{Z} \;\wedge\; \mathsf{finite}\,(f)$
$\sum x \cdot (x \in s \mid E)$	$\mathsf{sumf}\,(\lambda x \cdot (x \in s \mid E))$	$\forall x \cdot (x \in s \;\Rightarrow\; E \in \mathbb{Z})$ $\mathsf{finite}\,(s)$
$\sum x \cdot (x \in s \;\wedge\; P \mid E)$	$\mathsf{sumf}\,(\lambda x \cdot (x \in s \;\wedge\; P \mid E))$	$\forall x \cdot (x \in s \;\wedge\; P \;\Rightarrow\; E \in \mathbb{Z})$ $\mathsf{finite}\,(s)$
$\prod x \cdot (x \in s \mid E)$	$\mathsf{prodf}\,(\lambda x \cdot (x \in s \mid E))$	$\forall x \cdot (x \in s \;\Rightarrow\; E \in \mathbb{Z})$ $\mathsf{finite}\,(s)$
$\prod x \cdot (x \in s \;\wedge\; P \mid E)$	$\mathsf{prodf}\,(\lambda x \cdot (x \in s \;\wedge\; P \mid E))$	$\forall x \cdot (x \in s \;\wedge\; P \;\Rightarrow\; E \in \mathbb{Z})$ $\mathsf{finite}\,(s)$
$[E]$	$\{1 \mapsto E\}$	$E \in s$
$[L, E]$	$[L] \leftarrow E$	$[L] \in \mathsf{seq}\,(s) \;\wedge\; E \in s$
$t \uparrow n$	$(1\,..\,n) \lhd t$	$t \in \mathsf{seq}\,(s) \;\wedge\; n \in (0\,..\,\mathsf{size}\,(t))$
$t \downarrow n$	$\mathsf{plus}\,(n)\,;((1\,..\,n) \ntriangleleft t)$	$t \in \mathsf{seq}\,(s) \;\wedge\; n \in (0\,..\,\mathsf{size}\,(t))$
$\mathsf{first}\,(t)$	$t(1)$	$t \in \mathsf{seq}_1(s)$
$\mathsf{last}\,(t)$	$t(\mathsf{size}\,(t))$	$t \in \mathsf{seq}_1(s)$
$\mathsf{tail}\,(t)$	$t \downarrow 1$	$t \in \mathsf{seq}_1(s)$
$\mathsf{front}\,(t)$	$t \uparrow (\mathsf{size}\,(t) - 1)$	$t \in \mathsf{seq}_1(s)$

Syntax	Definition	Condition
$\mathrm{cmp}\,(f)$	$\lambda t \cdot (t \in \mathrm{seq}\,(s) \mid t\,;f)$	$f \in s \rightarrow u$
$\mathrm{cat}\,(u)$	$\lambda t \cdot (t \in \mathrm{seq}\,(s) \mid u \frown t)$	$u \in \mathrm{seq}\,(s)$
$\mathrm{sort}\,(s)$	section 3.7.4	$s \in \mathrm{seq}\,(\mathbb{Z})$
$\mathrm{sortset}\,(s)$	section 3.7.4	$s \in \mathbb{F}(\mathbb{Z})$
$\mathrm{squash}\,(f)$	$\mathrm{sortset}\,(\mathrm{dom}\,(f))\,;f$	$f \in \mathbb{Z} \nrightarrow s \,\wedge\, \mathrm{finite}\,(f)$
$s < t$	$s \neq t \,\wedge\, \mathrm{size}\,(s) = \mathrm{size}\,(t) \,\wedge\,$ $s(i) < t(i)$	$s \in \mathrm{seq}\,(\mathbb{Z}) \,\wedge\, t \in \mathrm{seq}\,(\mathbb{Z})$ where $i = \min\,(\{\,n \mid n \in \mathrm{dom}\,(s) \,\wedge\, s(i) \neq t(i)\,\})$
$s \leq t$	$s = t \,\vee\, s < t$	

C.10. Finite Tree Definitions (§3.8, §3.9, §3.10)

Syntax	Definition
FSN	$\mathbb{F}(\mathrm{seq}\,(\mathbb{N}_1))$
ins	$\lambda i \cdot (i \in \mathbb{N} \mid \lambda s \cdot (s \in \mathrm{seq}\,(\mathbb{N}) \mid i \rightarrow s))$
cns	$\lambda t \cdot (t \in \mathrm{seq}\,(\mathrm{FSN}) \mid \{\,[\,]\,\} \cup$ $\bigcup i \cdot (i \in \mathrm{dom}\,(t) \mid \mathrm{ins}\,(i)\,[t(i)]\,))$
gentree	$\lambda z \cdot (z \in \mathbb{P}(\mathrm{FSN}) \mid \mathrm{cns}[\mathrm{seq}\,(z)]\,)$
T	$\mathrm{fix}\,(\mathrm{gentree})$
sns	$\mathrm{cns}^{-1} \rhd \mathrm{seq}\,(\mathrm{T})$

Syntax	Definition	Condition
$\text{sizt}(t)$	$\text{succ}(\text{sum}(\text{sns}(t);\text{sizt}))$	$t \in \mathsf{T}$
$\text{mir}(t)$	$\text{cns}(\text{rev}(\text{sns}(t);\text{mir}))$	$t \in \mathsf{T}$
$\text{rep}(t)$	$(\ \rightarrow \text{conc}(\text{sns}(t);\text{rep}) \leftarrow\ )$	$t \in \mathsf{T}$
cons	$\lambda(x,t) \cdot ((x,t) \in s \times \text{seq}(\text{seq}(\mathbb{N}_1) \twoheadrightarrow s)\ \|$ $\{[]\mapsto x\} \cup \bigcup i \cdot (i \in \text{dom}(t)\ \|\ \text{ins}(i)^{-1};t(i)))$	
genltree	$\lambda z \cdot (z \in \mathbb{P}(\text{seq}(\mathbb{N}_1) \twoheadrightarrow s)\ \|\ \text{cons}\ [s \times \text{seq}(z)]\ )$	
$\text{tree}(s)$	$\text{fix}(\text{genltree})$	
top	$\text{cons}^{-1};\text{prj}_1(s,\text{seq}(\text{tree}(s)))$	
sons	$\text{cons}^{-1};\text{prj}_2(s,\text{seq}(\text{tree}(s)))$	
$\text{pre}(t)$	$\text{top}(t) \rightarrow \text{conc}(\text{sns}(t);\text{pre})$	$t \in \text{tree}(s)$
$\text{post}(t)$	$\text{conc}(\text{sns}(t);\text{post}) \leftarrow \text{top}(t)$	$t \in \text{tree}(s)$
$\text{sizet}(t)$	$\text{succ}(\text{sum}(\text{sns}(t);\text{sizet}))$	$t \in \text{tree}(s)$
$\text{mirror}(t)$	$\text{cons}(\text{top}(t),\text{rev}(\text{sns}(t);\text{mirror}))$	$t \in \text{tree}(s)$
$\text{rank}(t)(n)$	$\text{last}(n)$	$t \in \text{tree}(s)$ $n \in \text{dom}(t) - \{[]\}$
$\text{father}(t)(n)$	$\text{front}(n)$	$t \in \text{tree}(s)$ $n \in \text{dom}(t) - \{[]\}$
$\text{son}(t)(n)(i)$	$n \leftarrow i$	$t \in \text{tree}(s)$ $(n \leftarrow i) \in \text{dom}(t)$
$\text{subt}(t)(n)$	$\text{cat}(n);t$	$t \in \text{tree}(s)$ $n \in \text{dom}(t)$
$\text{arity}(t)(n)$	$\text{size}(\text{sons}(\text{subt}(t)(n)))$	$t \in \text{tree}(s)$ $n \in \text{dom}(t)$
$\text{bin}(s)$	$\{t \mid t \in \text{tree}(s) \wedge \forall n \cdot (n \in \text{dom}(t)\ \Rightarrow$ $\text{arity}(t)(n) \in \{0,2\})\}$	

Syntax	Definition	Condition
$\langle x \rangle$	$\text{cons}(x, [])$	$x \in s$
$\langle l, x, r \rangle$	$\text{cons}(x, [l, r])$	$x \in s \ \wedge \ l \in \text{bin}(s) \ \wedge \ r \in \text{bin}(s)$
$\text{left}(t)$	$\text{first}(\text{sons}(t))$	$t \in \text{bin}(s) \ \wedge \ \text{sons}(t) \neq []$
$\text{right}(t)$	$\text{last}(\text{sons}(t))$	$t \in \text{bin}(s) \ \wedge \ \text{sons}(t) \neq []$
$\text{infix}(\langle x \rangle)$	$[x]$	$x \in s$
$\text{infix}(\langle l, x, r \rangle)$	$\text{infix}(l) \frown [x] \frown \text{infix}(r)$	$l \in \text{bin}(s) \ \wedge \ r \in \text{bin}(s)$

C.11. Well-Founded Relation Definition (§3.11)

Syntax	Definition
$\text{wfd}(r)$	$\forall p \cdot (p \in \mathbb{P}(s) \ \wedge \ p \subseteq r^{-1}[p] \ \Rightarrow \ p = \varnothing)$

C.12. Generalized Substitution Definitions (§5.1.1)

Syntax	Definition
BEGIN S END	S
$x := E \ \| \ y := F$	$x, y := E, F$
$f(x) := E$	$f := f \lessdot \{ x \mapsto E \}$

Syntax	Definition
PRE *P* THEN *S* END	$P \mid S$
IF *P* THEN *S* ELSE *T* END	$(P \implies S) \;[\!]\; (\neg P \implies T)$
IF *P* THEN *S* END	IF *P* THEN *S* ELSE skip END
$x := \text{bool}(P)$	IF *P* THEN $x :=$ true ELSE $x :=$ false END

IF *P* THEN
  S
. . .
ELSIF *Q* THEN
  T
ELSE
  U
END
	IF *P* THEN
	  S
	ELSE
	  . . .
	  IF *Q* THEN
	    T
	  ELSE
	    U
	  END
	  . . .
	END

IF *P* THEN
  S
. . .
ELSIF *Q* THEN
  T
END
	IF *P* THEN
	  S
	. . .
	ELSIF *Q* THEN
	  T
	ELSE
	  skip
	END

CHOICE *S* OR $\cdots$ OR *T* END	$S \;[\!]\; \cdots \;[\!]\; T$

Syntax	Definition

SELECT P THEN
  S
  $\ldots$
WHEN Q THEN
  T
END
	CHOICE
	  $P \Longrightarrow S$
	OR
	  $\ldots$
	OR
	  $Q \Longrightarrow T$
	END

SELECT P THEN
  S
  $\ldots$
WHEN Q THEN
  T
ELSE
  U
END
	SELECT P THEN
	  S
	  $\ldots$
	WHEN Q THEN
	  T
	WHEN $\neg (P \vee \cdots \vee Q)$ THEN
	  U
	END

CASE E OF
  EITHER l THEN
    S
  $\ldots$
  OR p THEN
    T
  END
END
	SELECT $E \in \{l\}$ THEN
	  S
	  $\ldots$
	WHEN $E \in \{p\}$ THEN
	  T
	ELSE
	  skip
	END

CASE E OF
  EITHER l THEN
    S
  $\ldots$
  OR p THEN
    T
  ELSE
    U
  END
END
	SELECT $E \in \{l\}$ THEN
	  S
	  $\ldots$
	WHEN $E \in \{p\}$ THEN
	  T
	ELSE
	  U
	END

Syntax	Definition
ANY x WHERE P THEN S END	$@x \cdot (P \Longrightarrow S)$
$x :\in U$	ANY y WHERE $y \in U$ THEN $x := y$ END
VAR x IN S END	$@x \cdot S$
LET $x, \ldots, y$ BE $\quad x = E \ \wedge$ $\quad \ldots$ $\quad y = F$ IN $\quad S$ END	ANY $x, \ldots, y$ WHERE $\quad x = E \ \wedge$ $\quad \ldots$ $\quad y = F$ THEN $\quad S$ END
$x : P$	ANY x' WHERE $\quad [x_0, x := x, x'] P$ THEN $\quad x := x'$ END

C.13. Set-theoretic Models (§6.3, §6.4, §9.2.1, §9.2.2)

Syntax	Definition
$\mathrm{trm}(S)$	$[S](x = x)$
$\mathrm{prd}_x(S)$	$\neg [S] \neg (x = x')$

Syntax	Definition
fis (S)	$\neg\,[\,S\,]\,\neg\,(x = x)$
pre (S)	$\{\,x \mid x \in s \;\wedge\; \text{trm}\,(S)\,\}$
rel (S)	$\{\,x, x' \mid (x, x') \in s \times s \;\wedge\; \text{prd}_x(S)\,\}$
dom (S)	$\{\,x \mid x \in s \;\wedge\; \text{fis}\,(S)\,\}$
str $(S)(p)$	$\{\,x \mid x \in s \;\wedge\; [S]\,(x \in p)\,\}$
str $(S\hat{\ })(p)$	$\text{fix}\,(\lambda q \cdot (q \in \mathbb{P}(s) \mid p \;\cap\; \text{str}\,(S)(q)))$
WHILE P DO S END	$(P \implies S)\hat{\ }\,;(\neg\,P \implies \text{skip})$

C.14. Refinement Conditions (§11.1.2, §11.2.4)

$S \sqsubseteq T$	$\forall\, p \cdot (p \subseteq b \;\Rightarrow\; \text{str}\,(S)(p) \subseteq \text{str}\,(T)(p))$
	$\text{pre}\,(S) \subseteq \text{pre}\,(T) \;\wedge\; \text{rel}\,(T) \subseteq \text{rel}\,(S)$
$S \sqsubseteq_r T$	$\forall\, q \cdot (q \subseteq c \;\Rightarrow\; \text{str}\,(S)(\overline{v\,[\overline{q}]}) \subseteq \overline{v\,[\overline{\text{str}\,(T)(q)}]})$
	$v^{-1}[\text{pre}\,(S)] \subseteq \text{pre}\,(T) \;\wedge\; v^{-1}\,;\text{rel}\,(T) \subseteq \text{rel}\,(S)\,;v^{-1}$

APPENDIX D
Visibility Rules

D.1. Visibility of a Machine

D.1.1. Visibility of a Machine with Respect to its Own Objects (§5.2.2)

The tables in this appendixshould be read as follows: a clause in a certain column can use a certain object in a line if and only if the corresponding box is ticked. For example, in a PROPERTIES clause, you can use a *constant* and also a *set*, but not a *variable*. Notice that a line called *constants* or *variables* without extra information means both concrete and astract *constants* or *variables*.

	CONSTRAINTS	INCLUDES	PROPERTIES
parameters	√	√	
sets		√	√
constants		√	√
variables			

	INVARIANT	OPERATIONS
parameters	✓	✓
sets	✓	✓
constants	✓	✓
variables	✓	✓
operations		

D.1.2. Visibility of a Machine with Respect to the Objects of an Included Machine (§7.2.4)

	INCLUDES	PROPERTIES	INVARIANT	OPERATIONS
parameters (of included)				
sets (of included)		✓	✓	✓
constants (of included)		✓	✓	✓

	INCLUDES	PROPERTIES	INVARIANT	OPERATIONS
variables (of included)			√	read-only
operations (of included)				√

D.1.3. Visibility of a Machine with Respect to the Objects of a Used Machine (§7.3.3)

	INCLUDES	PROPERTIES	INVARIANT	OPERATIONS
parameters (of used)			√	√
sets (of used)		√	√	√
constants (of used)		√	√	√
variables (of used)			√	read-only
operations (of used)				

D.1.4. Visibility of a Machine with Respect to the Objects of a Seen Machine (§12.2.3)

	INCLUDES	PROPERTIES	INVARIANT	OPERATIONS
parameters (of seen)				
sets (of seen)	√	√	√	√
constants (of seen)	√	√	√	√
variables (of seen)				read-only
operations (of seen)				

D.2. Visibility of a Refinement

D.2.1. Visibility of a Refinement with Respect to the Objects of its Abstractions (§11.3.2)

	INCLUDES	PROPERTIES	INVARIANT	OPERATIONS
parameters (of machine)	√		√	√
sets (of abstractions)	√	√	√	√
concreteconstants (of abstractions)	√	√	√	√

D.2.2. Visibility of a Refinement with Respect to the Non-shared (Abstract) Variables or Abstract Constants of the Construct it Refines (§11.3.2)

	INCLUDES	PROPERTIES	INVARIANT	OPERATIONS
abstract variables			√	
abstract constants		√	√	

D.2.3. Visibility of a Refinement with Respect to the Objects of an Included Machine (§11.3.1)

	INCLUDES	PROPERTIES	INVARIANT	OPERATIONS
parameters (of included)				
sets (of included)		√	√	√
constants (of included)		√	√	√
variables (of included)			√	read-only
operations (of included)				√

D.2.4. Visibility of a Refinement with Respect to the Objects of a Seen Machine (§12.2.3)

	INCLUDES	PROPERTIES	INVARIANT	OPERATIONS
parameters (of seen)				
sets (of seen)	√	√	√	√
constants (of seen)	√	√	√	√
variables (of seen)				read-only
operations (of seen)				inquiry

D.3. Visibility of an Implementation

D.3.1. Visibility of an Implementation with Respect to its Abstractions (§11.3.2, §12.3)

	IMPORTS	VAL	PROP	INVT	OPER
parameters (of machine)	√			√	√
sets (of abstractions)	√	√	√	√	√
concrete constants (of abstractions)	√		√	√	√

D.3.2. Visibility of an Implementation with Respect to the (Abstract) Variables or Abstract Constants of the Construct it Refines (§11.3.2)

	IMPORTS	VAL	PROP	INVT	OPER
abstract variables				√	in loop invt
abstract constants			√	√	in loop invt

D.3.3. Visibility of an Implementation with Respect to the Objects of an Imported Machine (§12.1.5, §12.3)

	IMPORTS	VAL	PROP	INVT	OPER
parameters (of imported)					
sets (of imported)		√	√	√	√
concreteconst. (of imported)		√	√	√	√
abstractconst. (of imported)			√	√	in loop invariant only
concretevar. (of imported)				√	read-only
abstractvar. (of imported)				√	in loop invariant only
operations (of imported)					√

D.3.4. Visibility of an Implementation with Respect to the Objects of a Seen Machine (§12.2.3, §12.3)

	IMPORTS	VAL	PROP	INVT	OPER
parameters (of seen)					
sets (of seen)	√	√	√	√	√
concreteconst. (of seen)	√	√	√	√	√
abstractconst. (of seen)			√	√	in loop invariant only
concretevar. (of seen)					read-only
abstractvar. (of seen)					in loop invariant only
operations (of seen)					inquiry

Rules and Axioms

E.1. Non-freeness Rules (§1.3.3, §1.4, §1.5, §2.1.1)

	Non-freeness	Condition
NF 1	$x \setminus y$	x, y are distinct
NF 2	$x \setminus (P \wedge Q)$	$x \setminus P$ and $x \setminus Q$
NF 3	$x \setminus (P \Rightarrow Q)$	$x \setminus P$ and $x \setminus Q$
NF 4	$x \setminus \neg P$	$x \setminus P$
NF 5	$x \setminus \forall x \cdot P$	
NF 6	$x \setminus \forall y \cdot P$	$x \setminus y$ and $x \setminus P$
NF 7	$x \setminus [x := E] F$	$x \setminus E$
NF 8	$x \setminus [y := E] F$	$x \setminus y$ and $x \setminus E$ and $x \setminus F$

	Non-freeness	Condition
NF 9	$x \setminus (E = F)$	$x \setminus E$ and $x \setminus F$
NF 10	$(x, y) \setminus E$	$x \setminus E$ and $y \setminus E$
NF 11	$x \setminus (E, F)$	$x \setminus E$ and $x \setminus F$
NF 12	$x \setminus \forall(y, z) \cdot P$	$x \setminus \forall y \cdot \forall z \cdot P$
NF 13	$x \setminus (E \in s)$	$x \setminus E$ and $x \setminus s$
NF 14	$x \setminus \text{choice}(s)$	$x \setminus s$
NF 15	$x \setminus (s \times t)$	$x \setminus s$ and $x \setminus t$
NF 16	$x \setminus \mathbb{P}(s)$	$x \setminus s$
NF 17	$x \setminus \{ y \mid P \}$	$x \setminus \forall y \cdot P$
NF 18	$x \setminus \text{BIG}$	

E.2. Substitution Rules (§1.3.4, §1.4, §1.5, §2.1.1, §7.2.2)

	Substitution	Definition	Condition
SUB 1	$[x := E] \, x$	E	
SUB 2	$[x := E] \, y$	y	$x \setminus y$
SUB 3	$[x := E] \, (P \wedge Q)$	$[x := E] \, P \ \wedge \ [x := E] \, Q$	
SUB 4	$[x := E] \, (P \Rightarrow Q)$	$[x := E] \, P \ \Rightarrow \ [x := E] \, Q$	

	Substitution	Definition	Condition
SUB 5	$[x := E] \neg P$	$\neg [x := E] P$	
SUB 6	$[x := E] \forall x \cdot P$	$\forall x \cdot P$	
SUB 7	$[x := E] \forall y \cdot P$	$\forall y \cdot [x := E] P$	$y \setminus (x, E)$
SUB 8	$[x := x] F$	F	
SUB 9	$[x := E] F$	F	$x \setminus F$
SUB 10	$[y := E] [x := y] F$	$[x := E] F$	$y \setminus F$
SUB 11	$[x := D] [y := E] F$	$[y := [x := D]E] [x := D] F$	$y \setminus D$
SUB 12	$[x := C] (D = E)$	$[x := C] D = [x := C] E$	
SUB 13	$[x, y := C, D] F$	$[z := D] [x := C] [y := z] F$	$x \setminus y$ and $z \setminus F$ $z \setminus (x, y, C, D)$
SUB 14	$[x := E] (F \in s)$	$[x := E] F \in [x := E] s$	
SUB 15	$[x := E] \, \text{choice} \, (s)$	$\text{choice} \, ([x := E] s)$	
SUB 16	$[x := E] (s \times t)$	$[x := E] s \times [x := E] t$	
SUB 17	$[x := E] \, \mathbb{P}(s)$	$\mathbb{P} ([x := E] (s))$	
SUB 18	$[x := E] \{ x \mid P \}$	$\{ x \mid P \}$	
SUB 19	$[x := E] \{ y \mid P \}$	$\{ y \mid [x := E] P \}$	$y \setminus (x, E)$
SUB 20	$[x := E] \, \text{BIG}$	BIG	
SUB 21	$[x := E] (y := F)$	$[x := E] y := [x := E] F$	see Note
SUB 22	$[x := E] \, \text{skip}$	skip	

Note: In **SUB 21**, the substitution $[x := E] \, y$ must result in a *Variable*.

	Substitution	Definition	Condition
SUB 23	$[x := E](P \mid S)$	$[x := E]P \mid [x := E]S$	
SUB 24	$[x := E](S \mathbin{[\!]} T)$	$[x := E]S \mathbin{[\!]} [x := E]T$	
SUB 25	$[x := E](P \Longrightarrow S)$	$[x := E]P \Longrightarrow [x := E]S$	
SUB 26	$[x := E](@y \cdot S)$	$@y \cdot [x := E]S$	$y \setminus (x, E)$
SUB 27	$[x := E](S \,;\, T)$	$([x := E]S)\,;\,([x := E]T)$	
SUB 28	$[x := E]S\hat{\ }$	$([x := E]S)\hat{\ }$	

E.3. Basic Inference Rules ($\S1.1.4$, $\S1.2.2$, $\S1.3.5$, $\S1.4$)

	Antecedents	Consequent
Basic 1		$P \vdash P$
Basic 2	$\begin{cases} \text{HYP} \vdash P \\[1ex] \text{HYP included in HYP'} \end{cases}$	$\text{HYP'} \vdash P$
Basic 3	P occurs in HYP	$\text{HYP} \vdash P$
Basic 4	$\begin{cases} \text{HYP} \vdash P \\[1ex] \text{HYP}, P \vdash Q \end{cases}$	$\text{HYP} \vdash Q$

	Antecedents	Consequent
Rule 1	$\left\{\begin{array}{l} \text{HYP} \vdash P \\[4pt] \text{HYP} \vdash Q \end{array}\right.$	$\text{HYP} \vdash P \land Q$
Rule 2 Rule 2′	$\text{HYP} \vdash P \land Q$	$\left\{\begin{array}{l} \text{HYP} \vdash P \\[4pt] \text{HYP} \vdash Q \end{array}\right.$
Rule 3	$\text{HYP}, P \vdash Q$	$\text{HYP} \vdash P \Rightarrow Q$
Rule 4	$\text{HYP} \vdash P \Rightarrow Q$	$\text{HYP}, P \vdash Q$
Rule 5	$\left\{\begin{array}{l} \text{HYP}, \neg Q \vdash P \\[4pt] \text{HYP}, \neg Q \vdash \neg P \end{array}\right.$	$\text{HYP} \vdash Q$
Rule 6	$\left\{\begin{array}{l} \text{HYP}, Q \vdash P \\[4pt] \text{HYP}, Q \vdash \neg P \end{array}\right.$	$\text{HYP} \vdash \neg Q$
Rule 7	$\left\{\begin{array}{l} x \setminus H \quad \text{for each } H \text{ of HYP} \\[4pt] \text{HYP} \vdash P \end{array}\right.$	$\text{HYP} \vdash \forall x \cdot P$
Rule 8	$\text{HYP} \vdash \forall x \cdot P$	$\text{HYP} \vdash [x := E] P$
Rule 9	$\left\{\begin{array}{l} \text{HYP} \vdash E = F \\[4pt] \text{HYP} \vdash [x := E] P \end{array}\right.$	$\text{HYP} \vdash [x := F] P$
Rule 10		$\text{HYP} \vdash E = E$

E.4. Derived Inference Rules (§1.2.4, §1.3.7, §1.4)

	Antecedents	Consequent
DR 1	HYP ⊢ P	HYP ⊢ $\neg\neg P$
DR 2	HYP ⊢ P HYP ⊢ $\neg Q$	HYP ⊢ $\neg(P \Rightarrow Q)$
DR 3	HYP ⊢ $P \Rightarrow \neg Q$	HYP ⊢ $\neg(P \wedge Q)$
DR 4	HYP ⊢ $P \Rightarrow R$	HYP ⊢ $\neg\neg P \Rightarrow R$
DR 5	HYP ⊢ $P \Rightarrow (\neg Q \Rightarrow R)$	HYP ⊢ $\neg(P \Rightarrow Q) \Rightarrow R$
DR 6	HYP ⊢ $\neg P \Rightarrow R$ HYP ⊢ $\neg Q \Rightarrow R$	HYP ⊢ $\neg(P \wedge Q) \Rightarrow R$
DR 7	HYP ⊢ $\neg P \Rightarrow R$ HYP ⊢ $Q \Rightarrow R$	HYP ⊢ $(P \Rightarrow Q) \Rightarrow R$
DR 8	HYP ⊢ $P \Rightarrow (Q \Rightarrow R)$	HYP ⊢ $P \wedge Q \Rightarrow R$
GEN	$x \setminus H$ for each H of HYP HYP ⊢ P	HYP ⊢ $\forall x \cdot P$
DR 9	$x \setminus R$ $x \setminus H$ for each H of HYP HYP ⊢ $\neg P \Rightarrow R$	HYP ⊢ $\neg \forall x \cdot P \Rightarrow R$

	Antecedents	Consequent
DR 10	HYP $\vdash \neg\,[x := E]\,P$	HYP $\vdash \neg\,\forall x \cdot P$
DR 11	$\begin{cases} \forall x \cdot P \;\; \text{occurs in HYP} \\[6pt] \text{HYP} \vdash [x := E]\,P \;\Rightarrow\; R \end{cases}$	HYP $\vdash R$
DR 12	$\begin{cases} x \setminus R \\[4pt] x \setminus H \;\;\text{for each } H \text{ of HYP} \\[4pt] \text{HYP} \vdash P \Rightarrow R \end{cases}$	HYP $\vdash \exists x \cdot P \;\Rightarrow\; R$
DR 13	HYP $\vdash [x := E]\,P$	HYP $\vdash \exists x \cdot P$
DR 14	HYP $\vdash \forall x \cdot \neg P \;\Rightarrow\; R$	HYP $\vdash \neg\, \exists x \cdot P \;\Rightarrow\; R$
DR 15	HYP $\vdash \forall x \cdot \neg P$	HYP $\vdash \neg\, \exists x \cdot P$
DR 16	HYP $\vdash \exists x \cdot \neg P$	HYP $\vdash \neg\, \forall x \cdot P$
DB 1	P occurs in HYP	HYP $\vdash \neg P \Rightarrow R$
DB 2	$\neg P$ occurs in HYP	HYP $\vdash P \Rightarrow R$
BS 1	R occurs in HYP	HYP $\vdash P \Rightarrow R$
BS 2	P occurs in HYP	HYP $\vdash P$

		Antecedents	Consequent
EQL 1		$E = F$ occurs in HYP P occurs in HYP P is the same as $[x := E]Q$ $\text{HYP} \vdash [x := F]Q \Rightarrow R$	$\text{HYP} \vdash R$
EQL 2		$E = F$ occurs in HYP R is the same as $[x := E]P$ $\text{HYP} \vdash [x := F]P$	$\text{HYP} \vdash R$
EQL 3		$E = F$ occurs in HYP $\text{HYP}, F = E \vdash R$	$\text{HYP} \vdash R$
EQL			$\text{HYP} \vdash E = E$

E.5. Set Axioms (§2.1.2)

SET 1	$(E, F) \in (s \times t) \;\Leftrightarrow\; (E \in s \;\wedge\; F \in t)$	
SET 2	$s \in \mathbb{P}(t) \;\Leftrightarrow\; \forall x \cdot (x \in s \;\Rightarrow\; x \in t)$	$x \setminus (s, t)$
SET 3	$E \in \{x \mid x \in s \;\wedge\; P\} \;\Leftrightarrow\; (E \in s \;\wedge\; [x := E]P)$	$x \setminus s$
SET 4	$\forall x \cdot (x \in s \Leftrightarrow x \in t) \;\Rightarrow\; s = t$	$x \setminus (s, t)$
SET 5	$\exists x \cdot (x \in s) \;\Rightarrow\; \text{choice}(s) \in s$	$x \setminus s$
SET 6	infinite (BIG)	

E.6. Generalized Substitution Axioms (§5.1.3, §9.1.2)

SUBST 1	$[\text{skip}]\,R \;\Leftrightarrow\; R$	
SUBST 2	$[P \mid S]\,R \;\Leftrightarrow\; (P \wedge [S]\,R)$	
SUBST 3	$[S \,[]\, T]\,R \;\Leftrightarrow\; ([S]\,R \wedge [T]\,R)$	
SUBST 4	$[P \Longrightarrow S]\,R \;\Leftrightarrow\; (P \Rightarrow [S]\,R)$	
SUBST 5	$[@x \cdot S]\,R \;\Leftrightarrow\; \forall x \cdot [S]\,R$	$x \setminus R$
SUBST 6	$[S\,;T]\,R \;\Leftrightarrow\; [S]\,[T]\,R$	

E.7. Loop Proof Rules (§9.2.9, §10.0.2)

LOOP 1	$[T]I$ $\forall x \cdot (I \wedge P \;\Rightarrow\; [S]I)$ $\forall x \cdot (I \;\Rightarrow\; V \in \mathbb{N})$ $\forall x \cdot (I \wedge P \;\Rightarrow\; [n := V][S](V < n))$ $\forall x \cdot (I \wedge \neg P \;\Rightarrow\; R)$ $\Leftrightarrow$ $[T\,; \text{WHILE } P \text{ DO } S \text{ INVARIANT } I \text{ VARIANT } V \text{ END}]\,R$
LOOP 1′	$[T]I$ $\forall x \cdot (I \wedge P \;\Rightarrow\; [S]I)$ $\forall x \cdot (I \;\Rightarrow\; V \in \text{seq}(\mathbb{N}))$ $\forall x \cdot (I \wedge P \;\Rightarrow\; [s := V][S](V < s))$ $\forall x \cdot (I \wedge \neg P \;\Rightarrow\; R)$ $\Leftrightarrow$ $[T\,; \text{WHILE } P \text{ DO } S \text{ INVARIANT } I \text{ VARIANT } V \text{ END}]\,R$

LOOP 2	$[T\,;\text{WHILE } P \text{ DO } S \text{ INVARIANT } I \text{ VARIANT } V \text{ END}]\,R$ $[T]J$ $\forall x \cdot (I \;\wedge\; P \;\wedge\; J \;\;\Rightarrow\;\; [S]J)$ $\Rightarrow$ $[T\,;\text{WHILE } P \text{ DO } S \text{ INVARIANT } I \;\wedge\; J \text{ VARIANT } V \text{ END}]\,R$
LOOP 3	$[T\,;\text{WHILE } P \text{ DO } S \text{ INVARIANT } I \text{ VARIANT } V \text{ END}]\,R$ $\forall x \cdot (I \;\;\Rightarrow\;\; (P \;\;\Leftrightarrow\;\; H))$ $\Rightarrow$ $[T\,;\text{WHILE } H \text{ DO } S \text{ INVARIANT } I \text{ VARIANT } V \text{ END}]\,R$
LOOP 4	$[T\,;\text{WHILE } P \text{ DO } S \text{ INVARIANT } I \text{ VARIANT } V \text{ END}]\,R$ $\Rightarrow$ $[T\,;B\,;\text{WHILE } P \text{ DO } S\,;A \text{ INVARIANT } I \text{ VARIANT } V \text{ END}]\,R$

E.8. Sequencing Proof Rule (§9.1.3, §10.0.3)

SEQ	$[S]P$ $\forall x \cdot (P \;\Rightarrow\; [T]R)$ $\Rightarrow$ $[S\,;T]R$

Proof Obligations

F.1. Machine Proof Obligations (§5.2.5)

```
MACHINE
    M (X , x)
CONSTRAINTS
    C
SETS
    S ;
    T = {a, b}
(ABSTRACT_)CONSTANTS
    c
PROPERTIES
    P
(CONCRETE_)VARIABLES
    v
INVARIANT
    I
INITIALIZATION
    U
OPERATIONS
    u ⟵ O(w)  ≘  PRE Q THEN  V  END ;
    . . .
END
```

Abbreviation	Definition
A	$X \in \mathbb{P}_1(\text{INT})$
B	$S \in \mathbb{P}_1(\text{INT}) \;\wedge\; T \in \mathbb{P}_1(\text{INT}) \;\wedge\; T = \{a, b\} \;\wedge\; a \neq b$

$$A \;\wedge\; B \;\wedge\; C \;\wedge\; P \;\Rightarrow\; [U]I$$

$$A \;\wedge\; B \;\wedge\; C \;\wedge\; P \;\wedge\; I \;\Rightarrow\; J$$

$$A \;\wedge\; B \;\wedge\; C \;\wedge\; P \;\wedge\; I \;\wedge\; J \;\wedge\; Q \;\Rightarrow\; [V]I$$

F.2. INCLUDES **Proof Obligations** (§7.4.3)

MACHINE
$M_1(X_1, x_1)$
CONSTRAINTS
C_1
SETS
S_1 ;
$T_1 = \{a_1, b_1\}$
(ABSTRACT_)CONSTANTS
c_1
PROPERTIES
P_1
INCLUDES
$M(N, n)$
(CONCRETE_)VARIABLES
v_1
INVARIANT
I_1
ASSERTIONS
J_1
INITIALIZATION
U_1
OPERATIONS
$op_1(w_1) \;\widehat{=}\;$ PRE Q_1 THEN V_1 END ;
$\ldots$
END

MACHINE
$M(X, x)$
CONSTRAINTS
C
SETS
S ;
$T = \{a, b\}$
(ABSTRACT_)CONSTANTS
c
PROPERTIES
P
(CONCRETE_)VARIABLES
v
INVARIANT
I
ASSERTIONS
J
INITIALIZATION
U
OPERATIONS
$\ldots$
END

Abbreviation	Definition
A_1	$X_1 \in \mathbb{P}_1(\mathsf{INT})$
B_1	$S_1 \in \mathbb{P}_1(\mathsf{INT}) \ \wedge \ T_1 \in \mathbb{P}_1(\mathsf{INT}) \ \wedge \ T_1 = \{a_1, b_1\} \ \wedge \ a_1 \neq b_1$
A	$X \in \mathbb{P}_1(\mathsf{INT})$
B	$S \in \mathbb{P}_1(\mathsf{INT}) \ \wedge \ T \in \mathbb{P}_1(\mathsf{INT}) \ \wedge \ T = \{a, b\} \ \wedge \ a \neq b$

$$\overbrace{A_1 \ \wedge \ B_1 \ \wedge \ C_1 \ \wedge \ P_1}^{\text{Including}}$$
$$\Rightarrow$$
$$[X, x := N, n]\overbrace{(A \ \wedge \ C)}^{\text{Included}}$$

$$\overbrace{A_1 \ \wedge \ B_1 \ \wedge \ C_1 \ \wedge \ P_1 \ \wedge \ I_1}^{\text{Including}} \ \wedge$$
$$\underbrace{B \ \wedge \ P \ \wedge \ [X, x := N, n](I \ \wedge \ J)}_{\text{Included}}$$
$$\Rightarrow$$
$$J_1$$

$$\overbrace{A_1 \ \wedge \ B_1 \ \wedge \ C_1 \ \wedge \ P_1 \ \wedge \ I_1 \ \wedge \ J_1 \ \wedge \ Q_1}^{\text{Including}} \ \wedge$$
$$\overbrace{B \ \wedge \ P \ \wedge \ [X, x := N, n](I \ \wedge \ J)}^{\text{Included}}$$
$$\Rightarrow$$
$$[V_1] I_1$$

$$\overbrace{A_1 \ \wedge \ B_1 \ \wedge \ C_1 \ \wedge \ P_1}^{\text{Including}} \ \wedge$$
$$\overbrace{B \ \wedge \ P}^{\text{Included}}$$
$$\Rightarrow$$
$$[\overbrace{[X, x := N, n]U}^{\text{Included}} \ ; \ U_1] I_1$$

F.3. USES **Proof Obligations** (§7.4.4)

```
MACHINE
    M(X, x)
CONSTRAINTS
    C
USES
    M₁
SETS
    S;
    T = {a, b}
(ABSTRACT_)CONSTANTS
    c
PROPERTIES
    P
(CONCRETE_)VARIABLES
    v
INVARIANT
    I ∧ I'
ASSERTIONS
    J
INITIALIZATION
    U
OPERATIONS
    op  ≙  PRE  Q  THEN  V  END;
    . . .
END
```

```
MACHINE
    M₁(X₁, x₁)
CONSTRAINTS
    C₁
SETS
    S₁;
    T₁ = {a₁, b₁}
(ABSTRACT_)CONSTANTS
    c₁
PROPERTIES
    P₁
(CONCRETE_)VARIABLES
    v₁
INVARIANT
    I₁
ASSERTIONS
    J₁
INITIALIZATION
    U₁
OPERATIONS
    . . .
END
```

where $v_1 \setminus I$

Abbreviation	Definition
A	$X \in \mathbb{P}_1(\mathsf{INT})$
B	$S \in \mathbb{P}_1(\mathsf{INT}) \ \wedge \ T \in \mathbb{P}_1(\mathsf{INT}) \ \wedge \ T = \{a, b\} \ \wedge \ a \neq b$
A_1	$X_1 \in \mathbb{P}_1(\mathsf{INT})$
B_1	$S_1 \in \mathbb{P}_1(\mathsf{INT}) \ \wedge \ T_1 \in \mathbb{P}_1(\mathsf{INT}) \ \wedge \ T_1 = \{a_1, b_1\} \ \wedge \ a_1 \neq b_1$

$$\overbrace{A_1 \ \wedge \ B_1 \ \wedge \ C_1 \ \wedge \ P_1}^{\text{Using}} \ \wedge$$
$$\underbrace{A \ \wedge \ B \ \wedge \ C \ \wedge \ P}_{\text{Used}}$$
$$\Rightarrow$$
$$[U]I$$

$$\overbrace{A_1 \ \wedge \ B_1 \ \wedge \ C_1 \ \wedge \ P_1 \ \wedge \ I_1 \ \wedge \ J_1}^{\text{Using}} \ \wedge$$
$$\underbrace{A \ \wedge \ B \ \wedge \ C \ \wedge \ P \ \wedge \ I \ \wedge \ I'}_{\text{Used}}$$
$$\Rightarrow$$
$$J$$

$$\overbrace{A_1 \ \wedge \ B_1 \ \wedge \ C_1 \ \wedge \ P_1 \ \wedge \ I_1 \ \wedge \ J_1}^{\text{Using}} \ \wedge$$
$$\underbrace{A \ \wedge \ B \ \wedge \ C \ \wedge \ P \ \wedge \ I \ \wedge \ I' \ \wedge \ J \ \wedge \ Q}_{\text{Used}}$$
$$\Rightarrow$$
$$[V]I$$

F.4. Refinement Proof Obligations (§11.3.3)

MACHINE
  $M_1(X_1, x_1)$
CONSTRAINTS
  C_1
SETS
  S_1;
  $T_1 = \{a_1, b_1\}$
(ABSTRACT_)CONSTANTS
  c_1
PROPERTIES
  P_1
(CONCRETE_)VARIABLES
  v_1
INVARIANT
  I_1
ASSERTIONS
  J_1
INITIALIZATION
  U_1
OPERATIONS
  $u_1 \longleftarrow op_1(w_1) \quad \widehat{=}$
    PRE
    Q_1
    THEN
    V_1
    END;
    ...
END

...

REFINEMENT
  $M_n(X_1, x_1)$
REFINES
  M_{n-1}
SETS
  S_n;
  $T_n = \{a_n, b_n\}$
(ABSTRACT_)CONSTANTS
  c_n
PROPERTIES
  P_n
INCLUDES
  $M(N, n)$
(CONCRETE_)VARIABLES
  v_n
INVARIANT
  I_n
ASSERTIONS
  J_n
INITIALIZATION
  U_n
OPERATIONS
  $u_1 \longleftarrow op_1(w_1) \quad \widehat{=}$
    PRE
    Q_n
    THEN
    V_n
    END;
    ...
END

MACHINE
  $M(X, x)$
CONSTRAINTS
  C
SETS
  S;
  $T = \{a, b\}$
(ABSTRACT_)CONSTANTS
  c
PROPERTIES
  P
(CONCRETE_)VARIABLES
  v
INVARIANT
  I
ASSERTIONS
  J
INITIALIZATION
  U
OPERATIONS
  ...
END

Abbreviation	Definition
A_1	$X_1 \in \mathbb{P}_1(\mathsf{INT})$
B_i for i in $1..n$	$S_i \in \mathbb{P}_1(\mathsf{INT}) \;\wedge\; T_i \in \mathbb{P}_1(\mathsf{INT}) \;\wedge\; T_i = \{a_i, b_i\} \;\wedge\; a_i \neq b_i$
A	$X \in \mathbb{P}_1(\mathsf{INT})$
B	$S \in \mathbb{P}_1(\mathsf{INT}) \;\wedge\; T \in \mathbb{P}_1(\mathsf{INT}) \;\wedge\; T = \{a, b\} \;\wedge\; a \neq b$

$$
\overbrace{A_1 \;\wedge\; B_1 \;\wedge\; \cdots \;\wedge\; B_n}^{\text{Including}} \;\wedge\;
$$
$$
\overbrace{C_1 \;\wedge\; P_1 \;\wedge\; \cdots \;\wedge\; P_n}^{\text{Including}} \;\wedge\;
$$
$$
\overbrace{B \;\wedge\; P}^{\text{Included}}
$$
$$
\Rightarrow
$$
$$
[\overbrace{[X, x := N, n]U}^{\text{Included}} \;;\; U_n] \neg [U_{n-1}] \neg I_n
$$

$$
\overbrace{A_1 \;\wedge\; B_1 \;\wedge\; \cdots \;\wedge\; B_n}^{\text{Including}} \;\wedge\;
$$
$$
\overbrace{C_1 \;\wedge\; P_1 \;\wedge\; \cdots \;\wedge\; P_n}^{\text{Including}} \;\wedge\;
$$
$$
\overbrace{I_1 \;\wedge\; \cdots \;\wedge\; I_n \;\wedge\; J_1 \;\wedge\; \cdots \;\wedge\; J_{n-1}}^{\text{Including}} \;\wedge\;
$$
$$
\overbrace{B \;\wedge\; P \;\wedge\; [X, x := N, n]\,(I \;\wedge\; J)}^{\text{Included}}
$$
$$
\Rightarrow
$$
$$
J_n
$$

$$
\overbrace{A_1 \;\wedge\; B_1 \;\wedge\; \cdots \;\wedge\; B_n}^{\text{Including}} \;\wedge\;
$$
$$
\overbrace{C_1 \;\wedge\; P_1 \;\wedge\; \cdots \;\wedge\; P_n}^{\text{Including}}
$$
$$
\Rightarrow
$$
$$
[X, x := N, n]\,\overbrace{(A \;\wedge\; C)}^{\text{Included}}
$$

$$
\overbrace{A_1 \;\wedge\; B_1 \;\wedge\; \cdots \;\wedge\; B_n}^{\text{Including}} \;\wedge\;
$$
$$
\overbrace{C_1 \;\wedge\; P_1 \;\wedge\; \cdots \;\wedge\; P_n}^{\text{Including}} \;\wedge\;
$$
$$
\overbrace{I_1 \;\wedge\; \cdots \;\wedge\; I_n \;\wedge\; J_1 \;\wedge\; \cdots \;\wedge\; J_n \;\wedge\; Q_1}^{\text{Including}} \;\wedge\;
$$
$$
\overbrace{B \;\wedge\; P \;\wedge\; [X, x := N, n]\,(I \;\wedge\; J)}^{\text{Included}}
$$
$$
\Rightarrow
$$
$$
Q_n \;\wedge\; [[u_1 := u_1']\,V_n] \neg [V_{n-1}] \neg (I_n \;\wedge\; u_1 = u_1')
$$

F.5. **Implementation Proof Obligations** (§12.6.4)

MACHINE
  $M_1(X_1, x_1)$
CONSTRAINTS
  C_1
SETS
  S_1 ;
  $T_1 = \{a_1, b_1\}$
CONSTANTS
  c_1
ABSTRACT_CONSTANTS
  c_1'
PROPERTIES
  P_1
(CONCRETE_)VARIABLES
  v_1
INVARIANT
  I_1
ASSERTIONS
  J_1
INITIALIZATION
  U_1
OPERATIONS
  $u_1 \longleftarrow op_1(w_1) \;\; \widehat{=}$
    PRE
      Q_1
    THEN
      V_1
    END ;
    . . .
END

$\cdots$

IMPLEMENTATION
  $M_n(X_1, x_1)$
REFINES
  M_{n-1}
SETS
  S_n ;
  $T_n = \{a_n, b_n\}$
CONSTANTS
  c_n
PROPERTIES
  P_n
IMPORTS
  $M(N, n)$
VALUES
  $S_1 = E_1 \;\; \wedge \;\; S_i = E_i \cdots \;\; \wedge$
  $c_1 = d_1 \;\; \wedge \;\; c_i = d_i \cdots$
CONCRETE_VARIABLES
  v_n
INVARIANT
  I_n
ASSERTIONS
  J_n
INITIALIZATION
  U_n
OPERATIONS
  $u_1 \longleftarrow op_1(w_1) \;\; \widehat{=}$
    PRE
      Q_n
    THEN
      V_n
    END ;
    . . .
END

MACHINE
  $M(X, x)$
CONSTRAINTS
  C
SETS
  S ;
  $T = \{a, b\}$
(ABSTRACT_)CONSTANTS
  c
PROPERTIES
  P
(CONCRETE_)VARIABLES
  v
INVARIANT
  I
ASSERTIONS
  J
INITIALIZATION
  U
OPERATIONS
  . . .
END

Abbreviation	Definition
A_1	$X_1 \in \mathbb{P}_1(\text{INT})$
B_i for i in $1 \mathinner{\ldotp\ldotp} n$	$S_i \in \mathbb{P}_1(\text{INT}) \;\wedge\; T_i \in \mathbb{P}_1(\text{INT}) \;\wedge\; T_i = \{a_i, b_i\} \;\wedge\; a_i \neq b_i$
A	$X \in \mathbb{P}_1(\text{INT})$
B	$S \in \mathbb{P}_1(\text{INT}) \;\wedge\; T \in \mathbb{P}_1(\text{INT}) \;\wedge\; T = \{a, b\} \;\wedge\; a \neq b$

$$
\overbrace{A_1 \;\wedge\; B_1 \;\wedge\; \cdots \;\wedge\; B_n \;\wedge\; C_1 \;\wedge\; P_1 \;\wedge\; \cdots \;\wedge\; P_n}^{\text{Importing}}
$$
$$
\Rightarrow
$$
$$
[X, x := N, n]\,(\overbrace{A \;\wedge\; C}^{\text{Imported}})
$$

$$
\overbrace{A_1 \;\wedge\; B_1 \;\wedge\; \cdots \;\wedge\; B_n \;\wedge\; C_1 \;\wedge\; P_1 \;\wedge\; \cdots \;\wedge\; P_n}^{\text{Importing}} \;\wedge\;
$$
$$
\overbrace{I_1 \;\wedge\; \cdots \;\wedge\; I_n \;\wedge\; J_1 \;\wedge\; \cdots \;\wedge\; J_{n-1}}^{\text{Importing}} \;\wedge\;
$$
$$
\overbrace{B \;\wedge\; P \;\wedge\; [X, x := N, n]\,(I \;\wedge\; J)}^{\text{Imported}}
$$
$$
\Rightarrow
$$
$$
J_n
$$

$$
\overbrace{B \;\wedge\; P}^{\text{Imported}}
$$
$$
\Rightarrow
$$
$$
\exists\,(c'_1, \ldots c'_{n-1}) \cdot [S_1, c_1, \ldots, S_n, c_n := E_1, d_1, \ldots, E_n, d_n]\,(\overbrace{P_1 \;\wedge\; \cdots \;\wedge\; P_n}^{\text{Importing}})
$$

$$\overbrace{A_1 \ \wedge \ B_1 \ \wedge \ \cdots \ \wedge \ B_n \ \wedge \ C_1 \ \wedge \ P_1 \ \wedge \ \cdots \ \wedge \ P_n}^{\text{Importing}} \ \wedge$$

$$\overbrace{B \ \wedge \ P}^{\text{Imported}}$$

$$\Rightarrow$$

$$[\overbrace{[X, x := N, n]U}^{\text{Imported}} \ ; \ U_n] \neg [U_{n-1}] \neg I_n$$

$$\overbrace{A_1 \ \wedge \ B_1 \ \wedge \ \cdots \ \wedge \ B_n \ \wedge \ C_1 \ \wedge \ P_1 \ \wedge \ \cdots \ \wedge \ P_n}^{\text{Importing}} \ \wedge$$

$$\overbrace{I_1 \ \wedge \ \cdots \ \wedge \ I_n \ \wedge \ J_1 \ \wedge \ \cdots \ \wedge \ J_n \ \wedge \ Q_1 \cdots \ \wedge \ Q_{n-1}}^{\text{Importing}} \ \wedge$$

$$\overbrace{B \ \wedge \ P \ \wedge \ [X, x := N, n](I \ \wedge \ J)}^{\text{Imported}}$$

$$\Rightarrow$$

$$Q_n \ \wedge \ [[u_1 := u_1'] \, V_n] \neg [V_{n-1}] \neg (I_n \ \wedge \ u_1 = u_1')$$

Index